P9-EER-349

Brazil
a country study

Federal Research Division
Library of Congress
Edited by
Rex A. Hudson

Research Completed
April 1997

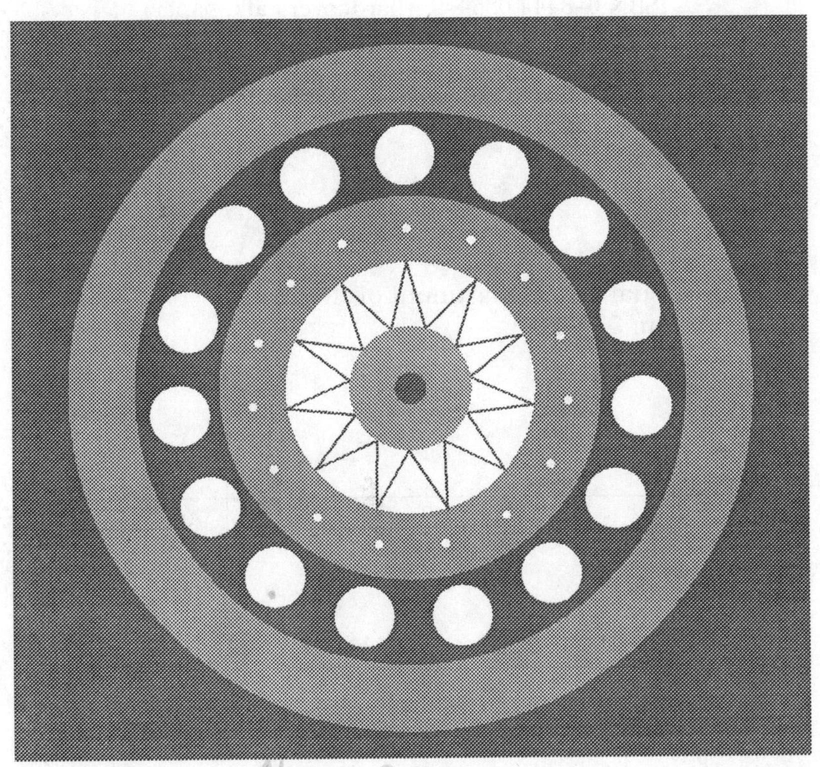

On the cover: A Xingu cosmological emblem with fifteen stars and fifteen moons

Fifth Edition, First Printing, 1998.

Library of Congress Cataloging-in-Publication Data

Brazil : a country study / Federal Research Division, Library of Congress ; edited by Rex A. Hudson. — 5th ed.
p. cm. — (Area handbook series, ISSN 1057–5294) (DA Pam ; 550–20)
"Supersedes the 1985 edition of Brazil : a country study, edited by Richard F. Nyrop."—T.p. verso.
"Research completed April 1997."
Includes bibliographical references (pp. 509–606) and index.
ISBN 0–8444-0854–9 (hardcover : alk. paper)
1. Brazil. I. Hudson, Rex A., 1947– . II. Library of Congress. Federal Research Division. III. Series. IV. Series: DA Pam ; 550–20.
F2508.B846 1997 97–36500
981.06'4—DC21 CIP

Headquarters, Department of the Army
DA Pam 550–20

For sale by the Superintendent of Documents, U.S. Government Printing Office
Washington, D.C. 20402

Foreword

This volume is one in a continuing series of books prepared by the Federal Research Division of the Library of Congress under the Country Studies/Area Handbook Program sponsored by the Department of the Army. The last two pages of this book list the other published studies.

Most books in the series deal with a particular foreign country, describing and analyzing its political, economic, social, and national security systems and institutions, and examining the interrelationships of those systems and the ways they are shaped by historical and cultural factors. Each study is written by a multidisciplinary team of social scientists. The authors seek to provide a basic understanding of the observed society, striving for a dynamic rather than a static portrayal. Particular attention is devoted to the people who make up the society, their origins, dominant beliefs and values, their common interests and the issues on which they are divided, the nature and extent of their involvement with national institutions, and their attitudes toward each other and toward their social system and political order.

The books represent the analysis of the authors and should not be construed as an expression of an official United States government position, policy, or decision. The authors have sought to adhere to accepted standards of scholarly objectivity. Corrections, additions, and suggestions for changes from readers will be welcomed for use in future editions.

Robert L. Worden
Acting Chief
Federal Research Division
Library of Congress
Washington, DC 20540–4840
E-mail: frds@loc.gov

Acknowledgments

The book editor would like to thank the chapter authors for reviewing and commenting on various chapters. Their country expertise contributed greatly to the overall quality of the book. Frank D. McCann, in particular, volunteered his expertise in Brazilian military history in the form of five subsections for the National Security chapter. The book editor would also like to thank Professor Roberto Patricio Korzeniewicz of the Department of Sociology at the University of Maryland at College Park for contributing the discussion of gender in chapter 2, The Society and Its Environment.

The authors are grateful to individuals in various agencies of the United States government, international organizations, private institutions, including nongovernmental organizations (NGOs) in Brazil, and Brazilian diplomatic offices who offered their time, special knowledge, or research facilities and materials to provide information and perspective. None of these individuals, is, however, in any way responsible for the work or points of view of the authors.

The book editor would like to thank the Rio Office of the Library of Congress—particularly Carmen Muricy, Senior Acquisitions Specialist; Pamela Howard-Reguindin, Field Director; and James C. Armstrong, former Field Director—for their bibliographical and other assistance. Thanks also go to Robert J. Olson, Department of the Army, for his efforts on behalf of the Country Studies/Area Handbook Program.

In addition, the book editor would like to thank members of the Federal Research Division who contributed directly to the preparation of the manuscript. These include Sandra W. Meditz, who reviewed all textual and graphic materials, served as liaison with the sponsoring agency, and provided numerous substantive and technical contributions; Marilyn L. Majeska, who managed editing and production; Andrea T. Merrill, who edited the tables, figures, and bibliography; and Barbara Edgerton, Janie L. Gilchrist, and Izella Watson, who did the word processing and initial typesetting. Thanks also go to Mary Ann Saour, who performed the copyediting of the chapters; Cissie Coy, who performed the final prepublication editorial review; Stephen C. Cranton and Janie L. Gilchrist, who prepared the camera-ready copy; and Sandi Schroeder, who compiled the index.

David P. Cabitto provided graphics support, including design of the cover and chapter illustrations. He was assisted by the firm of Maryland Mapping and Graphics, which prepared the book's maps and charts based on the editor's drafts.

The cover illustration is based on a nineteenth-century illustration from Antonio Bento, *Abstração na arte dos índios brasileiros,* Rio de Janeiro: SPALA Editora, 1979. The chapter illustrations are based on nineteenth-century Amazon Indian wood-carving designs reproduced in Theodore Menten, ed., *Amazon Indian Designs from Brazilian and Guianan Wood Carvings,* New York: Dover, 1994.

Finally, the book editor acknowledges the generosity of the individuals and the public, private, diplomatic, and international agencies—particularly the Inter-American Development Bank and the Office of the Military Attaché of the Brazilian Embassy in Washington—who allowed their photographs to be used in this study.

Contents

List of Figures

Preface

Like its predecessor, published in 1983, this study is an attempt to examine objectively and concisely the dominant historical, social, environmental, economic, governmental, political, and national security aspects of contemporary Brazil. This new edition also includes a chapter on science and technology. Sources of information included books, journals, other periodicals and monographs, official reports of governments and international organizations, and numerous interviews by the authors with Brazilian government officials and experts in academia and nongovernmental organizations (NGOs) in Brazil.

Chapter bibliographies appear at the end of the book; brief comments on sources recommended for further reading appear at the end of each chapter. To the extent possible, place-names follow the system adopted by the United States Board on Geographic Names (BGN). Measurements are given in the metric system; a conversion table is provided to assist readers unfamiliar with metric measurements (see table 1, Appendix). A glossary is also included.

The body of the text reflects information available as of April 1997. Certain other portions of the text, however, have been updated. The Introduction discusses significant events that have occurred since the completion of research, the Country Profile includes updated information as available, and the Bibliography lists recently published sources thought to be particularly helpful to the reader.

Table A. Selected Acronyms and Abbreviations

Acronym or Abbreviation	Organization or Term
ABACC	Agência Brasileiro-Argentina de Contabilidade e Contrôle de Materiais Nucleares (Brazilian-Argentine Agency for Accounting and Control of Nuclear Materials)
ABAL	Associação Brasileira de Alumínio (Brazilian Aluminum Association)
ABC	Agência Brasileira de Cooperação (Brazilian Cooperation Agency)
ABDD	Associação Brasileira de Defesa da Democracia (Brazilian Association for the Defense of Democracy)
ABERT	Associação Brasileira das Emissoras de Rádio e Televisão (Brazilian Association of Radio and Television Stations)
ABI	Agência Brasileira de Inteligência (Brazilian Intelligence Agency)
ABIN	Agência Brasileira de Inteligência (Brazilian Intelligence Agency)
ABINEE	Associação Brasileira da Industria Eletro-Eletrônica (Brazilian Electro-Electronic Industry Association)
ABONG	Associação Brasileira de Organizações Não-Governementais (Brazilian Association of Nongovernmental Organizations)
ADESG	Associações dos Diplomados da Escola Superior de Guerra (Associations of War College Graduates)
AEB	Agência Espacial Brasileira (Brazilian Space Agency)
AFA	Academia da Fôrça Aérea (Air Force Academy)
AGU	Advocacia-Geral da União (Office of the Federal Attorney General)
AIDS	acquired immune deficiency syndrome
ALADI	Associação Latino-Americana de Integração (Latin American Integration Association–LAIA)
ALALC	Asociación Latinoamericana de Libre Comercio (Latin American Free Trade Association–LAFTA)
ALCSA	Área de Livre Comercio Sul-Americana (South American Free Trade Association)
AMAN	Academia Militar das Agulhas Negras (Agulhas Negras Military Academy)
ANC	Assembléia Nacional Constituinte (National Constituent Assembly)
AP	Ação Popular (Popular Action)
Arena	Aliança Renovadora Nacional (National Renewal Alliance)
Avibrás	Avibrás Indústria Aeroespacial S.A. (Avibrás Aerospace Industry, Inc.)
Bacen	Banco Central do Brasil (Central Bank of Brazil)
Banerj	Banco do Estado de Rio de Janeiro (Rio de Janeiro State Bank)
Banespa	Banco do Estado de São Paulo (São Paulo State Bank)
BB	Banco do Brasil (Bank of Brazil)
BNDE	Banco Nacional de Desenvolvimento Econômico (National Economic Development Bank)
BNDES	Banco Nacional de Desenvolvimento Econômico e Social (National Bank for Economic and Social Development)
BNH	Banco Nacional de Habitação (National Housing Bank)

Table A. (Continued) Selected Acronyms and Abbreviations

Acronym or Abbreviation	Organization or Term
Bope	Batalhão de Operações Especiais (Special Operations Battalion)
Bovespa	Bolsa de Valores do São Paulo (São Paulo Stock Exchange)
Bradesco	Banco Brasileiro de Descontos (Brazilian Discount Bank)
Cacex	Carteira de Comércio Exterior (Department of Foreign Trade)
CAIC	Centro de Atenção Integrada à Criança (Center for Comprehensive Attention to Children)
CAPES	Fundação Coordenação de Aperfeiçoamento de Pessoal de Nível Superior (Council for Advanced Professional Training)
CBERS	Satélite Sino-Brasileiro de Recursos Terrestres (China-Brazil Earth Resources Satellite)
CBIA	Centro Brasileiro de Infancia e Adolescencia (Brazilian Center of Infancy and Adolescence)
CBPF	Centro Brazileiro de Pesquisas Físicas (Brazilian Center for Physics Research)
CDTN	Centro de Desenvolvimento de Tecnologia Nuclear (Center for Development of Nuclear Technology)
CEBs	Comunidades Eclesiais de Base (Ecclesiastical Base Communities)
CEF	Caixa Econômica Federal (Federal Savings Bank)
CEI	Comissão Especial de Investigação (Special Investigating Commission)
Cenimar	Centro de Informações de Marinha (Naval Intelligence Center)
Cenpes	Centro de Pesquisa e Desenvolvimento (Research and Development Center)
Cepel	Centro de Pesquisas de Energia Elétrica (Electric Power Research Center)
Cetem	Centro de Tecnologia Mineral (Mineral Technology Center)
CFN	Corpo de Fuzileiros Navais (Marines)
CIA	Centro de Informações da Aeronáutica (Air Force Intelligence Center)
CIAC	Centro Integrado de Assistência à Criança (Integrated Center for Assistance to Children)
CIE	Centro de Informações do Exército (Army Intelligence Center)
CLA	Centro de Lançamento de Alcântara (Alcântara Launching Center)
CMA	Comando Militar da Amazônia (Amazon Region Military Command)
CMFA	Comando Geral das Forças Armadas (Armed Forces Joint Command)
CNAE	Comissão Nacional de Atividades Espaciais (National Commission for Space Activities)
CNB	Comando Naval de Brasília (Brasília Naval Command)
CNBB	Conferência Nacional dos Bispos do Brasil (National Conference of Brazilian Bishops)
CNDM	Conselho Nacional de Direitos da Mulher (National Council on Women's Rights)
CNEN	Comissão Nacional de Energia Nuclear (National Nuclear Energy Commission)
CNI	Confederação Nacional das Indústrias (National Confederation of Industry)

Table A. (Continued) Selected Acronyms and Abbreviations

Acronym or Abbreviation	Organization or Term
CNM	Comando Naval de Manaus (Manaus Naval Command)
CNPCP	Conselho Nacional de Política Criminal e Penitenciária (National Council of Criminal and Prison Policy)
CNPq	Conselho Nacional de Pesquisas (National Research Council)
CNPq	Conselho Nacional de Desenvolvimento Científico e Tecnológico (National Council for Scientific and Technological Development) (original name)
Cobae	Comissão Brasileira de Atividades Espaciais (Brazilian Commission for Space Activities)
Cobra	Computadores e Sistemas Brasileiros (Brazilian Computers and Systems)
Conama	Conselho Nacional do Meio Ambiente (National Environmental Council)
Conasp	Conselho Nacional de Segurança Pública (National Council of Public Security)
Coppe	Coordenação dos Programas de Pós-Graduação em Engenharia (Coordinating Board of Postgraduate Programs in Engineering)
CPA	Conselho para Política Aduaneira (Customs Policy Council)
CPI	Comissão Parlamentar de Inquérito (Congressional Investigating Committee)
CPOR	Centro de Preparação de Oficiais da Reserva (Training Center for Reserve Officers)
CPqD	Centro de Pesquisa e Desenvolvimento (Research and Development Center)
CPT	Comissão Pastoral da Terra (Pastoral Land Commission)
CPTEC	Centro de Previsão do Tempo e Estudos Climáticos (Weather Forecasting and Climate Studies Center)
CSN	Companhia Siderúrgica Nacional (National Iron and Steel Company)
CSN	Conselho de Segurança Nacional (National Security Council)
CTA	Centro Técnico Aeroespacial (Aerospace Technical Center)
CTEx	Centro Tecnológico do Exército (Army Technology Center)
CTI	Fundação Centro Tecnológico para Informática (Computer Technology Center)
CTIC	Coordenadoria Técnica de Intercâmbio Comercial (Technical Coordinating Office for Trade)
CTT	Coordenadoria Técnica de Tarifas (Technical Coordinating Office for Tariffs)
CVRD	Companhia Vale do Rio Dôce (Rio Dôce Valley Company)
DAC	Departamento de Aviação Civil (Civil Aviation Department)
DAL	Diretoria de Apoio Logístico (Directorate of Logistical Support)
DASP	Departamento Administrativo do Serviço Público (Administrative Department of Public Service)
DCET	Departamento de Ciência e Tecnologia (Department of Science and Technology)
DEA	Drug Enforcement Administration (United States)
Depen	Departamento Penitenciário Nacional (Federal Prison Department)

Table A. (Continued) Selected Acronyms and Abbreviations

Acronym or Abbreviation	Organization or Term
DIAP	Departamento Intersindical de Assessorial Parlamentar (Interunion Parliamentary Advisory Department)
DIEESE	Departamento Intersindical de Estatística e Estudos Sócio-Económicos (Interunion Department for Statistics and Socioeconomic Studies)
DOI-CODI	Departamento de Operações Internas-Centro de Operações de Defesa Interna (Internal Operations Department-Internal Defense Operations Center)
DPD	Diretoria de Pesquisa e Desenvolvimento (Directorate of Research and Development)
DPF	Departamento de Polícia Federal (Department of Federal Police)
DRS	Diretoria de Radioproteção e Segurança Nuclear (Directorate of Radiation Protection and Nuclear Safety)
EC	European Community
ECEMAR	Escola de Comando e Estado-Maior da Aeronáutica (Air Force Command and General Staff School)
ECEME	Escola de Comando de Estado-Maior do Exército (Army General Staff School)
ECLAC	Economic Commission for Latin America and the Caribbean
ECT	Empresa de Correios e Telégrafos (Postal and Telegraph Company)
Eletrobrás	Centrais Elétricas Brasileiras S.A. (Brazilian Electric Power Company, Inc.)
Eletropaulo	Eletricidade de São Paulo S.A. (São Paulo Power, Inc.)
EMA	Estado-Maior da Armada (Navy General Staff)
EMAer	Estado-Maior da Aeronáutica (Air Force General Staff)
Embraer	Empresa Brasileira Aeronáutica (Brazilian Aeronautics Company)
Embrapa	Empresa Brasileira de Pesquisa Agropecuária (Brazilian Agriculture and Livestock Research Enterprise)
Embratel	Empresa Brasileira de Telecomunicações (Brazilian Telecommunications Company)
Embratur	Empresa Brasileira de Turismo (Brazilian Tourism Agency)
EMFA	Estado-Maior das Forças Armadas (Armed Forces General Staff)
EN	Escola Naval (Naval School)
Engesa	Engenheiros Especializados S.A. (Specialized Engineers, Inc.)
EPC	Escola Preparatória de Cadetes (Cadet Preparatory School)
EPCAr	Escola Preparatória de Cadetes do Ar (Air Cadets' Preparatory School)
ESA	European Space Agency
ESCA	Engenharia de Sistemas de Contrôle e Automação (Automation and Control Systems Engineering)
Escelsa	Espírito Santo Centrais Elétricas S.A. (Espírito Santo Power Plants, Inc.)
ESG	Escola Superior de Guerra (War College)
EsNI	Escola Nacional de Informações (National Intelligence School)
EsSA	Escola de Sargentos das Armas (School for Sergeants of the Services)
EU	European Union

Table A. (Continued) Selected Acronyms and Abbreviations

Acronym or Abbreviation	Organization or Term
FAB	Fôrça Aérea Brasileira (Brazilian Air Force)
FAPESP	Fundação de Amparo a Pesquisa do Estado de São Paulo (São Paulo State Federation to Support Research)
FBP	Frente Brasil Popular (Brazilian Popular Front)
FEB	Força Expedicionária Brasileira (Brazilian Expeditionary Force)
FEF	Fundo de Estabilização Fiscal (Fiscal Stabilization Fund)
FGTS	Fundo de Garantia do Tempo de Serviço (Severance Pay Fund)
FIESP	Federação das Indústrias do Estado de São Paulo (São Paulo State Federation of Industries)
Finep	Financiadora de Estudos e Projetos (Funding Authority for Studies and Projects)
FIP	Fôrça Interamericana de Paz (Inter-American Peace Force)
FNDCT	Fundo Nacional de Desenvolvimento Científico e Tecnológico (National Fund for Scientific and Technological Development)
FNMA	Fundo Nacional do Meio Ambiente (National Environmental Fund)
FSE	Fundo Social de Emergência (Social Emergency Fund)
FTA	Free Trade Agreement
FTAA	Free Trade Area of the Americas
Funai	Fundação Nacional do Índio (National Indian Foundation)
Funatura	Fundação Pró-Natureza (Pro-Nature Foundation)
Funcet	Fundo Estadual de Desenvolvimento Científico e Tecnológico (State Foundation for Scientific and Technological Development)
Furnas	Furnas Centrais Elétricas S.A. (Furnas Electric Power Plants, Inc.)
GATT	General Agreement on Tariffs and Trade
GDP	gross domestic product
GEAP	Grupo Evangélico de Ação Política (Political Action Evangelical Group)
GEF	Global Environment Facility
GNP	gross national product
GPI	general price index
G-77	Group of Seventy-Seven
GTA	Grupo de Trabalho Amazônico (Amazon Working Group)
HMO	health maintenance organization
IAE	Instituto de Atividades Espaciais (Space Activities Center)
IAEA	International Atomic Energy Agency
Ibama	Instituto Brasileiro do Meio Ambiente e dos Recursos Naturais Renováveis (Brazilian Institute for the Environment and Renewable Natural Resources)
IBASE	Instituto Brasileiro de Análise Social e Econômica (Brazilian Institute of Social and Economic Analysis)
IBGE	Fundação Instituto Brasileiro de Geografia e Estatística (Brazilian Institute of Geography and Statistics)
IBICT	Instituto Brasileiro de Informação em Ciência e Tecnologia (Brazilian Institute of Scientific and Technological Information)
IEAv	Instituto de Estudos Avançados (Institute of Advanced Studies)

Table A. (Continued) Selected Acronyms and Abbreviations

Acronym or Abbreviation	Organization or Term
IEM	Instituto de Engenharia Mecânica (Institute of Mechanical Engineering)
IEN	Instituto de Engenharia Nuclear (Nuclear Engineering Institute)
IMF	International Monetary Fund
IMPA	Instituto de Matemática Pura e Aplicada (Institute of Pure and Applied Mathematics)
INAMPS	Instituto Nacional de Assistência Médica da Previdência Social (National Institute for Medical Assistance and Social Security)
Inesc	Instituto de Estudos Sócio-Econômicos (Institute of Socioeconomic Studies)
Infraero	Empresa Brasileira de Infraestructura Aeroportuária (Brazilian Airport Infrastructure Firm)
INPA	Instituto Nacional de Pesquisas da Amazônia (National Institute of Amazon Research)
INPE	Instituto Nacional de Pesquisas Espaciais (National Institute of Space Research)
INT	Instituto Nacional de Tecnologia (National Institute of Technology)
Intelsat	International Telecommunications Satellite Organization
Interpol	International Criminal Police Organization
IPAM	Instituto de Pesquisa Ambiental da Amazônia (Environmental Research Institute of Amazônia)
IPEA	Instituto de Pesquisa Econômica Aplicada (Applied Economic Research Institute)
IPEN	Instituto de Pesquisas Energéticas e Nucleares (Institute for Nuclear and Energy Research)
IPES	Instituto de Pesquisas e Estudos Sociais (Institute for Research and Social Studies)
IPRI	Instituto das Pesquisas das Relações Internacionais (International Relations Research Institute)
IPT	Instituto de Pesquisas Tecnologicas (Institute for Technological Research)
IRBr	Instituto Rio Branco (Rio Branco Institute)
IRD	Instituto de Radioproteção e Dosimetria (Radiation Protection and Dosimetry Institute)
ISA	Instituto Sócio-Ambiental (Social-Environmental Institute)
ITA	Instituto Tecnológico de Aeronáutica (Aeronautical Technology Institute)
LAFTA	Latin American Free Trade Association
LAIA	Latin American Integration Association
LIBOR	London Interbank Offered Rate
Light	Serviços de Eletricidade S.A. (Power Services, Inc.)
LNA	Laboratório Nacional de Astrofísica (National Astrophysics Laboratory)
LNCC	Laboratório Nacional de Computação Científica (National Computer Science Laboratory)
LNLS	Laboratório Nacional de Luz Sincrotron (National Syncrotron Light Laboratory)

Table A. (Continued) Selected Acronyms and Abbreviations

Acronym or Abbreviation	Organization or Term
MAST	Museu de Astronomia e Ciências Afins (Museum of Astronomy and Related Sciences)
MDB	Movimento Democrático Brasileiro (Brazilian Democratic Movement)
MECB	Missão Espacial Completa Brasileira (Complete Brazilian Space Mission)
MEP	Movimento Eleitoral do Povo (People's Electoral Movement)
Mercosul	Mercado Comum do Sul (Common Market of the South)
MLRS	multiple-launch rocket system
Mobral	Movimento Brasileiro de Alfabetização (Brazilian Literacy Movement)
MPEG	Museu Paraense Emílio Goeldi (Emílio Goeldi Museum of Pará)
MPLA	Movimento Popular de Libertação de Angola (Popular Movement for the Liberation of Angola)
MR	Metropolitan Region
MST	Movimento dos Sem-Terra (Landless Movement)
MTCR	Missile Technology Control Regime
MUP	Movimento de Unidade Progressista (Progressive Unity Movement)
NAFTA	North American Free Trade Agreement
NASA	National Aeronautics and Space Administration (United States)
NDI	Núcleo de Direitos Indígenos (Center for Indian Rights)
NGO	nongovernmental organization
NPT	Nuclear Nonproliferation Treaty
Nuclebrás	Empresas Nucleares Brasileiras S.A. (Brazilian Nuclear Corporations)
OME	Ordem dos Ministros Evangélicos (Order of Evangelical Ministers)
ON	Observatório Nacional (National Observatory)
PADCT	Programa de Apoio ao Desenvolvimento Científico e Tecnológico (Program in Support of Scientific and Technological Development)
PAHO	Pan American Health Organization
PALOPs	Paises Africanos de Lingua Oficial Portuguêsa (Portuguese-Speaking African Countries)
PC	Polícia Civil (Civil Police)
PCB	Partido Comunista Brasileiro (Brazilian Communist Party)
PC do B	Partido Comunista do Brasil (Communist Party of Brazil)
PCDT	Programa de Apoio à Competividade e Difusão Tecnológica (Program for Competitiveness and Technological Diffusion)
PDC	Partido Democrático Cristão (Christian Democratic Party)
PDN	Plano de Defesa Nacional (National Defense Plan)
PDS	Partido Democrático Social (Democratic Social Party)
PDT	Partido Democrático Trabalhista (Democratic Labor Party)
Petrobrás	Petróleo Brasileiro S.A. (Brazilian Petroleum Corporation)
PF	Polícia Federal (Federal Police)
PFL	Partido da Frente Liberal (Liberal Front Party)

Table A. (Continued) Selected Acronyms and Abbreviations

Acronym or Abbreviation	Organization or Term
PGR	Procuradoria Geral da República (Office of the Solicitor General of the Republic)
PICD	Programa Integrado de Capacitação de Docentes (Faculty Improvement Integrated Program)
PJ	Partido da Juventude (Youth Party)
PL	Partido Liberal (Liberal Party)
Planasa	Plano Nacional de Saneamento (National Sanitation Plan)
PM	Polícia Militar (Military Police)
PMDB	Partido do Movimento Democrático Brasileiro (Brazilian Democratic Movement Party)
PND	Programa Nacional de Desestatização (National Privatization Program)
PNMA	Plano Nacional do Meio Ambiente (National Environmental Plan)
PP	Partido Popular (Popular Party)
PP	Partido Progressista (Progressive Party)
PPB	Partido Progressista Brasileiro (Brazilian Progressive Party)
PP-G-7	Programa Piloto para a Proteção das Florestas Tropicais do Brasil (Pilot Program for the Conservation of the Brazilian Rain Forest)
PPR	Partido Progressista Renovador (Progressive Renewal Party)
PPS	Partido Popular Socialista (Popular Socialist Party)
PRN	Partido da Reconstrução Nacional (National Reconstruction Party)
Prodes	Programa de Avaliação do Desflorestamento da Amazônia Brasileira (Brazilian Amazon Deforestation Appraisal Program)
Prona	Partido da Redefinição da Ordem Nacional (National Order Redefinition Party)
PSB	Partido Socialista Brasileiro (Brazilian Socialist Party)
PSBR	Public Sector Borrowing Requirement
PSC	Partido Social Cristão (Social Christian Party)
PSD	Partido Social Democrático (Social Democratic Party)
PSDB	Partido da Social Democracia Brasileira (Brazilian Social Democracy Party)
PST	Partido Social Trabalhista (Social Workers' Party)
PT	Partido dos Trabalhadores (Workers' Party)
PTB	Partido Trabalhista Brasileiro (Brazilian Labor Party)
PTR	Partido Trabalhista Renovador (Workers' Renewal Party)
PUC-RJ	Pontificia Universidade Católica do Rio de Janeiro (Pontifical Catholic University of Rio de Janeiro)
PV	Partido Verde (Green Party)
QCO	Quadro Complementar de Oficiais (Officers' Complementary Corps)
Radiobrás	Empresa Brasileira de Radiodifusão (Brazilian Radio Broadcasting Company)
RFFSA	Rêde Ferroviária Federal S.A. (Federal Railroad System, Inc.)

Table A. (Continued) Selected Acronyms and Abbreviations

Acronym or Abbreviation	Organization or Term
RHAE	Programa Nacional de Capacitação de Recursos Humanos para o Desenvolvimento Tecnológico (National Program for Human Resource Training for Technological Development)
RJU	Regime Jurídico Único (Single Judicial Regime)
SAE	Secretaria de Assuntos Estratégicos (Strategic Affairs Secretariat)
SAF	Secretaria de Administração Federal (Federal Administration Secretariat)
SBPC	Sociedade Brasileira para o Progresso da Ciência (Brazilian Society for Scientific Development)
SBT	Sistema Brasileiro de Televisão (Brazilian Television System)
SBTS	Sistema Brasileiro de Comunicação por Satélites (Brazilian Satellite Communication System)
SCCCMN	Sistema Comum de Contabilidade e Contrôle de Materiais Nucleares (Common System for Accounting and Control of Nuclear Materials)
SCD-1	Satélite de Coleta de Dados (Data-Collecting Satellite)
SCI	Secretaria de Contrôle Interno (Internal Control Secretariat)
SCTDE	Secretaria de Ciência, Tecnologia e Desenvolvimento Econômico (Secretariat for Science, Technology, and Economic Development)
SEE	Secretaria Especial de Entorpecentes (Special Secretariat for Drugs)
SEI	Secretaria Especial de Informática (Special Secretariat for Informatics)
Seplan	Secretaria de Planejamento e Coordenação da Presidência da República (Secretariat of Planning and Coordination of the Presidency of the Republic or Planning Ministry)
SEPNCD	Secretaria Especial da Política Nacional do Contrôle de Drogas (Special Secretariat for National Drug-Control Policy)
SFH	Sistema Financeiro de Habitação (Housing Finance System)
Sipam	Sistema de Vigilância da Amazônia (Amazon Region Surveillance System)
SIPRI	Stockholm International Peace Research Institute
Sisnama	Sistema Nacional do Meio Ambiente (National System for the Environment)
Sivam	Sistema de Vigilância da Amazônia (Amazon Region Surveillance System)
SLC	Superintendência de Licenciamento e Contrôle (Licensing and Control Superintendency)
SMA	Secretaria de Coordenação dos Assuntos do Meio Ambiente (Environmental Affairs Coordinating Secretariat)
SNDH	Secretaria Nacional dos Direitos Humanos (National Secretariat of Human Rights)
SNI	Serviço Nacional de Informações (National Intelligence Service)
SPI	Serviço de Proteção aos Indios (Indian Protection Service)
SPIA	Secretaria de Política de Informática e Automação (Secretariat for Computer and Automation Policy)
SSP	Secretaria de Segurança Pública (Secretariat for Public Security)
SSR-1	Satélite de Sensoriamento Remoto (Remote Sensing Satellite)

Table A. (Continued) Selected Acronyms and Abbreviations

Acronym or Abbreviation	Organization or Term
STF	Supremo Tribunal Federal (Federal Supreme Court)
STJ	Superior Tribunal de Justiça (Superior Court of Justice)
STM	Superior Tribunal Militar (Superior Military Court)
SUS	Sistema Único de Saúde (Single Health System)
SWAPO	South West African People's Organization
TCE	Tribunal de Contas dos Estados (State Accounts Court)
TCM	Tribunal de Contas Municipais (Municipal Accounts Court)
TCU	Tribunal de Contas da União (National Accounts Court)
Telebrás	Telecomunicações Brasileiras S.A. (Brazilian Telecommunications, Inc.)
TFP	Sociedade Brasileira de Defesa da Tradição, Familia e Propriedade (Brazilian Association of Tradition, Family, and Property)
TFR	Tribunal Federal de Recursos (Federal Court of Appeals)
TJ	Tribunal de Justiça (State Supreme Court)
TRE	Tribunal Regional Eleitoral (Regional Electoral Court)
TRF	Tribunal Regional Federal (Regional Federal Court)
TRT	Tribunal Regional do Trabalho (Regional Labor Court)
TSE	Tribunal Superior Eleitoral (Superior Electoral Court)
TST	Tribunal Superior do Trabalho (Superior Labor Court)
UDN	União Democrática Nacional (National Democratic Union)
UDR	União Democrática Ruralista (Ruralist Democratic Union)
UFRJ	Universidade Federal do Rio de Janeiro (Federal University of Rio de Janeiro)
UNCTAD	United Nations Commission on Trade and Development
UNDP	United Nations Development Programme
Unesp	Universidade Estadual Paulista (São Paulo State University)
Unicamp	Universidade Estadual de Campinas (Campinas State University)
UNICEF	United Nations Children's Fund
URV	Unidade Real de Valor (Real Value Unit)
USAID	United States Agency for International Development
Usiminas	Usinas Siderúrgicas de Minas Gerais S.A. (Minas Gerais Iron and Steel Mills, Inc.)
USP	Universidade de São Paulo (University of São Paulo)
Varig	Viação Aérea Rio Grande do Sul (Rio Grande do Sul Airline)
VLS	Veículo Lançador de Satélite (Satellite Launch Vehicle)
WWF	World Wildlife Fund

Table B. Chronology of Important Events

Period	Description
FIFTEENTH CENTURY	
June 7, 1494	Treaty of Tordesillas divides the world between Spain and Portugal, giving Portugal claim to eastern portion of as yet undiscovered continent of South America.
1500–1815	*Colonial Period*
SIXTEENTH CENTURY	
April 22, 1500	Pedro Álvares Cabral, en route to India, discovers Brazil.
1500–50	Logging of brazilwood.
1530	Expedition of Martim Afonso de Sousa, major captain of Brazil, to colonize and distribute land among captains (*donatários*).
1530	Beginning of sugar era.
1532	Founding of first colonies at São Vicente and Piratininga.
1536	Crown divides Brazil into fifteen donatory captaincies.
1542	Francisco de Orellana descends the Amazon.
1549	King names Tomé de Sousa first governor general of Brazil (1549–53). De Sousa establishes his capital at São Salvador da Bahia.
	Evangelization begins with arrival of Jesuit priests.
1551	Bishopric of Brazil created.
1555	French establish colony in Guanabara Bay.
1565	Governor Mem de Sá founds São Sebastião do Rio de Janeiro (Rio de Janeiro).
1567	Governor Mem de Sá expels French and occupies Guanabara Bay.
1580	Crown of Portugal passes to King Philip II of Spain, uniting Europe's two greatest empires under single ruler.
SEVENTEENTH CENTURY	
1603	Portuguese penetrate to Ceará.
1604	India Council established to oversee administration of Portuguese empire.
1615	Portuguese take over French town of São Luís do Maranhão.
1616	Portuguese found Belém.
1621	States of Maranhão (embracing the crown captaincies of Ceará, Maranhão, and Pará) and Brazil (centering on Salvador, Bahia) created.
1624–25	Dutch temporarily capture Salvador da Bahia.
1630	Dutch seize Recife, Pernambuco, and attempt unsuccessfully to conquer Northeast (Nordeste).
October 28, 1637–39	Captain Pedro Teixeira explores Amazon and founds Tabatinga.
1640	Portugal declares independence from Spain. Duke of Bragança takes throne as João IV.
1641	Victory of Jesuit-trained Guaraní in Battle of Mbororé.
1642	India Council renamed Overseas Council.
1654	Under Treaty of Taborda, Dutch withdraw from Brazil.

Table B. (Continued) Chronology of Important Events

Period	Description
1680	Colônia do Sacramento founded by Portuguese on Río de la Plata, across from Buenos Aires.
1693	Era of gold and diamond mining begins.
EIGHTEENTH CENTURY	
1705	Under Treaty of Spanish Succession, Portuguese give up Colônia do Sacramento.
1708–09	War of Outsiders over control of gold-mining areas.
1710–14	War of the Mascates (merchant class of Recife defeats planter class of Olinda).
1720	Governors general of Brazil renamed viceroys.
1727	Coffee introduced into Brazil.
January 13, 1750	Treaty of Madrid replaces Treaty of Tordesillas, and *uti possidetis* adopted to settle boundaries. José I (king of Portugal, 1750–77) assumes the throne in Portugal. Marquês de Pombal assumes effective power as José I's secretary of state.
1756	Guaraní War leads to expulsion of Jesuits.
1759	Pombal expels Jesuits from the empire.
1761	Treaty of El Pardo annuls Treaty of Madrid.
1763	Viceregal capital moved from Salvador, Bahia, to Rio de Janeiro.
1777	Treaty of San Ildefonso confirms Spain's possession of Banda Oriental (Uruguay) and Portugal's possession of Amazon Basin. Pombal dismissed.
February 1777	King José I dies.
1789	Minas Conspiracy (Inconfidência Mineira), first attempt to establish a republic, exposed.
April 21, 1792	"Tiradentes," Minas Conspiracy leader, is executed in Rio de Janeiro.
1798	Bahian conspiracy against Portugal exposed.
NINETEENTH CENTURY	
1807	French invade Portugal. Pedro de Alcântara de Bragança e Bourbon (King João VI) and son Pedro flee to Brazil with British naval escort.
1808–21	*Kingdom of Portugal and Brazil*
March 7, 1808	João VI arrives in Rio de Janeiro. Brazil's ports open to foreign trade.
1810	João VI signs treaties with Britain, giving it trade preferences and privileges of extraterritoriality.
1815	Portugal confers kingdom status on Brazil.
1817	Pernambuccan revolution against British regency fails but deepens anti-British sentiment.
1821	Uruguay annexed as Cisplatine Province.
April 25, 1821	João VI sails for Lisbon.
September 1821	Côrtes in Portugal votes to abolish Kingdom of Brazil.
1822–31	*The First Empire*
January 1822	Declaring Brazil independent, Pedro I forms new government headed by José Bonifácio de Andrada e Silva.
September 7, 1822	Pedro proclaims Brazilian independence.

Table B. (Continued) Chronology of Important Events

Period	Description
October 12, 1822	Brazilian independence proclaimed, with Pedro as constitutional emperor.
December 1, 1822	Pedro crowned emperor of Brazil.
1824	Pedro promulgates first constitution. United States recognizes Brazil.
1825–28	War with United Provinces of Río de la Plata (Cisplatine War).
August 29, 1825	Portugal recognizes Brazilian independence by signing treaty, and Britain follows suit.
1827	Britain consolidates commercial dominance of Brazil under Anglo-Brazilian Treaty.
1828	Argentina and Brazil agree to creation of Uruguay as independent nation.
1831–89	*The Second Empire*
April 7, 1831	Pedro I abdicates in favor of five-year-old son Pedro II. A three-man regency assumes control, ruling in Pedro II's name.
1834	Amendment of 1824 constitution institutes federalism (for six years) and one-man regency.
1835–37	Cabanagem rebellion in Pará.
1835–45	War of the Farrapos (ragamuffins), also known as the Farroupilha rebellion, in Santa Catarina and Rio Grande do Sul.
1837–38	Sabinada rebellion in Salvador, Bahia.
1838–41	Balaiada rebellion in Maranhão.
July 18, 1841	Coronation of Pedro II (emperor, 1840–89).
1842	Rebellions in Minas Gerais and São Paulo.
1844	Anglo-Brazilian Treaty expires and is not renewed.
1850	Land Law limits land acquisition to purchase. African slave trade outlawed.
1864–70	War of the Triple Alliance, allying Argentina, Brazil, and Uruguay against Paraguay.
1869	Brazilian forces defeat Paraguayan dictator Francisco Solano López and occupy Paraguay until 1878.
1870	Triple Alliance defeats Paraguay.
May 13, 1888	Golden Law abolishes slavery.
November 15–16, 1889	Army deposes Pedro II. Republic proclaimed. Deodoro da Fonseca assumes office as president. Pedro leaves the country.
1889–1930	*Old or First Republic*
1890	Church and State separated.
February 24, 1891	First constitution promulgated.
November 1891	Deodoro da Fonseca dissolves Congress and is ousted.
1893	A civil war erupts in South (Sul).
November 1894	First civilian president, Prudente José de Morais Barros, takes office.
TWENTIETH CENTURY	
August 1914	Contestado rebellion in South challenges colonel-dominated system.

Table B. (Continued) Chronology of Important Events

Period	Description
October 26, 1917	Brazil declares war on Germany and joins Allied powers.
July 5, 1922	*Tenente* (Lieutenants') Movement begins with Copacabana revolt.
1924–27	Prestes Column marches through backlands but fails to foment popular revolution.
1930–45	*Transitional Republic*
October 3, 1930	Revolts of 1930 bring Getúlio Dorneles Vargas to power.
July 9, 1932	São Paulo rebellion brings civil war.
July 16, 1934	A new constitution promulgated, and Congress elects Vargas to presidency.
November 10, 1937	Estado Novo (New State) established, and previously drafted constitution promulgated.
August 22, 1942	Brazil declares war on Axis powers.
1944	Brazilian Expeditionary Force sent to Italy. First steel mill opens.
October 29, 1945	Military deposes Vargas.
1946–64	*1946 Republic*
September 18, 1946	A new constitution promulgated.
October 1947	Brazil breaks diplomatic relations with Soviet Union.
January 1951	Vargas assumes office as reelected president.
August 24, 1954	Vargas commits suicide after armed forces and cabinet demand his resignation.
January 1956–January 1961	President Juscelino Kubitschek implements new economic strategy combining nationalist, developmentalist emphasis with openness to world economic system, creating economic boom.
1960	Capital moved inland to Brasília.
January 1961	Jânio Quadros assumes presidency.
September 2, 1961	A parliamentary system established.
August 1961	Quadros resigns presidency; replaced by João Goulart.
1963	National plebiscite ends parliamentary system and restores full presidential powers to Goulart.
March 31, 1964	Armed forces depose Goulart.
1964–85	*Military Republic*
April 1964	Marshal Humberto de Alencar Castelo Branco, elected by purged Congress, assumes presidency. First Institutional Act passed.
October 27, 1965	Second Institutional Act bans all existing political parties and imposes legal guidelines for new parties.
February 6, 1966	Third Institutional Act replaces direct election of governors with indirect elections by state assemblies and substitutes presidential appointees for mayors of capital cities.
March 1967	New constitution promulgated. General Artur da Costa e Silva inaugurated president.
September 1, 1967	Fourth Institutional Act gives military complete control over national security.
December 13, 1968	Fifth Institutional Act gives Costa e Silva dictatorial powers.
1975	Brazil signs nuclear energy accord with Federal Republic of Germany (West Germany).

Table B. (Continued) Chronology of Important Events

Period	Description
1977	Divorce legalized.
April 1977	Brazil renounces military alliance with United States.
January 1979	Decree ends Fifth Institutional Act, grants political amnesty.
1985	Military steps down from political power. Democracy restored.
1985–Present	*New Republic*
1988	"Citizen constitution" promulgated.
March 22, 1988	Presidential model reinstated.
November 15, 1989	First direct presidential election since 1960.
June 1992	United Nations Conference on the Environment and Development (UNCED), known as Earth Summit or Eco–92, held in Rio de Janeiro.
September 1992	President Fernando Collor de Mello impeached.
April 21, 1993	National plebiscite reaffirms presidential republic.
March 9, 1994	Congress approves constitutional reform reducing presidential term of office to four years, making it coterminous with term of congressional deputies.
July 1, 1994	New currency, the *real*, introduced at parity with United States dollar.
October 3, 1994	Fernando Henrique Cardoso wins presidential election in first round.
December 12, 1994	Former president Collor acquitted of corruption.
January 1, 1995	Cardoso assumes office as president.

Country Profile

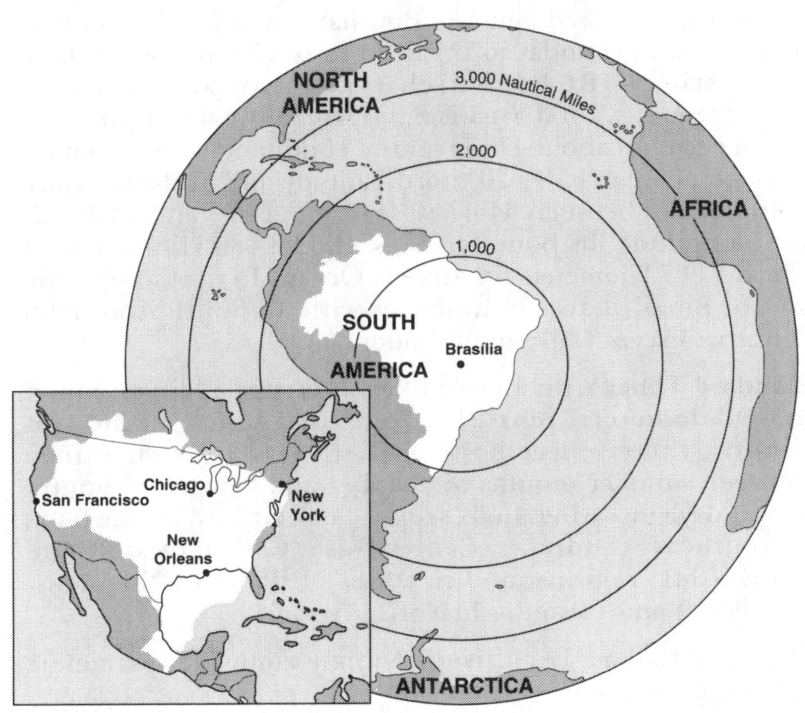

Country

Official Name: Federative Republic of Brazil (República Federativa do Brasil).

Short Name: Brazil (Brasil).

Term for Citizen(s): Brazilian(s).

Capital: Brasília.

Independence: September 7, 1822 (from Portugal).

Geography

Size and Location: Standard figure is 8,511,996 square

kilometers (including oceanic islands of Arquipélago de Fernando de Noronha, Atol das Rocas, Ilha da Trindade, Ilhas Martin Vaz, and Penedos de São Pedro e São Paulo). According to revised figure of Brazilian Institute of Geography and Statistics (Fundação Instituto Brasileiro de Geografia e Estatística—IBGE), which takes into account new measurements, total area is 8,547,403.5 square kilometers. Brazil occupies about 47 percent of continental area. Country situated between 05°16'20" north latitude and 33°44'32" south latitude, and between 34°47'30" east longitude and 73°59'32" west longitude. Its boundaries extend 23,086 kilometers, of which 7,367 kilometers on Atlantic Ocean. To north, west, and south, Brazil shares boundaries with all South American countries except Chile and Ecuador.

Standard Time: With an east-to-west territorial dimension of 4,319 kilometers, Brazil has four time zones. In most of country, time is three hours earlier than Greenwich time. Between summer months of October and February, country adopts daylight savings time, setting clock forward by one hour, in Southeast (Sudeste), Center-West (Centro-Oeste), and South (Sul) regions, and in states of Bahia in Northeast (Nordeste) and Tocantins in North (Norte).

Maritime Claims: Exclusive economic zone 322 kilometers (200 nautical miles).

Boundary Disputes: A short section of boundary with Paraguay, just west of Salto das Sete Quedas (Guairá Falls) on Paraná; and two short sections of boundary with Uruguay—Arroio Invernada area of Cuareim and islands at confluence of Quaraí and Uruguai.

Topography and Climate: Consisting of dense forest, semiarid scrub land, rugged hills and mountains, rolling plains, and long coastal strip, Brazil's landmass dominated by Amazon Basin and Central Highlands. Principal mountain ranges (Serra do Mar) parallel Atlantic coast. Climate varies from mostly tropical in North, where it is seldom cold, to more temperate in South, where it snows in some places. Also wide range of subtropical variations. World's largest rain forest located in Amazon Basin. Higher annual measurements (26°C to 28°C) occur in Northeast's interior and mid- and lower Amazon River. Lowest values (under 18°C) occur in hilly areas of Southeast and largest part of South. Highest absolute values, over 40°C, are recorded in Northeast's low interior lands; in

Southeast's depressions, valleys, and lowlands; in Center-West's Pantanal (Great Wetlands) and lower areas; and in South's central depressions and Uruguai Valley. Lowest absolute temperatures often show negative values in most of South, where frosts and snow usual. Rainy areas correspond to Pará's coastal lands and western Amazonas, where annual rainfall greater than 3,000 millimeters. In Southeast on Serra do Mar (São Paulo State), recorded annual rainfall exceeds 3,500 millimeters. Drought areas located in interior Northeast, where annual rainfall under 500 millimeters. Maximum precipitation occurs during summer-autumn in most parts of country, except for Roraima and north Amazonas, where rainy season occurs during winter because these two states are located in Northern Hemisphere.

Principal Rivers: Vast, dense drainage system consisting of eight hydrographic basins. Amazon and Tocantins-Araguaia basins account for 56 percent of total drainage area. World's greatest fluvial island, Bananal, located in Center-West Region on Araguaia. With ten of world's twenty greatest rivers, Amazon (Amazonas) is world's largest in volume of water and one of world's longest (6,762 kilometers, of which 3,615 kilometers are in Brazil), discharging 15.5 percent of all fresh water flowing into oceans from rivers. Union of Paraná and Iguaçu in South, at border between Brazil, Argentina, and Paraguay, forms Iguaçu Falls at Foz do Iguaçu.

Society

Population: 160,960,881, according to IBGE's February 14, 1998, count. Largest part of population lives in Southeast (63 million). Northeast has 45 million people; South, 23.1 million; North, 11.1 million; and Center-West, 10.2 million. Average annual population growth rate: 1.4 percent (1992–98), as compared with 3.15 percent in 1950–55. Urbanization rate: 80 percent (1997). Projected 169 million population in 2000 and 200.3 million in 2020. Population density, 18.38 people per square kilometer (1996), although majority crowd around coastal cities.

Age Structure and Aging: Although nearly half of Brazilians are in their mid-twenties, fraction under fourteen years of age has fallen from 43 percent to 34 percent, while fraction over sixty years of age has risen from 4 percent to 8 percent. Median age:

24.3 (1995, Pan American Health Organization—PAHO/ World Health Organization—WHO). Pension fund assets as percentage of gross domestic product (GDP—see Glossary): 10.

Birthrate: 21.16 births per 1,000 population (1995 estimate). Average for 1990–95: 24.6.

Death Rate: Eight deaths per 1,000 population (1995 estimate). Average for 1990–95: 7.5.

Net Migration Rate: Zero migrant(s) per 1,000 population (1995 estimate).

Infant Mortality Rate: According to 1991 census, 49.7 deaths per 1,000 live births, as compared with 69.1 per 1,000 in 1980. United Nations Development Programme (UNDP) figures: 57 per 1,000 in 1993; 59.5 per 1,000 in 1994. Rate in Northeast in 1995: 122 deaths per 1,000 live births.

Life Expectancy at Birth: In 1995, 67.1 years (men, 62.1; women, 68.9). Seniors over sixty years numbered 10.9 million in 1995, or 7.4 percent of the population.

Total Fertility Rate: About 2.3 children born per woman (1995 average estimate). Population growth curtailed sharply since 1975 with one of world's most successful family planning drives. Female sterilization (tubal ligation) and birth-control pills most common forms of contraception: 27 percent of women of child-bearing age have been sterilized, and 26 percent use birth-control pills. According to the new Family Planning Law of January 12, 1996, family planning is right of every citizen.

Health: Public expenditures on health as percentage of GDP: 2.5 percent (1995). Central government health expenditures as percentage of total central government expenditures: 6.7 percent. Total health expenditures as percentage of GDP: 5.8 percent. Physicians per 10,000 people: 13 (1990). Nurses per 10,000: 3.7 (1990). Hospital beds per 1,000 people: 3.6 (1990). Maternal mortality rate: 141 per 100,000 live births (1994). Mortality rate for cancer among women: 60 percent (1995). Cholera cases: 49,956 (1993), as compared with 30,054 in 1992. Malaria cases: 577,098 (1991). Cumulative cases of acquired immune deficiency syndrome (AIDS) reported to PAHO/ WHO as of September 1997: 10,845 (fourth highest rate in world); total AIDS deaths: 54,813. Human immunodeficiency virus (HIV) estimated prevalence in 1994: 550,000.

Housing and Sanitation: Country has serious problems resulting from growing demand for new housing and basic sanitation, in part because urbanization rate has increased from 47.0 percent in 1960 to 78.2 percent in 1991. In 1991, 70.7 percent of Brazilian households served by public water supply system, with 92.2 percent having indoor plumbing equipment. In urban areas, 95 percent of dwellings receive water and sewerage service, and 98 percent have electric power. Discrepancies, such as inadequate sanitation, exist between poor and better-off favelas. Disposal systems cover 84 percent of urban areas and 32 percent of rural areas. In rural areas, only 61 percent of dwellings have water and sewerage access, and only 55 percent have electricity. Roughly 70 percent of all Brazilian households have refrigerators. Approximately one installed telephone and one automobile for every ten Brazilians.

Ethnic Groups: Portuguese, who began colonizing in sixteenth century, and various European immigrant groups—mainly Germans, Italians, Spanish, and Polish—constitute about 55 percent; mixed Caucasian and African, 38 percent; African (brought to Brazil as slaves), about 6 percent; and others—Amerindian (principally Tupí and Guaraní linguistic stock), Japanese, and other Asians and Arabs—less than 1 percent. São Paulo has largest Japanese community outside Japan, except for Hawaii.

Amerindians: Indians do not have ownership of land that they occupy permanently. Brazil has 651 Indian reservations totaling 94.6 million hectares. Largest is Yanomami (Amazonas and Roraima states), with 9.6 million hectares and a population of 18,000 members. Guaraní total 20,000 members.

Language: Portuguese, official language, spoken by all but few isolated Amerindians, who retain their languages, and immigrants who have not yet acquired proficiency in Portuguese. There are no official regional dialects. Brazil only Portuguese-speaking country in South America.

Education: Investment in education (as percentage of government budget): 2.7 percent (1995). Education system organized on three levels: primary (eight years), secondary (three years), and higher education. States and municipalities largely responsible for primary education; states control secondary education; private institutions largely administer higher education, except for federal universities. School enrollment figures reported in last census (1990) were: preschool, 3.9 million in 57,614 schools; primary, 29.4 million in 206,817 schools; and secondary, 3.7 million in 10,928 schools. Primary school free and compulsory for children between ages of seven and fourteen. Average student in Brazilian public school receives four hours or less of class time per day, although national guidelines suggest six hours per day. Primary and secondary schools enroll only 88 percent of Brazil's children. High drop-out rates and grade repetition endemic problems. Only about a third of students enrolled in primary school finish eight-year "mandatory" schooling. Estimated 5 million children and 25 percent of poorest children do not attend school. Of sixty-eight major universities in Brazil, thirty-five are federal, twenty private or church-related, two municipal, and eleven state-supported. Nearly all states and Federal District have one or more federal universities, all of which operate directly under Ministry of Education. In many states, there are also one or more state universities and one or more Catholic universities. About 800 other colleges and institutions of higher education grant degrees in areas such as engineering, medicine, agriculture, law, economics, and business administration. Three military academies train officers of Brazilian Army (Exército Brasileiro), Brazilian Navy (Marinha do Brasil), and Brazilian Air Force (Fôrça Aérea Brasileira—FAB), granting diplomas equivalent to a B.A. degree. Only army and FAB schools of engineering grant graduate and postgraduate degrees.

Literacy: Of total number of Brazilians over fifteen years of age (100.7 million), 81 percent literate; 19 percent illiterate (1991 census), as compared with a 25.9 percent illiteracy rate in 1970. By 2000 illiteracy will be estimated 16 percent.

Religion: Official statistics: Roman Catholic, 70 percent; Protestant, 19.2 percent; other, 10.8 percent. Affiliations not necessarily mutually exclusive. Practice of folk religions and Afro-Brazilian cults based on animist beliefs and slave and Indian traditions—such as *umbanda* and *candomblé*—widespread among all ethnic groups. Also significant trend in evangelism among Catholic and Protestant groups, particularly in São Paulo area. Mormon Church of Latter-Day Saints and Jehovah's Witnesses active in Brazil as well. Important Jewish communities in states of São Paulo and Rio Grande do Sul, especially in respective capital cities of São Paulo and Porto Alegre, as well as in Rio de Janeiro.

Economy

Gross Domestic Product (GDP): Economist Intelligence Unit (EIU) estimated US$775 billion for 1997, as compared with US$387 billion for 1992. EIU's estimated GDP real growth rate for 1997, 3.7 percent; and 1998, 4.0 percent. Of 1995 GDP of US$717 billion, 47.3 percent generated by trade and services, 42.0 percent by industry, and 10.7 percent by agriculture.

Per Capita GDP and Minimum Wage: Per capita GDP US$5,128 (1997). GDP per capita average annual growth rate, 0.8 percent (1985–94). Minimum wage as of June 1995: US$108.46, or just over R$100 a month (for value of *real*—see Glossary), as compared with US$68.93, or R$70 a month, in July 1994, amounting to an actual increase of only 10 percent because of inflation. Minimum wage raised by 12 percent in May 1996.

Inflation: Inflation reached 50 percent per month by June 1994 and averaged 31.2 percent a month in 1994, for total of 2,294.0 percent that year. As result of *Real* Plan, declined to monthly rates of between 1 and 3 percent in 1995, for an annual rate of 25.9 percent. In 1996: 16.5 percent; 1997: 7.2 percent.

Employment and Unemployment: Estimated labor force in 1997: 65.5 million. Services sector employed 66 percent of women and 42 percent of men; industry, 14 percent of women and 23 percent of men; business, 15 percent of women and 15 percent of men; civil construction, 11 percent of men; other activities, 5 percent of women and 9 percent of men. Men held 61 percent of total jobs. Women's wages averaged 62 percent of those of men but declined to 54 percent in services sector. Recorded unemployment rate (includes only people actively looking for work and over age fifteen) in 1997: 5.5 percent.

Agriculture: One of world's leading exporters of agricultural products. Grain production in 1996: 73 million tons. According to estimates of Food and Agriculture Organization (FAO) of United Nations, Brazil produced 79.4 million tons of grains (record crop) in 1995, as compared with 56.1 million tons in 1990. Center-West and South and Rondônia account for 90 percent of crops. In 1995, 81.6 million tons of crops harvested, but producers saw their income reduced by about US$10.4 billion, or 26 percent, owing to price decreases.

Country has 46.5 million hectares under cultivation, 174.1 million hectares in grazing lands, and 140.6 million hectares in arable land. Crop year runs from June to May. From 1982 to 1992, total cultivated area fell by 30 percent, but production of certain grains, in tons per hectare, increased by 14.9 percent. Agricultural sector employed 29.4 percent of labor force in 1992. It accounted for 10.7 percent of GDP in 1996. It accounts for almost 40 percent of exports. Except for wheat, Brazil largely self-sufficient in food. Each farmer feeds 3.6 city dwellers, whereas 2.5 farmers were needed to feed each city dweller in 1940. Brazil is world's largest exporter of coffee, orange juice concentrate, and tobacco, and second largest exporter of sugar and soybeans. In addition to sugar, Brazil produces a large quantity of ethanol (mainly used as fuel) from crushed sugarcane. Other important crops: manioc, corn, and rice. In addition to oranges, principal fruits are lemons, mangoes, guavas, passion fruit, and tangerines.

Industry: Capital goods (see Glossary) production increased in 1970s with creation of new companies and large capital investments in transportation, communications, and energy infrastructure. New technologically sophisticated industries begun in that decade included weapons, aircraft, and computer manufacturing and nuclear power production. Industrial growth slowed by economic crisis of 1980s. After start of *Real* Plan, industrial production increased vigorously by 7.5 percent from 1993 to 1994. Manufacturing accounted for 62 percent of exports in 1996. Industrial growth in 1997 was 3.9 percent.

Energy: 94 percent of current energy capacity hydroelectric. Electricity consumption expanded by 7.6 percent in 1995 (versus 4.2 percent for GDP) and by 5.7 percent in first half of 1996 (versus projected GDP growth rate of 3 percent). A dozen hydroelectric and thermal plants being privatized because electricity demand expected to outstrip supply by 1999, and state unable to pay off energy-sector debts. A blackout in April 1997 affecting 20 million people expected to become an increasingly common occurrence. Predominance of highland rivers presents great potential for hydroelectric power production. Hydropower generating potential: 106,500 to 129,046 megawatts/year, of which 24.4 percent in operation or under construction, 35.8 percent inventoried, and 39.8 percent estimated (1994 estimate). In 1992, of 233,682 gigawatt-hours generated, 217,782 hydroelectric, 14,454 thermal, and 1,446 nuclear. Nuclear power generation in early 1998 was still negligible. About 60 percent of energy supply derived from renewable sources, such as hydroelectricity and ethanol. National oil production surpassed a record 840,000 barrels per day (bpd) in 1997. Petroleum imports in 1995: 760,000 bpd (442,000 bpd crude; 318,000 bpd derivatives). Brazil relies on natural gas for only 2 percent of energy needs. Produced more than 17 million cubic meters of natural gas per day in early 1990s.

Services: In 1994 services accounted for approximately 43.6 percent of work force.

Trade Balance: Total trade in 1997: US$109.4 billion, compared with US$77.3 billion in 1994. In ten years, 1985–95, foreign trade of Brazil accounted for US$521.8 billion, with surplus of US$129.3 billion. Foreign trade deficit in 1997: US$10.9 billion.

Imports: Totaled US$60.1 billion in 1997, as compared with US$20.5 billion in 1993. Average import duties dropped to 14 percent from 51 percent since 1988. Major suppliers in 1996: United States, 22.2 percent; Germany, 9.0 percent; Argentina, 12.7 percent; and Japan, 5.2 percent. Half of Brazil's imports of manufactured goods come from United States. Brazil only other major Latin American country besides Chile to import oil, which in 1996 cost an estimated US$6.4 billion.

Exports: Totaled US$49.2 billion in 1997, as compared with US$39.6 billion in 1993. Brazil's strengthened currency has made its exports less competitive. Brazil exports large part of world's production of tin, iron, manganese, and steel. Also one of world's largest exporters of food, mainly sugar, coffee, cocoa, soybeans, and orange juice. Major markets in 1996: United States, 19.5 percent; Argentina, 10.8 percent; Japan, 6.4 percent; and the Netherlands, 7.4 percent.

Tariffs: Average tariff rate: 14.0 percent; tariff ceiling: 70 percent on automobiles (imposed in mid-1995).

Reserves: International reserves in first quarter of 1998: US$63 billion.

Budget Deficit: Current account deficit in 1997: US$32.3 billion. EIU's current account deficit estimate for 1998: US$33.6 billion.

Internal Debt: Total debt of public sector (federal, state, and municipal governments): US$77 billion (1994). Totaled record US$213 billion (36.8 percent of GDP) in 1995, according to official figures, or US$267 billion (46 percent of GDP), if some unregistered existing debts included. IBGE calculated total domestic debt to be R$304.8 billion in September 1995, or 60.9 percent of estimated 1995 GNP. Public Sector Borrowing Requirement reached 5.6 percent of GDP in 1996, as compared with 5.1 percent in 1995.

External Debt: US$177.6 billion (public and private) in 1997; US$193.2 billion estimated by EIU for 1998. Total debt service: US$15 billion (1996). Debt-service ratio: 58.7 percent (1997).

Official Exchange Rate: On July 1, 1994, new currency, the *real* (pl., *reais*), introduced. As of January 31, 1996, government widened to 7.07 percent range within which value vis-à-vis United States dollar may vary. Exchange rate on April 13, 1998: R$1.140=US$1.

Foreign Investment: US$52 billion in 1996, US$38 billion in 1995, and US$25 billion in 1994.

Fiscal Year: Calendar year.

Fiscal Policy: Stabilization program in 1994–96 developed originally by Fernando Henrique Cardoso (president, 1995–) as minister of finance (May 1993 to April 1994). End of inflation in 1994 quickly increased demand and spending power of poorer Brazilians especially. Government endeavoring to dampen inflationary pressures. In order to consolidate stabilization program and put Brazil on path to long-term sustainable growth, government must implement wide-ranging structural reforms. Restrictive monetary policy has kept interest rates high and reduced aggregate demand and inflation, while improving trade balance. Fiscal position deteriorated considerably in 1995. Expansion of internal public debt a major threat to government's control over fiscal and monetary policy. Monetary policy somewhat more flexible since August 1995 because of lower level of economic activity, declining inflation rate, and abundance of foreign capital to finance current account.

Transportation and Communications

Roads: Since 1970s government has given funding priority to roads and highways. São Paulo, Rio de Janeiro, and other major cities have modern metropolitan expressways. Practically all state capitals linked by paved roads. Brazilian highways of modern design. Road network most developed, but maintenance remains problem. Highway transportation of passengers and freight leading form of transportation in Brazil, with highway system 1,670,148 kilometers in length (increase of more than 300 percent since 1970s), of which 161,503 kilometers paved. At least three-fourths of Brazil's population and goods transported by highway. Although Brazil borders all but two South American countries, only in southern regions are links to adjoining countries adequate; in North and Center-West, roads to adjoining countries barely passable or only planned. Large areas remain inaccessible. In part because of general disregard of traffic laws, automobile collisions claim lives of roughly 50,000 Brazilians per year, and drivers responsible for accidents rarely held accountable. New Transit Code took effect in January 1998, imposing a tough new set of traffic laws.

Railroads: Rail network, in proportion to highways, relatively small. Rail lines cover only 30,129 kilometers, of which 2,150 kilometers electrified. However, some special projects have been implemented, such as Steel Railroad (Ferrovia do Aço) to connect inland iron ore mining areas to steel mills and port facilities on Southeast's coast. Its western network sold to a foreign consortium in early 1996. Federal Railroad System, Inc. (Rêde Ferroviária Federal S.A.—RFFSA) has operated 73 percent of Brazil's suburban railroads, with 21,951 kilometers of track and 40,500 employees in nineteen states. In 1995 RFFSA hauled 85 million tons of cargo, and Southeastern Railroad Line accounted for 45 million tons. Central-eastern network 7,132 kilometers; western network 1,620 kilometers. Privatization of financially troubled RFFSA began in 1995.

Subways: Recife, Rio de Janeiro, and São Paulo have new urban subway systems. Although São Paulo needs a 200-kilometer network, it had only forty-three kilometers in 1996. Same US$0.60 fare takes one anywhere on São Paulo's Metrô network. New South Line of Rio de Janeiro's Metrô extends to Copacabana.

Ports: Thirty-six deep-water ports. Most, including Rio de Janeiro and Santos (largest in Latin America), being privatized.

Waterways: Some 50,000 kilometers navigable. Boats main form of transportation in many parts of Amazon Basin.

Amazon navigable by ocean steamers as far as 3,680 kilometers to Iquitos, Peru. Constitutional amendment ending state monopoly of domestic shipping approved August 15, 1995. Until regulations approved, foreign ships may carry only passengers.

Pipelines: Approximately 2,000 kilometers for crude oil, 465 kilometers for refined products, and 257 kilometers for natural gas. Planned Bolivia-Brazil gas pipeline targeted for completion in 1997; will be 3,415 kilometers in length, running from Santa Cruz, Bolivia, to São Paulo. Pipeline will also connect to states of Rio de Janeiro and Minas Gerais and link with existing refineries and production fields in São Paulo's Campos and Santos basins.

Air Transport and Airports: Vast network of air services in existence since 1930s. Direct air connections to all other countries in South America, several in Central America, and all three in North America, as well as to every continent. Routes—both at commuter and medium- to long-range level—operated by various commercial airlines, increasingly using airplanes designed and built in Brazil. All airlines registered in Brazil are private enterprises, some allowing foreign-equity participation. Major airlines include Rio Grande do Sul Airline (Viação Aérea Rio Grande do Sul—Varig) and São Paulo Airline (Viação Aérea São Paulo—VASP). Ten fully operational international airports.

Radio: Number of radios—about 30 million (1995). Number of radio stations: at least 2,751; 334 being installed. Range of radio stations: national/regional, 2,932; tropical (in tropical areas), eighty-two; shortwave, 151; and FM, 1,248. Estimated audience: 100 million. Government has ultimate control over radio stations through power to control licensing. Government broadcasts domestically for hour each night by requisitioning time on all national radio stations. Rádio Nacional (government's overseas radio service) transmits information and cultural programs supportive of Brazilian foreign policy and commercial activity to Europe, the Americas, Africa, and parts of Asia. Station's medium-wave and short-wave broadcasts in Portuguese to the Amazon Region. Brazilian Radio Broadcasting Company (Empresa Brasileira de Rádiodifusão—Radiobrás) became Brasília-based Brazilian Communications Company (Empresa Brasileira de Comunicações S.A.—

Radiobrás) in 1988. Radiobrás directs programming.

Television: Number of televisions increased by only 200,000 from 1985 to 1995, when total figure reached 26.2 million. Estimated potential audience: 80 million. TV programming run primarily by private enterprises. Licenses to operate issued by executive branch through Ministry of Communications and approved by Congress. Number of television stations, at least 257 and thirty-one under installation; commercial TV stations, 269; educational and university TV stations, twenty (owned by federal government, state governments, universities, and educational foundations). TV networks: Globo Television Network (Rêde Globo de Televisão), eighty-one stations; Rêde Bandeirantes, sixty-three stations; Brazilian Television System (Sistema Brasileiro de Televisão—SBT), seventy-seven stations; Rêde Manchete, thirty-six stations; TV Record, twelve stations. Domestic dissemination of signals beamed by all five national networks through two domestic Brasilsat satellites operated by Brazilian Telecommunications Company (Empresa Brasileira de Telecomuniçacões—Embratel), government's national communications corporation. Embratel also operates microwave system available to all stations. Various "cable" systems are also being developed in major Brazilian cities. Rather than actually transmitting by physical cable, these systems work via satellite to individual receiving dishes installed for subscribers. NET System, being installed in major cities, operates by cable. Every major television market in Brazil has five networks represented by affiliate station. Much of television programming entertainment, especially famous *telenovelas* (prime-time soap-opera-style dramas). Most cities also have educational TV channel, TV Educativa, which carries cultural, documentary, and sometimes foreign language programs.

Telephones: Number of telephones 13,237,852 (1995, IBGE). About half of telephones and one-third of installed cellular phone lines in São Paulo. Residents of São Paulo and Rio de Janeiro must pay about US$3,000 to obtain telephone line. Nine lines per 100 population. About 98 percent of rural properties have no telephone lines. Government plans to triple number of fixed phone lines to 40 million by 2003 and to increase number of cellular links from 800,000 to 8.2 million by 1999. In July 1996, Brazilian legislators formulating plans to privatize state-owned monopoly of Brazilian Telecommunications (Telecomunicações Brasileiras S.A.—Telebrás), which has 90 percent of Brazilian telephone subscribers and twenty-seven regional companies. Telebrás launched three cable systems but was facing stiff competition in cable market from publishing giants Grupo Abril (TVA Brasil) and Globo (Globocabo and NET Brasil). Sales of telecommunications products in 1995 accounted for US$2.1 billion. In 1997 Brazil had 7,600 kilometers of fiber optic cable; additional 7,400 kilometers scheduled for completion in 1999.

Telecommunications Organizations: Two main telecommunications organizations are National Department of Telecommunications (Departamento Nacional de Telecomunicações—Dentel), located within Ministry of Communications in Brasília; and Brazilian Association of Radio and Television Stations (Associação Brasileira de Emissoras de Rádio e Televisão—ABERT), also located in Brasília. Dentel supervises television and radio broadcasting.

Print Media: 333 newspapers published daily in Brazil in 1993. All newspapers privately owned and operated. Total daily circulation varies between 2.2 and 2.6 million. Leading newspapers: *Folha de São Paulo* (São Paulo; liberal, center-left; daily circulation 540,000 copies; Sunday circulation 1,200,000); *O Globo* (Rio de Janeiro; conservative; 280,000, daily; 525,000, Sunday); *O Estado de São Paulo* (São Paulo; independent; 320,000, daily; 650,000, Sunday); *Jornal do Brasil* (Rio de Janeiro; Catholic, conservative; 116,000, daily; 160,000, Sunday); weekday *Gazeta Mercantil* (São Paulo; business; 100,000, daily); *Correio Braziliense* (Brasília; 50,000, daily; 100,000, Sunday); *Jornal de Brasília* (Brasília; 22,000, daily; 26,000, Sunday). Periodicals: Of several hundred periodicals published in Brazil, most influential and widely circulated news and current affairs magazines are: *Veja* (1,207,521), *Visão,* and *IstoÉ* (491,752). Leading business news biweekly is *Exáme* (188,000). Leading illustrated general interest magazine is *Manchete* (130,000). All but Rio de Janeiro-based *Manchete* published in São Paulo. Domestic news agencies: Rio de Janeiro-based Agência Globo and Agência JB; Brasília-based Agência ANDA and Empresa Brasileira de Noticias; and São Paulo-based Agência Estado and Agência Fôlha.

Government and Politics

Administrative Subdivisions: Composed of 5,581 municipalities (1997) and 9,274 districts (1995). These subdivisions combined into twenty-six states and Federal District of Brasília. These states and Federal District form five major regions: North, including states of Acre, Amapá, Amazonas, Pará, Rondônia, Roraima, and Tocantins; Northeast, including Alagoas, Bahia, Ceará, Maranhão, Paraíba, Pernambuco, Piauí, Rio Grande do Norte, and Sergipe; Southeast, including Espírito Santo, Minas Gerais, Rio de Janeiro, and São Paulo; South, including Paraná, Rio Grande do Sul, and Santa Catarina; and Center-West, including Federal District, Goiás, Mato Grosso, and Mato Grosso do Sul. North Region, country's largest, covers 45.3 percent of national territory; Northeast, 18.3 percent; Southeast, 10.9 percent; South, smallest, 6.8 percent; and Center-West, 18.9 percent. Brasília seat of government, housing executive, legislative, and judicial branches.

Government: Federative republic with broad powers granted to federal government. Constitution, reenacted/revised on October 5, 1988, establishes presidential system with three branches—executive, legislative, and judicial. Chief of state and head of government is president. Fernando Henrique Cardoso won 1994 presidential elections in first round on October 3, taking 54 percent of vote, and assumed office on January 1, 1995. President assisted by vice president (elected with president) and presidentially appointed and headed cabinet. Cardoso may stand for reelection in 1998. Bicameral National Congress (Congresso Nacional) consists of Federal Senate (Senado Federal), with eighty-one members (three for each state and Federal District) popularly elected to eight-year terms, and Chamber of Deputies (Câmara dos Deputados), with 513 members popularly elected to four-year terms. Elections for both houses simultaneous and based on proportional representation weighted in favor of less populous states. Suffrage compulsory for Brazilians above age of eighteen. Highest court Federal Supreme Court (Supremo Tribunal Federal—STF), whose eleven justices, including chief justice, appointed by president to serve until age seventy. Each state has own judicial system. Federal revenue-sharing program, established by 1988 constitution, provides states with substantial resources. Framework of state and local government similar to federal government. Governors may stand for reelection to four-year terms in 1998. Federal District also governed by governor and vice governor. Governors have more limited powers than counterparts in United States because of centralized nature of Brazilian system and 1988 consutution, which reserves to federal government all powers not specifically delegated to states. States and municipalities have limited taxing authority.

National Election Dates: Presidential, congressional, and state elections occur simultaneously every four years in October and November; held in October–November 1994 and scheduled for 1998 and 2002. Dates of municipal elections: October–November 1996, 2000, and 2004.

Politics: Returned to democratic civilian government in 1985 after more than two decades of military rule (1964–85). President Fernando Collor de Mello elected in November 1989 and took office on March 15, 1990, first directly elected president in twenty-nine years. Chamber of Deputies impeached Collor in September 1992 on corruption charges, and he was removed from office by Senate vote that December. His vice president, Itamar Franco, then assumed presidency. In October 1994, Brazil held elections for presidency, state governorships, Chamber of Deputies, and two-thirds of Senate. Fernando Henrique Cardoso (president, 1995–) gained election on strength of heterodox alliance between his Brazilian Social Democracy Party (Partido da Social Democracia Brasileira—PSDB) and two center-right parties, Liberal Front Party (Partido da Frente Liberal—PFL) and Brazilian Labor Party (Partido Trabalhista Brasileiro—PTB). Alliance seen at time as strictly electoral, with little chance of lasting long into administration. Thus far, it has remained intact, with Cardoso adding Brazil's largest party, Brazilian Democratic Movement Party (Partido do Movimento Democrático Brasileiro—PMDB), to coalition immediately after election. Rivalries among parties for plum federal appointments in key states and regions have, however, plagued coalition, as has factiousness within parties. Congress uses committee system much like United States; there are six Senate committees and sixteen House committees. A notable distinction is absence of conference committees to work out differences between competing legislative texts; instead, bill modified by one house must be returned to originating house for up-or-down vote on modifications. Party leaders play key role in setting voting agenda. Also important are "rapporteurs" for individual bills; negative rapporteur's report can effectively kill bill before it reaches committee vote. Since Cardoso's inauguration, Congress has devoted itself largely to constitutional reform. Each constitutional amendment requires approval by margin of two-thirds, twice over, in each house (total of four votes). Despite obstacles, Congress has moved constitutional reform forward farther and faster than expected, particularly in economic area.

Political Parties: Fourteen political parties span most of political spectrum. PMDB (Brazilian Democratic Movement Party) Brazil's largest party; PFL (Liberal Front Party) is second largest party and largest on center-right; PTB (Brazilian Labor Party) is populist party confined to several western states; PSDB (Brazilian Social Democracy Party) includes President Cardoso and espouses a center-left social democratic agenda and free-market economy with greater involvement in health care and education; Brazilian Socialist Party (Partido Socialista Brasileiro—PSB) is leftist party; Communist Party of Brazil (Partido Comunista do Brasil—PC do B) still has Soviet-style platform. Other parties include Democratic Social Party (Partido Democrático Social—PDS) and Democratic Labor Party (Partido Democrático Trabalhista—PDT), populist party whose leaders, including Leonel de Moura Brizola, stress greater government role in addressing Brazil's social problems. Liberal Party (Partido Liberal) is also center-right party, popular among small businessmen at state and local levels in São Paulo and Rio de Janeiro; National Reconstruction Party (Partido da Reconstrução Nacional—PRN) is party of former President Collor de Mello; Popular Socialist Party (Partido Popular Socialista—PPS) is former Brazilian Communist Party, renamed in 1993; Progressive Party (Partido Progressista—PP) is center-right party supporting market-oriented policies; Progressive Renewal Party (Partido Progressista Renovador—PPR) is another center-right party supporting free-market reforms; and Workers' Party (Partido dos Trabalhadores—PT) is European-style leftist party headed by party founder Luis Inacio "Lula" da Silva.

Foreign Relations: Traditionally, United States-oriented but foreign policy increasingly diverse and pragmatic. Foreign policy dominated by trade concerns. Highly active and professional Ministry of Foreign Affairs popularly known as Itamaraty. Guiding principles of Brazilian diplomacy, as defined by President Cardoso, involve quest for greater democracy in international relations and support for economic multilateralism with clear and defined rules. Defense of principle of sustainable development (see Glossary) at Rio de Janeiro's Earth Summit in June 1992, conclusion in 1995 of

Uruguay Round of General Agreement on Tariffs and Trade (GATT—see Glossary), and desire for permanent seat on United Nations Security Council all part of these basic objectives. Parallel regional objectives include need for Brazil to seek regional options for increasing country's bargaining power. Brazilian proposal for creation of South American Free Trade Association (SAFTA) is important step in this direction.

International Agreements and Membership: Party to Inter-American Treaty of Reciprocal Assistance of 1947 (Rio Treaty) (see Glossary), Treaty of Tlatelolco (see Glossary), and Missile Technology Control Regime (see Glossary). Until June 20, 1997, Brazil refused to sign the Nuclear Nonproliferation Treaty (NPT). Memberships in international organizations many and varied, such as United Nations and specialized agencies; Organization of American States (see Glossary) and specialized agencies; regional trade and cooperation organizations, including Common Market of the South (Mercado Comum do Sul—Mercosul; see Glossary); international commodity agreements; and multilateral lending institutions.

National Security

Armed Forces: Total active-duty troops and officers: 314,700, including 132,000 conscripts (1997). Brazilian Army (Exército Brasileiro), largest service (accounting for 66 percent of total armed forces), has 200,000 active-duty officers and troops, including 125,000 conscripts. Brazilian Navy (Marinha do Brasil) totals 64,700 members, including 1,300-member Naval Aviation (Aviação Naval), 14,600-member Marines, and 2,000 conscripts; and Brazilian Air Force (Fôrça Aérea Brasileira—FAB), also 50,000, including 5,000 conscripts. Reserves: trained first-line: 1,115,000 (400,000 subject to immediate recall); second-line: 225,000.

Conscription: Twelve months officially; usually nine to ten months in practice, but can be reduced or extended by six months.

Defense Budget: Total 1997: US$12 billion. Investment in armed forces (as percentage of government budget): 1.7 percent (1995). Except 1990, military spending as percentage of federal budget has declined steadily since 1985. Fifth-ranked recipient of arms transfer agreements of developing nations in

1995, Brazil received US$800 million worth of arms.

Military Organization: Army divided geographically into eleven military regions, each with military headquarters. Military regions subordinate to seven military commands: Southern Command (Porto Alegre), Planalto Military Command (Brasília), Amazonian Command (Manaus), Eastern Command (Rio de Janeiro), Southeastern Command (São Paulo), Northeastern Command (Recife); Western Command (Campo Grande). Units include: eight divisions (three with regional headquarters); one armored cavalry brigade (two mechanized, one armored, one artillery battalion); three armored infantry brigades (each with two infantry, one armored, and one artillery battalion); four mechanized cavalry brigades (each with three infantry and one artillery battalion); thirteen motor infantry brigades (twenty-six battalions); one mountain brigade; four "jungle" brigades (seven battalions); one frontier brigade (five battalions); one airborne brigade (three airborne battalions and one special forces battalion); two coast and air defense artillery brigades; three cavalry guard regiments; twenty-eight artillery groups (four self-propelled, six medical, eighteen field); two engineer groups (each with four battalions, including two railroad battalions, to be increased to thirty-four battalions); helicopter brigade (forming, to comprise five helicopters per battalion). Navy best structured branch of armed forces in terms of quality of equipment and troop preparation. Two naval commands: Brasília and Manaus. Five oceanic naval districts: Rio de Janeiro (headquarters, 1st Naval District), Salvador (headquarters, 2d Naval District), Natal (headquarters, 3d Naval District), Belém (headquarters, 4th Naval District), and Rio Grande do Sul (headquarters, 5th Naval District). One riverine naval district: Ladário (headquarters, 6th Naval District). Air Force has three general commands—air, support, and personnel; organized into seven regional commands, as follows: 1st at Belém, 2d at Recife, 3d at Rio de Janeiro, 4th at São Paulo, 5th at Porto Alegre, 6th at Brasília, and 7th at Manaus. Five operational commands: Tactical Command (ten groups), Coastal or Maritime Command (four groups), Transport Command (six groups), Special Transport Group (VIP), and Training Command. Also one Administrative Command (one group) (IISS).

Police: Security forces, including state paramilitary Military Police (Polícia Militar—PM), under army control and considered an army reserve, totaled 385,600 in 1997.

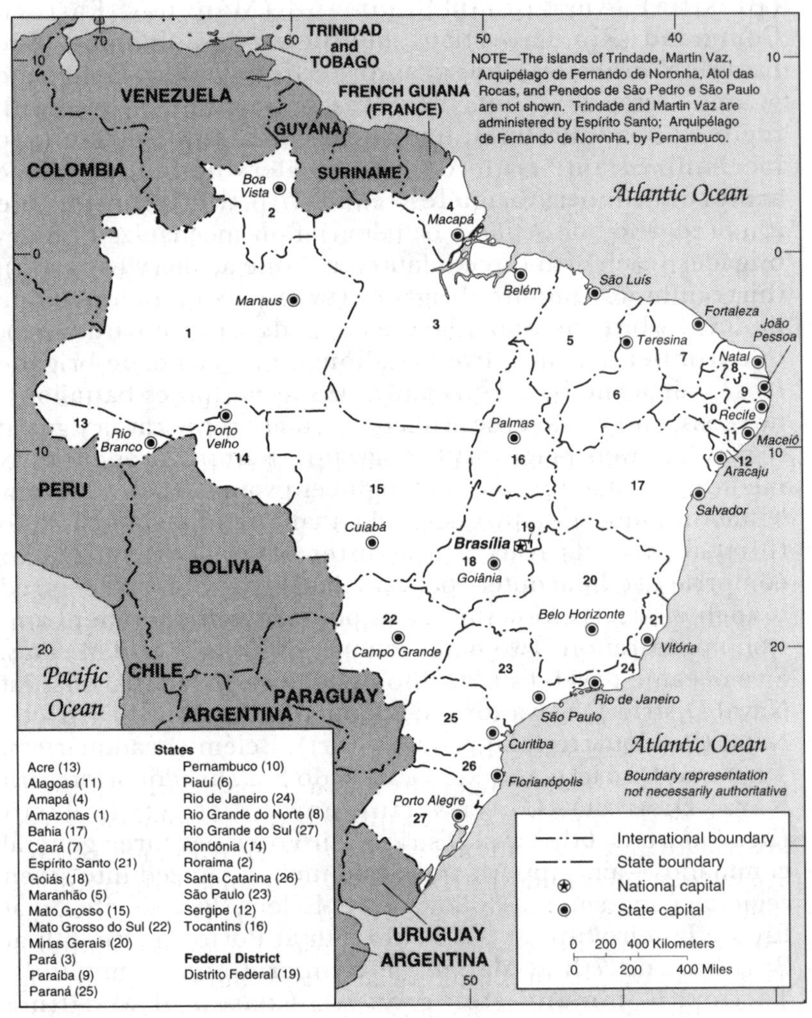

TRINIDAD and TOBAGO
VENEZUELA
GUYANA
SURINAME
FRENCH GUIANA (FRANCE)
COLOMBIA
NOTE—The islands of Trindade, Martin Vaz, Arquipélago de Fernando de Noronha, Atol das Rocas, and Penedos de São Pedro e São Paulo are not shown. Trindade and Martin Vaz are administered by Espírito Santo; Arquipélago de Fernando de Noronha, by Pernambuco.
Atlantic Ocean
Boa Vista
Macapá
Manaus
Belém
São Luís
Fortaleza
João Pessoa
Teresina
Natal
Recife
Maceió
Aracaju
Salvador
Palmas
Porto Velho
Rio Branco
PERU
BOLIVIA
Cuiabá
Brasília
Goiânia
Belo Horizonte
Vitória
Campo Grande
Rio de Janeiro
São Paulo
Curitiba
Florianópolis
Porto Alegre
Pacific Ocean
CHILE
PARAGUAY
ARGENTINA
URUGUAY
ARGENTINA
Atlantic Ocean
Boundary representation not necessarily authoritative
International boundary
State boundary
National capital
State capital
0 200 400 Kilometers
0 200 400 Miles
States
Acre (13)
Alagoas (11)
Amapá (4)
Amazonas (1)
Bahia (17)
Ceará (7)
Espírito Santo (21)
Goiás (18)
Maranhão (5)
Mato Grosso (15)
Mato Grosso do Sul (22)
Minas Gerais (20)
Pará (3)
Paraíba (9)
Paraná (25)
Pernambuco (10)
Piauí (6)
Rio de Janeiro (24)
Rio Grande do Norte (8)
Rio Grande do Sul (27)
Rondônia (14)
Roraima (2)
Santa Catarina (26)
São Paulo (23)
Sergipe (12)
Tocantins (16)
Federal District
Distrito Federal (19)

Figure 1. Administrative Divisions of Brazil, 1997.

Introduction

MORE LIKE A CONTINENT than a country, the Federative Republic of Brazil (República Federativa do Brasil) is geographically larger than the conterminous United States. It is the world's fifth largest nation in physical size, exceeded only by Russia, China, the United States, and Canada. By far the largest country in Latin America, Brazil occupies nearly half the land mass of South America and borders every South American country except Chile and Ecuador. With 90 percent of its territory lying between the equator and the Tropic of Capricorn, Brazil is the world's largest tropical country. The Amazon Region has the world's largest river system; the Amazon is the source of 20 percent of the world's fresh water.

Brazil's history prior to becoming an independent country in 1822 is intertwined mainly with that of Portugal. Unlike the other viceroyalties of Latin America, which divided into twenty countries upon attaining independence, the Viceroyalty of Brazil became a single nation, with a single language transcending all diversities and regionalisms. Brazil is the only Portuguese-speaking Latin American country, and its Luso-Brazilian culture differs in subtle ways from the Hispanic heritage of most of its neighbors. During the late nineteenth and early twentieth centuries, millions of Italians, Germans, Arabs, Japanese, and other immigrants entered Brazil and in various ways altered the dominant social system. Their descendants, however, are nearly all Portuguese-speaking Brazilians.

Except for a small indigenous Indian population, Brazilians are one people, with a single culture. Anthropologist Darcy Ribeiro attributes a "national ethnicity" to Brazil's melting-pot, disparate population, which has created a society that "knows itself, feels, and behaves as a single people." Unifying forces that have strengthened Brazilians' sense of national self-identity include the nation's multiracial society and its various religions; Brazilian Portuguese, music, and dance, particularly the samba and, more recently, Brazilian funk, a wildly popular version of the musical genres known in the United States as rap and hip-hop; the national soccer team, which won the World Cup championship for the fourth time in 1994; Edson Arantes do Nascimento (Pelé), widely acknowledged as the greatest soccer player ever, who won three World Cups with Brazil and was declared an official national treasure by Brazil's National Congress (Congresso Nacional; hereafter, Congress); world-renowned Brazilian Formula 1 auto racers, such as Emerson Fittipaldi and the late Ayrton Senna; and the country's television networks, with their widely viewed soap operas called *telenovelas*. Brazilian social scientists have used the concept of *homem cordial* (cordial man) to describe the Brazilian archetype. Brazilians are generally a friendly, warm, and spontaneous people.

With an estimated 161 million people in early 1998, Brazil is the world's largest Roman Catholic nation, and its population is the world's sixth largest. By 2000 Brazil will have an estimated 169 million people. Its population is largely urban; the urbanization rate soared from 47 percent in 1960 to 80 percent in 1996. Even the Amazon region is urbanized; 70 percent of its 18 million people live in cities. The Amazonian city of Manaus, which still lacks a sewerage system other than the river, now has a population of 1.5 million and a highway to Venezuela. Brazil has at least fourteen cities with more than 1 million people. Greater Rio de Janeiro's population totaled 10.3 million in 1995. Greater São Paulo, with 18.8 million people, is the world's third largest metropolitan area, after Tokyo and Mexico City. Although São Paulo's Metrô is clean and efficiently moves more people in one day than Washington's Metro does in two months, the megacity is disorienting and suffers from extreme traffic congestion and air pollution. To alleviate this situation, São Paulo State in January 1998 revived a fifty-year-old plan to build a US$2.5 billion beltway around the city.

The growth of Rio de Janeiro and São Paulo slowed during the 1980s and early 1990s, along with internal migration. Moreover, Brazil's demographic growth rate fell from about 3 percent a year in the 1960s to only an estimated 1.22 percent in 1995, even without the adoption of an official population-control program. During this three-decade period, Brazilian fertility rates decreased from 6.4 to about 2.3 children for each woman. The country's new demographic profile shows a generally young population; nearly 50 percent of Brazilians are younger than age twenty.

Some of Brazil's smaller cities, particularly those in the more developed South (Sul) and Southeast (Sudeste), have fared better than its megacities in their innovative approaches to urban ecology. Curitiba, the capital of Paraná, has earned a worldwide reputation as a model city, not only for the developing world but also the developed world, thanks to its former architect-mayor, Jaime Lerner (now governor of Paraná). In June 1996, the chairman of the Habitat II summit of mayors and urban planners in Istanbul described Curitiba as "the most innovative city in the world." Often compared with a city in Switzerland or Sweden, Curitiba is a city that functions, even though its budget of US$1 billion a year is the same as that of Lausanne, a city with only one-tenth of Curitiba's population. Curitiba has taken new approaches to urban ills such as illiteracy, homelessness, transportation and government service shortcomings, unemployment, pollution, and poverty. It has fifty-four square meters of green area per inhabitant, a widely praised trash-recycling system, and a world-class transportation system (used by 85 percent of the city's commuters). Curitiba's innovative professionals also include a heart surgeon, Randas J.V. Batista, who developed a revolutionary and potentially very important new heart-operation technique that surgeons around the world began learning about in June 1996.

Brazil has many other superlatives. The news media include highly professional, large-circulation newspapers and magazines and the powerful television network of Rêde Globo de Televisão (World Network), owner of TV Globo. Brazil has South America's most aggressive journalists. In the 1990s, they have investigated banking scandals, environmental abuses, massacres of Amazon Indians, murders of street children, and governmental corruption. Television reaches more than 80 percent of Brazilian homes. TV Globo is Latin America's largest network and the world's fourth largest television broadcasting system (after ABC, NBC, and CBS). Its *telenovelas* are watched by 70 million Brazilians nightly and in addition are sold to sixty-eight nations, earning the network US$30 million annually in foreign profits. In 1996 Brazil was the only Latin American country with a communications satellite in orbit. In the print media, *Veja*, with a circulation of 1.2 million, is Brazil's most influential magazine and the world's fifth largest weekly newsmagazine. All of these media have enabled Brazil to become the world's eighth largest advertising market, with US$4.5 billion spent on advertisements in 1994 and an estimated US$6 billion in 1995.

Brazil has enormous technological know-how and industrial capabilities. As President Fernando Henrique Cardoso explained to the *Wall Street Journal* in May 1997, "Our people are known throughout the world for their creativity, their ability to learn, to adapt to new circumstances, and to incorporate technical innovation on a daily basis."

Brazil is the most highly industrialized country in Latin America. Its huge industrial base includes steel, automobiles, military aircraft (including the AMX jet fighter), tanks, hydroelectric power, and a nuclear power program. Its industrial base is so developed that the country exports high-technology aviation components, such as aircraft engines and helicopter landing-gear systems. Brazil's Alberto Santos Dumont after all was the "father of aviation." Brazil will construct a small part of the international space station. Major manufactured products include motor vehicles, aircraft (including the internationally popular EMB–120 Brasília commuter turboprop and EMB–145 regional jetliner), helicopters (Brazil has the world's seventh largest helicopter fleet), electrical and electronic appliances, textiles, garments, and footwear. Since lifting its ban on computer imports in October 1992, Brazil has become the world's fastest-growing computer market and a major producer of computer software.

Brazil's major trading partners are the United States, Germany, Switzerland, Japan, the United Kingdom, France, Argentina, Mexico, and Canada. Exports represent 7.3 percent of Brazil's gross domestic product (GDP—see Glossary), and industry accounts for about 41 percent, a pattern found in some developed countries. Once an industrial powerhouse of the developing world, Brazil now counts on services for 48 percent of its GDP.

Brazil's economy, Latin America's biggest and the world's eighth largest, is greater than Russia's and twice as large as Mexico's. Its economy will be the sixth largest in the world by 2015, according to a Ministry of Finance prediction. In 1997 Brazil had an estimated GDP of US$775.5 billion, according to the Economist Intelligence Unit (EIU).

Brazil possesses enormous natural resources, including the world's largest rain forest. The country contains two-thirds of the endangered Amazon rain forest, a region representing 60 percent of the national territory. Sixty-six percent of Brazil's territory is still covered by forest. The Amazon rain forest and Pantanal (Great Wetlands) of Mato Grosso are two of the largest wildlife reserves on earth. The Amazon region is home to half of the earth's species and almost one-third of the world's 250 primates. Researchers in Brazil have identified a new primate species in Brazil six times in six years, including 1996. The

Pantanal, the world's largest freshwater wetland (larger than the state of Florida), contains flora and fauna that cannot be found anywhere else in the world, including eighty kinds of mammals, 230 varieties of fish, 650 species of birds, and 1,100 types of butterflies.

The country's vast river systems serve not only as a transportation network but also as an energy source. Brazil's hydroelectric plants provide 94 percent of the country's electricity. Its huge dams, including Itaipu, easily the world's largest hydroelectric power plant, generate vast amounts of hydroelectric power (a potential of at least 106,500 megawatts). Brazil is also the world's largest producer of bananas, coffee, and orange juice. It has the world's largest iron mine and vast stores of precious minerals. It is the world's largest exporter of iron and a major exporter of steel.

São Paulo, the financial center of Brazil, is an economic power in itself; the state's GDP of US$240 billion is larger than Poland's and the third largest economy in South America, after Brazil itself and Argentina. Its GDP per capita income of US$7,000 is nearly twice the figure for all of Brazil. São Paulo has half of the country's bank accounts. Its largest bank, with US$33.3 billion in assets and 1,900 branches, is the Brazilian Discount Bank (Banco Brasileiro de Descontos—Bradesco), Latin America's third largest and possibly most powerful bank holding company; Bradesco's profits in 1996 totaled US$800 million. The São Paulo Stock Exchange (Bolsa de Valores do São Paulo—Bovespa) has been one of the fastest growing in the world, at least until May 1997. Bovespa had a market capitalization of US$245 billion, far outranking the Mexican exchange's US$118 billion and five times that of the Buenos Aires exchange. In early 1997, the Bovespa index gained 86 percent, but by early November it had fallen 37 percent, a casualty of turmoil in world financial markets.

As a result of having to adjust to three decades of hyperinflation, Brazil has one of the world's most sophisticated and efficient banking systems. In 1993 the top forty Brazilian banks earned US$9 billion by lending inflation-eroded deposits to the government at high short-term rates. During the period of hyperinflation, the number of banks mushroomed from 106 institutions in 1988 to 246 in 1994. In 1996 Brazil had six of Latin America's ten largest banks, including the number-one ranked Federal Savings Bank (Caixa Econômica Federal—CEF), with US$90.8 billion in assets.

In 1995 Brazil was ranked third, after China and Mexico, for planned investments by American multinational companies. The second largest United States trading partner in the hemisphere in 1995–97, it is first in foreign direct investment from the United States, with US$41 billion. According to President Cardoso, foreign direct investment in Brazil in 1996 totaled US$9.4 billion, as compared with US$3.9 billion in 1995 and was expected to exceed US$14 billion in 1997. Multinationals based in Brazil remitted US$4 billion in dividends to their parent corporations during 1995. The energy, mining, petroleum, and telecommunications sectors expect investments of US$24 billion by the end of the 1990s.

Amid the chaos of inflation, Brazil's private sector had become the most dynamic in Latin America by 1994, with the automobile industry leading the country's economic upturn. Once the symbol of the "economic miracle" period of 1968–74 but declared all but defunct in the 1980s, the automobile sector—aided by tax breaks, an end to the list of banned imports, and the relaunching of the Volkswagen Beetle—was revived in 1990. Brazil's automobile industry, Latin America's biggest industrial complex, overtook Italy and Mexico in 1993 to become the tenth largest producer of cars in the world. Brazil produced 1.58 million cars in 1994 and 1.65 million in 1995, making it the world's ninth largest automotive manufacturer. Helped by a 70 percent tariff on imports by foreign automobile manufacturers, sales totaled about 1.7 million vehicles in 1996 and were expected to reach 2.5 to 3 million cars and trucks by 2000. However, the influx of new cars has made congestion and pollution in already clogged cities even worse. Furthermore, carmakers with manufacturing facilities in Brazil have been uncompetitive because of a tariff reduction on automobile imports mandated by the Common Market of the South (Mercado Comum do Sul—Mercosul; also known as Mercosur—see Glossary). General Motors was planning in 1997 to compete with a new US$9,000 automobile that would be the most affordable one in Brazil.

In the governmental realm, Brazil is the third largest democracy (after India and the United States). It has had civilian democratic rule since the end of the military dictatorship (1964–85). The period of military rule was relatively benign when compared with military dictatorships in the Southern Cone countries of Argentina, Chile, and Uruguay. In recent decades, Brazil has been relatively free from revolutionary violence and terrorism, with the exception of a left-wing terrorist campaign in the late 1960s and early 1970s. Indeed, the foreign image of Brazilians as a joyful, fun-loving, and nonviolent people began to fade as a result of the regime's repression, primarily from 1968 to 1972.

The constitution of October 5, 1988, Brazil's eighth, provides for a presidential system with several vestiges of a mixed parliamentary system. Although the 1988 constitution reestablishes many of the prerogatives of the Congress, the president retains considerable "imperial" powers. According to political scientist David V. Fleischer, Brazilian presidents may still have more "imperial" powers than their United States counterparts by being less accountable to Congress and being able to make innumerable political appointments.

Under a system of checks and balances similar to the United States system, the three branches of government operate with substantial harmony and mutual respect, but on rare occasions one of the branches may challenge or reject the interference of the others. However, as Professor Fleischer points out, executive-legislative conflict is inherent in the system because the president is elected directly by a national constituency, whereas Congress is elected by very parochial regional interests. Rural states of the North (Norte) and Northeast (Nordeste) elect proportionately more members of Congress than the industrial and more populous states of the South and Southeast, according to political scientist Ricardo Tavares.

The constitution continues the holding of municipal elections two years after presidential elections. Thus, municipal elections were held in 1988, 1992, and 1996 and are scheduled for 2000 and 2004, while both state and national elections are scheduled for 1998 and 2002. The number of political parties increased from eleven in 1987 to eighteen in 1996, of which eight are significant. Unlike in the United States, where two main parties are national organizations, Brazilian parties are regionally based.

A national plebiscite was held on April 21, 1993, to decide the form of government (a republic or, oddly enough, a constitutional monarchy) and the system of government (presidential or parliamentary), and it overwhelmingly reaffirmed Brazil as a presidential republic. However, a constitutional revision enacted in 1994 constrained the chief executive by shortening the presidential term from five to four years, as of January 1995, in exchange for allowing immediate reelection (approved by the Chamber of Deputies (Câmara dos Deputados) in January 1997 and the Federal Senate (Senado Federal; hereafter, Senate) in June 1997). In mid-1997 there were serious plans to set up a parliamentary government in Brazil by 2002.

With its modernistic capital of Brasília and its booming economy, Brazil was poised in the early 1970s during the "economic miracle" period (1967–74) to become "the country of the future." On being inaugurated on April 21, 1960, Brasília was referred to as "the city of the twenty-first century" and a "monument to the future." However, the US$10 billion needed to build and support the Federal District (Distrito Federal) started an inflationary spiral that was not tamed until late 1994. Far removed from the nation's realities, the sterile capital succeeded only in corrupting the political process by creating an enclave of privilege and self-interest. The 1990 census indicated that the wealthiest 10 percent of Brasília's population of about 500,000 residents earned 75 percent more than the top 10 percent in the rest of the country.

Although Lúcio Costa's jetliner-design for the futuristic capital was supposed to reflect Brazil's aspirations of *grandeza* (greatness), Brasília's once-dramatic architecture, designed in large part by Oscar Niemeyer, now inspires feelings of eerie alienation. Niemeyer, who is building a museum of modern art in the city, now refers to Brasília as "the city of lost hopes." More than half of the 1.2 million residents in the city's metropolitan area, including most of the capital's poor, live in more than a dozen satellite cities (*cidades satélites*), in favelas as far away as 150 kilometers from the city's center. Brasília is reputed to have the highest rates of divorce and suicide of any Brazilian city. In its favor, however, Brasília has little air pollution, its traffic congestion is tolerable, and its crime rate is relatively low.

Despite its many superlatives, the image of Brazil as a land of immense rain forest, cordiality, samba, political conciliation, and racial harmony has masked the reality of urban violence, chronic political instability and corruption, environmental depredation, highly unequal income distribution (the worst in the world, according to the World Bank—see Glossary), extraordinarily high levels of abandonment and abuse of children, and severe economic and social disequilibrium.

Beginning in the early 1970s, crime soared as the consumer expectations of poor Brazilians, raised by television advertising, were crushed. Violence has become an increasingly visible aspect of Brazilian society, in both rural and urban areas, and includes rising vigilantism by citizens. There has also been an epidemic of husbands killing their wives with impunity by invoking the "defense of honor" code. By the early 1990s, *homem cordial* no longer seemed to fit the Brazilian archetype, as news of massacres of Indians by miners, landless activists by landowners and police, and street children and prisoners by police became more frequent.

Death squads (*esquadrões de morte*) of off-duty or retired policemen target criminals in the favelas of Rio de Janeiro and São Paulo and street children, but to little effect. Their actions only seem to generate more crime. Civilian deaths at the hands of the São Paulo Police increased from an average of 34.1 per month in 1993 to 56 per month in the first half of 1996, according to the São Paulo Police ombudsman office. Between 1992 and 1996, São Paulo Police killed 2,203 persons. Military Police (Polícia Militar—PM) members were suspected in at least seventeen of forty-nine massacres in São Paulo in the first eleven months of 1995. Efforts to control the Military Police in metropolitan São Paulo supposedly improved their record of killings from 1,190 in 1992 to 106 in 1996.

Nevertheless, TV Globo's showing of videotapes of innocent civilians being shot, beaten savagely, or robbed by uniformed Military Police members in working-class suburbs of São Paulo in early March 1997 and Rio de Janeiro in early April shocked the country and caused profound soul-searching in Brazil. A poll taken in early April 1997 by *Folha de São Paulo* found that fewer than half of the people surveyed feared criminals more than they feared the police, and that 42 percent of all residents in the city of São Paulo had either experienced police violence first-hand, or knew someone who had. According to *Jornal do Brasil*, in the first half of 1996 the Rio de Janeiro police killed 20.5 civilians per month, as compared with an average of 3.2 persons per month prior to June 1995.

The world's ninth most violent city by 1979, Greater Rio de Janeiro reportedly has recorded more than 70,000 homicides since 1985. In the first nine months of 1995, there were 6,012 homicides in the city, a 10 percent increase over 1994. About 90 percent of Rio de Janeiro's violent crime is drug related and involves minors, whether as victims or perpetrators. In 1994–95 the military was deployed in Rio de Janeiro's favelas to carry out anti-drug-trafficking functions, normally a police responsibility. However, the temporary military presence in the favelas had no real impact on controlling the city's crime problem.

By 1996 kidnappings for ransom of leading businessmen and socialites in Rio de Janeiro and São Paulo had increased to an estimated fifty per month since 1994, in comparison with a reported seven in 1988. Kidnappings increased by 22.8 percent and bank robberies by 89.3 percent in Rio de Janeiro State in 1995, in relation to 1994, according to the Secretariat for Public Security (Secretaria de Segurança Pública—SSP). A poll conducted by the DataBrasil Research Institute (Instituto de Pesquisas DataBrasil) in late 1995 found that 76.5 percent of 600 *cariocas* (Rio de Janeiro residents) felt that the city had become more violent during 1995 than in 1994. On November 28, 1995, at least 70,000 *cariocas*, rallying under the slogan *Reage, Rio!* (React, Rio!), marched to protest the violence. By September 1996, Rio de Janeiro's crime rate was declining for the first time in years, with significant reductions in kidnappings and bank robberies, thanks to an energetic new command of the police force.

At the national level, homicide has had a major impact on Brazilian youths. A survey of 59.4 million Brazilian children, published on November 17, 1997, found that homicide had become the leading cause of death among fifteen- to seventeen-year-olds in Brazil, with its rate more than tripling since 1980. The survey, conducted by the Brazilian Institute of Geography and Statistics (Fundação Instituto Brasileiro de Geografia e Estatística—IBGE) and the United Nations Children's Fund (UNICEF), found that 25.3 percent of deaths in that age-group were homicides, as compared with 7.8 percent in 1980.

Police corruption has also been a growing problem. In late 1995, the *New York Times* reported that, according to an internal report on the notoriously corrupt Rio de Janeiro Police Department, an estimated 80 percent, or 9,600 members, of the 12,000-member force were dishonest and collected more than US$1 million a month in bribes or extortion from drug dealers and kidnappers. Brazilians have cited the need for a reformed and unified police force under federal control. On April 7, 1997, in an attempt to change the profile of Brazil's police forces, President Cardoso created a National Secretariat of Human Rights (Secretaria Nacional dos Direitos Humanos—SNDH), which is under the authority of the Ministry of Justice. The federal crackdown on human rights abuses and diminished earning power under the three-year-old national economic stabilization policy led to a wave of nation-wide police strikes in July 1997. As a result, Brazilian cities were hit by crime waves.

No issue has focused more world attention on Brazil since the 1970s than the destruction of the Amazonian jungle. Both Amazônia (the Amazon region) and the Pantanal are suffering the effects of human intervention from deforestation, slash-and-burn agriculture (see Glossary), highway construction, illegal mining, drug trafficking, and pollution. Tropical wood cutters have already bought up more than 4.5 million hectares of virgin forest in the Amazon Region, which holds about one-third of the world's remaining tropical woods. Dam building has also destroyed large swaths of rain forest. For example, the Tucuruí Reservoir inundated 2,000 square kilometers of tropical forest.

The topics of rapid deforestation and extensive burning of the Amazon rain forest and environmental pollution received unprecedented international attention in the late 1980s and early 1990s. Water and air pollution had also become a serious problem for Brazil. São Paulo State's Tietê is so polluted that in 1992 the state was forced to launch a US$2.6 billion program to revive it. In June 1992, Rio de Janeiro hosted the United Nations (UN) Conference on the Environment and Development (Eco-92). However, the Brazilian government's attention to the problems of deforestation and pollution waned following Eco-92, despite the creation in late 1993 of the Ministry of Environment and the Amazon Region.

In the mid-1990s, discussion of public policies intended to promote sustainable development (see Glossary) remained intense. One issue concerns the Pantanal, which is threatened by South America's massive waterway project, Hidrovia, a proposed 3,460-kilometer waterway along the world's fourth-largest river system, the Tietê-Paraná, intended to open the continent for the region's new free-trade bloc. According to a study by the Environmental Defense Fund, "channelization, dredging, channel simplification, and water control structures will drastically change the hydrology in the Pantanal region," causing the eventual "loss of biodiversity as habitats decline and exotic species are introduced via barge traffic and human migrations." However, Brazil shelved the project in early 1998.

As a result of deforestation and highway construction, Amazônia now consists of thirteen different regions that are in a critical political, social, economic, and environmental situation, according to a study begun in 1991 by the IBGE and the Strategic Affairs Secretariat (Secretaria de Assuntos Estratégicos—SAE) of the presidency of the republic. Since 1970 an area larger than 86 million hectares has been deforested. Marcio Nogueira Barbosa, director general of the government's National Institute of Space Research (Instituto Nacional de Pesquisas Espaciais—INPE), citing INPE statistics for 1995, told the *New York Times* on October 12, 1995, that "burnings in the Amazon Region appear to be approaching the worst levels ever."

During 1992–97 the Brazilian government claimed that destruction of the Amazon rain forest had slowed. However, Brazilian government information on the extent of forest clearing in the Amazon had dried up, and, five years after Eco-92, the government appeared unaware of what was happening in the Amazon rain forest. The *New York Times* reported that new data released in September 1996 showed that deforestation of the Amazon rose by 34 percent during 1991–94, from 6,913 square kilometers in the 1990–91 burning season to 9,253 square kilometers a year by 1994, consuming rain forest the size of Denmark. A study by the World Wildlife Fund (WWF) released in mid-1997 singled out Brazil as the nation with the highest annual rate of forest loss in the world. The *New York Times* reported on November 3, 1997, that burnings in the Amazon region were up 28 percent over 1996, according to satellite data.

Environmentalists have charged that tobacco and soybean cultivation, in addition to trans-Amazonian highway construction, has played a major role in Brazil's deforestation. Tobacco plantations occupied 271 million hectares of the nation's arable land in 1990. Brazil, which produced 450,000 tons of tobacco in 1994, is the world's fourth leading tobacco producer, after China, the United States, and India. Soybean cultivation has had a similarly devastating effect on the rain forest. The largest areas deforested in the first half of the 1990s from expanding soybean cultivation were in Mato Grosso State and the southern part of Maranhão State.

Ninety percent of Brazilians live on 10 percent of the land, mostly along the 322-kilometer-wide east coast region. The Atlantic Forest (Mata Atlântica) once stretched continuously along the entire coast of Brazil, extending far inland, and covering an area equivalent to France and Spain combined. Today, less than 7 percent of it remains, all in scattered fragments, and it is one of the world's two most threatened tropical forests. Many of Brazil's 303 species of fauna threatened with extinction are in the Atlantic Forest region, which contains 25 percent of all forms of animal and plant life existing on the planet. The region's biodiversity is forty times greater than the Amazon's.

Brazil's National Indian Foundation (Fundação Nacional do Índio—Funai) estimates that the indigenous Indian population, with about 230 tribes located in about 530 known Indian reservations in Brazil, totals 330,000 members. An estimated 10,000 to 15,000 Indians have never had contact with Brazilian government officials. About 62 percent, or 137,000, live in the Amazon region. They are the descendants of what could be the oldest Americans. According to a team of archaeologists led by Anna C. Roosevelt, radiocarbon dating of material in a cave located near Monte Alegre, between Manaus and Belém, shows that early Paleo-Indians were contemporaries of the Clovis people in the southwestern United States and had a distinctive foraging economy, stone technology, and cave art, dating back between 10,000 and 11,200 years ago.

One-tenth of Brazil's national territory is to be set aside for its Indian population, according to the constitution. However, fewer than half of the reservations have been demarcated, and the issue has continued to be controversial. Settlers and gold miners have massacred Indians. In May 1996, the Ministry of Justice published decrees recognizing the existence of seventeen indigenous areas in Brazil, totaling 8.6 million hectares. Each Brazilian Indian (including children) has on average an area of 400 hectares on which to live. By comparison, Native Americans in the United States live on only eighteen hectares per person. Some members of Brazil's Congress believe that the policy gives too much land to only two-tenths of the population.

A decree signed by President Cardoso in January 1996 did not include the Indians as one of his priorities. By permitting states, municipalities, and non-Indian individuals to contest demarcation of Indian land, the decree alarmed indigenous support groups. The executive order could end much of the violence against the Indians, by giving non-Indians a legal forum. However, official figures indicate that 153 of the 554 areas recognized by the government as Indian territories are liable to be revised under the decree. For example, in October 1996 a government decision on whether to uphold claims by

12,000 Indians, most of them from the 30,000-member Macuxí tribe, to more than 40 percent of 225,116-square-kilometer Roraima, Brazil's northernmost state, was put on hold indefinitely as a result of legal challenges by non-Indians.

Despite its vast natural resources and economic wealth, Brazil has an overwhelmingly poor population. Relatively few Brazilians have benefited from the economy. In a country with some of the world's widest social differences, grinding poverty and misery coexist with great industrial wealth; 20 percent of the population is extremely poor and 1 percent extremely wealthy. Brazil's Gini index (see Glossary) in 1991 was 0.6366. According to the UN, Brazil had the most uneven distribution of wealth in the world in 1995. The richest 10 percent of Brazilians hold 65 percent of Brazil's wealth (GDP), while the poorest 40 percent share only 7 percent. Brazil placed sixty-eighth out of 174 countries in the UN's 1997 human development index (see Glossary).

In the mid-1990s, at least one-fifth of the population, or about 32 million people, lived in extreme poverty (see Glossary), making less than US$100 a month. However, the anti-inflation policies of the Cardoso government helped pull 13 million Brazilians out of poverty, according to the Applied Economic Research Institute (Instituto de Pesquisa Econômica Aplicada—IPEA). During Cardoso's first three years in office, the number of people living below the poverty level dropped 9 percentage points to 21 percent. Thus, poverty in Brazil today is proportionately less, even though it is more visible and shocking, especially in the cities.

An estimated 45 million children and young people live in inhuman conditions, and the number of child workers has been as high as 10 million. Children from large poor families start working from the age of ten in order to help their parents. According to the IBGE, in 1995 there were 7.5 million Brazilian workers younger than eighteen, a group that represents 11.6 percent of the work force. However, the IBGE reported that the number of children between the ages of ten and fourteen who were employed decreased by 163,000 from 1993 to 1995. Some 3 million workers are between ten and fourteen years of age. Nongovernmental organizations (NGOs) estimate that anywhere from 500,000 to two million Brazilian children are forced into prostitution every year.

The vast substratum of the population lacks adequate housing, employment, education, health care, or any social security.

An estimated 10 million Brazilian families are homeless. The government spends only US$80 per person annually on public health, less than a third of what Argentina spends. Consequently, the health system is struggling to survive; its employees are often overworked and underpaid, and corruption is endemic. In this context, the new law that took effect January 1, 1998, mandating organ donations for transplants unless the person applies for an exemption, sparked fear and outrage.

Brazil stands out for its sharp regional and social disparities. Of Brazil's 39.1 million poor in 1990, 53.1 percent were in the poverty-stricken Northeast and 25.4 percent were in the prosperous Southeast. According to the IBGE, in 1996 the more developed Southeast and South regions had 63 million and 23.1 million people, respectively, who generated about 75 percent of the country's GDP. By contrast, the Northeast had 45 million residents and generated only about 13 percent of Brazil's GDP. The huge North and Center-West (Centro-Oeste) regions, which occupy 64.1 percent of Brazil's total area, had 11.1 million and 10.2 million residents, respectively, and also generated only about 13 percent of Brazil's GDP.

In 1988 the GDP per capita income of the Southeast was 43.6 percent higher than the national average, and that of the Northeast was 37.5 percent lower. Brazil's GDP per capita income was US$5,128 in 1997, as compared with US$3,008 in 1994, according to the IBGE. However, the 1997 GDP per capita was practically meaningless because of the vast disparity between north and south or, more specifically, the Southeast and Northeast. Whereas São Paulo State had a US$7,000 GDP per capita in 1994, Pernambuco, a relatively prosperous Northeast state, had only US$1,500.

Brazil's regional and social disparities are also reflected in the great inequalities of its education system. Illiteracy is widespread, particularly in the poor states of the Northeast and North. In 1995, according to Ministry of Education statistics, 18 percent of Brazilians over fifteen years of age could not read or write. Brazil will enter the twenty-first century with an estimated illiteracy rate of 16 percent. (Functional illiteracy in Brazil is as high as 60 percent.) Half of students nationwide repeat the first grade through a system of routine flunking. It takes an average of 11.4 years for students to complete the first eight years of education, and only 4.5 percent of all students who start school end up enrolling in a university. In 1994 UNICEF rated Brazil's basic education system as being in last place in world ranking, with large rates of nonattendance in poor states. As much as 68 percent of the electorate, or 65 million people, never finish primary school. In a hopeful development, however, primary education in Brazil is being radically reformed.

In 1995 the countrywide average salary was US$650 per month, and the minimum wage amounted to US$780 per year. In April 1995, the Cardoso government reluctantly raised the minimum monthly salary to 100 *reais* (R$100; Portuguese singular=*real*, pronounced hay-OW; for value—see Glossary). In 1994, when the minimum monthly salary was R$70 a month (about US$58), half the population earned less than US$240 a month, and about 15 million people, including 11.5 million pensioners, were on the minimum wage. The income of about 12 million Brazilians is less than US$65 per month.

Brazil's official statistics on employment, incomes, consumption, and living standards do not provide an accurate portrayal of the real Brazil. The black market enables millions of Brazilians to get by in a country where household appliances, automobiles, compact disks (CDs), restaurant food, and other consumer items cost more than in France, Germany, or the United States. The country's vast informal economy (see Glossary) produces from US$200 billion to US$300 billion per year, according to figures from the IBGE. Brazil's informal market, consisting of thousands of small to medium-size businesses that neither abide by government regulations nor pay taxes, is three times larger than the Portuguese economy and equal to that of Sweden. The illegal market provides an income for an estimated 30 million Brazilians. According to an early 1997 estimate by the weekly São Paulo newsmagazine *IstoÉ*, about half of the country's workforce is employed in the black market. In São Paulo only 52 percent of the workforce is employed in the formal economy, according to the Interunion Department for Statistics and Socioeconomic Studies (Departamento Intersindical de Estatística e Estudos Sócio-Econômicos—DIEESE). In Rio de Janeiro, one in every four persons works in informal jobs.

Brazil's regional income disparities have produced massive migration to favelas, particularly in Rio de Janeiro and São Paulo. By 1996 the country's poverty had become predominantly urban. The IPEA estimated that 23 million of the 30 million poor live in cities, with 9 million of them in big cities—half of them in Rio de Janeiro and São Paulo. In Rio de Janeiro, which has the largest concentration of poor migrants, 17 percent of the city's metropolitan population, or 1 million people, live in hillside favelas. Although rampant crime and disease remain entrenched in the favelas, steps have been taken to improve the living conditions. For example, Rio de Janeiro has slowed the growth of its favelas by prohibiting new settlements, and more than 300,000 residents have been moved to new homes. São Paulo's huge Cingapura project has been replacing 243 favelas, containing 500,000 people, with low-rise blocks of apartment buildings offering low-interest mortgages.

Brazil is steeped in five centuries of Roman Catholicism, but the religious affiliation of the Brazilian population has not remained unaffected by a decade of corruption, inflation, and economic hard times under civilian rule. About 93 percent of Brazilians identified themselves as Catholic in 1960; by 1993, however, the figure had dropped to 72.5 percent. Only an estimated 10 million of Brazil's Roman Catholics attend Mass regularly, and most Brazilian Catholics ignore the conservative Roman Catholic Church's teachings on family planning methods. The rapid growth and spreading influence of evangelical churches, such as the 3.5 million-member Universal Church of the Kingdom of God (Igreja Universal do Reino de Deus), have put into question the Vatican's characterization of Brazil as the world's largest Catholic country. Millions of Brazil's poor have turned away from the Roman Catholic Church and the liberation theology (see Glossary) that it began to espouse in the 1970s.

Instead, poorer Brazilians—more interested in spiritualism, hard work, sober living habits, and individual advancement than the political causes promoted by liberation theologists—have embraced Protestantism by the millions. By 1994 about 22 percent of the population (an estimated 35 million Brazilians) was Protestant, as compared with only 3.7 percent in 1960. Protestantism has swept the country because Brazilian culture, which is both spiritual and pragmatic, interacts readily with the Pentecostal message delivered by plain-speaking, blue-collar evangelical pastors, many of whom are blacks, in contrast to the Latin language of a Catholic Mass. The Pentecostal churches offer more social support in prayer groups and give rural migrants a feeling of security in large cities.

Competing with the evangelizing Protestants is the Catholic Charismatic Renewal, whose members practice an estatic prayer style, emphasizing lively music, "healings," and speaking in tongues. With a claimed 8 million active Charismatic Catholics, Brazil is considered to be the world's leading center of the movement.

Other former Roman Catholics have been lost to *espíritas,* a cult founded by a French mystic, and Afro-Brazilian religions, such as the Afro-centric *candomblé* and the twentieth-century cult more reflective of Brazilian urban life called *umbanda.* Owing to a Brazilian proclivity toward magic and mysticism, Afro-Brazilian cults have attracted members from all social classes, professions, and ethnic groups, including Brazilians of German, Italian, or Japanese ancestry. However, Christian evangelical churches have been drawing increasing numbers of former *candomblé* and *umbanda* worshipers.

At least 44 percent of Brazil's much-touted "racial democracy" is black (6 percent) or of mulatto (mixed) heritage (38 percent), while at most 55 percent is of European (mostly Portuguese) descent. In socioeconomic terms, the subsistence-level living standards of the black population reflect a long history of racial discrimination. Tens of millions of Brazilians living in poverty are overwhelmingly black, the descendants of slaves. Racial friction is a relatively new phenomenon. President Cardoso, author of a classic study on Brazilian blacks, admitted in November 1995 that discrimination against blacks is still a problem. For example, the Northeastern city of Salvador, which is 80 percent black, has never had a black mayor. Blacks are almost totally absent from high government and military posts, although President Cardoso's cabinet has a black member (soccer legend Pelé, the minister of sports). Two black women were elected to the Senate in 1994, but there were only eleven black federal deputies out of 513 in November 1995. Celso Pitta, a black, was elected mayor of São Paulo on October 3, 1996. Few blacks occupy high positions in business and other professions.

Largely marginalized (marginality—see Glossary), Brazil's blacks have an illiteracy rate twice that of whites and an average income less than half that of whites. Nearly 40 percent of nonwhites have four years or less of schooling. Very few blacks make it to the university; blacks and mixed-race people represent a mere 1 percent of the student body at the nation's largest university, the University of São Paulo (Universidade de São Paulo—USP). Black and mixed-race Brazilians were invisible in the print media until the founding of *Brasil Raça* (Brazil Race), a magazine geared to them, in September 1996 (300,000 copies of the first issue were sold).

Brazilian women, although constituting more than half of the population, traditionally have also been marginalized in politics. Only 868 women out of 12,800 candidates ran in the 1994 general elections. Only six of eighty-one senators and only thirty-four of 513 deputies are women. Only 171 of 4,973 mayors are women, and just 3.5 percent of 55,000 city council members nationwide are women. However, as a result of a 1995 quota law that requires at least 20 percent of the candidates of each political party to be women, an estimated 75,000 women participated in the October 3, 1996, election for mayors and members of city councils. According to Professor Fleischer, for the first time, two state capitals—Maceió and Natal—had exclusively female runoffs, and three other capitals had a woman in the runoff. He also noted that about 100,000 women ran for city council in 1996, as compared with only 869 in 1992.

In the countryside, land concentration, landlessness, homelessness, and joblessness are major issues. At least 500,000 rural jobs have been lost since the government formally ended its traditional protection of Brazilian-made goods in 1990. In the early 1990s, just under 2 percent of farms occupied 54 percent of arable land, while 15 million campesinos (see Glossary) worked farms with fewer than 10 hectares of land. Of Brazil's 3 million rural properties, only 58,000 account for about half the farmland. Moreover, about 42 percent of all privately owned land in Brazil lies idle.

Rural unions claim that 12 million peasants are landless, a figure that is disputed by government officials. The Landless Movement (Movimento dos Sem-Terra—MST), now Brazil's most powerful, grass-roots movement, is leading a pressure campaign on behalf of the landless. The MST claims that 4.8 million families have no land but want it and that Brazil has 78.9 million hectares of fallow lands, properties that mostly belong to wealthy farmers who live in cities and use the land for tax write-offs. Land reform has been promised since colonial days, but has yet to take place. Sociologist José de Souza Martins has described the landless situation as the "conflict between archaic Brazil and modern Brazil." Since its establishment in 1980, the MST has resettled permanently 150,000 families on land they originally occupied illegally. Led by more than 5,000 highly organized activists, the MST has 220,000 members and some 4 million followers. It reportedly enjoys the moral support of up to 90 percent of Brazil's population.

In 1995 the MST stepped up its aggressive occupations of land. Encouraged by trade unionists, left-wing politicians, and even Roman Catholic clergy, thousands of campesinos have resorted increasingly to land invasions to obtain a parcel to farm. After the Military Police massacred nineteen landless activists in El Dorado de Carajás, in northern Pará State, on April 17, 1996, the Cardoso government urged Congress to give priority to its agrarian reform measures. In addition, President Cardoso created a new cabinet-level ministry, the Special Ministry of Agrarian Reform. The government claims to have given land to more than 100,000 families. Although Cardoso promised to award land to 280,000 families by the end of 1998, and some 60,000 families had been granted land by the end of 1996, the Chamber of Deputies voted in May 1996 to halt his land-reform plans. Tension has continued to build in the many squatters' settlements in the countryside.

The Cardoso government found itself at odds with the Roman Catholic Church in the first half of 1997 as a result of President Cardoso's complaint to Pope John Paul II in February that Brazilian priests and bishops were actively abetting MST-organized land invasions. In late June 1997, Cardoso, exasperated with the MST, signed a decree making government land expropriations quicker and simpler but also penalizing occupation of land by peasants.

Landowners and miners have reacted violently to people who have gotten in their way. In Amazônia they have killed numerous peasants and rural labor leaders, including the renowned rubber tapper and rural union leader Chico Mendes, in 1988. Alarmed by the MST's activism, landowners have turned to hired guns (*pistoleiros*) and resurrected an organization linked in the past with strong-arm tactics, the Ruralist Democratic Union (União Democrática Ruralista—UDR). Apprehensive that the situation will only get worse unless there is an effective distribution of land, the military reportedly has been as anxious as the left to see rapid implementation of land reform. There has been intermittent violence resulting from land-reform problems, with much of it occurring in Pará State. About 1,000 people were killed in land conflicts during the 1985–95 period.

Since Brazil's recession began to be felt in 1989, many rural workers have fallen victim to another form of violence—slavery practices, involving imprisonment for debt and coercion to prevent workers from leaving their employers. According to the Pastoral Land Commission (Comissão Pastoral da Terra—CPT), a nonprofit group sponsored by the Roman Catholic Church, documented cases of forced labor in Brazil, mostly taking place on large estates called *fazendas,* rose from 4,883 in 1991 to 25,193 in 1994. The actual figure is believed to be closer to 85,000. In November 1995, Brazil, the last Western nation to abandon slavery (in 1888), celebrated the 300th anniversary of Zumbi, a seventeenth-century Afro-Brazilian. Zumbi led raids to free slaves from sugar plantations for more than twenty years, using Palmares, a fortress in Alagoas State, as his base of operations.

The huge, widening gap between Brazil's great potential and the reality of the large, poverty-stricken majority of its population has inspired national cynicism about the country's once-vaunted identification of its destiny with *grandeza.* During 1992–94 Brazilians reportedly were beset with self-doubt, disillusionment, and frustration at their country's lack of progress and were concerned that their grand future would never arrive. "Brazil is the country of the future—and always will be" has been a familiar Brazilian aphorism since the early 1960s.

Beginning with the economic crisis of the 1980s, many Brazilians, including scientists, already had given up on the Brazilian dream and moved abroad. In the second half of the 1980s, for the first time in the country's history, more people emigrated from Brazil than immigrated to the country; many moved to Canada and the United States (Brazilian migrants to the latter totaled an estimated 332,000 by 1994). An estimated 1 million Brazilians were living overseas by 1993.

Entering the 1990s with GDP per capita income no higher than it was in 1980 and monthly inflation raging at an unprecedented 30 percent, Brazilians were pessimistic about their economic future. Brazil was still squandering its riches, missing opportunities, and sinking deeper into misery. However, Fernando Collor de Mello (president, 1990–92)—young, athletic, and elegant—made Brazilians dream again with promises to make the country a developed world power through free-market policies that would bring inflation under control, create high economic growth, and attract foreign investment.

The 1992 presidential corruption scandal and subsequent impeachment of President Collor delayed action on economic reforms. In September 1992, Brazil became the world's first democratic country to impeach its president on charges of corruption. Collor's downfall reflected the endemic corruption that was undermining Brazilian democracy in the early 1990s. The principal result of a poll taken by the Gallup Institute in March 1991 was that 78 percent of Brazilians surveyed in the major cities remained convinced that Brazil was still a paradise—for corruption. The reputation of the judicial system was further undermined by Collor's acquittal on corruption charges. The crisis over Collor's impeachment nevertheless had a positive side. As President Cardoso explained in an address given in New York on October 23, 1995, it "clearly signaled the political maturity of a civic culture undergoing rapid consolidation."

Collor's replacement, his vice president, Itamar Franco (president, 1992–94), a civil engineer by profession, was out of step with the short-lived Collor administration's reform agenda. Initiatives to redress fiscal problems, privatize state enterprises, and liberalize trade and investment policies lost momentum. The Franco government continued timidly along a free-market course, while inflation soared to 50 percent a month. By the end of his first year in office, Franco nearly reached the *índice vaia*, or get-lost level, of unpopularity.

The same Congress that ousted Collor on corruption charges became engulfed in its own graft scandal in late 1993. Judges, lawyers, government officials, and politicians were accused of conspiring in a US$1.2 billion scheme to defraud the social security system through inflated labor court settlements. In a poll taken in Rio de Janeiro in June 1993, respondents ranked Congress near the bottom (15 percent) of a list of Brazilian institutions that earned their trust; political parties had the least credibility (5 percent), while the military ranked near the top, with 58 percent.

By the end of 1993, the National Accounting Court (Tribunal das Contas da União—TCU) had investigated and found that 1,500 current and retired politicians were unfit to hold office, again because of corruption. A report produced by the Congressional Investigating Committee (Comissão Parlamentar de Inquérito—CPI) named nine firms that it said had defrauded the government systematically since 1985. The CPI claimed that fifty-five politicians were part of the secret cartel, as well as all the governors of the sixteen North and Northeast states, with the exception of Ceará's governor, Ciro Gomes.

In December 1993, President Franco's fourth minister of finance, Fernando Henrique Cardoso, unveiled his controversial stabilization plan (Brazil's seventh since 1986), which caused a furor over its proposal to raise taxes. Nevertheless, Cardoso accomplished an essential first step in implementing this plan, restoring order to public finances, and eliminating the estimated US$22.2 billion budget deficit (5 percent of GDP). Cardoso pressured Congress in February 1994 to pass a constitutional amendment setting up a US$16 billion Social Emergency Fund (Fundo Social de Emergência—FSE), renamed the Fiscal Stabilization Fund (Fundo de Estabilização Fiscal—FEF), to be financed by tax increases. Official figures show how skewed the economy had become, thanks to the unbridled growth of bureaucracy.

A few days after announcing his presidential candidacy on March 30, 1994, Minster of Finance Cardoso launched the third phase of his financial package, the *Real* Stabilization Plan (Plano *Real*). It consisted of three stages: the introduction of an equilibrium budget mandated by Congress; a process of general indexation (prices, wages, taxes, contracts, and financial assets); and the introduction of a new currency, the *real*, pegged to the dollar, on July 1, 1994.

The legally enforced balanced budget would remove expectations of inflationary behavior by the vast public sector, which includes the national telephone company, many public utility companies, and several banks. By allowing a realignment of relative prices, general indexation would pave the way for monetary reform. Through monetary and fiscal adjustments, the *Real* Plan succeeded in reducing inflation, which was ascending at a stratospheric rate of 7,000 percent a year, to almost 2 percent by that October.

By September 1994, Cardoso had become the embodiment of Brazil's economic transformation. Cardoso's spectacularly successful *Real* Plan (which he coauthored with Pedro Malan, who later became his minister of finance) propelled him to a resounding presidential victory in the first round of the October 3, 1994, election. Voters were forced to choose between a social democratic, free-market model of modernization and a reworked model of corporatist (corporatism—see Glossary) or syndicalist socialism. The former was advocated by Cardoso of the Brazilian Social Democracy Party (Partido da Social Democrácia Brasileira—PSDB) and the latter by Luis Inácio "Lula" da Silva of the Workers' Party (Partido dos Trabalhadores—PT). Striking alliances to the right of his own PSDB, Cardoso marginalized the previously favored Lula.

The 82.2 percent voter turnout for the 1994 presidential election was impressive (as compared with the United States). Cardoso, a former *tucano* (São Paulo) senator and minister of finance, placed first in every state except the Federal District and Rio Grande do Sul, where Lula, a grade-school dropout and long-time lathe operator, was victorious. Cardoso was aided by the support of not only the poor but also conservative parties, São Paulo industrialists, and the powerful media network of Rêde Globo. In the congressional and gubernatorial elections, all 513 seats in the lower house, the Chamber of Deputies (Câmara dos Deputados), and fifty-four of the eighty-one Senate seats were up for reelection. However, Cardoso supporters were deprived of a first-round victory in São Paulo, Minas Gerais, and Rio de Janeiro, where abstentions and spoilt or blank votes accounted for more than half the total.

One of the most academically qualified presidents in history and a brilliant intellectual, Cardoso is a world-renowned sociologist and the author of more than 100 monographs, including two dozen books, many of them written in English. In addition to Portuguese, Cardoso speaks English, French, Spanish, and several other foreign languages. His wife, Ruth Corrêa Leite Cardoso, is a leading Brazilian urban anthropologist who specializes in studying community movements by women and blacks in São Paulo's favelas and who heads the Solidarity Community (Comunidade Solidária) social-action program.

For most of his life, Cardoso was a university professor. He taught at the USP until 1964, when the new military regime persecuted him and banned him from teaching. He then chose to go into exile in Santiago, Chile, from 1964 to 1968. During that period, he coauthored, with Chilean sociologist Enzo Faletto, *Dependency and Development in Latin America,* considered one of the most influential interpretations of twentieth-century Latin American structural dynamics. It attributes Latin America's underdevelopment to the once-influential doctrine that Cardoso cofounded, dependency theory (see Glossary), and the region's dependence on foreign capital and technology.

Cardoso also taught in France at the University of Paris (the Sorbonne), Britain (Oxford), and the United States (University of California-Berkeley, Princeton, Stanford, and Yale). In the 1970s, he became the best-known critic of the Brazilian nationalistic developmental model, which was based on the now obsolete strategy of state-led import-substitution industrialization (see Glossary). In the early 1970s, when Cardoso distributed pamphlets outside factory gates, Brazilian businessmen viewed him suspiciously as an unreliable leftist politician. Returning to São Paulo by the late 1970s, he established a think tank and entered politics in 1977. He served as a senator (1986–94), and, in 1988, helped to found the PSDB, a center-left party that opposed corruption.

As the son, grandson, and nephew of generals, Cardoso retains strong ties to the military. His father, General Leonidas Cardoso, was elected deputy by the Communist Party of Brazil (Partido Comunista do Brasil—PC do B) in the 1940s and was persecuted by the military. President Cardoso's grandfather, General Maurício Cardoso, was considered to have been the most brilliant officer of the Brazilian Army (Exército Brasileiro). Fernando Cardoso's uncle, General Henrique Assunção Cardoso, has been characterized as an extreme rightist. In 1969 Cardoso himself was arrested, blindfolded, and interrogated by the military.

After three civilian presidents of mediocre abilities, many Brazilians who had been despondent about their country's economic future viewed Cardoso's election as highly auspicious for Brazil, and most foreign observers agreed. Fellow sociologist Alain Touraine, a professor at the Maison des Sciences de l'Homme in Paris, commented to *O Estado de São Paulo* that Cardoso's election represented a victory of the future over the past at a moment in which the entire world is engaged in economic "globalization," a road that Brazil had rejected thirty years earlier. In addition to stabilizing the country economically, Cardoso was expected to stabilize Brazil's erratic record of incomplete presidencies. Not a single democratically elected Brazilian president had completed his term of office since 1926; the presidents either resigned, were forced from office, or, in one case (Getúlio Dorneles Vargas, president, 1930–45, 1951–54), committed suicide.

By the time Cardoso assumed office on January 1, 1995, at age sixty-three, the monthly rate of inflation was less than 1 percent, unemployment was low (about 5 percent), and Brazil had a comfortable and unprecedented level of foreign-exchange reserves, at a record US$40.8 billion, thanks largely to the influx of foreign capital into the local financial market. The conditions were favorable for essential reforms of the statist economy, the bloated federal government, and the overgenerous pension system. The latter had allowed privileged groups—teachers, airline pilots, soldiers, judges, journalists, and politicians (politicians after only eight years)—to qualify for 100 percent pensions in their fifties (some at age forty-five on a pension 20 percent higher than their last wage). One governor complained in October 1995 about a retired Military Police colonel who had accumulated twenty-six personal pensions and was drawing the equivalent of US$80,400 a month. By January 1995, the pension system was running an estimated annual deficit of 10 percent of GDP, or US$3 billion.

Whereas the public sector's wages accounted for only 3 percent of GDP in 1980, the government in 1993 employed one-third of the total workforce and paid 11 percent of GDP in wages. In 1995 the federal bureaucracy's wage bill rose by 40 percent, and states were spending 80 to 90 percent of their income on running the bureaucracy. The bloated bureaucracy is filled with thousands of nominal workers who receive salaries but do no work. The state governors, desperate to get thousands of civil servants off the state payrolls, have been Cardoso's most resolute allies in the battle for administrative reform and capping bureaucratic expenses at 60 percent of the government's revenues. However, privatization of state-owned companies is opposed by associations of civil servants reluctant to lose their privileges, particularly the officers (maharajas) in charge of state companies who are paid salaries (up to US$19,000 a month) that are high by Latin American corporate standards. (In late 1995, there were 6,471 civil servants in seven states earning more than President Cardoso's salary of US$8,800 a month.)

Cardoso's election also marked an ethical backlash to institutionalized corruption by traditional politicians, a reversal that began with the ouster of Collor. A report by government investigators published on January 1, 1995, noted that corruption within the Brazilian government was costing the country about US$20 billion and accounting for 40 percent of the national investment budget. Cardoso refused to trade 20,000 to 30,000 patronage jobs for congressional support, vowing to fill the jobs with qualified nonpoliticians to avoid corruption and to control spending. Cardoso's government sought to circumvent the corruption-ridden state and federal cronies by transferring most of the responsibility and funding of health, schools, and infrastructure to municipal authorities. Nevertheless, corruption has remained entrenched in the bureaucracy.

In his first 100 days in office, Cardoso was unable to deal effectively with the status quo forces in Congress, causing a further loss of public confidence in democracy. A poll conducted in April 1995 indicated that the percentage of Brazilians preferring democracy to any other form of government declined from 54 percent in the previous September to 46 percent, and the proportion regarding a dictatorship as better than democracy rose from 13 percent to 18 percent.

In 1996–97 President Cardoso attempted to further reform the constitution in order to reduce the state's role in the economy, revamp the federal bureaucracy, reorganize the social security system, redefine the federal-state relationship, simplify the tax system, and strengthen political parties. He succeeded in getting some major economic and political reforms enacted. Discarding the anticapitalist, theoretical nostrums that he had espoused during his academic career, he called for the implementation of a sweeping market-oriented reform, including public-sector and fiscal reform, privatization, deregulation, and elimination of barriers to increased foreign investment.

Cardoso's goals are to expand privatization measures, including elimination of constitutionally established monopolies. His initial economic reforms, adopted by the Congress in early 1995, permit the entry of foreign capital into previously exclusive areas, categorized as "strategic assets." These may include the oil extraction, mining, and telecommunications, and the banking, electricity, health, insurance, and retirement-plan sectors. Privatization sales in 1996 may have reached US$10.2 billion. On May 21, 1996, a consortium of Brazilian, French, and United States companies purchased a 34 percent share of the state-owned Power Services, Inc. (Serviços de Eletricidade S.A.—Light) in a transaction valued at US$2.2 billion, Brazil's then largest privatization. Cardoso administration officials hoped the sale of Light would revitalize Brazil's often criticized, delay-prone privatization program.

By April 1997, the government had sold fifty-five of 135 state-owned companies for a total of at least US$15 billion, since the inception of the program in 1991, including all of its steel companies. Most of those sales attracted little attention.

In early May 1997, however, in Latin America's largest, most historic privatization to date, the government sold its 45 percent controlling stake in the Rio Dôce Valley Company, Inc. (Companhia Vale do Rio Dôce S.A.—CVRD) to a consortium led by Brazil's largest steelmaker, the already privatized National Iron and Steel Company (Companhia Siderúrgica Nacional—CSN), for US$3.1 billion. Vale, as the firm is known, is the world's third largest mining company; it is the largest producer and exporter of iron ore (accounting for more than 18 percent of the global market, or 100 million tons annually, with reserves of 4 to 5 billion tons) and Latin America's biggest producer of gold (eighteen tons a year). Vale is also Brazil's largest exporter (US$1.2 billion in overseas sales in 1996) and a symbol of Brazilian nationalism. In addition to its railroad system, which carries almost two-thirds of Brazil's rail freight, Vale owns two ports (São Luís and Vitória). The government planned to sell its remaining 31.5 percent of ordinary shares in Vale, a company valued at US$11.7 billion, in late 1997. Some Brazilians protested the expected loss of Vale's tradition of providing jobs and grants for cultural and other activities.

Other giant state companies were slated for privatization, including São Paulo Power, Inc. (Eletricidade de São Paulo S.A.—Eletropaulo), which sells 15 percent of all of Latin America's electricity, and Brazilian Electric Power Company, Inc. (Centrais Elétricas Brasileiras S.A.—Eletrobrás), one of the world's top five power companies. Brazil's largest company, the Brazilian Petroleum Corporation (Petróleo Brasileiro S.A.—Petrobrás), with sales of US$18 billion, is the world's fifteenth largest oil and natural gas company and a world leader in deep-sea drilling. Nevertheless, the inefficient Petrobrás faced a process of accelerated deregulation in 1997 that may open the country's vast resources to joint exploration and development by foreign multinational oil companies.

The opening of the telecommunications sector to foreign private investment capital actually will not become effective until the next government takes office in 1999. Under the Cardoso government's proposed new regulations, as approved by the Chamber of Deputies in May 1996, foreign private companies would be permitted to purchase up to 49 percent in voting shares of state-owned telecommunications companies. Thus, new international joint ventures are changing the face of Brazil's long-introverted business world. The government expected to receive US$25 billion to US$30 billion from the privatization of telecommunications in 1997–99.

The telephone business is one of the largest Brazilian industries to be opened to foreign investors. In April 1997, in a move that was a precursor to the planned privatization in 1998 of the state-controlled telephone holding company, Brazilian Telecommunications, Inc. (Telecomunicações Brasileiras S.A.—Telebrás), which could establish Brazil as a major destination for foreign investment, the government auctioned off the regional cellular foreign investment concessions for minimum prices totaling US$3.6 billion. In addition to electrical generation and transmission companies, the government planned to sell banks, railroads, and the Rio de Janeiro Metrô in late 1997.

With its large and quite diversified economy, Brazil still has the potential to regain its former dynamism, despite the economy's considerable structural and short-term problems. According to some economists, radical fiscal reforms are crucial to the consolidation of Brazilian economic stability and to lay the groundwork for self-sustained economic growth. The goals of these reforms are to redefine the scope of the Brazilian nation, its functional profile, and the extent of interaction with the private sector. Reducing the unsustainable disparities in income distribution is considered to be an essential component of overdue structural reforms. However, political factors have slowed the Cardoso administration's progress on vital structural reform.

The *Real* Plan imposed a harsh new period of constricted profits and consolidation on Brazil's banks. The banking sector, employing 960,000, began to downsize. In 1994–95 the Franco and Cardoso governments intervened in many banks and closed more than a dozen others. In August 1995, the Central Bank of Brazil (Banco Central do Brasil—Bacen; see Glossary) was forced to take over the giant Economic Bank (Banco Econômico), Brazil's first private bank, based in the Northeast state of Bahia, after it ran up debts of US$3.6 billion. After his approval ratings and Brazil's stock market plummeted at the news of the federal bailout, Cardoso reversed course and instead sought to sell the bank to private investors. The Cardoso government also intervened to put the São Paulo State Bank (Banco do Estado de São Paulo—Banespa), which owed domestic and foreign lenders US$58 billion, under Central Bank control to save it from collapse and to put the Rio de Janeiro State Bank (Banco do Estado de Rio de Janeiro—Banerj) on the auction block. A US$12 billion government rescue package for private banks that was introduced in late 1995 laid the groundwork for a wave of mergers, privatizations, and liquidations.

By the end of 1995, President Cardoso, by employing pragmatic, free-market economics, had led Brazil's inflation-prone economy to its greatest stability in a quarter century. Cardoso's continued popularity resulted in large part from his ingenious handling of the economy. In the first twelve months of the new currency, the *real* and its associated fiscal measures brought strong growth, a flood of new investment, the creation of half a million new jobs, a temporary fall in unemployment, and an inflation rate of less than 25.9 percent a year. Nevertheless, the widening public deficit, combined with congressional resistance to the three reforms submitted by the Cardoso government in the second half of 1995—administrative, tax, and social security reform—threatened to undermine Cardoso's *Real* Plan. In the view of Cardoso's critics, he missed his chance for radical reform of the state by failing to move aggressively at the outset of his administration.

By 1996 Brazil's high public deficit (4 percent of GDP) from a rising public payroll, high interest rates, the mounting foreign debt-service costs (US$15 billion in 1996) and amortisations (US$18 billion), and the high level of social security payments were of increasing concern to investors. The cost of social security payments rose from US$25.4 billion in 1994 to US$32.9 billion in 1995. Social security showed a deficit of R$5 billion in 1996. Some analysts have expressed concern that the deterioration of the fiscal situation at the same time that credit is being regenerated to restart the economy adds up to a dangerous combination, considering that the pace of structural reform has apparently slowed down. In this view, Brazil faces a volatile situation reminiscent of Mexico in 1994. Economist Sebastian Edwards contended in a *Wall Street Journal* op-ed on November 7, 1997, that "without immediate action on the fiscal side, the *Real* Plan may be unsustainable." Other analysts believe that the deficit problem looks worse than it really is.

Cardoso's *Real* Plan succeeded in reducing inflation to 16.5 percent in 1996, the lowest in nearly half a century, thanks to an overvalued currency. Brazilians began to take economic stability for granted. However, since early 1996 some economists have warned that Brazil's exchange rate is too high. In June 1996, economist Rudiger Dornbusch, who predicted the 1994 Mexican peso crash, suggested that the *real* was overvalued by about 40 percent. In his analysis, which angered Brazilian officials and instigated a debate, Brazil has been controlling inflation by means of a highly overvalued currency and high interest rates. Conservative economists led by Deputy Antônio Delfim Netto (PPB), a former minister of planning, called for accelerated devaluation. In the view of these skeptical economists, the Cardoso government's economic policy dooms Brazil to remaining the country of the future. By some estimates, the *real* in early 1998 was overvalued by 15 percent. Whether Brazil can continue to sustain a monetary and exchange-rate policy that is inconsistent with its large and growing budget deficits without a major devaluation remains to be seen. Some economists expect a devaluation in 1998.

For much of 1997, Brazil continued to enjoy its greatest stability in three decades, with foreign reserves totaling US$57.5 billion by May. However, the growing trade deficit, which reached US$10.93 billion in 1997, had become a top concern of the government. In 1997 the current account deficit rose to US$32.3 billion. Of the main Latin American economies, only Brazil in 1997 had a fiscal deficit as high as 3.4 percent of its GDP.

Forced to choose between lower economic growth (estimated to be 3.2 percent in 1997) and a quick currency devaluation, which might aggravate inflation, Brazil's economic policy makers chose the former. In early November 1997, President Cardoso staved off financial speculators, who tried to force Brazil to devalue the *real*, by quickly raising interest rates and propping up the *real* with billions of dollars in reserves. He then unveiled an economic austerity package that will include higher taxes and reduced government spending. By announcing a series of fifty-one drastic measures to bolster revenues by as much as US$18 billion, Cardoso demonstrated decisive leadership and a willingness to take tough measures to maintain confidence in the *real*. To that end, his government won an important legislative victory on November 20 with the approval by the Chamber of Deputies of a key constitutional reform proposal to dismantle job protection for most civil service workers by giving the government new powers to dismiss them. The bill, which was expected to win approval in the Senate, would eventually cost about 280,000 of 537,053 public servants their jobs, thereby eliminating a major impediment to the country's fiscal health.

As a result of the 1996 municipal elections and strong opposition by powerful vested interest groups, the Cardoso administration's more challenging reforms—administrative, social security, and fiscal—languished in Congress and awaited passage in 1997. The opposition that Cardoso's bill to reform the deficit-ridden social security and pension systems encountered in Congress, among the state governors, and even in the Supreme Court has highlighted the constraints under which a

Brazilian president operates. In January 1998, the Cardoso administration estimated that Congress would approve the social security bill by April. In addition to the social security bill and a new labor reform proposal, the Cardoso government resubmitted its proposed administrative and fiscal reforms to Congress. The lower house approved the basic text of the administrative reform on November 19, 1997.

Despite congressional resistance to his reform proposals, President Cardoso further consolidated his power in early February 1997 when his candidates for the positions of speaker in both houses of Congress were elected. This led some observers to wonder whether the presidency was entering a de facto imperial era. Referring to "Emperor Cardoso," political analyst Villas-Boas Correia argued in a *Jornal do Brasil* article that no democratically elected president had ever accumulated so much power in Brazilian history.

In January 1997, the Chamber of Deputies passed an amendment allowing for immediate reelection of presidents, governors, and mayors. As a result of the Senate's approval of the amendment in June 1997, President Cardoso may stand for reelection in October 1998. His main opponent was Paulo Maluf, a right-wing populist and erstwhile presidential candidate of the Brazilian Progressive Party (Partido Progressista Brasileiro—PPB), as well as the largest party in Congress, the Brazilian Democratic Movement Party (Partido do Movimento Democrático Brasileiro—PMDB). However, Maluf decided that Cardoso was still too popular to run against, so he entered the race for governor of São Paulo State instead. On November 30, 1997, Luis Inácio da Silva announced officially that he will run for president on the Workers' Party ticket. But Cardoso's efforts to maintain a low rate of inflation, expand the economy, make progress in solving major socioeconomic problems, and reduce corruption and congressional immunity have lowered the left's chances of being elected to power in the October–November 1998 presidential, congressional, and state elections. Cardoso's reelection is generally considered likely.

Brazilian diplomacy had a landmark year in 1995 with Cardoso's assumption of office. The first former minister of foreign affairs to be elected president of Brazil, Cardoso personally led Brazil's most important diplomatic initiatives in 1995, bringing new credibility and respect to Brazilian foreign policy and the country's international relations profile. Having redefined Brazil's foreign policy objectives, the Cardoso government improved Brazil's relations with the United States and adopted a more assertive role within the South American region.

Brazil's priority in 1995–97 was to consolidate Mercosul (Common Market of the South) among Argentina, Brazil, Paraguay, and Uruguay. In the four years before Mercosul took effect on January 1, 1995, regional trade almost tripled, reaching US$10 billion by the end of 1994, as compared with only US$3.6 billion in trade among the four full member countries in 1990. Exports to Mercosul countries accounted for 15 percent of Brazil's total in 1995, as compared with 13 percent in 1994. Mean tariff rates were cut back from 32.2 percent in 1990 to 14.0 percent in 1994, while at the same time the tariff ceiling was brought down from 105 percent to 40 percent. Trade between Brazil and Argentina in 1995 was US$10 billion, amounting to 80 percent of all trade within Mercosul and making Argentina Brazil's second largest trading partner, after the United States.

In addition to removing trade barriers, Mercosul commits members to the coordination of policies on agriculture, industry, transport, finance, and monetary affairs. Argentina and Brazil see Mercosul primarily as a means of attracting foreign investment. Although Brazil's Mercosul partners were shocked when Brazil announced on March 25, 1997, its unilateral decision to impose restrictions on imports, Brazil alleviated fears of a trade shutdown by allowing an exemption for Mercosul goods.

Cardoso made a very successful state visit to Washington in April 1995. The Clinton administration welcomed Brazil's constitutional amendments opening up the Brazilian economy to increased international participation, especially the breaking up of state monopolies in the areas of petroleum and telecommunications, but intellectual property rights remained at issue. *Veja* reported in mid-April 1995 that United States firms were losing US$800 million a year as a result of piracy by Brazilian companies. However, the Cardoso government subsequently modified Brazil's intellectual property rights law to coincide with stricter trademark and patent provisions. The new Patents Law, enacted in 1996, meets international standards. Nevertheless, Brazil's software piracy rate was about 68 percent, accounting for nearly seven of every ten computer software programs sold in the country, according to a Price Waterhouse study released in May 1997. During his official visit to Brasília and

Rio de Janeiro in mid-October 1977, President Clinton emphasized trade, education, and environmental issues and succeeded in improving Brazilian-United States relations.

Brazil's history has been relatively free from major conflict with its ten contiguous neighbors, with the main exception of the War of the Triple Alliance (1864–70) with Paraguay. In the twentieth century, Brazil has been a gentle giant; the only major power with which Brazil has fought a war was Germany in World War II. After the war, however, 1,500 Nazis, including the infamous Josef Mengele, moved to Brazil, according to the World Jewish Congress. Moreover, Rio de Janeiro's *O Globo* reported in early 1997 that President Vargas, a Nazi sympathizer, confiscated US$46 million in assets from Brazilian Jews in 1947. In April 1997, President Cardoso created a special commission charged with investigating Nazi assets.

In the first half of the 1990s, Brazil's national security interests were reshaped not only by the new, post-regime civil-military relationship, but also by Brazil's greatly improved integration with Argentina and other South American countries through various security accords and a regional trade agreement, Mercosul. One of the Collor administration's most important national security actions aimed at the Brazilian Armed Forces (Forças Armadas Brasileiras) was to expose the military's secret nuclear bomb program, the so-called Parallel Program (Programa Paralelo), and bring it under civilian oversight and international monitoring. On December 13, 1991, Brazil reached a nuclear cooperation accord with Argentina, thereby accepting International Atomic Energy Agency (IAEA) safeguards.

President Collor also implemented other significant national security measures. He continued to reduce defense spending to the lowest level in decades and allowed the country's arms industry to collapse without any state intervention to sustain it. For example, the Collor administration announced that the Brazilian Aeronautics Company (Empresa Brasileira Aeronáutica—Embraer), the producer of planes such as the Tucano trainer and the subsonic AMX jet, would be privatized. In an attempt to demilitarize the government and institute a more democratic governmental structure more likely to help improve relations with the United States, Collor abolished the military-dominated National Intelligence Service (Serviço Nacional de Informações—SNI) and the National Security

Council (Conselho de Segurança Nacional—CSN) and formed the civilian-headed SAE (Strategic Affairs Secretariat).

However, the Collor government's policies soon reverted to a more pragmatic approach that was more independent of the United States. Prior to Operation Desert Storm against Iraq in January 1991, Brazil found itself aiding the wrong side, with controversial arms sales, construction contracts, and transfer of missile technology to Iraq. Brazil subsequently altered its close commercial relationship with Iraq.

In the second half of the 1990s, Brazil, strengthened by Mercosul, is evolving into a major intermediate regional power. Under Cardoso, Brazil has sought a more active international role, both in the UN and in bilateral relations. Traditionally, Brazil has played a leading role in collective security efforts and economic cooperation in the Western Hemisphere. For example, in early 1995 Brazil negotiated a cessation of border fighting between Ecuador and Peru. Cardoso believes that Brazil's international influence will be shaped by the extent to which regional cooperation in Latin America and the Caribbean, particularly the South Atlantic, is strengthened.

The Brazilian proposal for the creation of the South American Free Trade Association (Área de Livre Comércio Sul-Americana—ALCSA, or SAFTA), also known as the Free Trade Area of the Americas (FTAA), by 2005 is also an important step in Brazil's efforts to promote regional integration. At a May 13–15, 1997, meeting in Belo Horizonte of the thirty-four countries participating in the FTAA, Brazil opposed the United States preference for a faster timetable than 2005 and bilateral negotiations instead of discussions among trading blocs, such as Mercosul and the North American Free Trade Agreement (NAFTA—see Glossary).

Cardoso also sees a need for Brazil to develop alliances, coalitions, and partnerships on a global level, as distinct from a merely hemispheric level, be it with Asia, Europe, Africa, or the Middle East. The Cardoso government has focused on developing dynamic trade partnerships with the European Union (EU—see Glossary), Japan, and China as a counterweight to United States dominance. Brazilian exports to China of agricultural products and byproducts grew by 46 percent in 1995. In dollar terms, the figures rose from US$226.4 million in 1991 to US$1.2 billion in 1995, an increase of 430 percent.

In other national security areas, the Brazilian Armed Forces have been seeking a new role in the 1990s in the absence of any external threat to national security. They no longer have their two traditional "enemies": Argentina and communism. Since ending their regime in March 1985, the armed forces have continued to assert themselves politically under civilian rule. Their political influence, however, has diminished under the 1988 constitution, which places them under presidential authority, while the policy-making influence of the presidency, Congress, and civilian ministries has grown. In the absence of a defined security policy and a common project, the armed forces have been mired in bureaucratic rivalry.

Brazil's defense budget in 1997 totaled US$12 billion. The IBGE reported that investment in the armed forces as a percentage of the government budget declined sharply from 9.03 percent in 1985 to 1.70 percent in 1995. Not only is Brazil spending proportionately little on the military, some critics have argued, but the money is being spent badly and is being used to maintain an archaic and top-heavy bureaucracy. In the early 1990s, the army proportionately had more generals (164, of whom 141 were on active duty) than the United States Army. Critics have also singled out as "wasteful" the funds spent for the construction of a nuclear submarine, scheduled to be launched by 2007 at a cost of US$2.2 billion.

Brazil's new National Defense Plan (Plano de Defesa Nacional—PDN), approved on November 7, 1996, rules out "all possibilities" of conflict with Argentina. The PDN states that areas of future possible conflict are linked with "drug trafficking, narcoterrorism, and the presence of armed groups in Amazon regions bordering other countries." However, the "security and development" school of military thinking of a new generation of military strategists at the War College (Escola Superior de Guerra—ESG) disagrees with this threat assessment. It sees poverty and inequality as the main destabilizing influences.

The Clinton administration hoped that Brazil would significantly improve its efforts to stem international drug smuggling across its territory from Andean neighbors. The Amazon has become an international drug-trafficking route in the 1990s, and Brazil has become a major cocaine exporter. Increasingly, smugglers have been sending small shipments hidden in luggage or riverboat cargo. Under a new cooperation agreement signed in April 1995, the Clinton administration expected Brazil to improve coordination with the United States Drug Enforcement Administration (DEA). Stressing the threat posed by drug trafficking to Brazilian national security, President Cardoso announced on April 17, 1996, that the armed forces would join the drug enforcement effort in border areas, in the Northeast, and in the Amazon region. Mafia groups are gaining strength in Brazil. Nearly fifty Mafia kingpins were living in Brazil by mid-1997, either in Rio de Janeiro or São Paulo. Brazil had become the Italian Mafia's third area of activity, after Italy itself and the United States.

Brazil is becoming the largest market for money laundering in the world, according to the Federal Police (Polícia Federal) and Ministry of Justice. The Cardoso government calculated in 1996 that some US$490 billion evade taxes every year as a result of money laundering. In mid-1996 the government submitted a bill to Congress containing measures to combat money laundering.

Within Brazil, national sovereignty over the Amazon region has been a continuing security concern of the military, as evidenced by two projects: the Amazon Region Surveillance System (Sistema de Vigilância da Amazônia—Sivam) and the Amazon Region Protection System (Sistema de Proteção da Amazônia—Sipam). The Sipam and its sensor component, Sivam, involve superimposing a state-of-the-art surveillance system that will, by 2000, monitor 5 million square kilometers of the Amazon. It will transmit digital data from satellites, fixed and airborne radars, and other high-tech sensors (to be built under the Massachusetts-based Raytheon Company's US$1.4 billion contract with the Brazilian government) to computerized processing centers and hundreds of "user-nodes" dispersed throughout the Amazon region.

The concept of ecological security in regions such as the Amazon has become a major national security interest for Brazil. In the Cardoso government's view, the Sivam and Sipam projects are examples of how technology can be applied to rescue neglected regions. Sivam, which is coordinated by the Ministry of Aeronautics and the SAE (Strategic Affairs Secretariat), is promoted as an environmental initiative, with emphasis on the protection of the Amazon region, such as the monitoring of illegal logging and mining, forest burning, and even incursions into indigenous reserves. The system will be used to demarcate boundaries and monitor the use of Indian reservations, national parks, and other preserves. In addition to collecting ecological data, Sivam will monitor migration and settlement.

However, Sivam was conceived as a military project related to the development of an air traffic control network. Thus, Sivam will eliminate a radar blind spot for commercial airlines and facilitate the policing of illegal flights, estimated at as many as 3,000 daily. These illegal flights involve the smuggling not only of drugs, but also of consumer goods and ores. Most attention is focused on the 722 kilometers of the Brazilian-Colombian border, an area where most clandestine flights by drug traffickers take place.

The Sivam, which was signed in May 1995, was bogged down in the Senate throughout 1995 and much of 1996 amid objections over the cost, United States involvement, and allegations of influence peddling by a top aide to President Cardoso, whom the president subsequently fired. Ultimately, thanks to the personal intervention of President Cardoso and lobbying by the United States, the Raytheon Company's first financial contract with the Brazilian government to build Sivam was signed in October 1996. Raytheon signed Sivam contracts with two Brazilian firms on March 14, 1997.

Despite its efforts to monitor the Amazon region, one record set by the Cardoso administration has been in destruction of the Amazon rain forest. Deforestation in the first three years of the Cardoso administration reached 60,257 square kilometers, an area almost twice the size of Belgium. On January 26, 1998, Brazil's INPE (National Institute of Space Research), which is headquartered in São José dos Campos, released its report on deforestation of the Legal Amazon (the nine states in the North and Center-West regions), showing a declining trend in 1996–97 from a record level set in 1995. The new INPE figures, based on Landsat satellite images, show that, contrary to the government's claims that deforestation had slowed during 1992–97, the destroyed area in 1995 was 29,059 square kilometers of rain forest, the largest annual deforestation total recorded since the satellite monitoring began. The 1995 figure represented more than a doubling of the deforestation recorded in 1994 (14,896 square kilometers) and a rate even greater than that during the 1970s. The 1996 figure was well below the 1995 rate, but still a total of 18,161 square kilometers, an area almost as large as Israel, disappeared that year. The projection for 1997 is 13,037 square kilometers destroyed.

Another significant study, entitled *The Use of Fire in Amazônia: Case Studies Along the Arc of Deforestation,* was released in October 1997 by the Woods Hole Research Center in Massachussets and its newly established research center, the Institute of Environmental Research on Amazônia (Instituto de Pesquisa Ambiental da Amazônia—IPAM), based at the Federal University of Pará (Universidade Federal do Pará—UFPa) in Belém. This report found that cutting and burning have dried out the forest to the point that it could burn out of control.

On January 28, 1998, the Chamber of Deputies approved an environmental crimes bill to grant the "federal environmental agency" legal authority to enforce environmental protection laws. The "federal environmental agency" refers to the Brazilian Institute for the Environment and Renewable Natural Resources (Instituto Brasileiro do Meio-Ambiente e dos Recursos Naturais Renováveis—Ibama), which is under the Environmental Affairs Coordinating Secretariat (Secretaria de Coordenação dos Assuntos do Meio Ambiente—SMA) of the Ministry of Environment, Hydraulic Resources, and the Legal Amazon. The bill, which had languished in Congress for seven years, provides criminal penalties for damaging the environment and grants the "federal environmental agency" the right to levy fines, prosecute polluters, and order companies to correct environmental hazards.

Environmentalists supported the legislation, which includes significant provisions requiring companies to pay the cost of cleaning up environmental damage that they are proven to have caused (up to R$50 million), prohibiting proven polluters from signing government contracts, and setting daily fines for companies that refuse to clean up their damage. Although President Cardoso on January 30 disputed the results of the INPE's Brazilian Amazon Deforestation Appraisal Program (Programa de Avaliação do Desflorestamento da Amazônia Brasileira—Prodes), he signed the new Environmental Crimes Law on February 12. The president vetoed ten articles, including penalties for noise pollution, traditional slash-and-burn agricultural burnings, and automatic liability of companies to clean up their environmental damage and compensate victims. The watered-down law takes effect in April 1998.

Since the early 1990s, Brazil has actively sought to develop nonproliferation credentials. In September 1991, it signed the Mendoza Declaration prohibiting chemical and biological weapons. On February 9, 1994, Brazil began addressing international missile proliferation concerns by establishing a civilian space agency, thus ensuring that Brazil's space projects are exclusively peaceful. In addition, on May 30, 1994, Brazil finally ratified the 1967 Treaty for the Prohibition of Nuclear Weapons in Latin America (Treaty of Tlatelolco). Brazil was one of a half-dozen countries in the world that had not signed the 1968 Non-Proliferation Treaty (NPT). However, on June 20, 1997, President Cardoso submitted a request to Congress asking it to approve Brazil's adherence to the NPT.

In an attempt to overcome its reputation for transferring missile and nuclear technology to countries such as Iraq, Brazil signed the Missile Technology Control Regime (MTCR—see Glossary) in October 1995, committing itself to abide by the MTCR guidelines. Brazil hoped to convince MTCR members—such as the United States, France, the United Kingdom, and Germany—that Brazil can be trusted with sensitive technology.

Brazil's space program since 1991 has been restricted to creating satellite launchers for scientific and commercial purposes. Unlike Argentina, Brazil was able to join the MTCR without having to abandon its program for the development and construction of its Satellite Launch Vehicle (Veículo Lançador de Satélite—VLS). Production of the VLS got underway in May 1996. With MTCR membership, Brazil could reach new agreements with Germany, for example, in the field of space and nuclear technology cooperation and produce and export long-range rocket equipment and technology. However, Brazil's fledgling space program suffered a setback on November 2, 1997, when controllers were forced to destroy the rocket that was to carry the nation's second Data Gathering Satellite into Earth's orbit to collect information on the environment.

During then United States Secretary of State Warren Christopher's visit to Brazil on March 1, 1996, the Cardoso government reaffirmed Brazil's new attitude of partnership and cooperation with the United States. On that occasion, United States and Brazilian officials signed a new bilateral agreement for cooperation in space that emphasized the use of space technology for environmental research and analysis. Officials of both countries also pledged to cooperate in protecting the Amazon rain forest. In addition, a United States-Brazil Agreement for Cooperation on Peaceful Uses of Nuclear Energy was adopted.

The Cardoso government articulated a strategic vision of Brazil's future. This vision, as explained by Ronaldo Mota Sardenberg, secretary of the SAE, recognizes that the new world order is based on knowledge, communications technology, and services; Brazil must insert itself into the international community and South America by reducing social inequalities, increasing national integration, and emphasizing science and technology. Thus, the Cardoso government sees strategy as a long-term socioeconomic concept to overcome underdevelopment. It believes that Brazil will not maintain its status as a middle-income nation, much less climb into the developed world, if a large proportion of its population is excluded and entire regions of the country continue to be underdeveloped.

To better prepare Brazil for the strategic information needs of the twenty-first century, President Cardoso charged the SAE with collecting economic and political information and focusing on detecting social conflicts that could occur during his presidency. Cardoso also proposed the establishment of the Brazilian Intelligence Agency (Agência Brasileira da Inteligência Nacional—ABIN), an autonomous organization also under the Office of the Presidency. The ABIN is expected to replace the former SNI apparatus in 1998.

The new ministry of defense to be established by Cardoso in 1998 will merge the four military ministries. The current military ministries will be reduced to commands. The commanders of the army, air force, and navy will be directly subordinate to the minister of defense. The new ministry's budget for 1998 totalled 2.9 billion *reais,* almost US$3 billion, making it the third largest budget in the government. Sardenberg was expected to become the supervisor of the incumbent military ministers, thereby undermining the decision-making power of the military.

Cardoso succeeded in repairing Brazil's international image to reflect an economically and politically stable and reliable country that can achieve its development potential, compete for new markets, attract productive investment, and acquire foreign technology. He also appeared to have restored Brazilians' self-esteem and national pride. According to the results of a Vox Populi poll, reported in January 1996, a majority of people (2,000) questioned said they believed Brazil was well on its way to becoming a great power. In addition, 84 percent expressed pride in being Brazilian, and 79 percent said they had no wish to emigrate.

Brazil's 160 million inhabitants and rich resources make it a country of tremendous potential. Realization of Brazil's potential, however, will depend on implementation of the needed administrative, social, and tax reforms. According to a 1997 study by the University of São Paulo, their passage would result in annual GDP growth of 7 percent. By late 1997, little real progress had been made in the areas of health, education, homelessness, land squatting by rural peasants, transportation, and so forth. Nevertheless, Cardoso's Plano *Real* has aided the poor more than any other social class, raising their standards of living and their spirits by giving them greater purchasing power (as well as debts) and a sense of upward mobility. Although Brazil, with annual inflation of 7.2 percent in 1997, is clearly on a steadier course than it was in the first half of the 1990s, the country still has a long way to go in reversing the ever-widening socioeconomic inequities between rich and poor. Many regard Cardoso as the last, best hope for Brazil (at least in this century) to take the actions needed to get the country to realize its enormous potential and its destiny in the twenty-first century.

February 13, 1998

* * *

In the early months of 1998, rampant drug-trafficking and destruction of the Amazon rain forest rose to the forefront of threats facing Brazil. The country's drug trafficking and other drug-related crime have expanded much more rapidly and insidiously than the capability of Brazilian society to perceive the threat. Three laws enacted in late February 1998 demonstrate the higher priority to be accorded by the Cardoso government to drug enforcement. First, President Cardoso ordered the creation of the Special Secretariat for National Drug-Control Policy (Secretaria Especial da Política Nacional do Contrôle de Drogas—SEPNCD), directly subordinate to the presidency of the republic. The SEPNCD will give priority to border surveillance and control and coordinate the activities of state and local security agencies with fourteen federal agencies that combat drugs. It will also develop strategies and national policy on drug control. Second, Cardoso signed a newly passed money-laundering law, which will create mechanisms to identify "dirty money" and set prison terms of three to five years for money laundering. And third, Cardoso signed a law authorizing government agencies to shoot down hostile aircraft.

In the second half of March 1998, fires brought on by the worst drought in memory and *queimadas* (burnings) by slash-and-burn farmers swept Roraima, destroying vast swaths of savanna and the rain forests that were home to the Yanomami Indians. Roraima is the state with the lowest population density in Brazil (one inhabitant per square kilometer), but it has the largest indigenous community in the country, with about 14 percent of the nation's native American population. The conflagration was the worst in the history of the Amazon Region, according to the National Institute of Amazon Region Research (Instituto Nacional de Pesquisas da Amazônia—INPA). Indeed, in the assessment of the United Nations (UN) representative in Brazil, Walter Franco, the fires constituted an environmental disaster unprecedented on the planet. They consumed more than 36 million hectares, or 33,000 square kilometers, an area larger than Belgium and constituting 15 percent of Roraima's territory. Although the Brazilian military rejected a UN offer to help combat the fire as an intrusion into Brazil's sovereignty, the Cardoso government accepted it.

April 13, 1998

* * *

In the largest conservation step ever in the Amazon, on April 29, 1998, President Cardoso committed Brazil to tripling the area of Amazon forests under formal government protection by 2000. The agreement, to be carried out with the financial and technical assistance of the World Bank (see Glossary) and the World Wildlife Fund, would turn 10 percent of the Brazilian Amazon, or 25 million hectares, into parks and preserves.

May 11, 1998 Rex A. Hudson

Chapter 1. Historical Setting

A nineteenth-century wood carving made by an indigenous Brazilian tribe, from Hjalmar Stolpe, Amazon Indian Designs from Brazilian and Guianan Wood Carvings

EXPORTS, SLAVERY, AND PATRIARCHY have been the three constants of Brazilian history. The export orientation of the colonial economy shaped Brazil's society. Even the name "Brazil," like the country itself, is suggestive of commerce and the pursuit of wealth. Brazil's name derives from the brazilwood trees from which Europeans sought in the sixteenth century to make valuable red dyes. However, the central fact of the country's history was the exploitation of cheap labor, first as slaves, then as wage-earners. Indeed, Brazil's history is the story not only of conquest but also of the enslavement of its native peoples and of millions of imported African slaves.

Brazil's history can be divided into five economic periods, each characterized by a dominant export product. The first period, from 1500 to 1550, involved the logging of brazilwood along the coast of the Northeast (Nordeste). Brazilwood was the source of a red dye important to the expanding textile industry of sixteenth-century northern Europe, particularly Normandy and Flanders. The trees and the ready labor of the natives, who were eager to acquire metal products in return for cutting and hauling logs to the coast, attracted Portuguese and French ships. The French were quite successful because they sent young men to reside among the natives, to learn their languages, and to get them to bring the timber to the nearest bay or estuary. By contrast, the Portuguese, in the first few decades, traded from their ships or haphazard outposts. The Portuguese attempted to use the factory system that they were then employing along the African, South Asian, and Asian coasts. This system consisted of fortified trading posts that had minimal contact with the local population. The French, with deeper roots among the native peoples and more knowledge of their cultures, filled their waiting ships more quickly. France's activity convinced the Portuguese crown to undertake sustained settlement to protect its claim.

The Europeans struggled among themselves for control of the beachheads, anchorages, and bays. The Portuguese effort to gain effective control of the coast coincided with the onset of the sugar era, which extended from 1530 to 1650. Sugarcane cultivation was carried out in widely separated tidewater enclaves from São Vicente in the South (Sul—the present-day states of Paraná, Santa Catarina, and Rio Grande do Sul) to

Pernambuco in the Northeast; it became most successful around the Bahian Recôncavo and in Pernambuco. Enslaved natives and increasingly, after the 1560s, imported African slaves provided the labor for the mills (*engenhos*) and fields.

Sugar tied Brazil into the developing system of European capitalism, imposed a patriarchal social system on the country, and prompted Dutch attacks on Portugal's South Atlantic empire. The sugar economy's need for oxen and meat led to the accompanying growth of cattle raising in the dry interior hinterlands, known as the *sertão*. Cattle raising became so important to the economy and to the development of the interior as to almost constitute a phase in its own right. However, although cattle raising provided hides for export, it supplied principally local markets. The Dutch seizure of Recife in 1630 and their subsequent capture of Luanda on the Angolan coast, a principal source of slaves imported into Brazil, disrupted the Portuguese dominance over sugar. When the Hollanders (*holandeses*) withdrew from Brazil in 1654, they stimulated cane growing on the Caribbean islands and used their control of distribution in Europe to reduce Portuguese access.

The third period—mining of gold and diamonds from the 1690s to the 1750s—carried Portugal's effective occupation of the land far into the interior of what are now the states of Minas Gerais, Goiás, and Mato Grosso. The discoveries of alluvial gold on the Rio das Velhas in about 1693, throughout central Minas Gerais in the next years, and out into Mato Grosso in 1718 and Goiás in 1725, and then the growth of diamond mining along the Rio Jequitinhonha in Minas Gerais after 1730, shifted the colonial center away from the Northeast coast into the interior. Minas Gerais became the new jewel in Portugal's crown, although one that was difficult to keep in place. As more people spread to the distant interior, many of them were living beyond the reach of royal officials. Indeed, one of Brazil's distinctive features has always been the existence of people who live within the boundaries of the country but outside the limits of the society and the controls of the state.

The Northeast and the South were tied to Minas Gerais via the livestock trade. The *mineiro* (Minas Gerais) towns needed beef, as well as a seemingly endless supply of mules. Without good roads, mule trains became characteristic of the region, which was soon tied together by an extensive web of trails. The cattle came south from ranches along the Rio São Francisco, thereby linking the mines to the Northeast. The mules came from the pampas of Rio Grande do Sul via the market at Sorocaba in São Paulo, tying the South to the mining region. Because Paulistas (residents of the state of São Paulo) made most of the initial gold strikes, São Paulo was connected to all the mining areas. The importance of Minas Gerais and the mines farther inland led the crown to transfer the viceregal capital from Salvador, Bahia, to Rio de Janeiro in 1763.

Gold production declined in the later decades of the eighteenth century, and from about 1820 coffee cultivation provided a fourth period that lasted to the end of the 1920s. It began in the mountains behind Rio de Janeiro, moved along the Rio Paraíba Valley to the west across São Paulo State and out into Paraná. Coffee powered the rise of São Paulo and its port of Santos, and although it gradually took a secondary position to industrialization after the late 1930s, Brazil remained the world's major coffee producer.

The Amazon had an important era of its own from the 1880s to 1919, when it was the world's major source of rubber. The rubber boom drew world attention to the region, prompted Brazil to secure its boundaries, and lured thousands of rubber tappers from the drought-plagued *sertão* of the Northeast to the forests of Acre. It turned into a bust when the helter-skelter collection of wild rubber lost out to the massive production methods of British, Dutch, and French plantations in Southeast Asia.

The fifth period began in the 1930s with import-substitution industrialization (see Glossary) and extended into the 1990s. Industry's initial and heaviest concentration was in the triangle of São Paulo-Rio de Janeiro-Belo Horizonte. The period was perhaps best symbolized by the steel mills of Volta Redonda, built in 1944, and São Paulo's integrated industrial zone. Industrialization and its parallel urbanization attracted rural migrants from throughout the country, but especially from the drought-plagued Northeast. In the space of a generation after 1940, Brazil leaped from the age of the bull-cart to that of the internal combustion engine, changing the national map in the process.

Before the 1930s, despite the earlier incursions into the interior, Brazil still consisted of a series of enclaves connected by sealanes rather than by railroads or paved highways. Pan American Airway's introduction of the DC–3 on its run from Belém to Rio de Janeiro in 1940 vaulted Brazil directly into the air age. By the 1970s, it had the world's third largest commercial air fleet after the United States and the Soviet Union. The

1950s push to develop an automotive industry was followed in later decades by large-scale construction of long-distance highways, which by the 1980s made it possible to travel to all regions of the country on paved roads. Symbolic of this era was the building of Brazil's third capital at Brasília (1955–60) on the plains of Goiás. The internal combustion engine and the coinciding growth of the petroleum industry also made possible the mechanization of agriculture, which changed rapidly the face of the Brazilian west and made Brazil the second largest exporter of food in the 1980s. The combination of highways and automotive transport opened up Amazônia for the first time. The construction of the highway corridors from Brasília to Belém and from Cuiabá to Porto Velho to Manaus triggered large-scale migration, mining and agricultural development, timbering, land disputes, displacement of native peoples, and massive deforestation. The latter made Brazil's Amazon policies the subject of world debate, which in turn made Brazilians worry about the security of their immense North region (Amazônia).

The Indigenous Population

In 1500 Pedro Álvares Cabral's fleet, which was en route to India, landed at Porto Seguro in what is now the state of Bahia. The territory that comprises modern Brazil had a native population in the millions, divided among hundreds of tribes and language groups. Their ancestors had lived in this land for as long as 30,000 years. There is no way to be certain of the exact size of the population or its distribution. Many areas that were inhabited in 1500 were later stripped bare by epidemics or slave hunters. But scholars have attempted to make estimates based on contemporary reports and the supposed carrying capacity of the land. For Brazil's Amazon Basin alone, demographer William M. Denevan has suggested 3,625,000 people, with another 4,800,000 in other regions. Other estimates place 5 million inhabitants in Amazônia alone. More conservatively, British historian John Hemming estimated 2,431,000 people for Brazil as a whole. These figures are based on known tribes, although many unknown ones probably died out in the devastating epidemics of the colonial era.

Certainly, the indigenous population exceeded that of Portugal itself. The early European chroniclers wrote of multitudes along the coast and of dense populations in the Amazon Basin. Far from being awed by the newcomers, the indigenous inhabitants displayed curiosity and hospitality, a willingness to exchange goods, and a distinct ability at aggressive defense. However, they could not prevent the devastation caused by the diseases carried by the Europeans and Africans. Tens of thousands succumbed to smallpox, measles, tuberculosis, typhoid, dysentery, and influenza. Whole peoples were likely annihilated without having had direct contact with Europeans as disease was carried along the indigenous trade routes.

The Indians spoke languages that scholars have classified into four families: the Gê speakers, originally spread along the coast and into the central plateau and scrub lands; the Tupí speakers, who displaced the Gê on the coast and hence were the first met by the Portuguese; the Carib speakers in the north and in Amazônia, who were related distantly to the people who gave their name to the Caribbean; the Arawak (or Aruak) speakers in Amazônia, whose linguistic relatives ranged up through Central America to Florida; and, according to sociologist Donald Sawyer, the Nambicuara in northwestern Mato Grosso (see Language, ch. 2). These were not tribes but language families that comprised many language groups. Numerous tribes also spoke languages unrelated to any of the above. Warfare and migrations carried peoples from these linguistic families to various parts of Brazil. The Europeans took advantage of the cultural differences among the Indian peoples to pit one against the other and to form alliances that provided auxiliary troops in their colonial wars.

Portugal viewed the Indians as slave labor from the outset. When Portugal began its imperial ventures, it had a population of about 1 million. Indeed, in the mid-sixteenth century Portugal's population was so sparse that much of its territory was uncultivated and abandoned. African and native Brazilian slaves were common on the streets of Lisbon. Portugal's colonial economy in Brazil was based on slavery. Initially, the Portuguese bartered with the natives to bring brazilwood and other forest items to the coast. However, when the natives had accumulated all the tools and pots that they needed, they showed a lack of interest in continuing the arrangement. Consequently, the Portuguese turned to violent persuasion. The enslavement of the natives shaped much of the history that followed.

Just as Indian unrest had aided the Spanish conquerors of Mexico and Peru, so too did the Portuguese profit from arriving at a time of turmoil. The Tupí speakers had been shifting steadily from the south in a massive migration to coastal areas, displacing the resident Gê speakers, many of whom moved into the interior. This population shift had triggered continuous warfare against non-Tupí peoples and against Tupí subsets. It involved set battles that arrayed hundreds and, in some reports, thousands of warriors in fierce hand-to-hand combat. Some of the fighting went beyond struggles over control of land or resources to vendettas in which captives were sought and in some cases reportedly cannibalized. The Portuguese used these vendettas to keep the Indians from uniting against them and subsequently to obtain slaves. The conquest of Brazil was not a simple toppling of an organized empire as in Peru, but a drawn out, complicated process that spread over huge distances, different peoples, and centuries. Thus, it is not surprising that the Brazilian elites developed myths about racial harmony, peaceful change, and compromise that often have colored the interpretations of historians, thereby distorting understanding of Brazil's past.

Just as Portugal was different from the rest of Europe, so too would Brazil be different from the rest of the Americas. Portugal was both an agrarian and a maritime monarchy that used its control over land grants to discipline the nobility and its issuance of trading licenses to attract local and foreign investment in its overseas ventures. As merchant-king, the monarch supervised an economic system that imported timber, sugar, and wine from Madeira and the Azores, gold from the Guinea coast, spices from India, and dyewood and forest products, then sugar, gold, gems, and hides from Brazil. These products were then reexported to Europe.

The Portuguese established themselves on the Brazilian coast in their drive to control Europe's trade with India and East Asia. They secured "title" to what became eastern Brazil in their attempted division of the world with Spain in the Treaty of Tordesillas (see Glossary) of 1494. During the next centuries, the Portuguese, Spanish, French, English, and Dutch changed the South American continent's trade patterns, which previously had been focused internally. Seeking profits, the Portuguese marshaled Indian labor to provide exportable products. The commercial objective that initially had prompted overseas operations became the first principle of Portuguese colonization. Brazil was not to be a place where Europe's religious dissidents sought freedom of conscience. Rather, to paraphrase historian Caio Prado Júnior, the colonization of tropical Brazil would be "one vast commercial enterprise." Colonial Brazil's reason for being was to supply dyewood, sugar, tobacco, eventually gold and diamonds, cotton, coffee, and later rubber for the European and then world markets. The externally oriented colonial economy consisted of enclaves that faced seaward and that considered only their own commercial interests.

In his 1843 essay, "How the History of Brazil Should Be Written," Karl Friederich Philipp von Martius urged the study of the three basic racial groups—indigenous peoples, Europeans, and Africans—to obtain a clear understanding of the country's history. Yet when he discussed the interactions between the Indians and the Portuguese, he wrote that the former were only a few primitive tribes and that the "colonies developed and expanded almost without caring about these Indians." Although he could not have been more wrong, historians have echoed his attitude repeatedly. The natives, rather than being few, were in the millions, and the Portuguese determination to exploit their labor shaped frontier expansion and set Brazil's modern boundaries.

The Colonial Era, 1500–1815

Frontier Expansion That Shaped Brazil

Under the Treaty of Tordesillas, everything to the east of the line that ran from pole to pole 370 leagues west of the Cape Verde Islands was to be Portugal's to exploit. The exact reason for Portugal's interest in having the line so far to the west is debatable, but the Portuguese may have been trying to keep the Castilians away from the sure route to the East. Very practically, the line's placement gave Portuguese vessels en route to India ample room to pick up winds and currents that took them around the southern end of Africa, a feat carried out by Vasco da Gama on his voyage of 1497–99. The Portuguese also may have known that western lands or islands lay on their side of the line. On the modern map of Brazil, in the north the line cuts across the eastern end of the Ilha de Marajó, and in the south it passes through Laguna on the coast of Santa Catarina. Because most of present-day Brazil lies to the west of the line, clearly the Portuguese expanded successfully on this initial division.

The territorial aggrandizement, which is one of the main themes of Brazilian history, was both accidental and a matter of state policy. Uncertainty as to the detailed geography of South

America persisted into the twentieth century, so it is understandable that Portuguese officials professed to believe into the eighteenth century that the estuaries of both the Amazon and the Río de la Plata were on their side of the Tordesillas Line. The two river systems were, in the words of the Jesuit Father Simão de Vasconcellos, "two keys that lock the land of Brazil . . . two giants that defend it and demarcate between us [Portuguese] and Castille." Several centuries of penetration along these river systems gave Brazil its distinctive shape. It could be said that today's Brazil owes its vast territory to the native Indians who served as skilled trackers, warriors, porters, food suppliers, and paddlers for the Portuguese expeditions, and to the Indians whose potential as slaves lured the Portuguese inland.

The Portuguese empire at the outset was a commercial rather than a colonial one. Portugal lacked sufficient population to establish colonies of settlers throughout its maritime empire. The Portuguese practice was to conquer enough space for a trading fort and a surrounding enclave from which to draw on the wealth and resources of the adjacent country. A map of this maritime commercial domain would show a series of dots connected by sealanes rather than continuous stretches of territory. French competition forced the Portuguese shift to colonialism in Brazil. This shift involved the gradual move from trading for brazilwood to cultivating sugarcane, which required control of great expanses of land and increasing numbers of slaves. The first to burst past the Tordesillas Line were the slave hunters. The shift to colonialism was also facilitated by the union of the Spanish and Portuguese crowns between 1580 and 1640. Although the two governments on the Iberian Peninsula and in the Americas were kept separate, trade and travel controls became lax. An active contraband trade developed between Brazilian settlements and Buenos Aires, and Portuguese moving overland appeared in Asunción, Potosí, Lima, and even Quito.

Expansion along the Atlantic coast had been gradual. Using the model of the Atlantic islands, the crown in 1536 divided the Brazilian coast into fifteen donatory captaincies (*donatários*). To induce settlement, the crown offered ten leagues of coastline as personal property, a percentage of the dyewood trade, control over trade of enslaved natives, as well as the exclusive right to build mills. In 1580 Brazil comprised the area from Pernambuco in the north to São Vicente in the south. With

A view of Morretes, Paraná State, with the Pico do Marumbi in the background
Courtesy Jon Barlow Hudson

Spanish assistance thereafter, the Portuguese expanded north to Paraíba, then west through Ceará and Maranhão against the natives and the French, until they founded Belém in 1616. Beginning in 1621, these possessions were divided into the state of Maranhão (embracing the crown captaincies of Ceará, Maranhão, and Pará) and the state of Brazil, centering on Salvador, Bahia. The reassertion of Portuguese independence under the Braganças in 1640 led to sporadic conflict in frontier areas and to policies seeking to hold back Spanish advances. In the Amazon and Río de la Plata river basins, the Spanish rather than the Portuguese had been first on the scene. The Spaniards included Álvar Núñez Cabeza de Vaca, who journeyed from the coast of Santa Catarina to Asunción in 1540, and Francisco de Orellana, who descended the Amazon in 1542.

The most important Spanish advances were the mission settlements, where the Jesuits Christianized native peoples. Two areas of particular importance lay adjacent to the river systems that delimit Brazil in the south and in the north: the Paraná-Paraguay Basin in the south and the Mamoré-Guaporé Basin in the north. From 1609 to 1628, the Jesuits founded eight missions among the Guaraní peoples between the Paraná and

Paraguai rivers in what is now southern Paraguay. They pressed deep into what is today the state of Paraná, between the Ivaí and Paranapanema rivers, to establish fifteen more in what was called Guairá Province.

From 1629 to 1631, the Guairá missions were attacked by slave hunters, known as *bandeirantes* (see Glossary), from the Portuguese town of São Paulo. According to the governor of Buenos Aires, these attacks resulted in the enslavement of more than 70,000 Guaraní. Consequently, the Jesuits decided to evacuate some 10,000 survivors downriver and overland to sites between the Rio Uruguai and the Atlantic, in what became the state of Rio Grande do Sul. Other Jesuits fleeing the Guairá missions set up missions among the Itatín people on the eastern bank of the Rio Paraguai in what is now Mato Grosso do Sul, only to be destroyed brutally by *bandeirantes* in the 1630s and 1640s. By 1650 only twenty-two of forty-eight missions remained in the whole region. The Jesuits stopped the slave hunters in the south by arming and training the Guaraní, who dealt a significant blow to their oppressors in the Battle of Mbororé in 1641. This victory ensured the continued existence of the southern Spanish missions for another century, although they became a focal point of Portuguese-Spanish conflict in the 1750s. Broadly speaking, the Battle of Mbororé stabilized the general boundary lines between the Portuguese and the Spanish in the south.

In the north, the Spanish had established the town of Santa Cruz de la Sierra in 1561 and from there planted missions in the Mamoré-Guaporé Basin in about 1682. Called the Mojos and Chiquitos, these mission provinces were in what is now lowland Bolivia fronting on the states of Mato Grosso and Rondônia. By 1746 there were twenty-four mission towns in the Mojos and ten in Chiquitos. The *bandeirantes* again carried the flag of Portugal into the region, first attacking the Chiquitos missions for slaves and then discovering gold in Mato Grosso (1718–36). Unsure where these gold discoveries were in relation to the Spanish territories, the members of the Lisbon-based Overseas Council, which administered the colonies, ordered a comprehensive reconnaissance and the drawing of accurate maps. In 1723 Francisco de Melo Palhêta led an expedition from Belém to the Guaporé, reporting to Lisbon the startling news about the numerous prosperous Jesuit missions. Moreover, the question of fixing borders had become more urgent in 1722, when a respected French cartographer placed the mouths of the Amazon and the Río de la Plata on the Spanish side of the Tordesillas Line.

Because the Guaporé rises in Mato Grosso and flows into the Mamoré, which enters the Madeira, and then into the Amazon, these rivers formed a natural border. Moreover, the headwaters of the Paraguai were close and offered the possibility of linking the Amazonian and La Plata systems. In 1748 Lisbon created the Captaincy of Mato Grosso as its rampart on the Peruvian side and later in the century erected Fort Príncipe de Beira on the Guaporé. In northern Amazônia, in what were then the royal states of Maranhão and Pará, the Portuguese, worried about Dutch traders from Guiana (modern Suriname) and Spaniards from Venezuela, built fortifications at Óbidos, Manaus, Tabatinga, and on the Rio Branco and Rio Negro during the eighteenth century, thereby solidifying their claims. As it turned out, it was easier to secure the vast North region than it was the South.

In 1680 the Portuguese had built a fort at Colônia do Sacramento on the eastern La Plata shore opposite Buenos Aires to guard their claim and to capture a share of the contraband trade with silver-rich Potosí. According to the Overseas Council, Lisbon adopted the policy of fortifying and settling the coast below Santa Catarina, because "the continuation of these settlements will be the best means of deciding the question of limits . . . between the two crowns."

By the mid-eighteenth century, the Iberian powers were ready to admit the fiction of Tordesillas and to redraw their lines in South America on the basis of *uti possidetis* (that is, ownership by occupation rather than by claim). The Portuguese gave up Colônia do Sacramento, and in return received the lands of the Jesuit order's seven missions in western Rio Grande. This exchange led to the Guaraní War of 1756, which destroyed the missions and contributed to the Jesuit expulsion from Portuguese (1759) and Spanish (1763) possessions. With the Treaties of 1750, 1761, and 1777, Brazil took on its modern shape. The lines were drawn for the nineteenth-century struggles over the East Bank (Banda Oriental, or present-day Uruguay) of the Rio Uruguai and the Río de la Plata, the war with the United Provinces of the Río de la Plata (1825–28), and the Paraguayan War, also known as the War of the Triple Alliance (1864–70).

Thus, as a result of slave hunting, gold prospecting, and Portuguese royal policy, the Tordesillas Line became obsolete, and

Portugal obtained more than half of South America. When Brazil became independent in 1822, its huge territory was comparable in size with the Russian and Chinese empires.

Early Colonization

On April 22, 1500, the thirteen-ship fleet under Pedro Álvares Cabral anchored off the mouth of the Rio Buranhém (sweet bark in Tupí) on the Bahian coast. The chronicler of the discovery, Pêro Vaz de Caminha, wrote that immediately they saw men walking on the beach, and by the time a longboat reached the shore twenty or so had assembled. Entirely naked and dark skinned, they laid down their bows and arrows as a sign of peace, while responding to offers of Portuguese hats by giving over a parrot-feathered headdress and a long string of white seed pearls. Thus did the cultural exchange begin that would evolve over the next five centuries into the distinctive Brazilian culture.

In the nine days that the Portuguese stayed at the anchorage they called Porto Seguro, the natives were fascinated by the Catholic Mass, the iron tools, and alcoholic drink. Their seeming receptivity and lack of religious symbols that the Portuguese could understand caused Caminha to predict that these people quickly would turn Christian.

The natives helped fill a ship with fine-grained timber, dyewood, and presumably some of the *buranhém* wood or bark that gave the river its name. Cabral sent the ship back to Lisbon with Caminha's oft-quoted letter to the king, the first report on Brazil to reach Europe. As the rest of the fleet set sail from what Cabral called the Island of Vera Cruz for the Cape of Good Hope, two male convicts were left on the shore. Rather than execute such *degredados* (outcasts; see Glossary), the Portuguese were instinctively creating an advance guard that would learn the local language and via intermarriage would give them in another generation the means to penetrate both the indigenous societies and the Brazilian land mass.

After so many years of remarkable contacts with newly discovered lands, the Portuguese were a bit blasé about the news of this land of parrots, naked people, and brazilwood. At that time, peppers, spices, and silks were worth more than such exotica, and those products came from India and lands farther east.

With the exception of the New Christian (Jewish converts) investors, Brazil received little attention from Lisbon for three decades. The investors scouted and defended the coast and shared with the crown their monopoly contracts to harvest the brazilwood. The Portuguese monarchs followed the practice of holding legal title to lands and to certain commodities but issuing to others licenses to profit from these lands and commodities at their own expense, or with the backing of other investors. The custom was akin to the Castilian practice of *adelantado* (awarding of conquistador status—see Glossary) that developed during the reconquest of the Iberian Peninsula from the Moors, whereby the crown commissioned an agent to conquer a certain area at his own expense in return for rights to land, booty, and labor. The combination of royal licenses and private initiative that worked so well for Portugal along the African coast and in India was reshaped for Brazil.

But soon other Europeans were challenging Portugal's claims to exclusivity. Spanish captains edged their ships down the coast and up the Río de la Plata. From 1504 onward, French vessels from Brittany, Flanders, and Normandy were active in the dyewood trade. The reddish-purple dyes made from the wood brought good prices from tapestry and textile makers, and the French court ignored Portuguese protests. The Portuguese sent out naval expeditions to destroy French vessels and outposts, but by 1530 it was clear that mounting an effective coast guard along thousands of kilometers with countless coves, anchorages, and bays would be impossible; Portugal either had to take active possession or lose out to more interested rivals. Portugal took two steps, one immediate and the other long term. It dispatched a strong fleet under the command of Martim Afonso de Sousa, who was instructed to clear the coast of interlopers and to establish a permanent settlement. The result was Brazil's first European town, São Vicente, established in 1532.

The crown also may have wanted to follow up on the adventure in 1524 of Aleixo Garcia, a Portuguese shipwrecked on the southern coast who led about 2,000 Guaraní on a raid against Inca border towns in what is now Bolivia. Sousa sent a government-sponsored expedition (*entrada*) back over Garcia's route, only to meet death at the hands of the Carijó tribe of Indians. Such feeble results did little to attract investors, so the crown turned to the hereditary donatory captaincy system that had succeeded on the islands of Madeira and the Azores. Under this system, each donee was responsible for colonizing his own captaincy at his own expense. To help the lord proprietor attract settlers, he was given permission to issue land grants (*sesmarias*). This step was significant because it twisted a medieval Portuguese practice that placed conquered lands in the hands of peasants into one that gave some families holdings larger than Portugal's provinces. This practice in part led to the establishment of latifundia (see Glossary) in Brazil.

Nonetheless, the nobles were not interested in risking their lives or fortunes in a land of "naked savages," and most of those who received the grants were too ill-prepared, ill-financed, and ill-connected to succeed. The northern four captaincies never went beyond the planning stage, and the rest flourished or failed depending on the management skills and competence of the *donatário* in dealing with the native Brazilians. Sousa, who obtained the grant to São Vicente, prospered because he took advantage of João Ramalho, a castaway who had married the daughter of the chief of the Goiana Tupiniquin. Because of Ramalho, who lived until 1580, the Portuguese were able to obtain Indian labor, foodstuffs, and women. With his help, it was possible to establish a town at the village of Piratininga, which in time would grow into the metropolis of São Paulo. He was the key player in the Portuguese alliance with the Tupiniquin, who protected the colony from other Indians and who formed the basis for the future military power of the *bandeirantes*. The lack of European women facilitated assimilation and acculturation with the Indians. With the steady miscegenation, a substantial population of Tupí-speaking mestizos (*mestiços* or *mamelucos*—see Glossary) came into being.

Also important for São Vicente's success was Sousa's ability to attract investors for sugar mills, including an investor from Antwerp, which became the center of the European sugar market. Although Pernambuco in later years surpassed São Vicente in sugar production, its early success fixed Portuguese control on what centuries later would be the agricultural and industrial core of Brazil.

Similarly, the affluence of Pernambuco Province centering on Olinda resulted from successful interaction with the natives, the ability to draw investment capital (often from Italian merchants), and capable settlers. The *donatário*, Duarte Coelho Pereira, had married into the well-connected Albuquerque family, which helped him attract colonists and financial support to set up sugar mills. But he was especially fortunate because his brother-in-law, Jerônimo de Albuquerque, had married the daughter of chief Arcoverde (Green Bow) of the

Tobajara, thereby sealing an alliance that gave the Portuguese supplies of food and workers. The alliance also gave Coelho Pereira the military superiority to eventually defeat the French and their Indian allies. As the brazilwood stands were cut down, they were replaced with sugarcane plantations, which by 1585 were served by more than sixty mills or *engenhos.* The captaincy was so successful that there was reputedly more luxury in Pernambuco than in Lisbon. This strong beginning would make it the northern focal point of Portuguese America.

Porto Seguro failed to prosper as a captaincy. The constant fighting with the local Aimoré people may have been related to the presence of many married Portuguese couples and, consequently, little intermarriage with the natives. Likewise, Bahia failed at this stage because its *donatário* lacked managerial skills. Many of the Portuguese there were veterans of India, where abuse of the natives was routine. The Tupinambá finally tired of the mistreatment, and many of the Portuguese at Bahia, including the *donatário,* were captured and ceremonially killed and eaten. Ilhéus, Espírito Santo, São Tomé, Santo Amaro, and Santa Anna also failed because of poor management and hostile relations with the natives. The coast was now exposed to French incursions.

Such an outcome was not what the crown had in mind, and it decided wisely to listen to warnings. Rather than replace inept *donatários* with others, the king established direct royal control, except over Pernambuco and São Vicente. The crown may have acted at this juncture for several reasons: the Spanish discovery of the famed silver mountain at Potosí (1545), the decline of the Asian spice trade, and the crown's practice of reclaiming royal control after some years of leasing its rights. The enhancement of royal power was part of the general Iberian pattern of establishing royal control over the sprawling colonial ventures. In a larger sense, renewed royal control appears to have been linked to a new conservatism in Catholic Europe. The Council of Trent (1545–63) defined church dogma and practice, religious tolerance faded, and the Inquisition was emplaced in Portugal in 1547.

The king named Tomé de Sousa the first governor general of Brazil (1549–53). He ordered Sousa to create a capital city, Salvador, on the Bahia de Todos os Santos (Bay of All Saints) and to spread the royal mantle over the captaincies, defending the weaker ones and reestablishing the failed ones. Because Indian attacks were blamed for the failures, Sousa's orders amounted to a declaration of war on the indigenous peoples of Brazil. If they could be defeated, the French would have no allies and so would be less of a threat. In addition, Sousa was to increase royal revenues. The twin objectives of control and revenue were characteristic of royal policy for the rest of the colonial era.

Bahia, as the city and province would be known, was selected for its central location and its fine bay, and because the crown had purchased it from the heirs of the *donatário*. Sousa built fortifications, a town, and sugar mills. His knottiest task was forming a policy on the Indians, whose status remained unclear. Although he had treasury and coast guard officials with him, their roles were oriented toward Portuguese colonists and European interlopers.

As early as 1511, the crown had placed the Indians under its "protection," and it ordered Sousa to treat them well, as long as they were peaceful, so that they could be converted. Conversion was essential because Portugal's legal claims to Brazil were based on papal bulls requiring Christianization of the Indians. However, those who resisted conversion were likened to Muslims and could be enslaved. In fact, as historian Sergio Buarque de Holanda showed, by identifying Brazil as a destination of the wandering Apostle St. Thomas the Portuguese settlers were able to argue that all natives had their chance to convert and had rejected it, so they could be conquered and taken captive legitimately. Thus, a distinction was made between peaceful, pliable natives who as wards deserved crown protection and those resisters who wanted to keep their independence and on whom "just war" could be made and slavery imposed.

The dual mission of the governors was contradictory; how could they stimulate the economy using slave labor while converting the natives? To carry out the pacification and conversion of the natives, the crown chose the new Jesuit order of the Society of Jesus, which was international in membership and military in structure and which had the task of defending and spreading the Catholic Counter-Reformation. The Jesuits had a major impact on Brazil, despite their small numbers—128 by 1598. The Indians responded to the Jesuits with initial acceptance, then regression, evasion, and enmity. The objective of the Jesuits was to Europeanize the Indians by resettling them in Indian villages (*aldeias*). In a recurring pattern, the first *aldeia* near Bahia (1552) soon disintegrated as the Indians who sur-

The Lacerda elevator connecting the Upper City (Cidade Alta) with the Lower City (Cidade Baixa), Salvador, Bahia State Courtesy Jaklen Muoi Tuyen

vived the European-born diseases faded into the interior beyond the Jesuits' reach.

Europeanization was overcome by a sort of Brazilianization, as the Jesuits blended Indian songs, dances, and language into the liturgy and as the colonists adopted native foods, women, language, and customs. However, the first bishop of Brazil (1551), Dom Pêro Fernandes Sardinha, objected to the Jesuit accommodation with indigenous culture. He threw the weight of his authority behind subjugation and enslavement. At issue was the nature of the future of Brazilian society. The bishop, who had served in Goa and ironically had taught Ignatius Loyola, the Jesuit founder, insisted that Europeanization must precede baptism. He believed Brazil, like India, should have a dual society made up of heathen natives ruled by a small number of Portuguese.

The conflict between the Jesuits and the bishop had far-reaching significance for Brazil's future. To get away from his direct grasp, the Jesuits shifted their attention to the south, where they formed, in 1554, the *aldeia* of São Paulo de Piratininga on the plateau at the headwaters of the Rio Tietê high above São Vicente. Father José de Anchieta's mission village later became known as the city of São Paulo. The crown seemingly favored the Jesuit approach because it recalled Bishop

Sardinha. En route back, Sardinha was shipwrecked and then killed and reportedly eaten by Caeté people.

In 1557 the crown sent out a new bishop and a new governor to consolidate royal control and to bring organization to the far-flung settlements on the verge of collapse. The new crown representatives supported Jesuit methods and returned the Jesuits to Bahia. By protecting the Indians who lived in *aldeias* from enslavement, the crown representatives made the Jesuit towns more attractive. The pool of slaves available to the colonists dwindled, causing such protests that Mem de Sá (governor, 1558–72) approved a "just war" against the Caeté to punish them for killing Brazil's first bishop. However, the "just war" soon got out of hand as the closer and undefended *aldeias* were raided for slaves. The conflict damaged native trust in the missions, and the epidemics of influenza, smallpox, and measles in 1562 and 1563 decimated the Indian population and increased colonist competition for laborers. The famine that followed the waves of disease prompted starving Indians to sell themselves or their relatives in order to survive.

This situation led to a policy under which the Indians were considered free but could be enslaved in a sanctioned "just war," or for cannibalism, or if rescued from being eaten or enslaved by other natives. Government-sponsored expeditions (*entradas*) into the interior, sometimes ironically called rescues (*resgates*), became slave hunts under the guise of "just war." The Paulista expeditions (*bandeiras*), one of the major themes of Brazilian history in the 1600s and 1700s, would develop out of this practice. The eventual exploitation of the interior and the development of gold and gem mining in Minas Gerais, Goiás, and Mato Grosso have roots in the voracious appetite of coastal plantations for slave labor.

As Indian resistance, social disintegration, and flight into the interior increased in the last quarter of the sixteenth century, the Portuguese began to import more African slaves. In 1570 there were 2,000 to 3,000 such slaves in Brazil; by 1587 there were 14,000. Considering that the European population in 1570 was 20,760 and in 1585 was 29,400, the growth of African slaves from 14 percent of the number of whites to 47 percent is striking. Much of the commentary on native slavery holds that the Indians were unfit physically to be slaves, when actually it was their strong resistance to slavery and the colonial competition for their labor that led to the African slave trade. Also, the focus of many historians on Bahia and Pernambuco has left readers with the impression that Indian slavery gave way to African slavery throughout Brazil by 1600. This was not the case. Indians continued to be enslaved in Pará, which caused the depopulation of much of Amazônia by the mid-eighteenth century.

French and Dutch Incursions

In addition to dealing with labor supply, Mem de Sá, who was the consolidator of Portuguese Brazil, dealt successfully with the French threat. The French had continued to attack Portuguese shipping and to maintain interest in a permanent colony. Noting that Rio de Janeiro's Guanabara Bay had not been occupied, Vice Admiral Nicolas Durand de Villegaignon, a French navigator, led a mix of Huguenots and Catholics there in 1555 to establish a colony, France Antarctique, on Ilha de Sergipe. After a decade, his utopian dream of finding a religious refuge for Protestants and Catholics failed. Despite their good relations with the Indians, the French could not withstand the Portuguese assaults that began in 1565. That year, to ensure future control of the bay, Mem de Sá founded the city of Rio de Janeiro, which became the second royal captaincy. Expelled from Guanabara Bay in 1567, the French turned their efforts to the northern coast. They made alliances with the Indians and settled themselves on Ilha São Luís do Maranhão in 1612, where fierce fighting led to their expulsion in 1615. They kept active north of the Amazon delta, maintaining claims to Amapá.

By 1580 the Portuguese had overcome French threats and most indigenous resistance to their command of key ports. At this point, a more profound Spanish threat appeared with the passing of the crown of Portugal to King Philip II of Spain. This event had immediate and long-range consequences. Now Europe's two greatest empires were united under a single ruler and could well have been joined permanently, save for the determination of the Portuguese to maintain their identity. The Iberian union gave the Portuguese easier access to the Spanish domains. For Brazil, however, the most important result was that it made enemies of Portugal's former business associates, the Dutch. Portugal's commerce was more open than Spain's and perhaps more practical. Portugal recognized its need for shipping and for access to markets, both of which the Dutch provided for Brazilian sugar. The spirit of cooperation faded with the union of the crowns as the Dutch, long struggling for independence from the Spanish Habsburgs, were shut out officially from the Portuguese domains. This exclusion led to the formation of the Dutch West India Company in 1621 and the seizure of Brazilian sugar lands. After being unsuccessful in holding Salvador in 1624–25, the Dutch captured Pernambuco in 1630 and eventually extended their sway from the Rio São Francisco to São Luís do Maranhão until finally being forced out in 1654.

The Dutch incursion was the longest and most serious challenge to Portuguese control by a major maritime power. The struggle to drive out the Dutch had devastating effects on the sugar plantations and sugar mills. The Dutch, particularly Governor Johan Maurits, Count of Nassau, had worked to build good relations with the Portuguese planters in the interior, supplying them with credit, slaves, merchandise, and European markets. Nassau encouraged religious tolerance, constructed buildings and canals in the style of Amsterdam, and brought in artists, engineers, and scientists to embellish, record, and study the local flora, fauna, and peoples.

Portugal and its Brazilian subjects had divergent interests in responding to the Dutch. When the Duke of Bragança took the throne as João IV in 1640, his government faced the determination of Philip IV to reconquer Portugal, and he therefore needed to maintain peace with the rest of Europe. As much as the Portuguese economy needed the revenues from the sugar trade, the court had to face the reality that in Europe the Dutch dominated a good portion of that trade. Thus, if Portugal attacked Dutch-held Pernambuco, it would earn an enemy in Europe and lose access to the market. At the same time, the king understood the importance of Brazil when he called it his milk cow (*vaca de leite*). Indeed, historian Charles Boxer asserted that Portugal's independence depended chiefly on the Brazil trade, which centered on sugar and slavery.

The Dutch did not show the same hesitation. In 1641 they seized Luanda, an important source of African slaves, in violation of a truce with Portugal. Holland now held sugar and slave ports in the South Atlantic and the distribution system in Europe. Although Lisbon could not merely abandon its subjects in Brazil, it realized that it would be foolhardy to fight for the sugar area without also regaining the source of African slaves.

The colonists in the Dutch-occupied area played their own game of deception. They borrowed Dutch money to restore their war-torn plantations and *engenhos* and to buy slaves, but they realized that their long-term interests lay in expelling the Dutch and with them their indebtedness. After 1645, together with the governor general in Bahia, they conspired, rebelled, and fought against the Dutch. Their victories of 1648 and 1649 at the Battle of Guararapes in the Recife area of Pernambuco are commemorated today. However, after nine years of war the scorched-earth tactics had ravaged the region. Although sugar prices rose in Europe, Brazilian planters could not respond and permanently lost their leading market position. The Dutch and English set up plantations in Suriname and Barbados, taking advantage of the techniques developed in Brazil and their better access to capital, merchant fleets, and the northern European market. Although there were years of recovery (1665–80, 1698–1710), sugar was no longer the foundation of the Brazilian economy. Northeastern Brazil entered into a long stagnation, and Portugal, which now depended heavily on Brazil after its losses to the Dutch in the East Indies, watched its economy deteriorate.

Gold Mining Displaces Cane Farming

The decline in the sugar economy cut off the smaller Northeastern cane farmers from the customary paths to higher socioeconomic status, producing a situation in which this potentially powerful segment of the population no longer had reasons to support the traditional colonial society. The cane farmers had the same social origins as the wealthier planter and mill-owner class but generally were less independent financially, and now their future was darkened. As sugar prices fell, the planters and mill owners' response was vertical integration (see Glossary); stages of production were consolidated under the control of fewer firms. Purchases from independent cane farmers were reduced and their lands acquired. The situation was potentially explosive. Historian Stuart Schwartz commented that "at no time in Brazilian history had the conditions for a profound social upheaval been more suitable." But it did not occur for two reasons: the cane farmers did not rebel against the sugar barons for fear of encouraging a slave rebellion, and in addition, newly discovered gold fields to the south soon beckoned to free and slave populations. The removal of pressures for change solidified the hold of the great landowners on the coastal plantations.

Small deposits of alluvial gold had been exploited quietly for decades in São Paulo and to the south. The Paulistas likely found more than they revealed, fearing that the greed of the Portuguese authorities would soon strip them of their semi-independence. The discovery of gold by Paulistas in various parts of what is now Minas Gerais (General Mines), between the Serra de Mantiqueira and the headwaters of the Rio São Francisco, probably occurred between 1693 and 1695, but word filtered out slowly. The greatest concentration of deposits was along Brazil's oldest geological formation, the Serra do Espinhaço, lying in a north-south direction, throughout which it seemed that every river, stream, and brook glittered with gold. Mining camps that turned into the cities of Ouro Prêto, Mariana, and Sabará soon located in its southern end, and by 1730 diamonds were coming out of the northern reaches around Diamantina.

Word of the discoveries set off an unprecedented rush, the likes of which would not be seen again until the California gold rush of 1849. The Paulistas soon found themselves competing for control with adventurers from the Northeast who streamed down the Vale São Francisco, from Portugal, and from elsewhere. By 1709–10 the Vale São Francisco had become a lawless region filled with the dregs of the Portuguese world. Considerable violence broke out between the original Paulista *bandeirantes*, who considered the mines theirs, and the outsiders (*emboabas*). This fighting gave the crown authorities a reason for asserting royal control and arranging a settlement of the War of the Outsiders (Guerra dos Emboabas, 1708–09). Many Paulistas moved on to new gold discoveries in Goiás and Mato Grosso.

The discoveries shifted Brazil's center of gravity away from the Northeastern coast and toward the South and West. The loser would be Bahia, which in 1763 lost the viceregal capital to Rio de Janeiro, as power followed wealth. The population also shifted, as would-be miners and those who would profit from the mines arrived with their native or African slaves. The Jesuit Father André João Antonil (whose Italian name was Giovanni Antonio Andreoni) wrote the best contemporary study of Brazilian economic and social conditions. He said that by 1709 some 30,000 people were in Minas Gerais. In the next decades, the population swelled. The 1735 tax records showed a total of 100,141 slaves, among whom there were numerous natives. By 1782 Minas Gerais's population of 319,769 included 166,995

A colonial church in Diamantina, Minas Gerais State
Street scene in Diamantina, Minas Gerais State
Courtesy Inter-American Development Bank, Washington

blacks, 82,110 mulattoes, and 70,664 whites. The state had the largest concentration of population in the viceroyalty of Brazil: 20.5 percent of Brazil's 1,555,200 people.

The early population consisted predominantly of unruly males, who knew no law but their own whims and who drove their slaves hard in an existence that historian Charles Boxer tagged as "nasty, brutish, and short." Many African slaves reacted by running away to form hiding places called *quilombos* and were pursued by roughneck "bushwhacking captains" (*capitães do mato*). However, during the first decades life could not have been easy for anyone. Items such as meat, corn, flour, and rum were rare and costly. The first local supply of hogs and chickens appeared only in 1723, and a flask of salt could cost as much as half a pound of gold.

By the last decades of the eighteenth century, however, the cities of Minas Gerais were graced with impressive baroque and rococo churches, multistoried homes and shops, and grand public buildings. Poets and musicians enlivened the cultural scene. Some 3,000 musicians, mostly mulattoes, played fine baroque pieces, often in churches built by architect Antonio Francisco Lisboa (also known as "O Aleijadinho") and under ceilings painted by Manuel da Costa Ataíde.

The overland trails from São Paulo and from Paratí were superseded by ones connecting to Rio de Janeiro. The new viceregal capital sent African slaves and European merchandise to Minas Gerais and received the heavily laden chests of gold and diamonds en route to Lisbon. Rio de Janeiro also served as the supply base for the newly created captaincies of Santa Catarina and Rio Grande de São Pedro, passing their livestock products on to Portugal. Those captaincies were linked overland to São Paulo and Minas Gerais via the livestock trails that ran northeast from the pampas of what was later called Rio Grande do Sul to Sorocaba in São Paulo Province.

Ranching had developed in the Northeastern interior as an adjunct to the sugar economy and in the South as the legacy of the Jesuit missions. In the eighteenth century, ranching was an increasingly important part of the overall colonial economy. The moving frontiers that it created drew the interior into effective relationships with European-oriented Brazil. From the interior of Maranhão, southeast through Piauí, Ceará, Pernambuco, and Bahia, then west into Goiás, and on down to Rio Grande do Sul, a set of cowboy (*vaqueiro*) subcultures evolved that still mark local traditions. It was an age of leather in which the horse was the center of life. Many, perhaps most, of the *vaqueiros* were native Indians, mestizos, African slaves, and mulattoes. In the northern and central areas, slaves and free men worked together unsupervised for months at a time. In the South, the gaucho culture, mixing native, Spanish, and Portuguese bloodlines and traditions, took hold throughout the pampas of the Río de la Plata up into Rio Grande do Sul. In the latter state, by the mid-1820s cattle had driven out wheat farming, and the mounted gaucho with his bolas, knife, maté tea, and open-fire barbecued beef became characteristic.

Although gold mining weakened the dominance of sugar and seemingly stimulated the cattle industry, it did not totally supersede export agriculture. It displaced sugar as the colony's leading economic activity, but during the eighteenth century the value of gold exports never surpassed the value of sugar-led agricultural exports. Even so, gold did have serious long-term effects on Portugal. The fall in the value of Portugal's colonial products in the seventeenth century had made it difficult to obtain sufficient currency to purchase merchandise from northern Europe. In response, Portugal had begun to develop industries to meet its local and colonial requirements. The discovery of gold provided needed currency.

In 1703 Portugal signed the Methuen Treaty with England, giving English woolens preference in Portuguese markets in return for a favorable tariff on Portuguese wines. This seemingly simple arrangement ended the move toward industrial development, drained Brazilian gold out of Portugal, and gave England its increasing dominance over Portugal and Brazil. The gold and diamond chests arriving at the royal treasury in Lisbon immediately were dispatched north to pay for imported cloth and manufactured goods. Local Portuguese producers could not compete with cheaper foreign prices. Furthermore, English vessels anchored in the Tagus River in the Iberian Peninsula snatched large quantities of gold from under the noses of Portuguese authorities. Instead of Brazil's wealth being used to develop Portugal and its colonies, it helped finance the English industrial revolution and Portugal's eighteenth-century struggles to secure Brazilian boundaries.

Even though an immense amount of wealth was sent abroad, much stayed in Brazil to build urban public works, such as fountains, bridges, buildings, and churches; to endow some charitable foundations, such as hospitals; and to finance the elaborate contraband trade with the Río de la Plata and Alto

Perú (Upper Peru, or present-day Bolivia). However, it did not improve the condition of the poor; generate a prosperous middle class; improve agriculture, education, or industry; or produce lasting reform.

In 1732 António Rodrigues da Costa, a member of the Overseas Council, warned the crown that the heavy colonial taxes would one day lead the colonists to cast off their loyalty. It was obvious to Rodrigues da Costa that the "larger and richer" would not accept forever being ruled by the "smaller and poorer." In 1738 royal adviser Dom Luís da Cunha suggested secretly to King João V that he take the title "emperor of the west" and move his court to Rio de Janeiro, which he argued was better situated than Lisbon to control the Portuguese maritime and commercial empire. Rather than heed such advice, however, the monarchy tried at mid-century to gain more control, stop the massive outflow of gold, and contain the British. Beginning in 1755, Marquês de Pombal (Count Sebastião José de Carvalho e Melo), as secretary of state for overseas dominions, shaped a series of reforms that gave chartered companies a monopoly of the Brazil trade, encouraged national manufacturers, and worked to make commercial relations with Britain less dependent and more reciprocal. His goal was to revitalize the state and to break the stranglehold of British credit. He closed Brazilian ports to all foreign ships and hired foreign military experts to organize Brazil's defenses. To promote agricultural growth, Pombal distributed coffee and mulberry seedlings and also advocated production of indigo, flax, cotton, cocoa, and rice. Iron mining and smelting got underway in São Paulo, and shipbuilding and its attendant trades in Bahia and Rio de Janeiro increased. With the British seizure of Havana and Manila during the Seven Years' War (1756–63), the Portuguese wondered if Rio de Janeiro would be next. The crown responded with four goals: secure the borders, populate them for self-defense, defend the ports, and make the mines profitable.

Pombal distrusted the Jesuits, who controlled vast areas in the interior of South America. He suspected commercial links between their prosperous missions and the British, and in September 1759 expelled them from Brazil. The expulsion of the Jesuits caused the missions to fall to ruin and eliminated the strongest educational institutions in Brazil. Crown policy forbade any university or even a printing press in the colony, and modern Brazilian universities date only from the 1930s.

The crown's education policy was based on the idea that colonial and metropolitan elites would blend to shape an imperial elite united by ideology in support of the crown. During the colonial era, 3,000 Brazilians studied at Portugal's University of Coimbra, which in 1772 Pombal reformed with Enlightenment perspectives. Between 1772 and 1785, 300 Brazilians, many from Minas Gerais, were at Coimbra. Pombal placed these graduates and other members of the colonial plutocracy in judicial, administrative, and military posts. However, policy intention and outcome often clashed. Some of these students and officials would begin to think in terms of independence.

The production of gold began to decline about 1750 as the Minas Gerais society was solidifying and as the international situation was becoming more complicated. The more the Portuguese squeezed and tried to reduce the contraband in gold and diamonds, the more the divergence of interests grew. In the 1770s, as less gold reached royal coffers, the crown reacted by imposing a per capita tax (*derrama*) to make up the difference between the amounts expected and those received. Meanwhile, competition from British, French, and Dutch colonies pushed the price of Brazilian sugar down lower on the Amsterdam market, reducing still more Portuguese revenues. Moreover, the decline in available gold affected the contraband trade that the Brazilians had carried on with the Río de la Plata area, where they exchanged their illicit gold for Andean silver. The Brazilians then used the silver to buy illegal British goods, which they smuggled back into the Spanish domains. The elimination of the Jesuit missions, Spain's creation of the Viceroyalty of the Río de la Plata (1776), and the opening of direct trade between Spain and Buenos Aires further reduced the profitable trade in smuggled goods (see fig. 2). The decline in smuggling reduced transshipments of British goods through Portugal, reducing that country's overall level of trade with Britain catastrophically. The ensuing recession made it difficult to pay for the military expeditions sent to the southern borders during the 1770s, and the crown was unable to adjust expenditures in the face of declining revenues.

In Minas Gerais, landowners had manufacturing establishments on their properties turning out cotton, linen, and woolen items, and most of the other captaincies had "workshops and manufactories" that lessened the need to import from Portugal. The basis for a more complex textile industry was being laid.

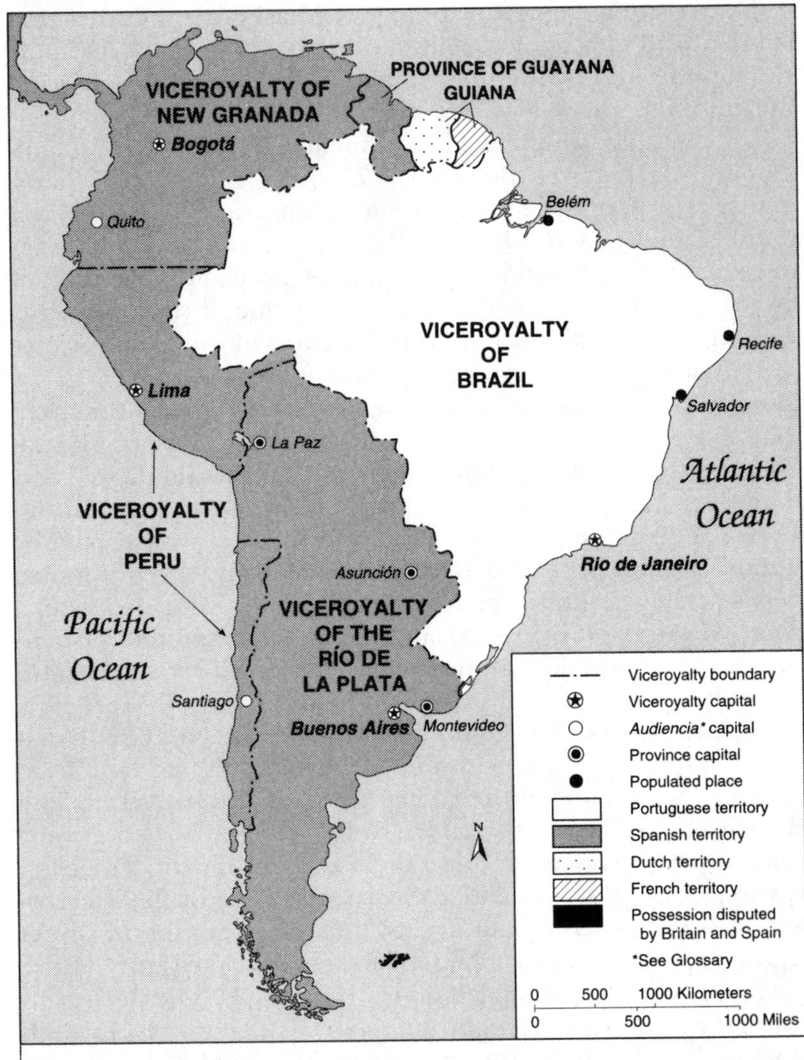

Source: Based on information from Barbara A. Tanenbaum, ed., *Encyclopedia of Latin America*, 5, New York, 1996, 408.

Figure 2. Four South American Viceroyalties, ca. 1800

Then, in February 1777, José I (king of Portugal, 1750–77) died, and with him went Pombal's hold on power and his common sense approach of encouraging industrial development. Pombal's successor as secretary of state for overseas dominions, Martinho de Melo e Castro, was alarmed that the nascent Brazilian factories could make the colony independent and warned that "Portugal without Brazil is an insignificant power." In January 1785, he ordered that they all be "closed and abolished."

In the early 1780s, Brazilian students at Coimbra had pledged themselves to seek independence. They were influenced greatly by the success of the North American British colonies in forming the United States of America. In 1786 and 1787, José Joaquim Maia e Barbalho of Rio de Janeiro, a Coimbra graduate studying medicine at Montpelier and a critic of the colonial relationship, approached Ambassador Thomas Jefferson in France. He told Jefferson that the students intended to break with Portugal and requested the aid of the United States. One of the Coimbra graduates was José Bonifácio de Andrada e Silva, the patriarch of Brazilian independence.

The failed Minas Conspiracy (Inconfidência Mineira) of 1789 involved some of the leading figures of the captaincy: tax collectors, priests, military officers, judges, government officials, and mine owners and landowners. Some had been born in Portugal, several had their early education with the Jesuits and later studied at Coimbra, a number wrote poetry that is still read and studied. But what they had most in common were financial problems caused by crown policies that required them to pay their debts, or that cut them out of lucrative gold and diamond contraband trade. They argued that Brazil had all it needed to survive and prosper and that Portugal was a parasite. They pledged to lift restrictions on mining; exploit iron ore; set up factories; create a university, a citizens' militia, and a Parliament; pardon debts to the royal treasury; free slaves born in Brazil; and form a union with São Paulo and Rio de Janeiro similar to that of the United States.

The history of the Minas Conspiracy is full of heavy drama. Revelation of the conspiracy turned brothers, friends, clients, and patrons against each other in an unseemly scramble to escape punishment. In one sense, the affair foreshadowed the nature of future Brazilian revolutionary movements in that it was a conspiracy of oligarchs seeking their own advantage, while claiming to act for the people. In the end, Lisbon decided to make an example of only one person, a low-ranked second lieutenant (*alferes*) of the Royal Mineiro Dragoons named Joaquim José da Silva Xavier ("Tiradentes"). His execution in 1792 in Rio de Janeiro might well have been forgotten if the nineteenth-century republicans had not embraced him as a symbolic counterpoise to Dom Pedro I, who declared Brazilian independence from Portugal in 1822. Later, with the establishment of the republic in 1889, every town and city in Brazil built a Tiradentes square, and the day of his execution, April 21, became a well-commemorated national holiday. Nonetheless, because the Minas Conspiracy was marked more by skulduggery than nobility and clarity, its value as a national symbol required selective interpretation and presentation.

Portugal resolved to watch Brazilians more carefully and reacted forcefully to a nonexistent but suspected plot in Rio de Janeiro in 1794, and to a real, mulatto-led one in Bahia in 1798. Meanwhile, the French Revolution, the resulting slave rebellion in Haiti, and the fear of similar revolts in Brazil convinced the Brazilian elites that the dream of a United States-style conservative revolution that would leave the slave-based socioeconomic structure intact and in their hands was impossible. The crown separated the residents of Minas Gerais from the revived coastal sugar producers through policies that set their interests at odds. Lisbon diverted Brazilian nationalism with greater imperial involvement.

The Transition to Kingdom Status

With the onset of the Napoleonic Wars, some Portuguese officials again raised the idea of moving the crown to the safety of Brazil. Dom Luís da Cunha's prophetic suggestion in 1738 that Rio de Janeiro was "safer and more convenient" made great sense as the French army approached Lisbon in November 1807. The British in 1801 had recommended transfer to Brazil in the event of an invasion and had promised to provide protection for the voyage and assistance in extending and consolidating Portuguese territory in South America. In 1803 the Lisbon government, faced with the increasingly deadly struggle between France and Britain, had reconsidered the idea. The choice was between losing Portugal to the French and having the British seize Brazil, or moving the crown to Brazil, from which the struggle for Portugal could be resumed. In any case, the royal government did not move until Portugal was actually invaded in late 1807.

At the time, the monarch was Queen Maria I, but because of mental illness triggered by her horror at the regicide in Paris, her son Dom João ruled as regent. His wife was Dona Carlota Joaquina, a Spanish princess and mother to their nine children, among whom the most important for Brazilian history was Pedro de Alcântara de Bragança e Bourbon. Dom João opened Brazilian ports to world commerce, allowing British goods to stream in, and eliminating the Portuguese middlemen. Rio de Janeiro substituted for Lisbon in a centralized system that placed the various captaincies in subservient positions to the new center. For the Brazilian elites, the transfer of the court meant that they could have conservative political change without social disorder. And best of all, depending on their proximity to the court, they had the chance to obtain the titles and honors that they felt their wealth had earned them. However, the pleasure of the elites was mixed with some frustration because now the monarch was close enough to keep an attentive watch on how they conducted their affairs. And with the court in Rio de Janeiro, the demands of international politics were more keenly felt.

Portugal and the Bragança dynasty were obligated deeply to the British. The British not only saved the royal family and some 15,000 courtiers but also lent US$3 million in 1809 to keep the government functioning. The British also liberated Portugal from the French and reorganized the Portuguese army. In addition, one of their officers ruled as regent in Lisbon. The Portuguese therefore had little with which to bargain when negotiating treaties. In 1810 Dom João signed agreements not only giving the British trade preferences and allowing them privileges of extraterritoriality but also promising to abolish the African slave trade. The last cut directly at the interests of the propertied classes, on whom the crown depended.

The crown had to duplicate, mostly from scratch, the government institutions it had left behind in Lisbon. It set up a Supreme Military Council (Conselho Militar Superior); boards of treasury, trade, agriculture, and industry; a Court of Appeals; a royal printing press and official newspaper; and the Bank of Brazil (Banco do Brasil). It created medical schools in Bahia and Rio de Janeiro, a school of fine arts, a museum of natural history, a public library, and the Botanical Garden (Jardim Botânico) in Rio de Janeiro. It also set up specialized courses of study in the Minas Gerais towns of Ouro Prêto and Paracatu. Most of the fleet had been transferred, but a new army was organized, naval and military academies were established, and arsenals created. The crown built a powder factory and an ironworks. It dealt with public safety by forming the Royal Police Guard, which brutalized slaves, sailors, drunks, gamblers, and prostitutes into submission. The crown also opened Brazil to European travelers, naturalists, scientists, and artists, who left a detailed picture of its life and landscape.

Curiously, by staying in Brazil after the British liberated Portugal from the French in 1811, the crown was keeping British influence under some control, because here it was removed both from Britain and the British-commanded Portuguese army. In 1815 the crown, determined to set its own course, raised Brazil to a kingdom equal with Portugal and acclaimed João as king when his mother died in 1816. The crown gained further maneuverability by arranging marriages between the two princesses and the Spanish King Fernando VII and his brother, and more important, between Crown Prince Pedro and the daughter of Franz I of Austria, the Archduchess Leopoldina.

The Kingdom of Portugal and Brazil, 1815–21

Portuguese businessmen who invested locally in Brazil, nobles and government officials who built expensive homes there, and those who married into provincial wealth shared a common interest in remaining. Indeed, what took shape was a new concept of a dual monarchy of Brazil and Portugal, which even under the best of circumstances would have been difficult to make work. It was an expedient idea that would founder because of resistance by those in Portugal who saw their status and that of the kingdom endangered; by the British, who wanted the king back in Lisbon, where he was more vulnerable; and by the unwillingness of Brazilians to suffer the indignity of being returned to colonial rank.

The centralization of power in Rio de Janeiro met with violent resistance in the Northeast. When Pernambuco raised the banner of republican rebellion in 1817, it was followed by Paraíba do Norte, Rio Grande do Norte, and the south of Ceará, each of which acted to defend local interests without thought of federating. They resented their loss of autonomy to Rio de Janeiro and the Portuguese who had settled in the Northeast since 1808. Significantly, although they sent envoys to secure recognition from Britain and the United States and to spread the revolt to Bahia, they did not send agents to central or southern Brazil. The revolt was crushed brutally. Although unsuccessful, the 1817 "Pernambuccan revolution" shook the monarchy's foundations because it had pushed aside authority and tarnished the crown's aura of invincibility. In desperation, the monarchy responded by banning all secret societies and by garrisoning Rio de Janeiro, Salvador, and Recife with fresh troops from Portugal.

Meanwhile, the monarchy was waging war in the Río de la Plata. King João regarded the East Bank of the Río de la Plata (present-day Uruguay) as the proper and true boundary of Brazil. Over British objections, he brought veteran troops from Portugal to seize Montevideo and to wage a wearing campaign (1816–20) against the forces of independence-minded José Gervasio Artigas, the father of Uruguay. The region was incorporated into the United Kingdom as the Cisplatine Province in 1821. Nonetheless, even as it was expanding, the United Kingdom, as the Rio de Janeiro royalists termed it, was suffering from pressures in Portugal itself.

The Pernambuccan revolution in 1817 encouraged army officers in Portugal to conspire against the regency of British Marshal William Carr Beresford. Twelve of the conspirators, including a general officer, were tried secretly and hanged. Anti-British sentiment deepened. In 1820, when a military revolt in Spain forced the revived absolutist regime of Fernando VII (1784–1833) to restore the liberal constitution of 1812, the Portuguese military followed suit by expelling the British officers and forming revolutionary juntas. The military petitioned the king's return and summoned a Côrtes (the Portuguese Parliament), the first since 1697 when the crown had dispensed with such bodies.

Unable to do more, João pardoned the juntas' usurpation of his prerogative to summon a Côrtes and acknowledged that a Côrtes could be useful in making proposals to him on how best to govern the United Kingdom. Then, in January 1821, Portuguese officers and troops, as well as Brazilian liberals, took over provincial governments in Bahia and Belém, and in late February, troops in Rio de Janeiro threw in with the movement and forced the king to take an oath to accept any constitution the Côrtes might write. In effect, Brazil was again being ruled from Portugal. A few days later, a royal decree announced that the king would return to Lisbon, leaving his twenty-four-year-old son Dom Pedro as regent in Brazil.

On April 25, 1821, twelve ships carrying the king and queen, 4,000 officials, diplomats, and families, as well as purloined funds and jewels from the Bank of Brazil, set course for Lisbon. The city and country that they left behind no longer constituted the closed colony of thirteen years before. Thanks to the surveys, expeditions, and studies that João had encouraged,

Brazil's resources would be exploited at a steadily increasing pace, but in a fashion that tied the country more closely to the rapidly expanding industrial capitalism of the North Atlantic. Nonetheless, João VI and Queen Carlota exemplified the fading absolutist regime; their son Pedro would seek to be more modern by embracing the new ideas of liberal constitutionalism.

During the thirteen years that João resided in Rio de Janeiro, international trade expanded as reflected by the growing number of foreign ships anchoring in the bay: from ninety in 1808 to 354 in 1820. By 1820 Rio de Janeiro had more than 3,000 foreigners among its 113,000 inhabitants.

Rio de Janeiro also had coffee houses serving the product that would become the backbone of the economy. Expanding from seedlings nurtured in the Jardim Botânico, coffee cultivation spread from the Rio de Janeiro area over the Serra do Mar into the fertile upland valley, through which the Rio Paraíba flows from São Paulo easterly to the sea, dividing the provinces of Minas Gerais and Rio de Janeiro. On both sides of the river, the tropical forests were cut to make way for the coffee groves. Mule trains that once brought gold from Minas Gerais to Rio de Janeiro now carried coffee in quantities that swelled from 2,304 kilos in 1792 to 7,761,600 kilos in 1820, and would reach 82,178,395 kilos in 1850.

São Paulo's entry into the coffee age lay in the future, but in 1821 it was providing herds of mules and horses for the coffee pack trains. The Cisplatine and Rio Grande do Sul were shipping abroad hides, tallow, and dried meat. In contrast, the Northeast and North were in decline because an 1815 treaty between Brazil and Britain forbade the African slave trade north of the equator, thereby reducing the demand for Bahian molasses-soaked rolled tobacco, and because Cuban competition slashed deeply into the Northeast's sugar market in the United States and Europe. Even cotton, which a few years before seemed a secure export for Maranhão, was overwhelmed by the post-War of 1812 expansion in the southern United States. The world demand for Amazonian nuts, cocoa, skins, herbs, spices, and rubber was still weak in 1821. Finally, in the Brazilian west (Mato Grosso and Goiás) gold mining had all but ended, and subsistence farming and livestock raising were predominant. Throughout the country, but more so from Bahia through Minas Gerais to Rio de Janeiro and São Paulo, the labor force was made up of African or locally born black slaves. The native heritage lived on in the substantial number of Tupí-speaking races and mixtures that lived in the tropical forest region.

The Empire, 1822–89

Emperor Pedro I, 1822–31

Dom Pedro meant to rule frugally and started by cutting his own salary, centralizing scattered government offices, and selling off most of the royal horses and mules. He issued decrees that eliminated the royal salt tax to spur output of hides and dried beef, forbade arbitrary seizure of private property, required a judge's warrant for arrests of freemen, and banned secret trials, torture, and other indignities. He also sent elected deputies to the Côrtes in Portugal. However, slaves continued to be bought and sold and disciplined with force, despite his assertion that their blood was the same color as his. In September 1821, the Côrtes, with only a portion of the Brazilian delegates present, voted to abolish the Kingdom of Brazil and the royal agencies in Rio de Janeiro and to make all the provinces subordinate directly to Lisbon. Portugal sent troops to Brazil and placed all Brazilian units under Portuguese command. In January 1822, tension between Portuguese troops and the Luso-Brazilians (Brazilians born in Portugal) turned violent when Pedro accepted petitions from Brazilian towns begging him to refuse the Côrtes's order to return to Lisbon. Responding to their pressure and to the argument that his departure and the dismantling of the central government would trigger separatist movements, he vowed to stay. The Portuguese "lead feet," as the Brazilians called the troops, rioted before concentrating their forces on Cerro Castello, which was soon surrounded by thousands of armed Brazilians. Dom Pedro "dismissed" the Portuguese commanding general and ordered him to remove his soldiers across the bay to Niteroi, where they awaited transport to Portugal. Pedro formed a new government headed by José Bonifácio de Andrada e Silva of São Paulo. This former royal official and professor of science at Coimbra was crucial to the subsequent direction of events and is regarded as one of the formative figures of Brazilian nationalism, indeed, as the patriarch of independence.

The atmosphere was so charged that Dom Pedro sought assurances of asylum on a British ship in case he lost the looming confrontation; he also sent his family to safety out of the city. In the following days, the Portuguese commander delayed embarcation, hoping that expected reinforcements would arrive. However, the reinforcements that arrived off Rio de Janeiro on March 5, 1822, were not allowed to land. Instead, they were given supplies for the voyage back to Portugal. This round had been won without bloodshed.

Blood had been shed in Recife in the Province of Pernambuco, when the Portuguese garrison there had been forced to depart in November 1821. In mid-February 1822, Bahians revolted against the Portuguese forces there but were driven into the countryside, where they began guerrilla operations, signaling that the struggle in the north would not be without loss of life and property. To secure Minas Gerais and São Paulo, where there were no Portuguese troops but where there were doubts about independence, Dom Pedro engaged in some royal populism.

Towns in Minas Gerais had expressed their loyalty at the time of Pedro's vow to remain, save for the junta in Ouro Prêto, the provincial capital. Pedro realized that unless Minas Gerais were solidly with him, he would be unable to broaden his authority to other provinces. With only a few companions and no ceremony or pomp, Pedro plunged into Minas Gerais on horseback in late March 1822, receiving enthusiastic welcomes and allegiances everywhere. Back in Rio de Janeiro on May 13, he proclaimed himself the "perpetual defender of Brazil" and shortly thereafter called a Constituent Assembly (Assembléia Constituinte) for the next year. To deepen his base of support, he joined the freemasons, who, led by José Bonifácio Andrada e Silva, were pressing for parliamentary government and independence. More confident, in early August he called on the Brazilian deputies in Lisbon to return, decreed that Portuguese forces in Brazil should be treated as enemies, and issued a manifesto to "friendly nations." The manifeso read like a declaration of independence.

Seeking to duplicate his triumph in Minas Gerais, Pedro rode to São Paulo in August to assure himself of support there and began a disastrous affair with Domitila de Castro that would later weaken his government. Returning from an excursion to Santos, Pedro received messages from his wife and from Andrada e Silva that the Côrtes considered his government traitorous and was dispatching more troops. In a famous scene at Ipiranga on September 7, 1822, he had to choose between returning to Portugal in disgrace or opting for independence.

Praça (plaza) Tiradentes, Ouro Prêto, Minas Gerais State
Courtesy Jaklen Muoi Tuyen
Street scene in Ouro Prêto
Courtesy Michaël Borg-Hansen

He tore the Portuguese blue and white insignia from his uniform, drew his sword, and swore: "By my blood, by my honor, and by God: I will make Brazil free." Their motto, he said, would be "Independence or Death!"

Pedro's government employed Admiral Thomas Alexander Cochrane, one of Britain's most successful naval commanders in the Napoleonic Wars and recently commander of the Chilean naval forces against Spain. Pedro's government also hired a number of Admiral Cochrane's officers and French General Pierre Labatut, who had fought in Colombia. These men were to lead the fight to drive the Portuguese out of Bahia, Maranhão, and Pará, and to force those areas to replace Lisbon's rule with that of Rio de Janeiro. Money from customs at Rio de Janeiro's port and local donations outfitted the army and the nine-vessel fleet. The use of foreign mercenaries brought needed military skills. The much-feared Cochrane secured Maranhão with a single warship, despite the Portuguese military's attempt to disrupt the economy and society with a scorched-earth campaign and with promises of freedom for the slaves. By mid-1823 the contending forces numbered between 10,000 and 20,000 Portuguese, some of whom were veterans of the Napoleonic Wars, versus 12,000 to 14,000 Brazilians, mostly in militia units from the Northeast.

Some historians have erred in supporting historian Manuel de Oliveira Lima's contention that independence came without bloodshed. In fact, although both sides avoided massive set battles, they did engage in guerrilla tactics, demonstrations, and countermoves. There is little information on casualties, but the fighting provided a female martyr in Mother Joana Angélica, who was bayoneted to death by Portuguese troops invading her convent in Bahia; and an example of female grit in Maria Quitéria de Jesus, who, masquerading as a man, joined the imperial army and achieved distinction in several battles.

Britain and Portugal recognized Brazilian independence by signing a treaty on August 29, 1825. Until then, the Brazilians feared that Portugal would resume its attack. Portuguese retribution, however, came in a financial form. Secret codicils of the treaty with Portugal required that Brazil assume payment of 1.4 million pounds sterling owed to Britain and indemnify Dom João VI and other Portuguese for losses totaling 600,000 pounds sterling. Brazil also renounced future annexation of Portuguese African colonies, and in a side treaty with Britain promised to end the slave trade. Neither of these measures pleased the slave-holding planters.

Organizing the new government quickly brought the differences between the emperor and his leading subjects to the fore. In 1824 Pedro closed the Constituent Assembly that he had convened because he believed that body was endangering liberty. As assembly members, his advisers, José Bonifácio de Andrada e Silva and Dom Pedro's brothers, had written a draft constitution that would have limited the monarch by making him equal to the legislature and judiciary, similar to the president of the United States. They wanted the emperor to push the draft through without discussion, which Pedro refused to do. Troops surrounded the assembly as he ordered it dissolved. He then produced a constitution modeled on that of Portugal (1822) and France (1814). It specified indirect elections and created the usual three branches of government but also added a fourth, the moderating power, to be held by the emperor. The moderating power would give the emperor authority to name senators and judges and to break deadlocks by summoning and dismissing parliaments and cabinets. He also had treaty-making and treaty-ratifying power. Pedro's constitution was more liberal than the assembly's in its religious toleration and definition of individual and property rights, but less so in its concentration of power in the emperor.

The constitution was more acceptable in the flourishing, coffee-driven Southeastern provinces than in the Northeastern sugar and cotton areas, where low export prices and the high cost of imported slaves were blamed on the coffee-oriented government. In mid-1824, with Pernambuco and Ceará leading, five Northeastern provinces declared independence as the Confederation of the Equator, but by year's end the short-lived separation had been crushed by Admiral Cochrane. With the Northeast pacified, violence now imperiled the South.

In 1825 war flared again over the Cisplatine Province, this time with Buenos Aires determined to annex the East Bank. The empire could little afford the troops, some of whom were recruited in Ireland and Germany, or the sixty warships needed to blockade the Río de la Plata. A loan from London bankers was expended by 1826, and Pedro had to call the General Assembly to finance the war. The blockade raised objections from the United States and Britain, and reverses on land in 1827 made it necessary to negotiate an end to the US$30 million Cisplatine War. The war at least left Uruguay independent instead of an Argentine province. In June 1828, harsh discipline and xenophobia provoked a mutiny of mercenary troops in Rio de Janeiro; the Irish were shipped home and the Germans sent to the South. The army was reduced to 15,000 members, and the antislavery Pedro, now without military muscle, faced a Parliament controlled by slaveowners and their allies.

As coffee exports rose steadily, so did the numbers of imported slaves; in Rio de Janeiro alone they soared from 26,254 in 1825 to 43,555 in 1828. In 1822 about 30 percent, or 1 million, of Brazil's population were African-born or -descended slaves. Slavery was so pervasive that beggars had slaves, and naval volunteers took theirs aboard ship.

Pedro had written that slavery was a "cancer that is gnawing away at Brazil" and that no one had the right to enslave another. He wanted to abolish slavery, but his own liberal constitution gave the law-making authority to the slavocrat-controlled Parliament. In Brazil liberal principles and political formulas were given special meaning. The language of social contract, popular sovereignty, supremacy of law, universal rights, division of powers, and representative government was stripped of its revolutionary content and applied only to a select, privileged minority.

After 1826 the slavocrat agenda was to control the court system; to provide harsh punishments for slave rebellion but mild ones for white revolt; to reduce the armed forces, cleansing them of foreigners unsympathetic to slavery; to keep tariffs low and eliminate the Bank of Brazil in order to deny the central government the ability to stimulate a rival, finance-based industrial capitalism; and to shape immigration policy in such a way as to encourage servile labor instead of independent farmers or craftsmen. Led by Bernardo Pereira de Vasconcelos of Minas Gerais in the assembly, slavocrats argued that slavery was not demoralizing, that foreign capital and technology would not help Brazil, and that railroads would only rust. Others, such as Nicolau de Campos Vergueiro of São Paulo, argued in favor of replacing slavery with free European immigrants. In the end, the Parliament established a contract system that was little better than slavery. There would be no liberal empire. Laws and decrees unacceptable to the slavocrats simply would not take effect, such as the order in 1829 forbidding slave ships to sail for Africa. These items of the slavocrat agenda were the roots of the regional rebellions of the nineteenth century.

After Dom João's death in 1826, despite Pedro's renunciation of his right to the Portuguese throne in favor of his daughter, Brazilian nativist radicals falsely accused the emperor of plotting to overthrow the constitution and to proclaim himself the ruler of a reunited Brazil and Portugal. They raised tensions by provoking street violence against the Portuguese of Rio de Janeiro and agitated for a federalist monarchy that would give the provinces self-government and administrative autonomy. Brazil's fate was in the hands of a few people concentrated in the capital who spread false stories and undermined discipline in the army and police. It would not be the last time that events in Rio de Janeiro would shape the future. When Pedro dismissed his cabinet in April 1831, street and military demonstrators demanded its reinstatement in violation of his constitutional prerogatives. He refused, saying: "I will do anything for the people but nothing [forced] by the people." With military units assembled on the Campo Santana, an assembly ground in Rio de Janeiro, and people in the streets shouting "death to the tyrant," he backed down. Failing to form a new cabinet, he abdicated in favor of his five-year-old son Pedro II, boarded a British warship, and left Brazil as he had arrived, under the Union Jack.

The Regency Era, 1831–40

The three regents that ruled in the young emperor's name from 1831 to 1840 witnessed a period of turmoil as local factions struggled to gain control of their provinces and to keep the masses in line. Out of desperation to weaken the radical appeals for federalism, republicanism, and hostility toward the Portuguese, and to protect against contrary calls for Pedro I's restoration, the regency in Rio de Janeiro gave considerable power to the provinces in 1834. Brazil took on the appearance of a federation of local *pátrias* (autonomous centers of regional power) with loose allegiance to the Rio de Janeiro government, whose function was to defend them from external attack and to maintain order and balance among them. The government's ability to carry out that function was impaired, however, by the low budgets allowed the army and navy, and by the creation of a National Guard, whose officers were local notables determined to protect their private and regional interests. The rebellions, riots, and popular movements that marked the next years did not spring as much from economic misery as from attempts to share in the prosperity stemming from North Atlantic demand for Brazil's exports.

Many of the disturbances were so fleeting they were all but forgotten. For example, in Rio de Janeiro alone there were five uprisings in 1831 and 1832. Another eight of the more famous revolts in the 1834–49 period included the participation of lower-class people, Indians, free and runaway blacks, and slaves, which accounts for their often fierce suppression. Republican objectives were apparent in some of these revolts, such as the War of the Farrapos (ragamuffins), also known as the Farroupilha Rebellion (1835–45), in Santa Catarina and Rio Grande do Sul. Others, such as the Cabanagem in Pará in 1835–37, the Sabinada in Salvador in 1837–38, the Balaiada Rebellion in Maranhao in 1838–41, and the ones in Minas Gerais and São Paulo in 1842, were propelled simultaneously by antiregency and promonarchial sentiments. Such unrest dispels the notion that the history of state formation in Brazil was peaceful. Instead, it shows the confrontation between the national government and the splintering *pátrias*, which would continue in varying degrees for the next century.

Pedro I's death from tuberculosis in 1834 had sapped the restorationist impulse and removed the glue that held uneasy political allies together. With the regency attempting to suppress simultaneous revolts in the South and North, it could not easily reassert its supremacy over the remaining provinces. Brazil could well have split apart in those years. It did not for three reasons. First, the military was reorganized as an instrument of national unity under the leadership of Luís Alves de Lima e Silva, who was ennobled as the Duke of Caxias (Duque de Caxias) and who would later be proclaimed Patron of the Brazilian Army. Second, the specter of slave revolt and social disintegration had become all too real. And third, the "vision of Brazil as a union of autonomous *pátrias*," in Roderick J. Barman's phrase, was replaced by the vision of Brazil as a nation-state. Rather than risk their fortunes and lives, the elites, longing for a focus of loyalty, identity, and authority, rallied around the boy-emperor, who ascended the throne on July 18, 1841, at age fifteen instead of the constitutionally specified age of eighteen. Thus, the second empire was born in the hope that it would be an instrument of national unity, peace, and prosperity.

The Second Empire, 1840–89

In the 1840s, the Brazilian nation-state coalesced as authorities suppressed revolts and rewrote Brazilian law. These laws, however, did not bode well for democracy because they shaped an electoral system based on government-controlled fraud. In 1842, on the advice of conservative courtiers, Pedro II used his constitutional moderating power to dismiss the newly elected liberal Chamber of Deputies and called new elections, which the conservatives won by stuffing the ballot boxes. In so doing, he set a pattern of favoring conservatives over liberals.

The constitution of 1824 had created the usual three governmental powers—executive, legislative, and judicial—and a fourth, the moderating power. The emperor held this power, which gave him the right to name senators, to dismiss the legislature, and to shift control of the government from one party to the other. In theory, he was to act as the political balance wheel. It should be noted that the parties were more groupings of members of Parliament than ideologically based movements dependent on distinct electorates. Historian Richard Graham observed that "No particular political philosophy distinguished one group from another." Then, as now, the political system had an artificial aspect to it; it did not relate openly to the real power structure of the country—the "lords of the land" (*senhores da terra*) who ran local affairs.

A good example of how the real power holders manipulated the system to protect their narrow interests to the detriment of the national interest was the Land Law of 1850, which set the pattern for modern landholding. The Land Law ended the colonial practice of obtaining land through squatting or royal grants and limited acquisition to purchase, thereby restricting the number of people who could become owners. By creating obstacles to landownership, the law's framers hoped to force free labor to work for existing landlords. However, proprietors sabotaged the law by not surveying their lands and not resolving their conflicting claims in order to keep titles cloudy and hence in their hands. One result of the uncertain titles was that slaves were used as collateral.

Also in 1850, British pressure finally forced the Brazilian government to outlaw the African slave trade. London, tiring of Brazilian subterfuge, authorized its navy to seize slave ships in Brazilian waters, even in ports. Rather than risk open war with Britain, paralyzation of commerce, widespread slave unrest, and destabilization of the empire, the government outlawed the African slave trade. It deported a number of Portuguese slavers and instructed the provincial presidents, police, judges, and military to crack down. Over the next five years, even clandestine landings stopped, and despite the tempting rise of slave prices in the coffee districts of Rio de Janeiro Province, the trans-Atlantic trade ended. Although the British claimed credit, it should be noted that for the first time a Brazilian government had the power to enforce a law along the length of the coast. Also, internal support for the trade had weakened. Most slave importers were Portuguese, who had been selling the ever more expensive Africans to landowners on credit at climbing interest rates, in some cases forcing the latter into insolvency and loss of property. Xenophobia and the debts of the landed classes combined to support the government action.

Ending the slave trade had a number of consequences. First, because labor needs increased in Rio de Janeiro and São Paulo as the world demand for coffee rose, Northeastern planters sold their surplus slaves to Southern growers. In addition, Parliament passed laws encouraging European immigration, as well as the Land Law of 1850. Second, ending the slave trade freed capital that could then be used for investment in transport and industrial enterprises. Third, it ensured that Britain did not interfere in Brazil's military intervention to end the rule in Buenos Aires of Juan Manuel de Rosas (president of Argentina, 1829–33, 1835–52).

Coffee dominated exports in the last half of the nineteenth century, going from 50 percent of exports in 1841–50 to 59.5 percent in 1871–80. But sugar exports also increased, and cotton, tobacco, cocoa, rubber, and maté were important. The vast cattle herds that grazed the Northeastern *sertão*, the plains (*cerrado*) of Minas Gerais, and the pampas of Rio Grande do Sul foreshadowed Brazil's status in 1990 as the world's second largest meat exporter. Meat-salting plants (*saladeros*) in Rio Grande do Sul shipped sun-dried beef to the expanding coffee-growing region to feed its slaves and freed tenant farmers (*colonos*). In addition to beef, Brazilians ate protein-rich beans, rice, and corn, much of which came from Minas Gerais or the immigrant colonies of Rio Grande do Sul. Interregional trade was budding, but for the most part local self-sufficiency was the norm. Indeed, more people produced food for the domestic market than labored on export crops.

Expanding coffee production in the 1850s and 1860s attracted British investment in railroads to speed transport of the beans to the coast. The Santos-São Paulo Railroad (1868)

Teatro Amazonas, the newly reopened, nineteenth-century belle époque opera house in Manaus, Amazonas State, was built with materials imported from Europe.
Courtesy Jaklen Muoi Tuyen

was the first major breach of the coastal escarpment, which had slowed development of the Southern plateau. Similarly, in the Northeast railroads began to cut into the interior from the coast. But generally the pattern was to connect a port with its export-oriented hinterland, creating a series of enclaves that were connected with each other by sea. Well into the twentieth century, Brazil lacked railroads and highways linking its major regions, urban areas, and economic zones. The country was laced together by intricate networks of mule trails that moved goods and people throughout the vast interior. Viewed as archaic by modern observers, the mule train trails nonetheless were important in Brazil's formation, tying the various regions together and spreading a common language and culture.

The empire had lost the East Bank of the Río de la Plata with the founding of Uruguay in 1828, but it continued to meddle in that republic's affairs. Brazil's most important businessman, Irineu Evangelista de Sousa, the Visconde de Mauá, had such heavy financial interests there that his company was effectively the Uruguayan government's bank. Other Brazilians owned about 400 large estates (*estancias*) that took up nearly a third of the country's territory. They objected to the taxes the Uruguayans imposed when they drove their cattle back and forth to Rio Grande do Sul, and they took sides in the constant fighting between Uruguay's Colorado and Blanco political factions, which later became the Colorado Party and the National Party (Blancos). Some of Rio Grande do Sul's gauchos did not accept Uruguayan independence in 1828 and continually sought intervention.

In the mid-1860s, the imperial government conspired with Buenos Aires authorities to replace the Blanco regime in Montevideo with a Colorado one. The Blancos appealed to Paraguayan dictator Francisco Solano López (president, 1862–70), who harbored his own fears of the two larger countries and who regarded a threat to Uruguay as a menace to Paraguay. A small landlocked country, Paraguay had the largest army in the region: 64,000 soldiers compared with Brazil's standing army of 18,000. In 1864 Brazil and Argentina agreed to act together should Solano López attempt to save the Blancos. In September 1864, wrongly convinced that he would not be so foolish, the Brazilians sent troops into Uruguay to put the Colorados in power. Each side miscalculated the intentions, capabilities, and will of the other. Paraguay reacted by seizing Brazilian vessels on the Rio Paraguai and by attacking the province of Mato Grosso. Solano López, mistakenly expecting help from anti-Buenos Aires caudillos, sent his forces into Corrientes to get at Rio Grande do Sul and Uruguay and found himself at war with both Argentina and Brazil. In May 1865, those two countries and Colorado-led Uruguay signed an alliance that aimed to transfer contested Paraguayan territory to the larger countries, to open Paraguayan rivers to international trade, and to remove Solano López. By September 1865, the allies had driven the Paraguayans out of Rio Grande do Sul, and they took the war into Paraguay when that country spurned their peace overtures.

Fiercely defending their homeland, the Guaraní-speaking Paraguayans defeated the allies at Curupaití in September 1866. The Argentine president, General Bartolomé Mitre (1861–68), took the bulk of his troops home to quell opposition to his war policy, leaving the Brazilians to soldier on. The famed General Lima e Silva, Marquis and later Duke of Caxias, took command of the allied forces and led them until the fall of Asunción in early 1869. With stubborn determination, the

Brazilians pursued Solano López until they cornered and killed him. They then occupied Paraguay until 1878.

The war dragged on for several reasons. First, the Paraguayans were better prepared at the outset and conducted an effective offensive into the territories of their adversaries, immediately handing them defeats. Even later, when pushed back onto their own land, they had the advantages of knowing the ground, of having prepared defenses, and of fielding stubbornly loyal troops. Second, it took the Brazilians considerable time to marshal their forces and considerable effort and cost to keep them supplied. Third, the Argentines, hoping to improve their postwar situation in relation to Brazil, delayed operations partly to force the empire to weaken itself by expending its resources. Fourth, this was the era of "unconditional surrender." It was militarily fashionable to pursue Solano López to the bitter end.

The war had important consequences for Brazil and the Río de la Plata region. It left Brazil and Argentina facing each other over a prostrate Paraguay and a dependent Uruguay, a situation that would soon turn into a tense rivalry that repeatedly assumed warlike postures. Historians debate the number of Paraguayan casualties, some asserting that 50 percent of Paraguayans were killed, others arguing that it was much less, possibly 8 to 9 percent of the prewar population total. Nonetheless, the losses from battle, disease, and starvation were severe and disrupted the development of the republic. In Brazil the war contributed to the growth of manufacturing, to the professionalization of the armed forces and their concentration in Rio Grande do Sul, to the building of roads and the settling of European immigrants in the southern provinces, and to the increased power of the central government. Most important for the future, the war brought the military firmly into the political arena. Military officers were keenly aware that the war had exposed the military's lack of equipment, training, and organization. Officers blamed these shortcomings on civilian officials. In the next decades, reformist officers seeking to modernize the army would criticize the Brazilian political structure and its peculiar culture as obstacles to modernization.

The end of the war coincided with the resurgence of republicanism as disenchanted liberals cast about for a new route to power. The 1867 collapse of the short-lived, French-sponsored Mexican monarchy of Maximilian left Brazil as the hemisphere's only monarchial regime. And because Argentina appeared to prosper in the 1870s and 1880s, it served as a powerful advertisement for republican government. The republican ideology spread in urban areas and in provinces, such as São Paulo and Rio Grande do Sul, where the people did not believe they benefited from imperial economic policies. The republican manifesto of 1870 proclaimed that "We are in America and we want to be Americans." Monarchy was, the writers asserted, hostile to the interests of the American states and would be a continuous source of conflict with Brazil's neighbors. The republicans embraced the abolition of slavery to remove the stigma of Brazil's being the only remaining slaveholding country (save for Spanish Cuba) in the hemisphere. It was not so much that they believed that slavery was wrong as that it gave the country an image distasteful to Europeans. Abolition, which would come in 1888, did not imply that liberals wanted deep social reform or desired a democratic society. Indeed, their arguments against slavery were weighted toward efficiency rather than morality. Once in power, the republicans looked to discipline the legally free work force with various systems of social control.

The Brazilian social system functioned through intertwined networks of patronage, familial relationships, and friendships. The state, capitalist economy, and institutions such as the church and the army developed within what historian Emília Viotti da Costa has called, "the web of patronage." Contacts and favor rather than ability determined success in virtually all occupations. Brazilian society was, and still is, one in which a person could not advance without friends and family; hence, the continued importance of kinship networks (*parentelas*), godfathers (*compadres*) and godmothers (*comadres*), and military school classes (*turmas*). Such a social system did not lend itself to reform.

The 1870s and 1880s saw a crisis in each of the three pillars of the imperial regime—the church, the military, and the slaveholding system. Together, these crises represented the failure of the regime to adapt without alienating its base. In the 1870s, Rome pressured Brazil's Roman Catholic Church to conform to the conservative reforms of Vatican Council I, which strengthened the power of the pontiff by declaring him infallible in matters of faith and morals. This effort by Rome to unify doctrine and practice worldwide conflicted with royal control of the church in Brazil. The crown had inherited the *padroado,* or right of ecclesiastical patronage, from its Portuguese predecessor. This right gave the crown control over the church, which imperial authorities treated as an arm of the state. Although some clerics had displayed republican sentiments earlier in the century, a church-state crisis exploded in the mid-1870s over efforts to Europeanize the church.

The importance of the military crisis is clearer because it removed the armed prop of the regime. After the Paraguayan War (1864–70), the monarchy was indifferent to the army, which the civilian elite did not perceive as a threat. The fiscal problems of the 1870s slowed promotions to a crawl, salaries were frozen, and officers complained about having to contribute to a widows' fund from their meager salaries. Moreover, the soldiers in the ranks were considered the dregs of society, discipline was based on the lash, and training seemed pointless. The gulf between the military and the civilian oligarchies broadened. The political parties were as indifferent as the government to demands for military reform, for obligatory military service, for better armament, and for higher pay and status. During the 1870s, the discontent was checked by the National Guard's reduced role; by an unsuccessful but welcomed attempt to improve the recruitment system; and, especially, by the cabinet service of war heroes, including the Duke of Caxias as prime minister (1875–78) and Marshal Manuel Luís Osório, the Marquis of Herval, as minister of war (1878). But the latter died in 1879 and Caxias the year after, leaving leadership to officers less committed to the throne. The junior officer ranks were filled with men from the middle sectors who had entered the army to obtain an education rather than to follow a military career. They were more concerned than their predecessors with social changes that would open opportunities to the lower middle class.

The officer corps was split into three generations. The oldest group had helped suppress the regional revolts of the 1830s and 1840s, had fought in Argentina in 1852, and had survived the Paraguayan War. The numerous mid-level officers were better schooled than their seniors and had been tested in combat in Paraguay. The junior officers had missed the war but had the most education of the three groups and had experienced the empire only when its defects had become clearly apparent. They were the least attached to the old regime and the most frustrated by the lack of advancement in a peacetime army cluttered with veterans of the great war.

Brazilian political tradition permitted officers to hold political office and to serve as cabinet ministers, thereby blurring the civil-military roles. As parliamentary deputies and senators, officers could criticize the government, including their military superiors, with impunity. In the 1880s, officers participated in provincial politics, debated in the press, and spoke in public forums. In 1884 a civilian minister of war attempted to impose order by forbidding officers to write or speak publicly about governmental matters. The subsequent punishments of offending officers led Field Marshal Manuel Deodoro da Fonseca and General José Antônio Correia de Câmara (Visconde de Pelotas) to head protests that eventually forced the minister to resign in February 1887 and the cabinet to fall in March 1888.

Even as the church and military crises were unfolding, the slavery issue shook the support of the landed elite. Members of the Liberal and Conservative Parties came from the same social groups: plantation owners (*fazendeiros*) made up half of both, and the rest were bureaucrats and professionals. The ideological differences between the parties were trivial, but factional and personal rivalries within them made it difficult for the parties to adjust to changing social and economic circumstances. As a result, the last decade of the empire was marked by considerable political instability. Between 1880 and 1889, there were ten cabinets (seven in the first five years) and three parliamentary elections, with no Parliament able to complete its term. The repeated use of the moderating power provoked alienation, even among traditional monarchists.

Attitudes toward slavery had shifted gradually. Pedro II favored abolition, and during the Paraguayan War slaves serving in the military were emancipated. In 1871 the Rio Branco cabinet approved a law freeing newborns and requiring masters to care for them until age eight, at which time they would either be turned over to the government for compensation or the owner would have use of their labor until age twenty-one. In 1884 a law freed slaves over sixty years of age. By the 1880s, the geography of slavery had also changed, and the economy was less dependent on it. Because of manumissions (many on condition of remaining on the plantations) and the massive flight of slaves, the overall numbers declined from 1,240,806 in 1884 to 723,419 in 1887, with most slaves having shifted from the sugar plantations in the Northeast to the south-central coffee groves. But even planters in São Paulo, where the slave percentage of the total population had fallen from 28.2 percent in

1854 to 8.7 percent in 1886, understood that to continue expansion they needed a different labor system. The provincial government therefore actively began subsidizing and recruiting immigrants. Between 1875 and 1887, about 156,000 arrived in São Paulo. Meanwhile, the demand for cheap sugarcane workers in the Northeast was satisfied by *sertanejos* (inhabitants of the *sertão*) fleeing the devastating droughts of the 1870s in the *sertão.*

The economic picture was also changing. Slavery immobilized capital invested in the purchase and maintenance of slaves. By turning to free labor, planter capital was freed for investment in railroads, streetcar lines, and shipping and manufacturing enterprises. To some extent, these investments offered a degree of protection from the caprices of agriculture.

Meanwhile, slaves left the plantations in great numbers, and an active underground supported runaways. Army officers petitioned the Regent Princess Isabel to relieve them of the duty of pursuing runaway slaves. Field Marshal Deodoro da Fonseca, commander in Rio Grande do Sul, declared in early 1887 that the military "had the obligation to be abolitionist." The São Paulo assembly petitioned the Parliament for immediate abolition. The agitation reached such a pitch that to foreign travelers, Brazil appeared on the verge of social revolution. The system was coming apart, and even planters realized that abolition was the way to prevent chaos.

The so-called Golden Law of May 13, 1888, which ended slavery, was not an act of great bravery but a recognition that slavery was no longer viable. The economy revived rapidly after a few lost harvests, and only a small number of planters went bankrupt. Slavery ended, but the plantation survived and so did the basic attitudes of a class society. The abolitionists quickly abandoned those they had struggled to free. Many former slaves stayed on the plantations in the same quarters, receiving paltry wages. They were joined by waves of immigrants, who often found conditions so unbearable that they soon moved to the cities or returned to Europe. No freedmen's bureaus or schools were established to improve the lives of the former slaves; they were left at the bottom of the socioeconomic scale, where their descendants remain in the 1990s. New prisons built after 1888 were soon filled with former slaves as society imposed other forms of social control, in part by redefining crime.

In the end, the empire fell because the elites did not need it to protect their interests. Indeed, imperial centralization ran counter to their desires for local autonomy. The republicans embraced federalism, which some saw as a way to counter the oligarchies, which used patronage and clientage to stay in power. In the early republic, however, they would find that the oligarchies adapted easily and used their accumulated power and skills to control the new governmental system. Taking advantage of cabinet crises in 1888 and 1889 and of rising frustration among military officers, republicans favoring change by revolution rather than by evolution drew military officers, led by Field Marshal Fonseca, into a conspiracy to replace the cabinet in November 1889. What started as an armed demonstration demanding replacement of a cabinet turned within hours into a coup d'état deposing Emperor Pedro II.

The Republican Era, 1889–1985

The history of the republic has been a search for a viable form of government to replace the monarchy. That search has lurched back and forth between state autonomy and centralization. The constitution of 1891, establishing the United States of Brazil (Estados Unidos do Brasil), restored autonomy to the provinces, now called states. It recognized that the central government did not rule at the local level, that it exercised control only through the local oligarchies. The empire had not absorbed fully the regional *pátrias*, and now they reasserted themselves. Into the 1920s, the federal government in Rio de Janeiro would be dominated and managed by a combination of the more powerful *pátrias* (São Paulo, Minas Gerais, Rio Grande do Sul, and to a lesser extent Pernambuco and Bahia). After the revolution of 1930, the trend would be strongly toward absorption of the *pátrias*, reaching a peak in the New State (Estado Novo) of 1937–45. Centralization extended into the smallest remote villages as the nation-state's bureaucracy and power grew to previously unknown levels. Renewed autonomy would come with the constitution of 1946 but would disappear under the military regime. The constitution of 1988 once again restored a degree of state autonomy but in the context of a powerful, all-embracing nation-state. In the 1990s, the *pátrias* are more folkloric vestiges than autonomous centers of power.

The history of the republic is also the story of the development of the army as a national institution. The elimination of the monarchy had reduced the number of national institutions to one, the army. Although the Roman Catholic Church continued its presence throughout the country, it was not national but rather international in its personnel, doctrine, liturgy, and purposes. By the time of the 1964 coup, the political parties were not national parties; they were oriented more along regional, personalist (personalism—see Glossary), and special-interest lines. Only in the struggle to reestablish civilian rule in the 1980s did a fitful process of creating national parties take shape. Thus, the army was the core of the developing Brazilian state, a marked change from the marginal role that it had played during the empire. The army assumed this new position almost haphazardly, filling part of the vacuum left by the collapse of the monarchy and gradually acquiring a doctrine and vision to support its de facto role. Although it had more units and men in Rio de Janeiro and Rio Grande do Sul than elsewhere, its presence was felt throughout the country. Its personnel, its interests, its ideology, and its commitments were national in scope (see The Military Role in Society and Government, ch. 5).

The republic's first decade was one of turmoil. It appears to be a pattern of Brazilian history that seemingly peaceful regime changes are followed by long periods of adjustment, often scarred by violence. Years of "regime change" in 1889, 1930, and 1964 introduced protracted adjustment that involved some authoritarian rule. Curiously, because the violence occurred over long periods, usually without overturning the government in Rio de Janeiro or Brasília, Brazil acquired an undeserved reputation for having a nonviolent history of political and social compromise.

The Old or First Republic, 1889–1930

The founders of the Brazilian republic faced a serious question of legitimacy. How could an illegal, treasonous act establish a legal political order? The officers who joined Field Marshal Deodoro da Fonseca in ending the empire were violating solemn oaths to uphold emperor and empire. The officer corps would eventually resolve the contradiction by linking its duty and destiny to Brazil, the motherland, rather than to transitory governments. In addition, the republic was born rather accidentally: Deodoro had intended only to replace the cabinet, but the republicans manipulated him into fathering a republic.

The Brazilian republic was not a spiritual offspring of the republics born of the French or American revolutions, even though the Brazilian regime would attempt to associate itself with both. The republic did not have enough popular support to risk open elections. It was a regime born of a coup d'état that maintained itself by force. The republicans made Deodoro president (1889–91) and, after a financial crisis, appointed Field Marshal Floriano Vieira Peixoto minister of war to ensure the allegiance of the military. Indeed, the Brazilian people were bystanders to the events shaping their history. In the last decades of the nineteenth century, the United States, much of Europe, and neighboring Argentina expanded the right to vote. Brazil, however, moved to restrict access to the polls. In 1874, in a population of about 10 million, the franchise was held by about 1 million, but in 1881 this had been cut to 145,296. This reduction was one reason the empire's legitimacy foundered, but the republic did not move to correct the situation. By 1910 there were only 627,000 voters in a population of 22 million. Throughout the 1920s, only between 2.3 percent and 3.4 percent of the total population voted.

The instability and violence of the 1890s were related to the absence of consensus among the elites regarding a governmental model; and the armed forces were divided over their status, relationship to the political regime, and institutional goals. The lack of military unity and the disagreement among civilian elites about the military's role in society explain partially why a long-term military dictatorship was not established, as some officers advocating positivism (see Glossary) wanted. However, military men were very active in politics; early in the decade, ten of the twenty state governors were officers.

The Constituent Assembly that drew up the constitution of 1891 was a battleground between those seeking to limit executive power, which was dictatorial under President Deodoro da Fonseca, and the Jacobins, radical authoritarians who opposed the Paulista coffee oligarchy and who wanted to preserve and intensify presidential authority. The new charter established a federation governed supposedly by a president, a bicameral National Congress (Congresso Nacional; hereafter, Congress), and a judiciary. However, real power was in the regional *pátrias* and in the hands of local potentates, called "colonels" (*coroneis*; *coronelismo*—see Glossary). Thus, the constitutional system did not work as that document had envisaged. It would take until the end of the decade for an informal but real distribution of power, the so-called politics of the governors, to take shape as the result of armed struggles and bargaining.

Article 14 on the military was particularly important for the future. It declared the army and navy to be permanent national institutions responsible for maintaining law and order and for ensuring the continuance of the three constitutional powers. Officers insisted on the statement of permanent status because they feared that the elites would disband their services. The armed forces were to be the moderator of the system, and military officers were Brazil's only constitutionally mandated elite. The article also required the military to be obedient to the president but "within the limits of the law." Thus, the armed forces were to obey only if they determined a presidential order to be legal. Oddly, military officials were less than enthusiastic about discretionary obedience, which they saw as subversive; the civilian politicians, however, wanted it as a check on presidential power. Interestingly, the constitutions of 1934 and 1946 kept the discretionary clause unaltered. However, the 1937 constitution of the dictatorial Estado Novo, which was a military regime in civilian dress, put the military securely under obedience to the president.

In the election that followed the adoption of the new constitution in 1891, Deodoro da Fonseca and Floriano Peixoto were elected president and vice president, respectively, but with the former gaining only 129 votes and the latter 153. The first president, Deodoro da Fonseca, had difficulty adjusting to sharing power with Congress and, in imperial fashion, dissolved it in November 1891, provoking rebellions in the navy and in Rio Grande do Sul. To mollify the opposition, he resigned in favor of Vice President Peixoto (acting president, 1891–94). Peixoto, known as the "Iron Marshal" (*marechal de ferro*), ousted all the state governors who had supported Deodoro, provoking violence in many parts of the country. One of the bloodiest of these struggles was the civil war that exploded in Rio Grande do Sul in 1893 and soon spread into Santa Catarina and Paraná, pitting former monarchist liberals against republicans. Concurrently, the fleet in Guanabara Bay at Rio de Janeiro challenged Peixoto, and the naval revolt quickly became linked to the struggle in the South. Peixoto's diplomat in Washington, Salvador de Mendonça, with the help of New York businessman Charles Flint, was able to assemble a squadron of ships with American crews, which proved decisive in ending the standoff in Guanabara Bay. The United States government, interested in Brazilian commerce and in the republic's survival, permitted this mercenary effort to occur and sent several cruisers to provide a barely concealed escort. This was the first documented American intervention in Brazil's internal affairs, and significantly it was organized privately.

Deodoro da Fonseca's dissolution of Congress, his resignation, Peixoto's assumption of power, and the outbreak of civil war split the officer corps and led to the arrest and expulsion of several senior officers. Although the power struggles that produced the fighting in Rio Grande do Sul during 1893–95 were local in origin, Peixoto made them national by siding with republican Governor Julio de Castilhos. The savage combat and the execution of prisoners and suspected sympathizers, in what historian José Maria Bello called the "cruelest of Brazil's civil wars," was shameful on both sides. Peixoto's fierce defense of the republic made him the darling of the Jacobins and from then on a symbol of Brazilian nationalism. In November 1894, because of his ill health (he died in 1895) and the military's disunity, Peixoto turned the government over to a spokesman for the agrarian coffee elite, São Paulo native Prudente José de Morais Barros, also known as Prudente de Morais, the first civilian president (1894–98). Prudente de Morais negotiated an end to the war in the South and granted amnesty to the rebels and the expelled officers. He weakened the army's staunchest republicans and sought to lower the military's political weight. He promoted officers committed to creating a professional force that would be at the disposal of the national authorities, who would determine how it was to be employed. A General Staff (Estado Geral), established in 1896 on the German model, was to shape this new army.

However, before the new army could take shape, it was used in 1897 to destroy the religious community of Canudos in the *sertão* of Bahia, which the Jacobins thought mistakenly was a hot-bed of monarchist sedition. The Rio de Janeiro government, which saw monarchists everywhere, threw a force of 9,500 against a population of perhaps 30,000. Some 4,193 soldiers were wounded between July and October 1897, and the townspeople were killed, taken prisoner, or fled. Canudos was erased in the same fashion that Indian villages had been and continued to be erased. Although the campaign's symbolic value as a defense of the republic faded as the reality became known, it remained a powerful warning to marginal (marginality—see Glossary) folk throughout Brazil that they would not

Naval station, Guanabara Bay, Rio de Janeiro
Courtesy Patricia A. Kluck

be permitted to challenge the hierarchical order of society. In this sense, Canudos was a step in creating mechanisms of social control in the postslavery era.

Canudos affected the political scene immediately when a returning soldier, the foil in a high-level Jacobin conspiracy, attempted to assassinate President Prudente de Morais but killed the minister of war instead, thereby acting as a catalyst for rallying support for the government. The abortive assassination made possible the election of Manuel Ferraz de Campos Sales (president, 1898–1902). In the army, the attempt consolidated the hold of generals who opposed Floriano Peixoto and were interested in professionalizing the institution.

The turmoil of the 1890s and particularly Canudos suspended the military's capability to exercise the moderating role that it supposedly inherited from the monarchy. By 1898 the rural-based regional oligarchies had regained command of the political system. Their fiscal policies reflected their belief that Brazil was an agricultural country whose strength was in supplying Europe and North America with coffee, rubber, sugar, tobacco, and many natural resources. Brazil produced 75 percent of the world's coffee. With competition increasing, however, prices fell continually, causing the government to devalue the currency against the British pound. This devaluation forced up the price of imported goods, thus lowering consumption and government tax revenues from imports. Those shortfalls led to suspension of payments on the foreign debt, and the generally poor economy caused half of the banks to collapse. The oligarchy responded to the situation by attempting to preserve its own position and by limiting national industry and infrastructure to that necessary to support the agricultural economy. The society that the economy underlay was one in which the elites regarded the majority of the people merely as cheap labor. The elites encouraged immigration to keep labor plentiful and inexpensive, although they also wanted to "whiten" the population. They considered public education of little use and potentially subversive.

The political system that took shape at the beginning of the twentieth century had apparent and real aspects. There was the constitutional system, and there was the real system of unwritten agreements (*coronelismo*) among local bosses, the colonels. *Coronelismo,* which supported state autonomy, was called the "politics of the governors." Under it, the local oligarchies chose the state governors, who in turn selected the president.

The populous and prosperous states of Minas Gerais and São Paulo dominated the system and swapped the presidency between them for many years. The system consolidated the state oligarchies around families that had been members of the old monarchial elite. And to check the nationalizing tendencies of the army, this oligarchic republic and its state components strengthened the navy and the state police. In the larger states, the state police were soon turned into small armies; in the extreme case of São Paulo, French military advisers were employed after 1906.

The "politics of the governors" kept a relative peace until the end of World War I. Urban Brazil, the one foreigners saw from the decks of ships, prospered. But there was no integrated national economy. Rather, Brazil had a grouping of regional economies that exported their own specialty products to European and North American markets. The absence of overland transportation, except for the mule trains, impeded internal economic integration, political cohesion, and military efficiency. The regions, "the Brazils" as the British called them, moved to their own rhythms. The Northeast exported its surplus cheap labor and saw its political influence decline as its sugar lost foreign markets to Caribbean producers. The wild rubber boom in Amazônia lost its world primacy to efficient Southeast Asian colonial plantations after 1912. The national-oriented market economies of the South were not dramatic, but their growth was steady and by the 1920s allowed Rio Grande do Sul to exercise considerable political leverage. Real power resided in the coffee-growing states of the Southeast (Sudeste)—São Paulo, Minas Gerais, and Rio de Janeiro—which produced the most export revenue. Those three and Rio Grande do Sul harvested 60 percent of Brazil's crops, turned out 75 percent of its industrial and meat products, and held 80 percent of its banking resources.

One factor that eventually would draw "the Brazils" closer together was the heightened sense of nationalism that developed among the urban middle and upper classes before World War I. This sense of nationalism can be explained partially by the Brazilian elite's focus on Rio de Janeiro as the center of their world. Although the national government was weak, it was still the source of prestige and patronage. Rio's sanitation projects and its remodeled downtown (1903–04) were soon copied by state capitals and ports.

The elites had reason to think that Brazil's status in the world was rising. In 1905 the archbishop of Rio de Janeiro received Latin America's first cardinalate. Brazil hosted the Third Pan-American Conference, raised its Washington legation to an embassy (1904), sent a notable delegation to the Second Hague Peace Conference (1907), gained possession via arbitration of hundreds of thousands of square kilometers of disputed territory, established the Indian Protective Service, tied together the far reaches of the country via telegraph, and purchased two of the world's largest dreadnoughts for its navy. Many cheered writer Afonso Celso when he asserted that the era was "the dawn of our greatness . . . . We will be the second or first power of the world."

However, the enthusiasm was not sufficient to overcome the resistance of Brazilians of all levels to military service. When an Obligatory Military Service Law was enacted in 1908, it went unenforced until 1916. Military service was unappealing because members were called on continually to take up arms. During the presidency of Marshal Hermes Rodrigues da Fonseca (1910–14), nephew of Deodoro da Fonseca, turmoil spread across Brazil. In 1910 sailors protesting extreme physical punishments in the navy seized the new dreadnoughts *São Paulo* and *Minas Gerais* and some smaller vessels in the bay at

Rio de Janeiro and threatened to bombard the city. Hermes da Fonseca was forced to grant the rebels their demands and to give them amnesty.

The image of national stability with which the earlier Campos Sales administration had tried to dazzle foreign bankers also was shattered by a series of military interventions, known as the Salvations, that replaced a number of state governments. The national government, somewhat against Hermes da Fonseca's inclination, sponsored what amounted to coups d'état against state governments in Sergipe, Pernambuco, Alagoas, Pará, Piauí, Bahia, and Ceará. In disorderly fashion, one oligarchic alliance substituted for another, often with an army officer in charge. In the disastrous case of Bahia, the local army commander bombarded the governor's palace and surrounding buildings. In 1911 São Paulo's French-trained Public Force (Força Pública) and civilian Patriotic Battalions saved the city from similar federal intervention.

Struggling to keep control of the army, Hermes da Fonseca replaced the minister of war three times in sixteen months and forced the retirement of about 100 colonels and generals. But to keep them from rebelling, they were all retired at higher ranks and salaries. The Brazilian political system was not so much one of compromise as of co-optation. With this internal army purge, the Salvationist Movement spent itself, and the tide turned away from federal military interventions to replace dominant regional oligarchies toward neutrality or preserving the status quo. The movement can be seen as a messy attempt to reduce state autonomy and to heighten the power of the central government.

Meanwhile, the vision of Brazilian order and progress as seen by the urban elite, intellectuals, and newspaper editorials was challenged again by the supposedly anarchic *sertão*, this time in the South. In August 1914, as world attention focused on the outbreak of war in Europe, a very different conflict burst forth in the Contestado region of Santa Catarina. A popular rebellion, also known as the Contestado, confronted the "colonel"-dominated socioeconomic and political system. Where the Salvationist Movement aimed at substituting one oligarchy for another, the Contestado rebels rejected the national system and wanted to remake their part of the Brazilian reality. As with Canudos, the response of state and federal authorities was pulverizing violence.

The region's economy was based on livestock, the collection of maté, and lumbering. Its social structure concentrated wealth and power in the hands of a few "colonels," around whom lesser landowners were arrayed. Most families lived at the sufferance of those men or had shaky land titles. A jurisdictional dispute between Santa Catarina and Paraná arose because each state issued deeds to the same land. The no-man's-land attracted fugitives from throughout Brazil. The construction of the São Paulo-Rio Grande do Sul Railroad and the timbering and colonization operations of United States capitalist Percival Farquhar added foreign elements to the already volatile mix. The Brazil Railroad and the Southern Brazil Lumber and Colonization Company forced Brazilians off their expropriated lands, imported European immigrants, and sawed away at virgin pine, cedar, and walnut trees. People whose families had lived in the region for a century suddenly saw their lands rented or sold to others. As if that were not enough, in 1910 the threat of war with Argentina loomed, and authorities speeded the railroad's construction and expanded labor crews to about 8,000. In this environment of tumultuous destruction of the forests, social tensions rose with evictions and the sudden introduction of foreigners and modern technology. The local "colonels" secured their own interests, abandoning their customary paternalism and leaving the mass of people adrift. The Contestado was afflicted with a collective identity crisis, which caused many to turn to messianic religion as solace.

The people of the Contestado followed a local healer, Miguel Lucena Boaventura, known as José Maria, who soon died in a confrontation with Paraná Military Police. His followers refused to accept his death, however, and believed that he was either alive or would rise again. His story mixed with the Luso-Brazilian belief in supernatural assistance in desperate times. This phenomenon, called Sebastianism, transformed the submissive population, accustomed to acting only with the "colonel's" approval, into a resolute fighting force. Their attacks on the railway and lumbering operations and the failure of negotiations with federal authorities led to an escalation of hostilities in 1912 and a fierce military campaign that in 1915 involved 6,000 troops, modern artillery and machine guns, field telephones and telegraph, and the first use of aircraft in a Brazilian conflict. The fighting was spread over a wide area, and the many redoubts of about 20,000 "fanatics," as the army called them, made suppression slow and difficult and also revealed the military's weaknesses. The number of casualties was uncertain but sizeable, and henceforth the army maintained a garrison in the region. The Contestado was subdued by the end of 1917.

Army reformers, a key group of whom returned from training in Germany by the end of 1913, wrote commentaries on the campaign in the new military monthly, *A Defesa Nacional.* They regarded the Contestado as "an inglorious conflict that discredited our arms." They blamed the republic for its "lack of elevated political norms, the abandonment of thousands of Brazilians . . . segregated from national society by the lack of instruction, by the scarcity of easy means of communication, by the want of energy, and by the poverty of initiative that, unhappily, has characterized the administrations generally since the time of the monarchy." They warned military leaders that "the lesson of the Contestado" was that the army's passivity in accepting poorly conceived political measures would only damage it "morally" and would bring Brazil "the most funereal consequences."

The Contestado joined Canudos as an important component in the army's institutional memory. Veterans played meaningful roles in military and national affairs in the next decades. Within a few years, the reformist critique would be part of the thinking that underlay the *tenente* or lieutenants' revolts of the 1920s, beginning with the Copacabana Revolt in 1922. The Salvationist Movement and the Contestado drew the army and the central government deeply into the internal affairs of the states, thereby whittling away at their coveted autonomy. The era's legacy of political intervention and suppression of dissent muddied the army's mission and self-image, but it amplified the power of the central government (Rio de Janeiro).

The growing power of Rio de Janeiro was reflected in Brazilian foreign affairs under the guidance of José Maria da Silva Paranhos, the Baron of Rio Branco, who served as foreign minister from 1902 to 1912, under presidents Francisco de Paula Rodrigues Alves (acting president, 1902–3; president, 1903–6), and Afonso Pena (1906–9), Acting President Nilo Peçanha (1909–10), and President Hermes da Fonseca. His vision shaped both the boundaries of the country and the traditions of Brazilian foreign relations. In the heyday of international imperialism, he was instrumental in negotiating limits over which the great powers were not to intrude. He argued for military reform to back up energetic diplomacy, and he began the process of moving Brazil out of the British orbit and into that of the United States. The latter was taking half of Brazil's total exports by 1926, but Brazil still owed Britain over US$100 million in the mid-1920s. British banks financed the country's international commercial exchange, and British investors provided 53 percent of the total foreign investment until 1930. But by the late 1920s, United States banks held nearly 35 percent of the foreign debt. Rio Branco's goal, which was pursued by his successors, was to diffuse the country's dependency among the powers so that none could intervene without being checked by another. Trade and financial ties with the United States were increased at British expense, and these would be balanced by military links with Germany and then France. France would continue for decades to provide a cultural model for the elites.

The Rio Branco years were the basis for what became known as the Itamaraty tradition (named after the building that housed the Ministry of Foreign Affairs in Rio de Janeiro), but not every administration grasped its purpose. Some confused its tactical aspects—reliance on foreign loans and investments, Pan-Americanism, and alliance with the United States—with its essential substance, the quest for independence and national greatness.

World War I found Brazil with nearly half of its army committed in the Contestado. The war in Europe was traumatic for the army, which was then beginning a reorganization under the influence of thirty-two officers who had recently returned from service in German army units. A German military mission had been expected, but pressure from São Paulo and from Paris resulted in a mission contract with France instead. Economics, Washington's decision to enter the war, and German submarine attacks on Brazilian merchant ships pulled Brazil into the conflict on the Allied side. The military mobilized, but the generals, feeling over-committed and ill-prepared, declined to send troops to Europe.

Pan-Americanism provided some outlet for Brazil's international status pretensions, but the period between the world wars often found its neighbor Argentina suspicious of harmless improvements in Brazil's armed forces. Brazil's obligatory military service, its construction of new barracks, its purchases of modern weapons, and its contracts for a French military mission and a United States naval mission were viewed by military officials in Buenos Aires as threatening. Brazilian leaders wanted their country regarded as the most powerful in South

America but understood that the public would not accept, and the constitution outlawed, a war of aggression. Regardless of what the Argentines thought, the military was not prepared to wage a foreign war. Tension between Argentina and Brazil and maneuvering for greater influence in Paraguay and Uruguay have been characteristic of their relations since the War of the Triple Alliance.

The interwar years in Brazil saw an increase in labor agitation as the economy expanded, industrialization and urbanization stepped up, and immigrants flowed into the country. Coffee overproduction by the turn of the century had provoked subsidization programs at the state and national levels that helped the planters but could not prevent the decline in the economy's capacity to pay for imported manufactured goods. Local industry began to fill the gap. World War I restricted trade further, and Brazilian industrial production increased substantially. The government stressed the need for more industrial independence from foreign producers and stimulated import substitution, particularly in textiles. Many of the factories were small, with an average of twenty-one workers. In 1920 about a million urban workers were concentrated in Rio de Janeiro and São Paulo. Brazil was just beginning to develop its industrial base, but it was still mainly an agricultural country with 6.3 million people working the soil.

The living conditions of urban workers were bad. Housing, transportation, sewerage, and water supply trailed far behind the rapid population growth and produced serious public health problems. The clean-up campaigns at the beginning of the century struck at the high incidence of yellow fever, malaria, and smallpox in Rio de Janeiro, Santos, and Northeastern seaports. The city centers were made safer, but the workers who crowded into sordid "beehives" (*cortiços*—small crowded houses) and favelas (shantytowns) suffered all sorts of ailments.

The federal and state governments subsidized immigration from Italy, Portugal, Spain, Germany, and Japan to provide workers for the coffee plantations. However, many immigrants soon fled the rough conditions in the countryside for better opportunities in the cities. They flooded the labor pools, making it difficult for unions to force factory owners to pay better wages. Women, who were the majority of workers in the textile and clothing industries, were frequently active in organizing factory commissions to agitate for improved conditions, freedom from sexual abuse, and higher pay. Strikes had occurred in 1903, 1906, and 1912, and in 1917 general strikes broke out in Rio de Janeiro, São Paulo, Recife, Santos, and Porto Alegre. Because the mentality of the industrialists was rooted in the slavery era and emphasized their well-being over that of the commonwealth and because they functioned on a thin profit margin, they tended to fire workers for striking or joining unions. The industrialists also blacklisted troublemakers, employed armed thugs to keep control inside and outside the factories, and called on the government to repress any sign of labor organization. There were no large massacres of strikers, as occurred in Mexico and Chile, but the physical violence was marked.

Some advocates of reform were heard. For example, economic nationalists like Roberto Simonsen argued for improved pay incentives to prevent individual workers from unionizing. During the 1920s, the Roman Catholic Church, as part of its effort to revive its status, organized the Young Catholic Workers and preached the example of the Holy Family accepting "the will of Providence, in pain and in happiness." By 1930 church societies, private charities, factory-sponsored recreational clubs, and government agencies strove for more control over workers' organizations and leisure time.

During the Old Republic, Brazil changed at a frightening rate. As its population increased 162 percent between 1890 and 1930, it became more urbanized and industrialized, and its political system was stretched beyond tolerance. Concern over the resurgence of labor activity in the late 1920s was one of the factors that led to the collapse of the Old Republic in 1930 and to the subsequent significant change in labor and social policy.

The Era of Getúlio Vargas, 1930–54

Just as the 1889 regime change led to a decade of unrest and painful adjustment, so too did the revolts of 1930. Provisional President Getúlio Dorneles Vargas ruled as dictator (1930–34), congressionally elected president (1934–37), and again dictator (1937–45), with the backing of his revolutionary coalition. He also served as a senator (1946–51) and the popularly elected president (1951–54). Vargas was a member of the gaucho-landed oligarchy and had risen through the system of patronage and clientelism, but he had a fresh vision of how Brazilian politics could be shaped to support national development. He understood that with the breakdown of direct relations between workers and owners in the expanding factories of Brazil, workers could become the basis for a new form of political power—populism. Using such insights, he would gradually establish such mastery over the Brazilian political world that he would stay in power for fifteen years. During those years, the preeminence of the agricultural elites ended, new urban industrial leaders acquired more influence nationally, and the middle class began to show some strength.

Tenentismo, or the lieutenants' rebellion against the army and governmental hierarchies, faded as a distinctive movement after 1931, in part because its adherents promoted the preservation of state autonomy when the trend toward increased centralization was strong. Individual lieutenants continued to exercise important roles, but they made their peace with the traditional political forces. In 1932 São Paulo, whose interests and pride suffered under the new regime, rose in revolt. The three-month civil war saw many officers who had lost out in 1930 or were otherwise disgruntled join the Paulistas, but federal forces defeated them.

A new constitution in 1934 reorganized the political system by creating a legislature with both state and social-sector representatives. It contained some electoral reforms, including women's suffrage, a secret ballot, and special courts to supervise elections. The Constituent Assembly elected Vargas president for a four-year term. However, the attempt to harness the revolution to the old system, somewhat remodeled, would soon fail completely and take Brazil into prolonged dictatorship. The left helped in that process by becoming a creditable threat. On misguided instructions from Moscow based on misinformation from Brazil, the Brazilian communists, led by a former *tenente,* staged a revolt in 1935, but it was rapidly suppressed.

In the 1930s, the civilian elites feared that Brazil would suffer a civil war similar to Spain's, and so for the first time in Brazilian history they supported a strong, unified military. The Estado Novo gave the army its long-held desire for control over the states' Military Police (Policia Militar) units. The elites of the old state *pátrias* gave up their independent military power in return for federal protection of their interests. This process was not always a willing one, as the Paulista revolt of 1932 showed, but federal monopoly of military force escalated the power of the central government to levels previously unknown.

A significant turning point in the history of Brazil had been reached.

Under the Estado Novo, state autonomy ended, appointed federal officials replaced governors, and patronage flowed from the president downward. All political parties were dissolved until 1944, thus limiting opportunities for an opposition to organize. In the process, Vargas eliminated threats from the left and the right. At the local level, "colonels" survived by declaring their loyalty and accepting their share of patronage for distribution to their own underlings. The Vargas years had their greatest impact on national politics and economics and their least impact at the local level where the older forms of power continued well into the 1950s. Even in the 1990s, local political bosses were tagged "colonels." Vargas took care to absorb the rural and commercial elites into his power base. He had the ability to make former enemies supporters, or at least neutrals.

The Vargas years saw the reorganization of the armed forces, the economy, international trade, and foreign relations. The government restored the old imperial palace in Petrópolis and encouraged the preservation of historic buildings and towns. The average annual rise in the gross domestic product (GDP—see Glossary) was nearly 4 percent. Brazil's first steel mill at Volta Redonda (1944) was the start of the great industrial output of the second half of the century. The 1930–45 era added corporatism (see Glossary) to the Brazilian political lexicon.

Even as it channeled investment into industry, the Estado Novo classified strikes as crimes and grouped the government-controlled unions into separate sector federations that were not allowed to form across-the-board national organizations. The idea was to keep the lines of control vertical (vertical integration—see Glossary). The government decreed regular wage and benefits increases and slowly expanded an incomplete social security system. Its minimum wage levels were never satisfactory. The regime's propaganda touted state paternalism and protection and depicted Vargas as the benefactor of the working classes. He also was the benefactor of the factory owners, who saw industry expand 11.2 percent a year throughout the 1930s, which meant that it more than doubled during the decade. Indeed, growth and repression were the twin orders of the day. Journalists and novelists were censored, jailed, and discouraged. The army restricted access to the military schools to those with acceptable racial, familial, religious, educational, and political characteristics.

As a result of these repressive measures, the suspension of political activities, and the government's support of rearming and modernizing the military, the army gained a coherence and unity that it had not experienced since before 1922. The popular status that the army won by participating in the Italian campaign (1944–45) of World War II also permitted the High Command, under General Pedro Aurélio de Góes Monteiro, a long-time supporter of Vargas, to step into the successionist crisis of October 1945 to depose Vargas and to cut short the political mobilization of the masses that the generals believed would upset the social order. Not to have acted would have violated the implicit agreement made with the elites when the latter surrendered their independent state military forces to federal control.

The elected government over which President Eurico Gaspar Dutra presided from 1946 to 1951 opened under the decree laws of the Estado Novo and continued under the new constitution of 1946. This charter reflected the strong conservative tendency in Brazilian politics by incorporating ideas from the constitution of 1934 and the social legislation of the Estado Novo. Over the next years, the various cabinet changes traced the government's steady movement toward the right. The Dutra administration was supported by the same conservative interventionist army that had backed the previous regime. Indeed, Dutra, who though retired from active duty, was inaugurated in his dress uniform and was promoted to general of the army and then to marshal while in office, made the point that he still belonged to the military class (*classe militar*), that he would not neglect its needs, and that he would guide the army politically.

More dispassionate observers see the ending of Vargas's productive leadership—during which the average annual rise in the GDP was nearly 4 percent—as the reaction of the landowning and business elite allied with the urban middle class against the processes of change. Dutra's years in office displayed a minimal level of state participation and intervention in the economy. It was indeed ironic that the man who led Brazil through the first steps of its "experiment with democracy" was a general who, in the early years of World War II, was so antiliberal that he had opposed aligning Brazil with the democratic countries against Nazi Germany. He was a fervent anticommunist, who quickly broke the diplomatic ties Vargas had established with the Soviet Union, outlawed the Brazilian Communist Party, and supported the United States in the opening phases of the Cold War. He exchanged official visits with President Harry S. Truman and sought American aid for continued economic development.

Dutra's government improved the railways, completed construction of roads that connected Rio de Janeiro to Salvador and São Paulo, and expanded the electrical generating and transmission systems. It also cooperated with the states in building more than 4,000 new rural schools and supported construction of new university buildings in various states. In 1951 it also created the National Research Council (Conselho Nacional de Pesquisas—CNPq), which would be important in developing capabilities and university faculties in coming decades (see Science and Technology as Modernization, 1945–64, ch. 6). His mandate was marked by heated disputes over the nationalization of oil and plans for an international institute to study Amazônia. The latter were shelved amidst emotional charges that they would lead to the loss of half of the national territory; and the campaign for the former was suppressed violently.

Dutra's military program included domestic arms production, sending many officers for training in the United States, expanding air force and naval schools and modernizing their equipment, and establishing the War College (Escola Superior de Guerra—ESG), which played such an important role in the political crises of the 1960s. Although Dutra could be criticized for not containing inflation and for allowing an importing frenzy that soon exhausted the savings of the war years, he managed to govern without declaring a state of siege, and he was the first elected president since 1926 to pass the office to his elected successor.

As a candidate for president in the 1950 elections, Vargas advocated accelerating industrialization and expanding social legislation, and he was rewarded with a sizeable 49 percent of the vote. Vargas's attempts to base his elected government (1951–54) firmly on populism induced military, elite, and United States fears of nationalism. Even so, it was a period of deepening political polarization. Anticommunist military officers saw red in every attempt to expand labor's influence and objected to wage increases for workers when the value of their own salaries was eroding steadily. The United States refused economic assistance that Brazilian leaders believed they deserved for providing bases, natural resources, and troops during World War II. The lack of postwar benefits, especially for the service of the Brazilian Expeditionary Force (Força Expedicionária Brasileira—FEB), caused Vargas and part of the military to reject the idea of sending troops to fight in Korea.

Although the United States government did not want to provide economic aid, it also did not want the Brazilian government to take an active role in developing the country's resources. Washington's desire to secure Brazil as a safe place for private United States investment clashed with Brazil's treatment of foreign-owned utilities. Foreign interests had been too slow in developing energy resources, so the Vargas government created the Brazilian Petroleum Corporation (Petróleo Brasileiro S.A.—Petrobrás) in 1953 and the Brazilian Electric Power Company (Centrais Elétricas Brasileiras S.A.—Eletrobrás) in 1961. The "Petroleum is Ours!" campaign of the nationalists caused arguments within the military over what was best to do. Some officers embraced the antistatist attitude that Washington was sponsoring. The bitterly fought, emotional debate over the creation of Petrobrás poisoned political life and contributed to the subsequent military interventions. The Vargas administration dissolved in frustration and charges of corruption; faced with military demands for his resignation, Vargas shot himself on August 24, 1954. His death produced considerable public sympathy, which in turn strengthened his reputation as "father of the poor." His influence in Brazilian politics was felt for decades.

The Post-Vargas Republic, 1954–64

If corporatism was the hallmark of the 1930s and 1940s, populism, nationalism, and developmentalism characterized the 1950s and early 1960s. Each of these contributed to the crisis that gripped Brazil and resulted in the authoritarian regime after 1964. At the core of the crisis was the continued unwillingness of the elite to share the benefits of Brazil's wealth with the majority of the people. By the early 1960s, the crisis was boiling in reverse, from the top down. The crisis had much more to do with elite fears of a mass uprising, supposedly instigated by international communism, than with the reality of social revolution. They, rather than the masses, believed the fiery rhetoric of leftist-populist politicians. What elites elsewhere might have seen as popular democratic mobilization, the Brazilian elites saw as revolutionary change that threatened their well-being. Because they portrayed their well-being as the same as the national well-being, and because they controlled the state and the instruments of power, they responded with a counterrevolution, what historian Joseph Page labeled "the revolution that never was."

Labor became more active in seeking to improve the status of the working class, and the population continued to grow beyond the state's ability to expand educational and social services. As a result, conservative elites feared that they were losing control of politics and of the state. The elites had opposed Vargas because he sought to use the state to spread benefits more broadly. The middle classes tended to identify with elite visions of society and to see the lower classes as a threat. Curiously, the term *povo* (people), which had meant the lowest class, the destitute, the squatters, the rural poor, had changed by the early 1950s to mean the politically active and economically mobile urban lower classes. Further, politicians appealed to the *povo* during election campaigns but once elected directed government benefits principally to the middle and upper classes.

Juscelino Kubitschek (1956–61), the only post-Vargas elected president to serve a full term, soothed opponents by avoiding the emotional appeals of the populists. Even so, his common touch reached millions, and his developmentalist and nationalist visions stirred the Brazilian imagination. Kubitschek coopted the military by involving it in the decision-making process and by adequately funding it. He pushed the creation of an automotive industry, which in a generation would result in Brazil's leaping from the bull cart and mule train era into that of the internal combustion engine. The new factories turned out 321,000 vehicles in 1960. The great highway network of the late twentieth century and the world's eighth-largest automobile production are his legacies. And he yanked Brazil away from its fascination with the coast by moving the capital to Brasília in a new Federal District (Distrito Federal) carved out of then-distant Goiás. Thanks to the changes in transportation and the growing availability of motorized farm equipment, the vast countryside of Goiás and Mato Grosso would be cultivated in the next decades, and Brazil would become the world's number-two food exporter. The overall economy would expand 8.3

percent a year. There was a lot of truth in his government's motto: "Fifty Years' Progress in Five."

Brazil of 1960 was very different from that of 1930. The population, which had been 33.5 million in 1930, was now 70 million, with 44 percent in urban areas. A third of all Latin Americans were Brazilian. Life expectancy had improved noticeably. The number of industrial workers had more than doubled from a 1940 level of 1.6 million to 2.9 million, and the industrial share of GDP was higher (25.2 percent) than that of agriculture (22.5 percent). The underside of such progress was a continuous swelling of urban slums and inflation. The annual rate of inflation rose from 12 percent in 1949 to 26 percent in 1959, and then zoomed to a shocking 39.5 percent in 1960. Savings depreciated, lenders refused to offer long-term loans, interest rates soared, and the government refused to undertake orthodox, anti-inflationary programs styled after those of the International Monetary Fund (IMF—see Glossary). Moreover, the disparities between rich and poor remained, with 40 percent of national income enjoyed by 10 percent of the population, 36 percent going to the next 30 percent, and 24 percent being divided among the poorest 60 percent of Brazilians. Before national wealth could be redistributed, however, development had to be maintained.

Brazil had the potential, but it lacked the hard currency necessary to pay for the imports needed to sustain swift industrialization. Either it could cut imports, thereby paralyzing factories and transportation, or it could stop repayments on foreign loans and profit remittances from foreign investments. With such unpalatable alternatives, it is not surprising that Brazilian governments had difficulty formulating an economic plan that would both satisfy creditors and keep trade flowing.

The populist administrations of Jânio Quadros (January–August 1961) and João Goulart (1961–64) expanded the term *povo* once again to embrace the rural poor, thereby producing the image of a budding proletariat ready to join a reformist government against elite privilege and United States imperialism. Quadros, a former governor of São Paulo, could not keep his promise to sweep out corruption, because his bid for more presidential power ended with his sudden resignation on August 25, 1961. He had assembled a makeshift political coalition that gave him an impressive electoral margin but did not give him enough influence in Congress to get his legislation passed.

Brasília
Courtesy Brazilian Embassy, Washington

Frustrated, he planned to restructure the government, but before he could act, Carlos Lacerda, governor of Guanabara (the old Rio de Janeiro Federal District), revealed that Quadros intended to close Congress, decree reforms, and get the people's blessing in a plebiscite. Quadros and Lacerda clashed over the issue of an independent foreign policy. Such a policy, which Quadros supported, emphasized new markets for Brazilian products and a strong stance in favor of the developing world, while maintaining relations with the United States but refusing to isolate Cuba. Lacerda was particularly critical of Quadros's pro-Cuba policy. Quadros resigned believing that the military would be unwilling to allow Vice President João Goulart, a populist and former minister of labor under Vargas, to assume the presidency. Quadros hoped that his action would shock the *povo* into taking to the streets to demand his reimposition and would spur the military into pressuring Congress. He then flew to São Paulo, where he spent the next day at a military base waiting for the summons to return, but instead the head of the Chamber of Deputies was sworn in as acting president. People were shocked, but they tended to feel betrayed by Quadros rather than believe that "terrible forces" had risen against him. On that Friday in August 1961, the republic of 1945 began its painful death.

Instead of worrying how to restore Quadros, the politicians and military leaders focused on Goulart's succession. An uneasy country awaited Goulart on his return from a trade mission to China. Congress refused to agree to the request of the military ministers that it disavow his right to the presidency. His brother-in-law, Leonel de Moura Brizola, the fiery governor of Rio Grande do Sul, and the regional army commander announced that their forces would defend the constitution. The threat of civil war was ominous. Instead, a compromise changed the constitutional system from a presidential to a parliamentary one (1961–63), with Goulart as president and Tancredo de Almeida Neves of Minas Gerais as prime minister. In the next months, Goulart, chafing at the attempt to turn him into a figurehead, made heated appeals to the masses to mobilize in his favor. Goulart secured victory in a 1962 plebiscite, which restored the presidential system in January 1963. Unhappily, Goulart interpreted the five-to-one margin as a personal mandate, as opposed to a mandate for the presidential system.

Goulart's relations with the United States went from uneasy, when he visited President John F. Kennedy and gave a speech to the United States Congress in April 1963, to frigid, when President Lyndon B. Johnson took over in Washington in November 1963. The United States, smarting from Fidel Castro's radicalization of Cuba, resented Brazilian unwillingness to isolate Havana and became obsessed with peasants organizing in the impoverished Northeast. Washington poured millions of dollars directly into that region's states, bypassing Goulart's government. The regional elites happily accepted United States aid to expand their autonomy vis-à-vis Brasília.

Goulart carried his populism too far when he backed proposals for noncommissioned officers to hold political office and when he appeared sympathetic to rebelling sergeants in September 1963. The officer corps believed that the president was undermining discipline, thereby threatening military institutions.

Minister of Army General Amaury Kruel complained that the army had been subjected to a "survival" budget since 1958 and that most of its armaments and equipment were either obsolete, beyond repair, or required replacement. In 1962 every regional army headquarters reported that it was not in condition to hold regular exercises, and many officers concluded that their efforts were useless because of a generalized "disbelief and lack of incentive." General Kruel alerted President Goulart that inadequate funding was creating a "calamitous situation" in which the army was being "economically and financially asphyxiated."

The right and the military charged that Goulart's call for reforming legislation was merely a cover for a radical nationalist takeover. Publicly, they organized study groups, formed a shadow government, orchestrated an intense press campaign, and staged street marches. Secretly, they armed large landowners (*fazendeiros*) in the countryside, developed plans to neutralize opposition and to topple the government, and sought help from the United States. The military was again about to break the bonds of obedience to a national government. The argument was that the armed forces should support any government as long as it was democratic.

Such logic grew more persuasive as political mobilization gripped the society. Peasant land seizures and urban food riots contributed to a sense of impending chaos. Brizola bragged foolishly that he had a 200,000-strong peoples' militia organized in groups of eleven. The opposition charged the government with arousing a "state of revolutionary war." In the months before March 1964, the staff and student officers of the Army General Staff School (Escola de Comando de Estado-Maior do Exército—ECEME) played a key role in convincing officers that they should support a move against Goulart. Even the highly respected chief of staff, Marshal Humberto de Alencar Castelo Branco, joined the conspiracy. Castelo Branco had served as FEB operations officer in Italy, director of studies at ECEME, and long-time head of the War College. The officers believed that rational economic development, internal security, and institutional well-being would occur only if economic and political structures were altered, and that the civilian leaders were unwilling to make the necessary changes. They believed that the left was so well-organized that the conspiracy might fail. They had plans to flee Brazil in that case, and United States officers had promised that they would receive training and logistical support to return to wage a guerrilla war.

Struggling to keep the impatient left on his side and to stave off the right, Goulart opted for a series of public rallies to mobilize pressure for basic reforms. In a huge rally in Rio de Janeiro on March 13, 1964, Goulart decreed agrarian reform and rent controls and promised more. A counter rally against the government, held six days later in São Paulo, put 500,000 people marching in the streets. Sailors and marines in Rio de Janeiro, led by an agent provocateur of the anti-Goulart conspiracy, mutinied in support of Goulart. However, Goulart mishandled the incident by agreeing that they would not be punished and that the navy minister would be changed. The uproar was immediate. Rio de Janeiro's *Correio da Manhã* published an unusual Easter Sunday edition with the headline "Enough!" It was followed the next day, March 30, with one saying "Out!" In the next two days, the military moved to secure the country, and Goulart fled to Uruguay. Brizola's resistance groups proved an illusion, as did the supposed arms caches of the unions and the readiness of favela residents to attack the wealthy. The period of the military republic had begun.

The Military Republic, 1964–85

The military held power from 1964 until March 1985 not by design but because of political struggles within the new regime. Just as the regime changes of 1889, 1930, and 1945 unleashed competing political forces and caused splits in the military, so too did the regime change of 1964. Because no civilian politician was acceptable to all the revolutionary factions, the army chief of staff, Marshal Humberto Castelo Branco (president, 1964–67), became president with the intention of overseeing a reform of the political-economic system. He refused to stay beyond the term of deposed João Goulart or to institutionalize the military in power. However, competing demands radicalized the situation; military hard-liners wanted a complete purge of left-wing and populist influences, while civilian politicians obstructed Castelo Branco's reforms. The latter accused him of dictatorial methods, and the former criticized him for not going far enough. To satisfy the military hard-liners, he recessed and purged Congress, removed objectionable state governors, and decreed expansion of the president's (and thereby the military's) arbitrary powers at the expense of the legislature and judiciary. His gamble succeeded in curbing the populist left but provided the successor governments of Marshal Artur da Costa e Silva (1967–69) and General Emílio Garrastazú Médici (1969–74) with a basis for authoritarian rule. Anti-Goulart politicians understood too late the forces they had helped unleash.

Castelo Branco tried to maintain a degree of democracy. His economic reforms prepared the way for the Brazilian eco-

Ministry of Army, Brasília
Courtesy Michaël Borg-Hansen

nomic "miracle" of the next decade, and his restructuring of the party system that had existed since 1945 shaped the contours of government-opposition relations for the next two decades. He preserved presidential supremacy over the military and kept potential coup-makers in check, but in the process he had to expand presidential powers in the infamous Second Institutional Act of October 1965, and he had to accept the succession of Minister of Army Costa e Silva.

As in earlier regime changes, the armed forces' officer corps was divided between those who believed that they should confine themselves to their professional duties and the hard-liners who regarded politicians as scoundrels ready to betray Brazil to communism or some other menace. The victory of the hard-liners dragged Brazil into what political scientist Juan J. Linz called "an authoritarian situation." However, because the hard-liners could not ignore the counterweight opinions of their colleagues or the resistance of society, they were unable to institutionalize their agenda politically. In addition, they did not attempt to eliminate the trappings of liberal constitutionalism because they feared disapproval of international opinion and damage to the alliance with the United States. As the citadel of anticommunism, the United States provided the ideology that the authoritarians used to justify their hold on power. But Washington also preached liberal democracy, which forced the authoritarians to assume the contradictory position of defending democracy by destroying it. Their concern for appearances caused them to abstain from personalist dictatorship by requiring each successive general-president to pass power to his replacement.

The role of the United States in these events was complex and at times contradictory. An anti-Goulart press campaign was conducted throughout 1963, and in 1964 the Johnson administration gave moral support to the campaign. Ambassador Lincoln Gordon later admitted that the embassy had given money to anti-Goulart candidates in the 1962 municipal elections and had encouraged the plotters; that many extra United States military and intelligence personnel were operating in Brazil; and that four United States Navy oil tankers and the carrier *Forrestal*, in an operation code-named Brother Sam, had stood off the coast in case of need during the 1964 coup. Washington immediately recognized the new government in 1964 and joined the chorus chanting that the coup d'état of the "democratic forces" had staved off the hand of international communism. In retrospect, it appears that the only foreign hand involved was Washington's, although the United States was not the principal actor in these events. Indeed, the hard-liners in the Brazilian military pressured Costa e Silva into promulgating the Fifth Institutional Act on December 13, 1968. This act gave the president dictatorial powers, dissolved Congress and state legislatures, suspended the constitution, and imposed censorship.

In October 1969, when President Costa e Silva died unexpectedly, the democratic mask fell off as the officer corps of the three services consulted among themselves to pick General Garrastazú Médici for the presidency. Costa e Silva and Médici represented the hard-line, antipolitics segment of the military, which seemingly was content to hold authority as long as necessary to turn Brazil into a great power. The Médici government illustrated how it was possible to remain in power without popular support, without a political party, and without a well-defined program. It was the era of terrorist actions in the cities, replete with kidnappings of diplomats, including the United States ambassador, and an extensive antiguerrilla campaign in northern Goiás. The repressive apparatus expanded into various agencies, which spied on political opponents and engaged in dirty tricks, torture, and "disappearings" (see The Military Role in the Intelligence Services, ch. 5). Those operations caused an open break between the government and the hierarchy of the Roman Catholic Church for the first time in Brazilian history. They also produced a deterioration in relations with the United States, whose leaders had expected the Castelo Branco vision of the revolution to win out.

The Médici administration wrapped itself in the green and gold flag when Brazil won the World Cup in soccer in 1970, began to build the Trans-Amazonian Highway through the northern rain forests, and dammed the Rio Paraná, creating the world's largest hydroelectric dam at Itaipu. From 1968 to 1974, parallel with the darkest days of the dictatorship, the military-civil technocratic alliance took shape as the economy boomed, reaching annual GDP growth rates of 12 percent. It looked as if Brazil's dreams of full industrialization and great-power status were possible. Sadly, in those years of the supposed "economic miracles," criticism and labor unrest were suppressed with arrests, torture, and censorship. Moreover, this apparent success of mixing authoritarian rule and economic growth encouraged officers in Argentina, Chile, Bolivia, and Uruguay to seize power in their countries.

It was in this atmosphere that retired General Ernesto Geisel (1974–79) came to the presidency with Médici's approval. There had been intense behind-the-scenes maneuvering by the hard-liners against him and by the more moderate supporters of Castelo Branco for him. Fortunately for Geisel, his brother, Orlando Geisel, was the minister of army, and his close ally, General João Baptista de Oliveira Figueiredo, was chief of Médici's military staff.

Although not immediately understood by civilians, Ernesto Geisel's accession signaled a move away from repression toward democratic rule. Geisel replaced several regional commanders with trusted officers and labeled his political program *distensão,* meaning a gradual relaxation of authoritarian rule. It would be, in his words, "the maximum of development possible with the minimum of indispensable security."

President Geisel sought to maintain high economic growth rates, even while seeking to deal with the effects of the oil shocks. He kept up massive investments in infrastructure—highways, telecommunications, hydroelectric dams, mineral extraction, factories, and atomic energy. Fending off nationalist objections, he opened Brazil to oil prospecting by foreign firms for the first time since the early 1950s. His government borrowed billions of dollars to see Brazil through the oil crisis.

Brazil shifted its foreign policy to meet its economic needs. "Responsible pragmatism" replaced strict alignment with the United States and a worldview based on ideological frontiers and blocs of nations. Because Brazil was 80 percent dependent on imported oil, Geisel shifted the country from a pro-Israeli stance to closer ties with oil-rich Saudi Arabia and Iraq. His government also recognized China, Angola, and Mozambique and moved closer to Spanish America, Europe, and Japan. The 1975 agreement with the Federal Republic of Germany (West Germany) to build nuclear reactors produced confrontation with the Carter administration, which was also scolding the Geisel government for the human rights abuses that it was fighting to stop. Frustrated with what he saw as United States highhandedness and lack of understanding, Geisel renounced the military alliance with the United States in April 1977.

In 1977 and 1978, the succession issue caused further confrontations with the hard-liners. Noting that Brazil was only a "relative democracy," Geisel attempted in April 1977 to restrain the growing strength of the opposition parties by creating an electoral college that would approve his selected replacement. In October he dismissed the far-right minister of army, General Sylvio Cueto Coelho da Frota. In 1978 Geisel maneuvered through the first labor strikes since 1964 and through the repeated electoral victories of the opposition Brazilian Democratic Movement (Movimento Democrático Brasileiro—MDB). He allowed the return of exiles, restored habeas corpus, repealed the extraordinary powers decreed by the Fifth Institutional Act, and imposed General João Figueiredo (1979–85) as his successor in March 1979.

The last military president, João Figueiredo, said that he took over the presidency more out of a sense of duty than political ambition. He signed a general amnesty into law and turned Geisel's *distensão* into a gradual *abertura* (the opening of the political system), saying that his goal was "to make this country a democracy." The hard-liners reacted to the opening with a series of terrorist bombings. An April 1981 bombing incident confirmed direct military involvement in terrorism, but Figueiredo proved too weak to punish the guilty. The incident and the regime's inaction strengthened the public's resolve to end military rule. Moreover, Figueiredo faced other significant problems, such as soaring inflation, declining productivity, and a mounting foreign debt.

Political liberalization and the declining world economy contributed to Brazil's economic and social problems. In 1978 and 1980, huge strikes took place in the industrial ring around São Paulo. Protesters asserted that wage increases indexed to the inflation rate were far below a livable level. Union leaders, including the future 1990 presidential candidate Luis "Lula" Inácio da Silva, were arrested for violation of national security laws. The IMF imposed a painful austerity program on Brazil. Under that program, Brazil was required to hold down wages to fight inflation. In the North, Northeast, and even in relatively prosperous Rio Grande do Sul, rural people seized unused, private land, forcing the government to create a new land reform ministry. Tension with the Roman Catholic Church, the major voice for societal change, peaked in the early 1980s with the expulsion of foreign priests involved in political and land reform issues.

To attack the soaring debt, Figueiredo's administration stressed exports—food, natural resources, automobiles, arms, clothing, shoes, even electricity—and expanded petroleum exploration by foreign companies. In foreign relations, the objective was to establish ties with any country that would contribute to Brazilian economic development. Washington was kept at a certain distance, and the North-South dialogue was emphasized.

In 1983 the economy leaped ahead with 5.4 percent GDP growth, but it was lost in the rising inflation and the failure of political leadership. Figueiredo's heart condition led to bypass surgery in the United States, removing him from control of the situation. In an impressive display, millions of Brazilians took to the streets in all the major cities demanding a direct vote (*diretas já!*) in the choice of the next president. In April 1984, Congress failed to achieve the necessary numbers to give the people their wish, and the choice was left to an electoral college. Figueiredo did not act forcefully to back a preference, so it became a scramble as candidates pursued the collegial votes.

On January 15, 1985, the electoral college elected Tancredo Neves of Minas Gerais, Vargas's minister of justice in the 1950s, and former federal deputy, senator, and prime minister. Neves was a sensible politician with a reputation for honesty. However, he collapsed the night before his inaugural, and the presidency passed to Vice President José Sarney (president, 1985–

90), long-time supporter of the military regime. Neves died on April 21. The hopes that 1985 would be a quick transition to a new regime faded as Brazilians watched this turn of events in a state of shock. Like the regime changes of 1822, 1889, 1930, 1946, and 1964, the 1985 change also proved to be long and difficult (see Politics, 1985–96, ch. 4).

* * *

Charles Wagley's *An Introduction to Brazil*, although dated, is still valuable for an understanding of Brazilian history. Darcy Ribeiro provides a stimulating overview in *O povo brasileiro*. For an examination of how race influenced thought and nationalism, see Thomas E. Skidmore's *Black into White*. E. Bradford Burns's *Nationalism in Brazil: Historical Survey* focuses on the creation of Brazilian nationalism. There are several general histories, such as Burns's *A History of Brazil*, Ronald M. Schneider's *Order and Progress: A Political History of Brazil*, and Leslie Bethell's two edited volumes for *The Cambridge History of Latin America*. *Modern Brazil: Elites and Masses in Historical Perspective*, edited by Michael L. Conniff and Frank D. McCann, sets contemporary Brazilian society into its historical context.

The starting point for the vast literature in English on the 322-year-long colonial era, is Francis A. Dutra's *A Guide to the History of Brazil, 1500–1822*. Not to be missed are books by Charles R. Boxer, Stuart B. Schwartz, Dauril Alden, and Kenneth R. Maxwell. The numerous books covering the period 1808–22, when the Portuguese crown ruled from Rio de Janeiro, into the independent Brazilian imperial era, include Roderick J. Barman's *Brazil: The Forging of a Nation, 1798–1852*; Clarence H. Haring's *Empire in Brazil*; Neill Macauley's *Dom Pedro: The Struggle for Liberty in Brazil and Portugal*; Roderick Cavaliero's *The Independence of Brazil*; and Emília Viotti da Costa's *The Brazilian Empire*. A fascinating study of Pedro II's Brazil is *O Brasil no tempo de Dom Pedro II, 1831–1889* by Frédéric Mauro. Slavery is a key topic of many studies, including Stanley J. Stein's *Vassouras*; Mary C. Karasch's *Slave Life in Rio de Janeiro, 1808–1850*; Joaquim Nabuco's *Abolitionism: The Brazilian Antislavery Struggle*; and Robert Conrad's *The Destruction of Brazilian Slavery, 1850–1888*.

An excellent overview of the 1889–64 period is in José Maria Bello's *A History of Modern Brazil, 1889–1964*. On the political economy of 1889–1930, see Steven C. Topik's *The Political Econ-*

omy of the Brazilian State, 1889–1930. For daily life, work, and the roles of women, see Ina von Binzer's *Os meus Romanos,* Maria Odila Silva Dias's *Power and Everyday Life,* and Joel Wolfe's *Working Women, Working Men.*

The military is the subject of José Augusto Drummond's fine study of *Tenentismo: O movimento tenentista;* Neill Macaulay's *The Prestes Column;* Stanley E. Hilton's *1932* and *A rebelião vermelha;* Alfred C. Stepan's *The Military in Politics, Authoritarian Brazil,* and *Rethinking Military Politics;* Frank D. McCann's "The Brazilian Army and the Problem of Mission, 1939–1964" in *Journal of Latin; American Studies;* and Amado Luiz Cervo and Clodoaldo Bueno's *História da política exterior do Brasil.* Foreign relations are the focus of E. Bradford Burns's *The Unwritten Alliance: Rio-Branco and Brazilian-American Relations;* Joseph Smith's *Unequal Giants;* McCann's *The Brazilian-American Alliance, 1937–1945;* Elizabeth A. Cobbs's *The Rich Neighbor Policy;* Ruth Leacock's *Requiem for Revolution;* Michael W. Weis's *Cold Warriors and Coups d'Étai;* and Amado Luiz Cervo (ed.), *O desafio internacional.*

The literature on politics after 1930 is extensive. Some suggestions are Thomas E. Skidmore's *Politics in Brazil, 1930–1964* and *The Politics of Military Rule in Brazil, 1964–85;* Ronald M. Schneider's *The Political System of Brazil;* Maria Helena Moreira Alves's *State and Opposition in Military Brazil;* and Stepan's *Democratizing Brazil.* For religion and the role of the Catholic Church, see Scott Mainwaring's *The Catholic Church and Politics in Brazil, 1916–1985* and Rowan Ireland's *Kingdoms Come.* (For further information and complete citations, see Bibliography.)

Chapter 2. The Society and Its Environment

A nineteenth-century wood carving made by an indigenous Brazilian tribe, from Hjalmar Stolpe, Amazon Indian Designs from Brazilian and Guianan Wood Carvings

THE FIFTH LARGEST country in the world, Brazil is the largest country in Latin America and has territory slightly larger than that of the continental United States. Its population, estimated officially at nearly 160 million in mid-1997, is the largest in Latin America and constitutes about half of the population in South America. With 80 percent of its population living in cities and towns, Brazil is one of the most urbanized and industrialized countries in Latin America. São Paulo and Rio de Janeiro are among the ten largest cities in the world. São Paulo, with its 18 million people, is the world's third largest city, after Mexico City and Tokyo. Yet, parts of Brazil's Amazon region, which has some of the world's most extensive wilderness areas, are sparsely inhabited by indigenous peoples still in the process of coming into contact with the modern world.

More than for its superlatives, however, Brazil stands out for its regional and social disparities. Brazil is noted for having one of the most unequal income distributions of any country. In the rural Northeast (Nordeste), there is poverty similar to that found in some African and Asian countries. Although increased urbanization has accompanied economic development, it also has created serious social problems in the cities. Even the wealthiest cities contain numerous shantytowns called favelas.

While in many ways this diversity or heterogeneity makes it similar to other developing countries in Latin America and elsewhere, Brazil is also unique. One of the fascinating elements of this uniqueness is that it is different things at once, presenting different faces or identities of a single coherent whole. Both local and foreign perceptions of Brazil tend to exaggerate particular features, lack a balanced view, and fail to grasp how the parts of the whole fit together. During the twentieth century, for example, Brazil came to be known to the rest of the world and to many of its own inhabitants in picturesque motifs that could best be fit together coherently in terms of a "land of contrasts." The country was considered a tropical paradise famed for its exports (coffee), music (such as Carmen Miranda, samba, and bossa nova), and soccer (thanks to Edson Arantes do Nascimento (Pelé)), as well as the nearly mythical Amazon rain forest. Rio de Janeiro was associated with Sugarloaf (Pão de Açucar), Copacabana, income tax fugitives, and even the mastermind of Britain's "Great Train Robbery" of 1963. On a more serious level, Brazil often was disparaged for its inability to solve basic political and economic problems, such as consolidating democratic institutions, controlling runaway inflation, and servicing the foreign debt. However, the nation is noted for being an emerging industrial power and for constructing giant public works, such as the new capital city of Brasília, the Trans-Amazonian Highway, and the world's largest hydroelectric dam (Itaipu). Brazil also stands out for its leadership role in Latin America and the developing world.

Most Brazilians saw the military regime (1964–85) as a repressive dictatorship, although others regarded it as having saved the country from communism. Brazilian society was viewed as conservative and male chauvinistic, yet simultaneously freewheeling or even licentious, as revealed in its Carnaval (Carnival) festivities. In the 1980s, much of the world saw the Amazon, the world's greatest store of biodiversity, and its native peoples as falling victim to unparalleled destruction. In the early 1990s, the news of massacres of Yanomami Indians, street children, and favela dwellers who inhabit Rio de Janeiro's hillsides sundered Brazil's image of cordiality. Although there were other reasons for pessimism and a continuing identity crisis (Brazil became the first democracy to impeach its president, in December 1992), there were reasons for pride as well (inflation was brought under control in 1994). Was Brazil a "serious country" destined to be a great power, or was it always to remain a land of the future?

One can find ample evidence for countervailing trends: unity and diversity, modernity and tradition, progressive government policies and deeply rooted inequality, tight control by elites and broadening popular participation, principles and pragmatism. There are no simple answers. This chapter examines Brazil's social and environmental complexity and its characteristic paradoxes and nuances of meaning, beginning with the physical setting and moving into the more mercurial social issues, with special attention to how society relates to nature.

The Physical Setting

Size and Location

With its expansive territory, Brazil occupies most of the eastern part of the South American continent and its geographic heartland, as well as various islands in the Atlantic Ocean. The only countries in the world that are larger are Russia, Canada, China, and the United States (including Alaska). The national territory extends 4,395 kilometers from north to south (5°16'20" N to 33°44'32" S latitude) and 4,319 kilometers from east to west (34°47'30" E to 73°59'32" W longitude). It spans four time zones, the westernmost of which, in Acre State, is the same as Eastern Standard Time in the United States. The time zone of the capital (Brasília) and of the most populated part of Brazil along the east coast is two hours ahead of Eastern Standard Time, except when it is on its own daylight savings time, from October to February. The Atlantic islands are in the easternmost time zone.

Brazil possesses the archipelago of Fernando de Noronha, located 350 kilometers northeast of its "horn," and several small islands and atolls in the Atlantic—Abrolhos, Atol das Rocas, Penedos de São Pedro e São Paulo, Trindade, and Martim Vaz. In the early 1970s, Brazil claimed a territorial sea extending 362 kilometers from the country's shores, including those of the islands.

On Brazil's east coast, the Atlantic coastline extends 7,367 kilometers. In the west, in clockwise order from the south, Brazil has 15,719 kilometers of borders with Uruguay, Argentina, Paraguay, Bolivia, Peru, Colombia, Venezuela, Guyana, Suriname, and French Guiana (see table 2, Appendix). The only South American countries with which Brazil does not share borders are Chile and Ecuador. A few short sections are in question, but there are no major boundary controversies with any of the neighboring countries.

Geology, Geomorphology, and Drainage

In contrast to the Andes, which rose to elevations of nearly 7,000 meters in a relatively recent epoch and inverted the Amazon's direction of flow from westward to eastward, Brazil's geological formation is very old. Precambrian crystalline shields cover 36 percent of the territory, especially its central area. The principal mountain ranges average elevations just under 2,000 meters. The Serra do Mar Range hugs the Atlantic coast, and the Serra do Espinhaço Range, the largest in area, extends through the south-central part of the country (see fig. 3). The highest mountains are in the Tumucumaque, Pacaraima, and Imeri ranges, among others, which traverse the northern border with the Guianas and Venezuela.

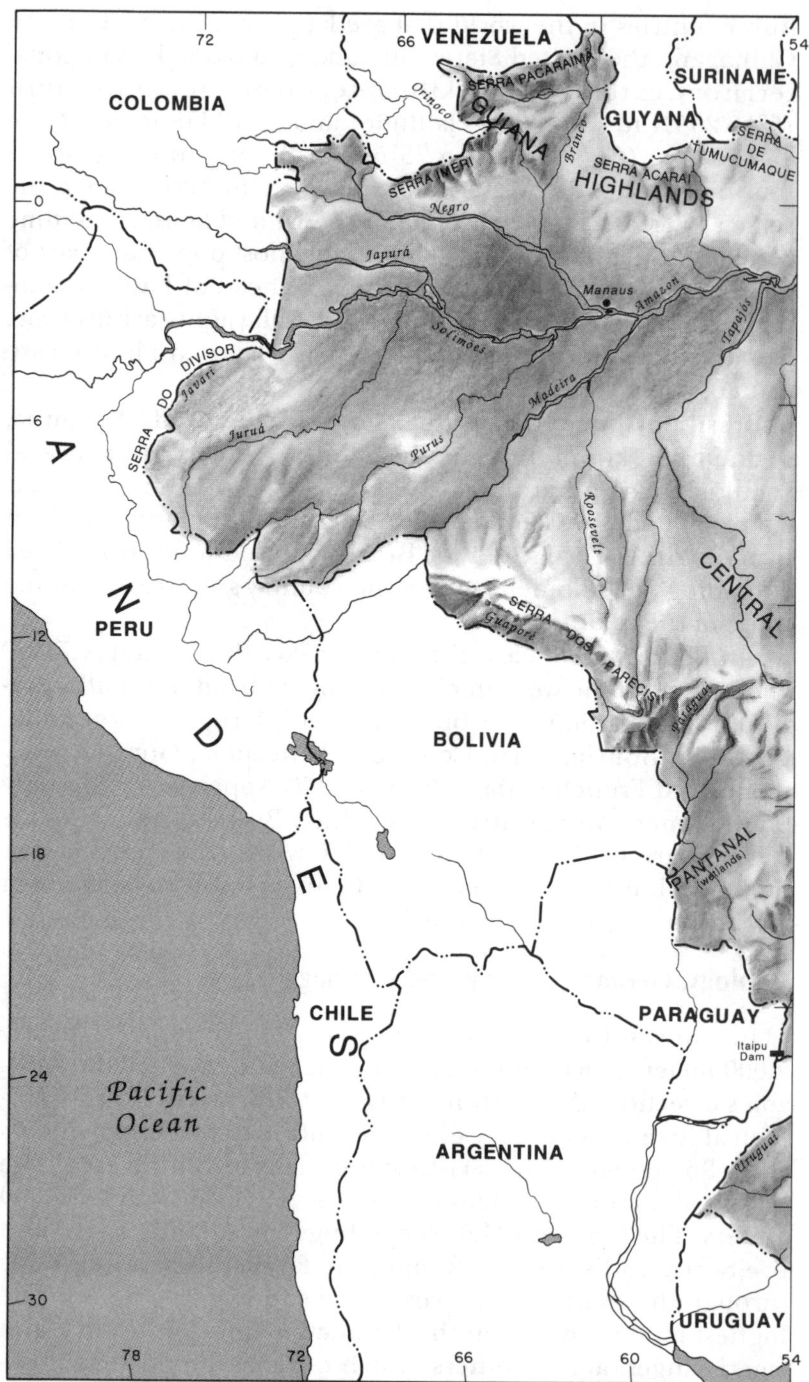

Figure 3. Topography and Drainage

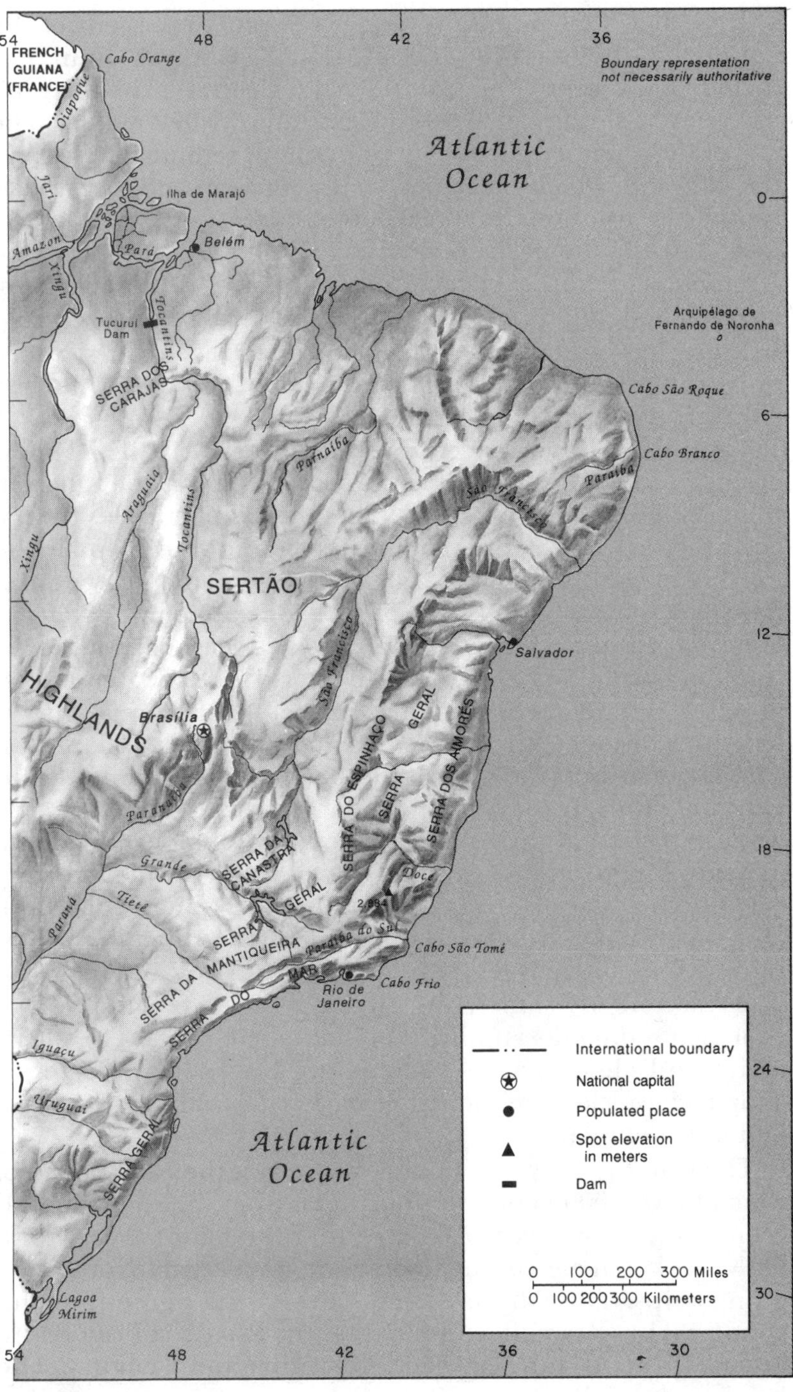
FRENCH GUIANA (FRANCE)
Cabo Orange
Boundary representation not necessarily authoritative
Atlantic Ocean
Oiapoque
Jari
Ilha de Marajó
Amazon
Pará
Belém
Xingu
Tucuruí Dam
Tocantins
Arquipélago de Fernando de Noronha
SERRA DOS CARAJÁS
Cabo São Roque
Parnaíba
Cabo Branco
Paraíba
São Francisco
Araguaia
Tocantins
Xingu
SERTÃO
Salvador
São Francisco
HIGHLANDS
Brasília
SERRA GERAL
SERRA DOS AIMORÉS
SERRA DO ESPINHAÇO
SERRA
Paranaíba
Grande
SERRA DA CANASTRA
Doce
Tietê
GERAL
2,884
Paraná
SERRA
SERRA DA MANTIQUEIRA
Paraíba do Sul
Cabo São Tomé
SERRA DO MAR
Rio de Janeiro
Cabo Frio
Iguaçu
Uruguai
SERRA GERAL
Atlantic Ocean
International boundary
National capital
Populated place
Spot elevation in meters
Dam
0 100 200 300 Miles
0 100 200 300 Kilometers
Lagoa Mirim
54
48
42
36
30
0
6
12
18
24
30

In addition to mountain ranges (about 0.5 percent of the country is above 1,200 meters), Brazil's Central Highlands include a vast central plateau (Planalto Central). The plateau's uneven terrain has an average elevation of 1,000 meters. The rest of the territory is made up primarily of sedimentary basins, the largest of which is drained by the Amazon and its tributaries. Of the total territory, 41 percent averages less than 200 meters in elevation. The coastal zone is noted for thousands of kilometers of tropical beaches interspersed with mangroves, lagoons, and dunes, as well as numerous coral reefs.

Brazil has one of the world's most extensive river systems, with eight major drainage basins, all of which drain into the Atlantic Ocean. Two of these basins—the Amazon and Tocantins-Araguaia—account for more than half the total drainage area. The largest river system in Brazil is the Amazon, which originates in the Andes and receives tributaries from a basin that covers 45.7 percent of the country, principally the north and west. The main Amazon river system is the Amazonas-Solimões-Ucayali axis (the 6,762 kilometer-long Ucayali is a Peruvian tributary), flowing from west to east. Through the Amazon Basin flows one-fifth of the world's fresh water. A total of 3,615 kilometers of the Amazon are in Brazilian territory. Over this distance, the waters decline only about 100 meters. The major tributaries on the southern side are, from west to east, the Javari, Juruá, Purus (all three of which flow into the western section of the Amazon called the Solimões), Madeira, Tapajós, Xingu, and Tocantins. On the northern side, the largest tributaries are the Branco, Japurá, Jari, and Negro. The above-mentioned tributaries carry more water than the Mississippi (its discharge is less than one-tenth that of the Amazon). The Amazon and some of its tributaries, called "white" rivers, bear rich sediments and hydrobiological elements. The black-white and clear rivers—such as the Negro, Tapajós, and Xingu—have clear (greenish) or dark water with few nutrients and little sediment.

The major river system in the Northeast is the São Francisco, which flows 1,609 kilometers northeast from the south-central region. Its basin covers 7.6 percent of the national territory. Only 277 kilometers of the lower river are navigable for ocean-going ships. The Paraná system covers 14.5 percent of the country. The Paraná flows south into the Río de la Plata Basin, reaching the Atlantic between Argentina and Uruguay. The headwaters of the Paraguai, the Paraná's major eastern tributary, constitute the Pantanal, the largest contiguous wetlands in the world, covering as much as 230,000 square kilometers.

Below their descent from the highlands, many of the tributaries of the Amazon are navigable. Upstream, they generally have rapids or waterfalls, and boats and barges also must face sandbars, trees, and other obstacles. Nevertheless, the Amazon is navigable by oceangoing vessels as far as 3,885 kilometers upstream, reaching Iquitos in Peru. The Amazon river system was the principal means of access until new roads became more important in the 1970s. The São Francisco was also used for transportation in the past. Dams and locks in the Paraná system have made it an important artery for interstate and international trade in the 1990s.

The various river systems descending from the shields have endowed Brazil with vast hydroelectric potential, estimated at 129,046 megawatts (MW), of which 30,065 MW were in operation or under construction in 1991. The largest hydroelectric projects are Itaipu, in Paraná, with 12,600 MW; Tucuruí, in Pará, with 7,746 MW; and Paulo Afonso, in Bahia, with 3,986 MW.

Soils and Vegetation

Brazil's tropical soils produce 70 million tons of grain crops per year, but this output is attributed more to their extension than their fertility. Despite the earliest Portuguese explorers' reports that the land was exceptionally fertile and that anything planted grew well, the record in terms of sustained agricultural productivity has been generally disappointing. High initial fertility after clearing and burning usually is depleted rapidly, and acidity and aluminum content are often high. Together with the rapid growth of weeds and pests in cultivated areas, as a result of high temperatures and humidity, this loss of fertility explains the westward movement of the agricultural frontier and slash-and-burn agriculture (see Glossary); it takes less investment in work or money to clear new land than to continue cultivating the same land. Burning also is used traditionally to remove tall, dry, and nutrient-poor grass from pasture at the end of the dry season. Until mechanization and the use of chemical and genetic inputs increased during the agricultural intensification period of the 1970s and 1980s, coffee planting and farming in general moved constantly onward to new lands in the west and north. This pattern of horizontal or extensive expansion maintained low levels of technology and productivity and placed emphasis on quantity rather than quality of agricultural production.

The largest areas of fertile soils, called *terra roxa* (red earth), are found in the states of Paraná and São Paulo. The least fertile areas are in the Amazon, where the dense rain forest is. Soils in the Northeast are often fertile, but they lack water, unless they are irrigated artificially.

In the 1980s, investments made possible the use of irrigation, especially in the Northeast Region and in Rio Grande do Sul State, which had shifted from grazing to soy and rice production in the 1970s. Savanna soils also were made usable for soybean farming through acidity correction, fertilization, plant breeding, and in some cases spray irrigation. As agriculture underwent modernization in the 1970s and 1980s, soil fertility became less important for agricultural production than factors related to capital investment, such as infrastructure, mechanization, use of chemical inputs, breeding, and proximity to markets. Consequently, the vigor of frontier expansion weakened.

The variety of climates, soils, and drainage conditions in Brazil is reflected in the range of its vegetation types. The Amazon Basin and the areas of heavy rainfall along the Atlantic coast have tropical rain forest composed of broadleaf evergreen trees. The rain forest may contain as many as 3,000 species of flora and fauna within a 2.6-square-kilometer area. The Atlantic Forest is reputed to have even greater biological diversity than the Amazon rain forest, which, despite apparent homogeneity, contains many types of vegetation, from high canopy forest to bamboo groves.

In the semiarid Northeast, *caatinga*, a dry, thick, thorny vegetation, predominates. Most of central Brazil is covered with a woodland savanna, known as the *cerrado* (sparse scrub trees and drought-resistant grasses), which became an area of agricultural development after the mid-1970s. In the South (Sul), needle-leaved pinewoods (Paraná pine or araucaria) cover the highlands; grassland similar to the Argentine pampa covers the sea-level plains. The Mato Grosso swamplands (Pantanal Matogrossense) is a Florida-sized plain in the western portion of the Center-West (Centro-Oeste). It is covered with tall grasses, bushes, and widely dispersed trees similar to those of the *cerrado* and is partly submerged during the rainy season.

Brazil, which is named after reddish dyewood (*pau brasil*), has long been famous for the wealth of its tropical forests. These are not, however, as important to world markets as those of Asia and Africa, which started to reach depletion only in the 1980s. By 1996 more than 90 percent of the original Atlantic forest had been cleared, primarily for agriculture, with little use made of the wood, except for araucaria pine in Paraná.

The inverse situation existed with regard to clearing for wood in the Amazon rain forest, of which about 15 percent had been cleared by 1994, and part of the remainder had been disturbed by selective logging. Because the Amazon forest is highly heterogeneous, with hundreds of woody species per hectare, there is considerable distance between individual trees of economic value, such as mahogany and *cerejeira*. Therefore, this type of forest is not normally cleared for timber extraction but logged through high-grading, or selection of the most valuable trees. Because of vines, felling, and transportation, their removal causes destruction of many other trees, and the litter and new growth create a risk of forest fires, which are otherwise rare in rain forests. In favorable locations, such as Paragominas, in the northeastern part of Pará State, a new pattern of timber extraction has emerged: diversification and the production of plywood have led to the economic use of more than 100 tree species.

Starting in the late 1980s, rapid deforestation and extensive burning in Brazil received considerable international and national attention. Satellite images have helped document and quantify deforestation as well as fires, but their use also has generated considerable controversy because of problems of defining original vegetation, cloud cover, and dealing with secondary growth and because fires, as mentioned above, may occur in old pasture rather than signifying new clearing. Public policies intended to promote sustainable management of timber extraction, as well as sustainable use of nontimber forest products (such as rubber, Brazil nuts, fruits, seeds, oils, and vines), were being discussed intensely in the mid-1990s. However, implementing the principles of sustainable development (see Glossary), without irreversible damage to the environment, proved to be more challenging than establishing international agreements about them.

Climate

Although 90 percent of the country is within the tropical zone, the climate of Brazil varies considerably from the mostly tropical North (the equator traverses the mouth of the Amazon) to temperate zones below the Tropic of Capricorn (23°27'

S latitude), which crosses the country at the latitude of the city of São Paulo. Brazil has five climatic regions—equatorial, tropical, semiarid, highland tropical, and subtropical.

Temperatures along the equator are high, averaging above 25°C, but not reaching the summer extremes of up to 40°C in the temperate zones. There is little seasonal variation near the equator, although at times it can get cool enough for wearing a jacket, especially in the rain. At the country's other extreme, there are frosts south of the Tropic of Capricorn during the winter (June–August), and in some years there is snow in the mountainous areas, such as Rio Grande do Sul and Santa Catarina. Temperatures in the cities of São Paulo, Belo Horizonte, and Brasília are moderate (usually between 15°C and 30°C), despite their relatively low latitude, because of their elevation of approximately 1,000 meters. Rio de Janeiro, Recife, and Salvador on the coast have warm climates, with average temperatures ranging from 23°C to 27°C, but enjoy constant trade winds. The southern cities of Porto Alegre and Curitiba have a subtropical climate similar to that in parts of the United States and Europe, and temperatures can fall below freezing in winter.

Precipitation levels vary widely. Most of Brazil has moderate rainfall of between 1,000 and 1,500 millimeters a year, with most of the rain falling in the summer (between December and April) south of the Equator. The Amazon region is notoriously humid, with rainfall generally more than 2,000 millimeters per year and reaching as high as 3,000 millimeters in parts of the western Amazon and near Belém. It is less widely known that, despite high annual precipitation, the Amazon rain forest has a three- to five-month dry season, the timing of which varies according to location north or south of the equator.

High and relatively regular levels of precipitation in the Amazon contrast sharply with the dryness of the semiarid Northeast, where rainfall is scarce and there are severe droughts in cycles averaging seven years. The Northeast is the driest part of the country. The region also constitutes the hottest part of Brazil, where during the dry season between May and November, temperatures of more than 38°C have been recorded. However, the *sertão*, a region of semidesert vegetation used primarily for low-density ranching, turns green when there is rain. Most of the Center-West has 1,500 to 2,000 millimeters of rain per year, with a pronounced dry season in the middle of the year, while the South and most of the Atlantic coast as far north as Salvador, Bahia, in the Northeast, have similar amounts of rainfall without a distinct dry season.

Geographic Regions

Brazil's twenty-six states and the Federal District (Distrito Federal) are divided conventionally into five regions—North (Norte), Northeast, Southeast (Sudeste), South, and Center-West (see fig. 4). In 1996 there were 5,581 municipalities (*municípios*), which have municipal governments. Many municipalities, which are comparable to United States counties, are in turn divided into districts (*distritos*), which do not have political or administrative autonomy. In 1995 there were 9,274 districts. All municipal and district seats, regardless of size, are considered officially to be urban. For purely statistical purposes, the municipalities were grouped in 1990 into 559 micro-regions, which in turn constituted 136 meso-regions. This grouping modified the previous micro-regional division established in 1968, a division that was used to present census data for 1970, 1975, 1980, and 1985.

Each of the five major regions has a distinct ecosystem. Administrative boundaries do not necessarily coincide with ecological boundaries, however. In addition to differences in physical environment, patterns of economic activity and population settlement vary widely among the regions. The principal ecological characteristics of each of the five major regions, as well as their principal socioeconomic and demographic features, are summarized below.

North

The equatorial North, also known as the Amazon or Amazônia, includes, from west to east, the states of Rondônia, Acre, Amazonas, Roraima, Pará, Amapá, and, as of 1988, Tocantins (created from the northern part of Goiás State, which is situated in the Center-West). Rondônia, previously a federal territory, became a state in 1986. The former federal territories of Roraima and Amapá were raised to statehood in 1988.

With 3,869,638 square kilometers, the North is the country's largest region, covering 45.3 percent of the national territory (see table 3, Appendix). The region's principal biome is the humid tropical forest, also known as the rain forest, home to some of the planet's richest biological diversity. The North has served as a source of forest products ranging from "backlands

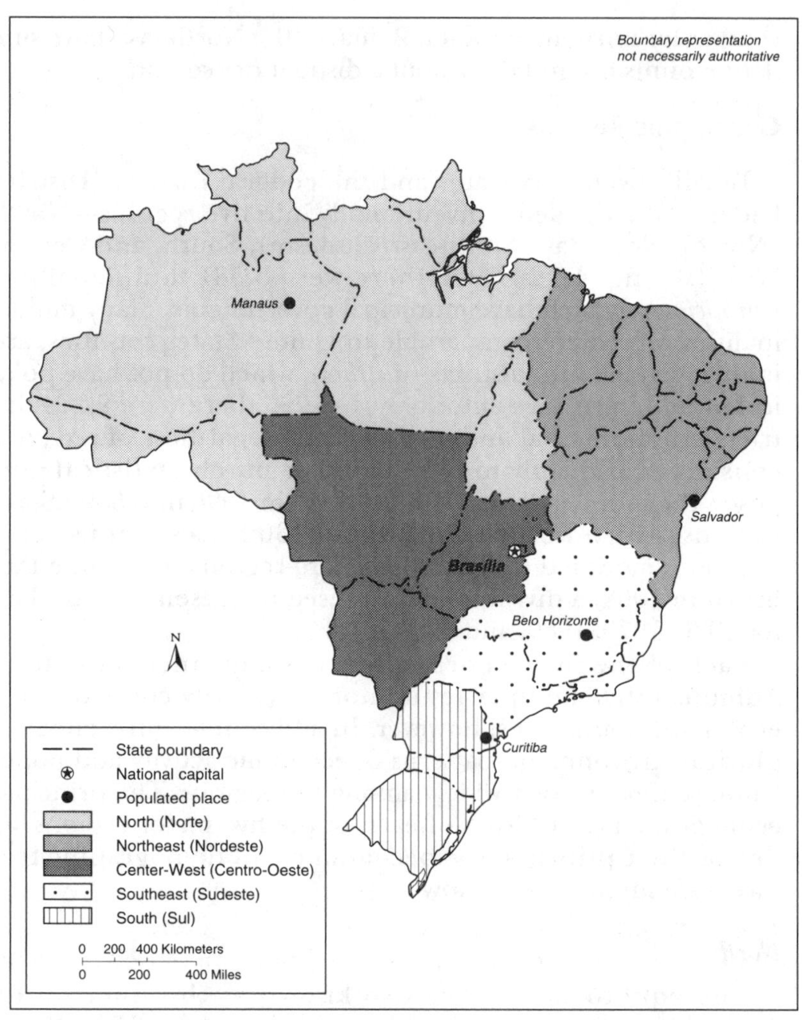

Figure 4. Geographic Regions, 1997

drugs" (such as sarsaparilla, cocoa, cinnamon, and turtle butter) in the colonial period to rubber and Brazil nuts in more recent times. In the mid-twentieth century, nonforest products from mining, farming, and livestock-raising became more important, and in the 1980s the lumber industry boomed. In 1990, 6.6 percent of the region's territory was considered altered by anthropic (man-made) action, with state levels varying from 0.9 percent in Amapá to 14.0 percent in Rondônia.

In 1996 the North had 11.1 million inhabitants, only 7 percent of the national total. However, its share of Brazil's total had grown rapidly in the 1970s and early 1980s as a result of interregional migration, as well as high rates of natural increase. The largest population concentrations are in eastern Pará State and in Rondônia. The major cities are Belém and Santarém in Pará, and Manaus in Amazonas. Living standards are below the national average. The highest per capita income, US$2,888, in the region in 1994, was in Amazonas, while the lowest, US$901, was in Tocantins.

Northeast

The nine states that make up the Northeast are Alagoas, Bahia, Ceará, Maranhão, Paraíba, Pernambuco, Piauí, Rio Grande do Norte, and Sergipe. The former federal territory of Fernando de Noronha was incorporated into Pernambuco State in 1988. For planning or ecological purposes, Maranhão west of 44° W longitude, most of which until recently was covered with "pre-Amazon" forest (that is, transition from the *cerrado* or *caatinga* to tropical forest), is often included in the Amazon region.

The Northeast, with 1,561,178 square kilometers, covers 18.3 percent of the national territory. Its principal biome is the semiarid *caatinga* region, which is subject to prolonged periodic droughts. By the 1990s, this region utilized extensive irrigation. In an area known as the forest zone (*zona da mata*), the Atlantic Forest, now almost entirely gone, once stretched along the coastline as far north as Rio Grande do Norte. Sugar plantations established there in colonial times persisted for centuries. Between the *mata* and the *sertão* lies a transition zone called the *agreste*, an area of mixed farming. In 1988–89, 46.3 percent of the region had been subjected to anthropic activity, ranging from a low of 10.8 percent in Maranhão to a high of 77.2 percent in Alagoas.

Because its high rates of natural increase offset heavy outmigration, the Northeast's large share of the country's total population declined only slightly during the twentieth century. In 1996 the region had 45 million inhabitants, 28 percent of Brazil's total population. The population is densest along the coast, where eight of the nine state capitals are located, but is also spread throughout the interior. The major cities are Salvador, in Bahia; Recife, in Pernambuco; and Fortaleza, in Ceará. The region has the country's largest concentration of rural population, and its living standards are the lowest in Brazil. In 1994 Piauí had the lowest per capita income in the region and the country, only US$835, while Sergipe had the highest average income in the region, with US$1,958.

Southeast

The Southeast consists of the four states of Espírito Santo, Minas Gerais, Rio de Janeiro, and São Paulo. Its total area of 927,286 square kilometers corresponds to 10.9 percent of the national territory. The region has the largest share of the country's population, 63 million in 1991, or 39 percent of the national total, primarily as a result of internal migration since the mid-nineteenth century until the 1980s. In addition to a dense urban network, it contains the megacities of São Paulo and Rio de Janeiro, which in 1991 had 18.7 million and 11.7 million inhabitants in their metropolitan areas, respectively. The region combines the highest living standards in Brazil with pockets of urban poverty. In 1994 São Paulo boasted an average income of US$4,666, while Minas Gerais reported only US$2,833.

Originally, the principal biome in the Southeast was the Atlantic Forest, but by 1990 less than 10 percent of the original forest cover remained as a result of clearing for farming, ranching, and charcoal making. Anthropic activity had altered 79.5 percent of the region, ranging from 75 percent in Minas Gerais to 91.1 percent in Espírito Santo. The region has most of Brazil's industrial production. The state of São Paulo alone accounts for half of the country's industries. Agriculture, also very strong, has diversified and now uses modern technology.

South

The three states in the temperate South—Paraná, Rio Grande do Sul, and Santa Catarina—cover 577,214 square kilometers, or 6.8 percent of the national territory. The population of the South in 1991 was 23.1 million, or 14 percent of the country's total. The region is almost as densely settled as the Southeast, but the population is more concentrated along the coast. The major cities are Curitiba and Porto Alegre. The inhabitants of the South enjoy relatively high living standards. Because of its industry and agriculture, Paraná had the highest average income in 1994, US$3,674, while Santa Catarina, a land of small farmers and small industries, had slightly less, US$3,405.

In addition to the Atlantic Forest and pine woods, much of which were cleared in the post-World War II period, the South contains pampa grasslands, similar to those of Argentina and Uruguay, in the extreme south. In 1982, 83.5 percent of the region had been altered by anthropic activity, with the highest level (89.7 percent) in Rio Grande do Sul, and the lowest (66.7 percent) in Santa Catarina. Agriculture—much of which, such as rice production, is carried out by small farmers—has high levels of productivity. There are also some important industries.

Center-West

The Center-West consists of the states of Goiás, Mato Grosso, and Mato Grosso do Sul (separated from Mato Grosso in 1979), as well as the Federal District, site of Brasília, the national capital. Until 1988 Goiás State included the area that then became the state of Tocantins in the North.

The Center-West has 1,612,077 square kilometers and covers 18.9 percent of the national territory. Its main biome is the *cerrado*, the tropical savanna in which natural grassland is partly covered with twisted shrubs and small trees. The *cerrado* was used for low-density cattle-raising in the past but is now also used for soybean production. There are gallery forests along the rivers and streams and some larger areas of forest, most of which have been cleared for farming and livestock. In the north, the *cerrado* blends into tropical forest. It also includes the Pantanal wetlands in the west, known for their wildlife, especially aquatic birds and caymans. In the early 1980s, 33.6 percent of the region had been altered by anthropic activities, with a low of 9.3 percent in Mato Grosso and a high of 72.9 percent in Goiás (not including Tocantins). In 1996 the Center-West region had 10.2 million inhabitants, or 6 percent of Brazil's total population. The average density is low, with concentrations in and around the cities of Brasília, Goiânia, Campo Grande, and Cuiabá. Living standards are below the national average. In 1994 they were highest in the Federal District, with per capita income of US$7,089 (the highest in the nation), and lowest in Mato Grosso, with US$2,268.

The Environment

The environmental problem that attracted most international attention in Brazil in the 1980s was undoubtedly deforestation in the Amazon. Of all Latin American countries, Brazil still has the largest portion (66 percent) of its territory covered by forests, but clearing and burning in the Amazon proceeded at alarming rates in the 1970s and 1980s. Most of the clearing resulted from the activities of ranchers, including large corporate operations, and a smaller portion resulted from slash-and-burn techniques used by small farmers.

Deforestation in the Amazon declined from levels averaging 22,000 square kilometers per year during the 1970–88 period to about 11,000 square kilometers per year between 1988 and 1991. There was controversy about the levels in the mid-1990s. Knowledgeable experts placed the level of accumulated deforestation at about 15 percent in 1996, as opposed to 12 percent in 1991. Although unseasonal rainfall patterns may explain some year-to-year variation, the basic cause for the decline in deforestation after 1987 was economic crisis. There was insufficient capital, credit, or incentive for large-scale clearing, as well as insufficient public investment to stimulate new migration. Migration to the Amazon also fell quickly in the late 1980s. More effective enforcement of government regulations and bad publicity for large offenders, both of which were associated with changes in public opinion about the environment, also played a part. Technical changes involved in the transition from horizontal expansion of agriculture to increasing productivity also accounted for decreasing rates of deforestation.

Desertification, another important environmental problem in Brazil, only received international attention following the United Nations Conference on the Environment and Development, also known as the Earth Summit, held in Rio de Janeiro in June 1992. Desertification means that the soils and vegetation of drylands are severely degraded, not necessarily that land turns into desert. In the early 1990s, it became evident that the semiarid *caatinga* ecosystem of the Northeast was losing its natural vegetation through clearing and that the zone was therefore running the risk of becoming even more arid, as was occurring also in some other regions.

In areas where agriculture is more intense and developed, there are serious problems of soil erosion, siltation and sedimentation of streams and rivers, and pollution with pesticides. In parts of the savannas, where irrigated soybean production expanded in the 1980s, the water table has been affected. Expansion of pastures for cattle-raising has reduced natural biodiversity in the savannas. Swine effluents constitute a serious environmental problem in Santa Catarina in the South.

In urban areas, at least in the largest cities, levels of air pollution and congestion are typical of, or worse than, those found in cities in developed countries. At the same time, however, basic environmental problems related to the lack of sanitation, which developed countries solved long ago, persist in Brazil. These problems are sometimes worse in middle-sized and small cities than in large cities, which have more resources to deal with them. Environmental problems of cities and towns finally began to receive greater attention by society and the government in the 1990s.

According to many critics, the economic crisis in the 1980s worsened environmental degradation in Brazil because it led to overexploitation of natural resources, stimulated settlement in fragile lands in both rural and urban areas, and weakened environmental protection. At the same time, however, the lower level of economic activity may have reduced pressure on the environment, such as the aforementioned decreased level of investment in large-scale clearing in the Amazon. That pressure could increase if economic growth accelerates, especially if consumption patterns remain unchanged and more sustainable forms of production are not found.

In Brazil public policies regarding the environment are generally advanced, although their implementation and the enforcement of environmental laws have been far from ideal. Laws regarding forests, water, and wildlife have been in effect since the 1930s. Brazil achieved significant institutional advances in environmental policy design and implementation after the Stockholm Conference on the Environment in 1972. Specialized environmental agencies were organized at the federal level and in some states, and many national parks and reserves were established. By 1992 Brazil had established thirty-four national parks and fifty-six biological reserves (see fig. 5). In 1981 the National Environment Policy was defined, and the National System for the Environment (Sistema Nacional do Meio Ambiente—Sisnama) was created, with the National Environmental Council (Conselho Nacional do Meio Ambiente—Conama) at its apex, municipal councils at its base, and state-level councils in between. In addition to government authorities, all of these councils include representatives of civil society.

The 1988 constitution incorporates environmental precepts that are advanced compared with those of most other countries. At that time, the Chamber of Deputies (Câmara dos Deputados) established its permanent Commission for Defense of

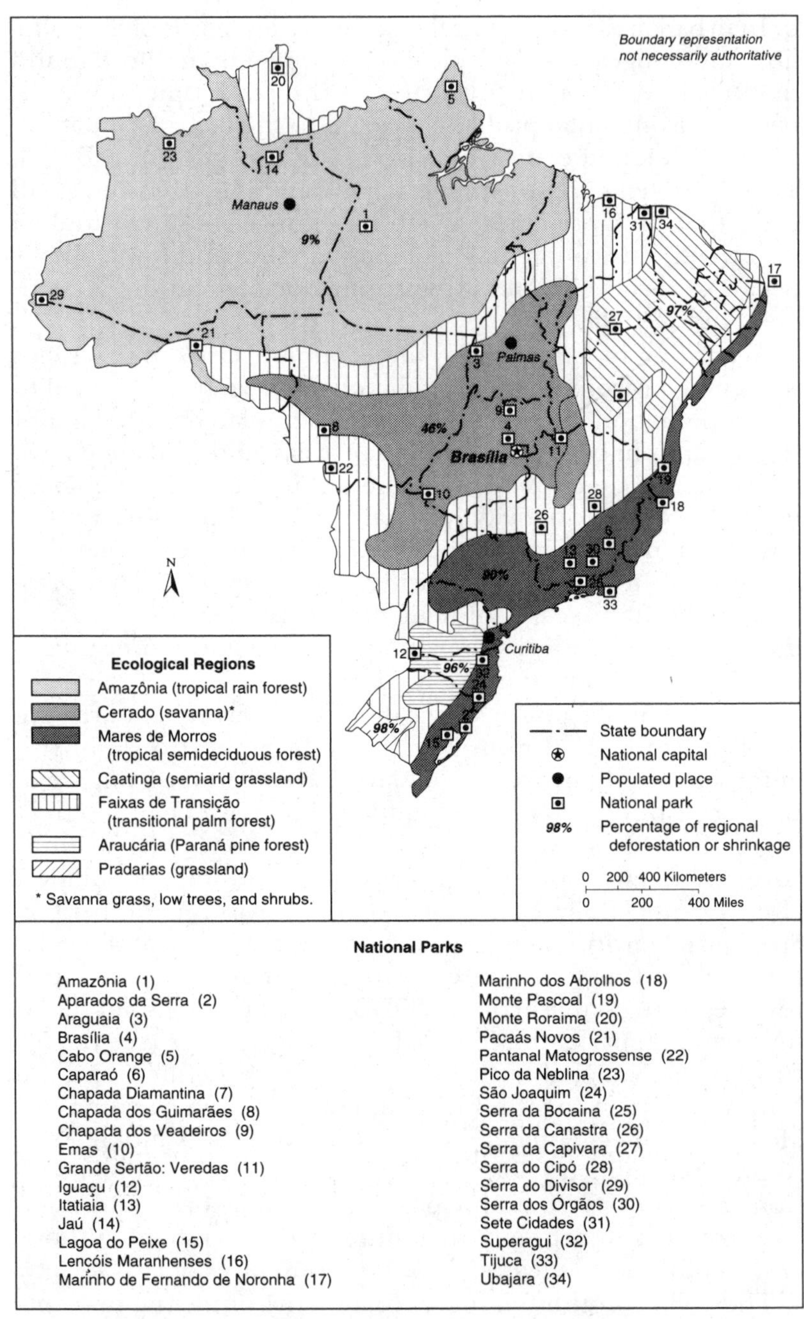

Source: Based on information from *Almanaque Abril 92,* São Paulo, 1992, 337.

Figure 5. Ecological Regions and National Parks, 1992

the Consumer, the Environment, and Minorities. In 1989 the creation of the Brazilian Institute for the Environment and Renewable Natural Resources (Instituto Brasileiro do Meio Ambiente e dos Recursos Naturais Renováveis—Ibama) joined together the federal environment secretariat and the federal agencies specializing in forestry, rubber, and fisheries. In 1990 the administration of Fernando Collor de Mello (president, 1990–92) appointed the well-known environmentalist José Lutzemberger as secretary of the environment and took firm positions on the environment and on Indian lands. In 1992 Brazil played a key role at the Earth Summit, not only as its host but also as negotiator on sustainable development agreements, including the conventions on climate and biodiversity. The Ministry of Environment was created in late 1992, after President Collor had left office. In August 1993, it became the Ministry of Environment and the Legal Amazon and took a more pragmatic approach than had the combative Lutzemberger. However, because of turnover in its leadership, a poorly defined mandate, and lack of funds, its role and impact were limited. In 1995 its mandate and name were expanded to include water resources—the Ministry of Environment, Hydraulic Resources, and the Legal Amazon—it began a process of restructuring to meet its mandate of "shared management of the sustainable use of natural resources." In 1997 the Commission on Policies for Sustainable Development and Agenda 21 began to function under the aegis of the Civil Household. One of its main tasks was to prepare Agenda 21 (a plan for the twenty-first century) for Brazil and to stimulate preparation of state and local agendas.

Institutional development at the official level was accompanied and in part stimulated by the growth, wide diffusion, and growing professional development of nongovernmental organizations (NGOs) dedicated to environmental and socio-environmental causes. The hundreds of NGOs throughout Brazil produce documents containing both useful information and passionate criticisms. Among the Brazilian environmental NGOs, the most visible are SOS Atlantic Forest (SOS Mata Atlântica), the Social-Environmental Institute (Instituto Sócio-Ambiental—ISA), the Pro-Nature Foundation (Fundação Pró-Natureza—Funatura), and the Amazon Working Group (Grupo de Trabalho Amazônico—GTA). The Brazilian Forum of NGOs and Social Movements for the Environment and Development and the Brazilian Association of Nongovernmental Organizations (Associacão Brasileira de Organizações Não-Governamentais—ABONG) are national networks, and there are various regional and thematic networks as well. The main international environmental NGOs that have offices or affiliates in Brazil are the World Wildlife Fund (WWF), Conservation International (CI), and Nature Conservancy.

Especially after the events of the late 1980s, international organizations and developed countries have allocated significant resources for the environmental sector in Brazil. In 1992 environmental projects worth about US$6.8 million were identified, with US$2.6 in counterpart funds (funds provided by the Brazilian government). More than 70 percent of the total value was for sanitation, urban pollution control, and other urban environmental projects. Thus, the allocation of resources did not accord with the common belief that funding was influenced unduly by alarmist views on deforestation in the Amazon.

Among the specific environmental projects with international support, the most important was the National Environmental Plan (Plano Nacional do Meio Ambiente—PNMA), which received a US$117 million loan from the World Bank (see Glossary). The National Environmental Fund (Fundo Nacional do Meio Ambiente—FNMA), in addition to budgetary funds, received US$20 million from the Inter-American Development Bank (see Glossary) to finance the environmental activities of NGOs and small municipal governments. The Pilot Program for the Conservation of the Brazilian Rain Forests (Programa Piloto para a Proteção das Florestas Tropicais do Brasil—PPG–7) was supported by the world's seven richest countries (the so-called G–7) and the European Community (see Glossary), which allocated US$258 million for projects in the Amazon and Atlantic Forest regions. The Global Environment Facility (GEF), created in 1990, set aside US$30 million for Brazil, part of which is managed by a national fund called Funbio. GEF also established a small grants program for NGOs, which focused on the *cerrado* during its pilot phase. The World Bank also made loans for environmental and natural resource management in Rondônia and Mato Grosso, in part to correct environmental and social problems that had been created by the World Bank-funded development of the northwest corridor in the 1980s.

Despite favorable laws, promising institutional arrangements, and external funding, the government has not, on the whole, been effective in controlling damage to the environment. This failure is only in small measure because of the opposition of anti-environmental groups. In greater part, it can be attributed to the traditional separation between official rhetoric and actual practice in Brazil. It is also related to general problems of governance, fiscal crisis, and lingering doubts about appropriate tradeoffs between the environment and development. Some of the most effective governmental action in the environmental area has occurred at the state and local levels in the most developed states and has involved NGOs. In 1994 the PNMA began to stress decentralization and strengthening of state environmental agencies, a tendency that subsequently gained momentum.

Population

Population Size and Distribution

At the turn of the century, Brazil's population was 17,438,434. By 1950 it had grown to 51,944,397, and in 1970 it reached 93,139,037. By 1991 Brazil was the world's sixth most populous country, with about 2.7 percent of the world's 5.3 billion people or 147,053,940 inhabitants. In July 1996, the population was counted as being 157,079,573, but estimated in 1997 to be nearly 160 million. Projections indicate a total population of 169 million in 2000 and 211 million in 2020, and population stability at about 250 million in 2050. The population growth rate for the 1992 to 2000 period is estimated at 1.5 percent per year. As a result of the decline in mortality and continued high fertility during the 1950s and 1960s, the average growth rate was nearly 3 percent per year. Subsequent to a decrease in total fertility, the growth rate dropped to 2.5 percent in the 1970s and 1.9 percent in the 1980s.

Average population density in Brazil in 1994 was 18.5 inhabitants per square kilometer. There was a wide variation between the densely populated Southeast and South, on the one hand, and the sparse North and Center-West, on the other, with the Northeast at intermediate levels. In comparison, in 1991 the United States (including Alaska) had an average of twenty-five inhabitants per square kilometer; France, 100; the United Kingdom, 100; China, 110; and Canada, three.

According to the 1996 count, the most populous region in the country is still the Southeast (63 million inhabitants), followed by the Northeast (45 million), the South (23.1 million), the North (11.1 million), and the Center-West (10.2 million). The most inhabited states are São Paulo, Minas Gerais, Rio de Janeiro, Bahia, Rio Grande do Sul, and Paraná. These states all lie along the Atlantic coast.

In some rural areas and many cities, particularly in major metropolitan areas, females outnumber males. The historical predominance of women over men in the Brazilian population has persisted. The 1996 count showed that there were ninety-seven men for every 100 women and that the total number of women exceeded the number of men by 5 million.

The average age of the Brazilian population has increased as a result of a continued decrease in mortality and fertility. Between 1980 and 1990, the proportional share of children from birth to age fourteen decreased from 38.2 to 34.7 percent, while the share for those of age fifteen to sixty-four increased from 57.8 to 61.1 percent. The proportion of elderly (age sixty-five or greater) increased from 4.0 to 4.2 percent and is projected to reach 9.0 percent by the year 2020. In all regions of the country, the count registered an increased number of people of ages fifteen to sixty-four and of older people over sixty-four years old. In the Southeast, for example, the proportion of people in the former age bracket increased from the 61.7 percent registered in 1980 to 63.6 percent in 1991, while the number of older people increased from 4.2 percent to 5.1 percent.

The demographic transition in Brazil becomes apparent as the bottom of the very wide-based pyramid, typical of developing countries with high birthrates, begins to narrow (see fig. 6). Further declines in the fertility rate, estimated at 2.44 children born per woman in 1994, eventually will lead to a pyramid that is shaped more like a bullet, with cohorts under age sixty of roughly equal size. Senior citizens will live longer, and the proportion of young people will decline. In the year 2000, young people will account for 28.3 percent of the population and senior citizens, 8 percent. Couples will have fewer children, and the fertility rate may be less than 2.2 children per woman, the replacement level.

Mortality

As is typical in demographic transitions, declines in mortality preceded declines in fertility in Brazil, but the process took only a few decades rather than centuries, as it did in developed countries. The death rate started to fall in the 1940s because of the expanding public health system, urbanization, and sanitation. The crude death rate in 1995 was eight per 1,000 population, a notable decrease from the 1960–65 rate of 12.3. The 1995 level, which is similar to that of developed countries, resulted from the age structure being still relatively younger.

Life expectancy at birth, which is a measure of mortality that is not affected by different age structures, began to rise in Brazil in the 1940s. It increased from 42.7 years in 1940 to 52.7 years in 1970 and 67.1 years in 1995. It is projected to reach 68.5 years in 2000 and 75.5 years in 2020. Life expectancy for women is about seven years greater than that for men, but the differential is decreasing.

A decline in mortality has occurred in all regions, but strong regional variations in life expectancy persist. The lowest levels are found in the Northeast (65.4 years in 1995) and the highest in the South (69.4 years in 1995), slightly higher than the Southeast. The North and Center-West regions have levels of life expectancy close to the national average. Within the socioeconomic strata, higher life expectancy is strongly associated with higher family income. Mortality is generally higher in rural than in urban areas, except for the lowest income groups.

In the past, the principal causes of death in Brazil were infectious and contagious diseases, especially diarrhea and intestinal parasites among infants, as well as tuberculosis, measles, and respiratory diseases (for a discussion of infant mortality, see Indicators of Health, this ch.). As these were brought under control in the postwar period, primarily in the more developed regions, degenerative diseases such as cardiovascular disorders and cancer became proportionately more prevalent. Deaths from external causes, including violence and traffic accidents, also gained importance.

Fertility

In 1996 the crude birthrate was estimated at 21.16 births per 1,000 population, a significant reduction from 42.1 for the 1960–65 period. As in the case of mortality, crude birthrates are affected by the age structure and, therefore, difficult to compare among countries and regions or over time. It is preferable to use the total fertility rate, a standardized measure that corresponds to the average number of children per woman at age forty-nine, the end of her reproductive life, assuming that she has survived and followed the fertility patterns characteristic of each age category.

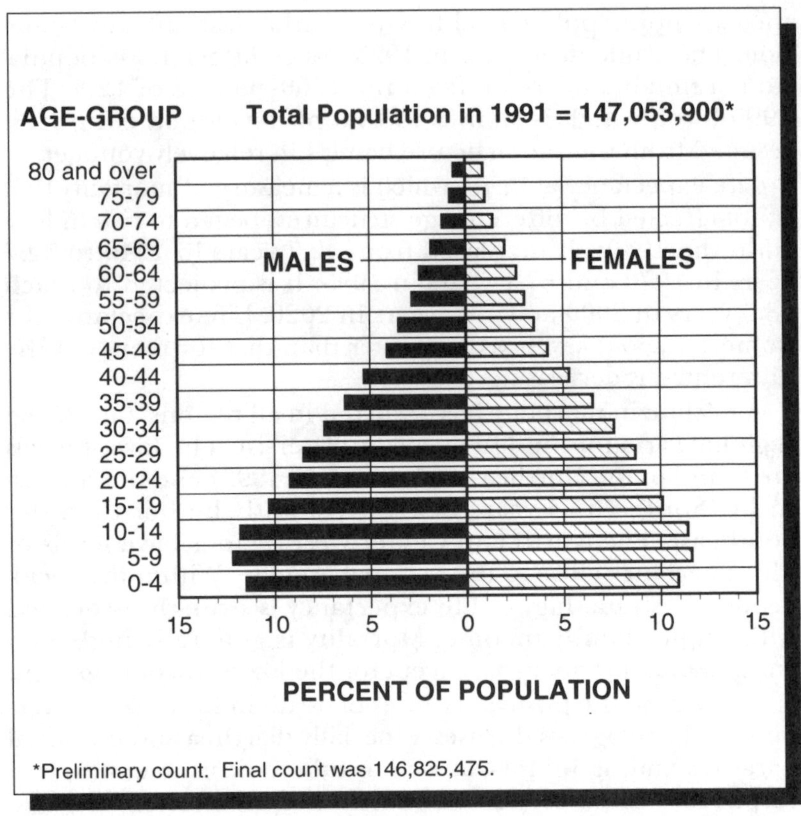

Source: Based on information from Fundação Instituto Brasileiro de Geografia e Estatística, *Anuário estatístico do Brasil 1993,* Rio de Janeiro, 1993, 2–25.

Figure 6. Population Distribution by Age-Group and Sex, 1991

Brazil's total fertility rate dropped from close to six in the 1940s and 1950s to 3.3 in 1986 to 2.44 in 1994, not much higher than the replacement level of 2.2. Fertility declined in urban and rural areas, in all regions, and among all socioeconomic strata, although the rates continued to vary. In large countries, such a rapid and generalized fertility decline had been observed previously only in China, where official policy placed intense pressure on couples to have only one child. Projections indicate a total fertility rate of 2.0 in the year 2000 and 1.8 in 2020, lower than replacement.

The Brazilian birthrate began to decline noticeably in the 1970s, by which time socioeconomic changes had made large families less affordable than in the traditional social and economic structure in rural areas. In the past, especially in rural areas, children started work early and supported their parents in old age, and the children did not cost much to raise. In the 1990s, they attend school for longer periods and cost more to support.

Meanwhile, new methods of birth control, primarily pills and female sterilization, became widely available in the 1970s. Oral contraceptives are sold over the counter without prescription. Surgical sterilization, which is practiced in Brazil more than any other country, is typically performed during cesarean deliveries. Such deliveries comprised nearly a third of all deliveries in the 1980s. Surgical sterilization is of questionable legality, but is often carried out by doctors who are paid for the cesarean section by the public health system and receive private payment for extra services on the side.

The number of Brazilian couples opting for sterilization as a means of contraception increased by more than 40 percent during the 1986–96 period, based on the Demographic and Health Survey carried out by Bemfam, an NGO. The survey, conducted between March and July 1996, interviewed 12,612 women between fifteen and forty-nine years of age as well as 2,949 men between fifteen and fifty-nine years. The survey found that 40.1 percent of married women or women living with partners had been sterilized, as compared with 26.9 percent in 1986. In 1986 only 0.8 percent of males had had a vasectomy, as compared with 2.6 percent in 1996. The Bemfam survey showed that the average age at which women are sterilized was 28.9 years in 1996, as compared with 31.4 years in 1986.

In the early 1990s, the use of birth-control pills and female sterilization (tubal ligation) continued to contribute to the fertility decline in Brazil. About 65 percent of Brazilian women used contraceptives, which is comparable with levels in developed countries. Of the women who used some method and were in union, 44 percent were sterilized. About 7 percent used rhythm, while other contraceptives or methods were rarer.

Abortion in Brazil is significant. In the early 1990s, some 1.4 million abortions were performed each year, almost all of which were technically illegal. This corresponds to approximately one abortion for every two live births. The only cases in which abortion is not subject to legal sanctions in Brazil are rape and danger to the mother's life, but the law is not enforced effectively. The practice of unsafe, clandestine abortions helps to explain why Brazil has the fifth highest maternal mortality rate in Latin America, estimated at 141 deaths per 1,000 births, in contrast to eight in the United States.

A fertility decline in Brazil occurred in the absence of any official policy in favor of controlling birthrates. The government's stance was one of laissez-faire. Although it did not promote family planning, largely because of the influence of the Roman Catholic Church, the government did little to interfere with the widespread practice of contraception among the population at large. Nor did the population pay much heed to religious dogma. In the case of fertility regulation, social change in Brazil occurred from the bottom up. Women took much of the initiative.

In the 1980s, the Ministry of Health included family planning services as part of an integrated women's health program. However, because of a severe lack of funds, the direct effects of the program were limited. Changing public opinion and the women's movement in Brazil favored changes in official policy, which were slow to come about. The 1988 constitution included the right to plan freely the number of children. A Family Planning Law took effect in 1997 in order to regulate sterilization, making it available in the public health network but forbidding it during deliveries, as well as provide birth-control alternatives through the same network.

Migration and Urbanization

Immigration from Europe and the African slave trade, which were the prime sources of population growth during much of Brazil's history, became demographically insignificant by the 1930s. Subsequently, there were massive transfers of internal migrants from the Northeast and Minas Gerais to the growing urban centers of São Paulo and Rio de Janeiro. Over time, there were successive waves of significant but less voluminous counterflows to frontier areas in Paraná, the Center-West, and finally the Amazon. The government's colonization plans, which included settlement along the Trans-Amazonian Highway, stimulated internal migration. However, the last cycle of frontier expansion came to a close, at least temporarily, in the late 1980s.

During the 1950s, 1960s, and 1970s, some 20 million people moved from rural to urban areas in Brazil. This population movement constitutes one of the largest of its kind in history. Brazil's urban population (by the official definition) grew at rates of about 5 percent per year and accounted for 56 percent of the total population in 1970, 68 percent in 1980, and 75 percent in 1991. During most of the post-World War II period, the largest cities grew fastest as a result of gradual migration to progressively larger cities. In the 1980s, however, the proportion of Brazil's population living in metropolitan areas dropped from 29 percent to 28 percent. The new pattern of population redistribution revealed by the 1991 census involved less interregional migration, with more people staying in their regions of origin or moving to large cities nearby rather than to megacities.

Numerous efforts have been made at the policy level to stimulate settlement in the interior, including colonization in the Amazon, and to limit the growth of the largest cities while strengthening middle-sized cities. Despite these efforts, however, most public policies have continued to favor population concentration in the Southeast and in large cities by promoting industry at the cost of agriculture and by providing services and benefits primarily to urban residents.

During the 1980s, as a result of economic crisis and improved transportation services, emigration from Brazil increased to other countries, including the United States, Canada, Portugal, and Japan. For the first time ever, Brazil became a net exporter of population and thus entered a new stage in its demographic history. Some of the emigrants sought employment in menial jobs in developed countries; others were skilled personnel, including scientists and engineers. However, a noteworthy reverse brain drain also took place, with skilled workers from other Latin American countries and Europe constituting a significant proportion of new immigrants. Immigration increased from neighboring countries, especially members of the Common Market of the South (Mercado Comum do Sul—Mercosul; see Glossary), including Argentina, Uruguay, and Paraguay, as well as from some countries in Africa and Asia.

Social Structure

Social Classes

Brazil inherited a highly stratified society from the colonial system and from slavery, which persisted for nearly three generations after independence in 1822. The legacy of sharp socioeconomic stratification is reflected in Brazil's highly skewed income distribution, among the world's worst (see Inequality and Poverty, ch. 3). The relatively high average per capita income (US$4,086 in 1995) masks deep inequality. During the postwar period, income concentration and regional disequilibrium did not change significantly despite numerous government policies aimed at greater equity. Poverty was widespread, reaching the lowest levels in the rural parts of the Northeast, but also including pockets of urban poverty in the largest cities in the developed regions. In 1990 the number of indigents suffering from extreme poverty (see Glossary) was estimated to be at least 32 million, about one-fifth of the country's total population. This included an estimated 9.6 percent of the residents of metropolitan areas, 18.4 percent of the population of other urban areas, and 42.8 percent of the rural population.

Socioeconomic inequality involves subtle forms of residential, educational, and workplace discrimination, in such ways that members of distinct socioeconomic strata tend to live, work, and circulate in different settings. The well-to-do live in chic neighborhoods, usually centrally located, go to private schools, drive or ride in cars, and shop at malls. The urban poor live in favelas or distant housing projects, take long bus trips to work, go to public schools or drop out, and shop at smaller supermarkets or local shops. The rural poor in the country's interior are practically invisible to the urban upper and middle classes.

Despite such social segregation, class solidarity is not strong. Instead of horizontal class ties, numerous cross-cutting vertical relationships involve personal dependence on individuals who have more property and prestige. Given the circumstances, these relationships of clientelism and paternalism are advantageous for both patrons and clients. Because of the lack of effective government services and real possibilities for class action, the poor have few alternatives but to seek the protection of patrons. The traditional rural forms of patronage have been described as colonelism (*coronelismo*—see Glossary), referring to the fact that rural bosses often had military titles (see The Old or First Republic, 1889–1930, ch. 1). Among other things, colonels (*coronéis*) used their influence over their clientele for electoral purposes. Such vertical interpersonal ties continue to be stronger in rural areas, especially in the Northeast, but they also persist in other forms in urban settings and at various levels of the socioeconomic scale. Even members of the modern middle class tend to have lower-income persons or families dependent on them for such things as domestic employment and economic or health emergencies. They, in turn, seek help from powerful friends and relatives.

Contrary to dualistic stereotypes of Latin American societies, Brazilian class structure cannot be reduced to a wealthy landed elite versus masses of poor peasants and workers. The middle sectors or classes have been significant at least since the nineteenth century. Sectors of Brazil's population that were neither slave owners nor slaves began to grow in the colonial period, when craftsmen, shopkeepers, small farmers, freed slaves, and persons of mixed racial origin began to outnumber slave owners and eventually slaves. During the twentieth century, the middle sectors continued to grow. The present middle class does not own large properties, industries, or firms but also is not destitute. It consists largely of a technical work force—clerks, professionals, teachers, salespersons, public servants, and highly skilled workers. Its position is based more on knowledge and skills than on property. A surge of upward mobility strengthened the middle class during the "economic miracle" in the late 1960s and early 1970s. At the same time, blue-collar workers with middle to low levels of skills constitute a lower middle class that is numerically very significant.

In addition to those formally employed, many workers are in the so-called informal economy (see Glossary), which includes self-employed businessmen and workers who do not have the legal protection of labor legislation. In 1990 the informal sector accounted for nearly half of the economically active population. The informal sector grows in times of recession because of unemployment and during times of prosperity, when opportunities for making money are more readily available. A survey released in 1996 by the Brazilian Institute of Geography and Statistics (Fundação Instituto Brasileiro de Geografia e Estatística—IBGE) showed that only 85 percent of those questioned wanted to seek formal employment.

Increasingly, the system of social stratification that was originally based on property (land or industry) has evolved in such a way that individuals who acquire special technical skills or know-how are able to earn reasonable incomes. Outside these two groups of propertied or skilled individuals lies a significant mass, perhaps a majority, that is excluded in the sense of limited participation in markets and poor access to government services, such as health, education, and sanitation.

Gender

For reasons of property transmission and religion, Brazilian society was originally strongly patriarchal, but there was also strong tension between rigid norms of Iberian origin and the extenuating circumstances of frontier life, where conditions were not favorable for compliance with the norms. The difficulty of putting Roman Catholic values into effective practice in the context of poverty, isolation, and unbalanced male/female sex ratios (number of men per 100 women) reinforced the Mediterranean double moral standard for men and women. Men were expected to demonstrate their masculinity, while proper women were supposed to remain virgins until marriage and to be faithful to their husbands. This double standard also favored frequent consensual unions, illegitimacy, and prostitution. Such behavior was not entirely acceptable but was tolerated more readily in Brazil, generally speaking, than in North America and the rest of Latin America.

Although women were allowed open access to schools and employment around the turn of the century and suffrage on a national level in 1933, they were not on an equal footing with men in family affairs. Men were automatically heads of households, and married women were legally subordinate to their husbands. Because of the inconvenience caused by informal remarriage, divorce was made legal in 1977. Under the constitution of 1988, women became entirely equal to men for all legal purposes.

Female participation in the labor force grew dramatically in the 1970s and 1980s, as a result of new employment patterns, especially the expansion of the services sector, and economic pressures on family income. Women are most commonly employed as domestic servants. The economic participation of women in Brazil rose from 18 percent in 1970 to 27 percent by 1980 and 30 percent by 1990 (although such figures might underestimate actual rates of participation by failing to include the informal activities that characterize small and/or household enterprises). More than 70 percent of women in the labor force are employed by the services sector (as compared with 42 percent of men), and women tend to be underrepresented among the formal labor force in agricultural and industrial activities. Patterns of labor force participation vary considerably by region. In the early 1990s, rates of female labor force participation ranged from 36.8 percent in Rio de Janeiro to 33.1 percent in the Northeast. In Brazil, as in most other coun-

A family on a nine-hectare farm at Hervalzinho near Almirante Tamandaré, Paraná State
Courtesy Inter-American Development Bank, Washington

tries in Latin America, rates of females participating in the job market appear to increase with education, especially the proportion of single educated women entering the formal sector rather than the informal and self-employed sectors.

There is a considerable wage gap between men and women. According to one recent estimate, the differential between women and men is less pronounced in urban areas (for example, women earn on average 77.8 percent of men's wages in Rio de Janeiro and 73.6 percent in São Paulo), and most pronounced in the Northeast (where, on average, women earn 63.5 percent of the wages of men). Average wages are also considerably lower in the Northeast, where women's average hourly wages are 42 percent of the prevailing average in Rio de Janeiro. According to recent economic studies, only a small portion (between 11 percent and 19 percent of wage differentials in the formal labor force) can be attributed to differences between men and women in their endowments (such as education or experience). For the most part, the wage gap probably reflects discriminatory practices.

Recent decades have also been characterized by significant changes in family structures. For example, the available data suggest a considerable increase over the past decades in female-headed households, which include the poorest of the poor, from 13 percent in 1970 to 16 percent in 1980 and 20 percent by the late 1980s. This process has been termed the "feminization of poverty." Once again, there are considerable differences among regions; in the urban North Region, for example, over 24 percent of households were headed by women in the late 1980s, while their relative share in the South was closer to 16 percent.

Despite persistent gender inequality, the status of women in Brazil is improving on various fronts. As a rule, there are as many females as males in schools, even at the highest levels, and professions that traditionally were dominated by males, such as law, medicine, dentistry, and engineering, are becoming more balanced in terms of gender, if there are not already more women students than men. More women than men are in the National Lawyers' Association (Associação Nacional dos Advogados). The attitudes and practices of young people are generally not as sexist as those of their parents, at least among youth of families with higher income and education.

Nevertheless, there are still relatively few women in positions of power. They have a significant, albeit limited, presence in high levels of federal government, although they have better representation at the state and municipal levels. Since the government of João Baptista do Oliveira Figueiredo (president, 1979–85), several female ministers have been in the cabinet, and in 1994 two women were candidates for vice president. By 1994 women made up only 7 percent of the Congress (see Women in Politics, ch. 4).

Women's movements grew in the 1980s, when a National Council on Women's Rights (Conselho Nacional de Direitos da Mulher—CNDM) was created. Originally, the feminist movement was closely connected to human rights movements and resistance to the military regime. In the 1980s and 1990s, attention shifted to violence against women, especially domestic violence and sexual abuse and harassment. One original response to this kind of problem was the creation of special police stations for women. Women's movements also mobilized support for reproductive health and rights, as defined in the 1994 International Conference on Population and Development, held in Cairo.

Youth

The population under age eighteen was only 30.7 percent of the total population in 1991. This significant decrease relative to previous decades—it was over 42.6 percent in 1960—was almost entirely the result of rapid fertility decline. Compared with developed countries, as mentioned above, Brazil still has a relatively young population.

Overall, school enrollment in the early 1990s reached about 90 percent of school-age children (seven to fourteen), although there was wide variation, with lower coverage among rural and low-income populations. There were also high levels of repetition, and only a minority of those who entered first grade completed the eight grades of fundamental schooling. One reason for the high dropout rate was child labor. In 1990, 18 percent of the children between the ages of ten and fourteen participated in economic activity.

Because of marital instability, unwanted pregnancies, and above all poverty, there are thousands of apparently homeless "street children" (*meninos de rua*) in Brazil. The numbers require cautious use because, in addition to about 10,000 children who actually live in the streets, this category also includes many children who work or otherwise generate income to help their families. Truly homeless street children constitute a small minority. They attracted considerable public and media attention nationally and internationally in the early 1990s because of their high visibility and frequent petty thievery, as well as cases of violent retaliation, including murder, by the police and local businesspeople.

At least officially, minors have long been protected by the Brazilian legal system. Judges in juvenile cases (*juizes de menores*) protect their interests, and a network of institutions, in theory, cares for their welfare. In 1990, in response to the problems of youth, the Collor government passed special legislation to establish children's rights, known as the Children's Statute, and created the Brazilian Center of Infancy and Adolescence (Centro Brasileiro de Infância e Adolescência—CBIA) to carry out special programs for children in these age-groups. The government also promoted the establishment of federal, state, and municipal councils of childhood and adolescence, which included participants from government agencies and civil society. The National Street Children's Movement is an NGO. The United Nations Children's Fund (UNICEF) developed the Pact for Childhood, and the National Conference of Brazilian Bishops (Conferência Nacional dos Bispos do Brasil—CNBB) supported the Children's Pastoral Service.

The Elderly

The proportion of elderly in the population increases as fertility declines and longevity increases. The absolute numbers grow faster than the total population. The proportion of the Brazilian population age sixty-five and older grew from 6.4 percent in 1960 to 7.6 percent in 1980 and 8 percent in 1991, or about 11.7 million. By 2020 the number is expected to increase to 15 percent of the population, or about 33 million. Brazil faces particular problems with the aged because of difficulties in employing them (younger and better trained workers are preferred over middle-aged workers) and a lack of appropriate means to care for them. As people live longer, the number of siblings and children drops, and population mobility increases. Consequently, older people are less likely to have children or other relatives living nearby who are willing and able to care for them. In 1996 the country was shocked by the number of deaths of elderly living in very poor conditions in publicly supported homes for senior citizens, especially the case of the Santa Genoveva Clinic in Rio de Janeiro.

The government-run social security system provides minimal pensions for retired people, including those in rural areas who did not contribute to the system as employees. However, health care becomes expensive in old age, especially for the so-called degenerative diseases, and the cost of private health insurance becomes prohibitive. Retired persons were successful in organizing pressure groups to protect the real value, after inflation, of their pensions in the early 1990s by keeping them pegged to the minimum wage. Nonetheless, these pensions were still far from being sufficient to care for the needs of most elderly persons.

Race and Ethnicity

The first European immigrants to Brazil were of Iberian origin, primarily Portuguese. Some Portuguese settlers were of

Two women using a public telephone in Salvador, Bahia State
Courtesy Inter-American Development Bank, Washington

Jewish or Moorish origin but most of them had converted to Christianity. There were also some Dutch immigrants to the Northeast in the sixteenth and seventeenth centuries. The Portuguese intermarried with the Amerindian population, which was decimated by conflict and disease.

During the colonial period, after Indian slavery proved difficult to enforce, the colonists imported hundreds of thousands of slaves from Africa for labor on the sugar plantations, in the mines, and later on coffee plantations. At first, slaves outnumbered the white settlers in many areas, but the balance eventually changed because of their high mortality and low fertility. However, as slavery became economically and politically less feasible after 1850 and the British blocked the slave trade, Italian immigrants began replacing the slaves on coffee plantations in São Paulo. During the same period, settlers from Europe, primarily Germany, Italy, and Poland, established farming colonies in parts of the South.

Brazil's racial mix was made more diverse with the arrival of Japanese and Middle Eastern immigrants in the early twentieth century. At first, the Japanese worked in agriculture in São Paulo and the Amazon, while the Lebanese, Turks, and Syrians became involved in commerce in many parts of the country. During the 1900s, the Japanese descendants, who constitute the largest community of Japanese outside of Japan, except for Hawaii, became primarily urban residents, especially in São Paulo. In the 1970s, intermarriage with non-Japanese became common.

As emphasized by anthropologists such as Gilberto Freyre and Darcy Ribeiro, all the racial and ethnic groups that arrived in Brazil intermingled and intermarried, with few exceptions. This led to increasing mixtures of all possible combinations and degrees. Many individuals are, therefore, difficult to classify in racial terms. Questions on color were included in the demographic censuses of 1940, 1950, 1980, and 1991. Although the answers involved self-classification and may not have been objective, it was clear that the proportion of blacks decreased while that of mulattoes increased. There was a simultaneous process of "whitening." The self-declared proportions in 1991 were 55.3 percent white, 39.3 percent mulatto, 4.9 percent black, and 0.6 percent Asian.

Because of the lack of a clear color distinction and a strong cultural tradition of tolerance and cordiality, as well as longstanding explicit laws against racial discrimination, Brazil has been touted as a "racial democracy." However, "racial democracy" is a myth. There is a very strong correlation between light color and higher income, education, and social status. Few blacks reach positions of wealth, prestige, and power, except in the arts and sports. Although discrimination is usually not explicit, it appears in subtle forms: unwritten rules, unspoken attitudes, references to "good appearance" rather than color, or simply placing higher value on individuals who are white or nearly white.

In the 1960s, black consciousness began to grow, although the very lack of a clear color line in biological or social terms weakened racial solidarity of the nonwhite population. The prevailing notion that Brazil was a "racial democracy" also made it easy to dismiss black movements as un-Brazilian. For the most part, the movements did not press for changes in government policy, which was already officially against racial discrimination. Instead, they emphasized racial pride and the struggle against subtle forms of discrimination and the often covert violence to which blacks were subject.

Amerindians

Estimates of the original Amerindian population of Brazil range from 2 to 5 million at the time of first contact with Europeans in the early sixteenth century. There were hundreds of tribes and languages. Now there are 230 tribes that speak more than ninety languages and 300 dialects.

Because of violence and disease, the original Amerindian population was reduced to about 150,000 by the early twentieth century. In 1910 the Indian Protection Service (Serviço de Proteção aos Indios—SPI) was established. Its leader, Marechal Cândido Rondon, was famous for stating that "one should die, if necessary, but never kill an Indian." In 1968 the National Indian Foundation (Fundação Nacional do Índio—Funai) replaced SPI, which was charged with corruption. The Indian Statute went into effect in 1973. The 1988 constitution provides that Indians are entitled to the lands that they traditionally occupy.

Despite the difficulties it faced, the Amerindian population began to recover its numbers and increased to 330,000 by the mid-1990s. In genetic terms, millions of Brazilians have some Amerindian ancestry, usually on the side of their grandmothers or great-grandmothers. The ancestry is especially strong in the Amazon region, where the inhabitants of mixed Indian and white descent are called *caboclos*. Because of such widespread miscegenation and acculturation, objective definitions of "Indian" are practically impossible in Brazil. The most useful definition, also used for official purposes, is subjective but pragmatic: Indians are those who consider themselves Indians and are considered by others as such. They include groups that are officially classified as isolated, in the process of integration, or integrated (although "integration" involves entry into the lowest ranks of Brazilian society).

Most of the Amerindian population is in the Amazon region, where Amerindian lands account for about 15 percent of the territory. Some of the largest areas were set aside during the Collor administration in 1992. The best known and largest of these is the 9.6-million-hectare Yanomami Indigenous Park, located in the northern states of Amazonas and Roraima, along Brazil's border with Venezuela. Gold miners and their diseases have had an adverse impact on the Yanomami. The Caiapó in southeastern Pará became widely known both for their traditional environmental management and their controversial concessions to gold miners and lumber companies. Other indigenous areas include the Xingu Indigenous Park and other parts of Amazônia, including the western section of the Amazon along the Rio Solimões, Roraima, northern Amazonas,

Rondônia, Acre, Amapá, and northern and southeastern Pará. The Northeast (Maranhão) and Center-West (western Mato Grosso, Mato Grosso do Sul, and Goiás) regions also have large indigenous areas.

Rural Groups

Some groups in rural Brazil merit special attention. Although there has been massive rural to urban migration in Brazil, nearly 40 million people still live in the countryside, and another 10 million live in towns with a population under 20,000. There are also signs of urban to rural migration as a result of exhaustion of employment and income opportunities in large cities.

Many of the inhabitants of the countryside are rural workers in agriculture, with permanent or, more typically, seasonal employment, particularly in harvesting, an activity in which women and children are also involved. Although a large number of small family farmers have land of their own, millions of rural workers are landless because land tenure is extremely concentrated in Brazil. In the face of slowness of official land reform, they began to invade unproductive properties in the 1990s. As a result of their organization and massacres of their activists in Rondônia and Pará, they entered the political limelight, and land reform was placed high on the political agenda.

In addition to farmers, Brazil has various kinds of traditional populations—including rubber tappers, Brazil nut collectors, *caboclos* and other traditional riverine dwellers, small fishermen, and others—who became a new social category in the late 1980s. Some of them received land from the government in the form of extractive reserves, meaning land containing valuable natural resources such as rubber-yielding trees, hardwoods, and so forth, ceded to their associations on the condition that they use their natural resources in a sustainable way. For some rural Brazilians, sustainable extraction presents an alternative to rural exodus and structural unemployment.

Cultural Unity and Diversity

Brazilian culture was never monolithic. Since the sixteenth century, it has been an amalgamation of traditional Iberian, indigenous, and African values, as well as more recent Western values, developed in northern Europe and the United States, such as equality, democracy, efficiency, and individual rights. At

A farmer buys food and supplies at a farm supply and food store, Agudos do Sul, Paraná State.
Courtesy Inter-American Development Bank, Washington

times there are subtle or open conflicts, especially between norms of Mediterranean and Anglo-Saxon origin, or between practices of European versus Amerindian or African origin. However, Brazil is remarkable for the way in which there is unity in cultural diversity. Sometimes the values and practices of different origins have blended with each other, as in the case of Afro-Brazilian religious syncretism or liberation theology (see Glossary).

Another way of reconciling diversity has been the often considerable distance between actual practices, which conform with tradition, and official norms, which generally follow the positivist (positivism—see Glossary) logic of "order and progress" that underlay the establishment of the republic in 1889. The difference between norms and behavior, or between theory and practice, is a constant throughout Brazilian history. In colonial times and during the empire, imported cultural values and social norms had to be reconciled with the extenuating circumstances and realities of a frontier situation. Getting married officially, for example, was difficult in the absence of priests or because of the high cost of service by the justices of the peace.

In the 1990s, many people ignore laws that are not enforced, or allege that doing the right thing would be fine but that they lack the *condições* (conditions). The aphorism that sums up a common attitude about doing one's duty is, "*Ninguém é de ferro*" (No one is made of iron). The relaxed attitude is reinforced by the fact that laws or norms are often seen as having been imposed from the outside, rather than being the result of a social contract established for the common good. Thus, Brazilians, who are known for pragmatism, have become adept at living with idealistic rules, on the one hand, and actual practices that are often quite divergent, on the other. They switch easily between different cultural codes ranging from "traditional" values, such as machismo and paternalism, to "modern" values and social norms that favor women and equality.

The Brazilian Way

Despite regional and social class variations, the Brazilian way of life has common traits that distinguish it from the customary ways of dealing with people and situations in North America and Europe and even in other Latin American countries. Its uniqueness seems to result from the peculiar blend of Portuguese, African, and Amerindian cultural influences in a setting in which central authority attempted, without great success, to exploit the people and resources and to enforce religious norms. Under these circumstances, it was preferable to appear to obey than actually to obey.

Many attempts have been made to explain what makes Brazilians different from their neighbors in the Americas, both North and South. In the late nineteenth century, Joaquim Maria Machado de Assis, one of Brazil's greatest writers, explored the subtleties of the Brazilian character, focusing on the attempts of the urban middle class to emulate European lifestyles and aspirations. In the 1920s, the writer Mário de Andrade, a leader of the modernist movement that broke with tradition and attempted to find an authentic Brazilian identity, created the archetypal Brazilian character, Macunaíma, a lazy but ingenious black-turned-white Amazonian who migrated to São Paulo and was a "man with no character." In the following decade, in books such as *The Masters and the Slaves* (Casa Grande e Senzala) and *The Mansions and the Shanties* (Sobrados e Mocambos), Gilberto Freyre emphasized the flexibility of the Portuguese, as well as the African roots of the Northeasterners. Other authors characterized the Brazilian as *homem cordial* (cordial man). In his novels and stories, João Guimarães Rosa, Brazil's greatest writer of the twentieth century, found universal themes in the contradictory characters and peculiar language of men and women deep in the *sertão* backlands. Novelist Jorge Amado focused on social conflict, local color, and sensuality in his native Bahia State. More recently, the Brazilian anthropologist Roberto da Matta explored tensions between the private and public spheres, spontaneity, and authority, as well as sentiment and order to which Brazilians have found their own characteristic solutions.

At the level of interpersonal relations, in contrast to what is usually found in Spanish-speaking Latin America, where behavior tends to be more formal and rigid, there are in Brazil strong cultural values in favor of conciliation, tolerance, and cordiality. To the extent possible, direct personal confrontation is avoided. This Brazilian style of behavior may be derived from an Iberian and colonial heritage of diverse ethnic groups living together, weaker central authority exercised by the Portuguese crown, and day-to-day practical forms of resistance to exploitation. It may also have an element of popular emulation of the genteel behavior of the elites. Whatever its origins, Brazilians are known for their informality, good nature, and charm (*simpatia*), as well as their desire not to be thought unpleasant or boorish (*chato*). They place high value on warmth, spontaneity, and lack of pomp and ceremony.

Though they are cordial and magnanimous at the interpersonal level, Brazilians as a whole are exploitative with regard to the environment. This attitude has been explained in terms of the *bandeirante* or conquistador mentality by authors such as Viana Moog and Jorge Wilheim. According to this interpretation, the general spirit of the colonizer of yesteryear or today is to accumulate as much wealth as possible as quickly as possible and then move on. Whatever its roots, the result of this kind of behavior is individualism, transience, and disregard for others and for nature as opposed to stability, solidarity, equilibrium, and equity. It has led to both human and environmental degradation.

In a similar fashion, Brazilians tend not to think in terms of the common good. Discourse invoking mutual benefit for all concerned is often mistrusted as a disguised justification for colonialism or exploitation. The result of widespread evasion of rules imposed by the central authority is a vicious circle involving crackdowns and inspections (*fiscalização*) to enforce ever-tougher rules and ever more sophisticated and ingenious ways of evading the rules (*burla*). This tendency often blocks the efforts of those who are well-intentioned, without creating major obstacles but rather making their work easier for the truly dishonest.

This nonconformity with illegitimate authority is probably an origin of one of Brazil's most characteristic and original concepts, summarized in the word *jeito*. The word is practically untranslatable but refers to ways of "cutting red tape," "bending the rules," "looking the other way," or an alternative "way out." In its worst form, it amounts to corruption. At its best, it means finding pragmatic solutions to difficult problems without making waves.

Many Brazilians regard soccer and Carnaval, for which Brazil is famous, as outlets for the frustrations of everyday life. Brazil's three world soccer championships led to great national pride until 1970; subsequent losses caused twenty-four years of frustration until the fourth World Cup was brought home in 1994. The yearly Carnaval festivities provide for short-lived release and relaxation.

Another form of release is through imported and native music, widely disseminated by modern communications. The bossa nova of the 1960s was replaced by the lively Brazilian rhythms and dance movement of *forró*, *lambada*, and *pagode*.

Language

Language is one of the strongest elements of Brazil's national unity. Portuguese is spoken by nearly 100 percent of the population. The only exceptions are some members of Amerindian groups and pockets of immigrants, primarily from Japan and South Korea, who have not yet learned Portuguese. The principal families of Indian languages are Tupí, Arawak, Carib, and Gê.

There is about as much difference between the Portuguese spoken in Brazil and that spoken in Portugal as between the English spoken in the United States and that spoken in the United Kingdom. Within Brazil, there are no dialects of Portuguese, but only moderate regional variation in accent, vocabulary, and use of personal nouns, pronouns, and verb conjugations. Variations tend to diminish as a result of mass media, especially national television networks that are viewed by the majority of Brazilians.

The written language, which is uniform all over Brazil, follows national rules of spelling and accentuation that are revised from time to time for simplification. They are slightly different from the rules followed in Portugal. Written Brazilian Portuguese differs significantly from the spoken language and is used correctly by only a small, educated minority of the population. The rules of grammar are complex and allow more flexibility than English or Spanish. Many foreigners who speak Portuguese fluently have difficulty writing it properly.

Because of Brazil's size, self-sufficiency, and relative isolation, foreign languages are not widely spoken. English is often studied in school and increasingly in private courses. It has replaced French as the principal second language among educated people. Because Spanish is similar to Portuguese, most Brazilians can understand it and many can communicate in it, although Spanish speakers usually have difficulty understanding spoken Portuguese.

Mass Communications

Under the military governments in the 1970s, Brazil's state-owned system of telecommunications became highly developed. The telephone system was modernized by means of massive government investments. Long-distance and international calls, which had been difficult to make and hear until then, were made accessible through direct dialing, at least to those who could afford the high price of telephone lines. The Postal and Telegraph Company (Empresa de Correios e Telégrafos—ECT) also became a model of efficiency. Some of the quality of telephone and postal services was lost in the 1980s and early 1990s.

The development of telecommunications in Brazil was originally part of a strategy of modernization with centralized control. However, the widespread flow of information contributed to democratization of society in the 1980s and 1990s, a process in which the uncensored press played a key role. Censorship imposed during the military regime was lifted during the Figueiredo administration. The press is owned by private enterprises, none of which can be owned or controlled by foreigners; it includes dozens of daily newspapers, several weekly magazines, and a myriad of other periodical publications.

Radio and television stations are licensed to private businesses owned by Brazilians. There are hundreds of radio stations all over the country. Television became widespread in the

1970s, with several national networks and numerous local stations in all states. Television sets are common even in low-income households. Soap operas (*telenovelas*) are widely watched and are a common topic of conversation. It is a sign of their high technical quality that these programs have been sold to countries all over the world. The news programs often include editorial comment. In the authoritarian period, this expression of opinion, sometimes in subtle ways, tended to support government. In the 1990s, it has contributed to clearer notions of good government and citizens' rights among strata that had not developed political consciousness, but it may also have contributed to disillusionment.

Family and Kinship

The Portuguese crown and ecclesiastical authorities in Brazil were not entirely successful in implanting their ideals with regard to marriage and the patriarchal family. Brazilians have limited enthusiasm for official norms and often resort to consensual unions, marital dissolution, serial unions, and what the Roman Catholic Church generally considers to be lax standards of behavior.

At the same time that many of them bend the rules, Brazilians place high value on family and kinship relations. These are especially valued in an environment in which authorities, on the one hand, and one's subordinates, on the other, are thought to be untrustworthy. Most Brazilians are genuinely fond of children and are attached to their parents, and they cultivate a wide circle of aunts, uncles, and cousins. In the past, relationships with godchildren, godparents, and ritual co-parents extended these networks, but they are losing their importance in modern urban society.

Marital separation and divorce as well as formal and informal remarriage are now commonplace. Women commonly head their own households, and families often include children from different marriages or unions. The new arrangements are socially accepted but have not become culturally institutionalized in the sense of devising new terminology for the various relationships.

Religion

Roman Catholicism

Brazil's strong Roman Catholic heritage can be traced to the

Iberian missionary zeal, with the fifteenth-century goal of spreading Christianity to the infidels. In the New World, these included both Amerindians and African slaves. In addition to conversion, there were also strong efforts to enforce compliance with Roman Catholicism, including the Inquisition, which was not established formally in Brazil but nonetheless functioned widely in the colonies. In the late nineteenth century, the original Roman Catholic populace of Iberian origin was reinforced by a large number of Italian Catholics who immigrated to Brazil, as well as some Polish and German Catholic immigrants.

According to all the constitutions of the republican period, there is no state or official religion. In practice, however, separation of church and state is weak. Government officials generally avoid taking action that may offend the church.

Brazil is said to be the largest Roman Catholic country in the world. In 1996 about 76 percent of the population, or about 122 million people, declared Roman Catholicism as their religion, as compared with 89 percent in 1980. The decline may have resulted from a combination of a real loss of influence and a tendency to be more objective in answering census questions about religion.

As in most dominant religions, there is some distance between nominal and practicing Catholics. Brazilians usually are baptized and married in the Roman Catholic Church. However, according to the CNBB (National Conference of Brazilian Bishops), only 20 percent of nominal Catholics attend Mass and participate in church activities, but the figure may be as low as 10 percent. Women attend Mass more often than men, and the elderly are more active in church than the young. In the 1990s, charismatic forms of Catholicism used unconventional approaches, along the line of those used by Pentecostal Protestant groups, to attempt revitalization and increase active participation.

Popular or traditional forms of Catholicism are widespread in the interior of the country. Many Brazilians pray to figures such as Padre Cícero (a revered priest who lived in Ceará from 1844 to 1934), make pilgrimages to the site of the appearance of Brazil's patron saint, our Lady of the Appearance (Nossa Senhora Aparecida), and participate in traditional popular rites and festivities, such as the Círio in Belém and the Festa do Divino in central Brazil. Some use expressions of religious origin, such as asking for a blessing on meeting someone older or responding "God willing" (*Se Deusquiser*) when someone says "See you tomorrow."

During the 1970s, the progressive wing of the church made an "option for the poor." They were influenced by the doctrine of liberation theology (see Glossary), in which Brazilian theologians such as Leonardo Boff played a leading role, and followed the decision of the Latin American Bishops' Conference in Medellín, Colombia, in 1968. The church organized Ecclesiastical Base Communities (Comunidades Eclesiais de Base—CEBs; see Glossary) throughout the country to work for social and political causes at the local level. During the military regime, the progressive clergy managed to make the church practically the only legitimate focus of resistance and defense of human rights. In the early 1990s, conservative forces, supported by Pope John Paul II, gained power in the church.

Other Religions

Syncretism, the combination of different forms of belief or practice, has been widespread in Brazil, where Roman Catholicism has blended with numerous Afro-Brazilian cults. Syncretism occurred partly because of religious persecution and partly because of the compatibility of the different belief systems. The most well-known and socially acceptable combinations are called *umbanda* or *candomblé*. At one extreme, *umbanda* blends in with Kardecian spiritualism (see Glossary). At the other extreme, there is a kind of black magic called *macumba*, which can be used for either good or evil purposes. Its practitioners leave offerings of chicken, rum (*cachaça*), flowers, and candles at crossroads, beaches, and other public places. Kardecian spiritists, as well as Mormons, Jehovah's Witnesses, Jews, and Buddhists, together account for about 3 to 5 percent of the population, while those declaring that they have no religion total 15 percent.

In recent decades, Protestantism has grown rapidly. The proportion of the population considered evangelical grew from 3.7 percent in 1960 to 6.6 percent in 1980. The 1991 census showed a proportion of 19.2 percent, or 28.2 million followers. Nearly half of Brazil's evangelicals, or 13 million, belong to the Assembly of God. This and other evangelical or Pentecostal varieties of Protestantism—Christian Congregation, Universal Church of the Kingdom of God, Quadrangular Evangelicals, Brazil for Christ, and God and Love—emphasize brotherhood and religious ceremonies that actively engage participants in

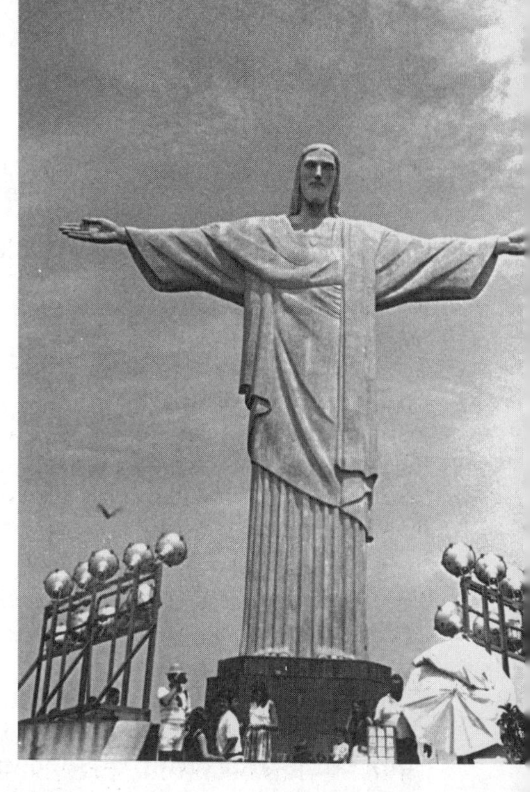

The forty-meter-high statue of Christ the Redeemer (Cristo Redendor) on Corcovado, Rio de Janeiro
Courtesy Jaklen Muoi Tuyen

The Catedral Metropolitana (Cathedral of Brasília), Oscar Niemeyer's modern rendition of the crown of thorns worn by Christ at his crucifixion
Courtesy Michaël Borg-Hansen

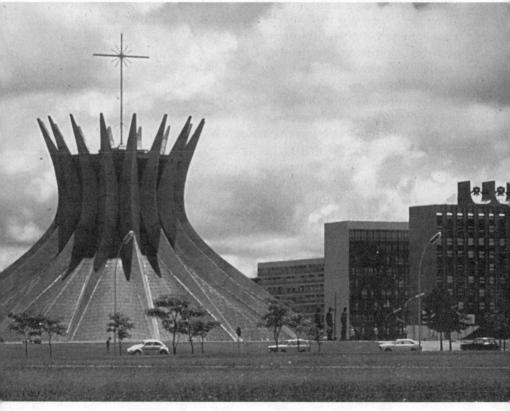

song and chants. The groups that have grown the most are fundamentalists with strict standards of personal behavior regarding dress, drinking, smoking, and gambling. They have special appeal among recent migrants to urban areas or to the frontier, who have had to adapt to new and difficult circumstances. In contrast to the formality and central control of the Roman Catholic Church, the fundamentalist Protestant groups grow rapidly and split and multiply frequently.

Health Status and Health Care

Indicators of Health

In 1996 the United Nations Development Programme (UNDP), which worked together with the Applied Economic Research Institute (Instituto de Pesquisa Econômica Aplicada—IPEA), released its *Human Development Report 1995* for Brazil. Using an index based on income, education, infant mortality, and other socioeconomic indicators, the report showed that Brazil was in a medium human development position as compared with other countries. It suggested that the national territory could be divided into three parts, with standards of living similar to those found in Belgium (the South and Southeast), Bulgaria (Center-West and North), and India (Northeast).

As in the *Human Development Report 1995*, infant mortality rates (deaths of children less than one year of age per 1,000 live births) often are used as indicators of living conditions. Since the denominator is births, they are not affected by the population's age structure. Because of underreporting of vital statistics, they must be estimated from census data. The overall average infant mortality rate for Brazil declined from 117 per 1,000 live births to eighty-eight, according to the 1960 and 1980 censuses, respectively. The 1991 census showed that the rate dropped to 49.7 in 1991. In 1995 the estimated rate was 44.4 per 1,000 live births.

As usual, national averages mask wide regional and socioeconomic variations. As in previous decades, infant mortality levels in 1995 were lowest in the South, at 21.1, and highest in the Northeast, where they reached 70.2, more than three times higher. In recent decades, infant mortality generally has been higher in rural areas, except for the poorest urban strata, whose mortality has been higher. State infant mortality rates fluctuate from year to year, depending on economic and public health conditions.

The sharp drop in infant mortality in recent decades did not necessarily reflect a commensurate general improvement in living conditions. To a large extent, the drop was the result of both the decline in fertility, which decreases the risk of infant deaths for biological and socioeconomic reasons, and specific health and sanitation interventions, primarily use of oral rehydration and extension of piped water.

Infectious and Chronic Diseases

Perinatal conditions were responsible for 47.1 percent of total infant mortality, ranking first among the causes of reported deaths for those under one year old in 1988. The leading cause of mortality among children one to four years of age, at 24.5 percent of all deaths in 1988, was infectious and parasitic diseases, particularly diarrheal diseases. External causes, specifically traffic accidents and homicide, accounted for the greatest share of registered deaths for the cohort aged five to forty-nine. Among the elderly population sixty years and above, deaths resulting from diseases of the circulatory system amounted to the highest percentage (50.3) of the total in 1989. Those diseases were also the leading cause of mortality for the entire nation, with higher ratios in the wealthier Southeast (36.2 percent) and South (37.2 percent), relative to the impoverished North (23.2 percent) and Northeast (29.3 percent). Although the proportion of deaths has shifted to older population groups, regional variations continue to hold, such that over a quarter of deaths afflicts the below-five age range in the North.

Expanded immunization coverage in recent years has favored a drop in mortality ascribed to vaccine-preventable diseases, from 12.9 percent in 1979 to 2.4 percent in 1988. In 1993 vaccination of Brazilian children less than one year old under the National Immunization Program reached 68.5 percent for diphtheria, pertussis, and tetanus, 92.3 percent poliomyelitis, 77.7 percent measles, and 98 percent tuberculosis. Although tuberculosis persists as a principal source of morbidity and mortality, particularly with the onset of the human immunodeficiency virus (HIV), its incidence and death rates have been steadily on the decline.

Control measures have proven effective in reducing the prevalence and outbreak of other infectious and endemic diseases, including cholera, Chagas' disease (American trypanosomiasis), yellow fever, and schistosomiasis (bilharzia). However, the number of registered cases of malaria, which 42.9 percent of the Brazilian population is at risk of contracting (mainly in the Amazon region), grew from 52,000 cases per year in 1970 to about 600,000 in the 1980s, with some improvement since then. Other communicable diseases either have been reintroduced, as in the case of dengue (breakbone fever) since 1986. Infectious tropical diseases reflect poor sanitary conditions as well as discrepancies in the standard of living between Northern and Southern Brazil, where such diseases ranked third and last, respectively, among the six leading causes of death in 1989.

Leprosy remains a serious problem in Brazil's high poverty areas, where the disease is spreading most rapidly. In October 1996, an average of 100 new cases were being reported each day. As many as half a million Brazilians are afflicted with leprosy.

The incidence of acquired immune deficiency syndrome (AIDS) in Brazil has also reached epidemic proportions, from 490 in 1985 to 103,262 cumulative cases by March 1, 1997, the fourth highest reported prevalence in the world. Based on 1996 data from the Pan American Health Organization (PAHO), homosexuals and/or bisexuals constitute 45 percent of the cumulative cases; intravenous drug users, 27 percent; heterosexuals, 20 percent; and others, 8 percent. The incidence was highest among young adults; 60 percent of those suffering from AIDS in 1994 were in the twenty-five to thirty-nine age-group. What began as a disease of homosexuals and recipients of blood transfusions quickly spread to heterosexuals and intravenous drug users. HIV infection attributed to needle-sharing during drug use increased from 3.0 percent of the cases in 1986 to 24.5 percent in 1992–93 and from 5.0 percent to 23.4 percent for heterosexual transmission, altering the male-to-female ratio from 100:1 in the 1980s to 4:1 in 1994. The surge in the proportion of women contracting the virus has resulted in part from a rise in perinatal transmission, the predominant mode of infection for the 12,000 infants and children diagnosed with AIDS in 1994.

The overall reduction in the number of new cases of the above infectious diseases, on the one hand, and the conspicuous rise in the incidence of chronic and degenerative diseases, on the other, indicate the occurrence of an epidemiological transition in Brazil. However, the transition is not complete; the two types coexist as major causes of death. Diseases of the circulatory system, including cerebrovascular and heart diseases, currently claim first place as the leading cause of death among the entire population (34.3 percent in 1989). The degenerative diseases have contributed to steep rises in the cost of health care, especially for the elderly.

Nutrition and Diet

Inadequate nutrition serves as a risk factor for morbidity and mortality from infectious diseases. Diarrheal and respiratory diseases, measles, tuberculosis, and malaria are the principal causes of death for malnourished children. The prevalence of malnutrition resulting from insufficient protein-energy diets among children under five years in Brazil in 1990 was 13.0 percent. Nevertheless, malnutrition within this age-group dropped substantially (61.4 percent) during the years 1975–88. Chronic malnutrition in 1989 characterized 15.4 percent of the entire population. The Northeast suffered from a greater rate of chronic malnutrition (27.3 percent) than the South (8.1 percent). The indigenous population's rate was twice that of low-income groups.

Improvement in nutrition has been accompanied by changes in the typical Brazilian diet. The staples of the traditional diet in Brazil are rice and beans, supplemented by whatever meat may be available, and few, if any, green vegetables. In the Amazon region, the staple carbohydrate is manioc meal, usually eaten with fish. Bread and pasta have become important parts of the diet of low-income families, especially in urban areas, because of government subsidies for wheat. Advances in poultry-raising have led to lower prices and greater consumption of chicken and eggs as sources of protein. Urban and rural workers often take their home-made rice and bean lunches to work, although this practice in urban areas is being replaced by employer-provided meal tickets for use in restaurants or luncheonettes, including fast-food outlets.

The Health Care System

The constitution of 1988 and the Organic Health Law (Lei Orgânica de Saúde) of 1990 universalized access to medical care, unified the public health system supported by the Ministry of Health and the National Institute for Medical Assistance and Social Security (Instituto Nacional de Assistência Médica da Previdência Social—INAMPS), and decentralized the management and organization of health services from the federal to the state and, especially, municipal level. Between 1985 and 1990, for example, the proportion of program funds managed by municipalities increased from 10 to 15 percent and by states from 23 to 33 percent. The sweeping health reforms that were initiated in the 1980s attempted to extend coverage to those outside the social security system.

The constitution grants all Brazilian citizens the right to procure free medical assistance from public as well as private providers reimbursed by the government. While the public domain oversees basic and preventive health care, the private nonprofit and for-profit health care sector delivers the bulk of medical services, including government-subsidized inpatient care (that is, private facilities owned 71 percent of hospital beds designated for government-funded health care in 1993). This publicly financed, privately provided health system continues to intensify its focus on high-cost curative care, driving hospital costs up by 70 percent during the 1980s.

Therapeutic treatment in hospitals tends to dominate funding at the expense of health promotion and disease prevention programs. Hospital-based assistance expanded from 44 percent (1985) to 77 percent (1990) of municipal health spending, while expenses for primary care decreased from 35 to 3 percent. Not only have basic and preventive health services for the entire population diminished, but the public health system also subsidizes expensive, high-technology medical procedures that consume 30 to 40 percent of health resources and often end up being used to attend affluent segments of the population. Despite an augmentation in hospital coverage, discrepancies in access and quality of health care among the five regions characterize the Single Health System (Sistema Único de Saúde—SUS); medical consultations average 1.3 per capita in the Northeast versus 2.3 in the Southeast.

Although states and municipalities rapidly acquired more responsibility in administering health funds and facilities, the federal government retained the role of financing public health outlays. As stipulated by the 1988 constitution, government subsidies for health services are derived from the social security budget, which is predominantly based on earmarked taxes and contributions from employee payroll and business profits. The federal government consistently underwrote over three-quarters of all public spending on health in the 1980s, a

The Sarah Kubitschek Rehabilitation Center, Brasília, named after the wife of former president Juscelino Kubitschek
Courtesy Inter-American Development Bank, Washington

sizable portion of which remunerated private medical charges. The percentage of total central government spending on health in 1990 was 6.7. Public health expenditures as a share of gross domestic product (GDP—see Glossary) in 1990 ranged from 2.1 to 3.1 percent, close to half of the total health expenditures of 5.8 percent.

Private sources finance the other half of total health expenditures. Perceptions of inefficiency in the government reimbursement schedule and deterioration in service quality of the public health system spurred a rapid growth in the private financing of health care during the 1980s, particularly in well-developed cities of the Southeast. The private sector covers 32 million citizens (roughly 20 percent of the Brazilian population) and consists of several hundred firms offering four principal types of medical plans: private health insurance, prepaid group practice, medical cooperatives, and company health plans. The group medical plans rank Brazil as the largest health maintenance organization (HMO) provider in Latin America; HMOs both finance and provide health care, but limit coverage to low-cost procedures and drive the burden of treating high-risk individuals to the publicly funded health system.

Health Professionals and Resources

Paralleling private insurance, human resources are disproportionately distributed in Brazil, with overrepresentation in the wealthy states. A strong demand for physicians persists in the Amazon region, while 61.5 percent of doctors are located in the Southeast. Physicians also dominate the health field, comprising 46.8 percent of the work force and serving an average of 847 people per doctor between 1988 and 1991, while nurses (one for every 3,448 people) and other auxiliary personnel lag behind in supply.

Although most health establishments belong to the public sector (65.2 percent public and 34.8 percent private), more private institutions (43.2 percent) provide inpatient care than public (6.8 percent). These establishments range from federal, state, municipal, and university hospitals and health posts to private clinics. The distribution of hospitals and outpatient facilities favors the South and Southeast, at levels two to four times higher per capita than in the North and Northeast, where health conditions are more precarious and the need for health care is greater. The ratio of hospital beds per 1,000 population has remained fairly constant between 1985 (3.9) and 1990 (3.6), and is 33 percent higher than predicted in relation to Brazil's gross national product (GNP—see Glossary).

Brazil has adopted new medical technologies from industrialized countries. However, specialized and high-technology services benefit a minority of privileged patients. Many poor Brazilians, unable to afford hospital-based medical care, rely on both prescription and nonprescription medication to relieve their ailments. The national pharmaceutical market in 1990 was valued at close to US$4 billion, 70.5 percent of which was earned by commercial pharmacies. Judging from the disproportionate availability of drugs and medical equipment to different income groups, universal and equitable access to health care remains a goal to be reached.

Public Health and Welfare

Social Security

The Ministry of Social Security, now separate from the Brazilian health system as discussed above, carries out the conventional mandate of ensuring old-age assistance. Until the 1940s, social security was limited to private plans organized by employers and employees. Over time, the components of the system became increasingly integrated and controlled by the federal government. More recently, health benefits and social security have become nearly universal, no longer depending on formal employment and contributions. Retirement and disability benefits are pegged to the official minimum wage. They weigh so heavily on government spending that they are one of the reasons the government resists raising the minimum wage for the active work force. At the same time, the middle class considers these benefits insufficient and, therefore, seeks private social security plans or makes investments in real estate, given the instability of financial markets in Brazil. The social security system will face even greater challenges as the age structure of the population changes, with a greater number of pensioners in relation to the number of contributing workers.

Sanitation and Public Utilities

The National Sanitation Plan (Plano Nacional de Saneamento—Planasa) of the 1970s did not keep pace with rapid urbanization in the development of safe drinking water supplies and waste disposal systems, particularly evident in the precarious metropolitan peripheries and favelas. Between 1988 and 1993, 87 percent had access to piped water and 72 percent to sewerage and waste disposal services, yet a 1989 study by the IBGE (Brazilian Geography and Statistics Institute) revealed that 92 percent of the municipalities did not treat domestic wastewater and only 27.6 percent of dwellings in a Northeast metropolis were linked to a sewerage system that passed quality standards.

The rural population receives far fewer water and sanitation services than its urban counterparts. Ninety-five percent of those in urban areas had adequate water supply during the 1988–93 period, as compared with 61 percent of rural dwellers; the levels for disposal systems were 84 percent and 32 percent, respectively (the rural figures refer to wells and privies, not service). To a certain extent, the urban-rural incongruity in the provision of environmental sanitation accounts for the higher percentage of deaths from diarrheal diseases in the rural North and Northeast than in the urban areas. The lack or deficiency of basic sanitation services has been associated with the persistence of diarrhea as well as outbreaks of contagious diseases, including cholera.

Housing

The National Housing Bank (Banco Nacional de Habitação—BNH) was established in the 1960s to finance public housing using funds from savings accounts and from the official employment guarantee system, known as the Severance Pay Fund (Fundo de Garantia do Tempo de Serviço—FGTS). Many thousands of basic houses (*casas populares*) were built, usually in projects at the edges or outside of cities. Because of the financial constraints of working with a low-income clientele, the federal Housing Finance System (Sistema Financeiro de Habitação—SFH) has been used primarily to provide low-cost mortgages for houses and apartments for the middle class.

Many poor people, without access to financing, find it necessary to build their own houses. The favelas on the hills of Rio de Janeiro are one well-known type. In other parts of Brazil, shantytowns on stilts are built over water (*alagados*), or in marshy areas (*baixadas*). In 1991 there were 3,221 medium- to large-size favelas (each with more than fifty-one households), which contained 2.9 percent of the country's households. The largest favelas, such as Rocinha in Rio de Janeiro, are home to hundreds of thousands.

Education

As in other areas of social life, education in Brazil is marked by great inequalities, with a highly developed university system at one extreme and widespread illiteracy at the other. Despite considerable progress in coverage, serious problems of quality remain. In 1995 the federal government was spending almost twice as much on the universities as on basic education, which is the primary responsibility of states and municipalities. Local governments often paid teachers wages that were well below the legal minimum.

In 1990 there were 37.6 million students, as compared with 10 million in 1964. Of the 1990 total, 3.9 million students were

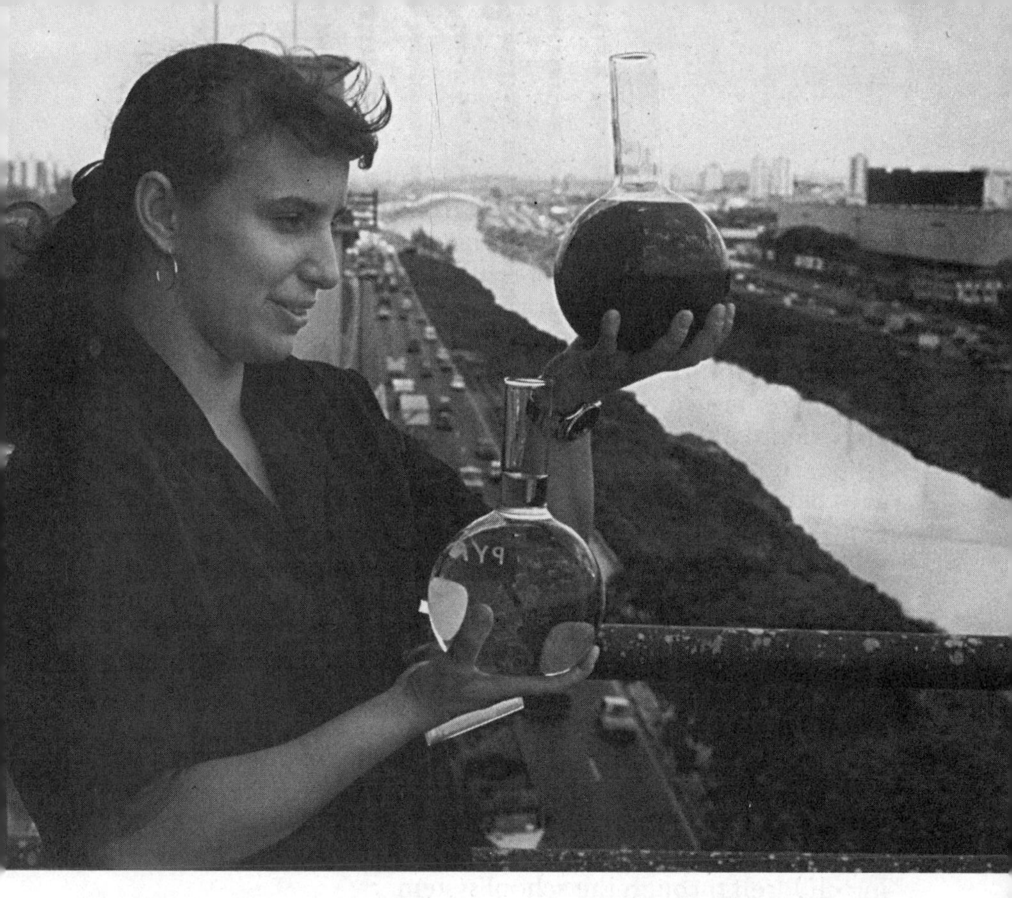

A São Paulo State Sanitation Authority technician compares a flask of polluted water collected from the Tietê (in background) with a flask of clean water.
Courtesy Inter-American Development Bank, Washington

in preschool, 29.4 million in elementary school, 3.7 million in secondary school, and 1.7 million in university. Despite this progress, less than 40 percent of the high school-age population was enrolled in school.

Because of the economic and social changes that have occurred in Brazil in recent decades, parents now place high value on education for their children. Availability of schools has become an important factor in deciding where to live and how to make a living, even in how many children to have.

Literacy

In 1990 it was estimated that 81 percent of the total population above age fifteen was literate, or 19 percent illiterate (based on the inability to sign one's own name). The level of functional illiteracy—that is, the inability to read newspapers and write letters—was not measured but was certainly much higher (an estimated 60 percent). As with most social indicators, illiteracy is highest in rural areas of the Northeast and North, where the figures are comparable to those in Africa, and lowest in urban areas of the Southeast and South, where the figures are comparable with those in the developed world. For example, southern towns had an adult illiteracy rate of only 10 percent in 1991, while the rate for children between the ages of eleven and fourteen was only 3 percent.

Literacy is strongly associated with income. When the population is divided into five income strata, illiteracy is ten times greater in the stratum with the lowest income. The illiteracy rate rises by age- group. The 1991 census also showed a strong racial gradient, with illiteracy levels of 11.6 percent among whites, 27.4 percent among mulattoes, and 29.9 percent among blacks. Differences by gender were not strong. Because of disappointing results when the federal government undertook a nationwide adult literacy campaign, the Brazilian Literacy Movement (Movimento Brasileiro de Alfabetização—Mobral), the emphasis shifted in the 1960s and 1970s to reaching children through the school system.

Primary and Secondary Schools

In theory, public education is free at all levels in Brazil and is compulsory for ages seven to fourteen, but coverage is incomplete and quality uneven. Private schools continue to meet a large part of the demand of those who can afford to pay. Generally speaking, the private primary and secondary schools are for the upper and middle classes, while the public schools at these levels are attended by those in the lower socioeconomic strata. During the 1990s, rising costs and economic pressures made it necessary for some of the middle class to shift from private to public schools.

The system of primary and secondary schools was restructured during the 1970s and 1980s to consist of eight years of basic ("fundamental") education and three years of secondary school. The public schools at these levels are run by municipalities and states. In 1990 the Collor government adopted a system of integrated educational centers, which included day care, school lunches, and health care, called Integrated Centers for Assistance to Children (Centros Integrados de Assistência à Criança—CIACs) and later renamed Centers for Comprehensive Attention to Children (Centros de Atenção Integrada à Criança—CAICs). These centers were based on the model developed in Rio de Janeiro State by the administration of Leonel de Moura Brizola, then governor of the state. However, because of limited funds they could not be implemented throughout the country, and the validity of concentrating resources on a small number of beneficiaries was questioned.

Between 1960 and 1990, enrollment rates for school-age children (seven to fourteen) increased from 50 percent to 90 percent for the country as a whole. They varied considerably from one region or state to another and within regions and states. Coverage was highest in the Southeast and South and lowest in the Northeast. There were also racial differences. According to 1985 data, 91.4 percent of white children ages seven to nine were in school, as compared with only 74.6 percent of black children of those ages.

One of the biggest educational problems in Brazil is school nonattendance. In wealthy states, 95 percent of children enroll from the start, while only 65 percent to 80 percent enroll in poor states. Approximately 25 percent drop out by the second year. UNICEF reported in mid-1994 that Brazil is in last place in a world ranking that compares the per capita income of each country with the rates of school nonattendance or absenteeism in the first five grades. Given Brazil's considerable economic strength, one would expect at least 80 percent of the children to complete the fifth grade, but only 39 percent finish, according to the UNICEF report. Often children from poor families start working from the age of ten in order to help their parents. Other reasons for school nonattendance include inadequate school facilities, the high examination failure rate, and malnutrition.

One of the government initiatives at the national level that has improved attendance and nutrition is the school lunch program. Some local governments, such as that of the Federal District, have experimented with providing payments to poor families of children who stay in school.

Colleges and Universities

The system of colleges and universities expanded rapidly in the 1970s and 1980s, reaching a total of 893 in 1993. Of these, ninety-nine were universities and 794 were isolated colleges or schools. Nearly all states have federal universities. The state universities are less widespread, while the few municipal universities or colleges are concentrated in large cities in the Southeast and South. The Southeast Region has nearly two-thirds of the country's colleges and universities. The number of undergraduate students admitted in Brazil in 1990 was 407,148, of which 14.1 percent were in federal universities, 10.9 percent in state universities, 5.9 percent in municipal universities, and 69.0 percent in private institutions. The total number of students enrolled was about 1.5 million, and the number of graduates was 230,000.

The best universities in Brazil generally include the University of São Paulo (Universidade de São Paulo—USP), the Campinas State University (Universidade Estadual de Campinas—Unicamp), the Federal University of Rio de Janeiro (Universidade Federal do Rio de Janeiro—UFRJ), the University of Brasília (Universidade de Brasília—UnB), and the Federal University of Minas Gerais (Universidade Federal de Minas Gerais—UFMG), all of which are public. The private Pontifical Catholic University of Rio de Janeiro (Pontifícia Universidade Católica do Rio de Janeiro—PUC-RJ) is also highly ranked. Public universities are free and do not charge tuition. Private colleges and universities, which charge tuition, grew very rapidly during the 1970s to meet the enormous demands of a growing middle class.

Because of the great demand for higher education and the limited resources, both public and private colleges (*faculdades*) and universities in Brazil require an entrance examination (*vestibular*). Passing these examinations often necessitates private college-preparatory courses, which only the upper and middle socioeconomic strata can afford. On completion of a full academic course of study, university students may obtain a bachelor's degree (*bacharelado*) and may also study an additional year to receive a teaching degree (*licenciatura*).

The choice of majors or specialties is not well-aligned with the job market. According to a 1993 IPEA study, two out of three students were in the social sciences or humanities, as opposed to scientific or technical fields. The study also concluded that four out of ten students dropped out before graduation and that those who graduated took an average of eight years to finish. Many of these had difficulty paying for tuition, or living expenses, and many who gave up before graduation realized that they were not being well prepared for the job market (see Research and Development, ch. 6).

Graduate study grew rapidly during the 1970s and 1980s. In 1991 Brazil had 973 master's programs in almost all areas, with 39,401 students, as well as 465 doctoral programs with 12,862 students. Because of this growth, along with budget constraints, the government restricted fellowships for university study abroad, which had made it possible for about 20,000 Brazilians to obtain their advanced degrees in the United States and Europe.

Principal Research Libraries

The strongest university libraries are at USP, UFRJ, and UnB. Researchers also have access to the National Library (Biblioteca Nacional) in Rio de Janeiro and the Library of Congress of Brazil (Biblioteca do Congresso do Brasil) in Brasília. The National Library is the equivalent of the United States Library of Congress, but the Library of Congress of Brazil is increasingly important. Brazilian libraries gradually are becoming computerized and linked to international information networks.

Social Conflict and Participation

Conflict and Nonviolence

While avoiding open conflict, Brazilian society has gone through transitions that in general have moved in the direction of modernization and democracy. Considering the decimation of Indian populations and the maintenance of African slavery long after it had been abolished elsewhere in the Americas, Brazil's colonial and imperial history was characterized by violence. At the same time, however, there is a strong Brazilian tradition of nonviolent resolution of conflicts. There was no war of independence against Portugal, but only local or regional conflicts, such as the Cabanagem (1835) in the Amazon, the War of the Farrapos (1845) in Rio Grande do Sul, and the São Paulo Civil War (1932) (see The Empire, 1822–89; The Republican Era, 1889–1985, ch. 1). Although Brazil participated in the Paraguayan War, also known as the War of the Triple Alliance (1864–70), most conflicts with neighboring countries were solved peacefully. The transition from empire to republic in 1889 was also relatively smooth. There was no generalized civil war, but there were isolated events, such as the resistance of a millenarian group at Canudos in the Northeast, described in Euclydes da Cunha's classic *Os sertões,* translated as *Rebellion in the Backlands.* In contrast to Spanish America, which fought protracted revolutionary wars and split into many separate countries, Portuguese America held together in one huge country. Although there were many violent episodes, Brazilian history, on the whole, has been remarkably peaceful.

Despite its nonbelligerent heritage at the national level, Brazilian life is marked by considerable violence on a day-to-day basis. Indians and slaves, or their descendants, have always been victimized. The rural bandits (*cangaceiros*) of the Northeast, of whom Lampião is the most famous, battled rival groups and backlands colonels in the early 1900s. In the post-World War II period, the struggle for land pitted rural workers and their leaders against the landowners and their hired gunmen, resulting in the murder of leaders and even priests, most notably in frontier areas. Chico Mendes, a rubber-tapper leader killed in Acre in 1988, was the most widely known among hundreds of victims. In 1995 and 1996, there were massacres of landless workers in Rondônia and Pará. In urban areas, especially the largest, violence has become commonplace, with frequent thefts, robberies, break-ins, assaults, and kidnappings. The police themselves are sometimes involved in criminal activities. In Rio de Janeiro, the government has little control over the favelas, which are dominated by gangs that control informal gambling (a numbers game called *jogo do bicho*) and drug trafficking as well as influence local politics.

For the most part, contemporary violence cannot easily be construed as a class struggle, at least as a struggle that involves collective consciousness and action. It is essentially particularistic and opportunistic at the individual level, although it often reflects perceptions of social injustice. Avoidance of more organized conflict between the privileged and the poor in Brazil can be attributed in part to the corporatist (see Glossary) system set up during the regime of Getúlio Dorneles Vargas (president, 1930–45, 1951–54) in the 1930s and 1940s. This system was designed to preempt direct class confrontation through well-controlled concessions to workers. The system of government-regulated labor unions and clientelism (see Glossary) reached its limits in the 1960s. In 1964 a bloodless military coup prevented it from going farther in the direction of the dispossessed.

The authoritarian military regime, which lasted from 1964 until 1985, used torture and killing to repress opposition, including cases of armed struggle between 1966 and 1975, but

The Catholic University of Petrópolis (Pontifícia Universidade Católica de Petrópolis), Rio de Janeiro State
Courtesy Jaklen Muoi Tuyen

was gradually worn down by democratic pressures and sheer fatigue. From 1976 until 1994, political efforts on the right and the left focused on redemocratization, with greater popular participation. Revolution and repression were set aside. Once again, a major transition occurred with relatively little violence, at least as compared with Chile and Argentina, for example.

Growth of Social and Environmental Movements

In contrast to developed countries, Brazil had few organizations—interest groups, associations, leagues, clubs, and NGOs—up until the 1970s. This lack of mediation between government and society was characteristic of a paternalistic and authoritarian social structure with a small but powerful elite and a dispossessed majority. During the 1970s and early 1980s, however, in part because of the growth of the middle class, a wide variety of social movements and local and national organizations appeared and expanded. Many engaged in some kind of political activity. Women's groups also appeared. Increasingly, social and political organizations reached into the lower classes. A significant number were connected directly or indirectly to the Roman Catholic Church, which sponsored CEBs (Ecclesiastical Base Communities) as part of its "option for the poor." Independent labor movements also grew during the 1980s. People took to the streets in 1984 to press for direct elections for president, as they did in 1992 to demand the impeachment of President Collor de Mello.

Once a new constitution was written in 1988 and a president was chosen through direct elections in 1989, opposition or resistance movements were forced to redefine their roles. Many of them made a transition from protest and denunciation to providing more constructive contributions in the areas of health, education, and social services. Others organized pressure on government agencies. A 1994 study showed that some 5,000 NGOs are dedicated to: the environment (40 percent), social change (17 percent), women's causes (15 percent), and racial issues (11 percent), among other causes (17 percent). As a rule, these movements are organized around the interests of neighborhoods or broad concerns that cut across social class lines. Most are small, voluntary organizations that operate at the local level and provide assistance, but there are also large professional NGOs, such as the Brazilian Institute of Social and Economic Analysis (Instituto Brasileiro de Análise Social e Econômica—IBASE) and the Federation of Social and Educational Assistance Agencies (Federação de Órgãos para Assistência Social). Some of the large NGOs are connected to international NGOs, and many receive donations from abroad (dues are not customary). Various associations of national and regional NGOs have also developed.

Collaboration between social and environmental movements, in what has been called "socio-environmentalism," reflects a Brazilian belief that concerns with the environment are inseparable from concerns with development, social equity, and justice. In this view, human and environmental degradation have common causes, and their solution requires the same sort of action.

Inclusion and Exclusion

Critical interpretations of Brazil's social situation in the 1980s and 1990s point to what is seen as a deepening of the economic crisis and the growth of misery and hunger. These interpretations are based on a series of observations and evidence that includes loss of value of the real minimum wage as a result of inflation, high unemployment levels, widespread informal economic activity, cutbacks in government spending on social programs, and mapping of indigence carried out by IPEA in 1990. They also take into account the more visible signs of discrimination and deprivation, such as favelas, camps of landless workers, urban violence, street children, and epidemics of diseases such as cholera and dengue.

However, social indicators on such phenomena as infant mortality, school enrollment, piped water, nutritional status, and protein consumption improved significantly in the 1980s and early 1990s. The improvements have resulted in no small measure from government investments in the social area since the 1970s. These have been called "compensatory social policies" because they seem to have been designed to compensate for the economic policies that favor income concentration. Although they were insufficient, the investments had unquestionably positive effects. To some extent, the benefits also can be attributed to fertility decline, which has biological and socioeconomic effects, and to technological development in the areas of health services and food production.

The apparent contradiction between negative and positive socioeconomic trends can be explained in part by the greater visibility of poverty, which has grown most in urban areas, while the above-mentioned benefits are more diffuse and less visible. However, the problems are not only because of perceptions or misreadings. The basic explanation for the contradiction is the coexistence of simultaneous processes of inclusion and exclusion. Inclusion resulted from extension to the lower middle class, by means of the labor and consumer markets and public services, of some of the benefits of development previously restricted to the upper and upper-middle strata. They have gained from participation in the labor market or markets for their goods and services and from government-provided services, such as education, health, and sanitation. In the simplest terms, the quantity of coverage has increased, although serious problems of quality remain, and the lowest strata continue to be excluded from integral participation in markets and full access to government services.

The perception of crisis is accentuated by the fact that social mobility slowed down considerably in relation to the rapid expansion of the upper middle class in the 1960s and 1970s. According to national surveys of household expenditures, 47 percent of the heads of household questioned in 1973 said that they were better off than their parents. In 1988 the proportion fell to 38 percent, and 60 percent responded that they were the same or worse off than their parents.

In sum, social polarization persists, but it is no longer a duality. Its boundaries are multiple and mobile, depending on the dimension, and remain poorly defined. There is a vast middle ground that defies simple analyses and explanations and includes the upwardly and the downwardly mobile.

Macroeconomic policies aimed at stabilization and competitive insertion of Brazil into global markets contribute to slower economic growth and structural unemployment, which in turn worsen exclusion. At the same time, government authorities have stated their intention to give priority to social equity, the reduction of regional inequalities, and the defense of human and citizen rights. Effective achievement of these goals, to the extent that economic conditions permit, depends on appropriate analysis, political will, and especially the ability of citizens to make their demands clear.

It is unclear whether never-ending economic and political crises, disasters, and scandals will provoke disillusionment with the redemocratization process and with Brazil's future, or whether Brazilian society will continue to change in the direction of greater equilibrium within society and between society and the environment. There are important signs that significant change is underway. The campaign against hunger and misery and for citizens' rights launched by Herbert "Betinho" de Souza, a sociologist, made many Brazilians aware of the poverty that surrounds them and made clear that economic growth or government benefits alone will not solve their problems. The process of decentralization opened up opportunities for participation but raised questions about pork-barreling, accountability, and the ability of local governments and civil society to make and implement informed decisions. The question is to what extent the progressive forces will prevail so that even if inequality persists, it will not be attributed to a failure of Brazilian society to respond.

* * *

While taking into account the contributions of foreign Brazilianists, this chapter draws heavily on the work (in Portuguese) of Brazilian authors. The most basic references in English are Thomas Lynn Smith's *Brazil: People and Institutions*, now quite dated; Charles Wagley's revised edition of *An Intro-*

duction to Brazil; Mark Carpenter's *Brazil: An Awakening Giant*; and Ronald M. Schneider's *Brazil: Culture and Politics in a New Industrial Powerhouse.*

For social aspects of the Amazon, in addition to the work of the geographers mentioned above, Wagley's *Amazon Town* is a classic. His *Man in the Amazon* and Marianne Schmink and Charles H. Wood's *Frontier Expansion in Amazonia* are useful edited volumes. The latter authors' study entitled *Contested Frontiers* and Alexander Cockburn and Susanna Hecht's *Fate of the Forest* provide some of the best analyses of recent social and environmental trends. Manoel Correa de Andrade has written classic analyses of the land and people of the Northeast. Albert O. Hirschman's *Journeys Toward Progress* describes government efforts to deal with the region's droughts.

Sociological perspectives on environmental problems and policies in Brazil are provided in *Dilemas sócioambientais e desenvolvimento sustentável*, edited by Daniel Hogan and Paulo Vieira da Cunha, and *População, meio ambiente e desenvolvimento,* edited by George Martine. Perceptions of environmental issues among leaders and the general public are analyzed in Samyra Crespo and Pedro Leitão's *O que o brasileiro pensa sobre meio ambiente.* Authors who have written about Brazilian environmental problems and policies in English include Martine, Hecht, Emílio Moran, Peter May, and John O. Browder.

The basic reference in English on various aspects of population in Brazil is Charles H. Wood and José Alberto Magno de Carvalho's *The Demography of Inequality in Brazil.* The historical record is presented by Thomas Merrick and Douglas Graham in *Population and Economic Development in Brazil: 1800 to the Present.* For specific aspects of population dynamics, see Merrick and Martine.

Economic and social trends are analyzed in Edmar L. Bacha and Herbert S. Klein's edited volume, *Social Change in Brazil, 1945–1985.* Brazilian social scientists, such as Fernandes and Fernando Henrique Cardoso, have produced excellent studies on social class in Brazil. Rural class relations are discussed by David Goodman and Michael Redclift. Urban class relations in Brazil have been dealt with mostly by numerous social scientists based in Rio de Janeiro and São Paulo, including Francisco Weffort and José Álvaro Moisés.

The starting point for analysis on race relations in Brazil is Gilberto Freyre's *The Masters and the Slaves,* followed by *The Mansions and the Shanties.* Thomas E. Skidmore's study, *Black into White,* dispels some of the ideology of racial democracy. *Race, Class and Power in Brazil,* edited by Pierre-Michel Fontaine, offers a political perspective.

John Hemming provides a detailed historical account of Amerindians in Brazil in *Red Gold,* and Shelton H. Davis criticizes the situation existing in the 1970s in *Victims of the Miracle.* A recommended 1992 study is Manuela Carneiro da Cunha's *História dos Índios do Brasil.* The indigenous languages are catalogued in Barbara F. Grimes's *Ethnologue.*

Wagley's *An Introduction to Brazil* is an authoritative starting point on unity and diversity of culture in Brazil in the postwar period. Family and kinship have been analyzed by, among others, Aspásia Camargo. Gender is a more recent concern. Authors who have written on this issue include Heleieth I.B. Saffioti. The volume *Mulheres Latinoamericanas em dados: Brasil* contains statistical data on women in Brazil. The Carlos Chagas Foundation in São Paulo publishes regularly on women's issues.

Studies of religion in Brazil have been limited for the most part to specific topics. In *Miracle at Joaseiro,* Ralph Della Cava writes on traditional Catholicism in the Northeast and the worship of Padre Cícero. Seth Leacock and Ruth Leacock's *Spirits of the Deep* is an example in English of the literature on Afro-Brazilian traditions.

The section on health status and health care draws heavily from studies by the PAHO. Statistical analyses of diseases, nutrition, and health-care resources are taken from reports published by the UNDP, the World Bank, and the Inter-American Development Bank. Foreign and Brazilian authorities on the national health-care system are also cited. (For further information and complete citations, see Bibliography.)

Chapter 3. The Economy

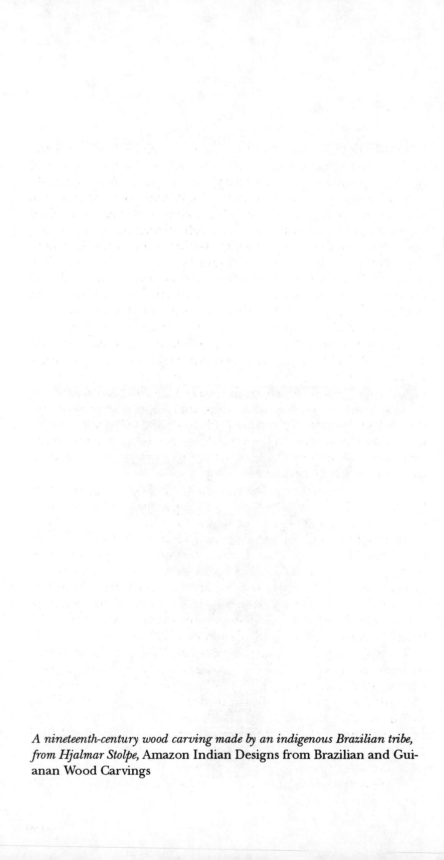

A nineteenth-century wood carving made by an indigenous Brazilian tribe, from Hjalmar Stolpe, Amazon Indian Designs from Brazilian and Guianan Wood Carvings

FROM PORTUGAL'S DISCOVERY of Brazil in 1500 until the late 1930s, the Brazilian economy relied on the production of primary products (see Glossary) for exports. Portugal subjected Brazil to a sternly enforced colonial pact, or imperial mercantile policy, which for three centuries heavily curbed development. The colonial phase left strong imprints on the country's economy and society, lasting long after independence in 1822. Measurable changes began occurring only late in the eighteenth century, when slavery was eliminated and wage labor was adopted. Important structural transformations began only in the 1930s, when the first steps were taken to change Brazil into a modern, semi-industrialized economy.

These transformations were particularly intense between 1950 and 1981, when the growth rates of the economy remained quite high and a diversified manufacturing base was established. However, since the early 1980s the economy has experienced substantial difficulties, including slow growth and stagnation. Nevertheless, Brazil still has the potential to regain its former dynamism. In the mid-1990s, it had a large and quite diversified economy, but one with considerable structural, as well as short-term, problems.

Socioeconomic transformation took place rapidly after World War II. In the 1940s, only 31.3 percent of Brazil's 41.2 million inhabitants resided in towns and cities; by 1991, of the country's 146.9 million inhabitants 75.5 percent lived in cities, and Brazil had two of the world's largest metropolitan centers—São Paulo and Rio de Janeiro. The rate of population growth decreased from about 3 percent annually in the 1950s and 1960s to 1.9 percent annually in the 1980–91 period, indicating that Brazil was in a demographic transition. By mid-1997 Brazil had an estimated population of 159.9 million.

The share of the primary sector (see Glossary) in the gross national product (GNP—see Glossary) declined from 28 percent in 1947 to 11 percent in 1992. Despite this reduction, the agricultural sector remains important. Although part of it is primitive and intensive, part is modern and dynamic. Brazil remains one of the world's largest exporters of agricultural products.

In the same 1947–92 period, the contribution of industry to GNP increased from less than 20 percent to 39 percent. The industrial sector produces a wide range of products for the domestic market and for export, including consumer goods, intermediate goods (see Glossary), and capital goods (see Glossary). By the early 1990s, Brazil was producing about 1 million motor vehicles annually and about 32,000 units of motor-driven farming machines. On an annual basis, it was also producing 1.8 million tons of fertilizers, 4.7 million tons of cardboard and paper, 20 million tons of steel, 26 million tons of cement, 3.5 million television sets, and 3 million refrigerators. In addition, about 70 million cubic meters of petroleum were being processed annually into fuels, lubricants, propane gas, and a wide range of petrochemicals. Furthermore, Brazil has at least 161,500 kilometers of paved roads and more than 63 million megawatts of installed electric power capacity.

Despite these figures, the economy cannot be considered developed. Although the economic changes since 1947 raised the country's per capita income above US$2,000 in 1980, per capita income in 1995 was still only US$4,630. Growth and structural change have not altered significantly Brazil's extremely unequal distribution of wealth, income, and opportunity. Despite impressive increments in economic growth and output, the number of poor has risen sharply. Most of the poor are concentrated in the rural areas of Brazil's Northeast (Nordeste) Region, or in the country's large cities or metropolitan areas. The economic and political troubles of the 1980s and early 1990s have only complicated the task of correcting the country's development pattern.

Historical Background and Economic Growth

The Colonial Period

Portugal's exploitation of Brazil stemmed from the European commercial expansion of the fifteenth and sixteenth centuries (see The Colonial Era, 1500–1815, ch. 1). Blocked from the lucrative hinterland trade with the Far East, which was dominated by Italian cities, Portugal began in the early fifteenth century to search for other routes to the sources of goods valued in European markets. Portugal discovered the maritime passage to the East Indies around the southern tip of Africa and established a network of trade outposts throughout Africa and Asia. After the discovery of America, it competed with Spain in occupying the New World (see the Indigenous Population, ch. 1).

Initially, the Portuguese did not find mineral riches in their American colony, but they never lost the hope of someday finding such riches there. Meanwhile, in order to settle and defend the colony from European intruders, the Portuguese established a pioneer colonial enterprise: the production of sugar in the Northeast. Beginning in about 1531, cattle began arriving in Brazil, and a cattle industry developed rapidly in response to the needs of the sugar industry for transportation and food for workers. The discovery of precious metals in the colony's Center-South (Centro-Sul), a relatively undefined region encompassing the present-day Southeast (Sudeste) and South (Sul) regions, came only in the eighteenth century.

The Sugar Cycle, 1540–1640

By the mid-sixteenth century, Portugal had succeeded in establishing a sugar economy in parts of the colony's northeastern coast. Sugar production, the first large-scale colonial agricultural enterprise, was made possible by a series of favorable conditions. Portugal had the agricultural and manufacturing know-how from its Atlantic islands and manufactured its own equipment for extracting sugar from sugarcane. Furthermore, being involved in the African slave trade, it had access to the necessary manpower. Finally, Portugal relied on the commercial skills of the Dutch and financing from Holland to enable a rapid penetration of sugar in Europe's markets.

Until the early seventeenth century, the Portuguese and the Dutch held a virtual monopoly on sugar exports to Europe. However, between 1580 and 1640 Portugal was incorporated into Spain, a country at war with Holland. The Dutch occupied Brazil's sugar area in the Northeast from 1630 to 1654, establishing direct control of the world's sugar supply. When the Dutch were driven out in 1654, they had acquired the technical and organizational know-how for sugar production. Their involvement in the expansion of sugar in the Caribbean contributed to the downfall of the Portuguese monopoly.

The Caribbean sugar boom brought about a steady decline in world sugar prices. Unable to compete, Brazilian sugar exports, which had peaked by the mid-seventeenth century, declined sharply. Between the fourth quarter of the seventeenth century and the early eighteenth century, Portugal had difficulties in maintaining its American colony. The downfall of sugar revealed a fragile colonial economy, which had no commodity to replace sugar. Paradoxically, however, the period of stagnation induced the settlement of substantial portions of the colony's territory. With the decline of sugar, the cattle sector, which had evolved to supply the sugar economy with animals for transport, meat, and hides, assimilated part of the resources made idle, becoming a subsistence economy. Because of extensive cattle production methods, large areas in the colony's interior were settled.

Realizing that it could maintain Brazil only if precious minerals were discovered, Portugal increased its exploratory efforts in the late seventeenth century. As a result, early in the eighteenth century gold and other precious minerals were found. The largest concentration of this gold was in the Southeastern Highlands, mainly in what is now Minas Gerais State.

The Eighteenth-Century Gold Rush

As a result of the mineral discoveries, settlers flocked to the gold region, and growing numbers of slaves were transferred from the sugar areas and brought in from Africa. Gold mining was mainly alluvial panning, a labor-intensive activity. The extraction of gold increased rapidly until the 1750s when gold exports peaked. After the gold deposits became depleted and exports declined sharply in the last quarter of the eighteenth century, the Brazilian economy entered another long period of stagnation.

The gold surge did not establish a basis for economic expansion after the depletion of the mines. The economic regression was especially bad because of the restrictions Portugal had imposed on the establishment of manufacturing in the colony. However, the gold rush had an important impact in shaping Brazil's territory. First, the various exploratory expeditions led to the incorporation of large areas originally belonging to Spain. In addition, the demand for food and animals for transportation and meat had major repercussions outside the mining region. The mines were located in inhospitable, mountainous terrain, and the movement of goods to and from the mines depended heavily on mules. Agricultural activities were expanded elsewhere in order to feed the miners. Thus, the gold rush brought about the occupation of, and interaction among, different geographical areas. Moreover, the colony's economic and administrative center of gravity moved to the Southeast Region. Gold was shipped through ports in or near Rio de Janeiro, prompting the transfer of the colonial administration from the Bahian town of Salvador to Rio de Janeiro.

The difficult period resulting from the depletion of the mines lasted well into the second quarter of the nineteenth century. The mainstays of the economy were in decline, and the colony fell into a state of depression and decadence. In the late eighteenth century, Brazil experienced a brief surge in cotton exports to Britain, as the War of Independence in America disrupted American trade temporarily; however, Brazilian cotton lost its place in the world market by the early nineteenth century.

The Economy at Independence, 1822

Despite Brazil's economic troubles, the early nineteenth century was a period of change. First, the Napoleonic Wars forced the Portuguese royal family to flee to Brazil in 1808, and for a short period the colony became the seat of the Portuguese empire (see The Kingdom of Portugal and Brazil, 1808–21, ch. 1). Moreover, in 1808 Britain persuaded Portugal to open the colony to trade with the rest of the world, and Portugal rescinded its prohibition against manufacturing. These events paved the way for Brazil's independence on September 7, 1822.

Brazil's early years as an independent nation were extremely difficult. Exports remained low, and the domestic economy was depressed. The only segment that expanded was the subsistence economy. Resources (land, slaves, and transport animals) made idle by the decline of the export economy were absorbed into mostly self-consumption activities.

The Coffee Economy, 1840–1930

The impact of coffee on the Brazilian economy was much stronger than that of sugar and gold. When the coffee surge began, Brazil was already free from the limitations of colonialism. Moreover, the substitution of wage labor for slave labor after 1870 meant an increase in efficiency and the formation of a domestic market for wage goods. Finally, the greater complexity of coffee production and trade established important sectorial linkages within the Brazilian economy.

Coffee was introduced in Brazil early in the eighteenth century, but initially it was planted only for domestic use. It took the high world prices of the late 1820s and early 1830s to turn coffee into a major export item. During the initial phase, production was concentrated in the mountainous region near Rio de Janeiro. This area was highly suitable for coffee cultivation, and it had access to fairly abundant slave labor. Moreover, the coffee could be transported easily on mule trains or on animal-drawn carts over short distances to the ports.

An entrepreneurial class established in Rio de Janeiro during the mining surge was able to induce the government to help create basic conditions for the expansion of coffee, such as removing transportation and labor bottlenecks. From the area near Rio de Janeiro, coffee production moved along the Paraíba Valley toward São Paulo State, which later became Brazil's largest exporting region. Coffee was cultivated with primitive techniques and with no regard to land conservation. Land was abundant, and production could expand easily through the incorporation of new areas. However, it soon became necessary to ease two basic constraints: the lack of transportation and the shortage of labor.

The cultivation of coffee farther away from ports required the construction of railroads, first around Rio de Janeiro and into the Paraíba Valley, and later into the fertile highlands of São Paulo. In 1860 Brazil had only 223 kilometers of railroads; by 1885 this total had increased to 6,930 kilometers. The main rail link between São Paulo's eastern highlands and the ocean port of Santos allowed for a rapid expansion of coffee into the center and northwest of the state.

After the initial coffee expansion, the availability of slaves dwindled, and further cultivation required additional slaves. However, by 1840 Brazil was already under pressure to abolish slavery, and a series of decrees were introduced, making it increasingly difficult to supply the new coffee areas with servile labor. In the 1870s, the shortage of labor became critical, leading to the gradual incorporation of free immigrant labor. The coffee expansion in the west-northwest of São Paulo State after 1880 was made possible largely by immigrant labor. In 1880 São Paulo produced 1.2 million 60-kilogram coffee bags, or 25 percent of Brazil's total; by 1888 this proportion had jumped to 40 percent (2.6 million bags); and by 1902, to 60 percent (8 million bags). In turn, between 1884 and 1890 some 201,000 immigrants had entered São Paulo State, and this total jumped to more than 733,000 between 1891 and 1900. Slavery was abolished in 1888.

The Brazilian economy grew considerably in the second half of the nineteenth century. Coffee was the mainstay of the economy, accounting for 63 percent of the country's exports in 1891. However, sugar, cotton, tobacco, cocoa, and, at the turn of the century, rubber were also important. During the first

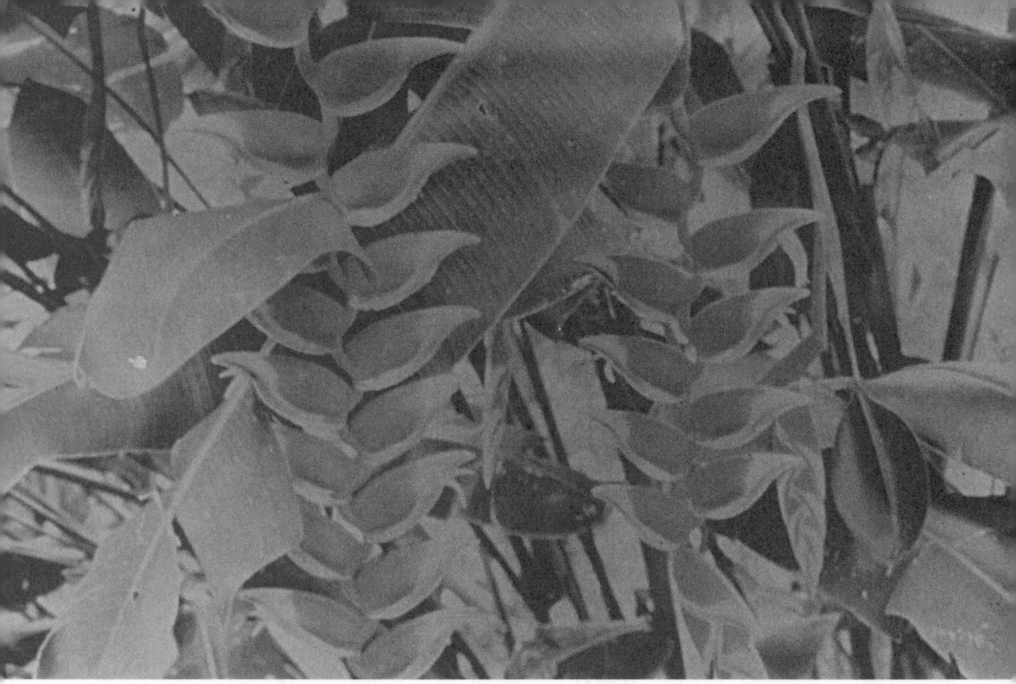

A platanilla (heliconia wagneriana-musaceae) *tropical plant on the Fazenda Marimbondo of conservationist Jorge Schweizer, Paraná State*
A tropical hardwood tree (ficus benjamin) on the Fazenda Marimbondo
Courtesy Jon Barlow Hudson

three decades of the twentieth century, the Brazilian economy went through periods of growth but also difficulties caused in part by World War I, the Great Depression, and an increasing trend toward coffee overproduction. The four-year gap between the time a coffee tree is planted and the time of the first harvest magnified cyclical fluctuations in coffee prices, which in turn led to the increasing use of government price supports during periods of excess production. The price supports induced an exaggerated expansion of coffee cultivation in São Paulo, culminating in the huge overproduction of the early 1930s.

The 1840 to 1930 period also saw an appreciable but irregular expansion of light industries, notably textiles, clothing, food products, beverages, and tobacco. This expansion was induced by the growth in income, by the availability of foreign exchange, by fiscal policies, and by external events, such as World War I. Other important factors were the expansion of transportation, the installed capacity of electric energy, increased urbanization, and the formation of a dynamic entrepreneurial class. However, the manufacturing growth of the period did not generate significant structural transformations.

Economic growth in the nineteenth century was not shared equally by the regions. Development and growth were concentrated in the Southeast. The South Region also achieved considerable development based on coffee and other agricultural products. The Amazon Basin experienced a meteoric rise and fall of incomes from rubber exports. The Northeast continued to stagnate, with its population living close to the subsistence level.

A Period of Sweeping Change, 1930–45

The decade of the 1930s was a period of interrelated political and economic changes. The decade started with the 1930 revolution, which abolished the Old Republic (1889–1930), a federation of semiautonomous states. After a transitional period in which centralizing elements struggled with the old oligarchies for control, a coup in 1937 established the New State (Estado Novo) dictatorship (1937–45) (see The Era of Getúlio Vargas, 1930–54, ch. 1).

To a large extent, the revolution of 1930 reflected a dissatisfaction with the political control exercised by the old oligarchies. The political unrest of the first half of the 1930s and the 1937 coup were influenced strongly by the onset of economic problems in 1930. The coffee economy suffered from a severe decline in world demand caused by the Great Depression and an excess capacity of coffee production created in the 1920s. As a result, the price of coffee fell sharply and remained at very low levels. Brazil's terms of trade (see Glossary) deteriorated significantly. These events, and a large foreign debt, led to an external crisis that took almost a decade to resolve.

The external difficulties had far-reaching consequences. The government was forced to suspend part of the country's debt payments and eventually to impose exchange controls. Excess coffee production led to increasing interventions in the coffee market. The state programs to support coffee prices went bankrupt in 1930. To avoid further decreases in coffee prices, the central government bought huge amounts of coffee, which was then destroyed. Central government intervention provided support to the coffee sector and, through its linkages, to the rest of the economy.

Despite the economic difficulties, the income maintenance scheme of the coffee support program, coupled with the implicit protection provided by the external crisis, was responsible for greater industrial growth. Initially, this growth was based on increased utilization of the productive capacity and later on moderate spurts of investment. The initial import-substitution industrialization (see Glossary) that occurred especially during World War I did not lead to industrialization; it became a process of industrialization only in the 1930s.

The 1930s also saw a change in the role of government. Until then, the state acted primarily in response to the demands of the export sector. During the first half of the decade, it was forced to interfere swiftly in an attempt to control the external crisis and to avoid the collapse of the coffee economy; government leaders hoped that the crisis would pass soon and that another export boom would occur. However, with the magnitude and duration of the crisis it became clear that Brazil could no longer rely solely on exports of primary goods (see Glossary) and that it was necessary to promote economic diversification. During the Estado Novo, the government made initial attempts at economic planning, and in the late 1930s began to establish the first large government enterprise, an integrated steel mill.

The World War II period saw mixed achievements. By the late 1930s, coffee production capacity had been reduced drastically, the worst of the external crisis had passed, and the Brazilian economy was ready to grow. However, the war interfered with development efforts. Output increased mainly through better utilization of the existing capacity but, except for the steel mill, there was little industrial and infrastructure investment. Thus, at the end of the war Brazil's industrial capacity was obsolete and the transportation infrastructure was inadequate and badly deteriorated.

Import-Substitution Industrialization, 1945–64

A review of the evolution and structural changes of the industrial sector since the end of World War II reveals four broad periods. The postwar period to 1962 was a phase of intense import substitution, especially of consumer goods, with basic industries growing at significant but lower rates. The 1968 to 1973 period was one of very rapid industrial expansion and modernization (between 1962 and 1967, the industrial sector stagnated as a result of adverse macroeconomic conditions). The 1974 to 1985 phase was highlighted by import substitution of basic inputs and capital goods and by the expansion of manufactured goods exports. The period since 1987 has been a time of considerable difficulties.

At the end of World War II, political and economic liberalism were reintroduced in Brazil. Getúlio Dorneles Vargas (president, 1930–45, 1951–54) was overthrown, democratic rule was reestablished, and the foreign-exchange reserves accumulated during the war made possible a reduction of trade restrictions. However, trade liberalization was short-lived. The overvalued foreign-exchange rate, established in 1945, remained fixed until 1953. This, combined with persistent inflation and a repressed demand, meant sharp increases in imports and a sluggish performance of exports, which soon led again to a balance of payments (see Glossary) crisis.

Pessimistic about the future of Brazil's exports, the government feared that the crisis would have a negative impact on inflation. Consequently, instead of devaluing the cruzeiro (for value of cruzeiro—see Glossary), it decided to deal with the crisis through exchange controls. In 1951 the newly elected government of Getúlio Vargas enforced a recently established system of import licensing, giving priority to imports of essential goods and inputs (fuels and machinery) and discouraging imports of consumer goods. These policies had the unanticipated effect of providing protection to the consumer goods industry. Early in the 1950s, however, convinced that the only

A welder helps to construct a plant to produce petrochemicals from natural gas at the US$2.5 billion petrochemical complex at Camacarí, sixty kilometers north of Salvador, Bahia State.
Courtesy Inter-American Development Bank, Washington

hope for rapid growth was to change the structure of the Brazilian economy, the government adopted an explicit policy of import-substitution industrialization. An important instrument of this policy was the use of foreign-exchange controls to protect selected segments of domestic industry and to facilitate the importation of equipment and inputs for them.

However, the move to fixed exchange rates together with import licensing drastically curtailed exports, and the balance of payments problem became acute. The system became nearly unmanageable, and in 1953 a more flexible, multiple-exchange-rate system was introduced. Under the latter, imports considered essential were brought in at a favored rate; imports of goods that could be supplied domestically faced high rates and were allotted small portions of the available foreign exchange. Similarly, some exports were stimulated with a higher exchange rate than those of traditional exports. This system continued to be the main instrument for the promotion of import-substitution industrialization, but the performance of the export sector improved only modestly.

Between 1957 and 1961, the government made several changes in the exchange-control system, most of which were attempts at reducing its awkwardness or at improving its performance with the advance of import-substitution industrialization. For this same purpose, the government also introduced several complementary measures, including enacting the Tariff Law of 1957, increasing and solidifying the protection extended to domestic industries, and offering strong inducements to direct foreign investment.

In the second half of the 1950s, the government enacted a series of special programs intended to better orient the industrialization process, to remove bottlenecks, and to promote vertical integration (see Glossary) in certain industries. The government gave special attention to industries considered basic for growth, notably the automotive, cement, steel, aluminum, cellulose, heavy machinery, and chemical industries.

As a result of import-substitution industrialization, the Brazilian economy experienced rapid growth and considerable diversification. Between 1950 and 1961, the average annual rate of growth of the gross domestic product (GDP—see Glossary) exceeded 7 percent (see table 4, Appendix). Industry was the engine of growth. It had an average annual growth rate of over 9 percent between 1950 and 1961, compared with 4.5 percent for agriculture. In addition, the structure of the manufacturing sector experienced considerable change. Traditional industries, such as textiles, food products, and clothing, declined, while the transport equipment, machinery, electric equipment and appliances, and chemical industries expanded.

However, the strategy also left a legacy of problems and distortions. The growth it promoted resulted in a substantial increase in imports, notably of inputs and machinery, and the foreign-exchange policies of the period meant inadequate export growth. Moreover, a large influx of foreign capital in the 1950s resulted in a large foreign debt.

Import-substitution industrialization can be assessed according to the contribution to value added by four main industrial subsectors: nondurable consumer goods, durable consumer goods, intermediate goods, and capital goods. Using data from the industrial censuses, the share of these groups in value added between 1949 and 1960 shows a considerable decline in the share of the nondurable goods industries, from nearly 60 percent to less than 43 percent, and a sharp increase in that of durable goods, from nearly 6 percent to more than 18 percent. The intermediate and capital goods groups experienced moderate increases, from 32 to 36 percent and from 2.2 to 3.2 percent, respectively.

A representative component of the nondurable group is the textile industry, the leading sector before World War II. Between 1949 and 1960, its share in the value added by industry as a whole experienced a sharp decline, from 20.1 percent to 11.6 percent. In the durable goods group, the component with the most significant change was the transport equipment sector (automobiles and trucks), which increased from 2.3 percent to 10.5 percent.

The lower increases in the shares of the intermediate and capital goods industries reflect the lesser priority attributed to them by the import-substitution industrialization strategy. In the early 1960s, Brazil already had a fairly diversified industrial structure, but one in which vertical integration was only beginning. Thus, instead of alleviating the balance of payments problems, import substitution increased them dramatically.

Stagnation and Spectacular Growth, 1962–80

Stagnation, 1962–67

As a result of the problems associated with import-substitution industrialization and the reforms introduced by the military regime after March 1964, the Brazilian economy lost much of its dynamism between 1962 and 1967. The average rate of growth of GDP in the period declined to 4.0 percent and that of industry to 3.9 percent. In part, stagnation resulted from distortions caused by the strategy. Moreover, political troubles negatively affected expectations and precluded the formation of a coalition to back the introduction of tough measures to control inflation and the balance of payments crisis. Political troubles also hindered the removal of obstacles to growth.

The 1964 coup dealt with the political obstacles by forcefully restraining opposition to the military agenda of change. With the objective of transforming Brazil into a modern capitalist economy and a military power, the regime implemented a series of reforms aimed at reducing inflation, at removing some of the distortions of import-substitution industrialization, and at modernizing capital markets. The regime gradually introduced incentives to direct investment, domestic and foreign, and tackled balance of payments problems by reforming and simplifying the foreign-exchange system. In addition, the regime introduced a mechanism of periodic devaluations of the cruzeiro, taking into account inflation. Finally, the military government adopted measures to attract foreign capital and to promote exports. It took steps to expand public investment to improve the country's infrastructure and later to develop state-owned basic industries.

Spectacular Growth, 1968–73

The post-1964 reforms and other policies of the military government, together with the state of the world economy, created conditions for very rapid growth between 1968 and 1973. In that period, the average annual rate of growth of GDP jumped to 11.1 percent, led by industry with a 13.1 percent average. Within industry, the leading sectors were consumer durables (see Glossary), transportation equipment, and basic industries, such as steel, cement, and electricity generation.

As a result of the post-1964 policies, external trade expanded substantially faster than the economy as a whole. There was a significant growth in exports, especially manufactured goods, but also commodities. Yet, imports grew considerably faster, rapidly increasing the trade deficit. This did not present a problem, however, because massive inflows of capital resulted in balance of payments surpluses.

The external sector contributed substantially to high growth rates, as did the rapid expansion of investment, including a growing share of public investment and investment by state-controlled enterprises. In addition, increased demand for automobiles, durable and luxury goods, and housing resulted from a rapid growth in income for the upper income strata and from credit plans created for consumers and homebuyers by the capital-market reforms.

The industrial sector generally experienced not only rapid growth but also considerable modernization. As a result, imports of capital goods and basic and semiprocessed inputs increased sharply. The share of intermediate goods imports in total imports increased from 31.0 percent in the 1960–62 period to 42.7 percent in 1972, and that of capital goods, from 29.0 to 42.2 percent. The total value of imports rose from US$1.3 billion to US$4.4 billion.

A comparison of the 1960 and the 1975 shares of the various industrial sectors in total value added by industry reveals a continuation in the relative decline of nondurable industries, notably textiles, food products, and beverages, and an increase in machinery, from 3.2 to 10.3 percent. The relative shares of most of the remaining industries, however, did not change significantly in the period.

As a result of the period's outward-looking development strategy, Brazil's industrial exports increased from US$1.4 billion in 1963 to US$6.2 billion in 1973. The composition of exports shows that whereas in 1963 processed and semiprocessed manufactured exports accounted for only 5 percent of total exports, in 1974 their share had reached 29 percent.

In the 1968–73 period, personal income became more concentrated and regional disparities became greater. Industrial expansion took place more vigorously in the Center-South Region, which had benefited most from the import-substitution industrialization strategy. Its per capita income considerably exceeded the national average, its infrastructure was more developed, and it had an adequate supply of skilled workers and professionals. The region was therefore able to take advantage of the opportunities and incentives offered by the military regime. Although a special regional development strategy existed for the Northeast, it promoted a distorted industrialization that benefited only a few of that region's large cities; the Northeast's linkages with the Center-South were stronger than its linkages within the region. The combination of a harsh climate, a highly concentrated land-tenure system, and an elite that consistently resisted meaningful change prevented the Northeast from developing effectively.

Growth with Debt, 1974–80

Brazil suffered drastic reductions in its terms of trade as a result of the 1973 oil shock. In the early 1970s, the performance of the export sector was undermined by an overvalued currency. With the trade balance under pressure, the oil shock led to a sharply higher import bill. Under such circumstances, a prudent course of action would have been to devalue the cruzeiro and to adopt growth-reducing policies in order to contain imports. However, Brazil opted to continue a high-growth policy. Furthermore, it adopted renewed strategies of import-substitution industrialization and of economic diversification. In the mid-1970s, the regime began implementing a development plan aimed at increasing self-sufficiency in many sectors and creating new comparative advantages (see Glossary). Its main components were to promote import substitution of basic industrial inputs (steel, aluminum, fertilizers, petrochemicals), to make large investments in the expansion of the economic infrastructure, and to promote exports.

This strategy was effective in promoting growth, but it also raised Brazil's import requirements markedly, increasing the already large current-account deficit. The current account (see Glossary) was financed by running up the foreign debt. The expectation was that the combined effects of import-substitution industrialization and export expansion eventually would bring about growing trade surpluses, allowing the service and repayment of the foreign debt.

Thus, despite the world recession resulting from other countries' adjustments to the oil shock, Brazil was able to maintain a high growth rate. Between 1974 and 1980, the average annual rate of growth of real GDP reached 6.9 percent and that of industry, 7.2 percent. However, the current-account deficit increased from US$1.7 billion in 1973 to US$12.8 billion in 1980 (see table 5, Appendix). The foreign debt rose from US$6.4 billion in 1963 to nearly US$54 billion in 1980.

Brazil was able to raise its foreign debt because, at the time, the international financial system was awash in petrodollars and was eagerly offering low-interest loans. By the end of the 1970s, however, the foreign debt had reached high levels. Additionally, the marked increase of international interest rates raised the debt service (see Glossary), forcing the country to borrow more only to meet interest payments (see table 6, Appendix). Productive capacity, exports, and the substitution of imports in various sectors expanded and became more diversified. However, the expected impacts on Brazil's current account were not to materialize until the mid-1980s.

Another feature of the 1974–80 period was an acceleration of inflation. Between 1968 and 1974, the rate of inflation had declined steadily, but afterward the trend was reversed. From 16.2 percent a year in 1973, the growth rate of the general price index (GPI—see Glossary) increased to 110.2 percent a year by 1980.

Stagnation, Inflation, and Crisis, 1981–94

The effect of the 1974–85 period's industrialization on the balance of trade was significant. The balance of trade moved from an average deficit of US$3.4 billion in the 1974–76 period to an average surplus of US$10.7 billion in the 1983–85 period. In 1985 the share of manufactures (processed and semiprocessed) of total exports reached 66 percent, and between 1971–75 and 1978–83 the share of basic input imports in total imports declined from 32.3 percent to 19.2 percent. The reces-

Loading soy beans and coffee onto a freighter for export,
Paranaguá State
Courtesy Inter-American Development Bank, Washington

sion and stagnation of the early 1980s had a role in reducing imports. However, import substitution was also important, as demonstrated by the few years of the 1980s that experienced a significant growth in GDP while the trade surplus was maintained.

Between 1981 and 1992, the GDP increased at an average annual rate of only 1.4 percent and per capita income declined 6 percent. Gross investment, as a proportion of GDP, fell from 21 to 16 percent, in part as a result of the fiscal crisis and the loss of public-sector investment capacity. The decline also reflected growing uncertainties regarding the future of the economy. The 1980s became known as the "lost decade," and its problems spilled over into the 1990s. Despite the stagnation of the 1981–92 period, inflation remained a major problem. It sometimes reached very high rates, prompting the implementation of short-lived shock-stabilization programs.

The 1981–84 Period

In 1979 a second oil shock nearly doubled the price of imported oil to Brazil and lowered the terms of trade further.

The rise in world interest rates increased sharply Brazil's balance of payments problem and the size of the foreign debt. Nevertheless, the government continued borrowing, mainly to face an increasing debt burden, while it tried vainly to maintain the high-growth strategy. At the beginning of the 1980s, however, the foreign-debt problem became acute, leading to the introduction of a program to generate growing trade surpluses in order to service the foreign debt. The program was achieved by reducing growth and, with it, imports, and by expanding exports. As a result, in 1981 real GDP declined by 4.4 percent. The 1982 Mexican debt crisis ended Brazil's access to international financial markets, increasing the pressure for economic adjustment.

The austerity program imposed by the International Monetary Fund (IMF—see Glossary) in late 1979 continued until 1984, but substantial trade surpluses were obtained only from 1983 on, largely as a delayed result of the import-substitution industrialization programs of the 1970s and the reduction in imports brought about by economic decline. The austerity program enabled Brazil to meet interest payments on the debt, but at the price of economic decline and increasing inflation.

Inflation accelerated as a result of a combination of factors: the exchange-rate devaluations of the austerity program, a growing public deficit, and an increasing indexation (see Glossary) of financial balances, wages, and other values for inflation. The first two factors are classical causes of inflation; the last became an important mechanism for propagating inflation and in preventing the usual instruments of inflation control from operating.

By the mid-1980s, domestic debt nearly displaced foreign debt as Brazil's main economic problem. During the high-growth 1970s, a significant portion of foreign borrowing had been by state enterprises, which were the main actors in the import-substitution industrialization strategy. Initially, they borrowed to finance their investments. However, toward the end of the decade, with the acute shortage of foreign exchange, the government forced state enterprises to borrow unnecessarily, increasing their indebtedness markedly. Their situation worsened with the sharp rise in international interest rates in the late 1970s, the devaluations of the austerity program, and the decreasing real prices of goods and services provided by the public enterprises stemming from price controls. Because the state enterprises were not allowed to go bankrupt, their debt burden was transferred gradually to the government, further increasing the public debt. This, and a growing disorganization of the public sector, transformed the public debt into a major economic problem. By the mid-1980s, the financial burden stemming from the debt was contributing decisively to its rapid expansion.

The 1985–89 Period

During the second half of the 1980s, it became increasingly clear that a large-scale fiscal reform, one that enabled noninflationary financing of the public sector, was needed not only to control inflation but also to restore the public sector's capacity to invest. Both were essential for an economic recovery. However, political obstacles prevented the reform from materializing. And, because inflation had become the most visible symptom of the public-sector disequilibrium, there were several attempts to bring inflation under control through what came to be known as "heterodox economic shocks." The period saw three such shocks: the Cruzado Plan (1986), the Bresser Plan (1987), and the Summer Plan (1989).

The objective of the Cruzado Plan was to eliminate inflation with a dramatic blow. Between 1980 and 1985, the rise in the GPI had escalated from 86.3 percent to 248.5 percent annually. Early in 1986, the situation became desperate, prodding the implementation of the plan. Its main measures were a general price freeze, a wage readjustment and freeze, readjustment and freeze on rents and mortgage payments, a ban on indexation, and a freeze on the exchange rate.

The plan's immediate results were spectacular: the monthly rate of inflation fell close to zero, economic growth surged upward, and the foreign accounts remained under control. However, by the end of 1986 the plan was in trouble. The wage adjustments were too large, increasing aggregate demand excessively and creating inflationary pressures. Moreover, the price freeze was maintained for too long, creating distortions and leading to shortages of a growing number of products. The plan could have been rescued if adjustments had been made at crucial moments. Instead, inflation accelerated again, and there was a return of indexation.

The two other stabilization plans amounted to renewed attempts at bringing inflation down from very high levels. It was soon clear that without a thorough reform of the public sector, controlling inflation would be impossible. Both plans introduced a price freeze and eliminated indexation, but there were differences between them, and with the Cruzado Plan. Neither was able to address the public-sector disequilibrium effectively. The objective of the Summer Plan, for instance, was mainly to avoid hyperinflation in an election year.

In fact, the public-sector disequilibrium became virtually locked in as a result of the 1988 constitution, which created advantages for various segments of society without indicating how these advantages would be paid for. Moreover, it transferred large portions of the tax revenues from the federal government to state and municipal governments, without requiring them to provide additional public services. With less revenue and more responsibility, the federal accounts experienced growing deficits. In addition, several subsidies were locked into the legislation. These factors and the financial burden of the public debt meant growing problems of public finance.

The 1980s ended with high and accelerating inflation and a stagnant economy, which never recovered after the demise of the Cruzado Plan. The public debt was enormous, and the government was required to pay very high interest rates to persuade the public to continue to buy government debt instruments (see also Trade Policies, this ch.).

The 1990–94 Period

The first post-military-regime president elected by popular suffrage, Fernando Collor de Mello (1990–92), was sworn into office in March 1990. Facing imminent hyperinflation and a virtually bankrupt public sector, the new administration introduced a stabilization plan, together with a set of reforms, aimed at removing restrictions on free enterprise, increasing competition, privatizing public enterprises, and boosting productivity.

Heralded as a definitive blow to inflation, the stabilization plan was drastic. It imposed an eighteen-month freeze on all but a small portion of the private sector's financial assets, froze prices, and again abolished indexation. The new administration also introduced provisional taxes to deal with the fiscal crisis, and took steps to reform the public sector by closing several public agencies and dismissing public servants. These measures were expected not only to swiftly reduce inflation but also to lower inflationary expectations.

However, few of the new administration's programs succeeded. Major difficulties with the stabilization and reform programs were caused in part by the superficial nature of many of the administration's actions and by its inability to secure political support. Moreover, the stabilization plan failed because of management errors coupled with defensive actions by segments of society that would be most directly hurt by the plan.

After falling more than 80 percent in March 1990, the GPI's monthly rate of growth began increasing again. The best that could be achieved was to stabilize the GPI at a high and slowly rising level. In January 1991, it rose by 19.9 percent, reaching 32 percent a month by July 1993. Simultaneously, political instability increased sharply, with negative impacts on the economy. The real GDP declined 4.0 percent in 1990, increased only 1.1 percent in 1991, and again declined 0.9 percent in 1992 (see table 7, Appendix).

President Collor de Mello was impeached in September 1992 on charges of corruption. Vice President Itamar Franco was sworn in as president (1992–94), but he had to grapple to form a stable cabinet and to gather political support. The weakness of the interim administration prevented it from tackling inflation effectively. In 1993 the economy grew again, but with inflation rates higher than 30 percent a month, the chances of a durable recovery appeared to be very slim. At the end of the year, it was widely acknowledged that without serious fiscal reform, inflation would remain high and the economy would not sustain growth. This acknowledgment and the pressure of rapidly accelerating inflation finally jolted the government into action. The president appointed a determined minister of finance, Fernando Henrique Cardoso, and a high-level team was put in place to develop a new stabilization plan. Implemented early in 1994, the plan met little public resistance because it was discussed widely and it avoided price freezes.

The stabilization program had three stages: the introduction of an equilibrium budget mandated by the National Congress (Congresso Nacional; hereafter, Congress); a process of general indexation (prices, wages, taxes, contracts, and financial assets); and the introduction of a new currency, the *real* (for value of the *real* (R$)—see Glossary), pegged to the dollar. The legally enforced balanced budget would remove expectations regarding inflationary behavior by the public sector. By allowing a realignment of relative prices, general indexation would pave the way for monetary reform. Once this realignment was achieved, the new currency would be introduced, accompanied by appropriate policies (especially the control of expenditures through high interest rates and the liberalization of trade to increase competition and thus prevent speculative behavior).

By the end of the first quarter of 1994, the second stage of the stabilization plan was being implemented. Economists of different schools of thought considered the plan sound and technically consistent.

The Labor Force and Income Levels

Substantial growth and structural transformations raised Brazil's per capita income from the low-income range in the late 1950s to the upper middle-income range in 1980. Despite the economic problems of the 1980s, per capita income remained in the upper middle-income range. Structural change had an important effect on employment and earnings and on income distribution and poverty.

Employment and Earnings

Employment

Since World War II, the level of employment in Brazil has coincided generally with the expansion of the country's labor force. However, there have been considerable changes in the occupational structure (see fig. 7). The period from 1950 to 1970 witnessed slow growth in agricultural employment and a rapid increase in typically urban occupations, notably commerce and services but also industry (manufacturing, construction, and mining). The period from 1970 to 1980 was one of very rapid growth in employment, led by industry, resulting from a decade of marked economic expansion. The period between 1980 and 1990 saw an expansion of employment, led by segments of the services sector, despite the sluggish economy.

In the 1950–70 phase, the employed population went from 17.1 million people to 29.6 million, increasing at a 2.7 percent annual rate, similar to the rate of population growth. This expansion was led by the services sector, with 4.6 percent annual growth. Industrial employment also expanded significantly, with 3.9 percent annual growth. However, industrial labor expansion was quite a bit slower than the sector's growth in real product in the period (7.9 percent annually). In turn, employment in the primary sector experienced only a small increase of 1.3 percent annually, much less than the sector's growth in real product in the period (4.5 percent annually). In the 1950s and 1960s, the output elasticity (see Glossary) of employment was very small, not only for agriculture but also for industry, the economy's dynamic sector.

The share of agriculture in total employment fell from almost 60 percent in 1950 to 44.3 percent in 1970, that of the industrial sector increased from 14.2 percent to 17.9 percent, and that of the services sector increased from 25.9 percent to 37.8 percent. Another change in the period was the increase in the number of women in the labor force, from 13.6 to 18.5 percent. The male participation rate declined from 80.8 to 71.8 percent.

The 1970–80 period saw very rapid economic expansion. In the 1970s, GDP grew 8.7 percent annually; industry, 9.5 percent; and agriculture, 4.4 percent. In the same period, the employed population increased 3.9 percent annually, from 29.6 million to 43.9 million persons. This time, the expansion in total employment was led by industry, with a 6.7 percent annual growth rate. The services sector's labor force grew 5.9 percent annually. As a result of conservative modernization, agriculture's labor force experienced a small reduction, from 13.3 million persons in 1970 to 13.0 million in 1980.

By 1980 the share of agricultural employment had fallen to 30.1 percent, that of industry had increased to 23.9 percent, and that of the services sector, to 46.0 percent. The number of women in the labor force continued to increase, from 18.5 percent in 1970 to 27.4 percent in 1980; the male participation rate changed little, from 71.8 to 72.4 percent.

During the 1980–90 period, total employment increased, despite the sluggish economy. Between 1981 and 1990, the average rate of GDP growth was only 1.6 percent annually; industry averaged only 0.5 percent annual growth; agriculture, 2.6 percent; and the services sector, 2.7 percent. Total employment, however, increased 2.8 percent annually, from 43.9 million to 62.1 million persons. The average rate of unemployment in the period jumped from around 4 percent in the still prosperous years of 1979 and 1980 to more than 6 percent (average for the nine major metropolitan regions) in the depressed 1981–84 period; thereafter, it declined, falling to

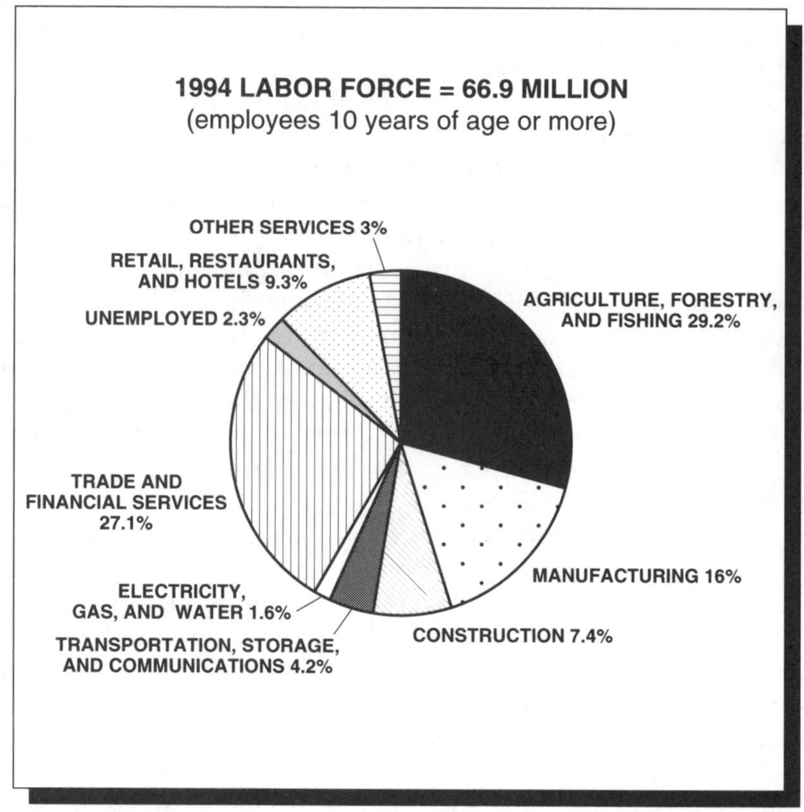

Source: Based on information from Economist Intelligence Unit, *Country Profile: Brazil, 1994–95* [London], 1995, 22, citing International Labour Organisation, *Yearbook of Labour Statistics.*

Figure 7. Employment by Sector, 1994

3.6 percent in 1986. However, even with the return of stagnation, open unemployment increased only slightly.

Despite a decline of 4.0 percent in GDP, the unemployment rate was only 4.3 percent in 1990, as opposed to 7.9 percent in 1981. Meanwhile, an extensive informal economy (see Glossary) expanded, acting as a cushion and absorbing a growing number of people that the formal sector failed to employ. The informal sector included not only large numbers of street vendors, peddlers, and providers of petty services but also large numbers of middle-class workers as artisans, self-employed agents, and backyard business operators. Moreover, established businesses used the informal sector as a means of avoiding taxes, increased regulations, and the costs associated with being registered as employed.

Brazil lacks precise data on informal-sector employment, but there are indications of its expansion since 1980. For instance, between 1980 and 1990 the share of employees in the total employed urban labor force fell from 78.7 percent to 74.6 percent, and the share of the self-employed (many in the informal sector) rose from 17.2 percent to 19.1 percent. Furthermore, the proportion of workers with formal labor contracts declined considerably in most urban economic segments. This was certainly true in areas where the informal sector traditionally has prevailed, such as personal services, entertainment, construction, and commerce; but, it was also true in the more organized sectors, such as manufacturing.

In the 1990–92 period, the economy deteriorated further, with a 1.3 percent annual decline in GDP and 4.1 percent decline in industrial output. Agriculture grew only 1.5 percent, and the services sector, only 0.4 percent annually. The overall unemployment rate increased from 3.4 percent in 1989 to 4.3 percent in 1990, 4.2 percent in 1991, and 5.8 percent in 1992. The labor absorption by the informal sector continued to be large and highly visible.

In 1992 the share of agriculture in the country's employed labor was 9.4 percent and that of industry, 16.0 percent. As a result of the swollen informal sector, employment in the services sector increased to 57.4 percent. The female participation rate continued to increase, from 27.4 percent in 1980 to 38.9 percent in 1990. In 1990 women made up 35.5 percent of the labor force compared with 15 percent in 1950. The male participation rate increased from 72.4 to 75.3 percent between 1980 and 1990.

Earnings

There are two constants regarding earnings in Brazil since World War II: the very low wages of unskilled labor and the wide disparity in the wage scale. An indication of the low wage levels for unskilled labor is the minimum wage. In 1961 the monthly minimum wage averaged only US$113.30 (in 1986 dollars). The index of the average real minimum wage exhibits a clear downward trend (see table 8, Appendix). The 1991 real average monthly minimum wage was less than one-third of the already low 1961 minimum wage.

It is interesting to observe the impact of recession and particularly inflation on the real minimum wage. The two periods of swift decline in the real minimum wage were characterized by recession and by a rapidly accelerating inflation. This was true in the 1961–65 period and especially so between 1982 and 1991. The prosperity and comparatively low inflation of the 1970s (notably during the first half of the decade) did not bring about a stronger recovery of the real value of the minimum wage only because of the repressive wage policy adopted by the military regime.

The 1990 household survey revealed that 30.8 percent (some 19.9 million persons) of the employed population earned one minimum wage or less. Even allowing for underestimations of earnings by the household surveys, the numbers living with very low wages in Brazil are indeed large.

Organized labor, which has substantially larger average earnings, has obtained considerable gains since the late 1970s. These gains are reflected in the index of average real wage in São Paulo, the core of the country's modern industrial sector. The index evolved from a level of 100 in 1978 to 125.1 in 1982, declined to 112.9 in 1983, but jumped to 175.9 in prosperous 1986. After this it decreased somewhat, reaching 165.9 in 1990 and 158.4 in 1992.

As for the disparity in the wage scale, according to the 1990 household survey, in September of that year 10.8 percent of the employed work force, or 6.5 million persons, earned one-half of a minimum wage, a monthly average of US$299; 49.2 percent of the employed work force, or 29.8 million persons, received two minimum wages or less. At the other extreme, 7.8 percent of the employed work force received more than ten minimum wages, a monthly average of US$1,941; 3.2 percent, or 1.9 million persons, earned more than twenty minimum wages, or a monthly average of US$4,000. In that year, more than 60 percent of the employed labor force earned less than the average monthly earnings of US$211.

Moreover, data on the distribution of monthly earnings reveal that the distributive disparity has increased over time. In 1960 the poorest 10 percent of the employed labor force with earnings received 1.9 percent of the total earnings, but in 1990 their share was only 0.8 percent. At the other extreme, the richest 10 percent increased their share of total earnings from 39.6 percent in 1960 to 44.1 percent in 1990.

Inequality and Poverty

Income inequality in Brazil has a personal and a regional dimension. The highly concentrated distribution of income worsened in the 1960 to 1990 period. The Gini coefficient (see Glossary) for the country as a whole increased from 0.50 in 1960 to 0.56 in 1970, 0.59 in 1980, and 0.63 in 1990. The 1990 coefficient means that the richest 5 percent of the population received 36.6 percent of the national income, while the poorest 40 percent received only 7.2 percent. Moreover, the pattern of income distribution was similar in all of Brazil's five regions. In 1988 the South had the lowest Gini coefficient (0.58) and the Northeast had the highest (0.64). The difference is not remarkable; inequality is pervasive.

A substantial number of Brazilians are poor because Brazil has a large population, a medium-range income per capita (as compared with the United States, which is in the high range), and a high level of inequality. Estimates indicate that in 1990 almost a third of Brazil's total population, or 39.1 million persons, were poor. Approximately half of these poor lived in rural areas and half in urban areas. In relative terms, however, the proportion of the urban poor (22.5 percent) was substantially lower than that of the rural poor (50.1 percent). The rural to urban migration since 1950 markedly reduced the rural population, but it did not improve the lot of those who remained behind.

As for regional inequality, in 1991 the more developed Southeast and South regions, which occupy 17.6 percent of Brazil's total territory, had 58.7 percent of the total population and generated 74.3 percent of the country's GDP (in 1985). By contrast, the poverty-stricken Northeast, which occupies 18.3 percent of the total area, had 28.5 percent of the total population and generated only 13.1 percent of Brazil's 1985 GDP. The huge North (Norte) and Center-West (Centro-Oeste) regions, which occupy 64.1 percent of Brazil's total area, had 12.8 percent of the total population and generated 12.6 percent of Brazil's 1985 GDP. The Southeast had the largest urbanization rate (88.3 percent in 1991); the Northeast had the second largest proportion of the population in rural areas (41.6 percent in 1991), slightly below that of the frontier North (43.9 percent).

As a result of the economic boom, Brazil's per capita income experienced a marked increase in the 1970s, from US$1,253 to US$2,266; in the stagnant 1980s, it declined, reaching US$2,154 in 1990. In 1970 the per capita income of the Southeast exceeded the national average by 53.2 percent, while that of the Northeast was 44.4 percent lower. This discrepancy has declined, but only marginally: in 1988 the per capita income of the Southeast was 43.6 percent higher than the national average, and that of the Northeast was 37.5 percent lower. Of Brazil's 39.1 million poor in 1990, 53.1 percent were in the Northeast and 25.4 percent were in the prosperous Southeast. In the Northeast, the majority of the poor lived in rural areas, while in the Southeast the largest portion of the poor lived in cities.

Brazil's major urban areas warrant examination, given the large and growing number of urban poor. In 1991 nine Metropolitan Regions (MRs), including Belém, in the North; Fortaleza, Recife, and Salvador in the Northeast; Belo Horizonte, Rio de Janeiro, and São Paulo in the Southeast; and Curitiba and Porto Alegre in the South, had a combined population of 42.7 million people, almost one-third of Brazil's total population. The smallest MR, Belém in the Amazon, had 1.3 million inhabitants, and the largest, São Paulo, had more than 15 million inhabitants. The three largest MRs were in the Southeast. They had a combined population of 28.6 million, nearly 67 percent of the total metropolitan population and almost 20 percent of Brazil's total population. The four MRs in the North/Northeast had a combined population of 9.0 million—a large number for an underdeveloped or frontier area. The South's two MRs had a combined population of 5.0 million.

The metropolitan Gini coefficients for 1970 and 1988 show that all the MRs except for Curitiba experienced a deterioration in income distribution. The coefficients for 1988 also show that the distribution of income was worse in the Northeast MRs and better in São Paulo and in the two Southern MRs, but the differences were not large.

The metropolitan average household real income shows that all MRs, except for Rio de Janeiro, had increases between 1970 and 1988. In 1970 and in 1988, the average household incomes of the North-Northeast MRs were significantly lower than those of the Southeast-South. However, the gap between the two groups has declined somewhat. In 1970 the average household income of Fortaleza (the MR with the lowest average) was only 36.6 percent of that of São Paulo (with the highest average); in 1988 this average had increased to 53.3 percent. This does not mean that the Northeast MRs were prospering. Rather, it means that São Paulo, flooded with migrants, had a sharp increase in the number of households, moderating the rise in its average household income.

Estimates indicate that in 1990 the nine MRs had a combined total number of poor of almost 12.3 million people, or 28.9 percent of the total population of the MRs. São Paulo and Rio de Janeiro had the largest absolute number of poor (over 3 million, or nearly 24 percent of the total MR poor each), but the highest levels of urban poverty were in the MRs of the North/Northeast.

In 1989 the proportion of the poor unemployed was 11 percent, while that of the rest of the work force was only 3 percent. The proportion of the poor employed in informal occupations was 38 percent, while that of the remaining population was 26 percent (still quite a high percentage). And, the proportion of poor children, age seven to fourteen, out of school was 14 percent, while that of the nonpoor was only 6 percent.

Structure of Production

The growth and diversification that took place after World War II brought considerable changes to the productive structure of the Brazilian economy. The share of the agricultural sector in GDP declined from 24.3 percent in 1950 to 11 percent in 1993. In the same 1950 to 1993 period, the share of industry increased from 24.1 percent to 29 percent, if this sector includes manufacturing, mining, and construction (see fig. 8). The share of agriculture in total employment dropped from 62 percent in 1950 to 29.2 percent in 1994, and that of services increased from 25 to 43.6 percent. (Taking into account the informal economy, the services sector totaled 56 percent of GDP in 1993, depending on the source of information.) Yet, despite the industrialization that took place, the share of industry in total employment increased only from 13 to 23.4 percent between 1950 and 1994.

Agriculture

When examining the behavior of the agricultural sector in the postwar years, it is possible to identify two distinct periods: horizontal (geographical) expansion from 1949 to 1969 and conservative modernization, from 1970 to the present. In the immediate postwar years, Brazilian agriculture included an export sector that relied heavily on coffee but also on cotton, sugar, and a few minor commodities, and a semisubsistence

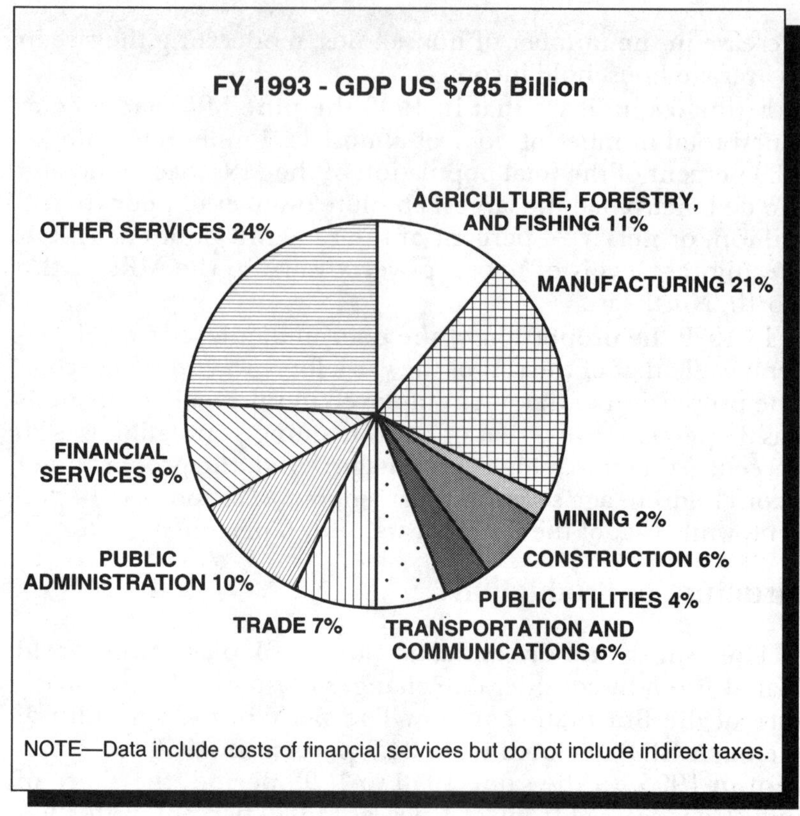

Source: Based on information from Fundação Instituto Brasileiro de Geografia e Estatística, *Anuário estatístico do Brasil 1993*, Rio de Janeiro, 1993, Annex supplement, table with data for 1993.

Figure 8. Gross Domestic Product (GDP) by Sector, 1993

sector that produced for the domestic market. At the time, the country's population, its per capita income, and its urban sector did not yet impose a large demand on the agricultural sector. With import-substitution industrialization, however, the situation changed drastically. This particular industrialization strategy required that the agricultural sector generate most of the economy's foreign exchange, produce growing outputs of food and some industrial inputs, and transfer resources for import-substitution industrialization. The transfer mechanism was a tax on the foreign exchange earned by coffee exports and the persistent implicit taxation of agriculture. The virtual exclusion of many agricultural products from the world market was caused by the highly overvalued cruzeiro, which resulted from this strategy. Consequently, the cheap domestic food policy that prevailed depressed prices in favor of the urban-industrial sector.

Paradoxically, the overall performance of agriculture during the horizontal expansion period was adequate. Agricultural GDP increased 4.2 percent a year between 1949 and 1969, a considerably higher growth rate than that of the population; between 1950 and 1959, food production increased 5.4 percent a year, and the production of exportables rose 4.1 percent annually. A major factor in this performance was horizontal expansion, that is, the incorporation of new land, especially along the agricultural frontier, made possible by an aggressive policy of road construction (see Frontier Expansion That Shaped Brazil, ch. 1). Moreover, the disincentives of the import-substitution industrialization policies were circumvented by maintaining ample access to land at concessionary terms for the landowning elite and for commercial farmers, reproducing a pattern established early in the colonial period.

By the late 1960s, it was clear that horizontal growth of agriculture was reaching its limits rapidly and that increases in productivity would be essential for a continued expansion of production. Moreover, the growth strategy of the military regime required a fast expansion of exports, including agricultural commodities. Thus, the government implemented a conservative modernization strategy consisting of technical change for a restricted number of subsectors and incentives for the formation of agribusiness complexes.

Technical change involved the development and adaptation of green-revolution technologies, geared mainly toward large agricultural operations that had important roles for mechanization and chemical inputs. Regarding the agribusiness complexes, the government provided strong incentives for the creation and expansion of processing industries and for the development and modernization of agricultural input industries. Moreover, the agricultural phase of the soymeal and oil, instant coffee, processed beef, poultry, orange juice, and sugar and alcohol agribusiness complexes received subsidized credit, guaranteed prices, and tax exemptions and subsidies when exported. Traditional, unprocessed, agricultural products, however, were subjected to heavy taxation and to price and other controls. As in the import-substitution industrialization phase, the production of cheap food was required, but only recently have government policies begun specifically to address this need.

Products benefiting from agricultural modernization responded well to the conservative modernization strategy. Their production methods underwent considerable technical change, and their production and yields increased markedly. Traditional products, however, failed to modernize and tended to perform poorly. They had scant access to credit and to the price-support policy. Moreover, they were frequently subjected to price controls, to a maze of regulations and export restrictions and quotas, and to competition from subsidized imports when they failed to supply the domestic market adequately.

At the beginning of the 1990s, the main crops in the modern segment were cocoa, cotton, rice, sugarcane, oranges, corn, soybeans, and wheat; those in the traditional segment included beans, manioc (cassava), bananas, peanuts, and coffee (see table 9, Appendix). Brazil is also one of the largest exporters of guavas, lemons, mangoes, passion fruit, tangerines, and tobacco. Crop production between 1970 and 1990 shows that the components of the modern segment grew considerably, both in production and in yield, while those of the traditional segment stagnated or declined. The growth in export crops allowed Brazil to become one of the world's largest soybean producers and to earn needed foreign exchange. It also allowed the substitution of sugarcane alcohol for imported oil.

Livestock

Brazil's livestock sector went through a similar process of selective modernization. Until the early 1970s, it remained quite backward; its expansion relied chiefly on the incorporation of more land and animals into production. Following the expansion of agribusiness complexes, livestock production processes also changed. However, major differences exist between the modern and the traditional segments of the beef-cattle, poultry, and swine subsectors—the country's main livestock subsectors.

Between 1970 and 1991, Brazil's beef-cattle herd grew at a 3.1 percent average yearly rate, from 78.5 million to 152.1 million head; the slaughter of beef-cattle increased from 9.6 million to 13.9 million head; and the total carcass weight increased from 1.8 million to 2.9 million tons. However, these numbers hide large regional differences (see table 11, Appendix). The beef-cattle industry in areas near the country's more developed core has experienced considerable modernization, interlocked with the expansion of a dynamic agribusiness sector, which supplies the industry with modern inputs and slaughters and processes its animals for domestic and world markets. As a result, Brazil's beef exports increased from 98,300 tons of chilled beef and 15,800 tons of processed beef in 1970, at a total value of US$298.6 million (in 1992 dollars), to 96,800 tons of chilled beef and 127,300 tons of processed beef in 1992, at a total value of US$618.1 million. A still substantial traditional beef-cattle industry can be found in the frontier areas or in the more backward parts of Brazil; its productivity remains very low, and it is plagued by serious sanitary and management problems.

The poultry subsector experienced spectacular improvements from 1970 to 1991, changing from a small, backyard-based production into a modern industry. This change is reflected in the fact that, while the poultry flock increased 2.8 times between 1970 and 1990, from 214.3 million to 594.3 million head, the total carcass weight of the fowl slaughtered commercially increased twenty-one times, from 85,400 to 1.8 million tons. Moreover, the export of poultry products, which in 1970 was negligible, in 1992 amounted to 378,000 tons, representing a total value of US$455.6 million. The transformation of the poultry subsector into a modern industry was achieved through the development of agribusiness complexes. These modern enterprises play a central role; they provide farmers with inputs, with genetic material, and with technical assistance, in addition to buying the finished poultry from the farmers.

As for pork, the swine herd increased only 33.9 percent between 1970 and 1991, from 25.6 million to 34.3 million animals. However, a small portion of this subsector experienced considerable changes, also induced by agribusiness. Until the early 1990s, the Brazilian swine herd was composed overwhelmingly of mixed breeds of low-quality, lard-producing animals. Moreover, the management of the herd was primitive, and poor sanitation was a problem. The growing modern segment of the pork industry has a high-quality herd of meat-producing animals. Management practices have improved considerably, and there is a similar interaction between farmers and commercial and industrial enterprises.

Fishing

With the exception of a few specialized subsectors geared to the world market, such as lobster fishing, Brazil's fishing industry has not developed well, despite the fiscal incentives it received during the 1970s. Even the specialized subsectors, including fish, crustaceans, and mollusks, only increased from 526,300 tons in 1970 to 798,600 tons in 1989.

In Brazil fishing is undertaken by businesses employing fairly modern equipment, and by thousands of independent fishermen spread along Brazil's immense coastal region. Independent fishermen employ primitive tools and fishing methods, producing for self-consumption and for sale in nearby markets. With some exceptions, the commercial segment has not expanded significantly, and in 1989 the production of fish and related catches amounted to a mere 5.3 kilograms per inhabitant.

Industry

After 1987 problems that had confronted industry earlier in the decade intensified, adverse macroeconomic conditions persisted, and political troubles affected expectations adversely. Until the end of the 1980s, industry relied heavily on government protection and favors, but it also faced pervasive regulations and extensive governmental interference. These factors had a deleterious effect on industrial investment and on the productivity of several industrial subsectors, increasingly blunting the competitive edge they had struggled to achieve in the world market. Moreover, as a result of the fiscal crisis, the government was hard-pressed to continue to provide support and subsidies for industry and to maintain and expand the country's infrastructure.

The Collor de Mello administration, inaugurated in 1990, introduced significant changes in Brazil's economic strategy. Regarding industry, the government implemented measures to eliminate regulations, to liberalize trade, and to markedly reduce governmental favors and subsidies. It also announced a series of actions aimed at increasing industry's competitiveness. Despite these efforts, political and macroeconomic difficulties prevented the effective implementation of the new strategy, and the mounting fiscal crisis dampened efforts to rebuild and improve the badly deteriorated infrastructure. Therefore, an important part of the industrial sector failed to recover and to modernize. With stagnation, the domestic market could not give industry a dynamic push. Moreover, the reduction in investment, coupled with the deteriorating infrastructure, led to declines in competitiveness. These developments, together with fewer import barriers, caused industry's balance of trade to decline, from a peak of US$16.3 billion in 1988 to US$11.1 billion in 1991. In the early 1990s, despite sectoral weaknesses, the industrial sector became a major contributor to the country's exports and trade surplus.

Mining

Since the early colonial period, expectations have loomed large about mineral riches hidden in Brazil's vast territory. However, the full extent of the country's mineral wealth is still unknown. Various efforts have been made to survey the country, one of which uncovered the Greater Carajás mineral province in the eastern Amazon (see fig. 9). Yet, at the beginning of the 1990s only 10 percent of the country's subsoil was known in sufficient detail. Correspondingly, the share of mining in GDP has increased but remains small; in 1950 it was only 0.4 percent, rising to 0.8 percent in 1970, to 1.0 percent in 1980, and to 2.5 percent in 1986, but declining to 1.5 percent in 1990.

The value of mineral production expanded from US$5.4 billion in 1980 to US$13.0 billion in 1990. However, only ten minerals—crude oil, iron, gold, calcium ore, natural gas, bauxite, phosphate, granite, cassiterite, and zinc—accounted for 85.5 percent of this total; crude oil alone accounted for 37.6 percent of the total, and both iron ore and gold accounted for 11.4 percent each. Apparently, the exploration of several other mineral substances has great potential, but such efforts have yet to be realized.

Advances in the early 1990s included the Greater Carajás project, which involves the production and export of iron ore, products of the bauxite-aluminum complex, and manganese, among other minerals. Overall, exports of mineral products expanded substantially, and there was a considerable import substitution of mineral inputs. In 1974 the trade balance of the mineral sector (primary, semiprocessed, and manufactured minerals) was a negative US$2.5 billion, and the deficit increased, reaching US$10.7 billion in 1980. However, by 1985 the deficit had declined to US$0.6 billion and thereafter the trade balance showed growing surpluses (US$1.1 billion in 1988, US$1.3 billion in 1989, and US$1.6 billion in 1990). This reversal was caused by an expansion of exports, especially of iron ore, products of the bauxite-aluminum complex, and

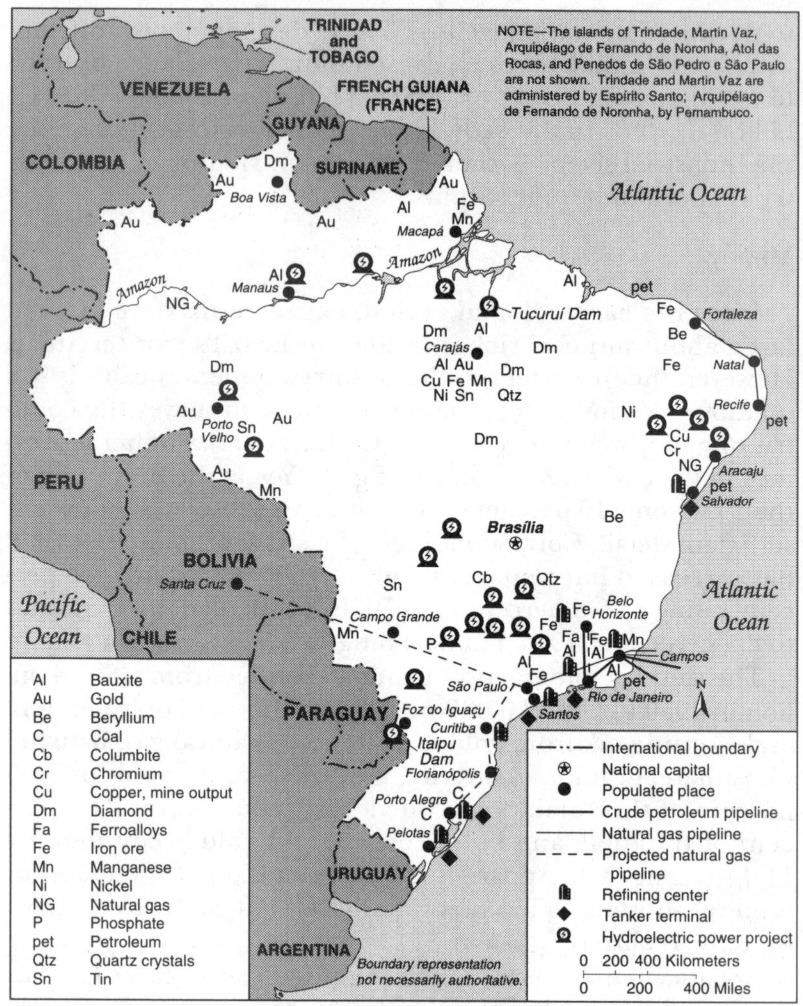

Source: Based on information from Orlando D. Martino, *Mineral Industries of Latin America*, Washington, 1988, 30; "Energy Map of Latin America," *Major Pipelines of the World* [London], 62, No. 3, March 1995; and "Amazonia: A World Resource at Risk," *National Geographic Magazine*, August 1992.

Figure 9. Petroleum, Natural Gas, Minerals, and Hydroelectric Resources, 1995

manganese, and to a significant extent by reductions in crude oil imports.

Brazil's mineral policy has been marked strongly by national security considerations. Until the early 1990s, foreign capital was mostly barred from the more attractive portions of the sector. Petroleum has been a state monopoly. Another state enterprise, the giant Rio Dôce Valley Company, Inc. (Companhia Vale do Rio Dôce—CVRD), has a large share of the iron ore deposits, and it has played an important role in the development of the bauxite-aluminum complex and of other minerals. CVRD is also a major railroad and shipping operator, by far Brazil's largest exporter, and its largest generator of foreign currency. In late 1994, foreign investment funds held about 10 percent of CVRD's stock. In 1995 there were still legal obstacles to foreign participation in Brazil's mineral sector.

Energy

The unfolding of Brazil's current difficulties in the energy arena constitutes a classic example of distortions arising from misdirected regulation combined with the action of interest groups. When import-substitution industrialization began in the early 1950s, the country's main sources of energy were firewood, charcoal, and bagasse (the dry residue from the processing of sugarcane). Because modern industrial expansion could not be based on these, a decision had to be made regarding the sources of energy to be used. Not surprisingly, electricity and petroleum products received special attention.

Electric Power

In 1950 Brazil's capacity to generate electricity was only 1.9 million kilowatts, and most of the required petroleum products had to be imported. An adequate supply of electric energy became critical, both for production and for a rapidly growing urban population. Petroleum requirements expanded quickly because of the decision to make the automobile industry the mainstay of import-substitution industrialization and because of the heavy reliance on trucks for short- and long-distance transportation. Ambitious road-building programs were implemented, and the domestic automobile industry quickly expanded the stock of motor vehicles, reaching 1.05 million units in 1960, 3.1 million units in 1970, and 10.8 million units in 1980.

Low electricity prices stemmed from the substitution policy and from the attempt to control inflation by restraining the increase in public-sector prices in nominal terms. Thus, the capacity of the electricity sector to generate resources for investment was affected considerably. As a result of federally induced borrowing in the late 1970s and early 1980s, the sector was also heavily indebted. Intermittent adjustments in electricity prices allowed the sector to generate profits and thus some resources for investment. However, on occasion, the government returned to the practice of manipulating consumer prices to contain inflation.

Although the federal treasury initially assumed many of the cost distortions of the energy policy, by the end of the 1980s the virtual bankruptcy of the public sector precluded this approach. In the early 1990s, the government implemented a series of measures to reduce its role. It introduced deregulation, market reforms, and privatization, but these reforms did not change the essence of the energy policy. Interest groups prevented the adoption of measures that would drastically alter the liquid combustible policy, and the agency controlling electric energy continued to lack resources for investments. Thus, the energy price structure was altered only marginally.

Low electricity prices induced a considerable substitution of electricity for other sources of energy and the expansion of electricity-intensive production, such as aluminum. The heavy investments in hydroelectricity of the 1970s and 1980s matured, creating a considerable generating capacity (50,500 million megawatts or 93.3 percent of the total generating capacity of electricity in 1993). One of the world's leading producers of hydroelectric power, Brazil has a potential of 106,500 to 127,868 megawatts, or, according to the *World Factbook 1996*, 55,130,000 kilowatts. The country's two largest operating hydroelectric power stations are the 12,600-megawatt Itaipu Dam, the world's largest dam, on the Rio Paraná in the South, and the Tucuruí Dam in Pará, in the North Region (see fig. 3).

In principle, an increase in the generating capacity for electricity should have been easy to achieve. Brazil has enormous hydroelectric potential, and investments in the sector were forthcoming, although with an initial delay. However, until 1995 nationalistic considerations excluded foreign capital from the electric energy sector, and regulatory obstacles prevented domestic private investment. The federal and state governments were therefore left with the task of expanding the generating capacity. As of the early 1990s, the government continued to control the sector's production end, as well as transmission and distribution, although privatization of the sector is under consideration.

Petroleum

The fast-growing requirements of petroleum and petroleum by-products were met initially by imports. However, foreign-exchange difficulties, coupled with strategic considerations, led to efforts to reduce the country's dependence on imports. In the early 1950s, the government granted a near monopoly of the exploration, production, refining, and transportation of oil to the Brazilian Petroleum Corporation (Petróleo Brasileiro S.A.—Petrobrás), the state-owned oil company, and made resources available for investments. Emphasis was placed on the expansion of a domestic refining capacity because world oil prices were low and no problems were envisaged with oil supply. Thus, an important refining sector developed gradually.

The oil crises of the 1970s placed Brazil in a vulnerable situation. In 1974 almost 80 percent of Brazil's total oil consumption was imported, and the increases in oil prices imposed a substantial burden on the country's balance of payments. Consequently, reducing dependence on imported energy, particularly petroleum, became the main objective of energy policy. This reduction was to be achieved by large investments in petroleum substitutes, notably electric energy and ethanol, and by a substantial expansion in the exploration and domestic production of petroleum. Although modest oil fields were not discovered until late in the 1970s, investments in the energy sector increased from around 10 percent of total investment in the early 1970s to a peak of 23.5 percent in 1982–83. As a proportion of GDP, investment in energy increased steadily, from 2.8 percent early in the 1970s, to a peak of 5.0 percent in 1982.

The government also implemented the energy price policy in reaction to the 1979 oil shock. The basic assumption was that the price of oil would remain at its high 1979 level. Thus, emphasis on promoting substitution was absolute. The problem, however, was that this emphasis did not change after oil prices began to decline. To encourage substitution, the government set energy prices. The price of gasoline was set at a high level, not only to reduce its use but also to finance Petrobrás's exploration effort and to subsidize other petroleum products. The prices of diesel fuel and propane (extensively used for cooking) were maintained artificially low, requiring subsidies. The low diesel price was intended to keep transportation costs from increasing sharply, and social arguments were used to justify the propane subsidy.

To induce the purchase of ethanol-propelled cars, the price of ethanol was maintained at 60 percent of that of gasoline. To finance this subsidy, a mixture of 20 percent of ethanol in the gasoline was established. The high gasoline prices exceeded the cost of ethanol, and the profits were used to cover the subsidy. Specially low prices for electric energy were established to encourage the replacement of fuel oil and other oil derivatives in production.

The combination of conservation and substitution, along with the expansion of domestic production, reduced the country's dependence on imported crude oil, from around 80 percent in the late 1970s to 45.6 percent in 1990. Domestic output of crude oil increased from an average 165,000 barrels a day in 1975 to some 800,100 barrels a day by 1996. By the end of 1995, Brazil's proven reserves had reached 4.8 billion barrels and potential reserves were at 8.8 billion barrels. About 64 percent of Brazil's domestic oil comes from the continental shelf in the Campos Basin, which accounts for 83 percent of proven reserves. The country's petroleum reserves may actually reach 20 billion barrels if as yet unproven discoveries in deep water off the Brazilian coast are included.

Despite these advances, however, the rigidity of the energy price policy brought about serious problems. The maintenance of the gasoline-ethanol price differential and other inducements led to a rapid increase in the purchase of ethanol-propelled automobiles and to a growing conversion of gasoline cars to ethanol. Moreover, the basic assumption that the price of oil would remain high was incorrect. Although world oil prices declined, the price policy remained in effect for ethanol producers, owners of ethanol-propelled cars, and the motor vehicle industry. Additionally, the real gasoline price was eroded gradually by the government's tendency to fight inflation by tampering with the prices of goods and services produced by the public sector. Also, the substitution of ethanol for gasoline caused a swift reduction in the sale of gasoline in the domestic market. Consequently, the profits Petrobrás obtained initially from gasoline dwindled quickly, and the company required assistance from the treasury for its exploration program and to cover various subsidies. The sharp increase in the use of diesel fuel for transportation, created by this fuel's subsidy, together with technical rigidities in refining, forced Petrobrás to produce much more gasoline than was required by the domestic market. This excess had to be sold abroad, often at

The 6 million-kilowatt Paulo Afonso Hydroelectric Project in Paulo Afonso, Bahia State
Courtesy Inter-American Development Bank, Washington

Transmission lines carrying electricity from the Paulo Afonso Hydroelectric Project past the town of Agua Verde, Ceará State
Courtesy Inter-American Development Bank, Washington

below-cost prices. Because the demand for diesel fuel continued to grow and the demand for gasoline to shrink, Petrobrás was forced to invest heavily in changing the product profile of its refineries. In the early 1990s, the government reduced the gasoline-ethanol price differential (in 1993 the price of ethanol was 78.4 percent of that of gasoline). The price of gasoline was maintained sufficiently high to prevent massive subsidies to ethanol. The prices of diesel fuel and propane were increased.

Natural Gas

Brazil meets only 2 percent of its energy needs with natural gas, but the country's natural gas consumption is likely to increase greatly. In May 1992, the state oil companies of Brazil and Bolivia signed an agreement outlining the route for a 2,270-kilometer, US$2 billion pipeline system to deliver natural gas from Bolivian fields to Brazil's Southeast. The pipeline was scheduled to begin supplying 8 million cubic meters a day of Bolivian gas in 1997, building up to 16 million cubic meters a day by 2004.

Nuclear Power

Nuclear energy provides an interesting chapter in Brazil's energy policy. In the early 1970s, nuclear energy was considered to have great potential, but it failed to develop. In 1975 Brazil signed an agreement with the Federal Republic of Germany (West Germany) under which that country would supply eight nuclear power reactors and transfer technology for the complete nuclear fuel cycle. A small nuclear power plant—the Angra I, which has a 626-megawatt capacity—was built near Rio de Janeiro, and work was programmed to start on two larger facilities on the same site (the Angra II and III units, which were to have a combined capacity of 3.1 million kilowatts).

The Angra I plant, which has a reactor supplied by Westinghouse Electric Corporation, was completed and trial runs were made in 1982, but reactor defects delayed operations until 1983. Moreover, technical problems allowed the facility to function only intermittently. Regarding the Angra II and III plants, construction was started on the first. However, the fiscal crisis, a slower than anticipated growth in the demand for electricity in the 1980s, the adverse United States reaction to the Brazil-West Germany agreement, and a growing environmental militancy in Brazil led to slowdowns in construction.

In 1985 the agreement with West Germany was revised, and the construction of the other reactors was postponed indefinitely, in part for financial reasons. Moreover, growing fiscal difficulties led to an interruption of construction on Angra II and further postponement of Angra III. In 1988 it was estimated that the completion of the two plants would require US$2.8 billion, which was not available. In the early 1990s, there were no indications of when the two facilities would be completed. Despite the delays, the technology transfer clauses of the agreement have been maintained, and Brazil has continued to receive West German nuclear technology.

In 1990 Brazil's uranium reserves were estimated at 301,500 tons, or the equivalent of 2.1 billion tons of petroleum. A yellow-cake (see Glossary) factory and a plant to produce nuclear fuel elements have been completed, and additional processing facilities are under construction or planned. These will allow for the enrichment of uranium and the reprocessing of spent fuel. However, as was the case with the power reactors, lack of resources has slowed down developments in this area. In early 1997, the Brazilian nuclear energy program was being supplied by the only uranium mine operating in Brazil, in Poços de Caldas, Minas Gerais State. That mine is being deactivated and replaced by the Lagoa Real/Caetité Mine in the Caetité District in southwestern Bahia State (see Nuclear Programs, ch. 6).

The Services Sector

In 1950 Brazil's services sector was still small and, except for certain segments associated with international trade, quite undeveloped. With industrialization, the sector expanded and underwent considerable changes. By the early 1990s, it had developed an important modern segment, mainly composed of parts of the subsectors of commerce, transportation, communications, finance, and professional services. However, other subsectors, especially education and public administration, failed to develop adequately.

Moreover, an informal economy, a large portion of which was in the services sector, expanded as a result of poverty, the rapid rise in population, the inadequate provision of education, and the succession of economic troubles since 1980. This expansion can be seen by examining the services sector's share of GDP and employment over time. Between 1950 and 1980, the services sector generated around 50 percent of the country's GDP; by 1993 the share had increased to at least 41 percent but possibly as high as 55.9 percent, in part because of industry's poor performance but also because of the informal sector's expansion. The share of the services sector in the absorption of manpower is also evidence of the recent growth of the informal sector. In 1950 the services sector employed only 22.5 percent of the total economically active population (see Glossary); this proportion rose to 33.3 percent in 1970, to 40.8 percent in 1980, and, in a sharp rise, to 57.4 percent in 1992.

Transportation

Before the 1930s, roads and railroads primarily linked production centers to seaports, and there were some connections among major urban centers. Rail links to the rest of South America were never developed in any measure comparable with those among European countries, or between the United States and Canada. Adequate international road links with neighboring countries existed only with Brazil's southern neighbors—Argentina, Uruguay, and Paraguay. By the 1980s, a start had been made on a national road system connecting the various parts of the country. However, construction and maintenance costs were high, slowing extensions to the system as well as the addition of feeder roads. In a country as large as Brazil, with its difficult terrain, a developed transportation system remains many years off (see fig. 10).

Highways

By 1992 Brazil's national highway network totaled 1,670,148 kilometers. Paved highway totals 161,503 kilometers; 1,508,645 kilometers are gravel or earth. Paved roads link the capital, Brasília, with every region of Brazil. Roads are the principal mode of transport, accounting for 60 percent of freight and 95 percent of passenger traffic, including long-distance bus service. Major projects include the 5,000-kilometer Trans-Amazonian Highway, running from Recife and Cabedelo to the Peruvian border; the 4,138-kilometer north-south Cuibá-Santarém Highway; and the 3,555-kilometer Trans-Brasiliana Project, which will link Marabá, on the Trans-Amazonian Highway, with Aceguá, on the Uruguayan border.

Railroads

Railroads total at least 30,129 kilometers, of which 24,690 kilometers consist of 1.000-meter gauge, 5,120 kilometers con-

sist of 1.600-meter gauge, 310 kilometers consist of mixed 1.600- to 1.000-meter gauge, 13 kilometers consist of 0.760-meter gauge, and 2,150 kilometers are electrified. Rail projects from mining areas to ports have accounted for the bulk of investment in the railroads since the mid-1980s. Mining companies operate several privately owned railroads. In 1987 the government announced controversial plans to build a 1,600-kilometer north-south railroad to link the city of Açailândia, in Maranhão State, with Brasília. The Federal Railroad System, Inc. (Rêde Ferroviária Federal S.A.—RFFSA) is responsible for suburban networks throughout Brazil. By 1994 the government had approved plans to privatize RFFSA. A new railroad running westward from Santos through agricultural lands, then north reaching near the Amazon's southwestern margin, is being built by a private entrepreneur's railroad company, Ferronorte.

Subways

Recife, Rio de Janeiro, and São Paulo have new urban subway systems. São Paulo's Metrô, the first in Brazil, began operating in 1975. It is clean, safe, cheap, and efficient. It has two main lines intersecting at Praça de Sé. One runs north-south from Santana to Jabaquara. Another runs east-west from Corinthians Itaquera to Barra Funda. A third line runs from Clinicas in the west, along Avenida Paulista, to Ana Rosa in the south, joining the Jabaquara line at Paraíso and Ana Rosa.

Rio de Janeiro also has a good, clean, and fast Metrô service. The nineteen-kilometer Line One operates between Tijuca and Botafogo, via the railway station and Glória. It is being extended one kilometer at the Tijuca end and seven kilometers on the new South Line from Botafogo to Ipanema and Leblon (Jardim do Allah) via Copacabana. Line Two runs past the Maracanã Stadium northward to Irajá and eventually will operate form Praça 15 de Novembro through the city center to Estácio.

Airports

Air travel is very important for a country the size of Brazil. It has 3,581 airports, 3,024 of which are usable. The airports include 436 with permanent-surface runways, two with runways more than 3,659 meters long, twenty-two with runways 2,440 to 3,659 meters, and 598 with runways 1,220 to 2,439 meters. Principal international airports include the Campo Grande Airport, the Rio de Janeiro Airport, the Guarulhos Airport in São Paulo, and the Guararapes Airport in Recife.

Ports

Brazil has thirty-six deep-water ports. The largest ones are Belém, Fortaleza, Ilhéus, Imbituba, Manaus, Paranaguá, Porto Alegre, Recife, Rio de Janeiro, Rio Grande, Salvador, Santos, and Vitória. With the possible exception of Argentina and Uruguay, ocean-shipping arrangements are easier to the United States and Europe than to the rest of Latin America. In January 1993, the Brazilian Congress approved legislation that could allow for the privatization of the nation's ports. Brazil's major port, in terms of the value of exports and imports, has long been Santos, São Paulo State, followed by the ports of Rio de Janeiro and Vitória. Although all three ports handle some trade with other Latin American countries, they traditionally have handled more trade with Europe and the United States, and the Japanese presence has been increasing. Santos is Latin America's largest port. Located seventy-two kilometers south of São Paulo, it handles a daily average of 50,000 tons cargo. In 1994 Santos handled its largest volume of cargo since it first started operations in 1892. A total of 3,960 ships with 31.4 million tons of cargo passed through the port in 1994.

Inland Waterways

River transport accounts for only a minor part of the movement of goods. In 1988 total freight carried was 7.7 million tons, as compared with 4.7 million tons in 1980. Brazil has 50,000 kilometers of inland waterways. The three major river systems are the Amazon, the Paraná, and the São Francisco. The Amazon is navigable for 3,680 kilometers to Iquitos, Peru. Oceangoing ships can reach as far as Manaus, 1,600 kilometers upstream. There are plans to link the Amazon and Upper Paraná. In addition, a 3,442-kilometer waterway system is being created by extending the Tietê-Paraná river network along the Paraguai and Paraná rivers as far as Buenos Aires.

Merchant Marine

The merchant marine, the largest in Latin America, has 220 ships totaling 5,139,176 gross ton weight (GTW) and 8,695,682 deadweight tons (DWT). It has five passenger-cargo, forty cargo, one refrigerator cargo, twelve combination ore/oil, sixty-five bulk, two combination bulk, and eleven vehicle carrier ships. In addition, one naval tanker is sometimes used commercially.

Telecommunications

Brazil has a good system of telecommunications, including extensive microwave radio-relay facilities. In 1995 the country had 13,237,852 telephones. It has as many as 3,171 broadcast stations. These include 1,265 FM, 1,572 medium-wave, and eighty-two tropical-wave radio stations and 257 television stations.

In 1995 the Roman Catholic Church organized a UHF satellite television channel broadcasting to eight states under the aegis of the Brazilian Institute of Christian Communication. The Brazilian government founded the Brazilian Radio Broadcasting Company (Empresa Brasileira de Radiodifusão—Radiobrás) in 1975 to unite all existing state-owned broadcasting stations and to create new radio and television services capable of reaching the Amazon region.

Until the 1988 constitution, the president had the exclusive prerogative to allocate radio and television concessions. In 1981, after canceling the Tupi Network concessions, the military government very capriciously selected political allies to set up new networks—Manchete, Bandeirantes, and the Brazilian Television System (Sistema Brasileiro de Televisão—SBT)—and passed over other communications enterprises (the newspaper *Jornal do Brasil* and the publisher Editora Abril, for example). From 1985 through 1988, television and radio concessions became the "currency of political negotiation" as President Sarney tried to maintain majorities in Congress. As a result, many evangelical (born-again Christian) organizations acquired radio and television concessions, much to the dissatisfaction of the Roman Catholic Church.

In 1988 Radiobrás and the official Brazilian News Agency became a single organization under the name Brazilian Communications Company (Empresa Brasileira de Comunicação), which retained the Radiobrás acronym. Today, Radiobrás stations can be heard all over the country and abroad. Its television programs also are transmitted throughout the country by Brazil Network (Rêde Brasil). Brazil has six principal television networks: Globo (owned by Roberto Marinho), Manchete (Adolfo Bloch), Bandeirantes (João Jorge Saad), the SBT (Sílvio Santos), Record (pentecostal Bishop Edir Macedo), and TV-Gaúcha S.A. There is also an embryonic system of pay television (cable, microwave, and satellite). Brazil is connected internationally by three coaxial submarine cables, three Atlantic Ocean International Telecommunications Satellite Organization (Intelsat) earth stations, and sixty-four domestic satellite earth stations.

Brazilian Telecommunications, Inc. (Telecomunicações Brasileiras S.A.—Telebrás), a state-owned company with monopoly control over Brazilian telecommunications, oversees Brazil's telecommunications. According to Telebrás, the Brazilian government is developing an indigenous cellular telephone project, called Eco–8, which by 1998 is supposed to enable telephone contact between anywhere in Brazil and some Central American countries. A 1995 constitutional reform proposal allowed for the privatization of Telebrás.

Brazil leads Latin America with at least 161 Internet networks; second-place Mexico has 105 networks. Almost 80 percent of Brazil's largest nongovernmental organizations (NGOs) are connected with each other and with the Internet. According to the Brazilian Telecommunications Company (Empresa Brasileira de Telecomunicações—Embratel), in early 1995 the Internet became available to any Brazilian with access to a telephone and a modem. Until then, the Internet had been available only to researchers linked to educational institutions or NGOs.

Tourism

Brazil's natural wonders include the Amazon; the wildlife-packed Pantanal wetlands; 8,850 kilometers of superb Atlantic coastline, including 3,200 kilometers of white sand beaches in the Northeast running from São Luís in the north to the Bahia Basin in the south; and the waterfalls at Foz do Iguaçu. Brazil has one of the world's most spectacularly located cities, Rio de Janeiro, which hosts the annual Mardi Gras Carnaval (Carnival); one of the largest cities, São Paulo; one of the most modernistic, Brasília; and one of the most ecologically advanced, Curitiba. Other popular cities include Salvador, Ouro Prêto, and Manaus.

Traditionally, Brazilian politicians have regarded travel and tourism as elitist and an unnecessary luxury. This view has been changing, however, as politicians have begun to see travel and tourism as a major industry. In the early 1990s, about 6 million jobs were linked to Brazil's travel and tourism industry. The industry is one of the country's biggest employers, involving one in every eleven workers. It contributes an estimated 8 percent to the country's GDP. This figure compares favorably with Latin America's average of 5.1 percent, but it is well below the world average of 10.2 percent.

Since the United Nations-sponsored Rio Earth Summit (Eco–92) in 1992, the Brazilian government has targeted ecotourism as a priority. For example, the government is encouraging foreign investment in tourist facilities in Amazônia. The Ministry of Commerce, Industry, and Tourism includes a cabinet-level official in charge of tourism policies. The National Secretary of Tourism and Services, the National Tourism Board, and the state and municipal tourist authorities are responsible for the day-to-day administration of the sector.

The development of tourism in the seven states that make up the impoverished Northeast has received special attention. More than 3 million Brazilian and foreign visitors boosted hotel occupancy in the Northeastern states from 43 percent in 1991 to 67 percent in 1993.

In 1992 some 2,235,000 passengers flew to Brazil, an increase of 14.5 percent from 1991, and the same number flew out of Brazil. About 513,000 of these visitors flew between Argentina and Brazil, and according to Brazil's Civil Aviation Department (Departamento de Aviação Civil—DAC), more than 541,000 passengers flew between the United States and Brazil, an increase of 10.4 percent from 1991. The Brazilian Tourism Agency (Empresa Brasileira de Turismo—Embratur) found that 72.6 percent of those who came to Brazil in 1992 came for tourism; the rest came for business, conferences, and conventions, including Eco–92. In 1993 about 1.6 million foreign visitors traveled to Brazil.

Privatization

The rise in interest in the privatization of state-owned enterprises in Brazil that began in the 1980s reflects similar trends worldwide. Although much of the rhetoric used by the advocates of privatization emphasized economic efficiency and competitiveness, much of Brazil's privatization experience since 1990 is better understood as a response to the fiscal pressures on the public sector, which worsened significantly in the 1980s.

The sale of state enterprises to private buyers, both domestic and foreign, offered an attractive means to reduce the fiscal pressures. First, the sale of an enterprise provided an immedi-

Iguaçu Falls, Foz do Iguaçu
Courtesy Larry Buzard

ate revenue gain for the government. Second, to the extent that the enterprise sold was operating at a loss, the future fiscal burden on the public sector was reduced. Finally, the conversion of a state enterprise into a profitable private one increased the future tax revenues of the government.

Implicit in these motives for privatization is a difficult choice for the government. The first reason suggests that the greatest immediate revenue effect would be obtained from the sale of the most profitable firms, such as the CVRD (Rio Dôce Valley Company), Brazil's iron mining and exploring complex. The second consideration, however, suggests that long-term revenue benefits would be more likely from the sale of enterprises that have had a long history of low or negative returns, such as the RFFSA (Federal Railroad System, Inc.). Brazilian privatization experience and policies since the 1980s reflects the difficulty of deciding which firms to privatize first.

Although some privatization occurred between 1980 and 1990, it was confined to cases in which the federal government had taken over firms in financial difficulties, and did not touch any of the major state-owned enterprises that had been established purposely by the federal government and by some state governments in the preceding three decades. In all, only thirty-eight enterprises were privatized by the federal government before 1990, and the total receipts of the government were only US$723 million.

Policy changed significantly with the entrance of the Collor government in 1990, which made privatization one of the major planks of its economic platform. The National Privatization Program (Programa Nacional de Desestatização—PND), which was created by the National Economic Development Bank (Banco Nacional de Desenvolvimento Econômico—BNDE), expanded the scope of privatization to include a number of the enterprises formerly considered as "strategic" by earlier governments. During the Collor government between 1990 and 1992, fifteen state-owned enterprises were privatized, yielding about US$3.5 billion in total proceeds. The most important sale was that of the Minas Gerais Iron and Steel Mills, Inc. (Usinas Siderúrgicas de Minas Gerais S.A.—Usiminas) steel company in October 1991, which alone accounted for nearly twice the revenue of all previous privatizations and sold for US$2.3 billion. The Japanese holding company Nippon Usiminas acquired about 18 percent of the shares. During this period, most sales were exchanges of equity in state-owned enterprises for different types of public debt or "soft money," rather than for cash.

Under the Franco government (1992–94), privatization continued but with a greater emphasis on sales for cash. Eighteen state-owned enterprises were sold, yielding over US$5 billion. Among the most important enterprises sold in this period was the Brazilian Aeronautics Company (Empresa Brasileira Aeronáutica—Embraer), an aircraft manufacturer, which had been established in 1969 and controlled by the Ministry of Aeronautics. By 1994 only twenty-five state-owned enterprises had been sold, mostly in exchange for debt certificates and little hard cash. Other enterprises included several chemical, fertilizer, and mining companies, with the steel sector wholly privatized by the end of 1994.

Privatization policy under the Cardoso administration, beginning in 1995, shifted focus to state-owned enterprises responsible for the major part of Brazil's economic infrastructure, among them enterprises in the energy, transportation, and communications sectors. The first major privatization was the sale of the Espírito Santo Power Plants, Inc. (Espírito Santo Centrais Elétricas S.A.—Escelsa), the federally owned power company serving the state of Espírito Santo, in July 1995. In a departure from earlier policy, the CVRD, one of Brazil's largest state enterprises, was included in the program by the new government. Although Brazil's largest state-owned enterprises, Petrobrás, remained outside the program because of constitutional restrictions, appraisals were begun of the RFFSA and of the remaining federally owned power companies.

Exchange-Rate and Balance of Payments Policies

Many of Brazil's economic difficulties since the 1970s have been blamed on external economic shocks. Brazil's heavy dependence on imported petroleum and on capital inflows from other countries made it highly vulnerable to sharp rises in oil prices and to increases in interest rates. Even when prices and interest rates declined in the late 1980s from their earlier peaks, Brazil's economic problems persisted. Brazil was surprisingly successful in adjusting its external payments after the foreign debt crisis, which began with the Mexican default in August 1982. However, Brazil paid a heavy domestic price for external adjustment. Short-term measures to alleviate the balance of payments, moreover, delayed long-term moves toward a more open and efficient economy.

Exchange Rates and Foreign Trade

The single most important policy tool for influencing Brazil's balance of payments is the exchange rate. Brazilian exchange-rate policy has evolved over the past several decades. Policy makers and Brazilian exporters believed that trade flows in the 1960s and 1970s were most effectively managed through trade policies such as tariffs (see Glossary), import controls, or export incentives. Beginning in the 1980s, they began to recognize that balance of payments adjustments may be more efficiently pursued using the exchange rate, rather than tariffs, subsidies, and direct controls on trade. This evolution in thinking reflects in part the increasing skepticism among many Brazilians, both economists and policy makers, about the government's ability to maintain external balance using trade policy without creating severe economic distortions.

Even more important, however, was the exchange-rate experience of the early 1980s. Following the onset of Mexico's debt crisis in 1982 and the resulting inability of Brazil to continue to finance its current-account deficit through external borrowing, the cruzeiro was devalued sharply against the dollar in February 1983. Unlike the earlier "maxidevaluation" of December 1979, which was soon undermined by rapid increases in internal cruzeiro prices, the real depreciation of the cruzeiro resulting from the 1983 adjustment was maintained for the next several years. Exports increased substantially in 1983 and 1984, and the value of imports fell by over US$5 billion between 1982 and 1984. Although some of this decline resulted from the fall in petroleum prices from their record levels in 1981, the response of the trade deficit to the large and sustained real depreciation of the cruzeiro provided clear evidence that Brazil's external adjustment problem could be addressed through exchange-rate policy. The experience of the early 1980s, in fact, led to the recognition that Brazil's real problem was not the private sector's lack of response to the exchange rate, but the inability of the domestic economy, particularly the public sector, to generate the net saving that is the counterpart of a current-account surplus.

Brazil's success in moving the current account into surplus after 1982 implied a corresponding adjustment in either net private saving (private saving minus private investment) or in public-sector saving (tax receipts and other public revenues minus public expenditures). Because net public-sector saving actually deteriorated in the 1980s, the burden of adjustment fell on the private sector, particularly on investment. The dramatic fall in investment after 1982 had important consequences for Brazilian competitiveness and hence for the potential benefits that Brazil would derive from trade reform.

Thus, the experience of the early 1980s suggests that the Brazilian economy had responded to real exchange rates (see Glossary) that facilitated external adjustment, but the policy also reduced domestic private investment and future economic growth. In retrospect, the delay among policy makers in using the exchange rate as the primary tool for achieving external balance is surprising. Their approach may have been influenced in part, however, by the success of the "crawling-peg" policy instituted in August 1968. This policy consisted of small but frequent adjustments in the nominal exchange rate in line with Brazilian inflation and price changes in Brazil's major trade partners, primarily the United States. It ushered in a long period of real exchange-rate stability, broken only a decade later by the December 1979 devaluation. The crawling-peg policy was a marked improvement over the earlier exchange-rate regime, in which the combination of domestic inflation and a nominal exchange rate fixed for long periods of time resulted in large fluctuations and uncertainty about the real exchange rate. The real rate may in fact have been too stable, however, leading Brazil to delay the appropriate exchange-rate response to the external shocks of the 1970s.

A rise in the real exchange rate represents an increase in Brazilian price competitiveness in international markets. Such an increase in price competitiveness could be caused by a depreciation of the cruzeiro against the dollar, a rise in United States prices, or a fall in Brazilian prices. A slowing of inflation in the 1970s made Brazil more competitive, while the rapid acceleration of inflation in the second half of the 1980s substantially eroded Brazil's price competitiveness. Unlike other episodes in which the actual effects of a devaluation were rapidly undercut by Brazilian inflation, the 1983 real devaluation was maintained through frequent adjustments in the nominal exchange rate, sufficient to maintain Brazil's price competitiveness in international markets until the 1986 Cruzado Plan froze the nominal exchange rate (see fig. 11; table 12, Appendix).

A number of implications for Brazil's balance of payments policy are clear from exchange-rate trends and movements in the current account. First, by the 1980s it was clear that Brazil-

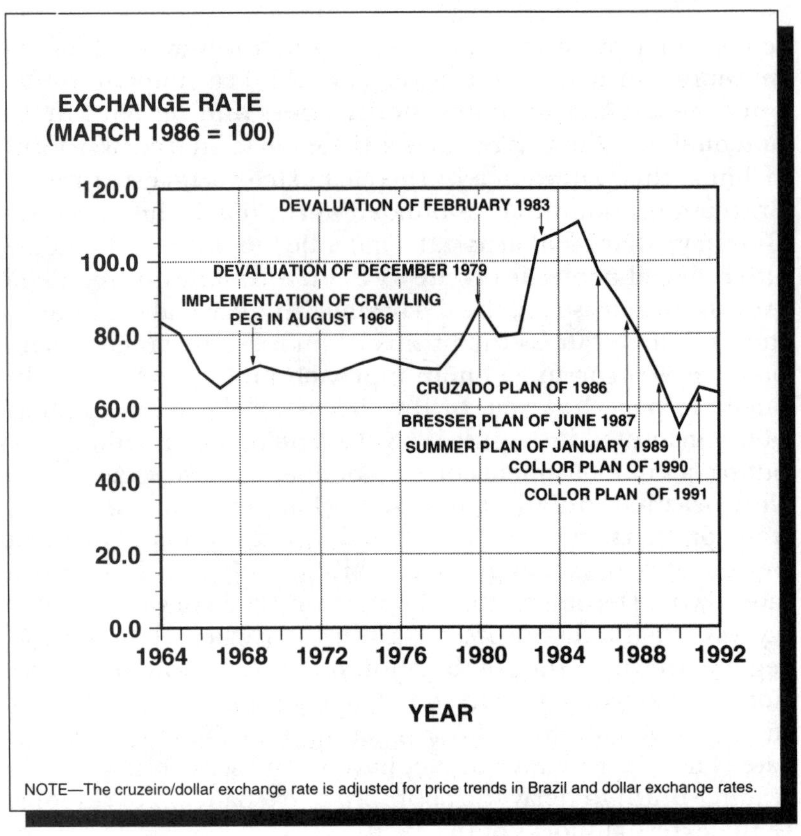

NOTE—The cruzeiro/dollar exchange rate is adjusted for price trends in Brazil and dollar exchange rates.

Source: Based on information from Donald V. Coes, "Macroeconomic Stabilisation and Trade Liberalization: Brazilian Experience and Choices," *World Economy* [Oxford], 17, No. 4, July 1994, 439; and an updated chart provided by the author.

Figure 11. Brazil's Real Exchange Rate and Government Intervention, 1964–92

ian trade flows were strongly responsive to the real exchange rate. If "elasticity pessimism," which hypothesizes that trade responses to relative prices are low, was ever justified in the Brazilian case, those days were long past. Since the late 1960s, Brazil has ceased to be a developing country in terms of its trade flows. Traditional primary products, such as coffee, cocoa, or sugar, in recent years have accounted for less than a third of the value of Brazilian exports. The increasing importance of manufactured exports, as well as the variety of local import substitutes, makes Brazil's trade balance responsive to real exchange-rate changes. This responsiveness removes one of the traditional justifications for extensive tariff and import restriction policies and for administrative intervention in trade to attain external balance. The evidence of the past several decades suggests that Brazil can attain external balance without extensive market intervention, however harsh the domestic effects of external adjustment.

Second, the introduction of a degree of indexation of the nominal exchange rate in the form of the crawling-peg policy has permitted the external sector to avoid some of the consequences of domestic inflation that would otherwise have produced much more severe external payments crises. Real exchange rates remained relatively stable for a decade after the policy's introduction in 1968. Unlike several other Latin American countries such as Argentina, Brazil avoided the sharp swings in the real exchange rate resulting from domestic inflation and infrequent adjustment of the nominal rate. When Brazil departed from this pattern, as it did in 1986 during the Cruzado Plan, policy makers soon learned that this was a mistake. Subsequent stabilization plans, even if they were failures for other reasons, at least did not succumb to the temptation to use the exchange rate as an anti-inflationary weapon.

Finally, and perhaps more negatively, Brazilian exchange-rate policy transformed Brazil's external adjustment problems of the early 1980s into more intractable domestic balance problems in the early 1990s. Contrary to the initial expectations of many observers, Brazil was able to solve its external balance problem after the 1982 debt crisis with surprising speed. The cost was a sharp increase in the demand for domestic saving to replace lost foreign capital inflows. With little increase in net public-sector saving or in private-sector gross saving, investment fell substantially, undercutting the growth of the Brazilian capital stock and the economy's potential growth in competitiveness.

Capital Flows and the External Debt

Much of Brazil's economic experience in the past two decades has been dominated by large capital inflows that attained record levels in the 1970s, only to collapse after 1983 in the wake of the Mexican debt crisis. For the rest of the decade, Brazil coped with the consequences of this collapse, and only in the 1990s did capital again begin to flow into the

Brazilian economy, with a substantial increase after the *Real* Plan.

The enormous inflow of external capital to Brazil that ended in 1982 had its roots in a number of policies and institutional changes in the preceding two decades. The military government that seized power in April 1964 quickly reformed existing laws governing direct foreign investments, including liberalizing restrictions on remittances of profits and simplifying procedures for reinvestment of profits. The changes did not address the effects of inflation in the currency of the lending country, however, so that the real returns on a direct investment were affected negatively by inflation in dollar prices. The negative effect of dollar inflation on a direct foreign investment in Brazil arose because the original investment was registered in a fixed dollar amount, on which allowances for profits and remittances were calculated. A million-dollar investment in 1964, for example, would still be registered as a million-dollar investment in 1974. Higher nominal dollar profits in 1974 would then result in a substantially higher nominal profit rate and a heftier Brazilian tax, thus lowering the real return.

Financial lending to Brazil was different because the interest rate on the loan, usually denominated in dollars, incorporated the market's expectations of inflation. The asymmetrical treatment of financial capital flows and direct investment was one of the reasons total capital flows to Brazil in the post-1964 period were dominated by bank lending, which at times was ten times as great as foreign direct investment.

Among the other changes that encouraged large financial capital flows to Brazil was Law 4,131, which allowed final borrowers to deal directly with foreign lenders after approval by the Central Bank of Brazil (Banco Central do Brasil—Bacen; see Glossary). Another vehicle for capital flows was Resolution 63, which permitted Brazilian banks and authorized subsidiaries of foreign banks to obtain dollar loans abroad and reloan the proceeds to one or more domestic borrowers. Finally, the increasing participation of the Brazilian government as a borrower itself, backed by explicit "full faith and credit" guarantees and by the implicit assumption that taxes could be levied to pay for loans to the government, made lending to Brazil an increasingly attractive option for foreign banks.

Equally important in explaining the sharp rise in financial lending to Brazil after the mid-1960s were changes in international financial markets. International banks began to negotiate variable interest rate loans, in which the borrower and the lender agreed to reset the loan's interest rate at specified intervals, usually six months, on the basis of a rate that neither the borrower nor lender controlled (usually the London Interbank Offered Rate—LIBOR), or the United States prime rate. Added to this underlying rate was a "spread," or premium charged to borrowers like Brazil, based on the market's assessment of any additional risk compared with the risks associated with prime borrowers. Finally, the rise in syndicated bank lending, in which one "lead" bank organized the loan and then sold portions of it to other international lenders, permitted banks to expand substantially their loans to borrowers like Brazil.

Together, these innovations cleared the way for lending on a scale that was unprecedented in Brazil's history and with few parallels elsewhere in the world. Because the loans were denominated in the creditor country's currency, they were isolated effectively from inflation in cruzeiro prices. As long as the value of Brazil's export revenues grew at rates exceeding the interest rates charged on the loans, an assumption that appeared valid throughout the 1970s, the burden of the external debt in relation to Brazil's capacity to repay it would fall.

Although it is easy from the vantage point of the 1990s to criticize the volume and terms of much of the bank lending to Brazil, at the time it appeared to be an extremely attractive option for a borrower like Brazil. When inflation in the currencies of the lending countries is subtracted from the rates charged on loans to Brazil, real interest rates on these loans in the 1970s were negligible and often negative. The nominal and real interest rates in the markets in which Brazilian external borrowing occurred do not include the spread paid by Brazil, which during the 1970s and early 1980s was generally between 1 percent and 2 percent. Nevertheless, these rates do show clearly why foreign borrowing appeared to be such an attractive option for Brazil.

The debt crisis that began in Mexico in August 1982 had an almost immediate impact on the ability of other Latin American borrowers to maintain capital inflows. Even though Brazil's trade balance and current account had improved slightly in 1981, loans from international lenders became increasingly scarce. Interest on new loans increased, and most lenders refused to roll over on existing loans. New lending dried up in the second half of 1982, reducing capital inflows, which had reached a peak in 1981, by more than a third. Private borrowers in Brazil encountered a total cutoff of loans from foreign lenders, while official borrowing dropped sharply. By 1984 net capital inflows (public and private) were negligible by comparison with earlier years, and by 1986 the country was experiencing a net capital outflow of US$7.3 billion, a sum nearly equal to Brazil's trade balance. The principal components of Brazil's balance of payments show this sharp drop in the net inflow of foreign capital after 1982 (see table 13, Appendix).

The 1982 crisis interrupted for many years private Brazilian external borrowing. Private loans contracted under Law 4,131 had leveled off in the late 1970s, and after 1982 net private borrowing under this law became negative. The fall in private borrowing under Resolution 63 was even more pronounced. After a rapid rise in such borrowing between 1979 and the 1982 debt crisis, this source of financing virtually collapsed, as the level of outstanding Resolution 63 debt was more than cut in half between 1982 and the end of 1987.

Part, if not all, of the increase in external debt reported by the Central Bank after 1982 was simply forced lending to finance interest payments. It did not have a real counterpart in the form of new resources entering the country through the capital account. As a result, Brazil's ability to tap external saving to finance either public-sector borrowing or private-sector investment collapsed after 1982.

A number of Brazilian economists have made the point that before 1982 net capital inflows more than covered service payments (net interest, profits and dividends, and reinvested profits). After 1982 interest payments alone far exceeded net capital inflows, which turned negative after 1985. Although 1982 is usually viewed as the turning point, the net capital transfer from the rest of the world actually began to decline in the mid-1970s. Brazil was only able to avoid an external payments crisis in the late 1970s because lenders were willing to finance debt service through further lending. After the Mexican debt crisis in 1982, Brazil's own crisis could no longer be postponed.

The 1986 Cruzado Plan exacerbated capital outflows. Real exchange-rate overvaluation, with increasing expectations of a future adjustment, was one factor. A second factor was the increase in uncertainty about future fiscal and monetary policy, as the shortages and informal markets produced by the price controls undercut the euphoria of the first few months.

During the rest of the 1980s, net capital outflow continued, further reducing Brazil's capacity to finance investments needed for future economic growth. In real terms, however, the external debt began to decline in the late 1980s, both as a result of debt renegotiation and a marking down of some of the debt by public and private lenders. Despite temporary interruptions in debt servicing, domestic political pressures in Brazil for a permanent repudiation of the external debt were rejected. As interest rates in international financial markets declined substantially in the early 1990s, the costs of servicing the remaining external debt were reduced further.

Although the debt crisis that exploded in Brazil in the early 1980s had not disappeared a decade later, it was no longer regarded as Brazil's central economic problem. Its effects, however, lingered on in several forms. First, the steep fall in the availability of international reserves (see Glossary) after 1982 sharply curtailed Brazilian investment. The resulting decline in capital formation was evident a decade later, as Brazilians faced the consequence of lower levels of investment in plant, equipment, and essential infrastructure. Second, international confidence in the financial soundness of external lending to Brazil remained low. When foreign capital began to return to Brazil in the early 1990s, it took a rather different form from the capital inflows of the 1970s. Foreign capital inflows to Brazil in the early 1990s were smaller and were no longer dominated by loans from international banks. Instead, foreign lenders sought equity investments in Brazilian enterprises. Foreign firms with the capacity to manage direct investments in Brazil began to replace commercial banks as the primary source of foreign capital.

Fiscal and Monetary Policy, the Public Sector, and Inflation

In the 1980s, most Brazilians were convinced that the huge foreign debt was at the heart of their economic difficulties. A decade later, as other heavily indebted developing nations reduced inflation to negligible levels and began to grow again, it was more apparent that some of Brazil's economic difficulties were homemade. By the early 1990s, a new consensus had emerged among Brazilian economists and policy makers. It emphasized the role of the public sector in the economy and, more specifically, the way in which public-sector expenditures are financed.

By the late 1980s, the overhang of public debt had placed a servicing burden on the public sector that would have strained any government. Given its huge debt to private Brazilian creditors and foreign creditors alike, the public sector came to be viewed as practically bankrupt. With new foreign credit virtually eliminated after 1982 and domestic credit increasingly costly, the government's only remaining recourse was to finance its deficit through the creation of money. This led in turn to an accelerating and unpredictable rate of inflation, which by the early 1990s was more than 4,000 percent at annual rates.

Fiscal Trends in the 1980s

In an inflationary economy like Brazil's, there are severe technical problems in quantifying fiscal trends. The basic difficulty stems from a large domestic public debt that is owed in cruzeiros. A large part of reported government expenditures is interest payments that simply compensate the debt holders for the effect of inflation (see table 14, Appendix). Government interest payments exploded in the 1980s, rising from less than 1 percent of GDP in 1980 to an unmanageable 6.1 percent in 1989, before being halted temporarily by the government freeze on payments in 1990. Despite the fact that new foreign resources were unavailable to Brazil after 1982, interest payments on the existing public-sector external debt also increased substantially over the 1980s.

An increase in domestic and foreign interest payments could be financed if other parts of the public sector's accounts were to change enough to create a "primary" budget surplus (approximately the difference between tax receipts and noninterest-related public expenditures). In Brazil the reverse happened. The noninterest-related surplus declined sharply, beginning in the 1970s and accelerating in the late 1980s.

A number of reasons account for this trend. Tax receipts as a share of GDP declined significantly in the early 1980s, partly as a result of the difficulties inherent in maintaining tax collections with accelerating inflation. By the late 1980s, tax receipts, net of transfers for such items as social security, were insufficient even to pay for public-sector wages and salaries and purchases of goods and services.

An Emb–120 Brasília on the final assembly line at the factory of the Brazilian Aeronautics Company (Empresa Brasileira Aeronáutica—Embraer) in São José dos Campos, São Paulo State
Courtesy Embraer

On the expenditure side, Brazil's return to a more open, democratic political system in the mid-1980s made it difficult, if not impossible, for political leaders to contain public expenditures for personnel costs, goods, and services. Between 1980 and 1990, the share of such expenditures in GDP mushroomed from 9.2 to 15.6 percent.

Grim as these trends were, they were probably underestimates of Brazil's true fiscal situation. In the early 1970s, the public enterprises were operated profitably, and the prices of their products and services at least kept up with inflation. With the acceleration of inflation after the two oil shocks in the 1970s, the fiscal position of the public enterprises began to worsen, although this trend was not recognized widely until the 1980s.

It was not until the 1980s that the Brazilian government, partly because of pressure from foreign creditors and multilateral organizations, such as the International Monetary Fund (IMF—see Glossary) and the World Bank (see Glossary), began to publish more extensive statements on the public sector's finances. In 1983 the government began preparing estimates of the Public Sector Borrowing Requirement (PSBR). These estimates included not only the expenditures of the federal, state, and local governments but also those of state enterprises, social security authorities, and a number of previously "off-budget" activities. These estimates clearly show that Brazil's fiscal imbalances worsened even more in the 1980s than is suggested by more traditional measures.

Had the worsening trend in the PSBR been simply the result of increases in nominal interest payments, inflation alone might have been blamed. In fact, many of the intellectual proponents of what became the Cruzado Plan made this argument in the 1980s. These proponents maintained that if inflation could be stopped (through a price freeze or other means), the public sector's deficit would disappear. Even if the effects of inflation were accounted for, however, Brazil would have had a large public-sector debt.

Pressures on Public-Sector Expenditures in the 1980s

Despite the popular image of Brazil's public sector as a profligate spender and intense consumer of resources, public expenditures as a share of national product remained relatively stable until the mid-1980s. The containment of public spending under the government of President João Batista de Oliveira Figueiredo (1979–85) at the federal level included limitations on hiring and expenditures on goods and services as well as cuts in public investment. Spending by state and local governments was limited by reductions in the revenues transferred to them by the federal government.

Total spending for public-sector wages and salaries, which had actually declined as a share of national product between the early 1970s and 1984, only began to increase when the government of President José Sarney (1985–90) took over, reaching almost 10 percent of GDP in 1989. Public-sector spending on goods and services as a share of GDP also increased under President Sarney. A fall in net subsidies to the private sector and a stable level of social security spending were not sufficient to offset a sharp rise in government spending on wages and salaries. The expansion of public spending after 1985 occurred at all levels of government. At the federal level, it was partly caused by the efforts of President Sarney to secure a full five-year mandate, reinforced by the misperception that Brazil's budget deficit would be negligible if the effects of inflation on it were discounted. At the state and local levels, greater revenues were available as a result of changes in federal transfers after 1985, a trend reinforced by the 1988 constitution. Much of this spending went for current expenses, primarily personnel, rather than investment in infrastructure. Even with this expansion in state and local spending, however, the federal government remained responsible for about two-thirds of total expenditures. State spending was primarily for education and health, and local government expenditures were devoted principally to housing and urban development. At all levels of government, however, much of this spending, whatever the announced function, was for personnel and administrative costs.

The worsening of Brazil's public-sector finances in the 1980s was in part the consequence of the political and administrative decentralization that took place following the return to civilian rule in 1985. In 1988 the new constitution made this decentralization explicit, transferring to state and local governments a substantial part of the revenues that were formerly received by the federal government. There was not, however, a parallel decentralization of expenditure responsibilities. The federal government retained most of its functional responsibilities, while losing a significant part of its revenues.

Trends in tax revenues after 1983 further aggravated Brazil's public-sector finances. Tax receipts as a share of GDP fell sharply after 1983, having averaged about 25 percent in the preceding decade. With the exception of the atypical year of 1986 (the Cruzado Plan), they did not regain such levels until the first years of the Collor de Mello government, when increases in income taxes and social security contributions, as well as taxes on manufactured goods and financial operations, slowed the decline in revenues.

Although the federal government in the early 1990s made determined efforts to maintain its income by enforcing tax collection, these efforts met with limited success. Public cynicism about the government's use of tax revenues, fed in part by the corruption scandal that forced Collor de Mello from office in September 1992, led to increased tax avoidance and in many cases to outright tax evasion. Although little firm evidence is available to quantify tax evasion, considerable anecdotal and fragmentary evidence suggests that it rose significantly in the 1980s and early 1990s. With the increased financial opening of the economy, many Brazilians sought to shelter income derived from financial assets by placing them outside Brazil, even when before-tax returns in Brazil were substantially higher. Capital flight from Brazil, which had not been as serious a problem as it had been for a number of other Latin American nations in the 1970s and early 1980s, accelerated significantly in the late 1980s. Other ways in which Brazilians evaded taxes included substantial understatement of income from professional and service activities and the widespread practice of making transactions without documentation for tax purposes.

The adoption of the new constitution in 1988 had a significant impact on public-sector finances. Many Brazilians viewed it as the vehicle through which to redress what they regarded as excessive concentration of powers at the federal level. Consequently, strong support existed for decentralizing government and shifting power from the presidency to the Congress. Many Brazilians also saw the new constitution as a way not only to guarantee civil rights but also to secure specific economic rights in the areas of health, education, employment guarantees, and social security.

The result was a document that is far more specific and lengthier than those of most other nations. Some advances were made in the arrangement of public finances, among them restrictions on off-budget spending by the executive and better defined procedures for the preparation and passage of an annual budget. In a larger sense, however, the 1988 constitution made the potential for fiscal deterioration more likely, especially at the federal level. It not only reduced the revenues that went to the federal government by transferring them to states and municipalities but also linked many revenue sources to specific objectives, further restricting the federal government's ability to allocate expenditures. In addition, the new charter actually expanded some federal responsibilities in a number of areas, among them law enforcement, education, and cultural affairs. Another provision granted tenure to public employees after two years. The constitution strengthened employment and pension guarantees and the explicitly maintained pension and retirement rights based on length of service—thirty-five years for men and thirty years for women—

without regard to age at retirement. Together, these provisions made fiscal equilibrium, especially at the federal level, even more difficult to attain than it had been before 1988.

A number of Brazilian economists and policy makers soon recognized the budgetary implications of the new constitution. The stabilization program of the new Collor de Mello government in 1990 temporarily halted the decline in federal government revenue through its price and wage freezes, but this was done at a very high cost. The dramatic freezing of most Brazilians' financial wealth under the first Collor de Mello plan raised basic legal and constitutional questions about the fiscal rights and responsibilities of the government. A number of Brazilian legal scholars questioned the right of the government to impose what they argued was a tax, not allowed for in the constitution, through the freezing of assets whose full real value would not be repaid to their holders.

By the early 1990s, a consensus had emerged that successful economic and price stabilization would require profound changes in Brazil's fiscal system and, if necessary, amendments to the 1988 constitution. Although such views were rejected vigorously if suggested by others, such as the IMF or foreign lenders, many Brazilians recognized that the 1988 constitution had created a number of fiscal problems. In October 1991, the Collor de Mello government submitted to Congress a series of proposals aimed at reducing the fiscal pressures at the federal level. Among the proposed changes were modifications of the constitutional obstacles to administrative reform, limitations on the constitutional guarantees for social security, and authority to create new sources of federal tax revenue. With the erosion of support for the Collor de Mello government during 1992, the proposals had little chance of passage, and the fundamental fiscal disequilibrium continued under the administration of Itamar Franco (1992–95), Collor de Mello's successor.

Fiscal Deficits and Inflation

The root of Brazilian inflation has been the monetization of the public sector's fiscal deficit, because deficits that are not financed by borrowing either from abroad or domestically must be covered by the creation of money. By the early 1990s, the old debate between the monetarists (see Glossary), who emphasized the central role of money supply growth in the inflationary process, and the structuralists (see Glossary), who attributed price increases to supply problems in developing economies like Brazil's, was viewed as an obsolete and largely sterile discussion. Instead, debate focused on the causal relationship between inflation and the money supply, and on how much freedom the government actually had in determining money-supply growth.

However important monetization of the public sector's fiscal deficit may have been in the past in either initiating or accelerating inflation, the reinforcement of the inflationary process by past inflation and by expectations of future inflation was an important part of the Brazilian experience in the 1980s and 1990s. In Brazil the feedback effect of past inflation has been institutionalized in an extensive indexation or "monetary correction" (*correção monetária*) system, which was developed and extended to most markets between 1964 and 1970. The result was an economy in which apparently modest initial shocks could be transformed into high and continuing inflation. Recognition of this feedback effect in the early 1980s played a role in the design of the 1986 Cruzado Plan, as well as in subsequent stabilization attempts, notably the *Real* Plan in 1994. The inflation indexation system, which in the 1970s had been virtually unquestioned, was increasingly blamed for contributing to the continuation and acceleration of inflation in the 1980s and early 1990s.

Although inflation accelerated significantly in the 1980s, it had long been a feature of Brazil's economy. The first major inflationary surge began in the late 1950s and continued until 1964, in part the result of the monetary accommodation of fiscal pressures resulting from a sharp rise in government expenditures. A second surge began in the 1970s, partly as a result of the external shocks caused by the rise in energy prices. The indexation system served as a vehicle for amplifying energy price increases into higher widespread price increases than might have occurred. Inflation worsened dramatically in the 1980s, however, as Brazil lost its access to foreign capital markets and domestic borrowing to finance the growing public-sector deficit became increasingly expensive (see table 15, Appendix). Inevitably, money creation became one of the primary ways to finance the deficit.

It is difficult for non-Brazilians to grasp the significance of double-digit inflation for forty years, with triple- and even quadruple-digit inflation in the 1980s. By the late 1980s, annual rates of inflation were almost meaningless, and Brazilians themselves routinely characterized inflation by its monthly rate, which in the early 1990s was over 35 percent. Between the end of World War II and Brazil's *Real* Plan in 1994, the price level had increased more than 100 billion times.

Not only did inflation accelerate over the 1980s, but the rate became more variable and less predictable. The frequency of price adjustments increased, and wage and salary adjustments that had once occurred annually were adjusted semiannually, then quarterly, and in some markets monthly, as inflation accelerated. In other markets, especially the capital markets, inflation had similar effects in shortening contract periods. Few borrowers or lenders would dare to make long-term commitments, and by the late 1980s most Brazilian firms, as well as most wealthier individuals, held any excess assets in short-term, highly liquid deposits that were literally known as the "overnight."

The rise in indexation in Brazil after 1964 had permitted the government to tap the supply of domestic saving by selling indexed government bonds to savers, who were thus protected against the effects of inflation on the value of such assets. Although indexed bonds were regarded as a great success in the 1960s and 1970s, the need to pay not only the interest but also the inflation adjustment became an increasing burden for the government in the 1980s.

Despite the burden that indexed bonds placed on government finances as inflation accelerated, inflation itself appears to have been an important source of revenue for the government. The "inflation tax," which is the real income that the government receives through the issuance of new money, tends to increase with inflation, because nonindexed money or partially indexed financial assets issued by the government lose their real value. This loss in spending power incurred by the holders of money is in effect a tax, because the government spending financed by money creation is paid for by the loss in value of the money held by the public. Attempts have been made to measure the income that the Brazilian government earned through the inflation tax, and some estimates suggest that income from this source in the 1980s was over 3 or 4 percent of GDP.

Brazil's *Real* Plan

On July 1, 1994, Brazil implemented the last, and to date, most successful of its economic stabilization programs to end inflation. Nearly three years later, the *Real* Plan was intact, far outliving its ill-fated predecessors. By late 1996, inflation by some measures approached an annual rate of less than 20 percent, a remarkable achievement in an economy that a few years earlier would have regarded even a monthly rate at this level a triumph. The new monetary unit created by the plan, the *real* (pl., *reais*; for value of the *real*, see Glossary), actually appreciated against the dollar in the months after its creation.

The design and implementation of the *Real* Plan also distinguished it from the earlier plans, and may help explain some of its success in its first years. Unlike the earlier plans, it did not depend on a general price and wage freeze to stop inflation. At the heart of the new plan was the de-indexation of the Brazilian economy, which was accomplished in part by converting salaries and a number of other prices in the months preceding the implementation of the *Real* Plan into Real Value Units (URVs), which were then linked to the United States dollar. After July 1, 1994, prices in URVs were converted into *reais*, which began officially at par with the dollar, but traded at a premium in the open market. Although the new plan made no guarantees of automatic price and wage adjustments to compensate for inflation, few restrictions were placed on employers and employees in private wage negotiations.

Although some observers characterized the *Real* Plan as a form of "dollarization" of the Brazilian economy, in which prices and wages that previously had been indexed to inflation were now linked to a foreign currency, there was a significant difference between Brazil's approach and that of countries like Argentina, which attempted to stabilize the value of their currencies through a formal and legal link to the dollar. Brazil did not make such a commitment, and despite the stability of the *real* against the dollar throughout the first year and a half of the *Real* Plan, there was a widespread expectation that the *real* eventually would depreciate.

This exchange-rate policy and the expectations that accompanied it had significant consequences for the domestic Brazilian economy. Expectations of an eventual depreciation of the currency, coupled with the short-term stability of the exchange rate and much greater mobility of financial capital between Brazil and world financial markets led to a strong appreciation of the *real* and painfully high domestic real interest rates. Lenders required interest rates that would protect them against a possible depreciation. With prices stable or even falling for some products, borrowers could not repay in currency that had

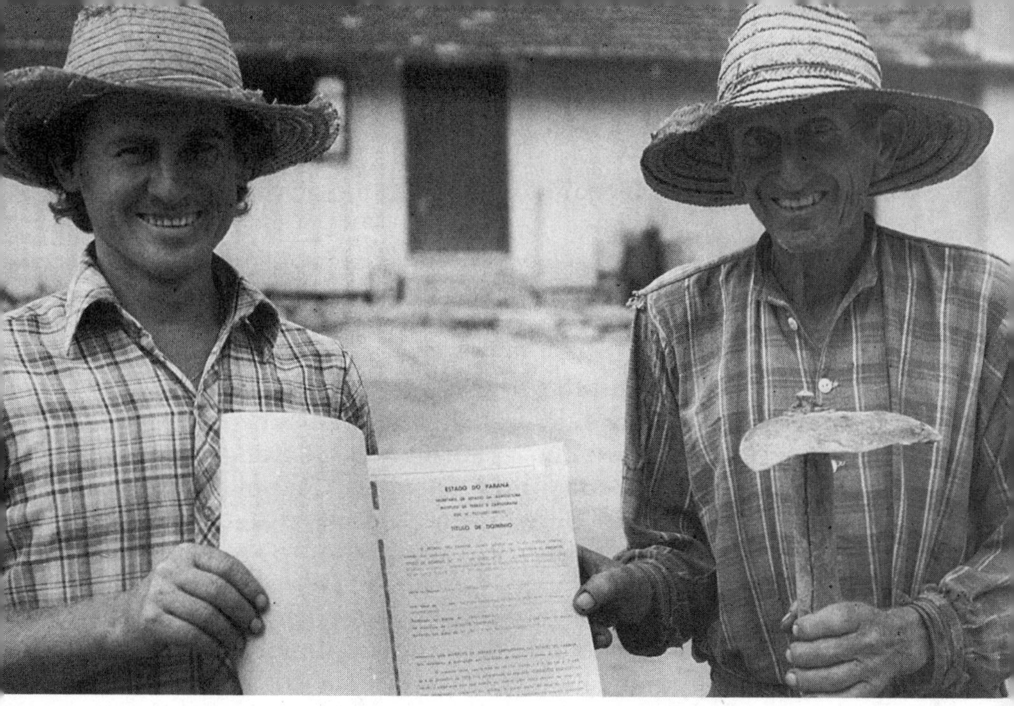

A young farmer and his father show the newly acquired title to their farm near Almirante Tamandaré, Paraná State.
Courtesy Inter-American Development Bank, Washington

lost its value through inflation, as they were accustomed to do in earlier years.

International enthusiasm for the *Real* Plan, reinforced by its apparent success in its first year, led to the resumption of large-scale flows to Brazil, permitting the government to maintain its policy of approximate exchange-rate stability. Despite the worries about a depreciation, and several speculative attacks against the *real* in its first year, the high level of capital flows to Brazil more than financed the high level of imports stimulated by the resumption of economic growth, leading to a sharp increase in Brazil's reserves of foreign currency. By late 1995, they totaled more than US$50 billion.

The fall in inflation, supported in part by the strong *real*, led to important changes in income flows within the Brazilian economy. Decades of inflation had produced a large financial sector, which flourished in part through the spread between borrowing and lending rated in a high-inflation environment. With the fall in this revenue, a number of financial intermediaries came under severe pressure, despite the high real interest rates. During 1995 there were bank insolvencies, with failures avoided by Central Bank intervention to merge these intermediaries with stronger ones.

The fall in inflation also had consequences for Brazil's income distribution. Lower-income groups, which had borne a disproportionately large share of the inflationary burden because of their relatively limited access to fully indexed savings opportunities and to the tendency of minimum salaries and other nominal wages to lag behind inflation, benefited significantly from the *Real* Plan. In the months following its implementation, sales of consumer durables, especially those purchased by lower-income groups, increased significantly, leading the government in 1995 to attempt to restrict consumption and reward saving. The rise in the real incomes of lower- income groups produced a level and depth of political support for the *Real* Plan that made it difficult for unions and other groups opposing many of the policies of the new Cardoso government to confront the *Real* Plan head on. It also may have helped the government in its efforts to secure the support of the Congress for a number of its proposed reforms.

The *Real* Plan's success in its first year strengthened the political support that the government needed to attack the underlying fiscal disequilibrium. By 1995 the operational budget of the federal government was significantly smaller than it had been in earlier years, and the attempts by some organized sectors, among them the employees of state enterprises, to overturn many of the policies of the *Real* Plan had been resisted. Further progress in reducing the pressures on the finances of Brazil's public sector rested on the rates of the first year of the *Real* Plan, as well as on the support of Congress for the fiscal reforms proposed by the Cardoso government.

By the end of 1996, the *Real* Plan appeared to have succeeded in its objective of ending decades of inflation and macroeconomic uncertainty. It had also bought valuable time for the government to attack the underlying fiscal imbalance that generated the inflationary pressures. There was little time to be lost, however, and the rise in public-sector expenditures, especially at the state and municipal levels, cast a cloud over the prospect for the long-run success of the *Real* Plan. This rise was the consequence of a number of factors, among them the surge in costs for public-sector employees created in part by the requirements of the 1988 constitution. In the short run, the rise in interest costs in the first year of the *Real* Plan was a heavy burden for many states and municipalities, some of which were unable in 1995 to pay employees their full salaries. Other pressures on the public sector included rising pension and social security costs, caused in part by demographic trends and by the generous promises of earlier governments to future retirees.

Trade Policies

Brazil's economic history has been influenced remarkably by foreign trade trends and policies. Successive cycles of export booms in such commodities as sugar, gold and diamonds, rubber, and coffee played major roles in Brazilian development before World War II. In the 1930s, the collapse of coffee prices signaled a turn inward, resulting in a nascent industrialization. In succeeding decades, industrial development was fostered deliberately through restrictive trade policies, making Brazil a relatively closed economy by the mid-1960s. Only in the early 1990s did Brazil begin significant liberalization of its trade policies, and even these reforms were modest by comparison with those in a number of other Latin American nations.

Government intervention in foreign trade has a long history in Brazil, reaching back to the colonial period when Portugal forbade Brazilian trade with other nations. Following independence in 1822, Brazil opened its ports and expanded its trade with other nations, particularly Britain. Extensive government regulation of trade continued, however, with tariffs providing over half of the government's revenue before World War I. Other forms of intervention in trade included the 1906 coffee price support plan, which was a sophisticated attempt to exploit Brazil's monopolistic position in the world coffee market.

Before World War II, trade policies were used mostly as a source of revenue or as a response to specific groups such as the coffee producers, rather than as a means of achieving national economic goals. In the early 1950s, Brazil began to use trade policy in a more deliberate way to promote industrialization. The forced reduction in Brazilian imports after 1929 had resulted in the first major industrial growth in Brazil, centered in São Paulo. Heeding this apparent lesson, policy makers in the 1950s argued that measures that deliberately reduced imports would stimulate domestic production, thereby encouraging technological development and increasing employment in activities that were regarded as more "modern" than Brazil's traditional agricultural and extractive activities.

Between 1953 and 1957, Brazil attempted to use multiple exchange rates to encourage some trade transactions and discourage others. In 1957 the country instituted a broad ad valorem tariff system under Law 3,244. The new system created not only a new tariff structure but also the administrative machinery to impose or revise tariffs in accord with national development objectives and requests by domestic producers for protection. Implementation of the system heavily favored domestic producers of manufactured consumer goods, while permitting the import of capital and intermediate goods at much lower tariffs. For some goods, protection was great enough to completely eliminate competing imports from the Brazilian market.

Following the imposition of military rule in 1964, Brazil once again modified its trade policies. The new government moved quickly to eliminate some of the restrictions on Brazilian exports, and it provided special incentives for exports of manufactures. In March 1967, it significantly cut tariffs, which fell to about half their former level in a number of sectors. Brazilian imports soon increased, but this was more the result of the acceleration of economic growth after 1967 than of the tariff reforms. During the "economic miracle" between 1967 and 1973, the GDP grew at record rates. Throughout this period, trade policy continued to be relatively open in comparison with Brazilian policies before or after the economic miracle.

The steep rise in world oil prices that began in late 1973 soon ended Brazil's move toward greater trade openness. The approximate balance between imports and exports in the early 1970s became an unprecedented US$4.7 billion deficit in 1974. Although record levels of external capital flows financed this deficit, Brazilian policy makers responded by restricting imports. In June 1974, import financing for many products was suspended, while tariff rates on more than 900 items were doubled. Over the year, restrictions were increased further, and in 1975 the government required that imports be paid for in advance with deposits that did not earn interest or any correction for inflation. On the export side, further measures were taken to promote exports, especially for manufactures. Despite these measures, Brazil's trade balance remained in deficit for most of the 1970s.

The worsening of Brazil's external payments position in the early 1980s forced policy makers to turn to other measures to attempt to restore external balance, among them adjustment in the exchange rate, which was devalued sharply early in 1983. Controls on trade were not relaxed, however, and the cessation of voluntary lending to Brazil following the Mexican debt crisis in 1982 had significant effects on trade policy. Import controls that had been introduced in response to the worsening trade balance in 1980 were strengthened by centralization of all foreign-exchange transactions in the Central Bank. A negative list, which enumerated items whose import was suspended, was expanded considerably, and financing for imports was further restricted.

The combination of tightened import controls, real depreciation, and the fall in domestic demand induced by the restrictive macroeconomic policies of the early 1980s resulted in a sharp adjustment in Brazil's external accounts. The magnitude of the adjustment appears to have surprised even many of its proponents, both in the Brazilian government and among creditors. After 1983 the massive trade surpluses averaged more than 3 percent of GDP, compared with negative or negligible levels through most of the 1968–82 period. In 1984, as the full effects of the adjustment program were felt, exports were about double imports, and Brazil's trade surplus reached an unprecedented 6.1 percent of GDP, far exceeding the comparable shares in other important economies such as Japan (3.5 percent of GDP) and West Germany (3.8 percent).

Most of the import controls that were used after 1982 were in place well before the cessation of voluntary external lending. One of these measures, introduced in 1980 following the worsening of the current account, was the financing requirement for specific imports. Another form of import control, much used after 1982, was the establishment of formal import programs, which were negotiated agreements between importing firms and the Department of Foreign Trade (Carteira de Comércio Exterior—Cacex). These agreements in effect turned the import decision into a process that depended more on administrative and political considerations than on economic merit. The high degree of administrative control that these agreements gave to Cacex created problems, because middle-level trade officials acquired extensive control over the fortunes of an enterprise through their ability to approve particular trade transactions.

By 1984 it was clear that the successful external adjustment had a domestic price, as inflation accelerated to more than 200 percent at annual rates. Trade policy consequently began to be viewed as a potential instrument for internal stabilization, with some import liberalization viewed as a potential contributor to reduced inflation.

In late 1984, a number of the direct controls on imports were cut back, and the number of products on the negative list was reduced substantially. Import financing requirements were also relaxed through exemptions, and tariff surcharges were replaced by smaller additions to the legal tariff. On the administrative side, the Cacex policy of import restrictions for balance of payments purposes was reduced.

In February 1986, following several months in which the prices accelerated at an average of more than 500 percent, the Sarney government decreed the now infamous Cruzado Plan. Although the plan was presented as a definitive program to deindex the economy and wipe out inflation, its main thrust was to freeze prices. Wages were not frozen and in fact were increased by 8 percent when the plan was announced. Foreign economic policy in the plan consisted primarily of fixing the exchange rate, and no trade policy changes were included in the plan.

The combination of increased domestic real income, a fixed nominal exchange rate, and a fall in nominal interest rates soon produced a sharp increase in excess demand. In sectors less affected by price controls, such as clothing or used automobiles, prices rose sharply. The effects on the trade balance were apparent within several months after the plan was decreed. The value of monthly exports fell by about 40 percent between March and November 1986, and imports rose rapidly beginning in May. For the year, exports fell by 12.7 percent from 1985 levels, and imports increased by 5.7 percent. Brazil's external payments problems, which had appeared to be largely resolved by the record trade balances after 1983, emerged once again, as the trade balance fell from US$12.5 billion in 1985 to US$8.3 billion in 1986.

The policy response to the worsening trade balance consisted of a small 1.8 percent devaluation in October 1986, accompanied by administrative tightening of import controls. In early 1987, the negative list was once again increased, and some of the loss in exchange-rate competitiveness was regained with nominal devaluations of the cruzado (for value of the cruzado—see Glossary) of 7.8 percent and 8.7 percent in May and June of 1987.

The three-lane Immigrants Highway climbs 700 meters from the Atlantic to the plateau in a continuous grade marked by a spectacular series of tunnels and bridges.
Courtesy Inter-American Development Bank, Washington

Brazil's second price-stabilization attempt, popularly known as the Bresser Plan, was announced by the new minister of finance, Luiz Carlos Bresser Pereira, in June 1987. In contrast to the ill-fated Cruzado Plan, the Bresser Plan did not attempt to use external economic policy as an instrument for internal stabilization. Brazil returned to its earlier and generally successful "crawling-peg" policy, which consisted of frequent small devaluations roughly in line with domestic inflation. The trade balance improved with the fall in domestic demand resulting from the Bresser Plan, and a current-account balance was attained by the end of 1987.

The improving external payments situation permitted some modest liberalization, beginning with a reduction of the negative list in September 1987. Import financing requirements were once again relaxed, and in late 1988 Cacex announced an expansion of import program levels for 1989. The 1988 reforms also simplified the existing tariff system. Average rates were lowered from over 50 percent to about 40 percent. Moreover, the dispersion or variability of rates was reduced; the highest tariffs were brought down from 105 to 85 percent, and the number of different rates was reduced from twenty-nine to eighteen. The reforms further simplified the tariff system by consolidating the rules covering import transactions, reducing the number of agencies directly involved in the approval of trade transactions, and establishing greater automaticity in the approval process.

The contrast between the favorable external payments situation and Brazil's internal deficit became even more marked in 1988, as export value increased to record levels. The favorable external situation permitted a continuation of import liberalization. In August 1988, Cacex permitted firms to exceed considerably their programmed imports of capital and intermediate goods. Despite this modest relaxation of import policy, there was no noticeable increase in total imports, which actually fell slightly in 1988 from their 1987 level.

In January 1989, the government announced the Summer Plan, which temporarily froze wages and the exchange rate. Despite the announcement of further fiscal tightening, expenditures declined little and the budget deficit worsened as a result of freezing prices for public-sector services. By mid-1989 most other prices were rising at more than 30 percent per month, ending the year with a monthly rate of about 50 percent. Imports began to increase significantly in mid-1989, and Brazil's 1989 trade surplus was US$16.1 billion, well below the record US$19.2 billion of the preceding year. Although some of the increase in the level of imports may be attributable to the modest loosening of some import controls in the preceding year, major factors behind the worsening trade balance were the recovery of industrial activity and increasing overvaluation of the new cruzado (cruzado novo). In late 1989, the Customs Policy Council (Conselho para Política Aduaneira—CPA) issued Resolution 1,666, which further cut tariffs. The effect of this change was to reduce the average legal tariff from 41 to 35.5 percent. Many of the changes occurred in sectors that had formerly enjoyed high levels of protection, among them electrical equipment, some capital goods, and chemicals (see table 16, Appendix).

At the end of the Sarney government, inflation rates were at the threshold of hyperinflation, with the monthly rates in the first two months of 1990 at over 70 percent. Although the trade balance had fallen to about a third of the levels of the preceding year, Brazilian policy makers were clearly focused on internal stabilization; trade policy reform was a recognized but secondary goal.

Collor de Mello succeeded Sarney in March 1990. During the election campaign, Collor de Mello had successfully portrayed himself as an opponent of an intrusive, interventionist bureaucracy. His rhetoric, which included attacks on corruption and highly paid officials (*marajás*), emphasized deregulation and greater openness to world markets. The consequences of this political and ideological change for Brazilian trade policy were not long in coming. One of Collor de Mello's early moves was to abolish Cacex, by that time the subject of widespread criticism and frequent allegations of corruption by the business community. The Technical Coordinating Office for Trade (Coordenadoria Técnica de Intercâmbio Comercial—CTIC), a slimmer and less powerful agency under the Ministry of Economy, Finance, and Planning, took over the Cacex's functions.

Although import licenses were not abolished, their approval became a relatively routine operation, and by 1991 most licenses were being issued within five working days. The CTIC became primarily a reporting and registration agency, which had little of the discretionary power formerly exercised by Cacex. The former CPA, which had been far overshadowed by Cacex, was replaced by an agency coequal with the CTIC, the Technical Coordinating Office for Tariffs (Coordenadoria Técnica de Tarifas—CTT). With the shift in emphasis in trade policy from discretionary administrative control to the automaticity of published tariffs, many of them limited by Brazil's treaty commitments, the CTT's role in formulating import policy became significantly greater than the CPA's had been.

Early in 1991, the Collor de Mello government announced a series of tariff reductions to be phased in over the 1991–94 period. These were among the most far-reaching and significant reductions in Brazilian trade protection in several decades. Earlier tariff reductions often had been largely cosmetic, only reducing rates that were prohibitive to high levels that still barred many imports. The 1991 reforms went much further, and in many sectors reduced rates to about a third of their level in the early 1980s. Equally important, the reforms reduced the wide variability or dispersion of tariff rates that were once characteristic of Brazilian trade policy. The overall trend in Brazilian trade policy is clear. By the mid-1990s, Brazil had become a much more open economy than it had been a decade earlier.

Trade Patterns and Regional Economic Integration

Underlying much of the debate over trade policy in Brazil in the 1990s is an implicit choice between regional trade arrangements or a more nonpreferential policy that would not discriminate by national origin or destination. Brazil's most important current regional trade initiative is the Common Market of the South (Mercado Comum do Sul—Mercosul; see Glossary). With the ratification of the North American Free Trade Agreement (NAFTA; see Glossary) among Canada, Mexico, and the United States in 1993, it was inevitable that Brazilian participation in even larger regional trade arrangements than Mercosul would be discussed increasingly.

Despite the rhetorical prominence of Latin American trade in debate over Brazilian trade policies, Brazilian trade flows do not reflect a particularly strong orientation to other Latin American countries. However, with Mercosul, other Latin American countries may gain in relative importance. By the mid-1990s, trade with the other Mercosul partners, particularly Argentina, was one of the most rapidly growing sectors of Brazilian foreign trade.

In the 1980s, Brazilian exports to the rest of South America had averaged less than 10 percent of all exports; exports to Mexico, Central America, and the Caribbean added another 2 percent. Brazilian exports were directed overwhelmingly to the United States and Canada (about 30 percent) and to Western Europe (about 30 percent).

Brazilian export patterns in the 1980s and early 1990s were little different from earlier decades, when they were also dominated by trade with the United States and with Europe. This trade orientation reflected several historical influences, including the structure of Brazilian international transportation channels and the composition of Brazilian exports. Only in the 1970s did Brazilian exports shift from being dominated by primary and semiprocessed products to manufactures. Major markets for all these products were primarily in high-income countries; for example, Brazil long depended on the United States as its major market for coffee. Other important primary products, such as sugar, soybeans, and iron ore, were also sold mainly in high-income countries (see table 17, Appendix).

Finally, and possibly most important, Brazilian export patterns reflected the relatively strong inward orientation of most of Brazil's Latin American trade partners during most of the early post-World War II decades. The strong influence of the import-substitution industrialization doctrines of the Economic Commission for Latin America and the Caribbean (ECLAC; see Glossary) in most of the Latin American economies in the 1950s had by the early 1960s led to extensive import-substitution industrialization, particularly in Brazil and its larger trading partners, notably Argentina and Mexico. The inevitable result was that the more open economies of Europe and North America continued to provide the most important markets for Brazilian exports. Only with the concurrent liberalization of trade in a number of other Latin American economies, especially Argentina, did Brazil's exports begin to reflect the importance of its Latin American trade partners.

Brazil's export orientation toward North America and Europe is also noticeable in its import pattern. In addition, the Middle East is a significant trade partner because of the high value of petroleum imports. The large trade deficit with this region was financed primarily by surpluses with other regions, notably the United States and Europe. Brazil's imports from the rest of Latin America accounted for only about 12 percent of the total value of its imports in the 1980s.

Despite the approximately equal shares of Latin American trade in both Brazil's exports and its imports, during most of the 1980s Brazil had a large trade surplus with the region, exceeding US$800 million in most years. This surplus, which was generated primarily in trade with Argentina, Bolivia, and Paraguay, helped finance Brazil's oil imports from two of the region's oil exporters, Mexico and Venezuela. The value of Brazilian imports of petroleum from these countries was greatest in the early 1980s and declined with the fall in petroleum prices.

Brazilian attempts to expand formal regional trade agreements beyond bilateral preferential trading arrangements date from 1958, when the government joined Argentina, Chile, and Uruguay in discussions that led to the Treaty of Montevideo, signed in February 1960. Under the treaty, which was expanded subsequently to most of the economies of South America and to Mexico, the members agreed to negotiate mutual tariff reductions on a permanent basis.

Despite its professed intentions, the organization created by the treaty, the Latin American Free Trade Association (LAFTA—also known as Asociación Latinoamericana de Libre Comercio—ALALC; see Glossary) was only a limited success. Part of the reason lay in the departures of many of the agreements from the nondiscriminatory provisions of Article 24 of the General Agreement on Tariffs and Trade (GATT—see Glossary), which regulates regional trade agreements. Although the intent of LAFTA was to create new trade rather than to divert trade flows from efficient sources outside the region, its success in this respect was minimal. Another provision of the agreement, which required the formation of a free-trade area within a specified time period, was ignored. The deadline for LAFTA to create such an area was first extended from 1972 to 1980; when the 1980 deadline was not met, LAFTA was replaced by the Latin American Integration Association (LAIA—also known as Associação Latino-Americana de Integração—ALADI), which had more modest goals. The real blow to LAFTA/ALADI trade came after 1982, when international capital markets were closed to most Latin American borrowers following the onset of Mexico's external debt crisis. Like most Latin American governments, Brazil reacted by sharply restricting its imports, including those from other ALADI members. As a result, intraregional trade fell significantly in the first half of the 1980s.

Argentina historically has been Brazil's most important Latin American trade partner by a wide margin, both in imports from Brazil and exports to it. For this reason, virtually all Brazilian regional trade initiatives have been based on this bilateral trade relationship. Well behind, and of comparable importance, are Chile, Mexico, and Venezuela. One feature of Brazil's regional trade is the substantial surpluses that it has run with several of its neighbors, among them Bolivia, Colombia, and Paraguay. In the case of Paraguay, this surplus may reflect an underreporting of imports as a result of the high value of contraband and unreported consumer good imports from Paraguay to Brazil. Another prominent feature of Brazil's trade with the rest of Latin America is the importance of imports from the temperate-zone Southern Cone countries. With the exception of the oil exporters, Brazilian imports from other tropical Latin American economies are relatively unimportant, despite the importance of several of them as markets for Brazilian exports.

A widened and paved section of Highway BR–367 108 kilometers north of Diamantina, Minas Gerais State, traverses plantations of eucalyptus trees, grown to produce charcoal for Minas Gerais iron and steel mills.
Courtesy Inter-American Development Bank, Washington

During the 1970s, Brazil's trade with the United States, historically its most important trade partner, declined in relative importance as trade with Western Europe and Japan grew. On the export side, this trend ended in the early 1980s, as the United States economy grew more rapidly than Europe's and the real appreciation of the dollar made the United States a relatively more attractive market in which to sell. The tendency toward a greater trade surplus was reinforced by Brazil's efforts after 1982 to restrict imports, especially from traditional suppliers like the United States.

Brazil's export-led growth (see Glossary) since the 1980s has been oriented decidedly toward the industrialized countries. As a result of their already large share of Brazil's export market and their rates of growth, the United States and Canada were responsible for nearly half of Brazil's export growth during the late 1980s and early 1990s. Brazil's most rapidly growing market in the period was the rest of South America, with annual growth exceeding 10 percent. However, its relatively modest initial share of the Brazilian export market placed South America behind Asia and the Pacific and Western Europe, as well as the United States and Canada, in its contribution to total Brazilian export growth.

Brazilian import growth in the 1980s and early 1990s presents a similar picture. The total value of Brazilian imports in this period grew very slowly, as the decline in the value of oil imports nearly offset the rise in the value of imports from Western Europe and North America. As was the case with exports, the industrialized countries were far more important trade partners for Brazil than were the less developed regions. Brazilian imports from other Latin American trade partners fell in value after 1983, as modest increases in imports from the rest of South America and the Caribbean were more than offset by the fall in imports from Mexico and Central America.

Until the early 1990s, both Brazil and Argentina had a tradition of inward-oriented industrial policy, and it is therefore not surprising that trade between the two economies fell far short of its probable potential. The 1986 trade agreement between Brazil and Argentina was a partial attempt to address this problem and formed the nucleus of the regional trade agreement for Mercosul.

President Sarney and Argentina's Raúl Alfonsín (president, 1985–89) signed twelve protocols in July 1986 and additional protocols in December 1986. Most of the protocols aimed at strengthening Argentine-Brazilian economic cooperation, although cooperation in other areas also was included. In November 1988, following extensive consultations between the two governments, Alfonsín and Sarney signed the final Argentine-Brazilian Agreement, which was ratified subsequently without modification by the congresses of the two countries in August 1989.

Both governments hailed the agreements as major steps toward economic integration, as well as a Latin American response to what was perceived as the formation of economic blocs, such as the plans of the United States-Canada Free Trade Agreement (FTA) and the European Community (EC; see Glossary). In reality, the protocols were more statements of intention than the detailed results of negotiations in the areas covered. The Argentine-Brazilian Agreement was a short, five-page general statement summarizing the objectives of the July 1986 protocols. Unlike the massive United States-Canada FTA, it in effect deferred much of the specific negotiation involved in the agreement's implementation to the future. It was nevertheless an ambitious document, appearing to promise a level of cooperation and coordination analogous to that of the EC.

The Argentine-Brazilian protocols signed between 1986 and 1988 paved the way for an even more ambitious regional trade agreement. Following negotiations with Uruguay and Paraguay, the foreign ministers of the respective governments agreed in March 1991 in Asunción, Paraguay, to establish a common market among the four countries by the end of 1994; the Treaty of Asunción, which established Mercosul, explicitly recognized the potential participation of additional members. Like the earlier bilateral Argentine-Brazilian agreements, the 1991 Mercosul agreements were long on promises and left much for future negotiations. The agreements envisioned a full common market. Article 1 of the treaty provides for free circulation of goods, services, and factors of production (see Glossary) among the member countries; elimination of tariff and nontariff barriers; establishment of a common external tariff; coordination of policies in regional and international forums; and coordination of macroeconomic and sectoral policies.

During the transition period from 1991 through 1994, the accord called for a progressive "linear and automatic" reduction in tariffs, which was to be accompanied by the elimination of nontariff barriers to trade among the contracting parties. The December 31, 1994, target was to be a zero tariff among the members. As more recent entrants, Paraguay and Uruguay were given an additional year to comply with the terms of the treaty.

Compared with some earlier declarations of intent, the Treaty of Asunción was considerably more specific about how the common market was to be created. A schedule for tariff reductions was established; cuts were to be made at six-month intervals between June 30, 1991, and December 31, 1994. These reductions were to be calculated as a percentage of the lowest tariffs applied to members outside the Mercosul group and were based on the ALADI tariff classification.

Several other provisions of the treaty give it a positive bias toward greater economic openness. Tariff reductions are based on the rates prevailing before the signing of the treaty. Any external tariff reductions that lower the base from which intra-Mercosul tariffs are calculated was to apply to all signatories. The treaty also contains a type of "most-favored-nation" clause, which guarantees that any trade concession extended to nonmembers of Mercosul by any member will be extended automatically by all other contracting members.

The Treaty of Asunción allowed each nation to submit a list of exceptions to the tariff reduction list. Brazil and Argentina submitted 324 and 394 tariff exceptions, respectively; Paraguay, allowed 439; and Uruguay, 960. Although it is impossible to quantify the degree to which these exemptions undercut the main thrust of the treaty, their most important feature was that they were temporary. Argentina and Brazil agreed to reduce their exception list by 20 percent annually, while Paraguay and Uruguay were allowed an extra year (to the end of 1995) to eliminate their lists.

Brazil and many of its neighbors have tended to view Brazilian trade preference options as geographically defined and relatively local. Whatever the outcome of the Mercosul regional initiative, the existing pattern of Brazilian trade flows suggests that Brazil's long-term trade interests extend well beyond such regional boundaries. Indeed, Mercosul and the European Union (EU, the former EC; see Glossary) have been discussing the creation of a free-trade area between the two groups. Two alternatives to Brazil's South American-focused regional trade policy are participation in a hemispheric FTA or more open, nonpreferential trade with the entire world. The former would follow the Mexican example by negotiating Brazil's entrance into the NAFTA, which is composed of the United States, Canada, Mexico, and potentially, Chile. The second strategy is to follow a Chilean approach, avoiding preferential trade liberalization and making Brazil more open to all trade flows, whatever their geographical source.

Compared with membership in an expanded NAFTA, Brazilian participation in Mercosul represents a much more modest regional trade arrangement. Canada alone has a larger GDP than do all of the Mercosul economies combined; the four Southern Cone members have a combined GDP totaling less than 10 percent of the total GDP of the NAFTA countries. Given recent rates of economic growth, this gap has actually widened in recent years.

The great disparity in the sizes of the two regional trade groups has a number of implications for alternative Brazilian trade strategies. Membership in the current group, in which Brazil is by far the dominant economy, offers political influence and the possibility of shaping many of Mercosul's external commercial policies to match Brazilian trade objectives. In many manufacturing areas, Brazil faces little competition from the other Mercosul countries. If Brazil were to become a member of the larger hemispheric trade group (NAFTA), the country would account for only about 5 percent of the association's joint product.

In addition to the size difference between Mercosul and a hemispheric FTA, other features of the two regional trade arrangements have important cost and benefit implications for Brazil. The Treaty of Asunción is in many ways more ambitious than is NAFTA. Its stated objective is the creation of a true common market similar to the EU. In such a regional trade arrangement, trade barriers among the member countries are eliminated and external tariffs against third countries, fiscal policies, and exchange-rate policies are integrated.

Brazilian participation in a hemispheric FTA would in principle require less coordination of fiscal, monetary, exchange-rate, and foreign capital policy than is required by the Treaty of Asunción. One may question how seriously the Brazilian government or other Mercosul members are prepared to implement the integration implied by a common market. The replacement of LAFTA by ALADI in 1980 suggests that in the choice between national sovereignty and the benefits of greater economic integration, the former may prevail. But, if the explicit commitments of the four governments in the Treaty of Asunción are to be taken at face value, it would appear that a relatively high degree of policy independence would be sacrificed for economic integration benefits, which are likely to be considerably more modest than those attainable by membership in a hemispheric FTA.

Another option for Brazil would be to follow a Chilean approach of greater trade openness on a nonpreferential basis. Such an approach has three main advantages, which in principle make it superior to other trade strategies. First, the possibility that inefficient trade diversion will occur is eliminated. The lowest cost or most efficient producers would be able to supply Brazil without facing trade barriers, because no such producer would be eliminated from among Brazil's potential suppliers under a nonpreferential open-trade policy. Brazilian demand would thus be supplied by the most efficient suppliers in the world market, rather than those in a more restricted area.

Second, a nonpreferential approach in Brazilian trade policy would be more easily administered because it is in effect a unilateral policy, not dependent on negotiations with potential trade partners. However, this approach may not be perceived as an advantage from a political standpoint, as it appears to sacrifice Brazil's "bargaining chips."

Third, a nonpreferential strategy may better position Brazil to respond to changes in world markets. Until the mid-1990s, Brazilian trade had not grown faster in the Mercosul region than in other areas. In fact, the United States, Canada, Western Europe, and Asia all contributed more to the growth of Brazilian trade until the mid-1990s than did other Latin American economies. Although Brazilian membership in a hemispheric FTA might ensure greater access to the United States, Canada, and Mexico, it would offer little prospect of trade expansion with Europe or Asia.

Economic Outlook

Brazil entered the 1990s with much less confidence about its economic future than it once had. The economic stagnation and uncertainty of the 1980s had exacted a high toll, and per capita income in 1990 was no higher than it was in 1980. Inflation, at monthly rates, was over 30 percent, unprecedented even by Brazilian standards. It is reasonable therefore to ask what has been learned from the experience of the 1980s and what are the prospects for an economic future brighter than the recent past.

As an object lesson, the economic experience of the 1980s made a contribution. Government is much less likely to be seen as a solution, and many more Brazilians see the public sector as the problem. The rather tiresome debate between the monetarists and the structuralists that dominated discussions of inflation in the1970s has been superseded by a recognition that money supply growth does indeed have a close relation to inflation, but that the underlying problem is the fiscal deficit that drives the money supply process. Although the monetization of deficits may be postponed, as was sometimes done in the 1980s, the inflationary consequences of public-sector financial imbalance cannot be avoided indefinitely. A part of the economic disorder of the 1980s was the consequence of populist attempts to ignore this point.

The external shocks of the 1980s have also shown Brazilians that their country cannot be isolated from the rest of the world. By the early 1990s, Brazil was on the path to becoming more open to trade than it had been for several decades. Despite the loss of Brazilian access to world capital markets in

Copacabana Beach, Rio de Janeiro
Courtesy Larry Buzard

the early 1980s, external capital was beginning to return to Brazil by the early 1990s. In contrast to the massive capital flows of the 1970s, much of which financed public borrowing, capital flows in the 1990s focused more on the private sector.

Brazilians also learned that price stabilization is not easy and that "magic" solutions centered on price freezes do not work without the more difficult fiscal adjustments that emerge from a political consensus. That consensus had not been developed by the early 1990s, even though political leaders and economists recognized that fiscal adjustment was essential for macroeconomic stability. The failure of successive stabilization plans that ignored the underlying fiscal disequilibrium also imposed long-term costs, because the credibility of government economic policies was undermined. The fall of the Collor de Mello government in 1992 under charges of massive corruption and the economically unrealistic provisions of the 1988 constitution have made the task of regaining government credibility even more difficult.

For Brazil to return to the kind of economic growth that many of its people once regarded as their birthright, a number of changes must occur. First, the public-sector deficit must be reduced substantially. This can be done in a number of ways without imposing heavy costs on Brazilian society. Privatization of economically inefficient state enterprises is one way, and in the first half of the 1990s some progress was made in this area. The complex system of tax and credit subsidies that was developed in preceding decades offers many opportunities for efficiency-improving reform, which would also contribute substantially to reduction of the fiscal deficit.

Second, Brazil's recent moves toward becoming a more open economy offer the prospect of increasing economic efficiency and ensuring that new resources flow into activities in which Brazil has a strong international competitive position. Decades of protectionism in a number of key sectors have imposed high costs on Brazilian consumers. Greater openness to world markets, either through regional trade initiatives or through unilateral reductions in trade restrictions, will make a noticeable contribution to Brazilian economic welfare.

Finally, Brazil could become an economically prosperous country if it can seriously address the enormous inequities in income distribution. Serious efforts to help Brazil's least privileged must focus on the provision of basic services and, above all, on education. Without substantial efforts to address the income distribution problem, the strains on the political system that have their economic counterpart in fiscal disequilibrium may make the country much harder to govern and may reduce the prospects for a successful and sustainable price stabilization.

* * *

A highly regarded analysis of the Brazilian economy's formulation from the early colonial period to the breakdown of the coffee economy in the 1930s is in Celso Furtado's *The Economic Growth of Brazil.* A succession of external shocks, failed stabilization plans, and significant changes in trade policy in the 1980s and early 1990s provided the raw material for literature on recent Brazilian economic problems. A classical treatment of the 1980s is Werner Baer's *The Brazilian Economy—Its Growth and Development,* the fourth edition of which was published in 1995. Some of the difficulties in the transition from a primary product economy to an important industrial power are examined in Edmar L. Bacha and Herbert S. Klein's *Social Change in Brazil, 1945–1985.* A parallel treatment of some of these problems in Brazilian economic development is given in Luiz Carlos Bresser Pereira's *Development and Crisis in Brazil, 1930–1983.*

Brazil's economic response to the external debt crisis of the early 1980s is the subject of various studies, several of them parts of larger studies on a number of developing nations. One is Eliana A. Cardoso and Albert Fishlow's *The Macroeconomics of the Brazilian External Debt.* Donald V. Coes's *Macroeconomic Crises, Policies, and Growth in Brazil, 1964–90* provides a detailed macroeconomic history of post-1964 policies and their consequences. An earlier treatment on Brazil's experience is James Dinsmoor's *Brazil: Responses to the Debt Crisis.* A former minister of finance, Marcílio Marques Moreira, provides an insider's view of the external debt problem in *The Brazilian Quandary.*

William G. Tyler's *Manufactured Export Expansion and Industrialization in Brazil* and Werner Baer's *Industrialization and Economic Development in Brazil* examine a number of the causes and consequences of import-substitution industrialization. A World Bank-sponsored study by Coes, *Liberalizing Foreign Trade: Brazil,* examines Brazil's trade policies between 1964 and the early 1980s. Changes in Brazil's capital markets in this period are the subject of John H. Welch's *Capital Markets in the Development Process.* Samuel A. Morley examines Brazilian labor markets and income distribution in *Labor Markets and Inequitable Growth: The Case of Authoritarian Capitalism in Brazil.* Thomas J. Trebat studies the role of state enterprises in *Brazil's State-Owned Enterprises.*

Among the useful sources on the Brazilian economy and its development that are available only in Portuguese are *A ordem do progesso,* edited by Marcelo de Paira Abreu. Numerous works in Portuguese discuss Brazilian inflation and the various attempts to deal with it. Ignácio Rangel's *A inflação brasileira* is a classic work. Contemporary treatments of stabilization attempts include *Plano Cruzado* by Fernando de Holanda and Mario Henrique Simonsen, the latter a former finance minister.

Data on the Brazilian economy are available from a number of sources, including various Brazilian economic journals, many of high quality. *Revista Brasileira de Economia,* edited by the Fundação Getúlio Vargas in Rio de Janeiro, is Brazil's oldest and perhaps most conservative economic journal. *Estudos Econômicos,* edited by the Economic School of the University of São Paulo, is an eclectic journal. *Pesquisa e Planejamento Econômico,* which emphasizes academic articles dealing with current problems of the Brazilian economy, is published by the

National Research Institute (Instituto Nacional de Pesquisa—INPES) and the Applied Economic Research Institute (Instituto de Pesquisa Econômica Aplicada—IPEA), a semi-independent research organization of the Ministry of Planning, based in Rio de Janeiro. *Revista de Economia Política* is a critical but widely respected economic journal edited by the Center for Political Economy of São Paulo. An interesting economic journalism magazine is the monthly *Conjuntura Econômica*, published by the Fundação Getúlio Vargas. It presents short articles on trends in the Brazilian economy and has a rich statistical compendium.

A long view is provided in *Estatísticas históricas do Brasil: Séries econômicas, demográficas e sociais, 1550 a 1988*, published by the Brazilian Institute of Geography and Statistics (Fundação Instituto Brasileiro de Geografia e Estatística—IBGE). The IBGE yearbook, *Anuário estatístico do Brasil*, provides a wealth of data on all aspects of the economy, albeit with a lag of several years. The *Boletim do Banco Central* is a valuable source of macroeconomic and financial data. A rich source of studies on the Brazilian economy is in a series of publications by INPES-IPEA called *Perspectivas da economia brasileira.* Dealing with virtually all aspects of the Brazilian economy, the volumes, issued at two- to three-year intervals, not only review recent events but also perform projections for the near future. Among the sources available in English are the periodic studies published by the British Economist Intelligence Unit and the statistical series by the IMF published for all member countries. The World Bank provides a number of summary statistics in its annual *World Development Report* and is also the source of a wealth of more detailed statistical information, both published and unpublished, on contemporary Brazil. (For further information and complete citations, see Bibliography.)

Chapter 4. Government and Politics

A nineteenth-century wood carving made by an indigenous Brazilian tribe, from Hjalmar Stolpe, Amazon Indian Designs from Brazilian and Guianan Wood Carvings

BRAZIL'S POLITICAL EVOLUTION from monarchy to democracy has not been smooth. Following independence in 1822, Brazil, unlike its South American neighbors, adopted constitutional monarchy as its form of government. The new nation retained a slave-based, plantation economy, and political participation remained very limited. After the coronation of Dom Pedro II (emperor, 1840–89) in 1840, a two-party system based on the British model—with conservative and liberal parties and frequent cabinet turnovers—evolved. Within this centralized unitary system, the emperor appointed the governors, using his prerogatives under the moderating power (*poder moderador*—see Glossary) granted by the 1824 constitution, and legislative elections were indirect. Brazil enjoyed considerable political stability until the 1880s, when the system proved incapable of accommodating military demands and pressure to emancipate slaves.

Brazil patterned the constitution of what is now called the Old Republic (1889–1930) on the United States constitution. However, colonelism (*coronelismo*—see Glossary), a political system based on economic power by large landowners in rural areas, persisted. Under the new constitution of February 24, 1891, the president, National Congress (Congresso Nacional; hereafter, Congress), state governors and legislatures, and local officials were chosen through direct elections.

Following World War I, when Brazil began to undergo rural-urban and agricultural-industrial transformations, its political system again was unable to cope with the demands of the urban middle classes and especially the working classes. The 1929 stock market crash further exacerbated the volatile situation, and elites from the states of Rio Grande do Sul and Minas Gerais staged a preemptive revolution and deposed the old regime. As a result of the revolts of 1930, Getúlio Dorneles Vargas became president (1930–1945, 1951– 54).

Violent clashes over conflicting ideologies of the left and the right erupted in the streets of Brazil's major cities in the 1930s. Vargas tried to strike a balance between the demands of labor and capital following Italian dictator Benito Mussolini's Carta di Lavoro (see Glossary) model established in the 1920s. The 1934 constitution incorporated this model and thus began the politics of corporatism (see Glossary) in Brazil. In close cooperation with the military, Vargas pushed for import-substitution industrialization (see Glossary) and a reduction of military forces under the command of state governments, in favor of the Brazilian Armed Forces (Forças Armadas Brasileiras). President Vargas closed Congress in 1937 and ruled as a dictator until 1945.

The 1945–64 period is known for its multiparty democratic politics, and four presidents were elected freely in 1945, 1950, 1955, and 1960. In the early 1960s, an explosive combination of slower economic growth, rising inflation, populism, and nationalism produced political instability and popular discontent. The major political parties lost their hegemony, and labor unions accumulated great political influence over the government of João Goulart (president, 1961–64).

The military seized power in April 1964 and began twenty-one years of rule. Under its model of "relative democracy," Congress remained open, but with greatly reduced powers. Regular elections were held for Congress, state assemblies, and local offices. However, presidential, gubernatorial, and some mayoral elections became indirect. Political parties were allowed to operate, but with two forced realignments. These were the replacement of the old multiparty system with a two-party system in 1965 and a system of moderate pluralism, with six (and later five) parties in 1980. The military regime employed massive repression from 1969 through 1974.

After the "economic miracle" period (1967–74), Brazil entered a "stagflation" phase concurrent with political liberalization. During the military period, Brazilian society had become 70 percent urban; the economy had become industrialized, and more manufactured goods than primary goods were exported; and about 55 percent of the population had registered to vote. Foreign policy oscillated between alignment with the United States and pragmatic independence. A transition to a civilian president took place in 1985. From 1985 to 1997, Brazil experienced four distinct political models: a return to the pre-1964 tradition of political bargaining, clientelism (see Glossary), and economic nationalism under José Sarney (president, 1985–90); neosocial liberalism with economic modernization under Fernando Collor de Mello (president, 1990–92); an erratic personal style of social nationalism under Itamar Franco (president, 1992–94); and a consensus-style social-democratic and neoliberal coalition under Fernando Henrique Cardoso (president, 1995–).

Under heavy accusations of corruption, President Collor was impeached in 1992. His vice president, Franco, used a pragmatic policy of "muddling through," but in mid-1994 achieved great popularity with the *Real* Plan (for value of the *real* (R$)—see Glossary), a stabilization program authored by then Minister of Finance Cardoso. In the 1994 election, Cardoso and the Brazilian Social Democracy Party (Partido da Social Democracia Brasileira—PSDB) expounded a social-democratic model of modernization, while Luis Inácio "Lula" da Silva of the Workers' Party (Partido dos Trabalhadores—PT) supported a reworked model of corporatist or syndicalist socialism. The *Real* Plan was instrumental in the election of Cardoso as president.

Cardoso was inaugurated as president on January 1, 1995. The transition to the new government was nearly perfect. Cardoso had won an outright victory in the first-round election. He had potentially strong support blocs in the Chamber of Deputies (Câmara dos Deputados) and Federal Senate (Senado Federal; hereafter, Senate). He had strong support from a majority of the newly elected governors, including those from the important states of Minas Gerais, São Paulo, and Rio de Janeiro, which elected governors from the president's own PSDB. Moreover, the December 1994 inflation rate was less than 1 percent; unemployment was low; and popular expectations were extremely high.

Perhaps the most important task of the Cardoso government in 1995 was to promote the reform of key sections of the 1988 constitution in order to reduce the role of the state in the economy, reform the federal bureaucracy, reorganize the social security system, rework federalist relationships, overhaul the complicated tax system, and effect electoral and party reforms to strengthen the representation of political parties. The new Cardoso government initiated constitutional reform (which requires a three-fifths majority of each house), but soon met with stiff congressional resistance. Because of the 1996 municipal elections and other political impediments, the other reforms—administrative, social security, and fiscal—were stalled in Congress, awaiting passage in 1997.

Political Culture

Many aspects of Brazil's political system may be explained by its political culture (see Glossary), the origins of which may be found in traditional rural society during the colonial and independence periods through 1930. This political culture evolved into three styles of politics. Under the more traditional style of politics, *coronelismo,* the local *coronel* (colonel), in alliance with other large farmers, controlled the votes of rural workers and their families. The local political chiefs in turn exchanged votes with politicians at the state level in return for political appointments and public works in their municipalities (*municípios*).

As rural-urban migration increased after 1930, a transitional style of clientelistic politics emerged in medium-size and large-size cities. Under this system, neighborhood representatives of urban politicians would help recent migrants resolve their problems in exchange for votes. These representatives were usually from "clientele professions," such as medical doctors, dentists, and pharmacists.

The third style of mass politics involved a direct populist appeal to the voter by the politician, without formal intermediation by clientelism or domination by *coronelismo.* Research in the early 1990s revealed that in most cases voter decision making has been influenced by a mixture of the second and third styles, as well as by peer groups, opinion leaders, and television soap operas (*telenovelas*).

Polling results since the early 1970s have revealed changing public opinion concerning the relative merits of military government versus democracy. For example, the proportion of Brazilians favorable to military government decreased from 79 percent in 1972 to 36 percent in 1990. Moreover, 70 percent of Brazilians agreed in 1990 that the government should not use troops against striking workers, as compared with only 7 percent in 1972. In a March 1995 poll conducted by the Datafolha agency, however, only 46 percent of Brazilians responded that "democracy is always preferred over dictatorship," as compared with 59 percent endorsing the same proposition in March 1993. The relatively low crime rates during the military period may be a factor in the shift in public opinion regarding democracy.

Brazil has a diversity of regional political cultures. Politics in the states of the Northeast (Nordeste) and North (Norte) are much more dependent on political benevolence from Brasília than are the states of the South (Sul) and Southeast (Sudeste). Because Brazil's southernmost state, Rio Grande do Sul, suffered three civil wars and was involved frequently in political conflicts in the Río de la Plata areas, its population holds strong political loyalties. As a result, the Liberal Front Party (Partido da Frente Liberal—PFL) and the PSDB have very limited penetration in Rio Grande do Sul. Both parties are considered traitors: the PFL had splintered from the military regime's Democratic Social Party (Partido Democrático Social—PDS) in 1984, and the PSDB had broken from the Brazilian Democratic Movement Party (Partido do Movimento Democrático Brasileiro—PMDB) in 1988.

In the Southeast state of Minas Gerais, politics is conducted in a very cautious, calculated manner. Politicians there are known for their ability to negotiate and cut bargains, and they have political "adversaries" rather than enemies. In the western frontier states, politics is constantly evolving, because of the continuous inward migration from other regions. Most politicians and voters are newcomers with no local political roots or traditions.

The Southeast states of Rio de Janeiro and São Paulo have received large influxes of rural-urban and north-south migration since the 1950s. Because of higher levels of industrialization, per capita income, labor union membership, and education, the level of political consciousness is higher in these states than in those to the north and west.

As a result of intense rural-urban migration since 1960, urban voters have increased from fewer than 30 percent to more than 70 percent of the population in 1994. In 1960 only 22 percent (15.5 million) of Brazil's population was registered to vote; by 1994 more than 60 percent (nearly 95 million) of the population was enfranchised. The new migrants to urban areas quickly enhanced their political consciousness through television, increased schooling, and membership in new associations, such as labor unions.

Constitutional Framework

Brazil has had eight constitutions since independence in 1822, beginning with the constitution of March 25, 1824. The republican constitution promulgated on February 24, 1891, was very similar to the United States constitution, containing separation of powers, checks and balances, a bicameral legislature, federalism, and direct elections. Concepts of corporatism and centralization from Italy and Portugal influenced the 1934 and 1937 constitutions. The return to representative democracy in 1945–46 produced a more balanced, liberal document, which maintained a considerable role for the state in the nation's economy. Military rule after 1964 forced an uneasy balance between "relative democracy" and the "safeguards of a national security state," reflected in the 1967 and 1969 constitutions.

After 1964 the government of Marshal Humberto de Alencar Castelo Branco (president, 1964–67) issued four institutional acts and a series of complementary acts and decrees that severely compromised the 1946 constitution. Outgoing President Castelo Branco also convoked a lame-duck Congress in December 1966 and January 1967 to approve a new constitution drafted by his legal team. The 1967 constitution removed some important autocratic powers accorded the first military president.

This 1967 constitution soon became an anathema to the military, and the government of General Arthur da Costa e Silva (president, 1967–69) decreed the Fifth Institutional Act in December 1968, which allowed the regime to close Congress and begin a third wave of political purges (*cassações*). Before his incapacitating stroke in August 1969, Costa e Silva and his vice president, Pedro Aleixo, had apparently begun drafting a new constitution. The fourth military president, General Ernesto Geisel (president, 1974–79), decreed the end of the Fifth Institutional Act in January 1979.

In 1985, the first year of José Sarney's term, Congress approved the convocation of the National Constituent Assembly (Assembléia Nacional Constituinte—ANC) to draft a new constitution. Elected on November 15, 1986, and seated in February 1987, the ANC adopted a "from scratch" participatory methodology. Using this methodology, the ANC divided itself into eight committees and twenty-four subcommittees to draft respective sections of the document, and it held public hearings on suggested content. After twenty months of deliberation and two rounds of voting, the ANC produced the 1988 "citizen constitution," which was promulgated on October 5, 1988.

The majority party, the PMDB, was not united during the ANC. After the drafting committee produced a "progressive" first draft, the PMDB's center and right wings joined conservatives from other parties to form the conservative coalition, the Big Center (Centrão), in December 1987, to alter the internal rules governing first-round voting. The Big Center prevailed on some crucial votes, such as maintaining the presidential system and making Sarney's presidential term five years rather than four. However, plagued with absenteeism it was defeated in other areas, such as the economic order.

The result is a mixed document with certain inconsistencies. Very liberal in the section dealing with basic human rights, the constitution also enhances "social rights," such as retirement after thirty-five years of service, job stability for public employees, and four months of paid maternity leave. It maintains a strong role for the state in the economy and distinguishes between foreign and national capital enterprises.

The ANC maintained the skewed representational plan favoring Brazil's underdeveloped regions. It also created three very small states—Amapá, Roraima, and Tocantins—with sixteen additional deputies and nine new senators, while granting São Paulo ten more deputies. The states have considerable autonomy in certain areas, such as maintaining state banks, but the federal constitution is very centralized regarding election of state officials, mandates, and government organization.

The ANC was able to pass many controversial articles using bland wording and a final reference to "future regulation by ordinary legislation." Some 300 areas of the new constitution were not automatically applicable and awaited such "regulation" in subsequent legislative sessions (1989–90, 1991–92, 1993–94, 1995–96, and 1997–98). Thus, the constitution is incomplete.

The first draft of the constitution was based on a mixed parliamentary presidential model similar to that of Portugal and France, but a crucial vote taken on March 22, 1988, reinstated the pure presidential model. The redrafting to incorporate this major change was incomplete, however, and several vestiges of the mixed parliamentary system remained. Most notable was the provisional measure (*medida provisória*—MP), a sort of temporary decree, which replaced the presidential decree law. Whereas the decree law took effect only after thirty days of inaction by the legislature, the MP takes effect immediately. Although the MP ceased to exist after thirty days of legislative inaction, the president could reissue it for successive thirty-day periods. This power was formidable, especially for a president not commanding an absolute majority in Congress. In early 1997, however, the Senate approved an amendment extending an MP's validity from thirty to ninety days but prohibiting additional extensions and the use of MPs to create ministries or other government entities.

The 1988 constitution required each state to rewrite its constitution within one year (during 1989) and each municipality to elaborate its Organic Law (during 1990), which defines how it operates. In 1991 the Federal District (Brasília) drafted its Organic Law, and the new states of Amapá, Roraima, and Tocantins drafted their new constitutions.

ANC members agreed that a very detailed constitution would require frequent revisions to keep pace with an ever-changing society and economy. Thus, Article 3 of the transitional provisions provided that after five years the Congress could be converted into a unicameral assembly for constitutional revision, deliberating by absolute majority instead of by the three-fifths margin in each house normally required for the amendment process. In addition, Article 2 of the transitional provisions called for a national plebiscite to decide on the form of government (republic or constitutional monarchy) and the system of government (presidential or parliamentary). A constitutional amendment formally setting the plebiscite for April 21, 1992, passed the Chamber of Deputies. However, in late 1991, during the second round of voting in the Senate, President Collor intervened to ensure defeat, fearing negative consequences for his already beleaguered government. The plebiscite was finally held on April 21, 1993, and the presidential republic was confirmed by a wide margin.

The revision of the constitution scheduled for late 1993 and early 1994 took place, but with meager results. Factors hindering constitutional revision included aftershocks from a congressional financial scandal ("Budgetgate") exposed by the Congressional Investigating Committee (Comissão Parlamentar de Inquérito—CPI); the October 3, 1994, elections; strong pressure from nationalist and corporatist groups in defense of state enterprises, job stability, and national firms; and nonparticipatory methodology (see Glossary). As of May 1994, the only major change to the constitution was to shorten the presidential term from five to four years. The next attempt to thoroughly revise the 1988 constitution was begun in February 1995, but by the regular amendment process (three-fifths majority in both houses). Some members would like to use the 1998 elections to again convoke (as in 1987–88) a "constitutional revision Congress" in 1999, to do a revision by a unicameral, absolute majority (see Constitutional Reform, this ch.).

Structure of Government

Brazil is a presidential and federative republic with considerable decentralized federalism. It is composed of twenty-six states and the Federal District (Brasília). In 1996 the states were subdivided into 5,581 municipalities (see fig. 1). The system is built on a directly elected president with a national constituency and a Congress elected by very parochial regional interests. Although the 1988 constitution reestablished many of the prerogatives of the bicameral Congress, the president retains considerable "imperial" powers. The federal judiciary enjoys considerable independence and autonomy. Under a system of checks and balances similar to the United States system, the three branches of government operate in harmony and with mutual respect. However, on rare occasions, one of the branches may challenge or reject the interference of the others.

Since the end of military rule in 1985, unionization, collective bargaining, and frequent strikes have become commonplace among federal employees in all three branches. The 1988 constitution grants job stability to all federal employees with more than five years of service, including those who had been hired without public examination. All new hiring must be by civil service examinations, and job stability comes after two years of probation. Mandatory retirement for all public servants, except for those elected to political office, is at age seventy.

In January 1995, the government employed (excluding state enterprises) 650,000 civilian (executive, 586,000; judicial 50,000; and legislative, 14,000) and 310,000 military personnel, totaling 960,000. A total of 723,000 were retired. State enterprises counted another 700,000 active employees.

The Executive

Executive-branch reorganizations are frequent in Brazil, as each president seeks to impose his personal style and to incorporate political bargains struck. President Sarney expanded the cabinet to a record twenty-seven ministries. His successor, President Collor, embarked on a massive reorganization, reducing the number of ministries to twelve, abolishing many agencies, and firing some 80,000 federal employees. In a reorganization of his cabinet in early 1992, Collor was forced to dismember several ministries to create new positions in an effort to enhance political support. President Franco again expanded the cabinet to twenty-seven positions in October 1992.

In January 1995, President Cardoso installed a cabinet with twenty-two ministers and the ministerial-rank chief of the Civil Household of the Presidency and implemented several important changes (see fig. 12). The Cardoso government charged the new head of the Joint Chiefs of Staff with creating a ministry of defense by the end of 1995 (a target that was not met). It also granted three ministerial positions—Planning, Civil Household, and Finance—superior status in terms of coordinating and monitoring the other nineteen. In addition, the government also created a Political Council (Conselho Político) to coordinate major political strategy and policy decisions. The council was composed of the presidents of the parties supporting the government.

Since João Baptista de Oliveira Figueiredo (president, 1979–85), most presidents have attempted to reduce and streamline the executive branch. President Sarney reorganized the Administrative Department of Public Service (Departamento Administrativo do Serviço Público—DASP), created in the 1930s, into the Federal Administration Secretariat (Secretaria de Administração Federal—SAF), which Presidents Collor and Franco revamped. By 1994 the SAF had achieved moderate success in consolidating the number of diverse public-service career structures and salary differentials. Congress passed a new executive-branch civil service law, the Single Judicial Regime (Regime Jurídico Único—RJU), in December 1990. In addition to the large number of state enterprises under government control, the executive branch also includes many autonomous agencies and financial institutions, such as the Bank of Brazil (Banco do Brasil) and the Federal Savings Bank (Caixa Econômico Federal).

A president must be a native Brazilian over age thirty-five. From 1945 to 1979, presidents had five-year terms. Following President Figueiredo's six-year term, the 1988 constitution again set the term at five years, but the 1994 constitutional revision reduced the mandate to four years. Although all of Brazil's constitutions since 1891 have prohibited immediate reelection of presidents, governors, and mayors, in June 1997 Congress approved an amendment allowing reelection. Thus, President Cardoso and the twenty-seven governors may stand for reelection in 1998, and the mayors elected in 1996 may be reelected in 2000.

The Brazilian president has the power to appoint some 48,000 confidence positions, of which only ambassadors, higher-court judges, the solicitor general, and Central Bank directors must have Senate approval. The president may also use the line-item veto, impound appropriated funds, issue decrees and provisional measures, initiate legislation, and enact laws.

Until 1964 the president and vice president were elected on separate tickets, which produced incompatible duos in 1950 and 1960. When Vargas committed suicide in 1954 and Jânio Quadros (president, January–August 1961) resigned in August 1961, the actions of their vice presidents produced severe institutional crises, leading to their respective ousters by military intervention. Since 1964 presidents and vice presidents have been elected on a single ticket, indirectly until 1989 and by direct popular vote in 1989 and 1994; a second round takes place if a majority is needed.

The return to civilian rule in 1985 occasioned important roles for vice presidents. President-elect Tancredo de Almeida Neves died before taking office, and his vice president, José Sarney, was allowed to complete his term. After President Collor was impeached in 1992, his vice president, Itamar Franco, completed his mandate. In the event that the president and vice president become incapacitated, the line of succession falls sequentially to the president of the Chamber of Deputies, the president of the Senate, and the president of the Federal Supreme Court (Supremo Tribunal Federal—STF). If less than half of the mandate has been completed, a supplementary election must be called within ninety days. If more than half the mandate has been completed, the Congress elects a new president and vice president within thirty days.

The Legislature

Brazil's national legislature is composed of the 513-member Chamber of Deputies and the eighty-one-member Senate. Congress has a basic four-year term, but senators serve for eight years. It meets from March through June, and from August through December. The states have unicameral legislatures elected simultaneously with Congress. The municipalities have city councils with four-year terms; municipal elections take place two years after state and national elections. Since 1930 Congress has been closed five times under authoritarian intervention: November 1930 to December 1933; November 1937 to

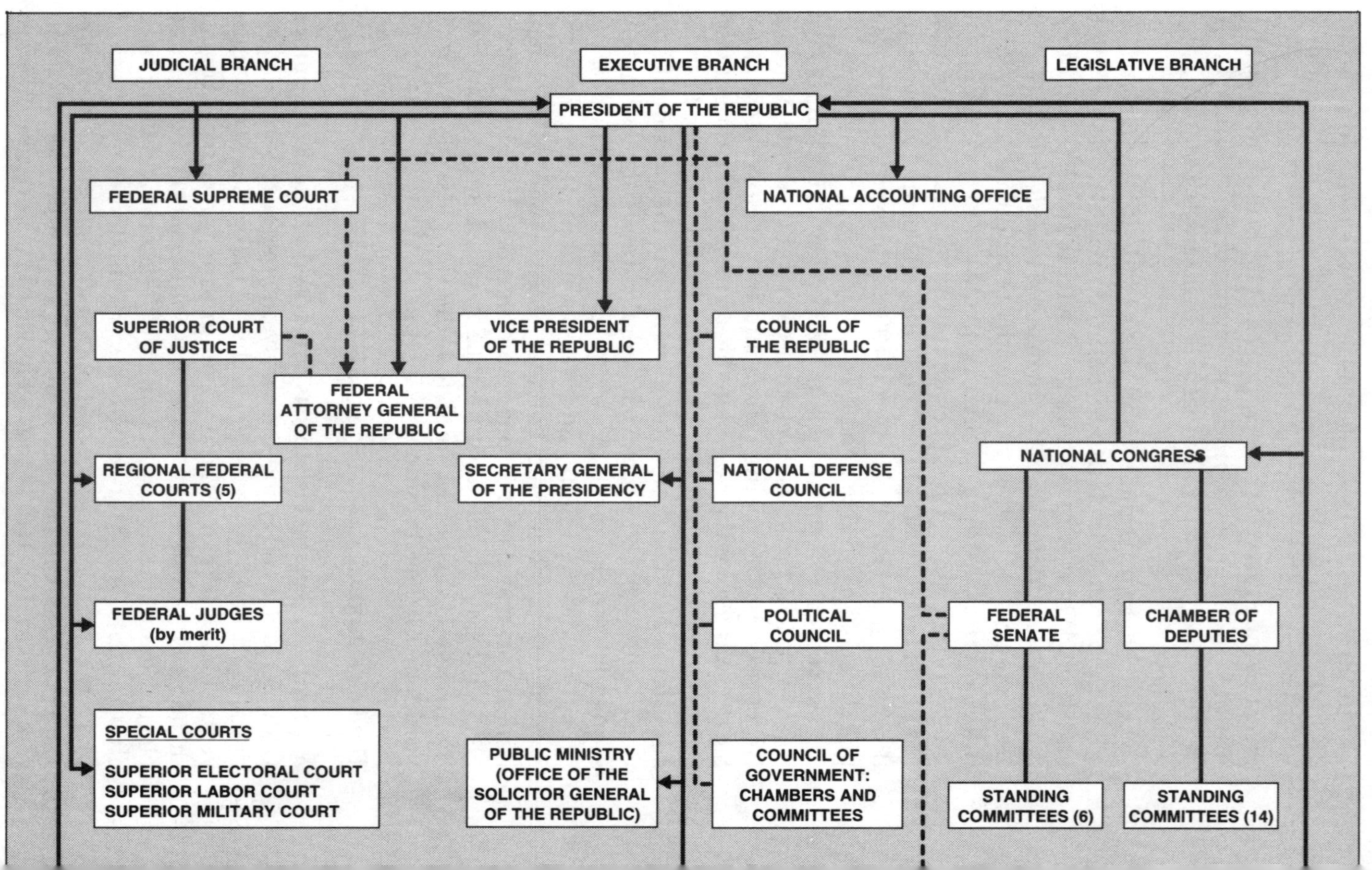
JUDICIAL BRANCH
EXECUTIVE BRANCH
LEGISLATIVE BRANCH
PRESIDENT OF THE REPUBLIC
FEDERAL SUPREME COURT
NATIONAL ACCOUNTING OFFICE
SUPERIOR COURT OF JUSTICE
VICE PRESIDENT OF THE REPUBLIC
COUNCIL OF THE REPUBLIC
FEDERAL ATTORNEY GENERAL OF THE REPUBLIC
NATIONAL CONGRESS
REGIONAL FEDERAL COURTS (5)
SECRETARY GENERAL OF THE PRESIDENCY
NATIONAL DEFENSE COUNCIL
FEDERAL JUDGES (by merit)
POLITICAL COUNCIL
FEDERAL SENATE
CHAMBER OF DEPUTIES
SPECIAL COURTS
SUPERIOR ELECTORAL COURT
SUPERIOR LABOR COURT
SUPERIOR MILITARY COURT
PUBLIC MINISTRY (OFFICE OF THE SOLICITOR GENERAL OF THE REPUBLIC)
COUNCIL OF GOVERNMENT: CHAMBERS AND COMMITTEES
STANDING COMMITTEES (6)
STANDING COMMITTEES (14)

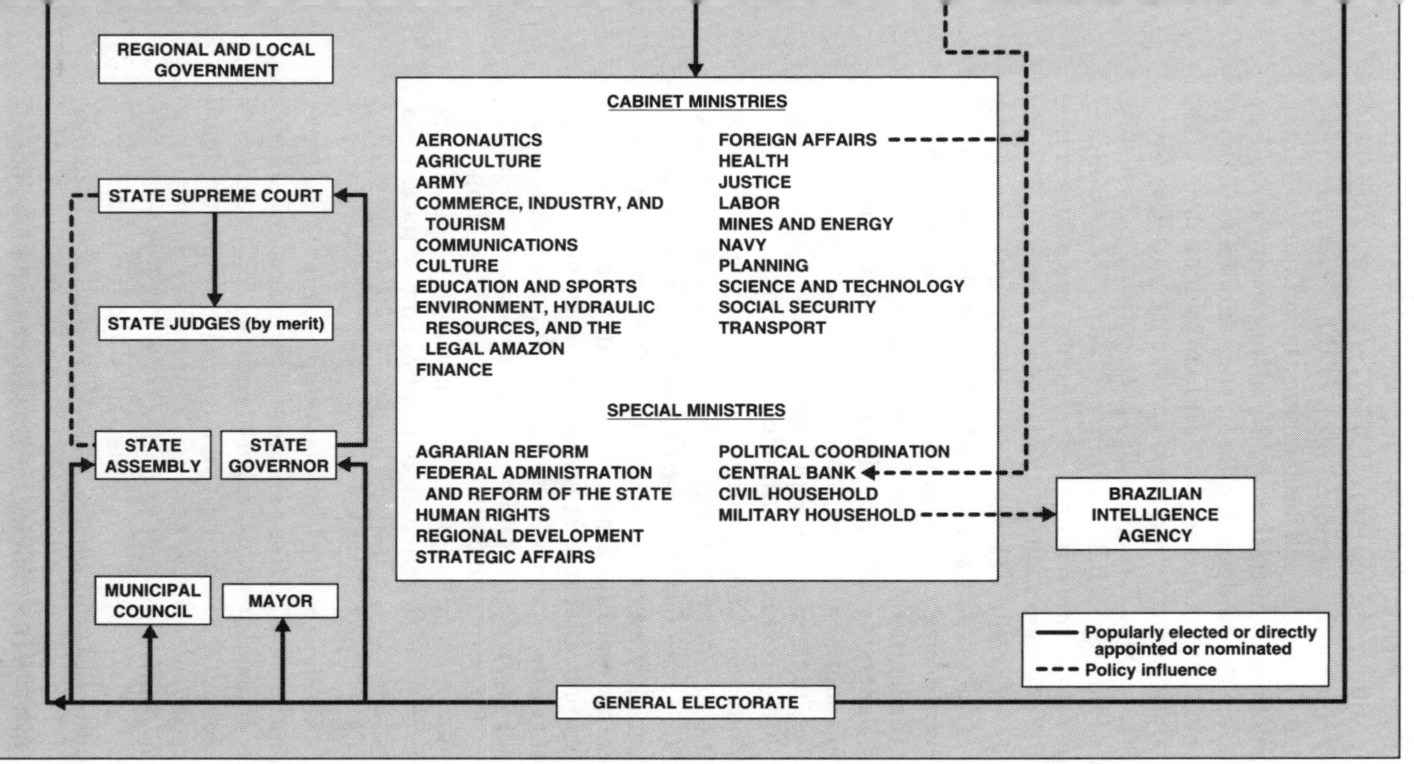

Figure 12. Structure of the Government, 1997

February 1946; November 1966; December 1968 to October 1969; and for fifteen days in April 1977.

The 1988 constitution restored most of the powers and prerogatives that Congress had lost during the military regime. Congress enjoys administrative and fiscal autonomy, as well as full power over the budget. Under certain circumstances, it may issue legislative decrees not subject to presidential veto. An absolute majority secret vote in Congress is required to override a presidential veto. Congress also has a very important role in setting national, especially economic, policies. For example, it must approve all international agreements, including renegotiation of the foreign debt.

Legislators enjoy almost total parliamentary immunity, even for capital crimes, such as homicide. Even if the respective chamber lifts the legislator's immunity by an absolute majority secret vote, the legislator retains the privilege of being tried by the STF. In December 1994, nearly 100 lawsuits (courts and prosecutors) sought to lift the immunity of deputies and senators. However, the legislative esprit de corps is so strong that only rarely does a case come to the floor for a vote.

Since 1950 federal and state legislators have been elected at regular four-year intervals. Senators must be at least thirty-five years old. Each state has three seats, and one or two seats are elected alternately every four years to eight-year terms. Election is by simple majority. Since 1946 deputies have had four-year terms and must be at least twenty-one years old. The 1946 constitution granted states with small populations a minimum delegation of seven deputies; larger states counted one additional deputy for every 150,000 inhabitants up to 3 million, and after that one for every 250,000. The small states imposed this system to reverse the dominance of the two largest states (São Paulo and Minas Gerais) in the Chamber of Deputies during the Old Republic (1889–1930).

In 1970, at the height of the military oppression, the balance was tipped in favor of the larger, more developed, urbanized states. State delegations were calculated based on the size of the electorate, rather than on population. The minimum delegation was reduced to three, and most of the states in rural Brazil had their contingents cut in half. These changes reduced the Chamber of Deputies to 310 deputies. Ironically, this system helped the Brazilian Democratic Movement (Movimento Democrático Brasileiro—MDB) elect a 44 percent minority in 1974; thus, in 1978 the military returned to calculations based on population. The 1988 constitution gave Brazil's largest state, São Paulo, seventy deputies, instead of the 115 it should have to be proportionate to its population.

Election of federal and state deputies and city council members is by proportional representation. Brazil uses one of the least-used variants of proportional representation, the open-list system (the d'Hondt method—see Glossary). Thus, there is virtually no conflict or competition among parties in the elections. The conflict is concentrated within each party or coalition list, and most deputies use their own resources (which may be considerable, up to US$5 million for a federal deputy) for campaigning. Therefore, they owe no loyalty to their party, and change labels frequently after their election (see table 18, Appendix). This produces very weak parties and low cohesion in Congress. The Workers' Party is an exception to this rule.

Those holding office (elective or appointive) in the executive branch who desire to become candidates for elective office must resign six months before the election. This requirement precludes a minister, governor, mayor, or state enterprise director from using the powers and resources of the office to favor his or her election.

The Senate and Chamber of Deputies have legislative initiative. The Senate and Chamber of Deputies have six and sixteen standing committees, respectively, plus a joint budget committee. The 1988 constitution gives the committees the power to approve or kill legislation.

To override a committee decision and bring the bill to the floor of the appropriate house requires a petition signed by a certain number of members. Once one house passes a bill, the other deliberates on it. If a different version of the bill is passed, it returns to the original house for a final vote on the differences. The internal rules of each house allow members and party leaders certain prerogatives of obstruction.

Party leaders distribute party quotas on committees proportionate to the party's size. Committee presidencies are apportioned among the parties on an annual rotational basis; thus, there are no longstanding powerful committee chairs, as in the United States Congress. There are no subcommittees, and legislative committees rarely conduct public hearings.

When a matter is very serious, at least one-third of the respective house or the full Congress may petition to initiate a CPI (Congressional Investigating Committee). The CPIs have full subpoena and investigative powers, such as the disclosure of bank, income tax, telephone, credit card, and other records. A CPI produced the evidence used to impeach President Collor in 1992 and uncovered the Budgetgate scandal of 1993–94.

Normally, the Chamber of Deputies has around 50 percent turnover at each election. In 1990 this figure rose to nearly 60 percent; in 1994 it returned to 54 percent. In years when two-thirds of the Senate stands for election and gubernatorial seats are being contested, turnover can also be high in the upper house (63 percent in 1994).

Senators tend to be older and have more established political careers. Most have served as federal deputies, and many have been governors. Deputies usually tend to have served in city councils, state assemblies, and as state cabinet secretaries. In the first half of the 1990s, the proportion of deputies elected with no prior political experience increased. In 1995 the largest contingents in the Chamber of Deputies by occupation were businessmen, 32 percent; lawyers, 20 percent; medical doctors, 11 percent; engineers, 7 percent; labor leaders, 6 percent; teachers, 5 percent; economists, 5 percent; public servants, 3 percent; journalists, 3 percent; and administrators, 2 percent.

Each house elects its presiding officers (one president, two vice presidents, four administrative secretaries, and four alternates) for two-year terms. The 1987–88 ANC (National Constituent Assembly) prohibited these legislative officers from being immediately reelected, a prohibition initially imposed by the military to break up "internal oligarchies." Traditionally, the largest party in each house has the prerogative of electing the president, but the PMDB (Brazilian Democratic Movement Party) was in such disarray in 1993 and 1995 that the Liberal Front Party (Partido da Frente Liberal—PFL), the second largest party, was able to build a coalition that elected the Chamber of Deputies president. By negotiation the PMDB returned to the Chamber presidency for the 1997–98 term, and the PFL won the Senate presidency for the first time since 1985. The presiding officers comprise an all-powerful Executive Board, which makes nearly all important political, administrative, procedural, and agenda-setting decisions. The Senate president is also the president of the Congress and presides over joint sessions.

During the 1987–88 ANC, an informal group called the College of Party Leaders developed. It became an important leadership group and was the forum for decisive bargaining on

Palácio do Planalto, the executive office building, and Palácio da Alvorada, the presidential residence, both designed by Oscar Niemeyer, Brasília
Courtesy Brazilian Embassy, Washington

crucial articles. This group has gradually acquired more power (especially agenda-setting) to the detriment of the formally elected officers, especially in the Chamber of Deputies.

The political role of Congress began to increase even before the demise of the military regime. In 1979 President Figueiredo took office without the extraordinary powers of the Fifth Institutional Act. In the 1982 elections, the government party lost its absolute majority in the Chamber of Deputies (see table 19, Appendix), and in 1983 the Chamber of Deputies defeated Figueiredo's initial decree laws, including one on social security.

Maximum political power accrued to Congress in 1985, when the vice president-elect, José Sarney (PMDB-Maranhão), assumed the presidency under less than auspicious circumstances. From March 1985 through February 1986, Chamber of Deputies President Ulysses Guimarães (PMDB-São Paulo) and PMDB Senate floor leader Fernando Henrique Cardoso (PMDB-São Paulo) more or less ruled with Sarney as informal "prime ministers." Sarney, however, recovered considerable presidential powers as a result of his cruzado (for value of the cruzado—see Glossary) economic stabilization plan, which began on March 1, 1986. Congress again assumed maximum power in 1992, when Brazil became the first nation in the world to constitutionally impeach a sitting, directly elected president.

The National Accounts Court (Tribunal de Contas da União—TCU) is the external control and oversight arm of Congress. The TCU conducts inspections, usually following newspaper exposés or requests from members of Congress, and audits the executive branch's annual accounts. Until the 1988 constitution, the president, with Senate approval, appointed members to the TCU. Retiring or defeated members of Congress or friends of the president in need of a sinecure usually filled the positions. With rare exceptions, TCU members have represented political factions and groups, and their main role is to protect allies who have been charged with corruption.

Under the 1988 constitution, recruitment criteria for the TCU became more specific. The president, with Senate approval, appoints three of the nine members. Two of the presidential appointees must be auditors or federal prosecutors from the TCU and must be chosen from a three-name list prepared by the TCU. Congress chooses the remaining six members. Each state has a State Accounts Court (Tribunal de

Contas dos Estados—TCE), but only the cities of Rio de Janeiro and São Paulo have a Municipal Accounts Court (Tribunal de Contas Municipais—TCM). The accounts of all other municipalities are reviewed by their respective TCE.

The Judiciary

The judicial branch is composed of federal, state, and municipal courts. By 1995 small-claims courts augmented some municipal courts. Only appointments to the superior courts are political and therefore subject to approval by the legislature. The minimum and maximum ages for appointment to the superior courts are thirty-five and sixty-five; mandatory retirement is at age seventy. These federal courts have no chief justice or judge. The two-year presidency of each court is by rotation and is based on respecting seniority.

The 1988 constitution produced five significant modifications in Brazil's judicial system. First, it converted the old Federal Court of Appeals (Tribunal Federal de Recursos—TFR) into the Superior Court of Justice (Superior Tribunal de Justiça—STJ). Second, it created an intermediate-level Regional Federal Court (Tribunal Regional Federal—TRF) system. Third, the federal general prosecutor was given a two-year renewable term, subject to confirmation by the Senate, without the possibility of removal by the president. Fourth, the STF (Federal Supreme Court) can issue a warrant of injunction (*mandado de injunção*) to ensure rights guaranteed by the constitution but not regulated by ordinary legislation. And fifth, the STF can decide on matters of constitutionality without waiting for appeals to come through the federal courts.

The judiciary came under criticism during the Collor and Franco administrations. The STF was harshly criticized during the Collor impeachment investigation and subsequent trials, particularly for the slow pace of the trials. In late 1993, former president Collor's appeal against the Senate's decision to strip his political rights for eight years ended in a four-four tie in the STF. Three judges had disqualified themselves: Collor's former foreign minister, Collor's first cousin, and the STF president who had presided over the Senate impeachment trial. Instead of throwing the case out after the tie vote, the STF called three substitute judges from the STJ, who broke the tie against Collor.

In addition, executive-branch public employees (especially in the armed forces) became discontented with the STF's utter disregard for parity salary scales among the three branches and with government austerity targets. To address these problems and to streamline the judicial process, the 1993–94 attempt at constitutional revision produced numerous proposals for reforming the judicial branch, including an external control body, the Penal Code (1941), and the 1916 Civil Code (revised in 1973). Significant reforms have yet to be enacted, however. The need for judicial reform in general is widely recognized because the current system is inefficient, with backlogs of cases and shortages of judges. Cases are frequently dismissed because they are too old. Lawyers contribute to backlogs by dragging out cases as long as possible because they are paid based on the amount of time they spend on a case. In addition, STF jurisprudence is not followed by lower courts. Some corrupt judges delay certain cases so that they can be dismissed. Vacancies on the bench are difficult to fill because of low pay and highly competitive examinations that often eliminate 90 percent of applicants.

Created in October 1890, the STF has eleven members appointed by the president with Senate approval. The STF decides conflicts between the executive and legislative branches, disputes among states, and disputes between the federal government and states. In addition, it rules on disputes involving foreign governments and extradition. The STF issues decisions regarding the constitutionality of laws, acts, and procedures of the executive and legislative branches, warrants of injunction, and writs of habeas corpus. Further, it presents three-name lists for certain judicial-branch nominations, and conducts trials of the president, cabinet ministers, and congressional and judiciary members. The president of the STF is third in the line of presidential succession and would preside over an impeachment trial held by the Senate.

The TFR (Federal Court of Appeals) was created under the 1946 constitution. It initially had thirteen members but expanded to twenty-seven members in 1979. In 1988 the TFR became the thirty-three-member STJ (Superior Court of Justice). As the last court of appeals for nonconstitutional questions, the STJ reviews decisions of the TRFs (Regional Federal Courts) and tries governors and federal judges. The president appoints its members with Senate approval on rotation. One-third are picked from the ranks of TRF judges; one-third from the ranks of State Supreme Court judges; and one-third from the ranks of state and federal public prosecutors.

The 1988 constitution created five TRFs—Recife, Brasília, Rio de Janeiro, São Paulo, and Porto Alegre. Each TRF must have at least six judges, appointed by the president and approved by the Senate. One-fifth must be from among lawyers or public prosecutors with at least ten years of professional experience. Members must be at least thirty years of age but no older than sixty-five.

Brazil's judicial system has a series of special courts, in addition to the regular civil court system, covering the areas of military, labor, and election affairs. The Superior Military Court (Superior Tribunal Militar—STM), created in 1808 by João VI (king of Portugal, 1816–26), is the oldest superior court in Brazil. It is composed of fifteen judges appointed by the president with Senate approval. Three members must have the rank of admiral in the Brazilian Navy (Marinha do Brasil), three must be general officers of the Brazilian Air Force (Fôrça Aérea Brasileira—FAB), four must be army generals, and five must be civilians. The latter must be over age thirty and under age sixty-five. Two of the civilians are alternately chosen from among military justice auditors and military court prosecutors; three are lawyers with noted judicial knowledge and ten years of professional experience.

The STM has jurisdiction over crimes committed by members of the armed forces. It was also used extensively to try civilians accused of crimes against "national security" during the military regime. States also have military courts to try cases involving state Military Police (Polícia Militar—PM). During the constitutional revision process of 1995, proposals were made to close down such courts at the state level. These proposals were renewed in 1997 after a series of revolts and strikes by Military Police in several states.

The government of Getúlio Vargas created the Superior Electoral Court (Tribunal Superior Eleitoral—TSE) in 1932 in an effort to end election fraud and manipulation. The TSE has jurisdiction over all aspects of elections and regulates the functioning of political parties. Its powers include supervising party conventions and internal elections; granting or canceling registration of parties; registering candidates and certifying those elected; regulating and supervising party access to free television and radio time during an election; and registering voters. All states have a Regional Electoral Court (Tribunal Regional Eleitoral—TRE); larger cities have municipal election judges, and smaller towns have local election boards.

The TSE has seven members, each with a two-year mandate. By secret ballot, the STF chooses three of its members to sit on the TSE, and the STJ chooses two of its members. The president appoints, with Senate approval, two lawyers from among a six-name list submitted by the STF. The TSE elects its president and vice president from among the members of the STF.

Since 1950 the TSE has made important decisions affecting Brazil's political system. In 1950 and 1955, the TSE decided in favor of the elections of presidents Getúlio Vargas (1951–54) and Juscelino Kubitschek (1956–61) by simple rather than by absolute majorities. In 1980 the TSE denied the "magic" label of the Brazilian Labor Party (Partido Trabalhista Brasileiro—PTB) to the Leonel de Moura Brizola faction, which was then forced to create the Democratic Labor Party (Partido Democrático Trabalhista—PDT). In 1994 the TSE prohibited noncandidates from appearing on the "free TV election hour," thus barring former President Collor from participating in the television campaign of the National Reconstruction Party (Partido da Reconstrução Nacional—PRN).

The system of labor courts was created by Getúlio Vargas in the 1930s to arbitrate labor-management disputes, which previously had been settled by police action. The 1946 constitution created the Superior Labor Court (Tribunal Superior do Trabalho—TST). Each state has a Regional Labor Court (Tribunal Regional do Trabalho—TRT), although São Paulo State has two TRTs, and each municipality has a set of labor conciliation boards. The labor court system has jurisdiction over all labor-related questions. It registers labor contracts, arbitrates collective and individual labor disputes, recognizes official union organizations, resolves salary questions, and decides the legality of strikes.

The president appoints, with Senate approval, twenty-seven judges to the TST. Seventeen of the judges—eleven career labor judges, three labor lawyers, and three labor court prosecutors—receive lifetime terms (to age seventy). Ten temporary judges are appointed from lists evenly divided between the confederations of labor and management.

The Public Ministry is an important independent body in Brazil's judicial system. Its principal component, the Office of the Solicitor General of the Republic (Procuradoria Geral da República—PGR), is composed of several public prosecutors selected by public examination. The PGR's headquarters is in Brasília, and it has branches in every state. The PGR is charged with prosecuting those accused of federal crimes, those accused of offending the president and his ministers, and all federal officials and employees accused of crimes. Before 1988 the president could appoint and dismiss the solicitor general at will. Under the 1988 constitution, the solicitor general has a fixed, renewable two-year term and is appointed by the president, with Senate approval, among the career prosecutors.

The Office of the Federal Attorney General (Advocacia-Geral da União—AGU), which was separated from the PGR by the 1988 constitution, defends the federal government against lawsuits and provides legal counsel to the executive branch. The AGU was organized and staffed under a provisional measure (MP) issued by President Franco.

Each state has a State Supreme Court (Tribunal de Justiça—TJ). The governor, with approval by the State Assembly (Assembléia do Estado), appoints the judges to the court. This court has the prerogative of appointing special state circuit judges to deal with agrarian problems. In addition, it is responsible for organizing and supervising the lower state courts. Each state is divided into district courts (*comarcas*).

State and Local Governments

Since independence Brazil has oscillated between centralization and state autonomy. During the empire (1822–89), Brazil had a centralized constitutional monarchy and little state autonomy. The emperor exercised the moderating power by appointing senators for life, presiding over a Council of State, removing and transferring police and judicial officials at will, and appointing provincial governors.

The Old Republic was established in 1889 in part because of state demands for greater autonomy. Until 1930 the larger and more powerful states enjoyed great autonomy under a federal system patterned after the United States model, but the smaller and poorer states constantly suffered interventions by the central government. "Young Turk" lieutenants (*tenentes*) rebelled against this system of state oligarchies in the 1920s and were prominent in the initial modernization strategies after the 1930 revolution. From 1930 to 1945, the national government centralized control over state and local governments by appointing governors, who in turn appointed all mayors. Except for the brief period of 1933–37, the national government closed legislatures at all levels. The 1946 constitution reestablished a more balanced federalism, but maintained central control over industrial, financial, labor, election, and development policies. In October 1965, the military regime began curtailing the autonomy of the states once again. From 1966 through 1978, the central government appointed state governors and mayors of state capitals and some 170 designated selected cities deemed vital to "national security." Active-duty army colonels were appointed as security chiefs in each state. As part of its "liberalizing opening," the military regime allowed direct elections for governors in 1982. In November 1985, President Sarney and Congress allowed direct elections for mayors of state capitals and selected cities deemed vital to "national security."

Until 1994 state governors and vice governors were elected to one four-year term, taking office on January 1 following their election. In 1998 those elected in 1994 may seek one consecutive second term. State deputies are also elected to four-year terms but are not restricted to one term. Governors have state cabinets, and their executive branch is organized in a manner similar to the federal executive branch. Likewise, state assemblies organize their legislative process like that of Congress. After 1988 state assemblies lost their salary autonomy; state deputies may receive up to 75 percent of the salary of a federal deputy.

State governments are responsible for maintaining state highway systems, low-cost housing programs, public infrastructure, telephone companies, and transit police. Both state and municipal governments are responsible for public primary and secondary schools and public hospitals. Municipal governments are also responsible for water, sewerage, and garbage services. State tax revenues are concentrated in sales taxes. State governments are allowed to operate state financial institutions, most of which are a constant problem for the Central Bank because they run heavy deficits, especially in election years. In 1995 the Central Bank intervened in some of the state banks with the worst deficits (São Paulo, Rio de Janeiro, Alagoas, and Mato Grosso) and sought to privatize others. In October 1996, Brazil had 5,581 municipalities, of which more than 15 percent had populations under 5,000. The municipal taxing authority is concentrated on property and service taxes.

Mayors and vice mayors must be at least twenty-one years of age and are elected to one four-year term. Reelection is now permitted as of the year 2000. City council members must be at least eighteen years of age and are elected to renewable four-year terms under a proportional representation system. From 1950 through 1970, municipal elections coincided with general federal and state elections. Local officials elected in 1970 were given two-year terms, so as to set local elections two years out of phase with general elections (the next local elections were held in 1972 and 1976). However, local officials elected in 1976 were given six-year terms to make municipal elections again coincide with general elections in 1982, but in turn the latter also got six-year terms to make local elections out of phase again (in 1988, 1992, and 1996).

The Political Party System

Historical Origins and Evolution

Shortly after Brazil's independence, the first political groups emerged with either pro-Brazilian or pro-Portuguese factions. During the second empire period (1831–89), the Conservative and Liberal parties alternated in power, and an embryonic Republican Party appeared in 1870. During the Old Republic (1889–1930), sections of the Republican Party in the larger states held political power. During the brief opening of representative politics between 1934 and 1937, attempts were made to organize national parties.

After 1945, when parties and elections again were permitted, local factions in the interior that had been allied with the Vargas government since 1930 organized the Social Democratic Party (Partido Social Democrático—PSD); the pro-Vargas groups in urban areas organized the PTB (Brazilian Labor Party); and all those opposed to Vargas initially formed the UDN (National Democratic Union). The PSD elected the president and an absolute majority to the 1946 Constituent Assembly. The Brazilian Communist Party (Partido Comunista Brasileiro—PCB), led by Luis Carlos Prestes, operated freely from 1945 through 1947, but the STF (Federal Supreme Court) canceled its registry in early 1948.

By 1960 Congress had thirteen parties. Confronted with adverse results in the direct gubernatorial elections of October 1965, President Castelo Branco (1964–67) decreed the end of this multiparty system and imposed a two-party system. His objective was to organize a strong majority support party and a loyal opposition. Thus, the National Renewal Alliance (Aliança Renovadora Nacional—Arena) and the MDB (Brazilian Democratic Movement) were born.

About 90 percent of the UDN, 50 percent of the PSD, and 15 percent of the PTB joined Arena. Although it held an absolute majority in Congress until its demise in 1979, Arena was plagued with regional and former party factionalism. The MDB suffered from ideological factionalism regarding the military government; the factions divided among the authentics (those most strongly opposed to the military government), the neo-authentics, and the moderates.

As a result of the voting trends of the 1974, 1976, and 1978 elections, which channeled protest votes to the MDB, General Golbery do Couto e Silva, the architect of much of the regime's political evolution from 1964 until his retirement in August 1981, called for a party realignment to achieve broader political maneuvering space for the government. A survey conducted among members of Congress in March 1979 showed that nearly three-fourths of Arena and two-thirds of the MDB desired a multiparty system. In December 1979, Congress approved government-sponsored legislation abolishing Arena and the MDB and permitting moderate party pluralism.

Initially, the realignment strategy was successful. The MDB became the PMDB (Brazilian Democratic Movement Party) but with half its 1979 size. Arena became the PDS (Democratic Social Party), and retained its majority position. MDB moderates and Arena liberals organized the government auxiliary Popular Party (Partido Popular—PP) led by Senator Tancredo Neves and Deputy Magalhães Pinto. Former deputy Ivette Vargas and former governor Leonel Brizola resurrected the PTB; and the new, more militant labor unions organized the Workers' Party.

In May 1980, this pluralism became less moderate when, in a highly political decision, the TSE (Superior Electoral Court) decided to give the PTB label to Ivette Vargas instead of Brizola, who had much broader organizational support within the party. Undaunted, Brizola immediately organized the PDT (Democratic Labor Party) and, in 1982, was elected governor of Rio de Janeiro, with twenty-three deputies versus Ivette Vargas's thirteen (see table 19, Appendix). Because of the harsh 1982 election rules imposed by the Figueiredo government, the Popular Party decided to dissolve itself and reincorporate with the PMDB, which greatly strengthened the latter in many states, especially in Minas Gerais and Paraná.

In 1985 Congress passed legislation easing the requirements for organizing new parties; thus, the ANC (National Constituent Assembly) seated eleven parties in 1987, nineteen in 1991, and eighteen in 1995. With the exception of the Workers' Party, traditionally all Brazilian political parties have been organized from the top down, with a compact group of professional politicians making major decisions. The party system suffered considerable fragmentation during the late 1980s and early 1990s, especially because of an exodus from the largest parties—PMDB and PFL (Liberal Front Party)—after 1988, similar to the factionalization in the 1950s and early 1960s. In 1987 the five largest parties accounted for 92.8 percent of the Chamber of Deputies. In 1989 this figure fell to 70.1 percent, and in 1992 it fell further to 61.4 percent. However, after the 1994 elections a "reconcentration" occurred, and by 1997 the five largest parties accounted for 83.6 percent.

In addition to strong internal cleavages, parties differ regionally. The Popular Party was almost totally concentrated in Minas Gerais and Rio de Janeiro. Initially, Brizola's PDT was concentrated in Rio de Janeiro and Rio Grande do Sul—the two states that had elected him in the 1947–64 period—but later expanded to more states and elected three governors in 1990 (see table 20, Appendix). The Workers' Party remains concentrated in São Paulo but has expanded to other states in the South and North. The PSDB (Brazilian Social Democracy Party) is highly concentrated in Ceará and São Paulo. The PFL has always been concentrated in the Northeast. In Rio Grande do Sul, the PFL and the PSDB have very limited penetration (see Political Culture, this ch.).

Major Parties in Congress

In 1995 eight political parties, constituting 89.7 percent of the total membership of the Chamber of Deputies, were considered major parties. Each held more than 5 percent of the Chamber. In 1997 the seven significant parties totaled 92.6 percent.

Progressive Renewal Party

The Progressive Renewal Party (Partido Progressista Renovador—PPR) was organized by the fusion of the PDS (Democratic Social Party) and the Christian Democratic Party (Partido Democrático Cristão—PDC) in April 1993. After the Workers' Party, the PPR has the most consistent ideology. It generally supports the interests of business and rural landlords. It has a radical position in favor of privatization, economic modernization, and reduction of the state's role in the economy. In 1994 the PPR elected three governors, two senators, and fifty-three federal deputies. The PPR contributed one minister (health) to Cardoso's cabinet, but the party does not automatically support government positions in Congress. In 1995 Paulo Maluf remained the main leader of the PPR, which attempted to form a bloc with the Progressive Party. In mid-September 1995, Maluf merged the PPR with the Progressive Party to form the Brazilian Progressive Party (Partido Progressista Brasileiro—PPB).

Brazilian Democratic Movement Party

The Brazilian Democratic Movement (Movimento Democrático Brasileiro—MDB), the political opposition to the military regime, began mobilizing national support in the late 1970s. Like the PTB (Brazilian Labor Party) in the early 1960s, the MDB was on the verge of becoming a mass political party when Congress dissolved it in 1979. The party president, Deputy Ulysses Guimarães, convinced the party to "add a P to the MDB" to preserve the hard-fought opposition image.

The Brazilian Democratic Movement Party (Partido do Movimento Democrático Brasileiro—PMDB) won nine governorships in 1982 and elected Tancredo Neves in the electoral college of January 1985 in alliance with the PFL. The centrist PMDB advanced to become the "catch-all, rainbow" party, electing a majority to the ANC (National Constituent Assembly), and all but one governor in 1986. Overloaded with joiners (many of whom migrated from the Arena/PDS), the PMDB acquired a more conservative profile, provided a base for the Big Center in the ANC, and projected an image of close collaboration with the Sarney government. These tendencies provoked the exodus of the more progressive members, such as the PSDB, in 1988. The party was less successful in the congressional and gubernatorial elections in 1988 and 1990, but made a slight comeback in the 1992 municipal elections.

In 1994 the PMDB's presidential candidate, former governor Orestes Quêrcia, placed fourth. Nevertheless, the PMDB managed to elect nine governors and remained the largest party in Congress, electing fourteen senators and 107 federal deputies. The PMDB had two important ministries (transport and justice), plus the Secretariat of Regional Development (now subordinate to the Ministry of Planning) in the Cardoso government. With the defeat of Quêrcia and the loss of São

Lagoa (lagoon) Rodrigo de Freitas, Rio de Janeiro
Courtesy Jaklen Muoi Tuyen

Paulo State, the party has no coherent national leadership, and the support of its sizable congressional delegation is uncertain. In 1997 the PMDB became the second largest party in Congress, losing its first-rank position to the PFL.

Liberal Front Party

A manifesto signed by three governors, ten senators, and sixty federal deputies in December 1984 officially launched the center-right Liberal Front Party (Partido da Frente Liberal—PFL). In the January 15, 1985, electoral college, the PMDB-Liberal Front-PDS ticket of Tancredo Neves and José Sarney received the votes of 102 federal deputies, fifteen senators, and fifty-one delegates still nominally affiliated with the PDS. In 1985 the PFL became the second largest party in Congress. It received a mere 8.8 percent of the votes in the municipal elections of November 1985, but when Sarney was able to reform the cabinet inherited from Tancredo Neves in February 1986, the PFL received six ministries. In 1992 the PFL elected nearly 1,000 mayors, second only to the PMDB.

Although the PFL is noted for its neoliberal ideology, it is always predisposed to pragmatic bargaining, such as in 1994, when it abstained from running its own presidential candidate and joined with the PSDB and PTB. Although it elected only two governors, it remained the second largest party in Congress, electing eleven senators and eighty-nine federal deputies (57 percent from the Northeast), in addition to the vice president. In Congress the PFL is known to have the most articulate and cohesive delegation, on a par with the Workers' Party. As a Cardoso coalition partner, the PFL received three ministries in 1995. It became the first-ranked party in 1997.

Brazilian Labor Party

The Brazilian Labor Party (Partido Trabalhista Brasileiro—PTB), a pre-1964 leftist party, was resurrected as center-rightist in 1980. Two factions—one led by Leonel Brizola and the other led by Ivette Vargas—vied for leadership of the PTB. Although twenty of the twenty-three federal deputies who originally joined the PTB were *brizolistas*, Ivette Vargas was allied with General Golbery do Couto e Silva, chief of Ernesto Geisel's Civil Household of the Presidency, who pressured the TSE (Superior Electoral Court) to give the label to Vargas's pro-government faction in May 1980.

The PTB elected thirteen deputies in 1982 and became the junior member in a coalition with the PDS to give the latter a majority in the Chamber of Deputies. In 1986 the PTB elected seventeen federal deputies, and in 1990 it elected two governors, four senators, and thirty-eight federal deputies. The party became a convenient election vehicle for politicians without space in the larger parties.

In 1994 the PTB formed a coalition with the PFL and PSDB in support of Cardoso's candidacy. In that election, the PTB elected one governor, three senators, and thirty-one federal deputies—a slightly worse record than in 1990. In 1995 the PTB remained loyal to its coalition with the PSDB and PFL in support of the Cardoso government and occupied two ministries.

Democratic Labor Party

Brizola founded the social democratic-oriented Democratic Labor Party (Partido Democrático Trabalhista—PDT) in May 1980 after losing the PTB label to Ivette Vargas. Over the ensuing fifteen years, many PDT members migrated to other parties. In 1990 the PDT elected three governors (Brizola included), five senators, and forty-seven federal deputies and became the third largest party in Congress. In 1994 Brizola placed fifth for president and was defeated by Enéas Carneiro in Rio de Janeiro, thus ending his forty-seven-year political career. The PDT elected only two governors, four senators, and thirty-three federal deputies that year.

Despite his massive defeat in 1994, Brizola refused to relinquish personal control of the party and tried to impose a systematic opposition posture on the congressional delegation, although the two PDT governors favored a more flexible position vis-à-vis the Cardoso government. Both the very dynamic governor of Paraná, Jaime Lerner, and Dante de Oliveira, governor of Mato Grosso, left the PDT in 1997.

Workers' Party

The Workers' Party (Partido dos Trabalhadores—PT), the country's first independent labor party, is a unique party in Brazil. Organized externally (outside Congress) from the grassroots up and based on the new trade unionism in São Paulo in 1979, the Workers' Party initially did not want any professional politicians or students in its ranks. However, to have a voice in Congress it accepted five deputies and one senator into its ranks in early 1980. Since then the Workers' Party has grown steadily, doubling its Chamber of Deputies delegation in 1982, 1986, and 1990, while tripling the number of its state deputies at each election, except in 1994. It has also won mayorships in several cities, including São Paulo (1988) (see Elections, 1988–96, this ch.).

The Workers' Party is divided into six factions along a left-right continuum. The right consists of Radical Democracy (Democracia Radical), which has a social-democratic orientation. The center consists of Unity and Struggle (Unidade e Luta), Catholic militants, and members of the right wing of Lula da Silva's former Articulation (Articulação) faction. The left consists of Option of the Left (Opção de Esquerda), which is divided into two subgroups—Hour of Truth (Hora da Verdade), the dissident left wing of the former Articulation group, former Stalinists, and Castroites; and Socialist Democracy (Democracia Socialista), the largest Trotskyite group, which existed before the Workers' Party. The extreme left consists of Workers' Party in the Struggle (Na Luta PT), which is divided into two subgroups—Socialist Force (Força Socialista), whose members are former militants from extreme left guerrilla groups from the 1960s: the People's Electoral Movement

(Movimento Eleitoral do Povo—MEP) and Popular Action (Ação Popular—AP); and The Work (O Trabalho), consisting of Trotskyites from two student movements of the 1970s—Freedom (Liberdade) and Struggle (Luta).

Until 1993 Lula's moderate Articulation group had a large absolute majority in the Workers' Party. This group conducted pragmatic coalition-building in the 1990 and 1992 elections, which resulted in the election of increasing numbers of deputies and city council members. However, in 1993 the extreme left and left elected an absolute majority (53 percent) of the national party directorate, took control, and imposed stricter criteria for coalition-building at the state level. In 1995 and 1997, the Articulation faction was again elected to the party presidency.

Brazilian Social Democracy Party

A center-left group of the PMDB (Brazilian Democratic Movement Party) organized the Brazilian Social Democracy Party (Partido da Social Democracia Brasileira—PSDB) in June 1988. Many of these PMDB members were associated with the Progressive Unity Movement (Movimento de Unidade Progressista—MUP). They had become discontented with the rainbow party, with the PMDB's participation in the conservative Big Center during the National Constituent Assembly, and especially with the politics of President Sarney. The principal leaders of the new party were from São Paulo, including Senator Cardoso (PMDB floor leader in the Senate).

The PSDB adopted a modernizing, social-democratic program and favored a parliamentary system of government. In 1988 it became the third largest delegation in Congress, although it elected only eighteen mayors that year (including Belo Horizonte).

The PSDB occupied three ministries in the Franco cabinet, including Senator Cardoso at the Ministry of Foreign Affairs. In May 1993, Cardoso moved to the Ministry of Finance, where he launched the *Real* Plan for economic stabilization in March 1994. With other major parties already engaged in different presidential alliances, the PSDB opted for a coalition with the more conservative PFL and PTB in the 1994 elections. The adoption of the new *Real* currency and the resulting near-zero inflation greatly boosted Cardoso's presidential candidacy in July and August and guaranteed his first-round victory with a margin of 54.3 percent on October 3. The PSDB also elected six governors (including Ceará, Minas Gerais, São Paulo, and Rio de Janeiro), nine senators, and sixty-two deputies, a much better performance than in 1990 (see General Elections, 1994, this ch). The Social Democrats occupied six ministries, including the powerful ministries of Planning, Finance, and Civil Household of the Presidency, in the Cardoso government.

Progressive Party

The Progressive Party (Partido Progressista—PP) grew out of the PTR (Workers' Renewal Party). In 1990 the PTR and the Social Workers' Party (Partido Social Trabalhista—PST) had elected just two federal deputies each. The new Progressive Party had thirty-seven deputies in 1993, and by 1994 had grown to forty-five, the fifth largest delegation in the Chamber of Deputies. In 1995 the Progressive Party became leaderless, with no clear political strategy. Thus, it merged with the PPR (Progressive Renewal Party) to form the PPB (Brazilian Progressive Party).

Minor Parties in Congress

In 1995 eleven smaller parties were represented in Congress, of which five are noteworthy.

Liberal Party

Deputy Alvaro Valle (PDS-Rio de Janeiro) founded the center-right Liberal Party (Partido Liberal—PL) in 1985. Dubbed the businessman's Workers' Party, the Liberal Party rapidly supplanted the Liberal Front Party (Partido da Frente Liberal—PFL) in São Paulo. In the elections of November 15, 1986, the Liberal Party secured seven seats in the Chamber of Deputies and one in the Senate. It received 4.8 percent of the national vote in 1990 and elected fifteen deputies. On taking their seats in February 1991, the new Liberal Party deputies joined the opposition bloc against Collor. In 1994 the Liberal Party elected no governors, one senator, and thirteen deputies.

Party of National Reconstruction

Created in February 1989 by a takeover of the Youth Party as an election vehicle for Collor's candidacy, the conservative Party of National Reconstruction (Partido da Reconstrução Nacional—PRN) immediately received twenty deputies and two senators. After Collor's election, the party increased its congressional delegation in 1990, but had a dismal performance in the October 3 elections that year: forty deputies and only 7 percent of the vote, and no governors. In 1994 the party, reduced to four deputies and four senators, elected one federal and two state deputies.

Brazilian Socialist Party

Resurrected in 1986 from the pre-1964 Socialist Party, the left-wing Brazilian Socialist Party (Partido Socialista Brasileiro—PSB) elected seven representatives to the ANC (National Constituent Assembly). It joined the Brazilian Popular Front (Frente Brasil Popular—FBP) coalition in 1989 in support of Lula, and again in 1994. With 2.3 percent of the national vote in 1990, the PSB elected eleven deputies, including twice governor of Pernambuco Miguel Arraes, PSB president. The PSB, which has a more pragmatic socialism than the Workers' Party, contributed two ministers to Franco's cabinet. In 1994 the PSB elected two governors (including Arraes), one senator, and fifteen federal deputies.

Brazilian Communist Party

In 1993 the Brazilian Communist Party (Partido Comunista Brasileiro—PCB), in a stormy national convention led by its president, Deputy Roberto Freire, removed Marxist-Leninist doctrine from the party statutes and the hammer and sickle from its flag, and changed its name to the PPS (Popular Socialist Party). The original PCB had been organized in 1922. At Moscow's initiative, Luis Carlos Prestes took over the PCB's leadership in the mid-1930s. Prestes presided over the party until the early 1980s, when he was ousted by a renovated Eurocommunist faction that had tired of his Stalinist line. During its illegal period (1948–85), the PCB was able to elect a few of its members under other party labels. The PCB regained legal registry in 1985, elected three representatives to the ANC in 1986, and again in 1990, always in coalitions. Deputy Freire carried the PCB banner as candidate for president in 1989, and became floor leader of the Franco government in 1992. In 1994 the PPS joined the FBP in support of Lula and elected one senator (Freire) and only two federal deputies.

Communist Party of Brazil

The Communist Party of Brazil (Partido Comunista do Brasil—PC do B) was created as an underground splinter from the

PCB in 1958, following Soviet leader Nikita Khrushchev's denunciations of Stalinist atrocities. The PC do B repudiated the new Moscow line and aligned itself with Maoism. When the People's Republic of China began making economic reforms in 1979, the PC do B aligned itself with Albania. When Albania held its first free elections in 1992, the PC do B became nonaligned. After the PC do B was legalized in 1985, under the leadership of former deputy and former guerrilla João Amazonas, it elected more deputies in 1986 and 1990 than its arch rival, the PCB. The PC do B joined the FBP in support of Lula in 1989 and 1994. The PC do B doubled its delegation from five to ten federal deputies, representing nine states, in 1994. This feat resulted from PC do B domination of student organizations in most states and astute use of coalitions.

Regional Strength of the Parties

Within the basic government coalition—the PFL (Liberal Front Party), the PSDB (Brazilian Social Democracy Party), and the PTB (Brazilian Labor Party)—the PFL is highly concentrated in the Northeast (Bahia and Pernambuco), and the PSDB to a lesser degree in the Southeast (São Paulo and Minas Gerais). Almost half of the PSDB deputies elected in the Northeast came from Ceará; the PTB elected only two deputies from the Northeast.

Those formally opposed to the new Cardoso government, led by the Workers' Party and PDT, are concentrated in the South and Southeast. The Workers' Party became the second largest delegation in the states of São Paulo and Rio Grande do Sul in 1994, and slightly expanded its delegations in the North, Northeast, and Center-West (Centro-Oeste) regions. Although reduced from its 1990 size, the PDT remained the largest delegation in Rio de Janeiro, but fell to fourth rank in Rio Grande do Sul, after the PMDB (Brazilian Democratic Movement Party), Workers' Party, and PPR (Progressive Renewal Party).

The PSB (Brazilian Socialist Party) is highly concentrated in the Northeast; nearly half of its fifteen deputies come from Pernambuco. The PC do B (Communist Party of Brazil) is the only small party to have elected deputies in all five regions of Brazil in 1994. It presents a very dispersed pattern, with ten deputies elected in nine states. The PC do B dominated student associations (university and high school) in almost all states and was able to mobilize these young voters to concentrate their preferences on one or two PC do B candidates in each state.

The delegations of the four parties considered potential allies of the government are mostly concentrated in the North, Center-West, and South. In 1994 the PMDB's two largest delegations came from the Southeast (thirty-two) and Northeast (thirty). Nonetheless, the PMDB was weakened in those regions in the 1994 elections, even though it elected four of the nine Northeastern governors (Piauí, Rio Grande do Norte, Alagoas, and Paraíba).

As a result of its electing three of the seven governors in the North, the PPR elected the second largest delegation from that region. Its second regional concentration was in the South, where it was tied with the Workers' Party with twelve deputies. The PPR became the second largest delegation in Rio de Janeiro with seven deputies. Leading defeated coalitions in the runoffs in Goiás and Brasília, the Progressive Party became the second largest delegation in the Center-West, after the PMDB. Its best performances at the state level were in Minas Gerais (seven deputies) and in Paraná (six deputies).

Party Legislation

Because Congress did not pass a new organic law for political parties in 1994, political parties until 1995 were regulated by a patchwork quilt of legislation: the 1988 constitution, the old Organic Law imposed by the military, and a host of individual laws passed over the past twenty years, including Election Law No. 8,713, passed on September 30, 1993. Parties are considered part of public law, and the state regulates and supervises them closely. Although Article 17 of the 1988 constitution states that parties are free to organize, fuse, incorporate, or dissolve themselves, Paragraph 2 of the same article states that after parties acquire a "legal personality" under civil law they may then register their statutes. Although Paragraph 1 states that parties are free to organize themselves internally, in reality they are governed by a detailed, complex, and often conflicting set of legal rules.

After 1985 provisional organization of new parties became easier: 101 members of the party sign a petition with bylaws, statutes, and a program, which are registered with the TSE (Superior Electoral Court). Definitive registry is more complicated; within a twelve-month period, the new party must organize state directorates in nine states and in one-third of the municipalities in each of these states.

In late August 1995, Congress finally passed the new Organic Law of Political Parties, which had been under consideration since 1989. This law imposed stiffer criteria for the registration of new parties, stated that party switchers might lose their mandate, and established a "weak" threshold of 3 percent for proportional elections (parties with less than 3 percent of the valid vote would not be allowed to operate in Congress, but those elected would be seated). Continuous party switching has been a problem in Congress. In the first five months of the 1995 legislature (February through June), more than forty federal deputies (8 percent) switched party labels at least once.

On the final deadline date of October 2, 1995, Law No. 9,100 was passed and published in the daily record; it regulated the municipal elections of October 3, 1996. Some minor changes were enacted: a 20 percent quota for female candidates for city councils; less transparency in campaign finance than in 1994; very high limits for campaign contributions (up to US$221,000.00 for businesses and US$51,500.00 for individual persons); and a return to the 1990 rules on free radio/television time.

Politics

Sarney's Presidency, 1985–90

The government's strategy of controlling the election of the first civilian president in the 1985 electoral college almost received a mortal blow on April 25, 1984. On that day, the *diretas já!* constitutional amendment, which called for direct elections for president on November 15, 1984, came just twenty-two votes shy of the necessary two-thirds majority (320 votes). In late June 1984, the Liberal Front dissident group split from the military government's PDS (Democratic Social Party) and joined the PMDB led by Governor Tancredo Neves (Minas Gerais). In the second half of 1984, massive rallies engulfed Brazil, as the Tancredo Neves-Sarney ticket consolidated its 300-vote margin over Paulo Maluf (PDS-São Paulo) in the January 1985 electoral college.

Sarney got his start in politics in his home state of Maranhão in the late 1950s as federal deputy in the progressive wing of the National Democratic Union (União Democrática Nacional—UDN). A staunch supporter of the 1964 revolution, he was able to defeat the PSD (Social Democratic Party) political machine in direct elections for governor in 1965, and was elected senator by Arena (National Renewal Alliance) in 1970. The military government never quite accepted Sarney and vetoed his attempts to return to the governorship in 1974 and 1978. He was also passed over several times for the presidency of the Senate and for the post of minister of justice in 1980. As a consolation prize, he became president of the PDS. In 1984 Sarney was one of the dissident leaders of the schism in the PDS, and he became Tancredo Neves's running mate.

Tancredo Neves took ill on the eve of his inauguration on March 14, 1985, and died on April 21. Sarney was first sworn in as vice president and then acting president within a very loose interpretation of the constitutional norms for presidential succession.

Deputy Ulysses Guimarães had been elected president of the Chamber of Deputies on February 1 and by right should have assumed the presidency because neither Tancredo Neves nor Sarney had been inaugurated. On the death of Tancredo Neves, a new indirect election should have been called within ninety days. Guimarães, perhaps sensing that the military would not accept this scenario, graciously declined in favor of Sarney.

Sarney's first year was very difficult. He was unprepared to assume the presidency and was assisted immediately by General Ivan Souza Mendes, director of the National Intelligence Service (Serviço Nacional de Informações—SNI). In effect, Brazil's government was an informal parliamentary system during 1985, with Deputy Guimarães and PMDB Senate floor leader Fernando Henrique Cardoso acting as informal prime ministers. The Sarney administration moved to consolidate representative democracy in 1985: it legalized the two communist parties, the PCB and the PC do B, allowed illiterates to vote, and called for direct elections for mayors of all capital cities and "national security" municipalities.

The PMDB performed poorly in the November 15, 1985, mayoral elections, when former president Jânio Quadros of the PTB (Brazilian Labor Party) narrowly defeated Cardoso for mayor of São Paulo. However, Sarney recovered national prestige and high standing in the polls following the introduction of the Cruzado Plan on February 28, 1986, and began to consolidate his power as president. The PMDB became the great "umbrella" party in the 1986 elections, leading a broad coalition to victory in all states but Sergipe, and electing an absolute majority in the ANC (National Constituent Assembly).

Rapid consolidation of democracy in Brazil after 1985 was in part slowed by some of the concessions negotiated by Tancredo Neves with the military to ensure their support. Tancredo Neves agreed that members of the armed forces who had been expelled for subversion after 1964 would not receive amnesty and reinstatement; that there would be no independent, non-congressional Constituent Assembly; and that before the new constitution was finished and promulgated, none of the authoritarian decrees—National Security Law, antistrike law, repressive press law, and limitations on Congress—would be canceled or modified.

By October 1988, Sarney, who was still a nominal member of the PMDB, had grown very unpopular because of increasing inflation and allegations of corruption. As a result, the PMDB lost many cities in the November 15, 1988, municipal elections—of the 100 largest cities, the party dropped from seventy-seven to twenty mayors, but in 1992 elected twenty-nine; in 1996 the number fell back to only sixteen (see table 21, Appendix). In addition, impeachment proceedings were initiated against Sarney on charges of corruption. The CPI (Congressional Investigating Committee) reported in favor of impeachment, but the measure was not transmitted to the floor of the Chamber of Deputies for deliberation.

During Sarney's presidency, Brazil suffered four austerity shock plans and used three currencies. Thus, for the December 17, 1989, runoff, voters selected the two presidential candidates who most vociferously criticized the Sarney presidency—Collor (PRN) and Lula (Workers' Party).

Collor de Mello's Presidency, 1990–92

Collor created extremely high expectations that he could solve Brazil's economic problems and that he could insert Brazil into the international economic arena. With one "silver bullet," he promised to rid Brazil of inflation, rampant corruption, and all *marajás* (literally maharajahs, or do-nothing, corrupt high government officials who draw huge salaries), while modernizing Brazil's economy and society.

Collor's ambitious program began by confiscating some US$50 billion in financial and bank assets from depositors and investors, thereby plunging the country into recession. He set about "taking the state apart," announcing that he would reduce the number of federal civilian employees from nearly 1 million to 300,000. Further, he would auction off government cars and housing in Brasília, sell all state enterprises, and begin a program to consolidate or eliminate the myriad of federal agencies. Collor's style of presidency was similar to that of developed countries and included well-orchestrated public relations campaigns and lavish entertaining.

Although he commanded a small minority bloc in Congress, Collor's high ratings in the polls and excellent television communication skills dissuaded many politicians from opposing his unusual proposals in an election year. Unlike the Cruzado Plan, which had helped Collor's election as governor of Alagoas in 1986, his 1990 stabilization plan did not produce positive economic results before the November 15 elections. Most of his allied gubernatorial candidates were defeated, and his coalition remained a minority in Congress. As inflation increased in 1991, the government began to flounder, and the opposition was able to thwart many of his proposals. Many of his initiatives in the international arena came to naught.

In late 1991, Collor counterattacked in a media blitz, blaming constitutional impediments for obstructing his modernization plan and boldly proposing a broad constitutional reform package of sixteen amendments. However, in March 1992, as new accusations of corruption mounted daily, Collor fired almost his entire cabinet (except for the military ministers and the ministers of health and education, who were not politicians) and brought in older, more experienced politicians who generally were considered "clean."

A month later, the president's younger brother, Pedro Collor, unleashed his bombastic accusations regarding the modus operandi of the corruption system, and on June 1, 1992, Congress installed the impeachment CPI. President Collor, together with his adviser, Paulo César Farias, and other cronies from Alagoas, had taken office with a "dynasty" strategy in mind. As described by Pedro Collor and other CPI witnesses, the Collor-Farias administration centralized all corruption, demanding 40 percent kickbacks for all government contracts and special policy decisions. With a war chest accumulating at nearly US$2 billion a year, they apparently expected to bribe their way into power for the next twenty years. As the 1993–94 Budgetgate CPI revealed, this conspiracy had numerous collaborators in Congress and the executive branch. Because the 1992 impeachment CPI threatened to widen its inquiry, the politicians decided to sacrifice Collor quickly to obscure their own involvement.

President Fernando Collor de Mello and President George Bush during a state visit to the White House, Washington, June 18, 1991
Courtesy The White House, Washington

Franco's Presidency, 1992–94

Senator Itamar Franco (Liberal Party-Minas Gerais) had been chosen as Collor's running mate for three reasons: Minas Gerais had the second largest electorate; Franco had led the impeachment CPI against Sarney's alleged corruption; and Franco was the ideal anti-impeachment "insurance" because of his idiosyncratic nature. During the 1989 campaign, Franco had threatened to resign several times and later voiced outspoken opposition to some Collor policies, especially concerning privatization. As president, Franco immediately installed a politically balanced cabinet and sought broad support in Congress.

Franco's presidential style was the opposite to that of Collor. A man of more simple habits and tastes, Franco refused the imperial, ceremonious presidential role. However, he proved to be quite temperamental, and many of his appointments were ill-conceived and short-lived. His most serious difficulty was defining an optimum economic strategy and selecting a minister of finance. He slowed Collor's privatization program to a near standstill and reverted to a developmentalist, nationalist model that was based on a national plan to guide the country through a series of stages of development, eventually culminating in modernization. After successively appointing two politicians and an academic economist to head the Ministry of Finance, Franco moved Senator Fernando Henrique Cardoso (PSDB-São Paulo) from the Ministry of Foreign Affairs to Finance in May 1993.

In October 1993, Congress installed a CPI to investigate its own members involved in a far-reaching scandal within the joint budget committee. The scandal had begun during the Sarney period and extended into Franco's government. In addition to investigating possible involvement of some fifty members of Congress and identifying the "corruptors" in the private sector, the investigations unmasked a conspiracy ring within the executive branch that involved several middle-level bureaucrats. Distraught by the scandal reaching the executive branch, President Franco contemplated resigning. However, cooler heads persuaded him not to, and instead the president appointed several distinguished citizens to a Special Investigating Commission (Comissão Especial de Investigação—CEI) headed by the SAF (Federal Administration Secretariat) chief. Some of those involved in corruption were fired. Franco also appointed several military officers to civilian positions in the Ministry of Transport, Federal Police, and Office of the Federal Budget Director, which had difficult problems.

With Cardoso's PSDB (Brazilian Social Democracy Party) team installed at Finance, the Franco government became less erratic, and the kitchen cabinet's influence somewhat diminished. However, inflation had increased from 25 percent to 45 percent by April 1994, when Cardoso resigned to run for president, a month after his new stabilization plan went into effect.

The economic stabilization plan took into account all the errors of the Cruzado Plan of 1986, and both Cardoso and his team were aware of its potential effect on the 1994 elections. Because of the great success of the *Real* Plan, President Franco's approval rating soared to nearly 80 percent at the end of his term. The Franco-Cardoso transition was the most tranquil in Brazilian political history.

Cardoso's Presidency, 1995–

Cardoso was inaugurated as president on January 1, 1995, under the most auspicious circumstances. He had won an outright victory in the first round of the election and had potentially strong support blocs in the Chamber of Deputies and Senate. He had strong support from a majority of the newly

President Fernando Henrique Cardoso
Courtesy Brazilian Embassy, Washington

elected governors, including those from the important states of Minas Gerais, São Paulo, and Rio de Janeiro, which had elected governors from the president's own PSDB. Further, the December 1994 inflation rate was less than 1 percent, unemployment was low, and popular expectations ratings were extremely high.

After his inauguration, Cardoso called the lame-duck Congress into session in an attempt to pass important legislation not acted on in 1994. President Cardoso abolished the CEI, which had not yet finished investigating corruption in the Franco administration, and transferred its mission to the new Internal Control Secretariat (Secretaria de Contrôle Interno—SCI). The Cardoso government pushed privatization and organized the sale of the Rio Dôce Valley Company (Companhia Vale do Rio Dôce—CVRD), one of the world's largest mining firms; the telecommunications system; and the electricity sector.

In 1995 Congress enacted major constitutional reforms, including economic deregulation, eliminating state monopolies, and changes in election and party legislation. By July 1995, the lower house had passed (and transmitted to the Senate) all five amendments dealing with the economic area. The amendments reduced to varying degrees state-held monopolies on coastal shipping, natural gas distribution, telecommunications, and petroleum, and eliminated the distinction between domestic and foreign firms in Article 171.

Perhaps the most important task of the Cardoso government in 1995 was to promote the reform of key sections of the 1988 constitution in order to reduce the role of the state in the economy, reform the federal bureaucracy, reorganize the social security system, rework federalist relationships, overhaul the complicated tax system, and effect electoral and party reforms to strengthen the political representation of political parties. In February 1995, the new Cardoso government moved quickly to initiate constitutional reform by a three-fifths majority of each house.

In the area of political reforms, Congress sought to improve Brazil's very weak party system. Congress proposed establishing a mixed system, prohibiting coalitions in proportional elections, establishing a minimum representation threshold (5 percent), permitting immediate reelection to executive office, imposing more rigid party fidelity norms, restricting party access to television and radio time, and establishing stricter regulations for campaign finance.

Women in Politics

The women's suffrage movement began in Brazil in the early 1900s. As in the United States, women were first fully enfranchised at the state level. In 1927 in Rio Grande do Norte, the state election laws were amended giving women the right to vote. A year later, Alzira Soriano was elected mayor of Lajes, Santa Catarina State. Finally, the new national election code, signed by President Vargas in 1932, allowed women to vote in the May 1933 elections for the 1934 Constituent Assembly. Two women were elected to that body.

Many women have been elected mayors. In 1985 Luiza Fontenelle (Workers' Party) was the first woman elected in a state capital (Fortaleza, Ceará). The most important elective office held by a woman in Brazil was the mayorship of São Paulo, which Luiza Erundina (Workers' Party) won in 1988.

Although women have become federal judges by public examination, none has ever been appointed to Brazil's superior courts. In 1988 President Sarney appointed the first woman to the National Accounting Court. However, this appointment was more related to the appointee's notorious journalist husband than to her judicial qualifications (see Gender, ch. 2).

By 1994 women constituted nearly half of the electorate. In August 1994, data from the TSE (Superior Electoral Court) showed that of 94,782,410 registered voters, 49.4 percent were women.

No women were elected to Congress in the 1946–51 period, but Getúlio Vargas's niece, Ivette Vargas, was elected federal deputy from São Paulo in 1950 at age twenty-three. Women continued to have minuscule representation in Congress and in state assemblies until the political opening (*abertura*) in 1982, when nine women were elected to the Chamber of Deputies, followed by twenty-six in 1986, twenty-three in 1990, and thirty-six in 1994. Among the latter, Vanessa Cunha (PSDB-Rio de Janeiro) was the youngest federal deputy at age twenty-two. Among state deputies, seventy-nine women were elected in 1994.

The first female senator assumed office in 1979 as an alternate on the death of her predecessor. Since then a few women have been elected to the Senate in successive elections. In 1994 fourteen women were candidates for the Senate, and four were elected.

In 1996 Congress adopted a quota system (20 percent) for female candidates for city council, and this policy increased the number of women elected. In 1997 Congress extended the mechanism to the 1998 general elections.

Until 1994 no women had been elected governor in their own right. When the governor of Acre resigned to run for the Senate in 1982, Yolanda Fleming was appointed governor to serve out the last ten months of the term. In 1994 eleven women ran for governor, and three made it into the second-round runoff—Angela Amin (PPR—Santa Catarina), Lúcia Vânia of the Progressive Party, and Roseana Sarney (PFL-Maranhão). Sarney, a daughter of the former president, was elected by a very small margin.

In 1994 women became candidates for vice president for the first time. The PMDB chose Iris Rezende, wife of the Goiás governor, to be Orestes Quêrcia's running mate. Although Rezende, a Protestant, had never held a formal political office, she was very active in politics while first lady of Goiás. With her candidacy, the PMDB hoped to attract the growing number of Protestant voters. Not to be outdone, the PPR chose Gardênia Gonçalves from Maranhão as a running mate for Senator Esperidião Amin. Gonçalves's husband had been a governor and senator from Maranhão, in opposition to the Sarney group, and in 1992 she was elected mayor of the capital city, São Luís.

Figueiredo (president, 1979–85) was the first president to name a woman to a cabinet position—Professor Esther Figueiredo Ferraz (no relation to the president) as minister of education and culture. His successors also appointed female cabinet ministers, the most famous of whom was Zélia Cardoso de Melo, President Collor's minister of economy. President Franco's cabinet included three women. President Cardoso appointed one woman during his first year in office, but she was replaced by a man in 1996.

The Electoral System

Since independence Brazil has experimented with almost every possible electoral system: single and multimember districts, and proportional representation with various formulas. Only the so-called mixed systems are yet to be tried. Election day is always a national holiday. Until 1965 national and state elections were held on October 3, but the military moved the date to November 15 (Day of the Republic, a military holiday). The constitution of 1988 reestablished October 3 (ninety days before the inauguration of executive-branch elected officials) for the first round of voting, and November 15 for runoff elections when needed. As of 1998, first-round elections will be held on the first Sunday in October and runoff second rounds on the last Sunday of October.

Brazilian election laws are very complex and detailed. The law requires that all candidates who hold executive positions resign six months before the election (see The Legislature, this ch.). No "write-in" candidacies are allowed; only candidates officially presented by a registered political party may participate. Parties choose their candidates in municipal, state, or national conventions. Although the legislation does not recognize party primaries officially, on occasion they have been used informally.

Voting is considered both a right and a duty in Brazil; thus, registration and voting are compulsory between the ages of eighteen and seventy. Illiterates vote, but their voting registration card identifies their status, and they sign the voting list with a fingerprint on election day. The 1988 constitution lowered the voting age, permitting sixteen- and seventeen-year-olds to vote on a voluntary basis. In 1994 these young voters (who cannot legally drink or drive) totaled 2,132,190 (2.2 percent of the electorate). For these reasons, turnouts for all elections in Brazil are very high, usually more than 85 percent. At certain times, voters have cast blank and void ballots as a means of protest, especially in 1970, when military oppression was at its height.

Before 1966 individual paper ballots were used for each office, and the voter placed the appropriate set in an envelope, which was inserted into the ballot box. Since 1966 unified single ballots have been used for simultaneous elections. In 1996 fifty-one of Brazil's largest cities used a new electronic voting machine with great success. In 1998 some 90 million voters will use this new technique, which may become a hot export item. For majority elections, candidates' names are listed in random order, and the voter must mark the respective box. For proportional elections, the voter can write the name or identification (ID) number of the candidate, or write the symbol or ID number of the party preference. There is no alternative to making a straight party vote for all offices on the ballot. This procedure is extremely complicated for voters with little schooling. In elections in the first half of the 1990s, many voted for one or two executive offices and left the rest of the ballot blank.

Before Congress adopted Law No. 8,713 in September 1993, there were few restrictions on campaign finances. Businesses and labor unions could not make political contributions. Individual persons could contribute to parties, but not to individual candidates. Parties were required to submit their accounting to the TSE (Superior Electoral Court), countersigned by each other. In 1994 contributions from individual businesses (but not labor unions) were legalized, and electoral bonus (*bônus eleitoral*) receipts were issued to contributors, who have often used them to evade taxes.

In 1994 Law No. 8,713 also required parties and candidates to submit to the electoral courts detailed balance sheets listing contributors and expenses. These reports were made public and hastily analyzed by the press. Cardoso's presidential campaign listed expenses of nearly R$32 million, about one *real* per vote, and contributions from banks, large construction firms, and businesses.

Brazil has four types of majority elections: the president, governors, and mayors are elected by absolute majorities; senators, by simple majorities. In elections for president, governors, and mayors of cities with more than 200,000 voters, a runoff is required between the top two candidates if no one receives an absolute majority in the first round (50 percent plus at least one vote). The president, governors, and mayors have their respective vice president, vice governors, and vice mayors, who are elected on unified slates.

The May 1994 constitutional revision reducing the presidential term from five to four years unified the terms of the president, state governors, and Congress. State and national elections are scheduled for 1998 and 2002, two years out of phase with municipal elections, which are set for 1996 and 2000.

Three senators are elected by simple majority to represent each of the twenty-six states and the Federal District. They are elected to alternating eight-year terms: one seat will be contested in 1998 and the other two in 2002. Each senator has an alternate elected on a unified ticket, usually from another party in the coalition. If the senator elected takes leave, dies, resigns, or is expelled, the alternate takes over.

Brazil uses an open-list d'Hondt proportional representation system to elect federal and state deputies and city council members. Each party or coalition selects its list of candidates, which is registered with the respective Electoral Court in June. Coalition partners lose their identity and compete in a single "basket" of votes. Coalitions are very important for proportional representation elections in Brazil. In 1962 nearly 50 percent of federal deputies were elected through coalitions. With the surge of new parties created after 1985, coalitions again appeared in the 1986, 1990, and 1996 elections. These coalitions accounted for nearly 90 percent of those elected.

In proportional representation elections, voters have the option of making a party vote. Usually, however, the proportional representation campaigns are so individualized (many candidates never mention their party label in their propaganda) that the party vote is very small (8 percent in 1994). An exception is the Workers' Party, which received 33 percent of its votes for federal deputy as party votes in 1994.

Elections

The Presidential Election of 1989

The 1989 presidential election, the first direct presidential election since 1960, was established by the 1988 constitution. The 1988 municipal elections were a preview of the 1989 elections for the PMDB, the nation's largest party, which lost in most cities with a population of more than 100,000. Leonel Brizola's PDT (Democratic Labor Party) and Lula's Workers' Party made considerable gains, as voters made plain their rejection of parties associated with the Sarney government.

As a result of more lenient legislation, twenty-two parties qualified candidates for the presidency in 1989. The PRN (Party of National Reconstruction) was hastily organized by a questionable takeover of the Youth Party (Partido da Juventude—PJ) to launch the candidacy of Alagoas governor Fernando Collor de Mello, who had been elected by the PMDB in 1986, and had a brief flirtation with the PSDB in late 1988. Six of the major candidates were closely associated with the Sarney period or with the Big Center in the ANC (National Constituent Assembly).

By June 1989, Collor, aided by numerous television appearances, had close to 50 percent of voter preference. His other advantages in this election included his antiparty and antiestablishment posture; his being relatively unknown politically; a huge war chest of campaign funds, efficiently collected by campaign treasurer, Paulo Cesar Farias; a fleet of fifteen Lear jets at his disposal for campaigning; a sophisticated campaign organization; and his good communication and oratory skills, acquired while working at the family television station in Maceió.

In the first round of voting, Collor received 28.5 percent of the votes and Lula, 16.1 percent, slightly edging out Brizola in a close third (see table 22, Appendix). In the second round, Lula managed to pull ahead of Collor in the polls by some 5 percent in the last ten days of the campaign. However, because of Collor's negative campaign attacks against Lula, the election swung in Collor's favor by a 5.7 percent margin (see table 23, Appendix). Collor's geographic vote distribution was very similar to that of the PDS (Democratic Social Party)—the smaller the city, the larger Collor's proportion of the vote.

Congressional and State Elections, 1990

Although President Collor had been able to pass most of his emergency legislation in 1990, he knew that his government needed to elect a solid majority to Congress, backed up by sympathetic governors. The economic stabilization plan adopted in March 1990 produced a deep recession, which was not reversed before the October 3 general elections. The 1988 constitution had created three new states—Amapá, Roraima, and Tocantins—and home rule came to Brasília, which elected its first governor. Thus, twenty-six states and the Federal District held simultaneous elections for governor, state assemblies, the full 503-member Chamber of Deputies, and thirty-one senators (the new states of Amapá and Roraima elected three senators each).

Seventeen of the gubernatorial races had runoffs on November 15. Among the twenty-seven governors elected, Collor had four staunch allies, eleven sometime allies, and twelve in opposition. Parties nominally aligned with Collor had elected close to an absolute majority (252) of federal deputies, but because of low party loyalty and cohesion, the president had great difficulty passing his legislative agenda in 1991 (see table 24, Appendix). The PMDB (Brazilian Democratic Movement Party) remained the largest party in Congress, retaining the presidency of the Senate. However, in 1993 the PMDB lost the presidency of the Chamber to a PFL-led coalition. Nineteen parties gained representation in the lower house.

Municipal Elections, 1992

The 1992 municipal elections were held five days after Collor's impeachment. The PMDB recovered some positions lost in 1988. The PFL (Liberal Front Party), PSDB, and PDS (Democratic Social Party) also made moderate advances.

General Elections, 1994

The 1994 elections were significant because the presidential election coincided with the general elections for governor, senator, and federal and state deputy for the first time since 1950. It was expected that a strong presidential showing would have strong coattails (see Glossary) at the state level. However, many thought that election results proved otherwise. Coalition-building was generally inconsistent between the national and state levels, because local political animosities and affinities were so diverse from state to state that none of the presidential coalitions could cover all the possible combinations. Among the major parties, the PFL, PTB (Brazilian Labor Party), and Progressive Party decided not to field separate presidential candidates. The PMDB, PDT (Democratic Labor Party), PPR (Progressive Renewal Party), Workers' Party, and PSDB decided to run their own candidates. Four minor parties—the Liberal Party (Partido Liberal—PL), National Order Redefinition

Brasília, at night
Courtesy Brazilian Embassy, Washington

Party (Partido da Redefinição da Ordem Nacional—Prona), PRN (Party of National Reconstruction), and Social Christian Party (Partido Social Cristão—PSC)—also nominated candidates.

Despite opposition from a minority, the PMDB nominated former São Paulo governor Orestes Quêrcia as its presidential candidate. The PDT again nominated Leonel Brizola. Lula's Workers' Party articulated a broad coalition on the left, including the Brazilian Socialist Party (Partido Socialista Brasileiro—PSB), Popular Socialist Party (Partido Popular Socialista—PPS), PC do B (Communist Party of Brazil), and Green Party (Partido Verde—PV). However, Marxist wings of the Workers' Party, having gained control of the party's Executive Committee, imposed a difficult, radical platform on the campaign.

Cardoso had become minister of finance in May 1993 and had assembled the same PSDB economic team that had formulated the Cruzado Plan in 1986. This time, however, the team put together a stabilization plan that included the components missing in 1986. The hope was that the initiative would boost Cardoso's potential candidacy into the second round. In February 1994, Congress approved the Real Value Units (Unidades

Reais de Valor—URVs; see *real* (R$) in Glossary) Stabilization Plan, which gave the minister of finance almost absolute power to impound or reallocate budgeted funds, reduce the fiscal deficit, and conduct a rescheduling of the foreign debt.

The impact of the *Real* Plan on the preference polls was even more dramatic than PSDB strategists had imagined. They had thought that, at best, if the plan were a success, Cardoso might pull even with Lula by the end of August, thus guaranteeing a second round in November. However, Cardoso surpassed Lula in the Datafolha firm's presidential preference poll results at the end of July by successfully branding the Workers' Party as against the *Real* Plan and for inflation. Cardoso went on to win the election outright on the first round with 54.3 percent of the valid votes cast (44.1 percent of the total vote, including blank and null ballots) (see table 25, Appendix). Lula placed second with 27.0 percent. Cardoso's PSDB-PFL-PTB coalition received additional support from the PMDB and PPR, which abandoned their candidates and climbed aboard the Cardoso bandwagon. In addition to electing the president and a majority of the governors, the Center coalition returned substantial majorities to Congress.

The social-liberal alliance, the Big Center, that elected Cardoso on the first round enjoyed only moderate presidential coattails at the state level (see table 26, Appendix). The PSDB-PFL-PTB alliance elected nine (33 percent) governors, twenty-four of fifty-four (44 percent) senators up for election, 182 of 513 (35 percent) federal deputies, and 324 of 1,045 (31 percent) state deputies. Cardoso placed first in every state except the Federal District (Brasília) and Rio Grande do Sul. Lula surpassed Cardoso in the Federal District and Rio Grande do Sul, where his coattails pulled the Workers' Party gubernatorial candidates into the second round.

The 1994 gubernatorial election was the fourth in a series of direct elections for governor since their reinstatement in 1982. Compared with 1990, the PSDB had the best performance of all parties in 1994. The PSDB was formed hastily in June 1988, and in 1990 elected only one governor (Ceará). In 1994 the PSDB won six governorships, including Minas Gerais, São Paulo, and Rio de Janeiro. These three states account for nearly 60 percent of Brazil's gross national product (GNP—see Glossary) and tax base. Certainly, presidential coattails and the *Real* Plan were important factors in these three second-round victories. Brizola's PDT lost the three states won in 1990, but in

1994 elected the governors of Paraná (Jaime Lerner) and Mato Grosso (Dante de Oliveira), both on the first round. The Workers' Party made it into the second round in three states and won in two: Brasília and Espírito Santo. The two victories gave the Workers' Party a chance to demonstrate how it would manage a state government. The party had already elected mayors in major cities (São Paulo, Porto Alegre, and Belo Horizonte) in 1988 and 1992.

Of the fifty-four Senate seats up for election in 1994, only nine incumbents were reelected. Six of the twenty-seven senators elected in 1990 were replaced by their respective alternates (five were elected to other offices and one died). Thus, in 1995 fifty-one of the eighty-one senators were new, although five of the latter had served in the Senate before 1990. The PMDB, PFL, and PSDB continued to have the largest upper-house delegations; and the PFL made substantial gains (see table 27, Appendix). The most significant change was the advance of the left. From only two senators in 1991, this group increased to seven (five from the Workers' Party). The PPS, the former PCB (Brazilian Communist Party), elected its first senator (Roberto Freire) since Luís Carlos Prestes was elected in 1945.

The Chamber of Deputies was enlarged in 1995 with the expansion of the São Paulo State delegation from sixty to seventy as mandated by the 1988 constitution. Turnover in the lower house in 1995 (275 new deputies out of 513, or 53.6 percent) was slightly lower than that in 1991. As in 1991, the Chamber of Deputies in 1995 continued to have two larger parties (PMDB and PFL) and six middle-sized parties. By electing deputies in all five regions of Brazil, these eight parties, as well as the PC do B, have a more national representation.

Voter turnout was lower in 1994 (82.2 percent) than in 1989 (88.1 percent), and blank and null votes were more frequent in 1994 than in 1989. These differences may have resulted in part from the fact that the 1994 election was more complicated, with two ballots and six offices.

Municipal Elections, 1996

On October 3, 1996, voters in 5,581 municipalities chose mayors and city councils. Only thirty-one cities held runoff elections on November 15. Big gains were made by the PSDB and the PFL, which took the cities of Rio de Janeiro, Salvador, and Recife for the first time, while a divided PMDB declined considerably. Paulo Maluf elected his successor as mayor of São

Paulo, thereby reinforcing his future political ambitions. On the left, the Workers' Party suffered reverses, and the PSB advanced.

Generally, issues were local and not national, and women had increased participation, boosted by the new 20 percent quota rule for proportional elections. About 142 federal deputies decided to run in these local elections, but only forty-two won and thus left the Congress. The apparent desire for administrative continuity enhanced the arguments in favor of the reelection amendment.

Interest Group Politics

Brazil has very intense and diversified interest groups. Before 1964 the most visible were labor unions, student organizations, and business groups, which exercised their pressures more on Congress than on the executive branch. During the military period, especially from 1969 to 1974, interest groups continued to operate but almost exclusively vis-à-vis the executive branch. In 1983, when it became apparent that a political transition would take place, Congress again became the focal point of interest groups. The most explicit example of this trend was the ANC (National Constituent Assembly), when literally thousands of lobbyists—one researcher catalogued 121 noninstitutional groups—descended on Brasília.

Interest Groups

Government institutions lobby the executive and legislative branches through their legislative liaisons and employee associations. The president's office maintains a Subsecretariat for Congressional Relations. State enterprise employee associations, such as those of the Brazilian Petroleum Corporation (Petróleo Brasileiro S.A.—Petrobrás) and the Brazilian Electric Power Company, Inc. (Centrais Elétricas Brasileiras S.A.—Eletrobrás), have very active lobbying organizations, as do federal employees. All states and many large cities maintain permanent representation offices in Brasília. Although strictly prohibited, military officers exerted heavy pressure on the government for better salaries in 1992–94 through protest marches by military families.

In 1983 the Interunion Parliamentary Advisory Department (Departamento Intersindical de Assessorial Parlamentar—DIAP) was founded to coordinate and unify the lobbying efforts of the labor movement. The DIAP represented 517 unions, nine confederations, and one central federation in 1992. The DIAP soon proved highly efficient in monitoring legislative activities, publishing profiles of the performance of congressional members, and identifying friends and enemies of workers. In the 1991–94 period, the party leadership's manipulations attempted to thwart DIAP monitoring by floor voting, and very few roll-call votes were taken during that session.

Since the 1930s, business groups have been organized into umbrella federations at the state level and confederations at the national level, such as the São Paulo State Federation of Industries (Federação das Indústrias do Estado de São Paulo—FIESP) and the National Confederation of Industry (Confederação Nacional das Indústrias—CNI). Other businesses are organized as national associations by sector: the Brazilian Association of Radio and Television Companies (Associação Brasileira das Empresas de Rádio e Televisão—ABERT), the Brazilian Electro-Electronic Industry Association (Associação Brasileira da Indústria Eletro-Eletrônica—ABINEE), and the Brazilian Aluminum Association (Associação Brasileira de Alumínio—ABAL). Business groups mounted a very efficient lobbying operation in support of the Big Center during the ANC.

Professional groups, such as associations of medical doctors, lawyers, pharmacists, and engineers, are usually more active regarding the regulation of their professions, but occasionally attempt to influence more generalized economic and social legislation. Since the 1970s, there has been a steady growth of urban social movements and groups concerned with issues such as the prevention and treatment of acquired immune deficiency syndrome (AIDS), racial prejudice, consumer rights, ecology, the homeless, Indians, mortgages, street children, and tenants. As a result, there has been a parallel growth of nongovernmental organizations (NGOs). Some NGOs are considered aggregative, such as the Brazilian Institute of Social and Economic Analysis (Instituto Brasileiro de Análise Social e Econômica—IBASE) in Rio de Janeiro, or the Institute of Socioeconomic Studies (Instituto de Estudos Sócio-Econômicos—Inesc) in Brasília. Some are more issue-focused, such as the Center for Indian Rights (Núcleo de Direitos Indígenos—NDI) in Brasília, or SOS Atlantic Forest (SOS Mata Atlântica) in Rio de Janeiro.

Religious groups are also important. The Roman Catholic Church acts officially through the National Conference of Brazilian Bishops (Conferência Nacional dos Bispos do Brasil—CNBB). However, it has an unofficial far right wing in the Brazilian Association of Tradition, Family, and Property (Sociedade Brasileira de Defesa da Tradição, Família e Propriedade—TFP), and an unofficial left wing of liberation theology linked to the Ecclesiastical Base Communities (Comunidades Eclesiais de Base—CEBs) (see Glossary). The center and left had always elected the president and general secretary of the CNBB since its inception. However, in May 1995 conservative Prime Bishop-Cardinal Lucas Moreira Neves was elected president of the CNBB, a consequence of Pope John Paul II's consistent appointment of conservative bishops in Brazil. The Protestants have their Order of Evangelical Ministers (Ordem dos Ministros Evangélicos—OME) and Political Action Evangelical Group (Grupo Evangélico de Ação Política—GEAP).

The Lobbying Process

Three basic styles of lobbying are found in Brasília: the interest group sends its own representatives to Brasília, when the legislative agenda warrants; the interest group has its own representatives permanently installed in Brasília; or the group contracts with lobbyists in Brasília to represent its interests. Professional lobbyists systematically monitor the activities of Congress and the executive branch regarding legislative agendas and procedures. Visits by groups and individual interests to strategic members of Congress are organized frequently. In some cases, the deputies' geographical vote profiles for the last election within their state are analyzed for the client. When the interest group has a large membership, bus caravans to Brasília are organized to pressure Congress or the executive branch.

As in many legislatures, the Brazilian Congress also has inside lobbyists; that is, Chamber of Deputies or Senate staff, and some members themselves (the so-called single-issue deputy or senator). Because staff are very important to the legislative process, they are cultivated assiduously by lobbyists, and many become sensitive to (or eventually agents for) certain interest groups. In response to these pressures, the Chamber of Deputies Research Staff Association began preparing a Code of Ethics in 1993.

Campaign contributions are local and are an integral part of the lobbying process. The Ministry of Finance issues electoral bonus receipts for campaign contributions. Many contributing businesses, however, have used these receipts to evade taxes by providing documentation for their bogus records, known as their *caixa dois* (second set of books). Several bills have been introduced to address this problem, but no legislation had been passed by early 1997. The Chamber of Deputies allows groups to receive lobbying credentials. In the 1991–92 session, thirty-nine groups (twenty-eight business groups) received credentials, in addition to all ministries and sixteen other public-sector agencies. The Senate does not offer credentials.

The Media

Print and electronic media play a very important role in Brazilian politics. Until the 1988 constitution, the president had the exclusive prerogative to allocate radio and television concessions. From 1985 through 1988, television and radio concessions became the "currency of political negotiation" as President Sarney tried to maintain majorities in Congress. Although "social control" over concessions and renewals is called for in the new constitution, no such action had been taken until Cardoso's new minister of communications, Sérgio Motta, served notice in 1995 that all pending concessions would be canceled and a National Social Control Commission would be established that would use different criteria.

Shortly after radio arrived in Brazil in the 1930s, President Vargas initiated weekday transmissions of the Voice of Brazil, as propaganda on government operations. The news show, which emphasizes activities in and around government and political circles, carries thirty minutes of news from the executive branch and thirty minutes from Congress and the judiciary.

Media owners have very definite political agendas and pursue them assiduously. Francisco de Assis Chateaubriand Bandeira de Melo built the first media empire in Brazil. He founded the Diários Associados newspaper chain in the 1930s, and in the 1950s established a media empire that included thirty-three newspapers, eighteen magazines, the Tupi Network (with twenty-five radio and eighteen television stations), and two news agencies. Chateaubriand exercised tremendous coercive power over businessmen, presidents, governors, and Congress. As a result of losing a political and judicial battle against the rise of the TV Globo Network, Tupi deteriorated after Chateaubriand's death in 1968. The military government finally confiscated and reallocated its concessions in 1981. The newspaper chain still exists but with less central coordination.

The second media empire and the most powerful one in 1997, Globo Organizations (Organizações Globo), began with the Rio newspaper *O Globo,* founded by Irineu Marinho in the 1920s. In 1931 the oldest son, Roberto Marinho, assumed control of the newspaper and still commanded the empire in 1997 at age eighty-five. Globo began radio transmissions in 1944, and TV Globo began in Rio de Janeiro in 1965, the latter under a controversial technical assistance agreement with the Time-Life Group that generated a CPI.

With the establishment of a microwave and later satellite national hookup by the Brazilian Telecommunications Company (Empresa Brasileira de Telecomunicações—Embratel) in 1970, the Globo network steadily advanced to cover all states. The network accounts for approximately 70 percent of television audience ratings and advertising billings in Brazil.

In 1993, 333 daily newspapers had a total circulation of about 2.5 million. Magazines sold 222 million copies in 1993 (1.47 per inhabitant), down 32 percent from 1991. Although per capita newspaper circulation and readership is very low in Brazil, research has shown that print media have considerable influence on politics because of very competent investigative reporting and exposés, influence among "opinion leaders," and influence on other media. Of the five national newspapers—*O Estado de São Paulo, Folha de São Paulo, Gazeta Mercantil, O Globo,* and *Jornal do Brasil*—members of Congress regarded *Gazeta Mercantil* as the least biased paper, according to a May 1995 survey.

Radio and especially television exert a tremendous direct influence over the voting behavior of the vast majority of Brazilians. When the TSE (Superior Electoral Court) completed a massive computerized voter registration before the 1986 elections, it classified 70 percent of those registered as "illiterate or semi-illiterate." Brazilian television has an insidious influence on these nearly 60 million voters. Political subplots are cleverly woven into television soap operas (*telenovelas*) and situation comedies to jaundice public opinion about certain political groups and types of politicians. Biased news coverage of political campaigns is commonplace.

Foreign Relations

The Foreign Service

The Rio Branco Institute (Instituto Rio Branco—IRBr) recruits from twenty to thirty candidates each year among college graduates. After four semesters of intensive study of language and diplomacy, graduates receive a certified bachelor of arts degree in diplomacy and begin their careers as third secretaries. In 1996 the IRBr began studies to upgrade the course to an M.A. program. The IRBr teaching staff is composed of senior diplomats and some academics from the University of Brasília (Universidade de Brasília). Some foreign students are admitted, mostly from Latin America and Africa.

After three or four years experience within several divisions of the Ministry of Foreign Affairs (known as Itamaraty, after the building it formerly occupied in Rio de Janeiro), the junior diplomat is posted overseas. Promotion to second and first secretary is by merit (evaluation by immediate superiors). Before promotion to minister second class, the diplomat goes through a mid-career course and produces a monograph, which is defended before an examining board. Many diplomats also acquire graduate degrees during their career. Promotion to the final positions of counselor (minister first class) and ambassador involves a combination of merit and political considerations; the president makes the final decision. Because Itamaraty has more diplomats than posts overseas and in Brasília, diplomats frequently fill key positions in other ministries, state enterprises, and the president's office. Brazilian diplomats generally are considered skilled and patient negotiators by their peers.

Foreign Policy Decision Making

Most foreign policy strategies and decisions originate within Itamaraty. A senior diplomat always occupies the position of foreign affairs adviser within the president's office, and diplomats occupy similar liaison positions in key ministries. Since the 1980s, Itamaraty, in response to the growing complexity of foreign policy issues, has established new divisions dealing with export promotion, environmental affairs, science and technology, and human rights. Itamaraty also established the International Relations Research Institute (Instituto das Pesquisas das Relações Internacionais—IPRI) as part of the Alexandre

Gusmão Foundation, which functions as a think tank and conference center and publishes foreign policy studies.

The Senate and Chamber of Deputies each have foreign affairs standing committees. Under the 1988 constitution, the Senate expanded its treaty approval prerogative to include all international financial agreements, such as negotiations with the International Monetary Fund (IMF—see Glossary) and international banks, which in the past had been the exclusive prerogative of the executive branch (see The Military in the Amazon, ch. 5). The Congress also has involved itself in major government contracts with foreign companies, such as the contract with Raytheon for an Amazon surveillance system.

The Brazilian Cooperation Agency (Agência Brasileira de Cooperacão—ABC), a foreign aid agency formally established in the late 1980s, coordinates all international technical cooperation and assistance received by Brazil from foreign donors (often, but not always, within the context of bilateral agreements). For example, in the absence of a United States-Brazil bilateral agreement, United States Agency for International Development (USAID) programs in Brazil are not coordinated through the ABC. The ABC also coordinates Brazilian international technical cooperation and assistance directed to other countries, mostly through South-South relationships conducted by Brazilian government agencies, universities, and NGOs.

At times other agencies may take the lead in foreign policy decision making. For example, in June 1995 the economic sector, led by the Ministry of Planning, made the initial decision to impose quotas on imported automobiles. This decision provoked a crisis within the Common Market of the South (Mercado Comum do Sul—Mercosul; see Glossary)—because Argentine automobile exports to Brazil would have been affected. Itamaraty intervened, and a solution was negotiated excepting Mercosul from the rigors of the measure.

The military had the final say on foreign policy during the 1964–85 period, when foreign policy was decided frequently within the National Security Council (Conselho de Segurança Nacional—CSN). Since then the military occasionally has exercised some influence. When the United Nations (UN) requested Brazilian troops for a peacekeeping force in Namibia during the delicate, pre-election phase of transition in 1991, Itamaraty was favorable, but the army vetoed the initiative. The reverse occurred in 1995. After a successful peacekeeping mission in Mozambique in 1993–94, the army, in search of new missions, approved sending a battalion to the peacekeeping operation in Angola. However, for reasons of economic austerity the ministries of Planning and Finance delayed the appropriation until 1996.

Multilateral Relations

Brazil was a founding member of the League of Nations (see Glossary) in 1920 and the UN in 1945, and has chaired the UN Security Council on several occasions. Brazil is also an active participant in the Organization of American States (OAS; see Glossary), IMF, World Bank (see Glossary), Inter-American Development Bank (IADB; see Glossary), African Development Bank (ADB), World Trade Organization (WTO, which now administers the General Agreement on Tariffs and Trade—GATT; see Glossary), International Commodity Organization (coffee, cocoa beans), and Antarctic Treaty. International pressures have been strong on Brazil to join certain agreements, such as the Non-Proliferation Treaty (NPT), which Brazil announced its decision to sign on June 20, 1997. Brazil joined the Missile Technology Control Regime (MTCR—see Glossary) in October 1995.

Brazil has participated in UN peacekeeping operations since the Suez Crisis in 1956. A Brazilian contingent participated in the UN observer force that guaranteed the October 1994 elections in Mozambique, and in the UN observer force in Bosnia in 1995. Regarding the latter, a Brazilian general commanded a force of 680 observers, of whom thirty-four were Brazilians. In May 1995, two Brazilian officers were among the several hundred UN observers captured by the Bosnian Serbs and used as human shields against further NATO bombings. The number of Brazilian personnel attached to UN peacekeeping operations has gradually declined from 1,166 in August 1996 to forty-eight in September 1997. Because of its active participation in UN activities and its status as a middle-level emerging economic and political power, Brazil aspires to a permanent seat on the Security Council, if and when membership in this body is expanded.

Latin America

Brazil's first circle of international relations is with its Latin American neighbors. Being the largest nation in the region makes this process somewhat delicate. Most border issues were settled in the late nineteenth and early twentieth centuries, but some questions concerning the borders with Bolivia, Colombia, Paraguay, and Venezuela remain. In 1995 Brazilian farmers and forest gatherers penetrated Bolivia's Pando Department, in an action reminiscent of the invasion of Acre by Brazilian rubber tappers in the 1890s. Brazil regularly extends export credits and university scholarships to its Latin American neighbors. A certain quota of Latin Americans are admitted to the Rio Branco Institute and the armed forces staff schools.

An active participant in regional security activities, Brazil hosted the conference that established the Inter-American Treaty of Reciprocal Assistance (Rio Treaty) in 1947. In addition, Brazil was a founding member of the OAS in 1948 and has participated in several OAS peacekeeping endeavors. Most notable was Brazil's participation in the Inter-American Peace Force (Fuerzas Interamericanas de Paz—FIP) in the Dominican Republic in 1965. In the 1980s, Brazil was an active participant in the Contadora Support Group (see Glossary), which sought a permanent peace in Central America. In June 1995, eighty-seven Brazilians were attached to peacekeeping operations in the Americas—thirty-seven in El Salvador, thirty-two in Nicaragua, ten on the Ecuador/Peru border, six in Honduras, and two in Guatemala.

The Treaty of Asunción—signed in 1991 by Brazil, Argentina, Uruguay, and Paraguay—was the culmination of a rapprochement between Brazil and Argentina after 160 years of regional rivalry (see Trade Patterns and Regional Economic Integration, ch. 3). It also incorporated Uruguay and Paraguay into Mercosul, and Bolivia and Chile joined Mercosul in 1996.

Europe

During the period from the 1970s to 1995, the relative importance of the European Economic Community (EEC; now the European Union—EU) as a trading partner with Brazil was reduced, but increased in the mid-1990s. By 1995 German investments in Brazil were second only to the United States, but Britain, Italy, and France also have important investments, mostly in industrial manufacturing, heavy equipment and automobiles, and consumer goods. In mid-1995 negotiations advanced toward establishing a free-trade association between the EU and Mercosul. In December 1995, the EU signed an important free-trade protocol with Mercosul, the first ever between two regional trading blocs. Since then Brazil has

A Brazilian Air Force Hercules C–130 transport plane
Courtesy Brazilian Embassy, Washington

adroitly used the EU card to force a slowdown of the United States pressure to "fast track" the Free Trade Area of the Americas (FTAA) expansion of the North American Free Trade Agreement (NAFTA).

Relations with the EU are economically important, but even more so from a North-South political perspective. Brazil and its Mercosul partners want to strengthen their trading bloc to include not only Chile but also Bolivia, Colombia, Ecuador, Peru, and Venezuela before 2005, to be able to negotiate as a bloc with NAFTA, as opposed to bilateral negotiations as favored by the administration of President William Jefferson Clinton. The United States view is that 2005 is the date for the FTAA to be "fully operational," whereas Brazil and its Mercosul partners view the year 2005 as a "starting point" for the FTAA process.

The Middle East

Immigrants from the Middle East began arriving in Brazil in large numbers in the twentieth century, especially following World War I. These immigrants spread throughout Brazil but can be found mostly in the Southeast region, where many are merchants.

Brazil's economic relations with the Middle East were accelerated by the 1973 petroleum crisis. Brazil tried to maintain a moderate stance vis-à-vis the Arab-Israeli conflict and supported all UN peace initiatives. In late 1973, Brazil established embassies in Iraq and Saudi Arabia and legations in Libya and Kuwait, and it signed cooperation agreements with Egypt, Israel, and Iraq.

However, in 1975, because of the deepening petroleum crisis and in search of petrodollar investments, Brazil tilted its foreign policy in favor of the Arab (Palestinian) cause in three crucial votes in the UN. Brazil's military government upgraded its representation in Iraq by appointing a succession of four-star generals as ambassadors to Baghdad. When the Iran-Iraq War broke out in 1979, nearly 35 percent of Brazil's oil imports were coming from Iraq. In 1981 it was reported that Brazil had sold low-grade uranium ore or yellow cake (see Glossary) to Iraq.

The Iraq-Kuwait conflict, which resulted in Operation Desert Storm in early 1991, placed Brazil in a very delicate position. United States congressional subcommittees accused Brazil of exporting technology and expertise to Iraq to develop a missile based on the Piranha missile (MAA–1). Retired Air Force Brigadier Hugo Oliveira Piva had taken a private group of Brazilian technicians to Baghdad to complete this project; under pressure, the Collor government ordered the group's return to Brazil.

At the time of Desert Storm, a Brazilian construction company, Mendes Júnior, had several hundred workers and technicians, as well as several million dollars worth of equipment, in southern Iraq working on railroad and irrigation projects. Thus, Brazil, unlike Argentina, did not participate in the Allied operation. The Brazilian government had to dispatch its key negotiator, Ambassador Paulo de Tarso Flecha de Lima, from his post in London to negotiate the release of the Mendes Júnior personnel from Iraq and the disposition of the equipment. Brazil had won a US$5 billion price and performance competition to supply its Osório tank to Saudi Arabia in 1990, but the Kuwait conflict changed the decision in favor of the United States Abrams tank.

Africa

Brazil's relations with Africa date from the beginning of the slave trade in the seventeenth century. By the middle of the nineteenth century, many former slaves had returned to West Africa and had become prosperous merchants and entrepreneurs, and regular shipping lines and commerce flourished from Bahia. After 1945 Brazil maintained a low-profile position in the anticolonialism debate in the UN, but supported the positions of Portugal, Belgium, France, and Britain. In 1961 President Jânio Quadros's new independent foreign policy made some timid advances in favor of independence for the remaining colonies in Africa. During the Goulart period (1961–64), Brazil took contradictory positions, especially regarding Portugal. Brazil's main contacts with the newly independent nations of West Africa involved price-fixing attempts within the International Coffee Organization. The Castelo Branco administration (1964–67) sent two commercial missions to Africa, the Costa e Silva administration (1967–69) opened an embassy in Abidjan (Côte d'Ivoire) and one in Kinshasa (Zaire).

Nonetheless, the opening to Africa really began during the presidency of Emílio Garrastazú Médici (1969–74). In November 1972, Foreign Minister Mário Gibson Barbosa visited nine West African countries. In 1973 Brazil voted in favor of anticolonialism measures in the UN. This vote and follow-up trade missions resulted in numerous bilateral agreements and Brazil's participation in the ADB (African Development Bank). South African companies made considerable investments in Brazil, especially in mining. Brazil's exports to Africa jumped from US$90.4 million in 1972 to US$1.96 billion in 1981, and its imports from US$152.9 million to US$1.98 billion.

Brazil's opening to Africa was consolidated during the Geisel period (1974–79), which coincided with the emancipation of the five Portuguese colonies in Africa. Brazil recognized the independence of Guinea-Bissau and Cape Verde in July 1974, before it was conceded by Portugal. In November 1975, Brazil became the first Western nation to recognize the independence of Angola, under the revolutionary government of the Popular Movement for the Liberation of Angola (Movimento Popular de Libertação de Angola—MPLA), and to establish an embassy in Luanda. Brazil's stance caused much consternation for the United States because the MPLA government in Angola was socialist and dependent on the communist bloc and Cuba at that time. That same month, Brazil established relations with the government in Mozambique because of its strategic importance in southern East Africa and the Indian Ocean. Within the context of the Cold War and Brazil's anticommunist military government, this decision was a bold move on the part of the Geisel government. However, Brazil placed considerable importance on establishing relations with African countries. It was hard hit by the 1973–74 petroleum crisis and desired access to West African oil exports in particular. The petrodollars thus earned were used to buy Brazilian exports of manufactured goods through Petrobrás International Trade, Inc. (Petrobrás Comércio Internacional S.A.—Interbrás).

Over the next twenty years, Brazil established very close relations with the lusophone or Portuguese-Speaking African Countries (Paises Africanos de Lingua Oficial Portuguêsa—PALOPs). In addition to Angola and Mozambique, these included São Tomé e Príncipe, Cabo Verde, and Guinea-Bissau. The Rio Grande do Sul Airline (Viação Aérea Rio-Grandense do Sul—Varig) established regular flights to Lagos, Nigeria; Abidjan; Luanda, Angola; and Maputo, Mozambique. However, in the early 1990s flights were suspended to Lagos (to control drug traffic) and Maputo. President Figueiredo (1974–85) was the first Brazilian president to visit Africa (five countries in November 1983). Brazilian construction companies undertook hydroelectric and infrastructure projects, and Petrobrás signed risk contracts for oil exploration.

By 1986 Brazil had twenty-two embassies in the region, and President Sarney continued the expansion of relations with Africa, visiting Cape Verde in 1986 and Angola in 1989. African heads of state from Algeria, Zaire, Cape Verde, and Mozambique, as well as Sam Nujoma of the South West African People's Organization (SWAPO), also visited Brasília. By 1985 commerce between Africa and Brazil had grown to US$3.3 billion.

In the context of the independence of Namibia in 1990, the UN requested a Brazilian battalion to participate in peacekeeping operations, but Brazil refused, saying that the army was not prepared and the government lacked resources for such a venture. However, when the UN asked for Brazilian army and police participants in peacekeeping operations during the October 1994 election in Mozambique, the Itamar Franco government was quick to oblige. In 1995 the Cardoso government sent a full engineering battalion to Angola to participate in UN

A Brazilian Army Peacekeeping Force embarking for Angola
A Brazilian Army patrol in Mozambique
Courtesy Brazilian Embassy, Washington

operations (minesweeping and infrastructure rebuilding). In 1996 President Cardoso made a short visit to Angola en route to a longer state visit to South Africa.

Asia

Before 1960 Brazil maintained diplomatic relations with three Asian nations: Japan, India, and Nationalist China (Taiwan). In that year, Brazil established ties with the Republic of Korea (South Korea) and Ceylon (now Sri Lanka). In August 1961, President Quadros sent his vice president, João Goulart, to the People's Republic of China as head of a commercial delegation. In August 1974, Brazil broke relations with Taiwan and established full relations with China, four years before the United States. The Nationalist diplomats were evicted unceremoniously from the Chinese embassy in Brasília to make way for the new tenants.

In the 1970s and 1980s, relations with Asia expanded to ten embassies in Brasília. Because of the growing importance of the newly industrialized countries in the Pacific Basin, Brazil installed a legation in Singapore. Although not a major trading partner, India became an important South-South ally in international forums, such as the UN Conference on Trade and Development (UNCTAD), GATT, and the Group of 77 (G–77).

With its gradual economic opening to the West, mainland China has become an important trading partner for Brazil since the 1980s. Petrobrás began oil exploration under risk contract, and engineering services were contracted for mining and hydroelectric ventures. In addition, the Chinese have purchased large quantities of Brazilian iron ore and steel plate.

However, Japan has received the highest priority within the region. Brazil established diplomatic relations with Japan in 1897. The first Japanese immigrants arrived in Brazil in 1908, as the São Paulo coffee planters sought alternative free labor after the abolition of slavery in 1888. This influx of Japanese immigrants continued until 1934, when the new constitution limited foreign immigration to 2 percent of the past fifty years. Diplomatic relations broke off during World War II, but resumed in 1952. Some 100 years after the first waves of immigration, Brazilians of Japanese descent constitute one of the largest ethnic segments of Brazil's population.

In the 1960s, Japan began to invest heavily in various sectors in Brazil, including mining, steel, aluminum, telecommunications, manufacturing, and agricultural ventures (the latter in the Central Highlands plateau region and the Amazon). In return, Japan imported large quantities of iron, other nonferrous ores, unfinished steel and aluminum products, and soybeans and other agricultural products.

In the 1980s, with cycles of recession and decreasing employment opportunities in Brazil, a reverse immigration flux began; some 200,000 Brazilians of Japanese descent traveled to Japan in search of jobs. Their monthly remittances to their families remaining in Brazil have become an important item in bilateral commerce.

In 1992 Japanese companies invested US$1.4 billion in Brazil in the areas of telecommunications, capital goods, mining, and metallurgy. The Japan International Cooperation Agency (JICA) has sponsored many rural colonization projects in Brazil since the 1950s. In 1995 JICA was using Brazilian technicians and installations to train people from developing countries in Latin America and Africa in industrial job training, community development, education, and so forth.

In mid-1995 the Socialist Republic of Vietnam signaled a desire for closer trade relations with Brazil, thus eliminating Thailand as middleman. President General Le Duc Anh visited Brazil and the Brazilian foreign minister visited Vietnam in the second half of 1995. Brazil's opening to Vietnam was made within the context of Brazil's general Southeast Asian strategy and its view that Vietnam may soon become an "Asian Tiger."

United States

The United States was the first nation to establish a consulate in Brazil in 1808, following the transfer of the Portuguese royal court to Rio de Janeiro and the subsequent opening of the ports to foreign ships. However, it was not until after World War II that the United States became Brazil's number-one trading partner and foreign investor. After 1945 United States-Brazil relations took on five basic dimensions: promoting and protecting United States investments in and exports to Brazil; promoting Brazil's exports of primary goods or products (see Glossary) and supporting Brazil's industrialization policies; garnering Brazil's support for United States policy positions in the hemisphere and in other world forums; promoting Brazil's emergence as a middle-level world power in Latin America and the developing world; and showcasing Brazil's successful independent foreign policy and autonomous development strategy among its peers in the developing world.

During the presidency of Enrico Gaspar Dutra (1946–51), Brazil's foreign policy was aligned closely with that of the United States. Brazil outlawed the PCB (Brazilian Communist Party) in 1947 and broke off relations with the Soviet Union. Vargas's return to power in 1951 signaled a cooling of relations. Vargas blamed the United States for his ouster in 1945 and appealed to Brazilian nationalism, which was growing in many sectors, including the armed forces. The Korean War and the European recovery were then high United States priorities. Brazil was not at the time threatened by communism, and United States arms sale policies equated formerly pro-Axis Argentina with Brazil. Brazil's foreign policy of actively promoting its agricultural exports, whose terms of trade (see Glossary) were diminishing, ran counter to United States interests. The establishment of the Petrobrás oil monopoly in 1953 crowned these nationalist sentiments and was hailed as an economic declaration of independence from United States oil companies. These sentiments were further fanned by charges of United States involvement in Vargas's ouster and suicide in August 1954. His suicide note blamed "international economic and financial groups."

President Kubitschek (1956–61) improved relations with the United States, while strengthening relations with Latin America and Europe, and exploring market possibilities in Eastern Europe. His industrial development policy attracted huge direct investments by foreign capital, much from the United States. He proposed an ambitious plan for United States development aid to Latin America in 1958 (Operation Panamerica). The outgoing administration of President Dwight D. Eisenhower found the plan of no interest, but the administration of President John F. Kennedy appropriated funds in 1961 for the Alliance for Progress (see Glossary).

Relations again cooled slightly after President Quadros announced his new independent foreign policy in January 1961. Quadros also made overtures to Cuba and decorated Cuban revolutionary Ernesto "Che" Guevara with Brazil's highest honor.

Severe economic problems, political and economic nationalism, union populism, and strained relations with the United States frustrated President Goulart, eventually causing his overthrow in 1964. Before assuming the presidency, Goulart was known for having been a Vargas protégé and for being pro-Fidel Castro, procommunist, and antiforeign capital. However, during the first parliamentary period (September 1961 to February 1963) of his presidency, Goulart tried to maintain close relations with the United States by naming strongly pro-United States Roberto Campos as ambassador in Washington and Deputy Santiago Dantas as minister of foreign affairs. Nonetheless, certain domestic and foreign policy issues clouded this relationship. First, Goulart's brother-in-law, Leonel Brizola, then governor of Rio Grande do Sul, insisted on expropriation of foreign-owned public utilities (electric power and telephones), and nationalists in Congress pushed for zero or minimum compensation. Second, Brazil joined Argentina, Bolivia, Chile, Ecuador, and Mexico in abstaining from a final vote on an OAS resolution expelling Cuba from that organization. Third, in August 1962, Congress approved a more restrictive law governing profit remittances, and new foreign investments dwindled to almost zero in early 1964.

In late 1963, Washington, alarmed that Brazil might become a hostile, nonaligned power like Egypt, reduced foreign aid to Brazil. The exact United States role in the March 31, 1964, military coup that overthrew Goulart remains controversial. However, the United States immediately recognized the new interim government (before Goulart had even fled Brazilian territory); a United States naval task force anchored close to the port of Vitória; the United States made an immediate large loan to the new Castelo Branco government (1964–67); and the new military president adopted a policy of total alignment with the United States.

The Castelo Branco regime broke off relations with Cuba (while enhancing them with the Soviet Union and Eastern Europe); purged or exiled leftists and alleged communists; adopted a more discreet position in the UN vis-à-vis Portuguese colonialism; duly compensated expropriated foreign capital investments; passed a new profit remittances law; and sent a 1,200-man battalion as part of the Interamerican Peace Force to the Dominican Republic in 1965. Brazilian foreign policy centered on combating subversion and contributing to the collective security of the hemisphere. Brazil ranked third after Vietnam and India as recipients of United States aid; it received US$2 billion from 1964 to 1970. Nonetheless, Castelo Branco's all-out support for United States policies only served to increase anti-Americanism rather than to lessen it.

Divergence and some hostility characterized relations during the Costa e Silva period (1967–69). Brazil perceived that

United States leadership in the global struggle was faltering because of the winding down in Vietnam, making it more difficult for Brazil to support United States positions in world forums. In 1969 the Richard M. Nixon administration assumed a low-profile policy with Latin America. Washington provided less economic aid and fewer arms shipments to Brazil and sharply reduced its military mission in Brazil (from 200 in 1968 to sixty in 1971).

Although Costa e Silva did not turn to economic nationalism and the climate for foreign investments remained generally favorable, Brazil asserted its independence in other ways. It withdrew support from the Interamerican Peace Force, declined to sign the NPT (Non-Proliferation Treaty), tried to organize a Latin American nuclear community, assumed a leadership role in the nonaligned G–77, and increased Soviet-Brazilian trade. Nevertheless, Costa e Silva paid a state visit to Washington in 1967, and in 1969 Brazil sided with the United States against the nationalization of oil properties by the Peruvian military government.

The Médici and Geisel governments (1969–79) generally followed the same course of increasingly independent foreign policy combined with friendly relations with the United States. Brazil sought to pursue its own advantages by leaving open its nuclear options, greatly expanding trade with the Eastern Bloc, recognizing the Beijing government four years before the United States normalized relations with mainland China, and asserting a 322-kilometer maritime zone (always referred to by Brazilians as "200 miles") contrary to United States policy and fishing interests.

Brazil's policies emphasized North-South issues over the East-West conflict. Brazil took the lead in organizing commodity cartels (coffee, sugar, and cocoa). In 1975 Brazil voted for the UN resolution equating Zionism with racism and did not condemn the Soviet and Cuban intervention in Angola.

The Nixon administration remained basically sympathetic to Brazilian hopes for growth and world power status, and considered Brazil to be one of the developing world nations most sympathetic to the United States. In February 1976, Secretary of State Henry Kissinger and Minister of Foreign Affairs Antônio Azeredo da Silveira signed a memorandum of understanding that the two powers would consult on all issues of mutual concern and would hold semiannual meetings of foreign ministers. Brazil had signed similar agreements with Brit-

President Fernando Henrique Cardoso meets with President William Jefferson Clinton during a state visit to the White House, Washington, April 20, 1995.
Courtesy The White House, Washington

ain, France, and Italy in 1975. Only Brazil and Saudi Arabia, aside from the major Western allies, had such an agreement with the United States. Although these agreements had no great practical consequences, they indicated a changed United States policy of wooing Brazil.

The Carter administration marked a definite cooling of United States-Brazil relations. The confrontation involved two very sensitive issues—human rights and nuclear proliferation. In 1967 Brazil had signed a contract with Westinghouse to build a 626-megawatt nuclear power station at Angra dos Reis, Rio de Janeiro State, to be completed in 1977. In 1973–74 the petroleum crisis jolted Brazil into a high-priority policy of seeking alternative energy sources (hydro, solar, alcohol, biogas, Bolivian natural gas, and nuclear). However, the United States Nuclear Regulatory Commission renounced its guarantee of delivery of enriched uranium, casting doubts on the value of nuclear cooperation with the United States, which had prohibited Westinghouse from constructing enrichment and reprocessing plants in Brazil.

Brazil, desiring independent control of the full cycle from ore to kilowatts, signed a broad nuclear agreement with West Germany in June 1975. It involved furnishing technology and equipment for eight nuclear power plants, plus enrichment and reprocessing facilities. Despite safeguard provisions, some thought this agreement opened the door for Brazil to construct nuclear weapons, if desired. The Ford administration reacted only mildly to the agreement, but from his first day in office, President Carter sought to prevent its implementation.

In 1975 the United States Congress mandated that the Department of State produce a general report on human rights performance by all recipients of United States military assistance. The section of the report dealing with Brazil noted some improvements and described violations as mildly as possible. This report might have gone unnoticed if the United States Embassy had not delivered a copy to the Foreign Office in Brasília just hours before its release in Washington. This gesture, intended as a courtesy, was interpreted as an intolerable interference in Brazil's internal affairs. The next day, Brazil renounced the United States-Brazil Military Assistance Agreement, which had been in effect since 1952, and some military nationalists pushed for breaking diplomatic relations. Formal relations between the two military organizations have still not been reestablished.

The Reagan administration made ostensible gestures to improve relations with Brazil. A former military attaché to Brazil during the 1964 coup, retired General Vernon Walters was dispatched to Brasília to express United States concern over the Cuban-supported guerrilla movement in El Salvador and to request support and assistance. Brazil listened politely, but then refused to join the military governments of Argentina, Uruguay, and Chile in support of the Salvadoran government. Moreover, it increased trade credits to Nicaragua and signed several large trade agreements with the Soviet Union.

In the early 1980s, tension in United States-Brazil relations centered on economic questions. Retaliation for unfair trade practices loomed on the horizon and threatened Brazilian exports of steel, orange juice, commuter aircraft, frozen chickens, shoes, and textiles. The United States criticized Brazil for its trade restrictions and unfair practices (in the area of pharmaceutical patents and restrictions on United States computer giants), and for its US$5 billion trade surplus with the United States. Brazil replied that it needed desperately to maintain large balance of payments surpluses to meet its foreign debt obligations.

When President Sarney took office in March 1985, political issues, such as Brazil's arms exports to Libya and Iran, again surfaced. Brazil's foreign debt moratorium and its refusal to sign the NPT caused the United States Congress to put Brazil on its mandated blacklist, thereby restricting Brazil's access to certain United States technologies (see Nuclear Programs, ch. 6). On taking office in March 1990, President Collor sought a quick rapprochement with the United States in order to begin an aggressive policy of inserting Brazil into the world economy and placing it at the negotiating table of world powers. Collor concluded a nonproliferation agreement with Argentina, which was registered with the International Atomic Energy Agency in Vienna. He moved to deactivate Brazil's autonomous nuclear project and the nuclear submarine project, as well as the air-to-air Piranha missile project. He also gained congressional approval for eliminating the market reserve on computer products and beginning tariff reductions. Collor abolished the National Intelligence Service (Serviço Nacional de Informações—SNI) and the National Security Council (CSN), and fashioned a Strategic Affairs Secretariat (Secretaria de Assuntos Estratégicos—SAE) with a civilian head. However, after a year in office the Collor government concluded that these overtures had been in vain. Reciprocity by the United States was not forthcoming, and Brazilian policies reverted to a more pragmatic, independent approach.

The Franco administration maintained an even more independent stance and reacted coolly to proposals by the Clinton administration for a Latin American free-trade zone. Brazil pushed ahead with its Satellite Launch Vehicle (Veículo Lançador de Satélite—VLS) program, based in Alcântara, Maranhão. Because Brazil wants to participate in the very lucrative satellite launching market, it had consistently refused, until October 1995, to sign the MTCR (Missile Technology Control Regime), which it believed restricted developing nations from attaining access to this technology. In June 1995, the Israeli military attaché in Brasília denounced Brazil for continuing sales of Astros II surface-to-surface missile launchers and heavy bombs to Libya, despite UN embargoes. In October 1995, after continuous pressure from the United States, Brazil finally met the conditions to join the MTCR and was accepted as a member. Brazil joined the MTCR because it was necessary to gain access to crucial rocket technology to finalize the VLS IV and to ensure that it would become operational in 1997.

Relations with the Cardoso government in 1995–97 were good. Cardoso made a very successful trip to Washington and New York in April 1995, and the Clinton administration was very enthusiastic regarding the passage of constitutional amendments that open the Brazilian economy to increased international participation. The United States was especially pleased with the break-up of state monopolies in the petroleum and telecommunications sectors. However, the United States called for increased efforts to stem international drug smuggling across Brazil's territory from Andean neighbors, and better coordination between the United States Drug Enforcement Administration (DEA) and Brazilian authorities. In April 1995, Brasília and Washington signed a new cooperation agreement.

Related to the problem of surveillance of drug smuggling across the Amazon region was the controversial Amazon Region Surveillance System (Sistema de Vigilância da Amazônia—Sivam) contract. In the 1970s and 1980s, Brazil had installed three air surveillance and traffic control systems in the South (Sul), Southeast, and Northeast, purchased from Thomson CSF, the French electronics manufacturer. In the 1990s, several international consortiums, including Thomson CSF, hotly contested the proposed Sivam contract (worth US$1.5 billion). A timely visit by United States Secretary of Commerce Ron Brown in June 1994 heavily influenced the decision, and two days after his departure, the Brazilian government decided in favor of a consortium led by the American firm Raytheon, instead of Thomson CSF. United States incentives included very favorable Export-Import Bank financing and assurance that Raytheon would participate in the privatization of the Brazilian Aeronautics Company (Empresa Brasileira Aeronáutica—Embraer), which never happened.

In 1995, before the final signing of the contracts with Raytheon, Brazil's Congress, under pressure from environmental groups and the governors of the Amazon region, decided to review the decision process and contract details. Under intense pressure from the United States Embassy in Brasília, however, the Brazilian Senate and Chamber of Deputies finally approved the plan in May 1995, over protests from the governors from the Amazon region.

In response to United States criticism over its unfair trade practices and its failure to protect intellectual property rights, Brazil finally signed a new patent protection law in March 1996. The new law includes protection for pharmaceutical patents and contains a "pipeline" mechanism. The United States also looks to Brazil to fulfill its longstanding commitments to enact legislation on computer software and semiconductor layout design, and to introduce amendments to its copyright laws.

* * *

The best general treatments of the Brazilian political scene are Ben Ross Schneider's *Politics Within the State: Elite Bureaucrats and Industrial Policy in Authoritarian Brazil,* Robert Wesson and David V. Fleischer's *Brazil in Transition,* Gláucio A.D. Soares's *Sociedade e política no Brasil,* Riordan Roett's *Brazil: Politics in a Patrimonial Society,* Ronald M. Schneider's *Order and Progress: A Political History of Brazil,* and Thomas E. Skidmore's *Politics in Brazil* and *The Politics of Military Rule in Brazil.*

Good descriptive works on the structure of the Brazilian government are not available. For a specific treatment of Congress, see Abdo I. Baaklini's *The Brazilian Legislature and the Political System.* There are few adequate treatments of state and local governments. There is also a dearth of publications on the process of the political opening (*abertura*) and transition in Brazil. Keith S. Rosenn's *Whither Brazil: The Consolidation of Democracy in Brazil after the Impeachment of President Collor* is a collection of papers on the Collor period. The only publication to record Itamar Franco's presidency was written by his stalwart adviser, Ferreira de Castro, and is entitled *Itamar: O homen que redescobriu o Brasil.* Although the influence of media on politics is extremely important in Brazil, few thorough analyses exist. Fernando Morais's *Chatô, o rei do Brasil* describes the empire built by Assis Chateaubriand in the 1940s and 1950s.

Hélgio Trindade edited a very good collection of papers on election reform in the 1990s, entitled *Reforma eleitoral e representação política no Brasil dos anos 90.* There has been considerable scholarship published on Brazilian political parties. Fleischer edited two volumes of studies on the 1945–79 period, entitled *Os partidos políticos no Brasil.* Maria D'Alva Gil Kinzo's *Brazil: The*

Challenges of the 1990s and Jairo Marconi Nicolau's *Multipartidarismo e democracia* are more recent analyses.

There is considerable scholarship on Brazil's international relations. In his memoirs, *A lanterna na pôpa,* former Ambassador Roberto Campos provides an overview since Bretton Woods. Mercosul has a growing bibliography, most notable of which is a compilation by the new Brazilian Council of International Affairs (Conselho Brasileiro de Relações Internacionais), entitled *Mercosul.* Other useful works on Mercosul include Luiz Alberto Moniz Bandeira's *Estado nacional e política internacional na América Latina,* and Rubens Barbosa's *América Latina em perspectiva.* Rubens Ricupero's *Visões do Brasil: Ensaios sobre a historia e a inserção internacional do Brasil* is an excellent account by one of Brazil's most distinguished diplomats. Finally, Brazil-United States relations have received considerable attention. Frank D. McCann's *The Brazilian-American Alliance* gives an overview from the early 1900s. W. Michael Weis's *Cold Warriors and Coups d'État* reviews the Cold War period. Maria Helena Tachinardi's *A guerra das patentes* analyzes the computer and intellectual property rights confrontations. (For further information and complete citations, see Bibliography.)

Chapter 5. National Security

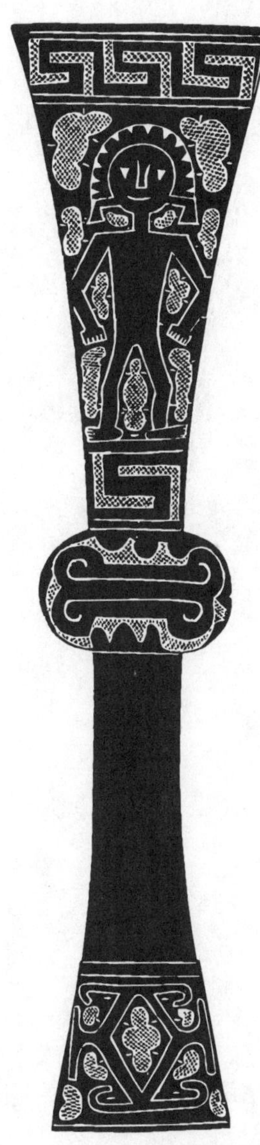

A nineteenth-century wood carving made by an indigenous Brazilian tribe, from Hjalmar Stolpe, Amazon Indian Designs from Brazilian and Guianan Wood Carvings

BRAZIL'S ARMED FORCES (Forças Armadas) have played an active political role ever since they helped overthrow the empire in 1889. From 1930 until 1964, they asserted their moderating power (*poder moderador*—see Glossary) and intervened frequently in the political process. In 1964 the military ousted the civilian president and governed for twenty-one years.

A national security doctrine, with two major elements, guided the military regime. The first element was a broad definition of security that included not only defense against external aggression but also internal defense against insurgency and communism. By using repressive measures, the military countered domestic insurgencies successfully from 1967 through 1973. The second element was economic development. Under the military, the role of the state in the economy grew considerably with the expansion of Brazil's industrial base. High economic growth rates of the 1968-73 period helped to legitimize military government.

The armed forces returned to the barracks in March 1985. Although they have continued to assert themselves politically, their political influence has been reduced substantially because of several factors. First, as Brazil has sought to consolidate its democracy, the National Congress (Congresso Nacional; hereafter, Congress) and civilian ministries have become more involved and influential in broadly defined security issues. Second, the military was forced to compete with civilian ministries for extremely limited resources and was unable to halt a continual decline in its share of government expenditures. And third, although the 1988 constitution preserves the external and internal roles of the armed forces, it places the military under presidential authority. Thus, the new charter changed the manner in which the military could exercise its moderating power (see The Military Mission since 1988, this ch.).

Furthermore, the armed forces were unable to promote and fund pet projects effectively in the nuclear, space, missile, and armament arenas. President Fernando Collor de Mello (1990–92) exposed Brazil's secret, military-sponsored nuclear bomb program, the so-called Parallel Program (Programa Paralelo). As a result, several of Brazil's nuclear programs were placed under international monitoring. Collor also placed the Brazilian space program controlled by the Brazilian Air Force (Força

Aérea Brasileira—FAB) under civilian oversight. In addition, the Brazilian government announced in early 1994 that Brazil would seek to join the Missile Technology Control Regime (see Glossary), and succeeded in doing so in October 1995. Brazil's armaments industry, supported by the military regime, collapsed without any major intervention by the state to shore it up.

Geopolitical changes and a shifting civil-military balance within Brazil recast the country's security interests. One geopolitical change in the early 1990s included a transformation from bipolarity toward multipolarity in the international system. Another change involved greater integration between Brazil and Argentina. Political and economic uncertainties in 1995 also influenced the Brazilian military's perceptions of the country's national security.

Since the 1950s, Brazil's rate of military expenditures has been among the lowest in the world. In 1993 this figure dropped to only 1.1 percent of the gross national product (GNP—see Glossary). This trend reflects the low level of external threat. Brazil is by far the largest country in Latin America and enjoys generally good relations with its ten South American neighbors. There is no threat to Brazil's internal security in the narrow sense of insurgencies. The politically inspired terrorism of the late 1960s and 1970s is nonexistent.

Despite the low level of defense expenditures, Brazil's armed forces are the largest in Latin America, with 314,000 active-duty troops and officers in 1997, including 132,000 conscripts. The Brazilian Army (Exército Brasileiro), the largest service (accounting for 66 percent of the total armed forces), has 200,000 active-duty troops and officers. The Brazilian Navy (Marinha do Brasil), totals 64,700 members, and the Brazilian Air Force (FAB), 50,000.

With no serious external or internal threats, the armed forces are searching for a new role. They are expanding their presence in the Amazon under the Northern Corridor (Calha Norte) program (see The Military in the Amazon, this ch.). In 1994 Brazilian troops joined United Nations (UN) peacekeeping forces in five countries. The Brazilian military, especially the army, has become more involved in civic-action programs, education, health care, and constructing roads, bridges, and railroads across the nation.

Debate in Brazil concerning national security policy has been practically nonexistent. Political dialogue is limited to discussion of the revisions of the constitution, where only modest changes in the role of the armed forces are expected. None of the political parties, except the Workers' Party (Partido dos Trabalhadores—PT), has articulated a position on defense matters. Although some civilians are experts in defense matters, their influence is negligible. There is no tradition of congressional oversight of the military, and the defense-related bureaucracy remains minuscule. Civil society continues to show a complete lack of interest in issues related to defense. The modest attempts by the armed forces to reevaluate their role, structure, doctrine, strategy, and tactics are conducted in a vacuum. Some analysts believe that the creation of a ministry of defense is a necessary condition for establishing civilian control of the military.

The Military Role in Society and Government

Early History

Throughout the colonial era, the Portuguese used military forces to defend their vast claims in South America. The typical practice was to depend on local fighters and on expeditionary forces sent to deal with particular crises. Such forces usually were led by nobles and large landowners who recruited, often forcibly, unemployed men for the ranks. In addition, the Portuguese long made use of mercenaries from various nationalities, a practice that would continue into the early nineteenth century. Colonial warfare against the French, and especially the Dutch (1624–54), the continuous wars and slave-raiding expeditions against the native peoples, and the famous *bandeirante* (see Glossary) expeditions produced a vibrant body of military traditions. However, the colonial era did not produce an institutionalized standing military force.

Thanks to the reforms of Marquês de Pombal, Portugal's emperor, in the mid-eighteenth century, more Brazilian-born men were drawn into colonial administration—more so than was the case in either the Spanish or the British colonies—including military affairs. Portugal did not have a navy or a large permanent army, so it had to depend on Brazilians to defend their lands. It was only after 1764 that regular royal troops were posted in Brazil, and even their ranks had to be filled out with local recruits. By the late eighteenth century, the officers of the regiments in Bahia were 60 percent Brazilian-born, but their attitudes, interests, and values were identical with the rest of the colonial elites; they were part of the Portuguese empire, not officers in a budding Brazilian army. Their identification was more with their local region or the greater Portuguese empire than with what is now Brazil.

The colonial units were segregated by color. Militia units called *Henriques* (see Glossary) were composed of free blacks, while those of mixed African-European ancestry, called *pardos,* had their own organizations and officers. Local bosses, then called *mestres de campo* (country masters), and later known as *coronéis* (colonels—see Glossary), organized the white elite and their hangers-on into urban and rural militia units. In the countryside, such units were really private armies that reinforced the power of the local elites. With royal authority behind them, the *mestres* and *coronéis* chased criminals and runaway slaves, kept track of who passed through their territories and how much their neighbors produced, and meted out justice as they saw fit. The viceroy was too far away to interfere with abuses.

Lieutenant Colonel Henrique Oscar Wiederspahn, in his study of Brazil's war with the United Provinces of the Río de la Plata (1825–28) over what is now Uruguay, observed that "the Brazilian Armed Forces have their origins in those [forces] that Dom João VI left us on returning with his Court to Lisbon. . . ." Dom Pedro I (emperor, 1822–31) used the army and navy to expel the Portuguese forces that remained loyal to the government in Lisbon after September 1822. In the campaigns of the 1820s to expel the Portuguese from Rio de Janeiro, Salvador, and Maranhão, the role played by foreign mercenaries, such as British Admiral Thomas Alexander Cochrane (Lord Dundonald) and Frenchman General Pierre Labatut, was pivotal in achieving victory. However, the political disputes of that decade placed the new emperor at odds with the regional elites. Their suspicion of the new imperial army (in 1828 it included a few thousand Irish and Germans recruited abroad) and of the Portuguese-born emperor and his Portuguese generals led to his abdication in 1831 and to the formation of the National Guard as a counterpoise to the army.

The army barely survived the 1830s and had to contend with the National Guard as a potential rival until early in the next century. What institutionalized the army were the fierce campaigns under the leadership of Luís Alves de Lima e Silva (later the famous Duke of Caxias (Duque de Caxias)) that crushed regional revolts (see The Regency Era, 1831–40, ch. 1) in the

Two Brazilian Air Force Northrop F–5Es, capable of in-flight refueling, pass over Rio de Janeiro's Corcovado.
Courtesy Brazilian Embassy, Washington

1830s and 1840s. Army organization was improved in the campaign against Argentine president Juan Manuel de Rosas in the upper Río de la Plata in 1852 and institutionalized as a result of the War of the Triple Alliance (1864–70) against Paraguay. That war provided the army's principal battle experience and heroes and fixed its main locus of operations on the South (Sul) for decades to come.

Brazil's involvement in the Paraguayan War proved to be a watershed for the army and navy. Brazil joined Argentina and the Uruguayan Colorados (members of the Colorado Party) and successfully resisted the expansionism of Paraguayan dictator Francisco Solano López. In March 1870, Solano López was defeated decisively. Although the number of Paraguayan casualties remains a topic of debate among historians, a majority of the Paraguayan adult male population supposedly was killed. The Paraguayan War rapidly expanded the size of Brazil's army. In 1864, prior to the war, Brazil had 17,000 soldiers in the army; by the end of the war, there were 100,000.

On returning to Brazil, many of the officers were restless with the deficiencies in their economy, such as the lack of an industry to supply the army adequately. Their leader, the Duque de Caxias, was loyal to Pedro II (emperor, 1840–89) and kept anti-imperialist sentiments under control, but after he died in 1880 officers became more active in the political arena. Although they were barred legally from debating government policies publicly, some military officers expressed dissatisfaction openly. For example, they resented their role in capturing runaway slaves. In 1879 officers reacted strongly to a bill that would reduce the size of the military. In 1883 they vehemently opposed compulsory payments to an insurance fund. In 1887 they founded Rio de Janeiro's Military Club (Clube Militar) to express their grievances. The Military Club provided a forum for open debate and criticism of government policies.

Field Marshal Manuel Deodoro da Fonseca, the first president of the Military Club, emerged as a vocal proponent of military interests. On November 9, 1889, Benjamin Constant, a leading advocate of positivism (see Glossary), spoke at the Military Club and called for "full powers to free the military from a state of affairs incompatible with its honor and its dignity." Less than a week later, on November 15, Deodoro led a bloodless coup, which ended the empire of Dom Pedro II, and ushered in the Old Republic (1889–1930). On November 16, he declared Brazil a federal republic.

Deodoro was the provisional leader of Brazil until February 25, 1891, when Congress elected him president. He served as president until November 23, 1891. Under Deodoro the army, which had decreased to 13,000 members in the aftermath of the Paraguayan War, increased its size to 20,000. Army officers governed half of Brazil's twenty states at the time. Cabinet members, however, were primarily civilians (exceptions included Colonel Constant, minister of war; and Vice Admiral Eduardo Wandenkolk, minister of navy).

Deodoro promulgated a new constitution on February 24, 1891, and a day later was elected president by Congress under that charter's provisions. Indicating their displeasure with what they perceived to be a fraudulent and manipulated constitution, Congress elected Deodoro's rival, Floriano Peixoto, to the vice presidency. On November 23, 1891, Deodoro resigned from the presidency because of strong resistance to his policies from Congress, some states, the navy, and a faction of the army led by Peixoto. Peixoto assumed the presidency on the same day, and ruled until November 15, 1894. Because of his strong personality, he was known as the Iron Marshal (Marechal de Ferro).

Peixoto was succeeded by Prudente José de Morais e Barros, also known as Prudente de Morais, the first civilian president of Brazil (1894–98), and the first elected by popular vote. Prudente de Morais was succeeded by Manuel Ferraz de Campos Sales (president, 1898–1902). Prudente de Morais and Campos Sales were the first of various presidents in what has been termed the Republic of the Oligarchies (República das Oligarquias), in which coffee growers in the Southeast (Sudeste) effectively controlled the presidency.

As presidents, Deodoro and Peixoto provided for the transition from empire to republic. In a matter of five years, the Brazilian presidency was turned over to a directly elected civilian. The governments between 1894 and 1930 were inherently conservative, but this was Brazil's first experiment with democracy.

Military Rebellion and the Revolution of 1930

Military planners in the late 1920s characterized the army as the central agent of Brazilian national unity and greatness. They believed that economic development, military preparedness, and national power were linked tightly. The national territory held immeasurable resources that had to be protected from covetous foreigners until Brazilians could exploit them. They pointed to Japan and Argentina as examples of countries building military and economic power simultaneously. Reformist officers (called "Young Turks" after the military reformers of Turkey) thought that the lack of national cohesion was a far greater threat to Brazil than was any foreign threat. The army, in their view, was the only instrument to hold the country together by being a school of citizenship, and by teaching the superiority of the collective over individual good in sacrifice for the motherland. Meanwhile, Brazilians of all classes fled from military service, and draft dodging was chronic.

Even so, obligatory military service resulted in the physical expansion of the army, which eventually gave it the ability to intervene in politics and in society more profoundly than in the past. To give the army a local image while eliminating the expense and supervisory burden of transporting draftees to distant training camps, garrisons were established in every state to train them. The new system also required expanding the number of personnel in the army (18,000 to 25,000 in 1916–17, 30,000 in 1920, 48,000 in 1930, 93,000 in 1940); indeed, during the Old Republic, it grew 52 percent faster than did the rapidly growing population.

In the 1920s, an intense struggle for control of the army was in part motivated by conflicting ideas of what the institution's role was to be in the increasingly consolidated Brazilian nation-state. The German-trained Young Turks sought modernization. After 1919 the French Military Mission also encouraged professionalization and enhancement of the army's self-image as the central institution of the Brazilian state. By 1929 the state had intensified its centralizing powers by expanding federal ownership of the country's railroads, shipping lines, ports, and banks. In the coffee-dominated economy, the federal government controlled coffee marketing and sought to influence world coffee prices. However, some officers were troubled by who was running the state and army during the presidencies of Venceslau Brás Pereira Gomes (1914–18), Delphim Moreira da Costa Ribeiro (acting, 1918–19), and Epitácio da Silva Pessôa (1919–22).

The lieutenants' rebellions (*tenentismo*—see Glossary) of the 1920s were complicated in that they involved a minority of officers who were as much in revolt against the army hierarchy as against the central government. There was to be no amnesty, and so faced with either giving up their careers or continuing to conspire, the *tenentes* chose the latter. The result was the 1924 uprising in São Paulo and Rio Grande do Sul, which led to the retreat of the *tenentes* into the interior and the long campaign of the Prestes Column, named after the romantic revolutionary Luis Carlos Prestes, across Brazil until it gave up and entered Bolivia in 1927. In that decade, many of the best of the officer corps became rebels to save their careers and to save the army from corrupt officers. Thus, during the 1920s, the army institution played a conservative role, while a determined, talented minority of its officer corps pursued revolution.

In the revolts of 1930, the *tenentes* joined with disgruntled former officers and anti-Paulista politicians who felt that their regional interests were suffering unduly from the São Paulo-centered national state. For the *tenentes*, joining the Liberation Alliance (Aliança Libertadora) was a compromise of their ideals because they were locking arms with the very politicians against whom they had rebelled—former presidents Pessôa and Artur da Silva Bernardes (1922–26). This course of action was necessary, however, if the *tenentes* hoped to win. The alliance also included their old civilian allies: the gaucho "libera-

Two 326 Xavante AT–26 aircraft, made by the Brazilian Aeronautics Company (Empresa Brasileira Aeronáutica—Embraer), overfly a colonial fortress.
Courtesy Brazilian Embassy, Washington

tors," Paulista democrats, and Federal District (Distrito Federal) opposition politicians.

In the past, the *tenentes* had always sought the support of higher ranking officers. In 1930 they failed to get any generals to join them, so they settled for an up-and-coming lieutenant colonel, Pedro de Góes Monteiro, who had fought against them. In the next decade, he would reshape the army. For its part, the Liberal Alliance, led by Getúlio Dorneles Vargas, governor of Rio Grande do Sul, embraced *tenente* demands—such as the secret ballot, better election laws, treatment of social problems, and especially amnesty. In this way, the *tenentes* became one of the strong arms of the dissident oligarchies of Rio Grande do Sul, Minas Gerais, São Paulo, and Paraíba.

The revolutionaries were successful in 1930 largely because the army lost its will to defend the regime. The command structure in effect imploded, and the rebels quickly gained control of fifteen of the twenty states. The senior generals in Rio de Janeiro realized that the government was finished, and that they would be too if they did not at least keep hold of what remained of the army in the capital. Also, they were nervous that the police would lose control of the streets, so they took President Washington Luís Pereira de Sousa (1926–30) into custody. Many texts speak incorrectly of the army staging a coup and turning the government over to Getúlio Vargas. In fact, the generals were looking at defeat and acted to gain some say in the future.

Nonetheless, the senior ranks were thinned by a massive purge. By the end of 1930, nine of the eleven major generals and eleven of the twenty-four brigadier generals were retired, and in 1931 twelve of the twenty brigadier generals, many of whom had been promoted recently, also were retired. The revolution of 1930 opened a decade of reform that made the army even more an instrument of the central government and its civilian leaders.

From Moderator to Director, 1930–85

There is a debate over whether the military appropriated the moderating power during the Old Republic (1889–1930). Many historians emphasize the moderating role as early as 1889, with the argument that the army claimed the emperor's moderating power, which had allowed him to intervene in and resolve political conflicts. Some argue that the military did not assume a moderating role until after 1930, primarily during the 1937-45 period of the quasi-fascist New State (Estado Novo) of Getúlio Vargas (president, 1930–45, 1951–54). According to the revisionist view, the army in 1889 did not intend to play a moderating role. However, after the collapse of the army in 1930 and its subsequent rebuilding, the military accepted the ideology of the *poder moderador*. The debate is important because the revisionist view suggests a more grudging acceptance by the military of the moderating role.

According to political scientist Alfred C. Stepan, the military played a moderating role in civil-military relations during the coups of 1930, 1945, 1954, and 1964; during the abortive intervention of 1961; and in 1953, when the minister of war, General Henrique Teixeira Lott, guaranteed President Juscelino Kubitschek's inauguration as the democratically elected president (1956–61) on January 31, 1956. The pro-Kubitschek faction within the military was actually the largest and most influential. The military viewed itself as "the people in uniform" (*o povo fardado*), inextricably a part of the political system. Civilians, in turn, generally accepted the military's moderating function as legitimate.

In the 1930 coup, military officers of a reformist bent supported Vargas after he declared the previous elections fraudulent and assumed the presidency. As the army reorganized itself, discipline was shaky. During the decade, there were sixteen barracks revolts and seventy-two other instances of agitation, conspiracy, and protest. Between 1931 and 1938, at least 624 officers and 1,875 soldiers were expelled from the army. Thus, one of the principal reasons for General Góes Monteiro and General Eurico Gaspar Dutra's support of the dictatorial Estado Novo in November 1937 was to reestablish control and discipline in the army. Whereas the turmoil of the 1890s had ended in the "politics of the governors," that of the 1930s ended in the imposition of Brazil's first long-lived authoritarian regime (1937–45).

Ironically, the second coup in 1945 was against Vargas. The military moved to intervene a third time in 1954, again to remove Vargas from office, an action that led to his suicide. In its fourth intervention, in 1955, an anti-Kubitschek faction of the military, defeated by the larger pro-Kubitschek military faction led by General Lott, failed to stop Kubitschek from assuming the presidency. In the fifth intervention, in 1961, three military ministers were unable to block João Goulart (president, 1961–64) from succeeding Jânio Quadros (president, January–August 1961). The sixth intervention came on March 31, 1964, when the military overthrew left-of-center Goulart. By that action, the military shifted from the moderator model of civil-military relations to direct military government.

The 1964 military coup was clearly different from that of the previous five military interventions. For the first time in the twentieth century, the Brazilian military assumed political power. As Stepan has noted, the military became the director and not the moderator of politics. Instead of maintaining the status quo, the military sought to transform the system. That transformation required a new professionalism (*profissionalismo novo*) for the military, which had no experience in long-term governing. The major vehicle for that new role was the War College (Escola Superior de Guerra—ESG). Emphasizing internal security and national development, the ESG is an advanced training program for senior officers and civilians.

Political scientist David V. Fleischer, referring to the security and development ideology of the military regime from 1964 to

1985, points out the continuity in the evolution of civil-military relations that can be traced to the nineteenth-century positivism of the military activists who founded the republic under the slogan of "Order and Progress." This continuity extends, Fleischer notes, through the growing economic nationalism in the 1930s and the Estado Novo to the Kubitschek era. In the latter era, autonomous development became a priority to ensure national security.

From 1964 to 1985, the military dominated the presidency. The army imposed its candidates for president and governor, and a docile Congress or an electoral college approved them. These candidates included Humberto Castelo Branco (president, 1964–67), Artur da Costa e Silva (president, 1967-69), Emílio Garrastazú Médici (president, 1969–74), Ernesto Geisel (president, 1974–79), and João Baptista de Oliveira Figueiredo (president, 1979–85). Both Médici and Figueiredo were former intelligence chiefs.

The military based its original plan of government on a moderate degree of civilian support and complete military unity. With time, military government exacerbated factionalism within the military. That division centered on adherents to and dissenters from the ESG ideology. The pro-ESG members of the military, the so-called Sorbonnists, were politically moderate and wanted to maintain democratic forms and institutions. They aided in returning the presidency to civilian government. Presidents Castelo Branco and Geisel best represented this faction. In contrast, the hard-liners within the military favored suspension of democratic processes and were more nationalistic. They argued against a high degree of foreign political and economic dependence in attaining the goals of security and development. The hard-liners were hesitant to return political power to civilians. Presidents Costa e Silva and Médici best represented this faction within the military.

The Internal Security Mission, 1964–85

A central feature of military government during the 1964–85 period was tension between external and internal defense roles. After World War II, an internal orientation became respectable as a result of the bipolar division of the world into Soviet and Western camps, the peacekeeping procedures of the Organization of American States (OAS; see Glossary), and the study programs of the ESG and the Army General Staff School (Escola de Comando de Estado-Maior do Exército—ECEME).

A Hawker Siddeley HS–125 EU/VU–93, Brazilian Air Force, takes off from Rio de Janeiro's Santos Dumont Airport on Guanabara Bay.
A Brazilian Army Aviation helicopter
Courtesy Brazilian Embassy, Washington

In the 1950s, the ESG expanded on the doctrines of the French Military Mission (1919–39) and the Joint Brazil-United States Defense Commission (1942–77), which emphasized the need for officers to study elements of the society and economy that contributed to socioeconomic and political stability. The ESG's military-civilian student body studied inflation, banking reform, agrarian reform, voting systems, transportation, and education, as well as counterinsurgency. Because of the interlocking of the ESG and ECEME, by the mid-1960s the ESG's doctrines were mirrored in the ECEME's and thus had been extended to the officer corps as a whole.

As Brazil's crisis deepened in the early 1960s, the military perceived the country as entering an era of subversive warfare. Military officers had studied this type of unconventional warfare in ECEME courses on internal security and irregular warfare. The ECEME played a key role in convincing officers to support the movement of 1964. In the months prior to March 1964, the staff and student officers distributed newsletters throughout the army, arguing the necessity of intervention. They had come to believe that internal security and rational economic development would occur only if various aspects of the economic and political structure were altered. They also believed that the civilian leaders were unwilling or unable to make the required changes.

For a military organization, mission and identity are tightly intertwined. It can therefore be argued that in seeking to clarify its mission, the Brazilian military was attempting to resolve its identity. Military analyst Edmundo Campos Coelho saw the military in the post-World War II era as suffering from a severe identity crisis. In his view, this crisis had its origin in the identity crisis of the Brazilian state, which lacked a focal institution that everyone could accept as the "incorporation of national authority."

In 1963 and early 1964, there was widespread acceptance in the officer corps of the need to act against the Goulart government. However, there was less of a consensus for maintaining military control once a stable government was established. Even though the hard-liners were able to impose authoritarian rule, an underlying sense of malaise followed. The military's organizational structure, field training, and weapon systems were geared for use against conventional forces or, to a lesser extent, guerrilla forces. Although the military was not structured to govern the country, military institutions adapted themselves to their assignments after 1964 (and especially after 1968). Nevertheless, many officers were ill at ease in their police-like internal security roles, and officers reacted angrily when names such as *milicia* (militia) were applied to them.

A power struggle in late 1965 and early 1966 led to the defeat of the Castelo Branco faction at the hands of the hard-line officers clustered around Minister of Army Arthur da Costa e Silva. It represented a victory for those who favored defining the military's mission as primarily one of internal security. In effect, this struggle may have produced two competing ideas of military professionalism: Stepan's "new professionalism" of internal security versus the other that sees the essence of the military profession as one in which troops are trained and equipped to fight foreign conventional forces as the essence of their profession. Some officers questioned the legitimacy of the internal security activities of their colleagues, even though they may have acknowledged the need for such activities. These officers regarded troop commands and normal staff assignments as being more "military" than internal security assignments.

The officer corps has split in a variety of ways over the years. After the rise of Geisel, if not before, some officers worried that a high level of political involvement was bad and distracted the corps from its main responsibility of protecting the country against foreign enemies. They argued in favor of a narrow definition of the military's mission, limiting it to external defense. They argued further that to mount a secure external defense, internal support and cohesion were necessary. Officers could not be seen imposing an unpopular government one day and appealing to the population's patriotism the next. Those who had long argued this way were nearly jubilant in pointing to the disastrous results of the failed Argentine invasion of the Falkland/Malvinas Islands in 1982.

Officers whose hands were tainted during the Military Republic (1964–85) were fearful of reprisals once civilian government returned. In August 1979, Congress approved Figueiredo's proposal for amnesty, for both the agents of repression and those who took up arms against the regime. The amnesty facilitated the military's return to the barracks but did not resolve the moral or legal issues involved. With the return of full democracy in 1985, the victims began seeking redress in the courts, while some officers with tarnished reputations were coming up for promotion to general. Many active and retired officers who were not involved directly in repression or torture tended to defend colleagues who were. The cleavages that the repression caused within the military and between the military and society have posed major problems for the army.

The hard-liners usually are very nationalistic and argue for stronger stances in foreign policy, for stronger controls over multinationals, and especially for stronger positions against the United States and the International Monetary Fund (IMF—see Glossary). On October 7, 1987, a group of retired hard-line generals and their civilian allies formed the Brazilian Association for the Defense of Democracy (Associação Brasileira de Defesa da Democracia—ABDD). The ABDD argued for a new military intervention "if the politicians did not turn back the chaos." The ABDD and similar groups, although populated by disgruntled retirees, have virtually no political influence.

The military has an elaborate ideology of nationalism and development, much of which has been incorporated into the thinking of civilian opinion makers and politicians. Essentially, this ideology holds that Brazil can be, and should be, a great power. The military sees its primary function as contributing to that objective.

Civil-Military Relations, 1985–94

Alfred C. Stepan has argued that although the Brazilian military ceded power to José Sarney (1985–90) in 1985, it retained significant prerogatives. President Sarney depended on the armed forces because of his weak political base. According to Professor Fleischer, Sarney was not well prepared to assume the presidency, so General Ivan Souza Mendes, the director of the National Intelligence Service (Serviço Nacional de Informações—SNI) "stepped in to fill the void" and helped him "organize his presidency." As a result of his dependence on the military, Sarney's administration made little progress in gaining greater control over the armed forces.

Congress, meeting as a Constituent Assembly (Assembléia Constituinte), redrafted the constitution from February 1987 until October 5, 1988, when it was promulgated. The 1988 constitution strengthened presidential control of the military by removing the clause that stated the military was only obedient to the executive "within the limits of the law." In late 1989, the first direct presidential election was held in almost three decades, and in March 1990 Fernando Collor de Mello took office.

Under President Collor de Mello, the prerogatives of the armed forces were reduced modestly, but erratically, in a "two steps forward, one step back" manner. Four examples of such reductions can be cited. First, Collor de Mello replaced the military-dominated SNI with the civilian-led Strategic Affairs Secretariat (Secretaria de Assuntos Estratégicos—SAE). Second, he cut defense spending to the lowest level in decades: approximately 0.3 percent of gross domestic product (GDP—see Glossary) in 1993, down from 0.9 percent in 1987. Third, he attempted to establish more effective control over Brazil's various nuclear and other strategic programs. And fourth, the government announced that the Brazilian Aeronautics Company (Empresa Brasileira da Aeronáutica—Embraer), which manufactures the Tucano trainer and the subsonic AMX fighter, would be privatized (Embraer was privatized in December 1994).

Furthermore, in 1990 Collor revealed publicly the secret atomic bomb project developed by the army. On September 5, 1991, Brazil and Argentina agreed to establish the Brazilian-Argentine Agency for Accounting and Control of Nuclear Materials (Agência Brasileiro-Argentina de Contabilidade e Contrôle de Materiais Nucleares—ABACC). This agreement permits the International Atomic Energy Agency (IAEA) to inspect nuclear installations in Argentina and Brazil. On that occasion, Brazil also signed, with Argentina and Chile, a treaty forbidding the development, manufacture, and use of chemical weapons. In December 1991, Collor participated in the signing of a comprehensive safeguards agreement among Brazil, Argentina, and the IAEA.

Collor created an interministerial group to formulate a more restrictive arms-control policy. He increased consultation with the United States on the conditions for gaining access to the technologies covered by the MTCR (Missile Technology Control Regime). He also announced that Brazil would create a space agency, under civilian control, to open up activities in this sector and to promote the commercial exploitation of the Alcântara rocket-launching base. That agency was established by his successor, Itamar Franco (president, 1992–94).

Under Collor civilian political institutions generally were strengthened. The government granted the Ministry of Foreign Affairs (Itamaraty) even greater autonomy on foreign policy issues, including some defense-related issues. Congress played a more assertive role, and in late 1990 conducted a major investigation into Brazil's nuclear program. The investigation, conducted by a Congressional Investigating Committee (Comissão Parlamentar de Inquérito—CPI), was extensive and included the testimony of former President João Figueiredo (1979–85).

Collor's political isolation after his first year as president led him to curry the support of the military. For example, Collor restored funding for Embraer's subsonic AMX fighter in mid-1991 after denying funding in 1990. In addition, the army announced that it would not allow a foreign firm to buy the nearly bankrupt Specialized Engineers, Inc. (Engenheiros Especializados S.A.—Engesa). Instead, Engesa, which had a debt of more than US$400 million and showed little hope for profitability, would be turned into a state-controlled enterprise.

President Franco established closer ties with the military. He named various retired officers to sensitive posts within the cabinet. On several occasions, he acquiesced to military requests for higher salaries. The government's relations with the military improved further after Fernando Henrique Cardoso became president on January 1, 1995.

Brazil and International Conflicts, 1917–95

Brazil's involvement in World War I did not include sending troops to Europe. In the early years of the war, the Brazilian authorities sought to maintain strict neutrality, and full diplomatic relations were continued with the Central (Axis) Powers. Pro-Allied sentiment was strong among the Brazilians, however, and by 1917, when German U-boats began torpedoing Brazilian freighters, Brazil broke diplomatic relations with and declared war against the Central Powers. Participation in the war was limited largely to naval patrols in the South Atlantic. As a belligerent, Brazil was represented at the Versailles peace conference, thereby securing a measure of prestige, as well as a share of German reparations. This led to Brazilian membership in the League of Nations (see Glossary).

At the outbreak of World War II, Brazil was again quick to announce its neutrality, and the Vargas government avoided any action that seemed to favor either side. The army's numerical growth, from a 1930 level of 47,997 to a 1940 level of 93,000, and its acquisition of modern weapons gave it the muscle to make its influence felt. Germany had become an important trading partner for Brazil during the 1930s and, because the United States was also neutral, Brazil did not feel uncomfortable in that category. Shortly after the Japanese attack on Pearl Harbor, Brazil broke diplomatic and trade relations with the Axis powers and supported the anti-Axis resolution of the Pan-American foreign ministers meeting in Rio de Janeiro in 1942. In the summer of 1942, a rash of U-boat sinkings of Brazilian freighters and ferries led to the abandonment of neutrality in favor of participation in the European war on the side of the Allies.

The Brazilian contribution to the World War II effort was considerably greater than it had been during World War I. For example, Brazil permitted the United States to establish air and naval bases in the Northeast (Nordeste) and to use Natal in Rio Grande do Norte as a staging area for transit to Africa. Brazil also made the islands of Fernando de Noronha available to Allied forces as a base of operations for patrolling South Atlantic sealanes. In addition, Brazil placed its navy under United States control in order to join other Allied navies in antisubmarine defense; Brazil provided corvettes and destroyers for Atlantic patrols and for convoy escort duty.

Unlike other Latin American countries, Brazil dispatched troop units to Europe to participate in combat. The Brazilian Expeditionary Force (Fôrça Expedicionária Brasileira—FEB) reached about 25,000 strong in Italy in the summer of 1944 to become part of the United States Fifth Army. The FEB's principal fighting unit, an infantry division, was committed to combat that September and remained in almost continuous action for more than 200 days, winning high praise from Allied leaders. World War II and the military alliance with the United States left the military with more equipment, enhanced its organizational and individual skills, increased its prestige, and ultimately gave it what it had lacked since 1870—combat seasoning against a foreign enemy. The experience of the FEB in the Italian campaign also gave the army a popular status somewhat separate from the Estado Novo and allowed the FEB veterans (Febianos) to return as heroes. After the war, an elaborate memorial was erected in Rio de Janeiro to honor the 451 servicemen who lost their lives during the conflict.

Since 1945 the armed forces have not engaged in international combat. However, Brazil did send units to the Suez Canal in 1956, to the Belgian Congo in 1960, and to the Dominican Republic in 1965. The first two instances were in response to

UN requests for multinational peacekeeping forces. The third was in answer to a call from the OAS, after President Lyndon B. Johnson sent the United States Marines to Santo Domingo to intervene in the civil war. Brazil complied by sending the largest contingent of non-United States troops (1,000), and a Brazilian general, Hugo Penasco Alvim, commanded the OAS forces. This was called the Inter-American Peace Force (Fôrça Interamericana de Paz—FIP).

Brazil has been reluctant to get involved in international conflicts that might require military action. In the early 1950s, Brazil politely declined the United States invitation to send troops to the Korean War. In September and October 1990, Brazil, anxious to win the release of 200 Brazilians being held in Iraq, refused to assist in the military blockade of Iraq, after Iraq invaded Kuwait. In stark contrast, Argentina sent two surface ships to the Persian Gulf. Brazil did, however, comply with UN Security Council Resolution 661 and cut off all exports to Iraq and Kuwait. The Central Bank of Brazil (Banco Central do Brasil—Bacen; see Glossary) suspended financial transfers to Iraq and Kuwait, and Brazil also observed the UN embargo of September 25, 1990, on air cargo.

In the early 1990s, Brazil became increasingly involved in UN peacekeeping operations. In 1993–94, for example, Brazil sent a company from the 26th Airborne to Mozambique for six months. By May 1994, 152 members of the Brazilian military and police were involved in five of the fourteen UN efforts—Angola, El Salvador, Mozambique, the former Yugoslavia, and on the Rwanda-Uganda border. These included eleven troops, sixty-six police, and seventy-five observers. A Brazilian brigadier general commanded the UN officer observer group in 1994–95. The officers were involved in nonmilitary assignments, in areas such as medical support, management, and observation. Typically, a Brazilian officer was assigned to one of the operations for one year, before being replaced by a fellow officer. Brazil's Congress had to approve any contributions to the peacekeeping forces. In 1995 Brazil sought to send a battalion to join the UN peacekeeping force in Angola. Although the ministries of planning and finance forced a delay because of budget constraints, a Brazilian battalion went to Angola.

Foreign Military Influence

The armed forces have been influenced by both European and United States doctrines. The French influence was stron-

Two Dassault-Breguet Mirage F–103s, Brazilian Air Force
A Bell 205 Iroquois UH–1H helicopter, Brazilian Air Force
Courtesy Brazilian Embassy, Washington

gest at the end of the nineteenth century, up to World War I. Brazil's navy was more heavily influenced by the British in the nineteenth century and by the Americans from World War I onward. Brazilian officers served on United States Navy vessels in World War I. In the early twentieth century, German influence grew in Brazil and in most of South America. From 1900 to 1914, many junior officers spent two-year assignments in Germany. During the interwar period, French influence again predominated, given Germany's defeat in World War I. With the reemergence of Germany in the mid-1930s, German influence challenged that of France.

United States-Brazilian security relations can be understood best in the context of the broader bilateral relationship. That relationship can be characterized as one of asymmetrical interdependence, in which Brazil depends more on the United States (especially its markets) than vice versa. Since the mid-1960s, Brazil has emerged as the dominant actor in South America, despite pressing political, economic, and social problems. As a result, Brazil has narrowed the asymmetries in its relationship with the United States and is more autonomous.

One implication of this change is that the United States has less influence in its relationship with Brazil. Another is that there cannot be a return to the status quo ante, when Brazil was perceived as a "junior partner." Brazil is a qualitatively different country than it was a generation ago. It has the world's ninth largest economy, a population of more than 160 million people, and a broad industrial base. Although the United States is still the dominant actor in the relationship, Brasília now has greater leverage in its dealings with Washington.

As a parallel to the changing bilateral relationship, the tenor of United States-Brazilian security relations has shifted over time. During World War II, Brazil supported the Allies, and Brazilian troops fought alongside their United States counterparts in the Italian campaign beginning in 1942. In the postwar era, United States security ties with Brazil were close, if somewhat paternalistic. Brazil and the United States signed a Military Assistance Agreement in 1952, through which the United States provided most of Brazil's major weapons and much of its military training. Relations between the two countries began to deteriorate in the late 1960s and early 1970s, as a result of Washington's restrictions on the transfer of arms to Latin America and Brazil's growing assertiveness in its foreign policy.

In April 1977, Brazil abrogated unilaterally the 1952 United States-Brazilian Military Assistance Agreement in reaction to pressure on Brazil by President Jimmy Carter's administration to improve its human rights record and to rescind its 1975 nuclear accord with West Germany. The abrogation curtailed the regular flow of United States arms to Brazil and reduced channels of interaction between United States and Brazilian officers, especially in the area of training. The termination of the agreement manifested a more aggressive and nationalistic foreign policy under President Ernesto Geisel. Moreover, this was reflected in Brazil's industrial prowess, its capabilities as an arms producer, and its diversified external ties.

In the 1980s, the United States and Brazil sought to improve security ties by developing structures and processes that reflected changes in both countries and in their overall relationship. The major change in Brazil was the continued political liberalization under President João Figueiredo (1979–85), with the eventual return of civilian government in March 1985. In the United States, the administration of President Ronald Reagan distanced itself from the Carter administration's human rights policies and took a more pragmatic approach, stressing good relations with Brazil's military. On August 31, 1983, the United States and Brazil signed a memorandum of understanding on industrial-military cooperation, and frequent meetings were held between high-level officials of both countries. Despite these and more recent efforts, security relations between the United States and Brazil have remained cool. A variety of tensions remain, encompassing broad spheres of the bilateral relationship, including technology transfers, and specifically nuclear proliferation—Brazil's nuclear and space programs and their potential for military applications. In addition, the United States has been concerned with Brazil's arms transfer policies. Increasingly, however, and much to the annoyance of the Brazilians, the issue of drug trafficking has dominated the agenda.

The transformation from bipolarity to multipolarity has pressed Brazil to further diversify its foreign relations and strengthen its ties with countries within Latin America and outside the region, such as France, Germany, Japan, China, and the countries of Central and Eastern Europe. The United States is unlikely to be displaced as the major external actor in Brazil. However, it will encounter growing competition from the rest of the world.

The traditional sources of equipment reflect the doctrinal influence on the respective service. Thus, the Brazilian Navy at the turn of the century depended primarily on British matériel. In contrast, army equipment came primarily from France and Germany. After 1942 Brazil depended primarily on the United States for its imported arms. During the 1970s, Brazil became more self-sufficient, as it produced a broad array of military equipment. In addition, Brazil diversified its sources of equipment, turning increasingly to Europe. In 1994 and 1995, Brazilians negotiated to purchase Russian military equipment at "cut-rate" prices. Nonetheless, in the early 1990s, the United States was still the most important source of imported matériel. In addition, the United States has participated since 1959 in annual naval exercises with Brazil (UNITAS) and has been involved in numerous fleet exchanges.

The Military Role in the Intelligence Services

The National Intelligence Service, 1964–90

The military-dominated SNI, which the Castelo Branco government created in 1964, was intended originally as a civilian agency of the executive branch. Initially, the SNI, under retired General Golbery do Couto e Silva, freed Castelo from dependence on army and Federal Police intelligence reports. The then head of the army, General Costa e Silva, feared that the new agency would weaken the army's secret service. However, by the end of 1968, with the triumph of the hard-liners, the SNI took on a military coloration. In 1973 it secured its dominance over the so-called intelligence community with the opening of the National Intelligence School (Escola Nacional de Informações—EsNI) in Brasília. The following year, the EsNI absorbed the ESG postgraduate intelligence course. Supposedly, the EsNI did not train police agents, and it selected its own students. By 1980 some officers were saying that the EsNI would be as useful as the ESG to their careers.

Alfred Stepan observed that the SNI differed from similar agencies in other countries in that it enjoyed a near monopoly over operations and training, and that the SNI chief had ministerial rank and therefore sat in the president's cabinet. In addition, he has pointed out that the SNI had an official in every government agency, in state-owned businesses, and at one point in the universities. These officials followed the daily functioning of the administrative machinery to ensure conformity with national security goals. Moreover, the SNI was autonomous, even regarding finances.

The SNI served as the backbone of the military regime's system of control and repression. Although there have been secret police in Brazil since at least the Vargas era, military involvement reached new heights with the creation of the SNI. The SNI grew out of the Institute for Research and Social Studies (Instituto de Pesquisas e Estudos Sociais—IPES), which General Couto e Silva had established to undermine the Goulart government. The SNI provided clearances for anyone seeking a government job or requesting to conduct research in the army archives. Using an elaborate system of informants and telephone taps, the SNI accumulated and analyzed reports on a wide range of people, organizations, and topics. One study by political scientists David V. Fleischer and the late Robert Wesson suggests that there were as many as 50,000 persons in the employ of the SNI during the 1964–85 regime. Furthermore, both Presidents Médici and Figueiredo had been SNI chiefs.

In theory, the SNI supervised and coordinated the intelligence agencies of the three services. However, in practice the service agencies maintained their autonomy. The service agencies included the Army Intelligence Center (Centro de Informações do Exército—CIE); the Air Force Intelligence Center (Centro de Informações da Aeronáutica—CIA); and the Naval Intelligence Center (Centro de Informações de Marinha—Cenimar).

The chief of staff of each of the army commands supposedly was responsible for the intelligence work in that command's territory. In practice, that officer was not necessarily informed of CIE activities, which followed a parallel chain of command. Each command also had an Internal Operations Department-Internal Defense Operations Center (Departamento de Operações Internas-Centro de Operações de Defesa Interna—DOI-CODI). The DOI-CODIs became centers of dirty tricks and torture.

From the outset, there was resistance to the idea of the CIE. In 1966 President Castelo Branco rejected the idea of creating an army intelligence service annexed to the minister of army's office, because it would weaken the General Staff's influence. The next year, the new minister of army, General Aurélio de Lyra Tavares, established the CIE over the objections of the chief of staff, General Orlando Geisel. As early as 1968, the CIE was exploding bombs in theaters, wrecking bookstores, and kidnapping people. When the left began terrorist violence in late 1968, the CIE expanded to about 200 officers and became the axis of repression, eliminating all signs of leftist violence in three years.

The SNI, CIE, and other intelligence agencies were the most dubious legacy that the military regime left to the New Republic. The scars of repression and violence, including the mistreatment, torture, and murder of prisoners, will mark the officer corps for years to come. During World War II, Brazilian officers serving in Italy with the FEB (Brazilian Expeditionary Force), the first Latin American military organization in history to participate in combat in Europe, prided themselves on the correct treatment they accorded German prisoners under the Geneva Convention. Their successors, however, were taught that international law did not apply in cases of internal security. Thus, they used massive intimidation, kidnappings, beatings, secret arrests and imprisonments, psychological and physical torture, murder, and secret burial. In the past, rebels or criminals from the margins of society and working-class people could expect brutal treatment from the forces of law and order. The military regime brought that experience to the opposition in the middle and upper classes. The "repressive apparatus," as it was often referred to, cast a shadow of fear and drew an invisible pale through Brazilian society to dissuade the educated classes from crossing it. It also served to dissuade opposition within the military itself.

The creation of the DOI network beginning in 1971 formed a parallel chain of command, one that did not necessarily end with the president of the republic. President Geisel, a retired general, struggled to have his orders fulfilled by the CIE system. Consequently, the CIE sought to undermine his government and to make Minister of Army Sylvio Couto Coelho da Frota the next president. The CIE also waged a pamphlet war against General Golbery do Couto e Silva, chief of Geisel's Civilian Household, who wanted to shut down the CIE.

The Strategic Affairs Secretariat, 1990–94

When Collor de Mello became president in 1990, he replaced the military-dominated SNI with the civilian-led SAE. One of his first acts as president was to dismiss 144 officers from the SNI. Under the Collor presidency, the SAE emerged as the most important actor in formulating Brazil's security policies. In part, its influence was derived from its direct access to

A Grajaú-class naval patrol boat, the P–44 Guajará
A Tupi-class "Tamoio" S–31 submarine, Brazilian Navy
Courtesy Brazilian Embassy, Washington

the president. The SAE's oversight responsibilities included Brazil's nuclear, space, missile, armaments, and intelligence programs. In an example of role expansion, however, the SAE drafted the 1992 Multiyear Plan, a document formulated previously by the Ministry of the Economy's National Planning Secretariat, and continued to have a strong military presence. Such broad activities led some to refer to the SAE as a "super ministry." In addition to the SAE, there are service intelligence agencies.

Despite attempts to make the SAE more open, there was virtually no congressional oversight of SAE activities. On September 26, 1991, President Collor submitted a bill for congressional supervision of the SAE's intelligence-gathering activities. According to the bill, the secretary of the SAE would be required to submit a confidential report to Congress every six months. Congress criticized several provisions, including the exemption from congressional oversight of intelligence activities of the armed forces and Federal Police; a penalty of imprisonment for three to ten years for breaches of confidentiality by Congress; and the formation of a joint congressional committee to monitor the SAE, thereby bypassing the committees that already existed within the Chamber of Deputies (such as the Committee on National Defense) and the Senate.

By mid-1992 it was clear that the SAE had not been "demilitarized," as suggested by Collor. Reserve and active-duty military officers continued to head most of the departments and coordinating sections. Nor did the SAE effectively oversee Brazil's intelligence apparatus. There was evidence that the intelligence branches of each service did not report to the SAE. In October 1992, President Itamar Franco appointed Admiral Mário César Flores to head the SAE. Some considered this military appointment a setback for the "demilitarization" of the SAE because Flores was Collor's minister of navy and was considered a leading proponent of Brazil's nuclear-powered submarine program.

In 1995 President Fernando Henrique Cardoso, who assumed the presidency on January 1, nominated Ambassador Ronaldo Mota Sardenberg to head the SAE. A seasoned diplomat, Sardenberg was a former ambassador to Moscow and the United Nations, and was widely published on issues relating to Brazil's foreign and security policies. President Cardoso also announced the creation of the Brazilian Intelligence Agency (Agência Brasileira de Inteligência Nacional—ABIN).

Defense Industries

Since the early twentieth century, the armed forces have pursued the goal of weapons self-sufficiency. Their intention was never to develop a large arsenal but to have the technical capability to produce the arms needed for Brazil's military. During World War I, the large navy was cut off from resupply of big gun shells and became a paper navy, thus reinforcing the drive for self-sufficiency. The rapid industrialization that took place after 1930 provided the infrastructure necessary for developing an arms industry. After World War II, Brazil developed a steel mill at Volta Redonda, in Rio de Janeiro State, and quickly became the largest steel producer in Latin America. In 1954 Brazil began manufacturing its first automatic pistols. The earliest armored personnel carriers (APCs) produced by Brazil, in the 1960s, benefited directly from some of the technology developed by Brazil's dynamic automotive industry. Brazil's push for nationalization of the computer-related industry in the 1970s also began with the navy, which could not decipher the "black box" computerized range-finding and firing mechanisms on the British frigates they had purchased, and did not want to be dependent on imported maintenance.

In the 1950s, Brazil set up the precursor to the Aerospace Technical Center (Centro Técnico Aeroespacial—CTA). Located in São José dos Campos, the CTA became the focal point for the arms industry. The CTA has trained a generation of engineers through its technical institute, the Aeronautical Technology Institute (Instituto Tecnológico da Aeronáutica—ITA). In 1986 it was estimated that 60 percent of 800 Embraer engineers had graduated from the ITA.

Brazil's three largest arms firms were established in the 1960s. Avibrás Aerospace Industry (Avibrás Indústria Aeroespacial S.A.—Avibrás) was established in 1961; Engesa, in 1963; and Embraer, in 1969. It was only in the subsequent period, from 1977 through 1988, that the three firms began to export arms on a large scale. In addition an estimated 350 firms were involved directly or indirectly in the arms production process in Brazil. The fourth largest Brazilian arms company was the War Matériel Industry (Indústria de Material Bélico do Brasil—Imbel), established on July 14, 1975, to unify the army's seven ordnance and ammunition factories.

Engineers associated formerly with the CTA created Avibrás as a private aerospace firm. In 1964 Avibrás was granted the Sonda I rocket contract and since then has been the major firm involved with the development of sounding rockets (Sondas II, III, and IV). It also has taken a leading role in developing missiles. In the 1980s and early 1990s, Avibrás worked almost exclusively with the manufacturing of rockets and multiple-launch rocket systems (MLRS), such as the Astros II, in addition to developing antitank and antiship missiles. At its peak, Avibrás employed 6,000 people.

Engesa also was formed as a private firm. Initially, it was involved in renovating World War II-vintage tanks. Engesa built wheeled APCs, such as the EE–11 Urutu amphibious APC, the EE–9 Cascavel armored reconnaissance vehicle, the EE–17 Sucuri tank destroyer, and the EE–3 Jararaca scout car, in addition to a wide range of other products. Engesa's APCs were all based on an indigenously designed suspension system. Engesa's weapons were exported almost exclusively to the developing world, especially to countries in the Middle East, Latin America, and Africa. By the mid-1980s, Engesa had expanded to a group of twelve subsidiaries and employed more than 5,000 people. By that time, the company had spent US$100 million on the development of the Osório, a main battle tank, but was unable to find a buyer for it. The Osório project came to an abrupt end with Operation Desert Storm against Iraq in 1991. In 1990 Engesa had won the evaluation process by the Saudis. After Desert Storm, Brazil was no match for United States competition, given the close ties that developed between Saudi Arabia and the United States during the war with Iraq.

By the mid-1980s, Embraer had become the largest aircraft manufacturer in the developing world, with sales of more than 4,000 aircraft. It has encountered great success with its Bandeirante and Brasília models, sold to the United States and other foreign countries. In 1988, at its height, it employed more than 12,000 workers. The Brazilian government owned about 5 percent of the company but controlled most of the voting stock. The government supported Embraer with generous interest rates on its loans, a reinvestment of profits into research and development, and purchases of its aircraft.

By 1980 Brazil had become a net exporter of arms. On the demand side, the rapid success resulted from a growing need in the developing world for armaments. On the supply side, Brazil's arms exports were designed for developing world markets and were noted for their high quality, easy maintenance, good performance in adverse conditions, and low cost. The product line was broad and came to include ammunition, gre-

EMB–312 Tucano T–27 trainers, Brazilian Air Force
Final assembly line of the EMB–312 Tucano, São José dos Campos
Courtesy Brazilian Embassy, Washington

nades, mines, armored personnel vehicles, patrol boats, navy patrol planes, turboprop trainers, tanks, and subsonic jet fighters.

In the early 1980s, Brazil emerged as one of the leading armaments exporters in the developing world. From 1985 to 1989, it was the eleventh largest exporter of arms. Brazil exported arms to at least forty-two countries, in all regions of the world. By far the largest regional market was the Middle East, to which Brazil sold approximately 50 percent of its arms from 1977 through 1988. According to an estimate by the Stockholm International Peace Research Institute (SIPRI), 40 percent of all Brazilian arms transfers from 1985 to 1989 went to Iraq.

Brazil's arms industry nearly collapsed after 1988, as a result of the termination of the Iran-Iraq War (1980–88), a reduction in world demand for armaments, and the decline in state support for the industry. In early 1990, the two major manufacturers, Engesa and Avibrás, filed for bankruptcy.

By late 1994, it appeared that Brazil's arms industry would not disappear completely. It was unlikely, however, that it would return to the robust form of the mid-1980s. Avibrás had paid off a substantial portion of its debt and was seeking ways to convert much of its production to civilian products. Engesa had been dismembered; some of its companies were sold to private interests, and its ordnance-related companies were taken over by the state and integrated with Imbel. Embraer was privatized in December 1994, and despite significant financial difficulties, it rolled out the new jet commuter plane prototype EMB–145 in 1995.

Mission of the Armed Forces

The Military Mission since 1988

Article 142 of the 1988 federal constitution states that "The armed forces, which consist of the navy, the army, and the air force, are permanent and normal national institutions organized on the basis of hierarchy and discipline under the supreme authority of the president of the republic." It adds that "Their purpose is to defend the fatherland, guarantee the constitutionally established powers and, on the initiative of any of said powers, law and order." Significantly, the 1988 constitution fails to include the clause that the military only be obedient to the executive "within the limits of the law." Thus, the armed forces have been placed more firmly under presidential control. According to Complementary Law No. 69 of July 23, 1991, the army's mission is also to cooperate in the national development and in civil defense.

According to Article 84 of the 1988 constitution, the president has the exclusive authority to appoint and dismiss the ministers of state, decree a state of emergency or state of siege, serve as supreme commander of the armed forces, promote their general officers, and appoint them to posts. The president may also declare war "in the event of foreign aggression and when authorized by the National Congress." He also presides over the National Defense Council.

There has been little debate in Brazil's civil society regarding the role of the armed forces. José Murilo de Carvalho, a political scientist, has called for such a debate, arguing that it is necessary to define the tasks of the armed forces before addressing issues of defense expenditures. Civilians, however, have not taken the initiative in defining those tasks.

The military has been seeking a new role, primarily to justify even its meager budget. The armed forces have seemed increasingly irrelevant, given the lack of an external threat (Brazil is involved in a common market, joint ventures, and nuclear cooperation with Argentina, its former rival); the lack of an internal threat (no political group in Brazil is calling for the use of violence to overthrow the government); and the demise of communism. In addition to a peacekeeping role, some of the potential new roles for the military include broader participation in the Amazon, involvement in the counter-drug war, and civic action. In late 1994 and 1995, the armed forces were involved intermittently in providing public security in Rio de Janeiro. On May 18, 1995, Governor Marcello Alencar appointed hard-line retired General Nilton Cerqueira, who was elected federal deputy in 1994, as state secretary of public security; General Cerqueira was well known as commander of the Rio de Janeiro DOI-CODI in the 1970s.

The Military in the Amazon

The Amazon region occupies more than half of Brazil's territory. In 1985 the army announced the Northern Corridor (Calha Norte) project, in an attempt to establish better control of Brazil's interests in the Amazon. The project has consisted of building a series of outposts along the Brazilian border with Colombia, Venezuela, Guyana, Suriname, and French Guiana.

Some of these outposts have been established. Calha Norte is therefore more than a military project. Its goals are to provide effective control of the border, improve the local infrastructure, and promote economic development of the region.

The army has increased the number of posts near the border from eight to nineteen. The posts are placed under five Special Frontier Battalions, with headquarters from west to east in Tabatinga, Rio Branco, São Gabriel da Cachoeira, Boa Vista, and Macapá. In addition, the army has been transferring battalions from the South and Southeast to the Amazon: the Seventeenth Motorized Infantry Battalion from Cruz Alta to the Seventeenth Jungle Infantry Battalion; the Sixty-first Motorized Infantry Battalion in Santo Angelo to the Sixty-first Jungle Infantry Battalion; and the Sixty-first Engineering and Construction Battalion at Cruzeiro do Sul to Rio Branco. The First Brigade in Petrópolis, Rio de Janeiro State, was moved to Tefé, Amazonas, except for one infantry battalion. Lastly, the army was planning to open two new garrisons in the Rio Negro region, at Tunui and Asuno do Içana.

Some Brazilian officers have warned against "foreign intervention" in the region. In July 1991, Army General Antenor de Santa Cruz Abreu, then chief of the Amazon Region Military Command (Comando Militar da Amazônia—CMA), threatened that the army would "transform the Amazon into a new Vietnam" if developed countries continued to "internationalize" the region. The vitriol subsided partially in January 1992, when General Santa Cruz Abreu was replaced by General Carlos Annîbal Pacheco, who dispelled some of the concerns about the "internationalization" of the Amazon.

In 1993 the Brazilian press reported on United States-Guyana military exercises near the Brazil-Guyana border. The proximity of the exercise to the Brazilian border provoked an angry response from many high-ranking Brazilian officers and government officials. United States joint exercises were also held with Colombia and Suriname, to the consternation of the Brazilians. In a show of force on October 4, 1994, the armed forces were involved in Operation Surumu, the largest combined and joint maneuvers ever carried out in the Amazon. The exercises were held north of the city of Boa Vista in the state of Roraima, over an area of 34,900 square kilometers. They included the participation of eight countries in a war against Cratenia, an imaginary enemy. The exercises involved 5,000 soldiers, thirty-seven aircraft, four ships, and two hospital ships. The army had the largest contingent with 3,000 men. The air force dropped 700 parachutists into the jungle and was involved in transporting most of the troops, many by civilian aircraft. The navy provided logistical support, using riverine patrol boats. The joint nature of the maneuvers indicated that whereas the army would continue to take the lead in the Amazon, the other two services (especially the air force) also would be involved.

However, such massive operations are specially staged affairs, giving an impression of military power that is not reflected in the day-to-day reality. The commanding general of the First Jungle Brigade, headquartered in Boa Vista, oversees two infantry battalions, whose units are spread from the Guyana border to that with Colombia. One battalion headquarters is located in Boa Vista, the other in São Gabriel da Cachoeira. The general does not have his own aircraft, and he must request transport from Manaus if he wishes to inspect his troops. Headquarters maintains contact with the units via radio. The first battalion maintains five Special Border Platoons (Pelotões Especiais de Fronteira—PEFs) at Bom Fim and Normandia on the Guyana side, at Pacarema (also called BV–8, for the eighth marker on the Brazil-Venezuelan line), Surucucu, and Auaris facing Venezuela. The second battalion at São Gabriel da Cachoeira has PEFs at Maturaca (near Pico da Neblina) and Cucui on the Venezuela border, and three more looking toward Colombia at Matapi, Uaupés, and Iauaretê.

The platoons consist of about seventy soldiers, corporals, and sergeants, and five officers, the most senior of whom is usually a lieutenant. Many of the soldiers are recruited locally. In Roraima many of the soldiers are Macuxí and Wapishana Indians.

In late 1993, the armed forces received presidential approval for the Amazon Region Surveillance System (Sistema de Vigilância da Amazônia—Sivam). Sivam will consist of a large network of radar, communication systems, and data processing centers and should assist the government in air traffic control and its efforts to curb deforestation and drug trafficking. The control centers of Sivam will be in Manaus, Belém, Porto Velho, and Brasília. It will take at least eight years to install the system, at a cost of US$1.55 billion. Sivam will include five Embraer EMB–120 Brasílias carrying Ericsson Radar Electronics Erieye airborne early warning and control system. Sivam is part of a larger plan called the Amazon Region Protection System (Sistema de Proteção da Amazônia—Sipam). The purpose of

Sipam is to provide a more sophisticated infrastructure for policing the Amazon.

The Sivam case was particularly controversial in 1994 and 1995 and involved Brasília, Paris, and Washington. In June 1994, two days after then United States Secretary of Commerce Ron Brown visited Brasília, President Itamar Franco decided to award the Sivam contract to a consortium led by Raytheon (United States), instead of to a group led by Thomson CSF (France). In December 1994, when many legislators already had left Brasília for the Christmas holidays, Brazil's Senate approved the financing of Sivam. A Brazilian senator reportedly received US$7 million to expedite congressional approval. In February 1995, the *New York Times* reported that the United States Central Intelligence Agency had discovered that Thomson CSF paid bribes to Brazilian officials. French diplomats countered that it was the United States that bribed Brazilian officials, paying US$30 million to obtain the contract. France charged the United States with industrial espionage and expelled five staff members from the United States Embassy in Paris.

In March 1995, Raytheon's Brazilian partner, Automation and Control Systems Engineering (Engenharia de Sistemas de Contrôle e Automação—ESCA), which was hired to manage Sivam and to develop the system's control software, was removed from the project because of fraud in social security contributions in Brazil. In its place, the Brazilian government proposed a team of Ministry of Aeronautics experts. However, wiretapping and alleged influence-peddling created the most serious crisis for the Cardoso administration in its first year in office, and threatened the very future of the Sivam project.

At least two dozen Brazilian government organizations deal with the Amazon, in addition to many nongovernmental organizations (NGOs) from both Brazil and abroad. The vast array of organizations reflects the many interests in the Amazon, which include concerns with national security, indigenous peoples, economic development, the environment, and drug trafficking. These interests often clash. In an attempt to coordinate Brazil's Amazon policies, President Franco created the Ministry of Environment and the Legal Amazon on August 18, 1993 (later renamed Ministry of Environment, Hydraulic Resources, and the Legal Amazon), and placed Rubens Ricúpero at the helm. Ricúpero, the chief negotiator of the

An Aérospatiale Super Puma CH–34 helicopter, Brazilian Air Force
Brazilian Army River Patrol commandos
Courtesy Brazilian Embassy, Washington

1977 Amazonian Cooperation Treaty, was brought from the post of ambassador in Washington.

President Collor established the Yanomami Indigenous Park, encompassing 9.5 million hectares of territory adjacent to Venezuela. The reservation is home to 25,000 members of the Yanomami tribe, 10,000 of whom live on the Brazilian side of the reserve. The 600 gold prospectors who lived on or near Yanomami land and ignored the extensive reservation were expelled. In 1992 President Collor demarcated the territory, and in the following year mining revenues dropped considerably.

The problems associated with competing interests in the Amazon became apparent in August 1993, when at least sixteen Yanomami Indians were massacred near the Brazil-Venezuela border. Twenty-three illegal gold prospectors were arrested and charged with the slayings. They were later acquitted, after investigations allegedly indicated that the Indians had died in conflict with other Indians.

The governors of Roraima, Amazonas, and Pará states have called for the reduction in the area of the reservations. According to one poll, 51 percent of Brazil's legislators agreed with that position. Many officers within the armed forces have also expressed their discontent with the size of the reservations. A common argument is that there are few Yanomami per square kilometer allotted to them.

In early 1994, there was a broad consensus in Brazil on the need to expand the military presence along the border. Such a presence was supported by Ministers Ricúpero and Flores. Brazilians have expressed concerns about sovereignty, particularly the encroachment by the United States and others via drug interdiction and environmentalism. Despite such consensus, however, only limited funding has been available to the Ministry of Environment, Hydraulic Resources, and the Legal Amazon, and the constant clash of interests has impeded a coordinated policy.

The Military Role in Counter-Drug Actions

The escalation of the war on drugs in the Andean region has led narco-traffickers to change their shipment routes, and Brazil increasingly is being used as such, especially for drugs sent to Africa and Europe. In addition, some drug producers in Colombia, Peru, and Bolivia have used Brazil as a shelter from security forces in their countries. Brazil is a major supplier of precursor chemicals. In the early 1990s, Brazil created the Special Secretariat for Drugs (Secretaria Especial de Entorpecentes—SEE) to coordinate the government's counter-drug actions.

Brazil's military has been reluctant to become involved in the war against drugs. Officers argue that, according to the constitution, it is the responsibility of the Federal Police to pursue such a war. The armed forces consider their involvement to be potentially corrupting and are loathe to become entangled in a "no-win" war. Furthermore, Brazilians, like other Latin Americans, are sensitive to United States involvement in the region and fear the United States may use the antidrug role as a rationale for an expanded presence in Brazil. From 1990 through 1993, the United States provided Brazil with approximately US$1 million a year for antidrug activities. As a result of United States Attorney General Janet Reno's visit to attend President Fernando Henrique Cardoso's inauguration on January 1, 1995, the antidrug agreement was renewed in April 1995, just before Cardoso's official visit to the United States.

The armed forces have been willing to provide logistical and intelligence support to the Federal Police in the war against drug trafficking. They have also become increasingly involved in countering the spread of armaments among the drug traffickers. In 1994 there were an estimated 40,000 illegal weapons in Rio de Janeiro. The constitution gives the army the responsibility for supervising armaments. In addition, the army's Eastern Command has provided the Military Police (Polícia Militar—PM) of Rio de Janeiro State with many weapons, long-range vision goggles, and bulletproof vests for countering the well-armed drug traffickers. In October 1993, the army provided the police forces with 7.62-millimeter FAL assault rifles—the first time such rifles were used by police forces in Brazil. The army also trained members of the Special Operations Battalion (Batalhão de Operações Especiais—Bope).

In October 1993, some police officers were implicated in the smuggling of arms to the traffickers, and as a result the army was called on to take firmer measures. All weapons seized in police operations were to be put under army control in military arsenals. In addition, special army agents were to work with the Civil Police, Military Police, and Federal Police forces to identify the traffickers' arms sources.

Drug trafficking and domestic consumption are, by all accounts, on the rise. Some of the groups involved in drug trafficking control entire shantytowns (favelas) and are far better armed than the Federal Police or State Police. In October 1994, there were reports that up to 70 percent of the police force was receiving payoffs by the heavily armed drug-trafficking gangs in the favelas. Growing public demands that law and order be restored in Rio de Janeiro prompted the Itamar Franco government to order the army to launch an offensive against the gangs and to oversee a purge of the police force. The army, under the command of a general, mobilized as many as 70,000 soldiers for the operation in the favelas.

The task force that identified the corruption was led by António Carlos Biscaia, attorney general of Rio de Janeiro State. Corruption in Rio de Janeiro was widespread, and included the Civil Police, Military Police, judges, and prosecutors. In addition, the Rio de Janeiro governor, Nilo Batista, was induced to sign an agreement with the federal government allowing for federal intervention through the army, which took over the security command of Rio de Janeiro prior to the 1994 gubernatorial elections. By mid-1995 the army had largely pulled out, but the security situation was little improved.

Civic Action

With the possible exception of military officers in Peru, the officers in Brazil have been the most involved in civic action in South America. To a certain extent, the civic-action role has been appropriated because the officers consider themselves responsible for the guidance and development of the nation. Civic action is not a new role for the armed forces. Under Vargas the army, which felt responsible for helping modernize the country through a more elaborate infrastructure, was involved in development and reconstruction projects. Construction battalions built roads and railroads in the interior of the country. Officers were placed in high positions within state enterprises such as the Volta Redonda steel plant and the Brazilian Petroleum Corporation (Petróleo Brasileiro S.A.—Petrobrás), the petroleum monopoly. The air force and navy were involved in transport to remote areas, and in health care assistance to those regions. As Professor Fleischer notes, "This new mission reinforced the doctrine of industrial development as a basis for national strength and security and the positivist ideology of a technocratic scientific approach to national problems."

In the early 1980s, the army was again extensively involved in civic-action projects, such as building roads in the Northeast and a railroad in Paraná State. Despite the reluctance of some officers to embrace such a role, cutbacks in defense funding make civic-action programs attractive.

Defense Expenditures

Data on Brazil's military expenditures need to be approached with caution. Their accuracy is complicated by high rates of inflation since the late 1950s, by secrecy surrounding the funding of various military-related projects, by personnel costs that are sometimes hidden in other budgets, and by the common practice of mixing the accounts of the national treasury, the Central Bank, and the Bank of Brazil (Banco do Brasil—BB). However, even if the figures generally attributed to Brazilian defense expenditures understate their true value, there is consensus that Brazil is among the countries with the lowest levels of military expenditures, and that those levels have declined in the last three decades. For example, the rate of military expenditures in relation to GDP has dropped steadily: in the 1960s, it averaged 2 percent; in the 1970s, 1.5 percent; in the 1980s, 1 percent; and in the early 1990s, less than 0.5 percent. In 1993 that rate reached a mere 0.3 percent. Brazil in 1993 ranked 133d out of 166 countries in military expenditures as a share of government expenditures. Within South America, only Guyana and Suriname ranked lower.

Political scientist Paulo S. Wrobel notes that these data point to a correlation between the type of government (military or civilian) and military expenditures. That correlation is made even clearer if one examines military expenditures as a share of the federal budget: in 1970 that figure was 20 percent; in 1993 it was only 1.3 percent (see table 28, Appendix). The 1993 figure was the lowest since independence in 1822. The highest figure was in 1864 and 1865, at the early stages of the Paraguayan War, when defense expenditures accounted for 49.6 percent of all government expenditures.

Brazil's low level of military expenditures can be attributed to the perception that the country has few external threats and to Brazil's large size in relation to its neighbors. In terms of threats, the deepening integration process with Argentina since the early 1980s virtually has removed the only potential external threat to Brazil.

Despite its low rate of military expenditures, in absolute terms Brazil is by far the largest military power in Latin America. In 1993 it ranked nineteenth among 166 countries in total military expenditures; the next highest in Latin America was Argentina, which ranked twenty-fourth. From 1988 through 1993, Brazil's military expenditures totaled US$43.12 billion (in constant 1993 dollars; an average of US$7.19 billion per year). They totaled US$10.6 billion in 1996. The defense budget in 1997 totaled US$12 billion.

The armed forces have had some minor triumphs on budget issues. In early 1994, the Franco administration announced that it would cut US$22 billion in the federal budget, dividing the cuts equally across ministries. The military ministers reacted quickly, going directly to the president to criticize the proposed reductions. They succeeded in lowering the proposed military cuts by at least US$300 million.

In late 1993 and early 1994, the armed forces were more vocal in their criticism of the low levels of military expenditures. They pointed out, for example, that the air force work week began on Monday afternoon, after lunch, and ended at Friday noon, before lunch, in order to save on the cost of feeding the officers and troops.

Military salaries were raised substantially in mid-1991 and in April 1992. According to one report, before the second raise, a four-star general with forty years in the service was earning about US$1,700 a month, and many soldiers earned only a few hundred dollars a month. In contrast, a congressional deputy earned more than US$6,000 a month.

The armed forces have been trying to protect their priority projects: the army—Calha Norte and the "defense" of the Amazon; the navy—its nuclear-powered submarine; the air force—its AMX subsonic fighter. Each project has had special funding from the federal government, aside from the general military budget. Additional funding has sometimes been available through various government agencies.

In essence, the armed forces are being squeezed in an unintended fashion by a neoliberal economic model that stresses cuts in government expenditures and privatizations. Not only has their budget been cut, but they no longer have the ready-made sinecure of state enterprises in which to work at the time of retirement. Indeed, under the military regime, state enterprises became bloated with retired military officers. A 1983 study by political scientist Walder de Góes identified more than 8,000 retired officers who were in positions within the state enterprises and federal bureaucracy.

What the defense spending levels suggest is that the military is having to compete with virtually every civilian ministry and, in many cases, is coming up short. Moreover, even though the military is still the most influential player on some issues, the number of civilian actors involved in the decision-making process has increased. In many cases, the military has been displaced by civilians. The Ministry of Finance has become the dominant actor on budget issues. Although the armed forces can try to appeal directly to the president, such an approach is not guaranteed to succeed. Also, the armed forces must deal directly with a Congress responsible for approving the budget.

Organization of the Armed Forces

Command and Control

The three services are separate from each other, except in three areas: the Armed Forces General Staff (Estado-Maior das Forças Armadas—EMFA), the National Defense Council (Conselho de Defesa Nacional—CDN), and the Armed Forces High Command (Alto Comando das Forças Armadas—ACFA) (see fig. 13). The EMFA, which is involved in planning and coordination, interprets interservice views about policy and comes the closest to functioning as a ministry of defense. It is headed by a four-star general, and the chair rotates among the services. The ACFA is involved with more immediate, day-to-day problems. It is composed of the ministers of the three services, their chiefs of staff, and the EMFA chief.

According to Article 91 of the constitution, the CDN is "the consultative body of the president of the republic in matters related to national sovereignty and the defense of the democratic state." The members of the CDN are the president, the vice president, the president of the Chamber of Deputies, the president of the Senate, the minister of justice, military ministers, the minister of foreign affairs, and the minister of planning. The CDN has authority to "express an opinion in instances of declaration of war and the celebration of peace" and to "express an opinion on the decreeing of a state of emergency, state of siege, or federal intervention." In addition, the CDN is authorized to "propose the criteria and conditions for the use of areas that are vital to the security of the national territory and express an opinion on their continued use, especially in the strip along the borders, and on matters related to the conservation and exploitation of natural resources of any

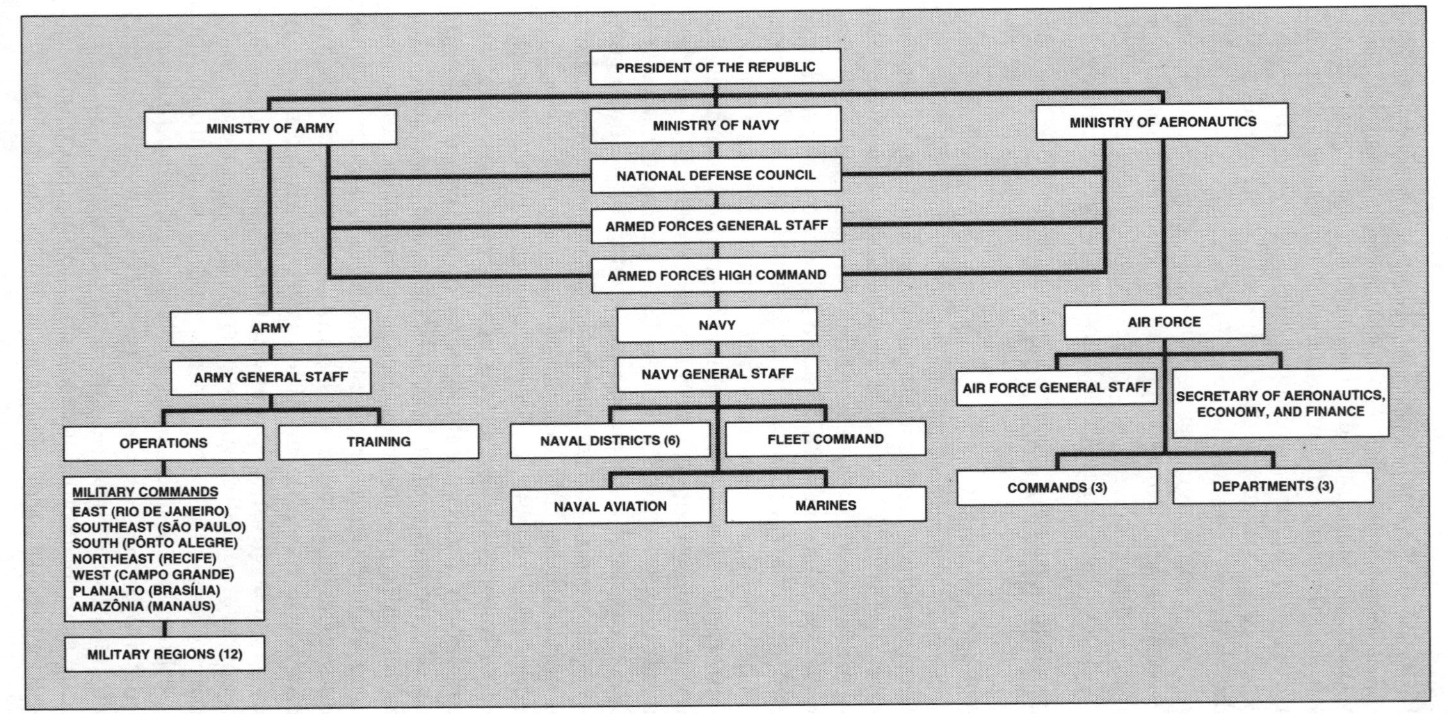

Figure 13. Organization of the Armed Forces, 1996

kind." The CDN also may "study, propose, and monitor the progress of initiatives necessary to guarantee national independence and the defense of the democratic state."

Interestingly, the highest level consultative body available to the president is the Council of the Republic (Conselho da República). This body does not include any military minister or officer, although the president may call on a military minister to participate if the matter is related to the respective ministry's agenda. According to Article 89 of the constitution, the Council of the Republic has authority to make declarations of federal intervention, a state of emergency, and a state of siege (all security-related issues).

Army

As in most Latin American nations, the Brazilian Army has been the most influential of the services because of its size, deployment, and historical development. Not only did senior army generals occupy the presidency from 1964 until 1985, but most of the officers who held cabinet posts during that time were from the army. In 1997 the army totaled 200,000 members.

Considering the short conscript tour (usually nine to ten months), the army has a high number of conscripts: 125,000. Because of the need for literate and skilled young men to handle modern weapons, the army has served as a training ground for a large reserve force. Its highly professional officer corps serves as a nucleus around which the trained service would be mobilized if required.

The noncommissioned officer (NCO) corps is not well developed. NCOs have virtually no autonomy or authority. Emphasis on training and professional development is for officers only. The NCOs account for slightly more than one-third of the total army strength. About half of the NCOs are sergeants, who serve as command links between officers and ranks. Some also serve as middle-level technicians.

In the early 1990s, the army began to undergo a generational change. The generals of the early 1990s had been junior officers in the early 1960s and had witnessed the military coup in 1964. Their worldview was shaped and influenced by the anticommunism of that time. These generals were being replaced by colonels who had entered the army in the early 1970s and whose view of the world had been shaped less by ideology and more by pragmatism. The United States, particularly through its counterinsurgency doctrines of the early 1960s, was more influential with the older group of officers.

The Army General Staff (Estado-Maior do Exército—EME) directs training and operations (see fig. 14). The EME has expanded from four sections in 1968 to fifteen sections in 1994. It is headed by the EME chief, except in the event of a war.

From 1946 through 1985, the army was divided into four numbered armies: the First Army was centered in Rio de Janeiro, the Second Army in São Paulo, the Third Army in Porto Alegre, and the Fourth Army in Recife. Historically, the First Army was the most politically significant because of Rio de Janeiro's position as the nation's capital through the 1950s. The Third Army was also important because of its shared border with Argentina (Brazil's traditional rival in Latin America) and Uruguay. In 1964, for example, close to two-thirds of the Brazilian troops were in the Third Army, and somewhat fewer than one-third were in the First Army. The rest were sprinkled throughout the Second and Fourth Armies. The Planalto Military Command (Comando Militar do Planalto—CMP), comprising the Federal District and Goiás State, and the Amazon Military Region Command (Comando Militar da Amazônia—CMA) supplemented the four armies.

On January 1, 1986, the army was restructured from four numbered armies and two military commands into seven military commands. The major addition was the Western Military Command (Comando Militar do Oeste—CMO), whose territory encompasses the states of Mato Grosso and Mato Grosso do Sul (previously under the Second Army territory), and Rondônia (previously under the CMA). Each of the seven military commands has its headquarters in a major city: Eastern Military Command (Comando Militar do Leste—CML), Rio de Janeiro; Southeastern Military Command (Comando Militar do Sudeste—CMSE), São Paulo; Southern Military Command (Comando Militar do Sul—CMS), Porto Alegre; Northeastern Military Command (Comando Militar do Nordeste—CMN), Recife; CMO, Campo Grande; CMP, Brasília; and CMA, Manaus. The CMP and CMO are led by major generals (three-star); the other five are headed by full generals (four-star). The army is divided further into eleven military regions. The CMSE is made up of only one state, São Paulo, and is in charge of protecting the industrial base of the country.

The changes were instituted as part of a modernization campaign to make the army better prepared for rapid mobilization. The reorganization reflected Brazil's geopolitical drive to "occupy the frontier" and the growing importance of Brasília, the Amazon, and western Brazil. In 1997 there were major units around Brasília, four jungle brigades, and five jungle battalions extending from Amapá to Mato Grosso do Sul. A tour with jungle units is a coveted assignment and is considered career-enhancing.

The move to occupy the Amazon and the short-term political implications of the army's reorganization should not be overstated. The army's geographic organization and distribution have continued to reflect a concern with internal rather than external defense. In what is perhaps an anachronism, the CML in Rio de Janeiro continues to have some of the best troop units and the most modern equipment (see table 29, Appendix). Command of the CML is still a coveted assignment, and the Military Village (Vila Militar), Rio de Janeiro's garrison or military community, is still considered one of the most important centers of military influence in the entire country. Principal army schools are located there or nearby. The CML is also important in countering the trafficking of drugs and armaments.

In a significant political development, the army established a formal High Command in 1964. Before that time, a clique of generals residing in Rio de Janeiro controlled major decisions of the army. Throughout the authoritarian period, tensions often existed between the High Command and the five generals who served as president. This tension was such that President Geisel dismissed Minister of Army Sylvio Frota in 1977. Since the January 1986 restructuring, the High Command has been composed of the seven regional commanders, the chief of staff, and the minister of army. The High Command meets to discuss all issues, including those of a political nature, and is responsible for drawing up the list of generals from which the president chooses those who will be promoted to four stars.

Navy

The navy traces its heritage to Admiral Cochrane's mercenary fleet and to the tiny Portuguese ships and crews that protected the earliest coastal colonies from seaborne marauders. The navy is the most aristocratic and conservative of the services and draws a larger share of its officers from the upper

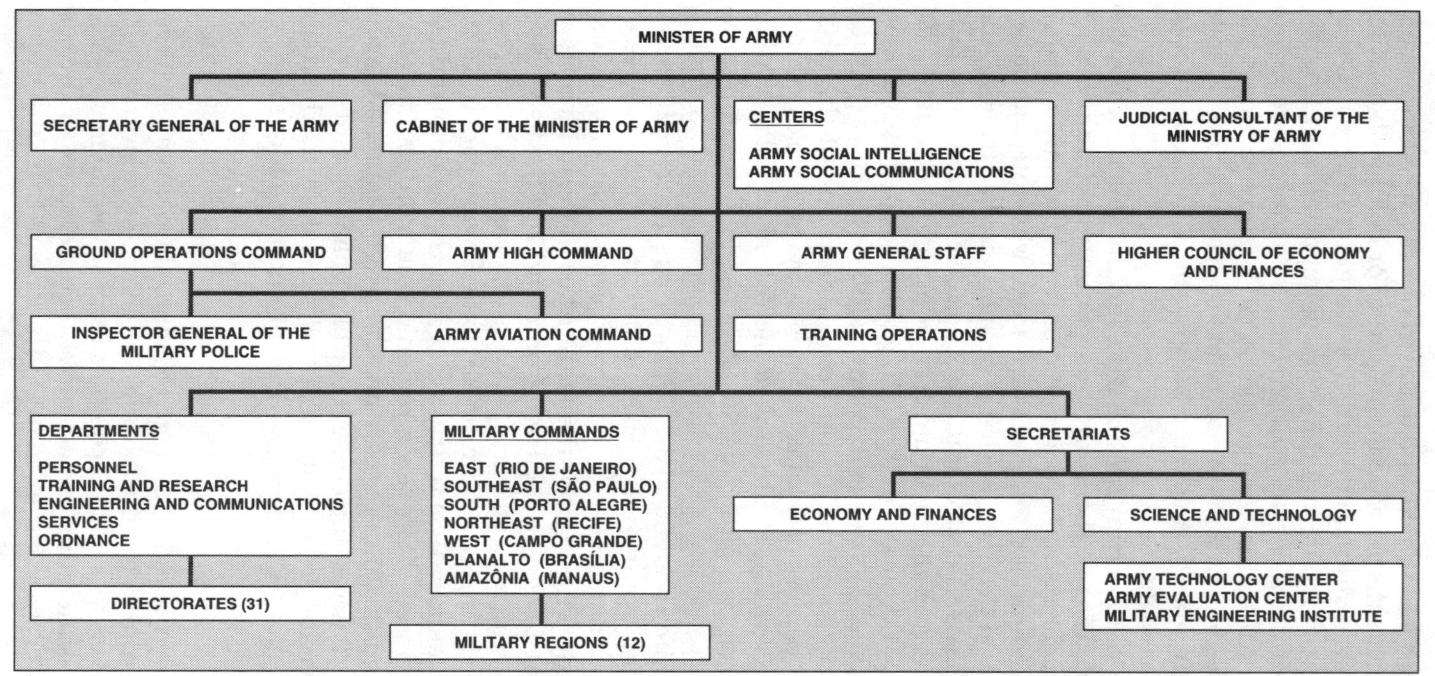

Source: Based on information from *Noticiário do Exército* [Rio de Janeiro], No. 8958, April 19, 1995, 2.

Figure 14. Organization of the Army, 1995

middle class and upper class. Although it is involved in "brown-water" (riverine and coastal) operations, the navy's primary goal has been to become an effective "blue-water" navy, able to project power on the high seas. Given its "blue-water" bias, the navy is even less inclined to become involved in counterdrug operations than the army or air force.

The total naval strength of 64,700 in 1997 included Naval Aviation (Aviação Naval) with 1,300 members, the Marines (Corpo de Fuzileiros Navais—CFN) with 14,600 members, and only 2,000 conscripts. Naval operations are directed from the Ministry of Navy in Brasília through the Navy General Staff (Estado-Maior da Armada—EMA), six naval districts (five oceanic and one riverine), and two naval commands—Brasília Naval Command (Comando Naval de Brasília—CNB) and Manaus Naval Command (Comando Naval de Manaus—CNM). The 1st Naval District is located at the country's main naval base in Rio de Janeiro; the 2d Naval District is in Salvador; the 3d, Natal; the 4th, Belém; and the 5th, Porto Alegre. The 6th Riverine District has its headquarters in Ladário, near Corumbá on the Rio Paraguai.

Until the 1980s, the flagship of the ocean-going navy was the aircraft carrier *Minas Gerais* (the ex-British H.M.S. *Vengeance*), which has been in service since 1945. Purchased from Britain in 1956, the *Minas Gerais* was reconstructed in the Netherlands in 1960 and refitted extensively in Brazil in the late 1970s, and again in 1993. In 1994 Mário César Flores, a former minister of navy, declared in an interview that the navy would be hard-pressed to defend the *Minas Gerais* in a conflict. Nevertheless, the *Minas Gerais* is not likely to be replaced until the next century. The navy's priority reequipment plans for the 1990s include the receipt of new Inhaúma-class corvettes, the construction of Tupi-class submarines, the refurbishing of the Niterói-class frigates, the acquisition of nine new Super Lynx and up to six former United States Navy Sikorsky SH–3G/H Sea King helicopters, the construction of the conventional SNAC–1 submarine prototype, and the development of nuclear-propulsion technology. In addition, the navy contracted in late 1994 to acquire four Type 22 British Royal Navy frigates and three River-class minesweepers for delivery in the 1995–97 period (see table 30, Appendix).

After years of intense rivalry between the navy and the air force for the control of naval aviation, President Castelo Branco decreed in 1965 that only the air force would be allowed to operate fixed-wing aircraft and that the navy would be responsible for helicopters. According to many critics, such an unusual division of labor has caused serious command and control problems. The complement of aircraft carried by the *Minas Gerais* includes six Grumman S–2E antisubmarine planes, in addition to several SH–3D Sea King helicopters and Aérospatiale Super Puma and HB–350 Esquilo helicopters. In accordance with the Castelo Branco compromise, the S–2E aircraft are flown by air force pilots and the helicopters by navy pilots. A crew of the *Minas Gerais* with full air complement consists of 1,300 officers and enlisted personnel.

The navy's most ambitious program is the development of a nuclear-powered submarine. The program enjoys broad political support, including from the political left, in part because of the perceived technological benefits that may be derived from the project. As minister of navy, Flores gave the development of nuclear propulsion for Brazil's submarines the highest priority.

Air Force

Established in 1941, the FAB (Brazilian Air Force) is the newest of the services and gradually has gained a larger share of the budget. The strength of the FAB—50,000 members in 1997 (including 5,000 conscripts), 272 combat aircraft, and forty-five armed helicopters—makes it the largest air force in Latin America (see table 31, Appendix). The FAB's budget is relatively large because of its civil air budget.

The minister of aeronautics, in addition to commanding the air force, controls all civil air activities: the construction and operation of airports through the Brazilian Airport Infrastructure Firm (Empresa Brasileira de Infraestructura Aeroportuária—Infraero), and air traffic control through the Civil Aviation Department (Departamento de Aviação Civil—DAC). The line of military command extends from the minister through his chief of staff, who heads the Air Force General Staff (Estado-Maior da Aeronáutica—EMAer), down to the commanders of the three general commands: General Air Command (Comando Geral do Ar), General Support Command (Comando Geral de Apoio), and General Personnel Command (Comando Geral do Pessoal) and three departments: Research and Development, Civil Aviation, and Training. There are also seven regional air commands under the General Air Command that cover the entire country. Numbered from one to seven, the headquarters of the regional air commands include Belém, Recife, Rio de Janeiro, São Paulo, Porto Alegre, Brasília, and Manaus.

Personnel and Training

Conscription

According to Article 143 of the 1988 constitution, military service is obligatory for men, but conscientious objection is allowed. Women and clergymen are exempt from compulsory military service. At age seventeen, men are required to register for the draft and are expected to serve when they reach age eighteen. About 75 percent of those registering receive deferments. Generally, those from the upper class and upper middle class find ways to defer, and as a result the ranks are made up primarily of lower-class and lower-middle-class recruits. A growing number of recruits are volunteers, accounting for about one-third of the total. Those who serve generally spend one year of regular enlistment at an army garrison near their home. Some are allowed six-month service terms but are expected to complete high school at the same time. These are called "Tiros de Guerra," or "shooting schools," which are for high school boys in medium-sized interior towns, run by army sergeants. The army is the only service with a large number of conscripts; the navy and air force have very few.

The conscript system is primarily a means of providing basic military training to a sizable group of young men who then return to civilian life and are retained on the reserve rolls until age forty-five. The army recognizes that it provides a public service by teaching large numbers of conscripts basic skills that can be valuable to the overall economy when the young men return to civilian life.

Ranks, Uniforms, and Insignia

The three armed forces use several different uniforms, including full dress, dress, service, and fatigue. The army service uniform is green; the navy, navy blue; and the air force, a lighter blue. The senior commissioned rank (four stars) in the army is general (*general de exército*); in the navy, admiral (*almirante de esquadra*); and in the air force, general (*tenente-brigadeiro*) (see fig. 15). In time of war, or in exceptional circumstances, a fifth star may be worn by the highest-ranking officer in the army (*marechal*, or general of the army) navy (*almirante*, or fleet admiral), and air force (*marechal do ar*, or general of the

BRAZILIAN RANK	ASPIRANTE-A-OFICIAL	SEGUNDO-TENENTE	PRIMEIRO-TENENTE	CAPITÃO	MAJOR	TENENTE-CORONEL	CORONEL	GENERAL DE BRIGADA	GENERAL DE DIVISÃO		GENERAL DE EXÉRCITO	MARECHAL*
ARMY												
U.S. RANK TITLES	2D LIEUTENANT	1ST LIEUTENANT		CAPTAIN	MAJOR	LIEUTENANT COLONEL	COLONEL	BRIGADIER GENERAL	MAJOR GENERAL	LIEUTENANT GENERAL	GENERAL	GENERAL OF THE ARMY
BRAZILIAN RANK	ASPIRANTE-A-OFICIAL	SEGUNDO-TENENTE	PRIMEIRO-TENENTE	CAPITÃO	MAJOR	TENENTE-CORONEL	CORONEL	BRIGADEIRO	MAJOR-BRIGADEIRO		TENENTE-BRIGADEIRO	MARECHAL-DO-AR*
AIR FORCE												
U.S. RANK TITLES	2D LIEUTENANT	1ST LIEUTENANT		CAPTAIN	MAJOR	LIEUTENANT COLONEL	COLONEL	BRIGADIER GENERAL	MAJOR GENERAL	LIEUTENANT GENERAL	GENERAL	GENERAL OF THE AIR FORCE
BRAZILIAN RANK	GUARDA-MARINHA	SEGUNDO-TENENTE	PRIMEIRO-TENENTE	CAPITÃO-TENENTE	CAPITÃO-DE-CORVETA	CAPITÃO-DE-FRAGATA	CAPITÃO-DE-MAR-E-GUERRA	CONTRA-ALMIRANTE		VICE-ALMIRANTE	ALMIRANTE DE ESQUADRA	ALMIRANTE*
NAVY												
U.S. RANK TITLES	ENSIGN	LIEUTENANT JUNIOR GRADE		LIEUTENANT	LIEUTENANT COMMANDER	COMMANDER	CAPTAIN	REAR ADMIRAL LOWER HALF	REAR ADMIRAL UPPER HALF	VICE ADMIRAL	ADMIRAL	FLEET ADMIRAL

*In time of war, or in exceptional circumstances, a fifth star may be worn by the highest ranking officer in the army, air force, and navy.

Figure 15. Officer Ranks and Insignia, 1996

air force). Army and air force officers wear rank insignia on shoulder boards; navy officers wear them on sleeve cuffs. Each service has ten officer grades, excluding officer candidates.

Army officer grades from second lieutenant to colonel equate directly with counterparts in the United States Army, but thereafter the systems diverge. A Brazilian brigadier general (*general de brigada*) wears two stars, and the next higher rank, known as major general (*general de divisão*), wears three; their United States counterparts have only one and two stars, respectively. The next higher rank, designated by four stars, is general (*general de exército*). The marshall wears five stars, but that rank is rarely attained on active duty. There is no rank that corresponds to United States lieutenant general.

Brazil's army has strict up-or-out retirement rules, which were developed in the mid-1960s by President Castelo Branco. The internal command structure determines all promotions through the rank of colonel. The president is involved in the promotions to general and chooses one candidate from a list of three names presented to him by the High Command. Once passed over, the colonel must retire. All colonels must retire at age fifty-nine; and all four-star generals must retire at age sixty-six, or after twelve years as general.

Despite the up-or-out system, under President Sarney the army became top-heavy as generals began to occupy many positions that previously had been reserved for colonels. In 1991 there were fifteen four-star, forty three-star, and 110 two-star generals. The figure for four-star generals did not include four who were ministers in the Superior Military Court (Superior Tribunal Militar—STM). Thus, in the mid-1990s the army sought to reduce the number of active-duty generals.

Air force ranks have the same designations as those of the army through colonel, and there is also no rank corresponding to lieutenant general. Air force general officer ranks are brigadier, major brigadier, lieutenant brigadier, and air marshal; the five-star rank is seen rarely. Navy ranks correspond directly to the United States Navy counterparts, except that there is no one-star rank, equivalent to rear admiral (lower half) in the United States. The flag ranks are rear admiral, vice admiral, admiral, and fleet admiral.

The highest army enlisted rank is *subtenente*, which is the equivalent of the United States master sergeant and sergeant major ranks (see fig. 16). The navy's highest enlisted rank is *suboficial*, which is the equivalent of the United States senior

BRAZILIAN RANK	SOLDADO	NO RANK	CABO	TERCEIRO-SARGENTO		SEGUNDO-SARGENTO	PRIMEIRO-SARGENTO		SUBTENENTE			
ARMY	NO INSIGNIA	NO RANK										
U.S. RANK TITLES	BASIC PRIVATE	PRIVATE	PRIVATE 1ST CLASS	CORPORAL/SPECIALIST		SERGEANT	STAFF SERGEANT	SERGEANT 1ST CLASS	MASTER SERGEANT	FIRST SERGEANT	SERGEANT MAJOR	COMMAND SERGEANT MAJOR
BRAZILIAN RANK	SOLDADO-DE-SEGUNDA-CLASSE	SOLDADO-DE-PRIMEIRA-CLASSE	CABO	TERCEIRO-SARGENTO		SEGUNDO-SARGENTO	PRIMEIRO-SARGENTO		SUBOFICIAL			
AIR FORCE												
U.S. RANK TITLES	AIRMAN BASIC	AIRMAN	AIRMAN 1ST CLASS	SENIOR AIRMAN	SERGEANT	STAFF SERGEANT	TECHNICAL SERGEANT	MASTER SERGEANT	SENIOR MASTER SERGEANT		CHIEF MASTER SERGEANT	
BRAZILIAN RANK	RECRUTA	MARINHEIRO	CABO	TERCEIRO-SARGENTO		SEGUNDO-SARGENTO	PRIMEIRO-SARGENTO		SUBOFICIAL			
NAVY	NO INSIGNIA											
U.S. RANK TITLES	SEAMAN RECRUIT	SEAMAN APPRENTICE	SEAMAN	PETTY OFFICER 3D CLASS		PETTY OFFICER 2D CLASS	PETTY OFFICER 1ST CLASS	CHIEF PETTY OFFICER	SENIOR CHIEF PETTY OFFICER		MASTER CHIEF PETTY OFFICER	

Figure 16. Enlisted Ranks and Insignia, 1996

chief petty officer and master chief petty officer. In the air force, the top enlisted rank is also *suboficial*, which is comparable with the United States senior master sergeant and chief master sergeant.

Education and Training

For the enlisted personnel in the three services, training is a constant in their military careers. Much of their time is devoted either to retraining others or to being trained themselves in various military institutions. Like officers, NCOs who aspire to higher ranks are expected to complete advanced training and educational courses. Technical courses given by army branches, for example, are open to all who qualify, and competition is strong for the courses that are prerequisites for advancement. The navy and air force also have educational institutions to train technicians to operate modern weapons and equipment. These training courses also accept some foreign students, mostly from Latin America.

Officers are selected and promoted through a rigid system of competitive examinations, mandatory experience, and review. The army has been considered a vehicle for upward mobility. Officers were recruited traditionally from the urban middle class, mostly from white, Roman Catholic families. They were primarily from the center-south of the country. According to historian Frank D. McCann, data from the Agulhas Negras Military Academy (Academia Militar das Agulhas Negras—AMAN) show a trend in the army in recent decades to reach farther down the socioeconomic scale for officer candidates. As a result, by the early 1990s, few entrants were from the upper middle class and upper class; rather, they were from middle- and lower-middle-class and lower-class backgrounds. There was a corresponding increase in black and mulatto cadets.

An example of the importance placed on education by the military is the School for Sergeants of the Services (Escola de Sargentos das Armas—EsSA) (see fig. 17). The EsSA acquired a reputation for excellence in the post-World War II period, when the drive for professionalization of the military was particularly strong. Like officer-candidate schools, the EsSA is open to civilian applicants, as well as to lower-ranking enlisted personnel who aspire to become career NCOs. Although qualifications for admission are high and the entrance examination is difficult, competition for admission has remained strong. The year-long course of instruction is weighted toward techni-

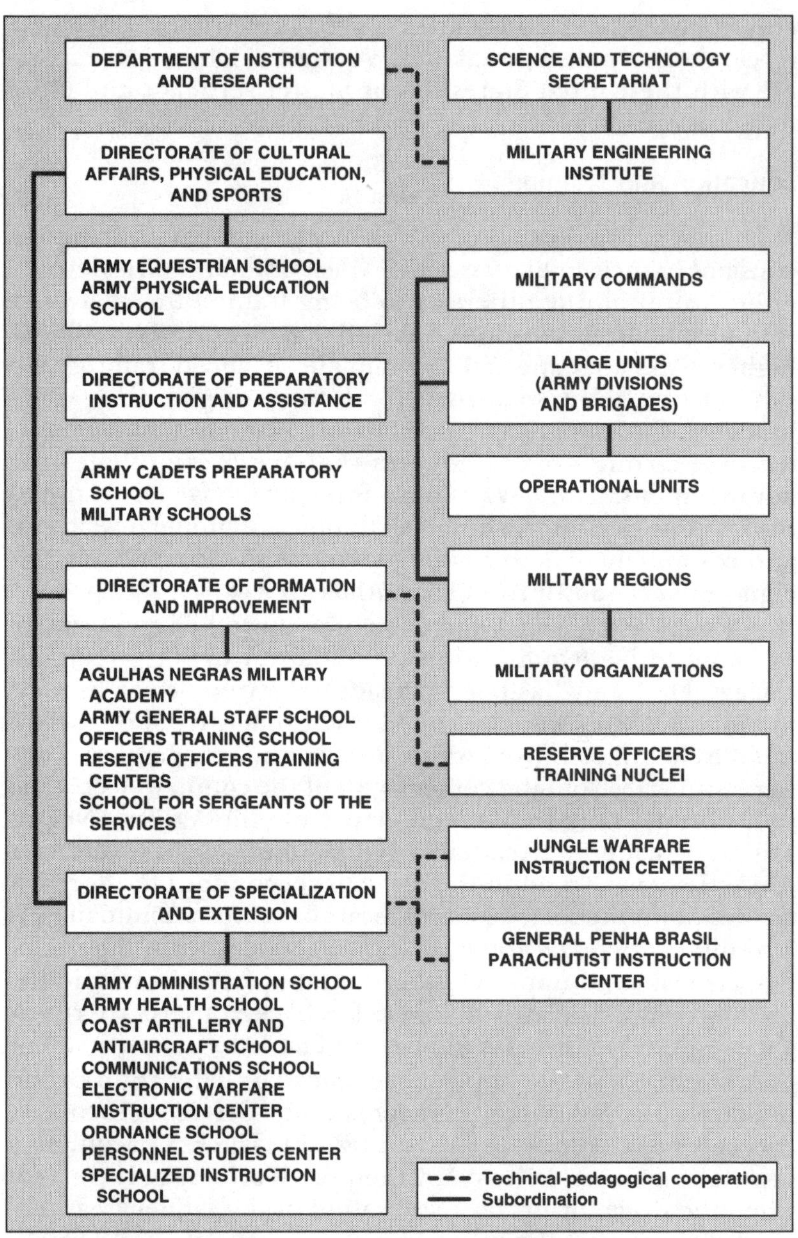

Source: Based on information from "Formação Militar: O ensino no Exército," *Revista do Exército Brasileiro* [Rio de Janeiro], 127, No. 2, April–June 1990, 71.

Figure 17. Organization of Military Instruction, 1996

cal subjects to meet the demands of advancing technology in the services. One of the side effects of professionalization of the NCO corps came after the military takeover of the government, when NCOs demanded and received the rights to vote and to run for office. The constitution of 1967 included those rights for NCOs, whereas previous constitutions had granted them only to officers.

Brazilians consider the educational systems developed for the armed forces, particularly in the army, to be better than most in the world. Many officers on active duty enter the system at the secondary level, beginning at one of the military preparatory schools that are supervised and directed by the armed forces. The navy, for example, has a preparatory school in Angra dos Reis. These officers, therefore, begin their military careers at about age fourteen. Qualified graduates of these schools and other secondary schools are permitted to take the written examination that determines who will be admitted to the AMAN, which provides a full four-year course. The navy has its counterpart at the Naval School (Escola Naval—EN) in Rio de Janeiro; the Air Force Academy (Academia da Fôrça Aérea—AFA) is in Pirassununga, São Paulo.

There has been an important change in the AMAN's recruitment policy. Now only those doing their third year of high school at the Campinas Cadet School may take the AMAN entrance examination. Those enrolled in the Brasília Military School (Colégio Militar—CM) and all others must transfer to Campinas for their third year. Also since the 1970s, an increasingly higher percentage of cadets at the AMAN are sons of military officers and NCOs.

Those who survive the competition for admission to the AMAN enroll as cadets to face a difficult four-year course leading to an army commission. Since 1964 the curriculum has stressed the national security doctrine, but more emphasis has also been placed on social science courses in addition to the engineering and science subjects that have always been given priority. Midway through the course, cadets indicate the branch to which they desire assignment (such as infantry, artillery, armor, or engineering), and during the last two years at the academy they receive intensive specialized branch training.

For the officer who aspires to high rank in the army, successful completion of each step in the educational system is essential. For those who would be generals, finishing each academic step in the highest percentile is required; high standing in graduating classes is among the most important criteria for promotion. After initial branch assignments, the system begins for company-grade officers with attendance at the Officers Training School (Escola de Aperfeiçoamento de Oficiais—EsAO), which offers a one-year Advanced Course that is required for promotion to field grade. Routinely during their careers, officers maintain contact with branch schools through correspondence or refresher courses. The army's premier engineering school is the Military Engineering Institute (Instituto Militar de Engenharia—IME), which is in Rio de Janeiro, and offers technical courses, including accredited graduate courses. The IME is the army's counterpart to the air force's ITA (Aeronautical Technology Institute).

The prize achievement for any army officer climbing the rungs of the educational system, however, is admittance to the Army General Staff School (Escola de Comando de Estado-Maior do Exército—ECEME), which is at Praia Vermelha beach in Rio de Janeiro. The ECEME's stiff entrance examination weeds out about 75 percent of the field-grade applicants, and without successful completion of the two-year course (reduced from three years in 1992), promotion to general officer rank is impossible. Appointment to faculty positions at military schools, including the ECEME, and attainment of the highly coveted general staff badge also require completion of the Command and General Staff Course.

In the navy, an officer's education begins at the Naval Academy (Escola Naval—EN) in Rio de Janeiro. The Naval Academy provides midshipmen with a four-year academic course equivalent to that given to cadets at the Military Academy. Graduation is followed by a year of shipboard training, and naval officers also attend a network of specialist schools, similar to the branch schools of the army. In addition naval officers attend courses at the Naval Research Institute (Instituto de Pesquisas Navales—IPqN), which focuses on naval science and technology and on research in advanced concepts. They also attend civilian institutions in Brazil and the Naval Postgraduate School in the United States. The Naval War College (Escola de Guerra Naval—EGN), the navy's highest educational institution, offers various programs for qualified officers, depending on rank. The EGN is located at Praia Vermelha.

The education of air force officers follows two different paths, depending on whether a cadet will become a flying officer or a technical officer. The Air Force Academy is primarily a flight training school to which students are admitted after completing one year of training at the Air Cadets' Preparatory School (Escola Preparatória de Cadetes do Ar—EPCAr) in Barbacena, Minas Gerais. Technical officers are trained at the CTA (Aerospace Technical Center) in São José dos Campos. Before attaining field grade, all officers attend the EsAO for courses in command, leadership, and administration. The next step is attendance at the Air Force Command and General Staff School (Escola de Comando e Estado-Maior da Aeronáutica—ECEMAR) at Galeão Air Base, in Rio de Janeiro, but admission requirements and the entrance examination eliminate many applicants. Among its graduates are the relatively small number of officers who will be promoted to general officer rank. Other air force schools include the Air Force University (Universidade da Fôrça Aérea), the Aeronautics Specialists School (Escola de Especialistas de Aeronáutica), the Adaptation and Instruction Center (Centro de Instrução e Adaptação), and the ITA.

Some Brazilian officers are sent to military schools abroad. Brazilian officers have attended United States basic and advanced service schools, and many senior officers have attended the command and staff schools, as well as the service war colleges, the national War College (Escola Superior de Guerra—ESG), and the Inter-American Defense College. In the 1960s and early 1970s, many Brazilian officers joined their Latin American counterparts at the School of the Americas, in Panama. During the period of strained relations between Brazil and the United States from 1977 through 1980, Brazilian students were rare on United States military bases, but in 1981 they began returning to the United States for training.

The top of the educational ladder for armed forces officers is the ESG in Rio de Janeiro. Students are selected from among colonels and generals or navy captains and admirals, as well as from among civilians who have attained high government status or prominence in varied fields, such as business and industry, education, medicine, economics, and even religion. Since 1973 a few civilian women have also been admitted to the ESG.

The ESG academic year is divided into segments of varying length, during which lectures and seminars cover national security doctrine as it pertains to all aspects of Brazilian life. Several weeks of discussions on basic doctrine are followed by a longer period devoted to national and international affairs as they affect security and development. Lecturers include senior military officers, cabinet ministers, key government officials, academic specialists, and occasionally, foreign diplomats.

The idea of establishing the ESG grew out of the close association of Brazilian and United States army officers during World War II and the experience of the FEB (Brazilian Expeditionary Force). After the war, several high-ranking FEB veterans, dissatisfied with their own staff operations and particularly with joint service staffs, requested that a United States mission be sent to Brazil to help establish a war college. A United States mission arrived in 1948, helped with the founding of the ESG in 1949, and remained in an advisory capacity until 1960. The chief of the United States mission held faculty status at the ESG.

Unlike the National War College in the United States, the ESG has placed greater emphasis on internal aspects of development and security and on civilian participation. The ESG philosophy, in which development and security are inseparably linked, influenced the military regime from 1964 to 1985.

The influence of the ESG on its alumni has been extended by the Associations of War College Graduates (Associações dos Diplomados da Escola Superior de Guerra—ADESG), which maintains contact with graduates and keeps them informed of ESG policies and events. The ADESG was a powerful force in the military governments, always keeping the ideology of the school foremost in the minds of the many graduates who had attained positions of power. The school's philosophy was incorporated into the curricula of all service schools, including the army's influential ECEME.

The ADESG holds short training courses (mini-ESG courses) each semester and recruits ESG candidates. However, the ESG is not as prestigious as in the 1970s, is shunned by most civilians, and is not as important to the military career.

Sociology of the Officer Corps

Throughout the period since 1930, officers have been drawn largely from the urban middle class. Although the middle and upper classes have always gone to great lengths to avoid having their sons serve as common soldiers, the opportunity for a free education has also attracted young men without better alternatives to the officer corps. Because of its emphasis on education, merit, and performance, the officer corps offers more opportunities for advancement than is the case in the political and socioeconomic spheres where family ties, friendships, connections, and money play a larger role.

A key factor shaping officers' attitudes has been the military educational system. However, changes in location, number, and function of the military schools, as well as changes in curricula, teaching staffs, equipment, and living and training facilities, have made it difficult to develop lasting traditions and a sense of commonality among the graduates. Moreover, the changes have deepened generational divisions.

Under Brazil's military education system, officers in a particular class form a *turma*, which is often a lifelong association. The *turmas* that officers are in at graduation are monitored carefully thereafter. Since World War II, the socialization process has involved the deliberate reinforcement of *turma* ties, including the interlinking of *turmas* by the Armed Forces General Staff. For some officers, the process may have begun in one of the twelve Military Schools (CMs) at the age of fourteen or fifteen. From the day they enter the AMAN, marching through the new cadets' gate, until they leave through the aspirants' (*aspirantes*) gate, the educational and training experience brings them together in a world that emphasizes unity and performance.

Spread over forty-two weeks each year, the AMAN curriculum blends military training with postsecondary studies. First-year cadets receive eight hours per week of military instruction, while second- and third-year cadets receive twelve and sixteen hours, respectively. The rest of their time is devoted to physical education, academic subjects, and study. In January and February, fourth-year cadets are sent to units in the states of Rio de Janeiro, São Paulo, or Minas Gerais to help train recruits for four weeks; they return to the same units for two weeks in June and a week in October to gain experience with the same soldiers further along in the training cycle.

In the first year at the AMAN, cadets are housed by *turma*, and thereafter they are quartered in multi-*turma* groups by service and branch—infantry, artillery, cavalry, engineering, quartermaster, communications, and war matériel. This early branch selection mirrors Brazilian civilian university procedure, which also forces career or professional selection at the outset. Considering that AMAN enrollment averages 1,400 and that graduating *turmas* tend to be between 300 and 400, it is relatively easy to know a large number of contemporary cadets. As the officer progresses from *aspirante* to colonel, the *turma* becomes an increasingly important identification.

The army's educational system reinforces the *turmas* and seeks to knit them together across generations. The army's personnel department tries to form the new class at the EsAO from the same AMAN *turma;* the same is true for those who pass the competitive examinations for the ECEME. In the intervening years, they have served together in units throughout Brazil and have formed close bonds with commanders and subordinates from other *turmas.*

Student officers reach the ECEME in early middle age as majors and lieutenant colonels. They usually are married and have children. However, many officers in the ECEME cannot afford to bring their families to Rio de Janeiro for the two years. Except for the few who have their own quarters, the student officers live in apartments next to the school on Praia Vermelha for the two-year course, forming tight relationships that embrace whole families. Thereafter, the ECEME relationship takes precedence, for only command school graduates move upward. The ECEME has the effect of producing midcareer male bonding, and it turns out articulate, active, and well-prepared administrators, planners, and commanders.

Within the *turma,* ties are maintained informally by birthday and promotion telegrams and by meeting for discussions, when a number of members are stationed near each other. As the *turma* members progress through their careers, they tend to expand the group's contacts. *Turmas* may attach themselves to an upwardly mobile officer, or such an officer may seek ties with a *turma* in which he has trusted men (*homens de confiança*) on whom he can call when he has openings in his command.

ECEME instructors, who are often appointed for their academic achievements and staff performance and who are upwardly mobile by definition, establish ties with the *turmas* they teach. Often when these instructors hold command positions, they turn to their former students to fill subordinate slots. For example, João Figueiredo was a student of Ernesto Geisel at the ECEME. There is a structural link between the ECEME and the AMAN in that many of the field-grade officers assigned to the AMAN are customarily ECEME graduates, and by regulation the history and geography courses must be given by officers wearing the command school insignia. In this fashion, the officer generations get knitted together, thereby contributing to institutional unity. ECEME graduates shape and execute military doctrine. They are the military elite, filling

The V–33 Frontim, an Inhaúma-class corvette, Brazilian Navy
A new U–27 Brazilian Navy training ship being inaugurated
Courtesy Brazilian Embassy, Washington

staff positions in the national and regional commands. From their ranks come all the general officers.

Officer Recruitment

Because the only entry into the regular officer corps is the AMAN, its records provide an accurate picture of the officer corps. In the decades following World War II, cadets from middle-class families increased, while those from upper-class and unskilled lower-class families declined. The total number of applicants also declined as a result of economic development diversification, which gave high school graduates more attractive options than entering the military. Increasingly, AMAN cadets came from among the graduates of the army-supported Military Schools, which sons of military personnel attended tuition free. Many of these students were sons of NCOs whose own origins were not middle class, so a form of intra-institutional, upward mobility existed.

The trend in the 1960s to recruit from civilian sources has abated. The mental, health, and physical aptitude tests excluded large numbers of civilian school graduates: in 1977 of 1,145 civilians attempting the tests, only thirty-four, or 3 percent, were admitted. In 1985 only 174, or 11 percent, of the AMAN's 1,555 cadets were graduates of civilian schools; the rest were from the army's Military School system, the Cadet Preparatory School (Escola Preparatória de Cadetes—EPC), or air force or navy secondary schools. In the early 1990s, AMAN cadets were drawn exclusively from those who had completed the EPC. By the mid-1990s, the AMAN's cadet population was about 3,000.

In the twentieth century, the officer corps has been composed predominantly of men from the Southeast and South of Brazil, where military units and greater educational opportunities have been concentrated. In 1901–02 the Northeast contributed 38 percent of students at the army's preparatory school in Realengo, whereas in 1982 it provided only 13 percent to the preparatory school in Campinas. In the same years, the Southeast supplied 40.4 percent and 77 percent, while the South gave 8.6 percent and 6.3 percent. Although São Paulo, according to Alfred Stepan and other observers, has not been noted for sending its young men into the officer corps, its contribution increased from 4.3 percent of students in 1901–02 to 33.5 percent in 1982. Regional origins of cadets at the AMAN were fairly consistent in the 1964–85 period. By far the largest contingent came from the state and city of Rio de Janeiro.

Although social theorists might be pleased with indications that the army is serving as a vehicle for social mobility, army leaders are concerned. Officers have remarked on the trend toward lower-class recruitment in the Training Center for Reserve Officers (Centro de Preparação de Oficiais da Reserva—CPOR) and the problems associated with such officers. In a 1986 interview, the former minister of army, General Leônidas Pires Gonçalves, observed that he did not want officers who would give only five or ten years to the army; he wanted individuals with a military vocation, who would stay for a full thirty-plus-year career. Many officers have expressed concern that those seeking to use the army to improve their status are not sufficiently dedicated to the institution. Indeed, some officers seek the earliest possible retirement in order to get a second job (second salary) to make ends meet.

A female officer serving in the Brazilian Army
Courtesy Brazilian Embassy, Washington

Women in the Armed Forces

Women did not participate in Brazil's armed forces until the early 1980s. The Brazilian Army became the first army in South America to accept women into the permanent and career ranks. In 1992, for example, 2,700 women out of 5,000 candidates competed for 136 positions within the Officer's Complementary Corps (Quadro Complementar de Oficiais—QCO).

To begin a career with the army, women must have completed a bachelor's degree in areas such as law, computer science, economics, or accounting. The competition is national in scope, and no applicant may be more than thirty-six years of age. Those accepted into the program study at the army's School of Administration in Salvador, beginning as second lieutenants (reserve). The School of Administration is also open to men. At the end of the one-year course, the graduate is promoted to first lieutenant in the permanent ranks. Generally, the officer is assigned to Brasília.

The navy and air force have incorporated women in their ranks, but in the Women's Reserve Corps. Although their positions are temporary in nature, with regular renewal of contracts these women can rise to officer status. The navy and air force had about 3,200 female troops and officers in 1991. In 1992 the navy promoted its first women to the rank of lieutenant commander. The three services are committed to admitting women in their military academies by the late 1990s. The FAB began accepting women at its academy in 1996, but not as pilots.

In 1991, 25,000 women were serving in state Military Police (Polícia Militar—PM) units. The largest number (2,500) were in the Military Command of the Southeast, in São Paulo. The women generally serve in health and administrative positions, and at all levels of the hierarchy.

Security Forces

Article 144 of the 1988 constitution states that the public safety function is to be exercised through the following agencies: on a national level, the Federal Police (Polícia Federal—PF), the Federal Highway Police, and the Federal Railroad Police; and on a state level, the Civil Police (Polícia Civil—PC), the Military Police, and military fire departments. In practice the Federal Railroad Police are nonexistent, and federal highways are under Federal Police control. State highways and traffic police are under state Military Police control. The Federal Police force is very small and plays only a minor role in maintaining internal security. Police forces in Brazil are controlled largely by the states. Of the two principal state police forces, the Civil Police have an investigative role, and the uniformed Military Police are responsible for maintaining public order.

Federal Police

The purpose of the Federal Police is to investigate criminal offenses of an interstate or international nature; to prevent and suppress illicit traffic in narcotics and related drugs; to perform the functions of a coast guard (enforcement only), air police, and border patrol; and to perform the functions of the judicial police. The Federal Police force is structured as a career service.

Officially, the Federal Police force is known as the Department of Federal Police (Departamento de Polícia Federal—DPF) and is headquartered in Brasília. In addition to the Federal District, DPF units are distributed throughout the states and territories. The DPF headquarters provides technical services relating to data processing, collection and dissemination of police intelligence, and scientific assistance to the Military Police. The DPF headquarters is also responsible for Brazil's input to and cooperation with the Paris-based International Criminal Police Organization (Interpol). Among the many agencies subordinate to the DPF are the National Police Academy, the National Institute of Criminology, and the National Institute of Identification, all in Brasília.

The DPF is headed by a general director, who is appointed by the president. Under the military regime, the general director was usually an active-duty army general. Since the return to civilian rule, the general director usually has been a civilian. On July 8, 1993, President Franco appointed a retired army officer to be general director of the DPF. Many within the DPF were outraged and started an unsuccessful six-day strike. They requested the removal of the appointee, in addition to better equipment and better salaries. Fifteen of twenty-four regional superintendents and 270 police chiefs resigned in protest. The strike ended when Franco promised to look into various complaints. The appointee, however, kept his position.

Indeed, the DPF force was experiencing deteriorating working conditions in the early 1990s. In 1992 it had a major budget deficit. The entire 1993 budget was spent by June of that year, and the force was threatened with eviction from all thirty-one buildings that it rented. The DPF office complained that the drug traffickers were better equipped than they were.

State Police

The State Police forces, nominally under the supervision of the state governors, are in fact associated closely with federal authorities. The State Police, by definition, are powerful forces in their states because municipal police generally do not exist (although municipal guard forces are allowed, according to Article 144 of the constitution). The city of São Paulo is a notable exception. Its mayor, Jânio Quadros (elected in 1985), created a municipal police force. All police functions not performed by DPF personnel are responsibilities of the state forces. State Police consist generally of two separate forces: the Civil Police and the Military Police, sometimes referred to as the State Militia (Polícia Militar do Estado). The Secretariat for Public Security (Secretaria de Segurança Pública—SSP), an important agency of each state government, supervises police activities. The SSPs are subordinate to the National Council of

Public Security (Conselho Nacional de Segurança Pública—Conasp).

Each state also maintains a Civil Police force, which, according to Article 144 of the constitution, is responsible for "the duties of a judicial police force and for investigating criminal offenses, except military criminal offenses." Given that there are virtually no municipal police, the state forces are stationed in populated areas and are responsible for all police functions. Cities are divided into precincts through which the Civil Police operate, using methods familiar to police squads in most other countries. Police chiefs are known as delegates (*delegados*), and the force is usually commanded by the general delegate (*delegado general*), whose rank is equal to that of the commandant of the Military Police. A *delegado* must have a law degree, and is selected by public examination. Lower-ranking officers are known as investigators. Promotion to the higher ranks of the Civil Police usually requires a law degree.

In 1997 there were 385,600 members of state Military Police organizations in Brazil. They are ultimately under army control and considered an army reserve. A Military Police Women's Company was established in Rio de Janeiro in 1982. According to Article 144 of the constitution, the function of the Military Police "is to serve as a conspicuous police force and to preserve public order." The Military Police of any state are organized as a military force and have a military-based rank structure. Training is weighted more heavily toward police matters, but counterinsurgency training is also included. Arms and equipment of state forces include machine guns and armored cars, in addition to other items generally associated with police.

Article 144 of the constitution stipulates that: "The Military Police forces and the military fire departments, and the auxiliary forces and the Army Reserve are subordinate, along with the civilian police forces, to the governors of the states, the Federal District, and the territories." Since 1969 the Ministry of Army has controlled the Military Police during periods of declared national emergency. Before 1930 these forces were under individual state control, and known as "the governors' armies." They sometimes outnumbered regular troops in many states. In the 1930s, the Federal Army took steps to reverse this situation. In 1964 most Military Police members were on the side of the successful conspirators.

The Military Police are auxiliary army forces that can be mobilized quickly to augment the armed forces in an emergency. In the past, Military Police units were often commanded by active-duty army officers, but that has occurred less frequently as professional police officers have achieved higher ranks and positions. The commandant of a state's Military Police is usually a colonel. The command is divided into police regions, which deploy police battalions and companies. Firefighting is also a Military Police function; firefighters are organized in separate battalions. State traffic police are either the State Highway Police (Polícia Rodoviária Estadual), or the Traffic Police (Polícia de Trafêgo) in the larger cities. Both are part of the state Military Police.

Elements within the Military Police in some states have been notorious for their vigilantism and death-squad activities, many against minors. On July 19, 1993, sixteen Military Police members were arrested in the state of Alagoas and accused of killing sixty-nine people. On July 23, 1993, eight street children were killed outside of Candelária Church (Igreja da Candelária), in Rio de Janeiro. The international response was one of outrage. Four military policemen, including a lieutenant, were arrested and eventually convicted. On August 30, 1993, thirty armed men wearing hoods entered Vigário Geral, a favela in Rio de Janeiro, and set fires, destroyed homes, and shot randomly, killing twenty-one people. Favela residents claimed that the assassins were Military Police avenging the killing of four of their members by drug traffickers in the shantytown. Later investigations substantiated those charges. Because of such activities, the Federal Police have been called in to investigate.

Various studies conducted in Brazil and abroad have linked the Military Police to the death squads. Social scientist Paulo Sérgio Pinheiro, of the University of São Paulo's Center for Studies of Violence (Núcleo de Estudos de Violência—NEV), stated in 1993 that "Brazil's Military Police are among the most violent police forces in the Third World." According to one explanation, vigilantism is an expression of frustration with a legal system that is perceived to be inefficient and corrupt, a court system that is backlogged, and jails that are overcrowded. Indeed there is significant popular support for death-squad activity.

Crime and Punishment

Crime

There are few reliable statistics on the incidence of crime in

Brazil. The United States Department of State, in its *Country Reports on Human Rights Practices for 1995*, concluded that "A high crime rate, a failure to apprehend most criminals, and an inept criminal justice system all contribute to public acquiescence in police brutality and killings of criminal suspects. Acts of intimidation, including death threats against witnesses, prosecutors, judges, and human rights monitors, often hindered investigation into these incidents." Intimidation seems to be most prevalent in the rural areas of the North and Northeast, where large landowners often threaten police, judges, lawyers, and reporters.

The skewed distribution of income in Brazil (one of the most unequal in the world) may be partially responsible for an endemic and increasing problem of nonpolitical crime. Since returning to civilian government, Brazil has experienced a dramatic increase in the level of crime. In 1992 Brazil's homicide rate of 37.5 per 100,000 residents surpassed that of the United States, with 22.76 per 100,000. Rio de Janeiro registered 4,253 murders in 1993, up from 3,545 in 1992. Rio de Janeiro had seventy-two murders per 100,000 residents in 1993, compared with thirty per 100,000 in New York City. Meanwhile, Rio de Janeiro State spending on security dropped from 15 percent of the state budget in 1984 to 8 percent in 1994.

As discussed earlier in this chapter, the rapid increase in the level of drug trafficking in Brazil raises numerous security issues. One has to do with the very control of national territory, as drug traffickers operate in the vast expanses of the Amazon and other regions. Indeed the threat of drug trafficking was used to justify the costly Sivam (Amazon Region Surveillance System) project. A second issue has to do with state control of entire favelas in Rio de Janeiro and possibly in other cities, where drug traffickers have a virtual monopoly over force. A third issue is that of potential corruption of the security forces, at all levels.

The shortcomings of the judicial system lead the public to tolerate vigilantism, in the form of lynching of suspected criminals. In Bahia State, for example, eighty-four documented cases of lynching occurred in 1993. In at least one case, the lynching occurred while the police watched.

Penal Code

The Penal Code has been amended considerably since its adoption in 1940 as a replacement for an older code. The

Penal Code has two sections. The first distinguishes between felonies and misdemeanors and outlines the individual citizen's responsibilities under the law. The 1988 constitution proscribes capital punishment, except in case of war. The second section defines criminal behavior more comprehensively, spelling out crimes against persons, property, custom, public welfare, and public trust. Misdemeanors are also defined.

In addition to the power arising from judicial warrant, decree laws empower the police to make arrests. These decree laws provide that any member of the public may, and the police must, arrest anyone found in flagrante delicto. The privilege of not being subject to arrest unless caught in the act of committing a crime or by judicial warrant derives from the 1891 constitution and has been included in subsequent versions. Article 5 of the 1988 constitution states: "No one shall be arrested except in the act of committing a crime or by written and substantiated order of a proper judicial authority." It states further that an arrest must be communicated immediately to a judge who, if he or she finds the arrest to be illegal, must order the release of the arrestee. In practice, there have been many violations of the constitutional guarantees, particularly in the late 1960s and early 1970s.

The process of bringing violators or suspected violators of the law to justice usually begins in one of three ways. The first and most simple occurs in cases of flagrante delicto. The second method is followed when illegal activity is uncovered during routine investigative work, after which a judge issues a warrant for the persons involved and arrests are made. The third method involves complaints from private citizens that, if borne out by evidence or otherwise deemed reasonable, result in the issuance of a warrant.

The handling of arrestees varies according to the nature of the crime, the nature of the charges, and the social status of the accused. An arrestee who holds a university degree cannot be held in a cell with those of a lower educational status, but has the right to a special cell and privileged treatment. Felonies that are punishable by imprisonment and for which the arrestee must be detained require thorough investigation followed by trial in an appropriate court. Offenses punishable by ordinary confinement of thirty days or less, or by small fines, usually are disposed of quickly at the lowest court level possible. A judge may direct that a prisoner be held in custody pending a preliminary hearing, or the judge may allow bail depending on the severity of the case. Prisoners may also be released on writs of habeas corpus.

According to law, within twenty-four hours of arrest, a prisoner must be given a copy of the complaint, signed by an authority and containing not only the details of the charge or charges but also the names of accusers and witnesses. To comply with these provisions, the police immediately must initiate an investigation; they must visit the scene of the incident, collect available evidence, interrogate witnesses, and compile a coherent account of what actually occurred. This information is presented as a police report to a judge, who then sets a date for a hearing.

The first step in the legal process is a hearing, popularly known as an instruction session, to identify the parties involved and to determine whether a punishable offense occurred. Except for misdemeanors, the instruction session is not a trial but rather a hearing at which both the prosecution and the defense are heard in presentation, rebuttal, and final argument. If the offense is a misdemeanor, the judge is permitted to turn the proceeding into a summary court and pronounce sentence. If the case involves a felony, no judgment is possible at the instruction session. If the judge believes that there is evidence of probable guilt, the accused is indicted and a trial date is set.

There are constant tensions between the Civil Police and the Military Police in most states, and sometimes these forces get involved in shootouts. The Military Police are under the jurisdiction of special police courts, which are independent of ordinary courts. The courts consist of five judges—one civilian and four ranking Military Police officials. Congressional legislation that would place the Military Police under ordinary courts remained stalled in 1995.

According to *Country Reports on Human Rights Practices for 1994*, "The Military Police courts . . . are overloaded, seldom conduct rigorous investigations of fellow officers, and rarely convict them. The separate system of state Military Police courts creates a climate of impunity for police elements involved in extrajudicial killings or abuse of prisoners, which is the single largest obstacle to altering police behavior to eliminate such abuses." Punishment remains the exception rather than the rule.

Various studies have supported the United States Department of State's conclusions. One study of police crimes against

Embraer-made 111 Bandeirante P–95 aircraft, Brazilian Air Force
P–21 Rapôso Tavares River Patrol boat, Brazilian Navy
Courtesy Brazilian Embassy, Washington

civilians in the Northeast, between 1970 and 1991, found that only 8 percent of the cases resulted in convictions. A separate study in São Paulo found that only 5 percent of similar crimes resulted in convictions.

In his first year as president, Fernando Henrique Cardoso sought to address some of the human rights violations in Brazil by unveiling a national human rights plan and creating a division within the Federal Police tasked with investigating human rights abuses. In April 1995, Cardoso established an interministerial commission to address the problem of forced labor. In addition, Cardoso sought to compensate the families of those who were killed by state-sponsored agents during military rule. Separately the federal Chamber of Deputies created a Human Rights Commission within the Chamber of Deputies.

The 1988 constitution prohibits arbitrary arrest or detention, limiting arrests to those caught in the act of committing a crime and those arrested by order of a judicial authority. Temporary detention is allowed for up to five days, under exceptional circumstances. Judges are permitted to extend that period. In practice, police sometimes detain street youths without judicial authority.

Penal Institutions

The two general categories of penal institutions are correctional and detention. The first category includes penitentiaries, houses of custody and treatment, penal and agricultural colonies, and houses of correction. Of Brazil's approximately 5,000 penal institutions, fifty-one are correctional institutions, including twenty-seven penitentiaries, six houses of custody and treatment, twelve agricultural colonies, and six houses of correction. The second category includes military prisons, houses of detention, and juvenile correctional institutions.

The Federal Prison Department (Departamento Penitenciário Nacional—Depen) is responsible for operating the penal system. Depen is subordinate to the National Council of Criminal and Prison Policy (Conselho Nacional de Política Criminal e Penitenciária—CNPCP), which is under the Ministry of Justice. Places of detention include twelve military prisons, 1,580 prisons, 2,803 jails, and five institutions for minors. The separate women's penal institutions are usually operated by nuns. Prisoners in penitentiaries are assigned to work units in maintenance shops and in light industrial plants that produce and maintain the clothing and furnishings used in the institutions.

In some minimum security agricultural colonies, inmates have their families live with them during their incarceration.

Prison conditions generally range from poor to harsh, and include overcrowding, a lack of hygiene, poor nutrition, and even instances of torture. In 1995 Brazil's overcrowded prisons held 129,169 inmates in space designed for 59,954. That compares with 23,385 inmates in 1965, nearly a sixfold increase. Often there are six to eight prisoners in a cell meant for three. The Ministry of Justice reported that thirty-three prison rebellions occurred in 1994, while attempted or successful escapes averaged almost nine per day.

Internal security in Brazil is primarily the responsibility of state governments. The Federal Police play only a minor role and are limited by their small force. The largest and most important State Police force is the Military Police, whose members are uniformed and responsible for maintaining order. They also serve as army reserves. The Civil Police constitute a much smaller force, and are responsible for investigations.

Toward the Future

As Brazil looks toward the future, it will have to adjust its national security policies to new international and domestic conditions. In the international arena, Brazil probably will continue its integration with nations in the Southern Cone of South America (especially Argentina, Paraguay, and Uruguay) and the rest of the continent, creating new linkages and reducing any perception of external threat. At the same time, there is increasing demand for Brazil's participation in operations other than war, such as peacekeeping. Although Brazil has resisted major involvement in such operations, the country's desire for greater recognition by the international community (for example, a seat on the Security Council of the United Nations) may force it to be even more fully involved.

Democratic rule in Brazil is being consolidated. The return of the armed forces to the barracks did not eliminate them from the decision-making process, but they were forced increasingly to share power with civilians. Unlike their counterparts in Argentina, the armed forces retained some of their prerogatives. And yet, as Alfred Stepan concludes: "It is clear that the attraction of military rule—its presumed stability, unity, and fixity of purpose—has been largely illusory. Even more importantly, the difficulties encountered by the highly professional army in Brazil, with its technocratic civilian allies, illustrate that there can be no apolitical solution to the problems of political development."

Major issues concerning Brazil's national security include the revision of the constitution, the role of intelligence, protection of the Amazon, and an increasing number of actors in the national security arena. There is a debate over whether a revised constitution should give the military responsibility for both external and internal defense, as was granted in the 1988 constitution. Weak political institutions in Brazil have created a vacuum in which the armed forces continue to play a somewhat influential political role. Although the military has resisted greater involvement in civic-action and counterdrug activities, it may have little choice but to increase its involvement in some of these areas. The military's dominant role in national security (especially in the nuclear, space development, and arms industries) may be eclipsed by an expanding roster of actors. It remains to be seen how the military will respond to its displacement by civilian actors in the political system.

The neoliberal economic model introduced by Fernando Henrique Cardoso poses major challenges for those involved with national security issues in Brazil. The economic model imposes severe financial constraints on all state-related sectors, including the security forces, and calls into question the size, roles, and missions of the armed forces. By late 1995, the armed forces had managed to curb any further erosion in defense expenditures, suggesting that the impact of the neoliberal economic model on the military would not be as severe as in Argentina. The economic model, with its emphasis on privatization, reduces state support for defense and other industries previously considered "strategic." The privatization of Embraer, for example, symbolized a new era of reduced state support for defense-related industries.

Although the neoliberal economic model has reduced the means for security in Brazil, the demand for security has not necessarily declined. On the external front, as seen above, participation in peacekeeping continues to strain resources. On the internal front, growing criminality, increased drug trafficking, and similar problems also strain the security apparatus. In conclusion, the need to balance means and ends in the security arena, at a time of major international and domestic changes, will challenge Brazilian policy-makers into the twenty-first century.

* * *

The rich literature on the Brazilian military is exemplified by Alfred C. Stepan's classic, *The Military in Politics,* and his *Rethinking Military Politics.* Thomas E. Skidmore provides a thorough review of the military regime in *The Politics of Military Rule in Brazil, 1964–85.* See also his *Politics in Brazil, 1930–64.* Stanley E. Hilton's works include "The Brazilian Military: Changing Strategic Perceptions and the Question of Mission" in the journal *Armed Forces and Society.* David V. Fleischer contributes excellent sections on the Brazilian military in *The Latin American Military Institution,* edited by Robert Wesson. Wendy Ann Hunter provides sophisticated analysis of the Brazilian military since 1985 in her doctoral dissertation, "Back to the Barracks? The Military in Post-Authoritarian Brazil."

Comprehensive coverage of the subject of defense in Brazil is contained in Adrian J. English's two books, *The Armed Forces of Latin America* and *Regional Defence Profile: Latin America,* both now somewhat dated. For a study of Brazil's defense industry from an economist's perspective, see Patrice Franko-Jones, *The Brazilian Defense Industry.* In the field of geostrategy, good and concise coverage is provided by Robert J. Branco's *The United States and Brazil: Opening a New Dialogue,* which takes a political-economic point of view, and by Orlando Bonturi's *Brazil and the Vital South Atlantic,* which deals mainly with Brazil's geostrategic importance.

From an historian's perspective, an overview of Brazilian military history from colonial times to the mid-1980s is Robert Ames Hayes's *The Armed Nation.* Frank D. McCann's *The Brazilian-American Alliance: 1937–1945* analyzes an important period in Brazil-United States military relations, including Brazil's participation in the Italian campaign of World War II. Hernani Donato's *Dicionário das batalhas brasileiras* provides a good synoptic outline of Brazilian military history, from the colonial period until World War II.

In the case of the individual armed forces, the history of the navy is better documented than that of the army and air force, thanks to the indefatigable efforts of the navy's own Historical Section. Apart from the navy's publications, Arthur Oscar Saldanha da Gama's two books on the Brazilian Navy in the two world wars provide excellent coverage not only of this aspect of the subject but also of the period immediately preceding each conflict. The public relations departments of the army and the navy publish monthly newsletters (*O Verde Oliva* and *No Mar,* respectively) on their respective forces, and these can be useful sources of up-to-date information on current developments. Informative dissertations done in the early 1990s include Scott D. Tollefson's "Brazilian Arms Transfers, Ballistic Missiles, and Foreign Policy" and Jorge Zaverucha's "Civil-Military Relations During the Process of Transition."

Deoclecito Lima de Siqueira's *Fronteiras: A patrulha aérea e o adeus do arco e flecha,* although dealing ostensibly only with the maritime patrol and antisubmarine warfare activities of the Brazilian Air Force during World War II, merits attention for the light it throws on the early development of Brazilian military aviation, the impact of United States military assistance, and the important role played by the Brazilian Navy and Air Force in the latter stages of the Battle of the Atlantic during World War II.

Useful magazines include *Tecnologia e Defesa* and *Flap,* which deal with general defense and aviation subjects on a bimonthly and monthly basis, respectively. Security and defense issues are discussed in *Segurança e Defesa.* The best sources of up-to-date and relatively objective information on Brazilian defense are the Spanish monthly magazine *Defensa* and the two German-published Spanish-language magazines *Tecnologia Militar* and *Iberoamericana de Tecnologias.* (For further information and complete citations, see Bibliography.)

Chapter 6. Science and Technology

A nineteenth-century wood carving made by an indigenous Brazilian tribe, from Hjalmar Stolpe, Amazon Indian Designs from Brazilian and Guianan Wood Carvings

IN THE 1970s, BRAZIL undertook a major effort to establish a strong scientific and technological base that would make the country self-sufficient economically, powerful militarily, and better able to withstand international pressures and constraints. Heavy investments were made in the country's infrastructure for the production of steel, machine tools, energy, communications, and transportation. A few high-technology projects with expected civilian spinoffs were started in atomic energy, aeronautics, and space research. Universities were reformed along the so-called United States model of graduate education and departmental organization, although they also retained strong European characteristics of separate faculties. Financing agencies for science and technology were set up and endowed generously. Several hundred graduate programs were organized, and several thousand fellowships were awarded each year for study at universities in the United States and Europe. Brazil's effort to strengthen its scientific base attracted international attention and was considered an example of how a country might move from underdevelopment, poverty, and international dependency to economic growth, better living standards, and self-reliance.

During the 1980s, however, Brazil's fast-growing economy lost momentum and entered a period of stagnation. The investments in science and technology of the previous years were insufficient to ward off the forthcoming debt crisis and uncontrolled inflation. The crisis resulted from a combination of factors, including the outmoded pattern of domestic economic growth through import-substitution industrialization (see Glossary), the increase in international interest rates and oil prices, and the uncontrolled increase in public expenditures resulting from decentralization of government and extensive patronage. Key questions for the 1990s are what went wrong, and how the capabilities created in the 1970s can best be used to regain economic growth and improve social conditions in a profoundly transformed international context.

Modern science and technology are products of Western culture and tradition and are not transposed easily to other societies and cultures. Nevertheless, the examples of Japan, the Republic of Korea (South Korea), and Taiwan show that this transposition is possible. A comparison between Brazil and the

Asian countries points to important differences in the two experiences and possible explanations for the different outcomes of their science and technology policies.

Science and technology in Western Europe, and more recently in the United States, developed along two parallel and mutually reinforcing lines: as part of a broader scientific culture, linked to education, the development of modern professions, and a growing and prestigious scientific community; and as part of the increasingly effective industrial and military establishments. The term *science* is usually applied to the first, while *technology* is used for the latter, with the assumption that they are two sides of the same coin.

The Asian countries, however, followed a strikingly different path. They introduced modern technology but little of modern science in their universities and other similar institutions; and most of their investments in technology were made in industrial firms, rather than in large, isolated governmental agencies, including the military sector. Brazil, by contrast, developed most of its scientific capabilities in universities, while investments in technology went to a few large-scale government projects under the military and to a handful of state-owned corporations.

The assumption in Brazil was that science and technology eventually would spill over from higher education and sophisticated technological projects into society as a whole. In practice, the introduction of scientific research and graduate education in universities happened at a time of rapid expansion of higher education enrollment, leading to declining quality in scholastic standards. The consequence was that, while a handful of universities and departments reached levels of quality similar to those in the developed countries, most higher education institutions, private and public, lagged behind. In technology the large military-based projects in atomic energy, space research, and aeronautics helped in the development of a few, highly qualified networks of local suppliers and partners, but they did not enhance the quality and competence of the industrial system as a whole.

In the early 1980s, the policy of technological nationalism and self-sufficiency had narrowed to the computer sector, where protective legislation tried to shield the Brazilian mini- and microcomputer industries from foreign competition. Here again, the policy allowed for the growth of local industry and a few well-qualified firms, but the effect on the productive capabilities of the economy as a whole was negative; and the inability to follow the international market in price and quality forced the policy to be discontinued.

There are other features found in the Asian countries that did not exist in Brazil and that help to explain the different outcomes of their development drives. These features include an emphasis on basic and secondary education, leading to a competent and well-educated manpower base; lower levels of social inequality, thereby strengthening the internal market for local products; a sustained effort toward international competitiveness that requires high levels of industrial efficiency and quality control; and competent and powerful public bureaucracies working in close association with a few large and well-endowed private firms.

Historical Evolution

A brief, historical sketch explains how Brazil's research and development institutions were shaped. In very broad terms, this history can be divided into seven periods, some of which overlap.

Colonial Science

"Colonial science" covered the period from the discovery of Brazil by the Portuguese in 1500 until the beginning of the nineteenth century. Contrary to what happened in many regions of Spanish America, the Portuguese did not bring their universities to the New World. Whatever existed in terms of scientific research in those years was done by European explorers, who incorporated their findings in the European collections of natural history. Economic activities in those years were restricted to the production of sugar, gold, and coffee; slave labor existed almost to the end of the nineteenth century, and work tended to be labor- and land-intensive and unskilled.

Imperial Science

The "imperial science" period lasted from 1808, when the seat of the Portuguese crown moved to Rio de Janeiro because of the Napoleonic Wars, until the beginning of the republican period in 1889. The first higher education schools—a military academy in Rio de Janeiro, two medical schools, and two law schools—were created in the first years of the "imperial science" period, and a few scientific institutions started to appear.

The search for new mineral riches and the effort to adapt agricultural products known in Europe and other regions to Brazil led to the creation of the first botanical gardens and mineralogical collections.

Brazil became independent formally in 1822 and enjoyed a period of political stability between 1840 and 1889, during the reign of Emperor Pedro II (1840–89). New scientific institutions were created in this post-independence period, such as the Museum of Natural History, the Astronomical Observatory of Rio de Janeiro, and the Imperial Geological Commission. Foreign scientists were invited to head these institutions, and Pedro II himself was very active not only in creating Brazilian institutions but also in supporting science in Europe. The kind of science being developed in Brazil in those years, although similar to that being developed in Europe, was not subject to the same standards of quality as its European model. The main economic activity in Brazil was the production of coffee for the international market, based on slave labor. After the 1850s, slave labor was replaced gradually by European and Japanese immigrants, and a domestic market for food, textiles, and other basic products started to develop.

Applied Science in Agriculture and Health

The "applied science in agriculture and health" period covers the first decades of the republic, from 1889 to the mid-1930s. As a republic, Brazil became more decentralized. The country's economic pole shifted gradually to São Paulo State—the center of coffee production and the destination of massive European immigration, second only to Buenos Aires in Latin America. Most of the new higher education and research institutions in those years were created in the city of São Paulo. They addressed the two main areas of concern in those years: public health, particularly the sanitation of the country's main port cities, Santos and Rio de Janeiro; and agricultural research. The main São Paulo State institutions from those years were the Agronomic Institute of Campinas (Instituto Agronômico de Campinas), the Biological Institute for Animal Protection (Instituto Biológico de Defesa Animal), the Butantan Institute (Instituto Butantan) for snake-venom research, the Geological Commission of São Paulo State (Comissão Geológica do Estado de São Paulo), and the Vaccine Institute (Instituto Vacinogênico). Also during this period, the scientific professions expanded and tried to find their place in the modernization of Brazilian society.

The most significant scientific institution in this period, however, was the Manguinhos Institute (Instituto Manguinhos), now the Oswaldo Cruz Foundation (Fundação Oswaldo Cruz) in Rio de Janeiro. This institute played a central role in the control of tropical diseases, such as yellow fever, malaria, and parasitic diseases. It developed important research lines in zoological fields such as helminthology (worms) and entomology (insects), and its researchers were the first to identify the full etiology of Chagas' disease. The Manguinhos Institute provided the link between Brazilian researchers and the international scientific community. Most of Brazil's leading scientists in human biology, public health, and related fields were trained there. The Manguinhos Institute's success is attributed to the ability of its leadership to combine a clear sense of short-term objectives with a commitment to the values of scholarship and research.

The Search for Alternatives

In the "search for alternatives" period in the 1930s, political centralization and the first attempt to provide Brazil with modern administrative, military, and educational institutions took place. The main initiatives included the University of São Paulo (Universidade de São Paulo—USP), which was created in 1934 as the country's first university. Its nucleus was a School of Philosophy, Sciences, and Letters, with professors coming from France, Italy, Germany, and other European countries. The USP also brought together several research and higher education institutions in the state, such as the School of Medicine (Faculdade de Medicina), the Polytechnical School (Escola Politécnica), and the School of Law (Faculdade de Direito). (The Polytechnical School includes civil, electrical, mechanical, mining, metallurgical, naval and oceanographic, and chemical engineering departments.) The USP became and still is Brazil's main academic and research institution. Along the same pattern, a national university, the University of Brazil (Universidade do Brasil), was created in Rio de Janeiro in 1939. Today, it is called the Federal University of Rio de Janeiro (Universidade Federal do Rio de Janeiro—UFRJ). A third university created in Rio de Janeiro in 1935, the University of the Federal District (Universidade do Distrito Federal), was closed down by the federal government a few years later.

This model of institutional modernization was also applied to the rest of the country. Except for the USP and a few sectors at the UFRJ, however, the philosophy schools (Faculdades de Filosofia) functioned as teacher colleges and conducted little or no research. The traditional professional schools remained independent and dedicated to their traditional degree-granting activities.

Deep conceptual differences between the USP and the University of Brazil help to explain the different institutional development. The São Paulo elites created the USP as part of an emerging tradition of cultural enlightenment. By contrast, the University of Brazil was the product of a centralized and authoritarian government, under the direct influence of the more conservative sectors of the Roman Catholic Church.

The first institutions for technological research were created in the 1930s. They included the National Institute of Technology (Instituto Nacional de Tecnologia—INT) in Rio de Janeiro and the Institute for Technological Research (Instituto de Pesquisas Tecnológicas—IPT) in São Paulo. They were supposed to provide technical support to an emerging national industry. The INT was involved in the first studies on the use of sugar cane alcohol for engine combustion and coal from Santa Catarina State for the steel industry.

Economic nationalism became dominant by the end of the 1930s. The 1934 Code of Mines declared as government property all resources under the soil; the first steel plant, the National Iron and Steel Company (Companhia Siderúrgica Nacional—CSN), was established in Volta Redonda in 1942, with United States support, and was linked to Brazil's entry into World War II; oil exploration became a state monopoly, and restrictions were placed on foreign and national private interests.

As the federal administration became more centralized and bureaucratized, some of its research institutions suffered. The Oswaldo Cruz Foundation went through a crisis for lack of autonomy and support. The INT gradually turned into an agency that merely provided training courses for the public bureaucracy.

Science and Technology as Modernization, 1945–64

After World War II, it was generally believed that Brazil was becoming a modern, industrial society, and science and technology were to be important components of this trend. Two

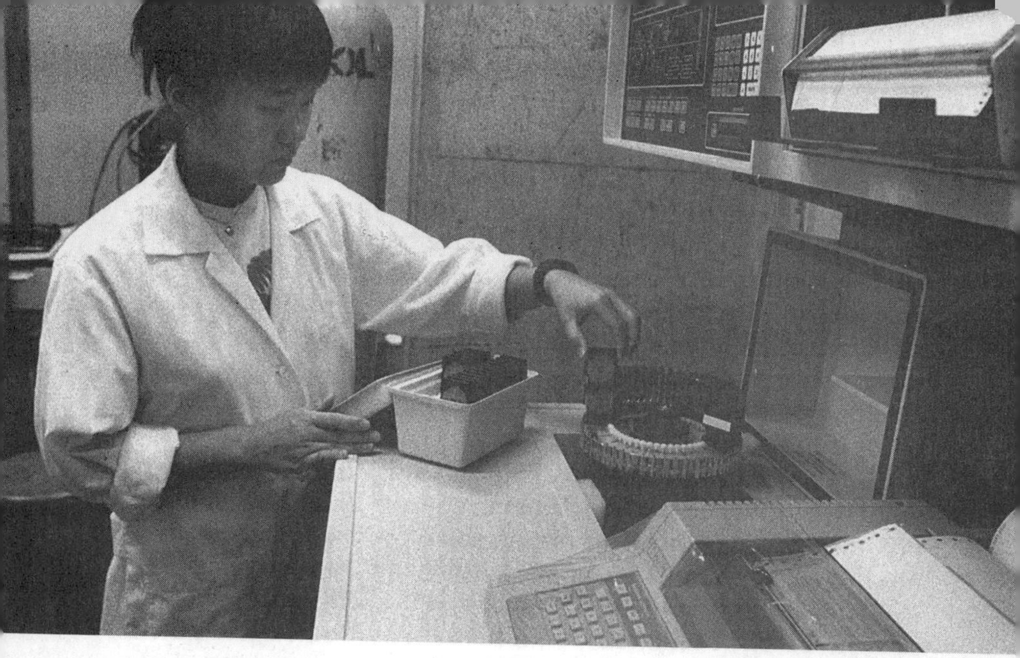

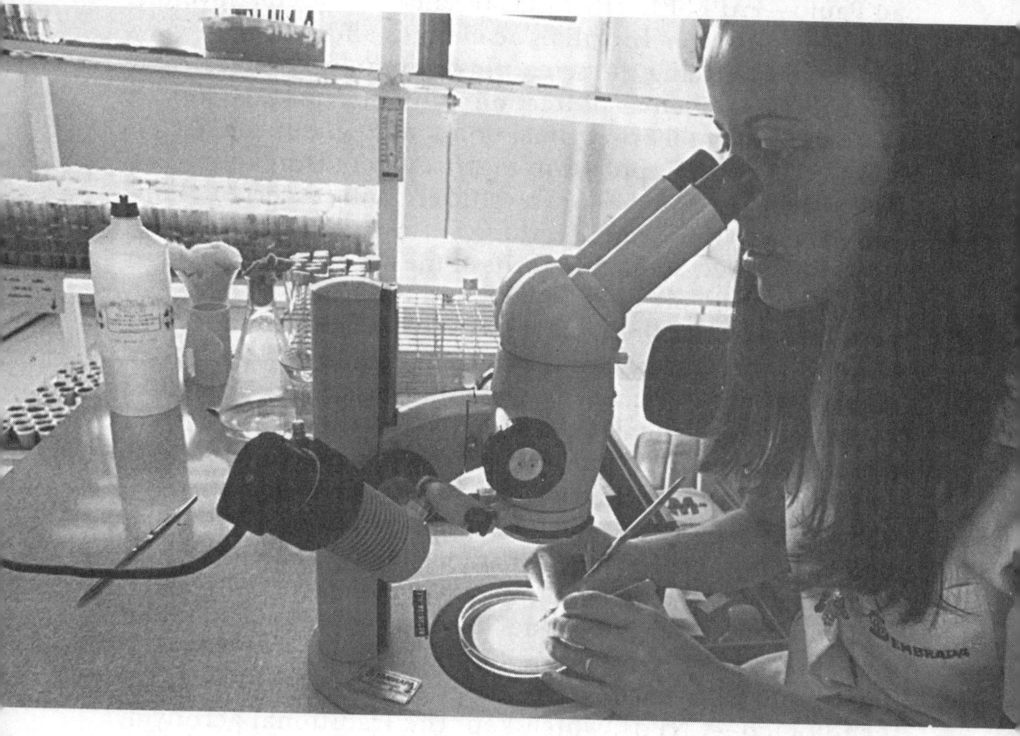

A pharmaceutical student prepares to place samples into an amino acid analyzer.
A lab technician trims plant tissue from cassava plants in order to reproduce disease-free clones of these plants in test tubes.
Courtesy Inter-American Development Bank, Washington.

diverging patterns were already taking shape in the development of science, technology, and higher education in Brazil, roughly corresponding to the broad cleavage in Brazilian society between the economic and political centers of São Paulo and Rio de Janeiro. The first was more entrepreneurial and associative, with strong civilian institutions. The second was more hierarchical, relying on the civilian and military bureaucracies, and was linked to the country's poorer regions through patronage.

São Paulo already had the country's main university, and after World War II the Southeast (Sudeste) Region's scientists organized two leading institutions, the Brazilian Society for Scientific Development (Sociedade Brasileira para o Progresso da Ciência—SBPC) and the São Paulo State Federation to Support Research (Fundação de Amparo à Pesquisa do Estado de São Paulo—FAPESP). The SBPC became Brazil's main voluntary association for Brazilian academics and has been very influential in voicing the scientific community's concerns on national issues, such as protection of intellectual freedom in the years of the military regime, promotion of a national computer industry, and opposition to strict patent legislation. The FAPESP was organized as a very efficient and respected grant-giving agency, which ran according to strict peer-review procedures. It received about 1 percent of the state tax revenues. In addition to the USP, FAPESP, IPT, and SBPC, the state of São Paulo had sixteen other research institutes linked to different branches of the state administration. It also had another research-oriented university, the Campinas State University (Universidade Estadual de Campinas—Unicamp), and a statewide university devoted to professional education, São Paulo State University (Universidade Estadual Paulista—Unesp).

The national government, meanwhile, embarked on its first attempt to muster the power of atomic energy. This effort was made through the combined creation of the National Research Council (Conselho Nacional de Pesquisas—CNPq), now called the National Council for Scientific and Technological Development (Conselho Nacional de Desenvolvimento Científico e Tecnológico—CNPq), which kept the traditional acronym, CNPq; the National Nuclear Energy Commission (Comissão Nacional de Energia Nuclear—CNEN); and the Brazilian Center for Physics Research (Centro Brasileiro de Pesquisas Físicas—CBPF). Together, these three institutions were supposed to develop the full cycle from the production of nuclear fuel to its application in energy generation, and eventually the technology of atomic weaponry. Beleaguered by limited resources, lack of qualified leadership, and international pressures, the atomic energy project was effectively abandoned at the end of the second Getúlio Dorneles Vargas government (president, 1930–45, 1951–54) in 1954. The CNPq was turned into a small, underfunded, grant-giving agency. After its reorganization in the 1970s, the CNPq absorbed the CBPF, by then an academic research center, as one of its institutes (see Nuclear Programs, this ch.).

One of the most successful institutes of the 1950s, the Aeronautical Technology Institute (Instituto Tecnológico de Aeronáutica—ITA), was placed in the city of São José dos Campos, between Rio de Janeiro and São Paulo. The Brazilian Air Force (Fôrça Aérea Brasileira—FAB) organized the ITA with the support of the United States government, working in close association with the Massachusetts Institute of Technology. However, the ITA was not restricted to military students and subjects; it became Brazil's leading engineering school, recruiting students from all over the country. ITA graduates went on to occupy central positions in Brazil's industries, research institutions, and main science and technology agencies. The ITA's research branch, the Aerospace Technical Center (Centro Técnico Aeroespacial—CTA), became the basis for Brazil's airplane industry and made São José dos Campos the hub of Brazil's most sophisticated technological industries. What was unique about the ITA was this combination of strong government support, qualified institutional leadership, and civilian orientation. The latter gave it the ability to tap some of the best talent among the country's researchers and students. As a result of the military governments after 1964, the ITA gradually lost its autonomy and civilian character and entered a period of decline.

The Great Leap Forward, 1968–79

In the so-called "great leap forward" period, the Brazilian military government, which took power in 1964, embarked on its ambitious program of scientific and technological self-sufficiency. In the first years, the military government entered into conflict with a significant part of the country's scientific leadership, because of the latter's real or assumed socialist stands. The two sides later reconciled, however, because of their shared nationalism and concern with social and economic development. The move toward scientific self-sufficiency reached its climax during Ernesto Geisel's presidency (1974–79), which scientist Reinaldo Guimarães describes as a period of "enlightened despotism." The main initiatives in this period included the university reform in 1969 that introduced graduate education and organized the universities into departments and institutes.

In the "great leap forward" period, science and technology became linked institutionally to the economic authorities. The federal government created support agencies and programs under a newly created Planning Ministry or the Secretariat of Planning and Coordination of the Presidency of the Republic (Secretaria de Planejamento e Coordenação da Presidência da República—Seplan). The National Bank for Economic and Social Development (Banco Nacional de Desenvolvimento Econômico e Social—BNDES), Brazil's main investment bank, created a special fund for science and technology, which led to a new agency, the Funding Authority for Studies and Projects (Financiadora de Estudos e Projetos—Finep). The Finep was organized as a private corporation under ministerial supervision and was responsible for the administration of the National Fund for Scientific and Technological Development (Fundo Nacional de Desenvolvimento Científico e Tecnológico—FNDCT), which has provided institutional grants for technological projects for research and development in public and private nonprofit institutions. The FNDCT's annual budget in the mid-1970s was around US$200 million but was reduced gradually to about US$40 million by the early 1990s.

The 1968–79 period also saw the establishment of two large research and graduate institutions in science and technology: the Coordinating Board of Postgraduate Programs in Engineering (Coordenação dos Programas de Pós-Graduação em Engenharia—Coppe) at both the UFRJ and Unicamp. Both institutions were oriented toward research and training in advanced engineering (chemical, mechanical, biomedical, electric, metallurgical, nuclear, and naval) and in new technologies derived from recent advances in solid-state physics and lasers. Other institutions also benefited, such as the Technology Center (Centro de Tecnologia) of the Pontifical Catholic University of Rio de Janeiro (Pontifícia Universidade Católica do Rio de Janeiro—PUC-RJ), the Polytechnical School at the USP, and the ITA. The PUC is Brazil's only private university that produces a significant amount of scientific research.

The Brazilian Air Force's AMX ground-attack fighter, made by Brazilian Aeronautics Company (Empresa Brasileira Aeronáutica—Embraer)
Courtesy Embraer

Initiatives in the 1968–79 period also included the cooperation agreement with the Federal Republic of Germany (West Germany) for the development of nuclear technology, followed by the development of the so-called Parallel Program (Programa Paralelo), a secret program for nuclear weapons development; the beginning of the space program, with the development of a satellite launch vehicle and a satellite; the development of a subsonic military jet aircraft (the AMX project, in association with Italy); the adoption of a market protection policy for the computer industry; and the writing of three successive national plans for scientific and technological development. Another initiative included the creation of research and development centers within the country's main state-owned corporations, such as the Brazilian Petroleum Corporation (Petróleo Brasileiro—Petrobrás), Brazilian Telecommunications, Inc. (Telecomuniçòes Brasileiras S.A.—Telebrás), and the Brazilian Electric Power Company, Inc. (Centrais Elétricas Brasileiras S.A.—Eletrobrás). In addition, a national system for agricultural research was reorganized and strengthened through the Brazilian Agriculture and Livestock Research Enterprise (Empresa Brasileira de Pesquisa Agropecuária—Embrapa), under the Ministry of Agriculture.

On the positive side, these initiatives were characterized by abundant funding resources, quick-decision mechanisms, and some relative flexibility in the use of the grants. Even for large projects, resources were provided whenever possible to the group leader, in a deliberate bypass of the traditional, cumbersome, and ineffectual procedures of public administration. On the other hand, the absence of well-defined peer-review procedures, particularly at Finep, allowed for the support of less than worthy groups and projects, which became permanent clients of FNDCT resources.

More serious was the lack of consistency that existed between science and technology policies, oriented toward self-sufficiency and a strong presence of the public sector, and the economic policies of the same period, which opened Brazil to multinational corporations and the acquisition of ready-made, turnkey technologies from abroad. The result was that the research seldom benefited the productive sector, except in three main areas: in agriculture, mostly through the development of new varieties of sugar cane, corn, soybeans, coffee, fruits, and other crops; in a few sectors where government research and development centers—such as the Army Technology Center (Centro Tecnológico do Exército—CTEx), the CTA, and those of Eletrobrás, Petrobrás, and Telebrás—linked with industry and established technical standards for communications equipment and other products; and in the area of computing, where the government tried to link research and production by Brazilian private firms under the umbrella of market protection.

Science and Technology as a Pressure Group, 1979–90

In the "science and technology as a pressure group" period, which started at the beginning of the last military presidency of João Baptista de Oliveira Figueiredo (1979–85) and included the first civilian government of José Sarney (1985–90), the picture changed completely. The Planning and Economy ministries were unified, and the science and technology sector lost its privileged access to the higher echelons; no resources were available to correspond to the increasing expectations of the previous years; scientists, engineers, and public employees in the science and technology sector became one among many different interest groups competing for resources from a government concerned only with its political survival and the administration of a mounting external debt and inflation.

The Computer Industry Policy

The "informatics" policy started in the late 1960s and early 1970s as an effort to develop a Brazilian personal computer (with the USP's Engineering School working on hardware and the PUC-RJ on software, and with support from the navy and the Finep). Technology was to be transferred to a state-owned corporation, Brazilian Computers and Systems (Computadores e Sistemas Brasileiros—Cobra), and to private firms owned by Brazilians. With the development of personal computers, a policy was devised that restricted this new market to Brazilian firms but allowed for the continuous presence of multinational corporations, particularly in the area of mainframe computers. Congress approved the policy in 1985. The central tenet of the legislation was the strict ban, for seven years, on the import of microcomputers and on the establishment of foreign firms producing microcomputers and software. The Computer Technology Center (Fundação Centro Tecnológico para Informática—CTI) was established in 1983 to encourage the development of scientific and technological research in the computer sector. A national office for the computer industry, the Special Secretariat for Informatics (Secretaria Especial de Informática—SEI), was established in Brasília. It had the power to control the import of equipment and components, to set targets for increasing Brazilian participation in joint ventures with foreign firms working in Brazil, and to decide about government purchases of computer equipment.

The policy was conceived not only to limit the small computer market to national firms but also to stimulate the local production of products and components, which was part of a broader policy of import substitution. Both Brazilian and multinational firms were required to increase the share of domestic content in their products. This requirement boosted the development of local competence but also led to higher costs and a loss of competitiveness, given the lack of scale in the local market. This strategy of mandatory high percentages of local components in all items, including disk drives and printers, contrasts with that of South Korea, for example, which concentrated on a few components, such as monitors, where the local industry could compete internationally in terms of quality and price.

To protect the local industry, the government introduced mechanisms to prohibit the transfer of technologies that were similar to ones being developed or that already had been developed by Brazilian companies. This policy was applied to both hardware and software, and Brazilian firms developed emulators of MS-DOS and Unix computer operating systems for the local industry. As a result, companies that could bypass this legislation and get the original software were in a better position than those that remained attached to much less advanced local products.

This protectionist policy was very controversial and drew strong opposition from the United States government and multinational firms, in the name of free trade. It also drew opposition from Brazilian firms and corporations that thought their access to high technology had been curtailed. Supporters argued that the policy generated technological competence in Brazilian firms and created employment for researchers and engineers at little cost to industry or Brazil. Detractors argued that the whole industrial sector suffered from restrictions on access to state-of-the-art electronics and, more generally, that Brazil was delayed in entering the microcomputer culture. In practice, the civilian government under Sarney did not invest in research and development for the computer industry, and a large part of that industry remained limited to the assemblage of microcomputers with imported components. A few firms have specialized in some market niches (such as bank automation) and, after 1992, entered into associations with multinational corporations for the development and distribution of international microcomputer brands in Brazil.

Science for Industrial Competitiveness

The World Bank (see Glossary) approved a US$72 million sector loan in 1985 (with another US$107 million to be provided by the Brazilian government) to increase the country's competence in selected areas of science and technology. The underlying assumption had been that the government would maintain the historical levels of expenditures for the sector as a whole. This expectation was not fulfilled, and the World Bank's program, called the Program in Support of Scientific and Technological Development (Programa de Apoio ao Desenvolvimento Científico e Tecnológico—PADCT), became one of the few sources of support for scientific research, although it did not contribute directly to an improvement in Brazil's industrial competitiveness.

The brief Fernando Collor de Mello presidency (1990–92) called for making science and technology more directly relevant to industrial effectiveness, in an economy that was being deregulated and subjected to international competition. It was also a period of high inflation, economic depression, and political crisis. The main initiatives and proposals, some dating from the previous years, included the continuation of the World Bank sector loan to science and technology; the transformation of Finep into an agency concerned almost exclusively with loans for the development of industrial technology; a sharp reduction in the FNDCT's budget; the end of market protection for the Brazilian computer industry; major reductions in the resources available to the CNPq, which became restricted to the administration of fellowships; proposals to create strong links between universities and the productive sector through "technological parks" and other mechanisms of university-industry cooperation; the closing down, phasing out, or revising of large military projects, such as the Parallel Program and the space program; and the privatization of most publicly owned corporations.

Several measures related to the opening of Brazil's economy were carried out and are still in effect. However, little progress was made in turning the science and technology sector in new directions. Economic depression limited industrial investments, while inflation channeled available resources to the financial markets. The scientific community viewed the Collor government with distrust.

The Itamar Franco government (1992–94), which succeeded Collor de Mello after his impeachment on corruption charges, was unable to overcome the country's runaway inflation until mid-1994 and did not have a chance to devise a science and technology policy. The minister of science and technology, José Israel Vargas, an internationally respected physicist with considerable credibility in Brazil, worked to keep the issues of science and technology high on the government agenda. He sought to pass legislation that would create incentives for technology investments in industry and that would revive Brazil's space program. In addition, he was committed to ensuring the bare minimum of resources for the daily activities of the government's main science and technology agencies. No long-term policy seemed to exist, however.

Administration of Science and Technology

The Ministry of Science and Technology

The central agency for science and technology in Brazil is the Ministry of Science and Technology, which includes the CNPq and Finep. This ministry also has direct supervision over the National Institute of Space Research (Instituto Nacional de Pesquisas Espaciais—INPE), the National Institute of Amazon Region Research (Instituto Nacional de Pesquisas da Amazônia—INPA), and the National Institute of Technology (Instituto Nacional de Tecnologia—INT). The ministry is also responsible for the Secretariat for Computer and Automation Policy (Secretaria de Política de Informática e Automação—SPIA), which is the successor of the SEI (see fig. 18).

The Ministry of Science and Technology, which the Sarney government created in March 1985, was headed initially by a person associated with the nationalist ideologies of the past. Although the new minister was able to raise the budget for the science and technology sector, he remained isolated within the government and had no influence on policy making for the economy. In addition, inflation brought the science and technology budget to extremely low levels.

With the new ministry, the science and technology agencies increased in size but lost some of their former independence and flexibility, and they became more susceptible to patronage politics. Most of the resources of the CNPq were channeled to fellowship programs that had no clear procedures for quality control and no mechanisms to make the fellows active in the country's science and technology institutions. New groups competed for resources and control of the country's agencies of science, technology, and higher education. These groups included political parties, unionized university professors and employees, scientific societies, and special interest groups within the scientific and technological community. The SBPC (Brazilian Society for Scientific Development) shed its image as a semi-autonomous association of scientists to become an active lobbyist for more public resources and the protection of national technology from international competition.

National Council for Scientific and Technological Development

The National Council for Scientific and Technological Development (Conselho Nacional de Desenvolvimento Científico e Tecológico—CNPq) is a complex structure with about 2,500 employees. It runs an extensive program of fellowships and research grants; several special programs, such as the National Program for Human Resource Training for Technological Development (Programa Nacional de Capacitação de Recursos Humanos para o Desenvolvimento Tecnológico—RHAE) and the Program for Competitiveness and Technological Diffusion (Programa de Apoio à Competividade e Difusão Tecnológica—PCDT); and integrated programs, such as those on endemic diseases, virology, genetics, agricultural development, and humid and semiarid tropical regions. Fellowships and research grants are provided under peer-review evaluations, whereas most of the resources for the special programs, when available, are managed directly by the administration.

The CNPq also has several research institutes of its own: those in Rio de Janeiro include the Brazilian Center for Physics Research (Centro Brasileiro de Pesquisas Físicas—CBPF), the Mineral Technology Center (Centro de Tecnologia Mineral—Cetem), the Institute of Pure and Applied Mathematics (Instituto de Matemática Pura e Aplicada—IMPA), the National Observatory (Observatório Nacional—ON), the Museum of Astronomy and Related Sciences (Museu de Astronomia e Ciências Afins—MAST), and the National Computer Science Laboratory (Laboratório Nacional de Computação Científica—LNCC). Others include the Brazilian Institute of Scientific and Technological Information (Instituto Brasileiro de Informação em Ciência e Tecnologia—IBICT) in Brasília, the National Astrophysics Laboratory (Laboratório Nacional de Astrofísica—LNA) in Itajuba (Minas Gerais), the Emílio Goeldi Museum of Pará (Museu Paraense Emílio Goeldi—MPEG) in Belém, and the National Syncrotron Light Laboratory (Laboratório Nacional de Luz Síncrotron—LNLS) in Campinas. These institutes vary in quality and size, and many of them have their own graduate education programs. The minister of science and technology appoints the president and directors of the CNPq, and a twenty-member Deliberative Council (Conselho Deliberativo), which includes numerous scientists, supervises it.

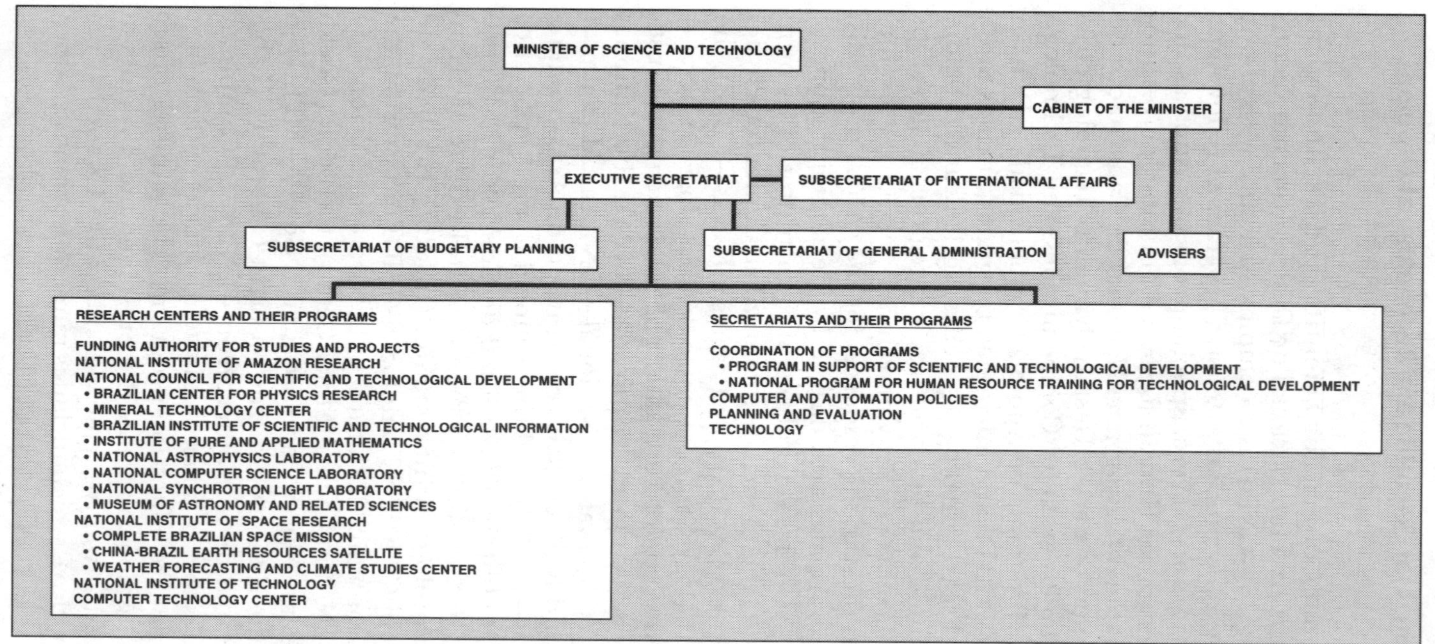

Source: Based on information from *Ministério da Ciência e Tecnologia: Relatório de atividades, 1992–94*, Brasília, 1994, 65.

Figure 18. Organization of the Ministry of Science and Technology, 1996

The activities of the CNPq are divided formally into fellowships and grants, research, information, and dissemination activities. The CNPq spent about US$350 million in all its activities in 1990, and US$371 million in 1991. About 70 percent of the total is used for development, 10 percent for research, and 20 percent for administrative and other expenses. Eighty-one percent of development funds go to fellowships. Most of the fellowships are given to a small number of undergraduate and M.A.-degree students, reflecting the limited demand that exists for advanced degrees (see table 32, Appendix).

The Funding Authority for Studies and Projects

The second main agency in the Ministry of Science and Technology is the Funding Authority for Studies and Projects (Financiadora de Estudos e Projetos—Finep). The minister of science and technology appoints the president and directors of the Finep, without any external peer review. The Finep traditionally has worked along two different lines: it administers the FNDCT, and it serves as a specialized bank that makes loans to the private sector for technological development and innovation. In practice, the Finep's activity in the early 1990s was limited mostly to loan contracts for research and development projects in industry. However, because of the economic recession and market interest rates, there were few takers (see table 33, Appendix).

The Coordination of High-Level Personnel Training

Another important agency involved in science and technology is the Council for Advanced Professional Training (Fundação Coordenação de Aperfeiçoamento de Pessoal de Nível Superior—CAPES) at the Ministry of Education. The CAPES provides fellowships for graduate education in Brazil and abroad and for several years has run a peer-reviewed evaluation system for the country's graduate programs. The fellowship program is divided into two parts: one responds to individual applications and the other to the Faculty Improvement Integrated Program (Programa Integrado de Capacitação de Docentes—PICD) (see table 34, Appendix). The CAPES also has administered some FNDCT grants.

Other Activities by the Federal Government

Together, the CNPq, CAPES, and Finep are responsible for

the administration of the World Bank-supported PADCT program, under the coordination of the Ministry of Sciene and Technology. Generally, the agencies under the ministry do not handle more than a third of the country's total science and technology federal budget, with another third going to projects in the military sector (see table 35, Appendix). Another major agency is the Brazilian Agriculture and Livestock Research Enterprise (Embrapa), which has a budget equivalent to that of the CNPq. The traditional Oswaldo Cruz Foundation in Rio de Janeiro remains an important research institution in public health and related fields.

Science and Technology in the States

State budgets allotted about US$300 million for science and technology in 1991, with the state of São Paulo accounting for 40 percent of spending, and the states of Minas Gerais, Rio de Janeiro, and Bahia accounting for 35 percent. After 1988 most Brazilian states established in their constitutions a fixed percentage of their budgets to be given to the state-level science and technology sector. They followed the example of São Paulo, which provides the FAPESP (São Paulo State Federation to Support Research) with about 1 percent of state tax revenues (this amounted to about US$60 million in 1991). However, São Paulo is the only state where the constitutional rule is followed strictly.

The São Paulo Science and Technology System

The FAPESP is just one part of a large science, technology, and higher education sector run by the state of São Paulo that includes three public universities and several research institutes. These activities are coordinated by the state Secretariat for Science, Technology, and Economic Development (Secretaria de Ciência, Tecnologia e Desenvolvimento Econômico—SCTDE). However, most of the institutions under the SCTDE—the three universities, the FAPESP, and the IPT (Institute for Technological Research)—are autonomous. The Institute for Nuclear and Energy Research (Instituto de Pesquisas Energéticas e Nucleares—IPEN), located on the USP campus, is also linked formally to the SCTDE but in practice is run by the federal government. The SCTDE also runs the State Foundation for Scientific and Technological Development (Fundo Estadual de Desenvolvimento Científico e Tecnológico—Funcet), which provides loans to the private sector, cooperatives, and associations, in collaboration with the São Paulo State Bank (Banco do Estado de São Paulo—Banespa). Funcet has a budget of about US$20 million and a grant program through its Department of Science and Technology (Departamento de Ciência e Tecnologia—DCET) (see table 36, Appendix).

Research and Development

A comparison between science in Brazil and science in other Latin American countries and in Israel helps to place Brazilian scientific research in a broader context. According to a 1994 study prepared by scientist Thomas S. Shott, Brazil performs less than 1 percent of the scientific research in the world. No Brazilian scientist was mentioned in a survey that cited nearly 3,000 scientists as principal contributors or as influential. Brazilian research amounted to a little less than half the research performed in Latin America and about a third of that performed in Israel, where scientific performance is high.

In economy and population, Brazil is roughly half the size of the rest of Latin America. However, Brazil is a whole order of magnitude larger than Israel in terms of the economy and even more in terms of population, and yet far less research is performed in Brazil than in Israel. Brazilian specialization emphasizes the disciplines of physics, biology, and mathematics. Brazilian research focuses on biomedicine and earth and space science and de-emphasizes clinical medicine and chemistry. Within medicine, however, tropical medicine and parasitology are fields of strong specialization in Brazil, as in the rest of Latin America. Brazilian growth has been highest in technological science, especially in computing.

Brazilian scientists are tied to colleagues, both Brazilian and foreign, who have influenced their research and who are collaborators or competitors in research. Cooperation and collaboration between Brazilian researchers and the scientific establishment in the rest of Latin America are also higher. Additional factors promoting scientific ties are social and cultural linkages between Brazil and the rest of Latin America.

Although regional integration is noticeable, it is overshadowed by the influence of scientific centers in North America and Western Europe. Brazilian scientists value their visits to these centers. The involvement of Brazilian scientists with the centers, however, has been slightly less than the participation of other Latin American scientists and much less than that of Israeli scientists.

University Research and Graduate Education

Most of Brazil's research and development activities take place in its main public universities. There are about 1.5 million higher education students, around 10 percent of the age cohort, distributed in federal (21.1 percent), state (12.7 percent), municipal (5.1 percent), and private institutions (61.1 percent). There are about 15,000 active scientists and researchers in Brazil, and about 1,000 graduate programs in most fields of knowledge.

Research in universities usually is associated with graduate education, although relatively few university professors hold a doctoral degree. These professors are concentrated in the São Paulo State system, which is responsible for more than 50 percent of the doctoral degrees granted, and in some of the best federal universities (see table 37, Appendix).

Most academics in public institutions have full-time contracts, and their salaries are equivalent to those obtained in private schools. The assumption is that they should combine teaching with research, but in practice few have the necessary training for research work. The universities provide physical space and salaries for research, but little else; the researcher, or the research group, has to seek out support money and research grants. In most cases, the researcher applies for grants from the CNPq and FAPESP or from some private foundation in Brazil or abroad. Equipment and library holdings in the universities usually are obtained through special grants and projects from Finep or from occasional programs run by the government, in some cases with resources from the World Bank or the Inter-American Development Bank (see Glossary). Researchers can also enter into cooperative research projects with public and private corporations, or with the government itself. Unicamp (Campinas State University), for instance, had an important cooperative agreement with Telebrás, Brazil's communications holding; and the Coppe (Coordinating Board of Postgraduate Programs in Engineering) has worked with Petrobrás in the development of technologies for deep-sea oil drilling. The Federal University of Santa Catarina is well known for its Institute of Mechanical Engineering (Instituto de Engenharia Mecánica—IEM) and has a large portfolio of research and development contracts with private institutions. The more entrepreneurial and competent departments and institutes obtain resources that enable them to work according to high standards of efficiency. Others, in the same institution, may not have the means to purchase a computer or even to renew journal subscriptions.

Research in State-Owned Corporations

About 10 percent of the public investments in research and development in Brazil are made by a small group of state-owned corporations and holdings in the fields of telecommunications, oil, electric energy, mining, metallurgy, and aeronautics. Several of these corporations have created their own research and development centers, the best known being Petrobrás's Research and Development Center (Centro de Pesquisa e Desenvolvimento—Cenpes), Telebrás's Research and Development Center (Centro de Pesquisa e Desenvolvimento—CPqD), Eletrobrás's Electric Power Research Center (Centro de Pesquisas de Energia Elétrica—Cepel), the Technology Center (Centro de Tecnologia) of the Rio Dôce Valley Company (Companhia Vale do Rio Dôce—CVRD), and the CTA (Aerospace Technical Center), associated with the Brazilian Aeronautics Company (Empresa Brasileira Aeronáutica—Embraer), the state-owned aircraft manufacturer.

At their best, these research centers are linked with the companies' suppliers and are responsible for establishing standards of quality and providing technical know-how. They also communicate with other research and development groups in government and universities in order to exchange ideas and information and bolster professional competence. These research centers played important roles in the 1970s and early 1980s. They saved foreign currency that would have been spent on technical assistance and royalties, improved their companies' operational capabilities, better utilized Brazil's natural resources, strengthened the private sector's competence, and provided resources to universities through research contracts and programs of technical assistance and training.

The oldest and largest of these centers is Cenpes, which, under different names, has existed since the creation of Petrobrás in the mid-1950s. Cenpes's most significant achievement was the development of state-of-the-art technologies for deep-sea oil drilling, in association with Coppe at the UFRJ (Federal University of Rio de Janeiro) and several other Brazilian universities. Cenpes, which is located on the UFRJ campus, maintains links with research institutions in the United States, Britain, and other countries and provides research services for other clients. Nonetheless, the proportion of resources spent by Petrobrás on research and development is significantly lower than the international average for large oil companies. In 1994 Cenpes had 1,656 employees. Its annual budget has ranged from US$134.2 million in 1987 to US$102.7 million in 1991, which corresponds to a figure of between 0.5 percent and 0.8 percent of Petrobrás's gross revenues.

Telebrás's research center, the CPqD, has played an important role in setting the standards for Brazil's telecommunication systems. Foreign companies in Brazil are requested to adopt these standards, local companies receive support to train personnel and to develop technological competence, and the government guarantees the purchase of products that meet Telebrás's standards. The consequence has been the creation of several dozens firms linked to the Telebrás system and protected from competition. The CPqD's budget is around US$50 million a year, and it has 1,200 employees.

These research centers usually are much better endowed with equipment, staff, and resources than research groups in universities and academic institutes. However, because they are shielded from outside review and from financial constraints, it is uncertain whether their performance is commensurate with their costs. Because of economic stagnation, their budgets were reduced in the late 1980s, and lower salaries led to the loss of their best researchers. In the new environment, they have been compelled to redefine their functions in two ways. First, they have had to stay much closer to the direct operational needs of their institutions and forsake long-term and technologically more ambitious projects; second, they have had to look for independent sources of support, whether by selling their services or by establishing associations with the private sector and other research and development institutions. Privatization has led to the shutdown of some of these research groups, as happened in some steel companies.

Technological Research in the Private Sector

Research and development in the private sector in Brazil take place among companies that participate in the international market and among those working in areas where the government has required or supported the development of local technology. "Required" areas include telecommunications and computers; "supported" areas include agriculture and military equipment. In addition, a few companies have adopted medium- and long-term strategies based on technological inno-

Technicians at a 3,200-kilowatt impulse generator of the Electrical Engineering and Electronics Central Laboratory's High Voltage Testing facility, Curitiba, Paraná State
Courtesy Inter-American Development Bank, Washington

vation. An estimated 200 companies have significant investments in research and development in Brazil. In 1985, 1,241 firms were on record as having declared some investment in research and development, totaling about US$300 million. These firms were responsible for 30 percent of the total revenues of the private industrial sector. Detailed surveys have shown that only 0.5 percent of persons with Ph.D. degrees in the country work in the private sector, that few firms have defined budgets for research and development, and that projects tend to be small and short-lived.

Centers of Excellence

Scientist Jacques Marcovitch conducted a detailed 1992 study, entitled *Centers of Excellence in PeD in Brazil*, on a small group of high-quality research centers in an attempt to identify the reasons for their success. They were Petrobrás's Cenpes, in Rio de Janeiro; the Institute of Mechanical Engineering of the Federal University of Santa Catarina, in Florianópolis; the Heart Institute (Instituto do Coração) at USP; the Butantan Institute, belonging to São Paulo State's SCTDE; IMPA (Institute of Pure and Applied Mathematics), associated with the CNPq, in Rio de Janeiro; the research center of Light Metal,

Inc. (Metal Leve S.A.), a leading Brazilian manufacturer of car and airplane components; the research center of Rhodia-Poulenc, a French chemical industrial group, in Paulínia, São Paulo; and the soybean research program at the Federal University of Viçosa, Minas Gerais.

Despite their different contexts and purposes, all these centers of excellence—government institutes, university research centers, and research and development units in private and public corporations—shared a common set of features. First, they benefited from their external environment, including the availability of financial support, different types of incentives, market niches, or well-identified local opportunities. A well-established and competent leadership identified these opportunities and put them to proper use. Second, they made world-class contributions in their fields of knowledge. This was true even for IMPA, which works in the most abstract fields of mathematics but still has an important impact on the teaching of mathematics at all levels in Brazilian education. Third, the leaderships of these centers shared an entrepreneurial spirit. The most outstanding researchers or institution-builders all shared the ability to identify successful goals for their institution, to garner resources, and to identify talent. Fourth, the leaders of these institutions had an ability to find a proper organizational model. According to Marcovitch, these entrepreneurs found innovative mechanisms that freed them from bureaucratic labyrinths, and they adopted institutional frameworks that supported the achievement of their goals. Constant organizational adaptations, specialized, task-oriented units, efficient decision making, and consensus among the leaders and the researchers were key features of success.

These conditions of success also help to explain why the centers of excellence are the exception rather than the rule among Brazilian research institutions. Most research centers in universities and government institutions follow civil service rules, which favor fixed procedures and conformity rather than entrepreneurship and managerial flexibility. Protected until recently by strong trade barriers or state monopolies, Brazilian companies did not make efficiency and innovation their priorities, and either did not invest in research and development or did not use products derived from their research and development units. If Brazilian science is to play a significant role in the country's future, Brazil's institutions need an environment of entrepreneurship, quality, and institutional flexibility that is typical of its centers of excellence. Only then can these centers become the rule rather than the exception.

Policy Perspectives

Brazil has developed a significant infrastructure for research, development, and innovation. Nevertheless there is a clear need to redirect the entire science and technology sector from the patterns established in the 1970s to others more in line with the realities of the 1990s. This new pattern should bring this sector much closer to the educational and productive sectors.

The fact that most Brazilian researchers and research projects are in the universities does not mean that they are as involved with professional, technical, and general education. Areas in need of improvement include establishing closer links between science and technology and the productive sector and stimulating the private sector to increase its share of the country's research and development efforts. Both cases require moving from a vertical approach, concerned with graduate education, leading-edge technology, and large science projects, to a more horizontal one, aimed at increasing the general level of competence of the population and the productive system as a whole. This change in emphasis requires that the institutions providing support and incentives to science also be changed. The two traditions of research and education that exist in Brazil—one more associative, based on the civil society, and more entrepreneurial; the other more hierarchical, centralized, and bureaucratic—point to the main direction of change, from the second to the first. Research groups and institutions need to increase their autonomy and flexibility. There is also a need for the government to establish general guidelines and incentives and for its policy decisions to be more pragmatic, ad hoc, and goal-oriented.

Traditionally, Brazil's technological community has restricted knowledge to a few sectors rather than used it for the benefit of the whole society. The Brazilian science and technology sector was subject to an extensive review in 1993. According to the main conclusions and recommendations of the study, which was published in 1994 by the Getúlio Vargas Foundation (Fundação Getúlio Vargas), science and technology are more important than ever for Brazil. If the country is to raise living standards, consolidate a modern economy, and participate as a significant partner in an increasingly integrated and global world, the economy must modernize and adjust to an internationally competitive environment. Education should be expanded and improved at all levels. As the economy grows and new technologies are introduced, new challenges will emerge in the production and use of energy, environmental control, public health, the management of large cities, and changes in the composition of the labor force. Strong indigenous competence will be necessary for Brazil to participate as an equal in international negotiations and in the setting of international standards that may have important economic and social consequences for Brazil.

According to the study, any new science and technology policy should stimulate the researcher's initiative and creativity; establish strong links between the researcher's work and the requirements of the economy, the educational system, and society as a whole; make Brazilian science and technology truly international; and strengthen the country's educational and science and technology capabilities. To fulfill these tasks, Brazil's technology policies need to be redirected in line with new economic realities. In the short run, policies need to be geared to the reorganization and technological modernization of the industrial sector. Permanent policies need to be established to induce the more dynamic sectors of the productive system to, as a main priority, enter a continuous process of innovation and incorporation of new technologies into the productive process and to keep in step with technical progress in the world economy.

The study also concluded that research groups in universities and government institutes should be strongly encouraged to link to the productive sector and to engage in applied work, while maintaining a high level of academic and basic research activities. The resources for applied work should not come from the budget for basic activities but from specific sources in government agencies, special programs, private firms, and independent foundations. Applied projects need to be evaluated in terms of their academic quality, as well as their economic viability and social and economic significance.

Globalization requires a profound rethinking of the old debate between scientific self-sufficiency and internationalism, which are not necessarily contradictory. Brazil has much to gain as it increases its ability to participate fully as a respected partner in the international scientific and technological community. To meet this objective, fellowship programs of the

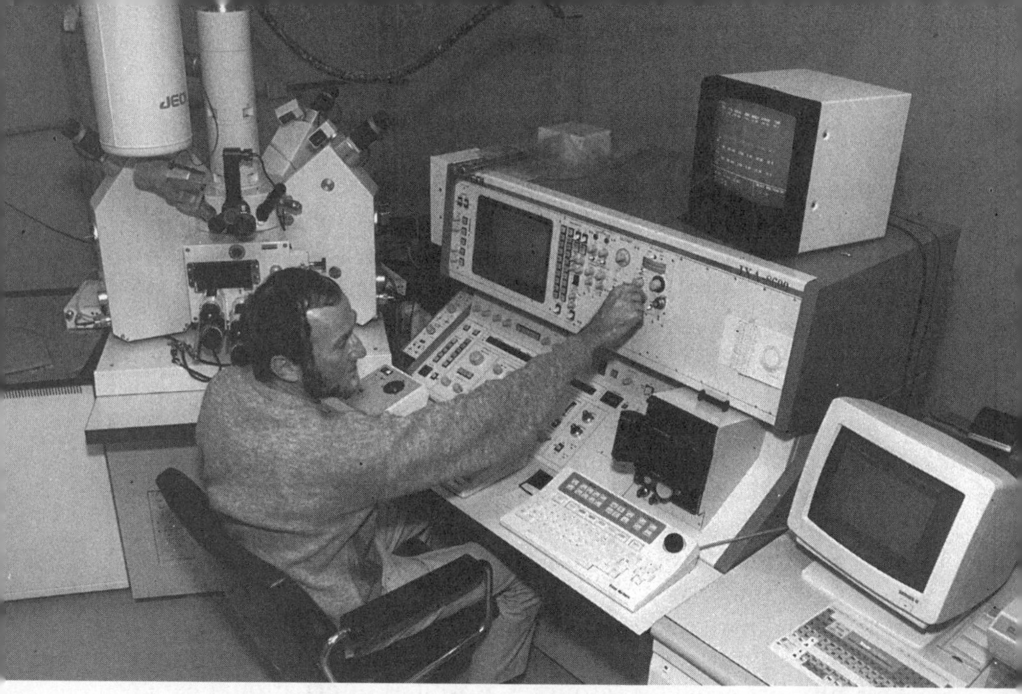

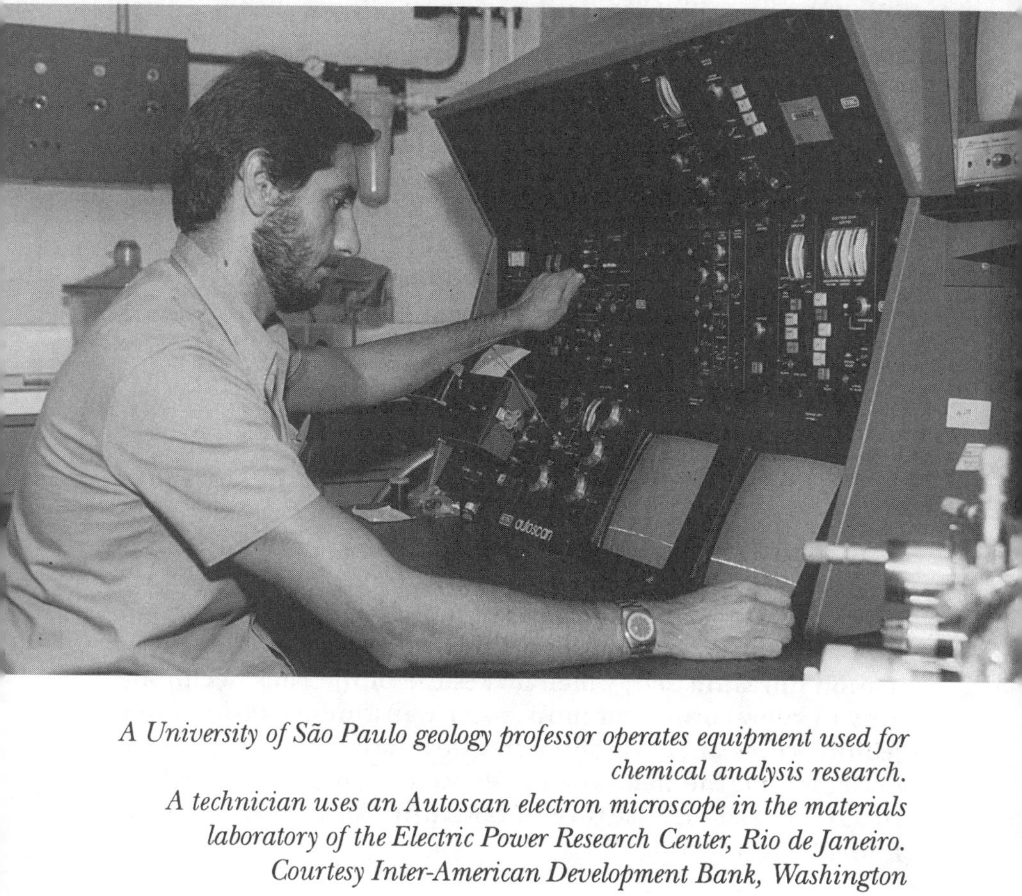

A University of São Paulo geology professor operates equipment used for chemical analysis research.
A technician uses an Autoscan electron microscope in the materials laboratory of the Electric Power Research Center, Rio de Janeiro.
Courtesy Inter-American Development Bank, Washington

CAPES (Council for Advanced Professional Training) and of the CNPq for studies abroad need to be revised and expanded eventually. Brazil will benefit most fully from a studies-abroad program by awarding fellowships to first-rate students. Provisions also need to be made for postdoctoral programs both abroad and in Brazil and to bring top-quality scholars from other countries for extended periods, or even permanent appointments, in Brazilian university and research institutions.

The channels for cooperation among Brazilians, international agencies and institutions, and the international scientific community need to be expanded. The World Bank, the Inter-American Development Bank, and the United Nations Development Programme (see Glossary) have played important roles in providing resources for capital investment, research support, or the development of Brazilian institutions. This support provides resources as well as international expertise and exposure. One possible future role for international agencies might be to stimulate the process of institutional reform.

The issues of protectionism versus market competitiveness loom large in Brazil's relations with industrialized countries. In particular, scientific and technological developments demonstrate a need to emphasize pragmatism over ideology. Brazil's instruments of technological and industrial policy include tax incentives, tariff protection, patent legislation, government procurement, and long-term investments in technological projects in association with the private sector. All of these serve a useful purpose, but adequate patent and intellectual property protection remains key to the normalization of Brazil's relations with the industrialized countries.

New and systematic means to incorporate technology into the industrial process are needed to emphasize the development and dissemination of norms, standards, and procedures for technological transfer and quality improvement. Easy access of scientists to libraries and databases in the country and abroad can ensure a well-organized and properly funded information infrastructure, which makes use of the latest technologies in electronic communication and networking. New technologies and competencies developed elsewhere have underscored the need to reevaluate the role of the CNPq's IBICT (Brazilian Institute of Scientific and Technological Information).

Nuclear Programs

Brazil's nuclear capabilities are the most advanced in Latin America; only Argentina has provided serious competition. Brazil has one nuclear power plant in operation (Angra I) and two under construction (Angra II and III). Its nuclear-enrichment program is multifaceted, with the military services involved in separate projects: the navy, centrifuge enrichment; the air force, laser enrichment; and the army, gas graphite enrichment.

The history of Brazil's nuclear programs can be traced back to the early 1930s, with the initial research in nuclear fission. Much of that early research was conducted at the USP (University of São Paulo), some by scientists who had been contracted from abroad. By the mid-1930s, Brazil had discovered vast deposits of uranium. In 1940 President Getúlio Vargas signed an agreement with the United States for cooperative mining, including mining for uranium and monazite. During the 1940s, Brazil signed three additional agreements with the United States. In exchange for monazite, the United States transferred nuclear technology.

In the early 1950s, President Vargas encouraged the development of independent national nuclear capabilities. He offered to sell uranium or thorium to the United States in exchange for nuclear technology. Under Vargas Brazil sought to purchase three ultracentrifuge systems for uranium enrichment from West Germany. After Vargas's death, Acting President João Café Filho (1954–55) reversed the nationalistic nuclear policy and allowed the United States to control uranium research and extraction for two years.

President Juscelino Kubitschek (1956–61), a pro-Vargas politician, sought to develop indigenous nuclear capabilities by appointing a Congressional Investigating Committee (Comissão Parlamentar de Inquérito—CPI) to examine United States nuclear ties with Brazil. The CPI urged Brazil to adopt an independent nuclear posture. As a result, Kubitschek in 1956 created the IPEN (Institute for Energy and Nuclear Research). Kubitschek's successor, Jânio Quadros (president, January–August 1961), continued the independent nuclear policy, which was based on natural uranium, as did his successor, João Goulart (president, 1961–64).

As part of that independent nuclear policy, the CNEN (National Nuclear Energy Commission) was created formally on August 27, 1962. The CNEN is under the direct control of the Strategic Affairs Secretariat (Secretaria de Assuntos Estratégicos—SAE) of the Brazilian presidency. According to the 1988 constitution, the CNEN is responsible for the orientation, planning, supervision, and control of Brazil's nuclear programs.

The CNEN is located in Rio Janeiro, and is divided into three directorates: Directorate of Research and Development (Diretoria de Pesquisa e Desenvolvimento—DPD), Directorate of Radiation Protection and Nuclear Safety (Diretoria de Radioproteção e Segurança Nuclear—DRS), and Directorate of Logistical Support (Diretoria de Apoio Logístico—DAL). The DPD is further subdivided into three scientific and technological institutes: the IPEN, in São Paulo; the Center for Development of Nuclear Technology (Centro de Desenvolvimento de Tecnologia Nuclear—CDTN), which was created in 1952 in Belo Horizonte as Brazil's first nuclear research institute; and the Nuclear Engineering Institute (Instituto de Engenharia Nuclear—IEN), in Rio de Janeiro. The DRS is composed of the Radiation Protection and Dosimetry Institute (Instituto de Radioproteção e Dosimetria—IRD), in Rio de Janeiro; the Licensing and Control Superintendency (Superintendência de Licenciamento e Contrôle—SLC), with its major laboratory in Poços de Caldas, Minas Gerais State; and various regional units.

The most important of the CNEN's research institutes is the IPEN, a civilian agency that is associated with the SCTDE (São Paulo State's Secretariat for Science, Technology, and Economic Development), and linked to the USP (University of São Paulo) (the IPEN provides teaching and graduate education). The IPEN has a broad infrastructure of laboratories, a research reactor (IEA–R1), an industrial accelerator of electrons, and a compact cyclotron of variable energy. The IPEN is involved primarily in conducting research in the areas of nuclear materials and processes, nuclear reactors, applications of nuclear techniques, and nuclear safety. The IPEN is noted for its production of radioisotopes for nuclear medicine.

Despite Brazil's search for autonomy in the nuclear sphere, it continued to receive technical assistance from the United States. In 1957 Brazil built the first of two nuclear research reactors in São Paulo, with United States support under the Atoms for Peace Program. That program had its origins in the Dwight D. Eisenhower administration (1953–61). Under the program, the United States agreed to share nuclear technology for peaceful purposes, but retained ultimate control over the processes. A second reactor was developed in Belo Horizonte in 1960. In 1965 Brazil built its first indigenous research reactor in Rio de Janeiro. The United States supplied the medium-grade enriched uranium for the reactor.

The construction of these reactors was controlled strictly by the United States. Brazil provided natural uranium to the United States and paid to have it processed. In turn the United States supplied Brazil with the enriched fuel required for its reactors. As envisioned by the Atoms for Peace Program, the United States retained control of the technology and by-products created by Brazilian reactors.

Based on the success of these research reactors, plans were made for a nuclear reactor to produce electricity. In 1968 the CNEN and Eletrobrás were tasked with building a nuclear power plant at Angra dos Reis, Rio de Janeiro State. Three years later, the Westinghouse Electric Corporation agreed to supply the technology for the power plant, and construction of Angra I began. However, Brazilian authorities were dissatisfied with the Westinghouse accord, because it barred the transfer of United States nuclear technology to Brazil, made Brazil dependent on United States uranium for the reactor, and required that all Brazilian nuclear facilities be safeguarded by the International Atomic Energy Agency (IAEA).

Brazil's military governments continued to assert autonomous nuclear strategies. These regimes were frustrated by restrictions imposed by the United States on its nuclear programs, concerned with Argentina's rapid nuclear development, and facing energy shortages (accentuated by the petroleum crisis of October 1973). A turning point was the inauguration of President Ernesto Geisel in March 1974. A former president of Petrobrás, the petroleum monopoly, Geisel was concerned with the country's pressing energy needs. In December 1974, he created the Brazilian Nuclear Corporations (Empresas Nucleares Brasileiras S.A.—Nuclebrás), a state company tasked with expanding the nuclear programs.

Brazil was faced with a technical dilemma: it could switch to natural uranium technology, which could be pursued independently; or it could continue to pursue the more costly and advanced enriched uranium technology, but with external assistance. Brazilian policy makers opted for the latter, but given that the United States had been an unreliable supplier, Brazil was forced to look elsewhere for assistance.

Brazil made a radical change in 1975, when it opted for nuclear technology from West Germany, despite strong protests from the United States. The agreement, signed on June 27, called for West Germany to transfer eight nuclear reactors (each of which could produce 1,300 megawatts), a commercial-scale uranium enrichment facility, a pilot-scale plutonium reprocessing plant, and Becker "jet nozzle" enrichment technology. West Germany's Kraftwerk Union, an affiliate of Siemens, was hired to construct the power plants. The projected cost of the program was US$4 billion, to be paid over a fifteen-year period. The most important element of the agreement was that it called for the first-ever transfer of technology for a complete nuclear fuel cycle, including enrichment and reprocessing. The United States government opposed the accord vigorously. Although it was unable to revoke the agreement, the United States convinced West Germany to enact stringent safeguards.

Many experts have questioned the cost-effectiveness of Brazil's nuclear power plants. The Angra I power plant cost US$2 billion to build, and it began to operate commercially in 1983. When Angra I is in full operation, it produces 20 percent of the electricity used in the city of Rio de Janeiro. From 1985 through 1993, however, Angra I was turned off more than thirty times because of technical problems and legal challenges, earning it the nickname "firefly." Furnas Electric Power Plants, Inc. (Furnas Centrais Elétricas S.A.—Furnas), the state company that administers Angra 1, lost US$100 million in operating costs in 1993 alone because the plant was closed down most of the year. The plant is expected to be torn down in 2009, at a cost of US$200 million.

Angra II, under construction since 1977, was projected to be ready by 1993, but in early 1996 its completion date was still uncertain. The construction of Angra II had cost at least US$4.6 billion through 1993, and it was estimated that at least an additional US$1.5 billion would be necessary to complete the project. Various experts projected that the total cost of the plant construction would exceed US$10 billion. Still in its early phases of construction, Angra III cost US$1 billion through 1993. On October 18, 1994, President Itamar Franco (1992–94) requested that US$400 million in funding that had been allocated to Angra III be transferred to Angra II. Given the severe budget constraints, the construction of Angra III and additional power plants appear doubtful.

West Germany did not require IAEA safeguards, and following the 1975 agreement Brazil transferred technology from its power plant projects to a secret program to develop an atom bomb. Code-named "Solimões," after a river in the Amazon, the secret program was started in 1975 and eventually came to be known publicly as the Parallel Program. In 1987 José Sarney (president, 1985–90) announced that Brazil had enriched uranium successfully on a laboratory scale to 20 percent. At that time, some observers predicted that Brazil would have a nuclear-weapons capability by the turn of the century. President Fernando Collor de Mello took bold steps to control and restrict Brazil's nuclear programs. In September 1990, he symbolically closed a test site at Cachimbo, in Pará State. That October, he formally exposed the military's secret plan to develop an atom bomb.

Within Brazil's Congress, a CPI looked into the Parallel Program. Members visited numerous facilities, including the Institute of Advanced Studies (Instituto de Estudos Avançados—IEAv) at the Aerospace Technical Center (Centro Técnico Aeroespacial—CTA) in São José dos Campos. They also interviewed key players in the nuclear program, such as João Figueiredo (president, 1979–85) and retired Army General Danilo Venturini, the former head of the National Security Council (Conselho de Segurança Nacional—CSN) under Figueiredo. The CPI investigation exposed secret bank accounts, code-named "Delta," which were managed by the CNEN and used for funding the program. The most disturbing revelation in the CPI report was that the IEAv had designed two atomic bomb devices, one weighing twenty to thirty kilotons and a second weighing twelve kilotons. It was also revealed that Brazil's military regime secretly exported eight tons of uranium to Iraq in 1981.

Through a series of agreements, Brazil and Argentina have defused the issue of nuclear rivalry. On May 20, 1980, while under military rule, both countries signed the Brazilian-Argentine Agreement on the Peaceful Use of Nuclear Energy, establishing technical cooperation in developing the nuclear fuel cycle and coordination of nuclear policy. President Sarney and Argentine president Raúl Alfonsín strengthened this cooperation in 1985, with the Joint Declarations on Nuclear Policy of Foz do Iguaçu. After the 1985 agreement, the presidents and technical staffs made reciprocal visits to nonsafeguarded nuclear installations in both countries. The heads of state made subsequent joint declarations in Brasília (1986); Viedma, Argentina (1987); Iperó, Brazil (1988); and Buenos Aires (1990).

On November 28, 1990, Presidents Collor de Mello and Carlos Saúl Menem of Argentina signed the second Foz do Iguaçu declaration (Argentine-Brazilian Declaration on Common Nuclear Policy of Foz do Iguaçu), in which both governments pledged their commitment to an exclusively peaceful use of nuclear energy and established a Common System for Accounting and Control of Nuclear Materials (Sistema Comum de Contabilidade e Contrôle de Materiais Nucleares—SCCCMN). On July 18, 1991, Presidents Collor de Mello and Menem agreed to establish the Agreement on the Exclusively Peaceful Use of Nuclear Energy, which created the Brazilian-Argentine Agency for Accounting and Control of Nuclear Materials (Agência Brasileiro-Argentina de Contabilidade e Contrôle de Materiais Nucleares—ABACC). That agreement entered into force on December 12, 1991, after ratification by the legislatures in both countries. With headquarters in Rio de Janeiro, the ABACC provides on-site inspections of nuclear facilities in Argentina and Brazil and maintains an inventory of nuclear material in each country.

The most important nuclear accord between Brazil and Argentina was signed on December 13, 1991, in a meeting attended by Presidents Collor de Mello and Menem at the headquarters of the IAEA in Vienna. The accord is referred to as the quadripartite agreement, because it was signed by Brazil, Argentina, the IAEA, and the ABACC. The agreement allows for full-scope IAEA safeguards of Argentine and Brazilian nuclear installations. It also allows the two countries to retain full rights over any "technological secrets" and to develop nuclear energy for the propulsion of submarines. Brazil's Senate ratified the agreement on February 9, 1994, but only after considerable pressure by Brazil's Ministry of Foreign Affairs (Itamaraty).

On May 30, 1994, Brazil ratified the Treaty of Tlatelolco (see Glossary), following the lead of Argentina and Chile, which had ratified it on January 18, 1994. In Brazil there was an active lobby against the quadripartite agreement and the Treaty of Tlatelolco. Indeed, it took Brazil considerably longer than Argentina to approve those pacts. Brazilian diplomats have argued that the Non-Proliferation Treaty (NPT) is discriminatory because it excludes capabilities of those already in the club. Furthermore, some Brazilians have argued that the NPT is an infringement on sovereignty and that the current agreements are sufficient and even stronger than the NPT. Nevertheless, Brazil finally agreed in 1997 to ratify the NPT.

Some observers have argued that Brazil is still seeking the technological capability to produce a nuclear bomb, despite the 1991 quadripartite agreement, the full ratification of the Treaty of Tlatelolco, and a provision in Brazil's 1988 constitution that bars the development of nuclear energy for anything but peaceful purposes. They note that Brazil's nuclear program is under the primary control of the military, which resents IAEA inspections. Brazil's Senate required a "supplementary adjustment" to the treaty that protects "industrial secrets," possibly the nation's Aramar centrifuge enrichment facilities, from on-site inspections. The Aramar Experimental Center was inaugurated in 1988 and is the only uranium enrichment plant in Brazil. It is located in the interior of São Paulo, in the town of Iperó. A further amendment was added that bans IAEA inspections outside the normal schedule. Finally, Brazil was allowed to provide an accounting of the uranium that has already been enriched, but the IAEA and ABACC have no way to verify that amount. The dual nature of nuclear energy allows it to be used for both peaceful and military purposes. The military application of Brazil's nuclear programs, therefore, depends less on technological considerations than on political will.

Most observers, however, are more optimistic about Brazil's nuclear intentions. Argentine diplomat and nuclear expert Julio César Carasales has argued that Brazil's nuclear programs need to be understood in the context of Brazil's rapprochement with Argentina. In that context, he concluded that, "Extraordinary accomplishments already have been achieved and have been generally welcomed; there is no danger that the process will be reversed or undermined; the time has come to consolidate the bilateral arrangements; the nuclear control agency, the ABACC, is performing in a satisfactory matter; new substantial agreements are not to be expected; and some policy divergence is possible, as in the case of the NPT, although there are reasons to predict that in the long run Brazil will join that treaty." Indeed, in 1997 Brazil announced its adherence to the NPT.

Brazil's nuclear programs have experienced severe financial constraints since 1990, when Collor de Mello was president. The Aramar Experimental Center dismissed 700 of its 1,600 employees between August 1994 and March 1995. The completion date for the navy's nuclear-powered submarine was postponed several times, from 1995 to 2010. Until 1995 that project had cost an estimated US$1 billion. The submarine program, rarely scrutinized in the past, was the subject of scathing criticism by *Veja*, the leading weekly news magazine, in December 1994. The magazine raised allegations of corruption and exposed technical difficulties with the program.

Despite such financial and technical hurdles, it is likely that Brazil will continue to fund efforts to develop more autonomous nuclear programs. Indeed, the administration of Fernando Henrique Cardoso (president, 1995–) in mid-1995 placed a high priority on completing the Angra II nuclear power plant. Such programs will be pursued in a more open environment, given the many bilateral and multilateral nuclear accords signed by Brazil.

The Space Program

Brazil has the most advanced space program in Latin America, with significant capabilities in launch vehicles, launch sites, and satellite manufacturing. In an attempt to build a Satellite Launch Vehicle (Veículo Lançador de Satélite—VLS), Brazil has since 1964 developed a series of sounding (research) rockets, named Sonda I, II, III, and IV. The early Sondas were test-launched from Barreira do Inferno (literally, "Barrier of Hell") Launch Center (Centro de Lançamento da Barreira do Inferno), near the city of Natal in the Northeast (Nordeste). The Sonda IV rocket was tested successfully on April 28, 1989. Subsequent launches were made from the Alcântara Launching Center (Centro de Lançamento de Alcântara—CLA), in Maranhão, President Sarney's home state. The CLA, officially dedicated on February 21, 1990, cost more than US$470 million to develop. It is the closest launch center to the equator in the world (2.3 degrees south of the equator), making it attractive for launches of geostationary satellites. For example, because it is so close to the equator it provides a 25 percent fuel savings compared with Cape Kennedy.

On February 9, 1993, the first satellite developed entirely in Brazil, the Data-Collecting Satellite (Satélite de Coleta de Dados—SCD–1), was launched from a United States B–52 plane carrying a Pegasus rocket made by the American Orbital Science Corporation. The SCD–1, sometimes referred to as the "green" satellite, is used by INPE agencies, such as the Weather

An Ansat–10 satellite earth station, ten-meter antenna of Avibrás Aerospace Industry, Inc. (Avibrás Indústria Aeroespacial S.A.—Avibrás)
Courtesy Avibrás

Forecasting and Climate Studies Center (Centro de Previsão do Tempo e Estudos Climáticos—CPTEC), for collecting meteorological and environmental data on the Amazon region, including the levels of carbon monoxide and carbon dioxide in the atmosphere. The data are transmitted to the INPE (National Institute of Space Research) and are used for monitoring forest fires. More than thirty companies were involved in the construction of the SCD–1, with the INPE providing most of the electronic hardware equipment. The SCD–2, which was scheduled to be launched by a Brazilian-made rocket, will also be used to collect environmental data. Brazil is also developing the Remote Sensing Satellite (Satélite de Sensoriamento Remoto—SSR–1).

On July 6, 1988, Brazil signed an agreement with China that calls for the joint development (between the INPE and the Chinese Space Agency) of two earth-imaging satellites to be launched by a Long March Chinese rocket from the Shanxi Launching site. Known as the China-Brazil Earth Resources Satellite (Satélite Sino-Brasileiro de Recursos Terrestres—CBERS), the high-resolution CBERS will collect data from the entire planet and will be used for agriculture, geology, hydrology, and the environment. The Sino-Brazilian agreement was inactive from 1988 through 1991 because of Brazil's lack of funds. In October 1991 and November 1994, Brazil and China signed additional agreements for the construction of the satellites, worth US$150 million. The CBERS–1 was scheduled to be launched in May 1997.

The Brazilian Telecommunications Company (Empresa Brasileira de Telecomunicacões—Embratel), a state-controlled agency in charge of the Brazilian Satellite Communication System (Sistema Brasileiro de Comunicação por Satélites—SBTS), owns and operates a series of satellites that are positioned in geostationary orbit over the equator. Arianespace, a French space and defense partner of France's Aérospatiale group, launched the first two Brasilsat satellites in February 1985 and March 1986.

Until 1994 the military directed most of the space program through the Ministry of Aeronautics, which is in charge of the CTA. Created in 1950, the CTA is involved in research and development for the aerospace programs of the FAB (Brazilian Air Force). In 1965 the FAB created the Space Activities Center (Instituto de Atividades Espaciais—IAE), one of several institutes within the CTA, to develop rockets. Since its creation, the IAE has tested more than 2,000 rockets.

In 1971 a joint civilian-military committee, the Brazilian Commission for Space Activities (Comissão Brasileira de Atividades Espaciais—Cobae), was established and placed under the CSN (National Security Council). Cobae was chaired by the head of the Armed Forces General Staff (Estado-Maior das Forças Armadas—EMFA) and was in charge of the Complete Brazilian Space Mission (Missão Espacial Completa Brasileira—MECB). The MECB was created in 1981 to coordinate launch vehicles, launch sites, and the manufacturing of satellites.

On the civilian side, the MECB is headed by the INPE. Established in 1971, the INPE replaced the National Commission for

A Brazilian Air Force AMX tactical fighter made by Embraer
Courtesy Brazilian Embassy, Washington

Space Activities (Comissão Nacional de Atividades Espaciais—CNAE). The INPE is subordinate to the Ministry of Science and Technology and roughly the CTA's counterpart. The INPE develops satellites and conducts space and meteorological research. It has also been developing engines using liquid propellants since 1988, but with mixed results.

Within Brazil's MECB, civilians have been primarily responsible for satellite production, and the armed forces have been in charge of developing launch pads and rockets. Despite this division of labor, the armed forces were the dominant actors in the MECB, at least through 1993. Military officers occupied most of the high-ranking positions in the MECB.

In an attempt to place the MECB more firmly in the hands of civilians, Brazil's President Itamar Franco signed a bill on February 10, 1994, creating the Brazilian Space Agency (Agência Espacial Brasileira—AEB). The AEB replaced Cobae, which acted merely as an advisory body and had no staff. The AEB, a semi-autonomous agency, has its own staff and responsibilities for policy implementation. It is led by a civilian, who is under the direct control of the president. The AEB oversees the MECB, but the Ministry of Aeronautics is still in charge of launch facilities and launch vehicles, and the INPE continues to direct the development of satellites. It remains to be seen, therefore, whether the AEB can effectively oversee the various ministries involved in the MECB.

The AEB was created in part to deflect criticism from the United States government, which viewed with alarm the involvement of Brazil's military in the MECB. The United States played a central role in the development of Brazil's MECB, beginning with its financial and technological support for the CTA and the INPE. In 1966 the United States supplied sounding rockets, which were launched subsequently by Brazil. Based on that technology, Brazil later developed larger boosters of its own.

The ties between Brazil and the United States were generally along functional lines within the two governments. The United States National Aeronautics and Space Administration (NASA) worked with the INPE, sharing data, helping to develop and implement scientific experiments, and training the institute's technicians and scientists. Likewise, the United States Air Force worked with Brazil's Ministry of Aeronautics and established a number of data-exchange agreements with the CTA that covered such matters as weather forecasting.

Brazil no longer relies as heavily on the United States for space technology. In 1981 it unveiled the MECB, an ambitious US$1 billion program with the aim of attaining self-sufficiency in space technology. At that time, Brazil committed itself to launching a series of four Brazilian-made satellites (two for weather forecasting and two for terrain photography) from Alcântara.

In further moves away from dependence on the United States, in the 1980s Brazil took steps to become self-sufficient in the production of ammonium perchlorate, an oxidizer for solid fuels. In addition to its indigenous research and development, Brazil now cooperates in its space program with Canada, the European Space Agency (ESA), Russia, France, and especially China. One joint satellite project with China is the China-Brazil Earth Resources Satellite. Brazil is also seeking space cooperation with new partners, such as Israel.

In the mid-1980s through the early 1990s, many United States policy makers were concerned with Brazil's MECB because of the possibility of diverting space-launch technology to a ballistic missile program. Although by mid-1997 Brazil had not produced a ballistic missile, its military had given high priority to the development of several missile systems, including the Piranha missile (MAA–1). Brazil's space-launch program,

The Avibrás-made Astros II artillery saturation rocket system fires an SS–60 rocket.
Courtesy Avibrás

coupled with its artillery rocket technology, suggests that the country has the potential to develop advanced missiles, including ballistic missiles.

From 1987 to 1994, the United States sought to stifle the development of Brazil's ballistic missile program through the Missile Technology Control Regime (MTCR—see Glossary), formed on April 16, 1987. Given Brazil's advanced nuclear program, the United States was especially concerned that a potential Brazilian ballistic missile could eventually serve as a vehicle for a nuclear warhead. The United States restrictions on space technology to Brazil stalled Brazil's VLS (Satellite Launch Vehicle) program and ballistic missile research and development, strained United States security relations with Brazil, and prompted Brazil to explore closer ties with China, Russia, and various countries in Europe and the Middle East (especially Iraq). In October 1995, for example, Brazil offered Russia the use of its Alcântara base, to launch rockets.

On February 11, 1994, Brazil announced that it would comply with MTCR guidelines. Such compliance would include export controls on Brazilian space and missile goods and technology. Brazil's accession to the MTCR coincided with various attempts by the United States to cooperate in space activities and seemed to signal a new era in space relations. Brazil's application for MTCR membership was accepted in October 1995. Thus, by the end of 1995 Brazil's space capabilities were improving, although they were modest by the standards of countries such as the United States and Russia.

Missile Programs

The potential military applications of Brazil's MECB center around the Sonda IV and its VLS, which could be used for a ballistic missile. Sonda IV has a range of 600 kilometers and can carry a 500-kilogram payload, and is therefore subject to MTCR restrictions. The transformation of the Sonda IV into an intercontinental ballistic missile (ICBM) would require several more successful launches and a major technological leap, especially in payload shielding and guidance.

Many of the factors that drove Brazil's nuclear programs also have driven the space and missile programs. In the mid-1980s, Brazil was concerned with Argentina's Condor II ballistic missile program, which received substantial technological assistance from Europe and funding from Iraq. In the late 1980s and early 1990s, however, Argentina dismantled its Condor missile program and removed that rationale for Brazil's MECB. Brazil's quest for advanced technology drives much of the space and ballistic missile programs. For example, Brazilian authorities considered the April 1990 purchase of follow-on satellites for the Brazilian Satellite (Brasilsat) program an opportunity to receive valuable technology. The Brazilian government specifically required that the transfer of satellite technology be a precondition for the purchase of the satellites. In sum, an attempt by Brazil to produce a ballistic missile is driven primarily by a search for technological autonomy, although political, security, and economic motives are also important.

The government of Brazil has stated that it supports the peaceful applications of space technology and denies any intention of developing a ballistic missile. It argues that the Sonda IV is only a satellite launcher and lacks the required accuracy for military use. At least one missile expert, Steven M. Flank, has argued that if Brazil had intended to develop a ballistic missile it would not have chosen the Sonda technological path. He notes, for example, that the VLS employed in the Sondas are solid-propellant systems, which are not as effective as liquid-propellants for launching ballistic missiles.

The armed forces have even greater control over missile production than they do over the MECB. Following a meeting in June 1986 among six companies, the Armed Forces General Staff (EMFA), and the three military ministries, missile production was placed under the authority of the Armed Forces Joint Command (Comando Geral das Forças Armadas—CMFA). All missile manufacturers are required to submit programs to the CMFA, which evaluates them and awards contracts.

The most important Brazilian company involved in incipient missile technology is Avibrás Aerospace Industry, Inc. (Avibrás Indústria Aeroespacial S.A.—Avibrás). The Astros II, a multiple rocket launcher, is the most profitable weapon produced by Avibrás. It can launch rockets of different caliber: SS–30 rockets up to thirty kilometers; SS–40 rockets, forty kilometers; and SS–60 rockets, sixty kilometers. In the 1980s, Avibrás sold an estimated sixty-six Astros II artillery systems to Iraq and an unspecified number to Saudi Arabia, Bahrain, and Qatar. Total sales of the Astros II between 1982 and 1987 reached US$1 billion.

In the late 1980s, Avibrás was involved in the development of the SS–150 (based on the Astros–II), the SS–300, and the SS–1000 (based largely on the Sonda rockets). All Avibrás programs were "put on hold" in January 1990, when the company filed for bankruptcy. Its employee roster had fallen from 6,000 to 900, and the company had US$90 million worth of unsold rockets. Although Avibrás improved its financial health in the early 1990s, by the end of 1995 the SS–150 and the SS–300 had not passed the initial stages of development, and the SS–1000 had not even been designed.

In the mid-1980s, the armed forces became frustrated by delays in the development of self-guided missiles. Following the June 1986 meeting between private industry and the military, a consensus was reached that standardization in missile production was necessary. As a result, a new firm, Orbital Aerospace Systems, Inc. (Órbita Sistemas Aerospaciais S.A.), was created in February 1987 to coordinate Brazil's missile program. Órbita was tasked with developing guided missiles, rockets, and satellite launchers for civilian applications. Órbita, however, collapsed in the early 1990s because of inadequate funding, technological constraints, and restrictions placed by the United States and other MTCR signatories on the transfer of sensitive technology to Brazil.

By mid-1997, therefore, Brazil could be placed in a fourth tier of ballistic missile producers. The first tier includes the United States and Russia, which have ICBMs. The second comprises nations such as France, China, Britain, and Israel, which have ballistic missiles of more limited range and accuracy. A third group includes developing countries, such as Iraq, India, and South Africa, which have advanced missile programs with modest ranges. A fourth category includes countries such as Argentina, Brazil, Egypt, Pakistan, and South Korea, which have artillery rockets and embryonic ballistic missile capabilities. Brazil's capabilities clearly pale in comparison with those of the first two tiers and are even modest when compared with those in the third tier. Nonetheless, its programs indicate that it aspires to a third- and perhaps a second-tier status. Finally, it should be noted that Brazil's space and missile capabilities are sophisticated in relation to those of most developing nations. In summary, Brazil's ballistic missile program, which faces formidable constraints, is largely in the preplanning stages and not engaged in serious research and development.

*   *   *

The main source of information about Brazilian science is Fernando de Azevedo's *As ciências no Brasil*, a collection of essays written by leading Brazilian scientists in the early 1950s. Simon Schwartzman's *A Space for Science: The Development of the Scientific Community in Brazil* is a sociological interpretation of the institutionalization of scientific and technological activities in the country. It is based on extensive interviews with leading scientists and a review of written sources. *Science and Technology in Brazil* by Schwartzman et al discusses the need for a strategic role by science and technology in Brazil.

A few key institutions have been the subject of detailed studies that have illuminated the social, economic, and political climate of the times. Noteworthy are those on the Ouro Prêto School of Mines (Escola de Minas de Ouro Prêto) in the nineteenth century and on the Oswaldo Cruz Foundation in the early twentieth century. Most institutional histories, however, are just laudatory tales of names and achievements and have little analytical content. Works on the Brazilian Association for the Progress of Sciences appeared in 1987 and 1990 by Ana Maria Fernandes and Antônio José Botelho, respectively. The association's journals, *Ciência e Cultura* and *Ciência Hoje*, are important repositories of historical and contemporary information.

The ambitious project of technological development since the 1970s has generated several analytical and comparative studies from economic and political perspectives. Emanuel Alder has compared the computer and nuclear policies in Brazil with those in Argentina, linking their different results with the ideologies and social groups behind these policies. For the broad policies, see the writings of Fábio Stefano Erber; for the computer industry, see Paulo Bastos Tigre. The main source for publications on the economic dimensions of scientific and technological policies in Brazil is the Applied Economic Research Institute (Instituto de Pesquisa Econômica Aplicada—IPEA), an agency of Brazil's Ministry of Planning. The ministry also publishes *Revista de Pesquisa e Planejamento Econômico.* The Brazilian Science and Technology Policy Project, conducted by the Getúlio Vargas Foundation in São Paulo in 1993, has published about forty studies on different aspects of Brazilian science and technology through the Editora da Fundação Getúlio Vargas in Rio de Janeiro.

A series of working papers resulted from three science and technology policy studies carried out in Brazil in 1993 and 1994, with the support of the Ministry of Science and Technology, the World Bank, the Inter-American Development Bank, and the UNDP (United Nations Development Programme). One of the studies was carried out at the University of Campinas under the coordination of Luciano G. Coutinho. It focused on the conditions and possibilities for strengthening Brazil's industrial competitiveness. A second study under the coordination of Francisco Biato was a joint project of the Ministry of Science and Technology, the Brazilian Academy of Sciences, and the UNDP. The third science and technology study was conducted at the Getúlio Vargas Foundation under the coordination of Simon Schwartzman, with the support of the Ministry of Science and Technology and the World Bank. The program of science and technology at the University of São Paulo has published a series of books on the management of science and technology research units and related subjects, with a special emphasis on the private sector.

Brazil's nuclear programs have received considerable academic and journalistic attention. The most insightful analysis is provided by Etel Solingen in her various journal articles and in her book, *Industrial Policy, Technology, and International Bargaining: Designing Nuclear Industries in Argentina and Brazil.* Some of the most vociferous critics of Brazil's nuclear development are Brazilians themselves. Luiz Pinguelli Rosa, a nuclear scientist who was a major opponent of the Brazilian-German nuclear accord, criticizes the role of Brazil's military in nuclear development in *A política nuclear e o caminho das armas atômicas.* Frederico Füllgraf provides critical and historical analysis in *A bomba pacífica: O Brasil e a corrida nuclear.* Tania Malheiros, a journalist, offers a provocative account of Brazil's nuclear program in *Brazil, a bomba oculta: O programa nuclear brasileiro.*

Brazil's space program has received much less attention than its nuclear programs. Steven M. Flank provides an excellent comparative analysis in his Ph.D. dissertation "Reconstructing Rockets: The Politics of Developing Military Technology in Brazil, India, and Israel." Brian G. Chow examines the difficulties in attaining space-launching capabilities in *An Evolutionary Approach to Space Launch Commercialization.* Péricles Gasparini Alves assesses Brazil's space program in "Access to Outer Space Technologies: Implications for International Security." (For further information and complete citations, see Bibliography.)

Appendix

Table

Table 1. Metric Conversion Coefficients and Factors

When you know	Multiply by	To find
Millimeters	0.04	inches
Centimeters	0.39	inches
Meters	3.3	feet
Kilometers	0.62	miles
Hectares	2.47	acres
Square kilometers	0.39	square miles
Cubic meters	35.3	cubic feet
Liters	0.26	gallons
Kilograms	2.2	pounds
Metric tons	0.98	long tons
	1.1	short tons
	2,204	pounds
Degrees Celsius (Centigrade)	1.8 and add 32	degrees Fahrenheit

Table 2. Extent of Brazil's Borderline Shared by Neighboring Countries and the Atlantic Ocean

Neighboring Countries and Atlantic Ocean	Extent of Border In Kilometers	Extent of Border As Percentage of Total
Neighboring countries		
Argentina	1,263	5.5
Bolivia	3,126	13.5
Colombia	1,644	7.1
French Guiana	655	2.8
Guyana	1,606	7.0
Paraguay	1,339	5.8
Peru	2,995	13.0
Suriname	593	2.6
Uruguay	1,003	4.3
Venezuela	1,495	6.5
Total neighboring countries	15,719	68.0
Atlantic Ocean	7,367	31.9
TOTAL[1]	23,086	100.0

[1] Figures may not add to totals because of rounding.

Source: Based on information from the World Wide Web home page of the Fundação Instituto Brasileiro de Geografia e Estatística (http://www.ibge.gov.br), Diretoria de Geociências, Departamento de Cartografia, Rio de Janeiro, 1996.

Table 3. Territory by Region and State, 1996

Region and State	Area in Square Kilometers	As Percentage of Brazil	As Percentage of Region
Center-West			
Federal District	5,822	–[1]	0.4
Goiás	341,290	4.0	21.2
Mato Grosso	906,807	10.6	56.3
Mato Grosso do Sul	358,159	4.2	22.2
Total Center-West[2]	1,612,077	18.9	100.0
North			
Acre	153,150	1.8	4.0
Amapá	143,454	1.7	3.7
Amazonas	1,577,820	18.5	40.8
Pará	1,253,165	14.7	32.4
Rondônia	238,513	2.8	6.2
Roraima	225,116	2.6	5.8
Tocantins	278,421	3.3	7.2
Total North[2]	3,869,638	45.3	100.0
Northeast			
Alagoas	27,933	0.3	1.8
Bahia	567,295	6.6	36.3
Ceará	146,348	1.7	9.4
Ceará-Piauí[3]	2,977	–	0.2
Maranhão	333,366	3.9	21.4
Paraíba	56,585	0.7	3.6
Pernambuco[4]	98,938	1.2	6.3
Piauí	252,379	3.0	16.2
Rio Grande do Norte	53,307	0.6	3.4
Sergipe	22,050	0.3	1.4
Total Northeast[2]	1,561,178	18.3	100.0
South			
Paraná	199,709	2.3	34.6
Rio Grande do Sul	282,062	3.3	48.9
Santa Catarina	95,443	1.1	16.5
Total South[2]	577,214	6.8	100.0
Southeast			
Espírito Santo	46,184	0.5	5.0
Minas Gerais	588,384	6.9	63.5
Rio de Janeiro	43,910	0.5	4.7

Table 3. (Continued) Territory by Region and State, 1996

Region and State	Area in Square Kilometers	As Percentage	
		of Brazil	of Region
São Paulo	248,809	2.9	26.8
Total Southeast[2]	927,286	10.9	100.0
Trindade and Martin Vaz Islands[5]	10.4	n.a.[6]	n.a.
TOTAL BRAZIL[2]	8,547,404	100.0	

1 — means negligible.
2 Figures may not add to totals because of rounding.
3 Area under litigation between Ceará and Piauí.
4 Includes area of State District of Fernando de Noronha (18.4 square kilometers).
5 Administered by Espírito Santo.
6 n.a.—not available.

Source. Based on information from the World Wide Web home page of Fundação Instituto Brasileiro de Geografia e Estatística (http://www.ibge.gov.br), Diretoria de Geociências, Departamento de Cartografia, Rio de Janeiro, 1996.

Table 4. Real Rate of Growth of Gross Domestic Product (GDP) and of Agriculture, Industry, and Services Sectors, 1950–96
(in percentages)

Year	GDP	Agriculture	Industry	Services
1950	6.8	1.5	11.3	7.1
1951	4.9	0.7	6.4	9.9
1952	7.3	9.1	5.0	10.8
1953	4.7	0.2	8.7	-0.1
1954	7.8	7.9	8.7	13.0
1955	8.8	7.7	10.6	3.5
1956	2.9	-2.4	6.9	4.7
1957	7.7	9.3	5.7	9.0
1958	10.8	2.0	16.2	5.4
1959	9.8	5.3	11.9	1.2
1960	9.4	4.9	9.6	13.0
1961	8.6	7.6	10.6	11.9
1962	6.6	5.5	7.8	3.3
1963	0.6	1.0	0.2	2.9
1964	3.4	1.3	5.2	2.0
1965	2.4	12.1	-4.7	1.3
1966	6.7	-1.7	11.7	5.8
1967	4.2	5.7	3.0	5.8
1968	9.8	1.4	13.2	8.9

Table 4. (Continued) Real Rate of Growth of Gross Domestic Product (GDP) and of Agriculture, Industry, and Services Sectors, 1950–96
(in percentages)

Year	GDP	Agriculture	Industry	Services
1969	9.5	6.0	12.2	8.4
1970	10.3	5.6	10.4	10.2
1971	11.3	10.2	11.8	11.2
1972	11.9	4.0	14.2	12.4
1973	14.0	0.1	17.0	15.6
1974	8.2	1.3	8.5	10.6
1975	5.2	6.6	4.9	5.0
1976	10.3	2.4	11.7	11.6
1977	4.9	12.1	3.1	5.0
1978	5.0	–2.7	6.4	6.2
1979	5.8	4.7	6.8	7.8
1980	9.2	9.5	9.2	9.0
1981	–4.4	8.0	–8.9	–2.2
1982	0.7	–0.5	0.0	2.0
1983	–3.4	–0.6	–5.8	–0.8
1984	5.0	3.4	6.6	4.1
1985	8.3	10.0	8.3	6.5
1986	7.5	–8.0	11.8	8.3
1987	3.6	15.0	1.0	3.3
1988	–0.1	0.8	–2.6	2.3
1989	3.3	2.9	2.9	3.8
1990	–4.0	–3.7	–8.0	–0.8
1991	0.3	2.8	–1.8	1.6
1992	–0.8	5.4	–3.7	0.0
1993	4.2	–1.0	6.9	3.5
1994	6.0	9.3	7.0	4.2
1995	4.3	5.1	2.1	6.0
1996	2.9	3.1	2.3	3.0

Source: Based on information from Fundação Getúlio Vargas, *Conjuntura Econômica* [Rio de Janeiro], various issues; Fundação Instituto Brasileiro de Geografia e Estatística, *Estatísticas históricas do Brasil*, Rio de Janeiro, 1990; and Fundação Instituto Brasileiro de Geografia e Estatística, *Sistema IBGE de Recuperação Automática—SIDRA 97* (Internet address: http://www.sidra.ibge.gov.br).

Table 5. Principal Components of the Current Account, 1970–96
(in millions of United States dollars)

Year	Exports[1]	Imports[1]	Trade Balance[2]	Net Services	Current Account[2]
1970	2,739	2,507	232	–815	–562
1971	2,904	3,245	–341	–980	–1,307
1972	3,991	4,235	–244	–1,250	–1,489
1973	6,199	6,192	7	–1,722	–1,688
1974	7,951	12,641	–4,690	–2,433	–7,122
1975	8,670	12,210	–3,540	–3,162	–6,700
1976	10,128	12,383	–2,255	–3,763	–6,017
1977	12,120	12,023	97	–4, 134	–4,037
1978	12,659	13,683	–1,024	–6,037	–6,990
1979	15,244	18,084	–2,840	–7,920	–10,742
1980	20,132	22,955	–2,823	–10,152	–12,807
1981	23,293	22,091	1,202	–13,135	–11,734
1982	20,175	19,395	780	–17,083	–16,311
1983	21,899	15,429	6,470	–13,415	–6,837
1984	27,005	13,916	13,090	–13,215	45
1985	25,639	13,153	12,486	–12,877	–241
1986	22,348	14,044	8,304	–13,694	–5,304
1987	26,224	15,052	11,172	–12,678	–1,436
1988	33,789	14,605	19,184	–15,104	4,174
1989	34,383	18,263	16,120	–14,800	1,564
1990	31,414	20,661	10,753	–15,369	–3,782
1991	31,620	21,041	10,579	–13,542	–1,407
1992	35,793	20,554	15,239	–11,339	6,143
1993	38,597	25,256	13,341	–15,585	–592
1994	43,545	33,079	10,466	–13,542	–1,689
1995	46,506	49,621	–3,115	–11,339	–17,742
1996	47,747	53,286	–5,539	–15,585	–24,347

[1] Free on board.
[2] Figures may not add to balances because of rounding. Current account balance includes unilateral transfers (not shown).

Source: Based on information from Fundação Instituto Brasileiro de Geografia e Estatística, *Estatísticas históricas do Brasil*, Rio de Janeiro, 1964–86; Fundação Instituto Brasileiro de Geografia e Estatística, *Anuário estatístico do Brasil*, Rio de Janeiro, 1990; and Fundação Getúlio Vargas, *Conjuntura Econômica* [Rio de Janeiro], May 1991.

Table 6. Nominal and Real Interest Rates in International Markets, 1970–96[1]
(in percentages)

Year	Nominal LIBOR[2]	Nominal United States Prime Rate	WPI Industrial Countries[3]	Real LIBOR	Real United States Prime Rate
1970	8.9	7.7	4.1	4.8	3.6
1971	7.1	5.7	3.3	3.8	2.4
1972	6.0	5.3	4.0	2.0	1.3
1973	9.4	8.0	12.4	-3.0	-4.4
1974	10.8	10.8	21.0	-10.2	-10.2
1975	7.8	7.9	8.3	-0.6	-0.4
1976	6.1	6.8	7.1	-1.0	-0.3
1977	6.4	6.8	7.2	-0.8	-0.4
1978	9.2	9.1	5.7	3.5	3.4
1979	12.2	12.7	10.9	1.3	1.8
1980	14.0	15.3	13.8	0.2	1.5
1981	16.7	18.9	9.0	7.7	9.9
1982	13.6	14.9	5.4	8.2	9.5
1983	9.9	10.8	3.3	6.6	7.5
1984	11.3	12.0	3.6	7.7	8.4
1985	8.6	9.9	1.5	7.1	8.4
1986	6.9	8.4	-3.3	10.2	11.7
1987	7.3	8.2	0.9	6.4	7.3
1988	8.1	9.3	3.0	5.1	6.3
1989	9.3	10.9	4.4	4.9	6.5
1990	8.4	10.0	2.7	5.7	7.3
1991	6.1	8.5	0.6	5.5	7.9
1992	3.6	6.0	0.5	3.1	5.5
1993	3.4	6.0	0.5	2.9	5.5
1994	5.1	7.7	1.1	4.0	6.6
1995	5.9	9.0	3.1	2.8	5.9
1996	5.7	8.3	1.0[4]	4.7	7.3

[1] Interest rates are averages for the year.
[2] The LIBOR (London Interbank Offered Rate) is the rate on six-month deposits in United States dollars.
[3] The WPI (Wholesale Price Index) is a weighted average for twenty-two industrialized countries.
[4] Preliminary estimate.

Source: Based on information from International Monetary Fund, *International Financial Statistics*, Washington, various issues.

Table 7. Index of Real Gross Domestic Product, 1950–96
(1970=100)

Year	Index (in percentages)	Year	Index (in percentages)
1950	28.7	1974	155.1
1951	30.4	1975	163.2
1952	33.0	1976	179.1
1953	33.9	1977	187.4
1954	37.3	1978	196.5
1955	39.9	1979	210.6
1956	41.1	1980	229.9
1957	44.4	1981	219.8
1958	47.9	1982	221.1
1959	50.5	1983	213.5
1960	55.4	1984	224.8
1961	60.2	1985	242.7
1962	64.4	1986	261.1
1963	65.4	1987	270.5
1964	67.3	1988	270.3
1965	69.1	1989	279.2
1966	71.7	1990	267.9
1967	75.2	1991	270.8
1968	83.6	1992	268.4
1969	91.9	1993	279.7
1970	100.0	1994	295.8
1971	111.5	1995	308.5
1972	124.8	1996	317.4
1973	142.3		

Source: Based on information from Fundação Instituto Brasileiro de Geografia e Estatística, *Estatísticas históricas do Brasil,* Rio de Janeiro, 1990; Fundação Instituto Brasileiro de Geografia e Estatística, *Anuário estatístico do Brasil,* various issues; and Fundação Instituto Brasileiro de Geografia e Estatística, *Sistema IBGE de Recuperação Automática—SIDRA 97* (Internet address: http://www.sidra.ibge.gov.br).

Table 8. Index of Average Real Minimum Wage, 1960–96
(1980=100)

Year	Index (in percentages)	Year	Index (in percentages)
1960	129.94	1979	97.51
1961	149.25	1980	100.00
1962	127.14	1981	98.69
1963	114.95	1982	99.12
1964	119.89	1983	87.86
1965	113.68	1984	81.24
1966	102.40	1985	83.90
1967	98.14	1986	82.29
1968	98.80	1987	64.04
1969	97.43	1988	63.23
1970	95.56	1989	68.47
1971	95.82	1990	46.72
1972	92.69	1991	45.12
1973	96.24	1992	45.46
1974	90.83	1993	47.47
1975	77.36	1994	36.09
1976	95.52	1995	35.85
1977	95.83	1996	36.39
1978	97.92		

Source: Based on information from Donald V. Coes, *Macroeconomic Crises, Policies, and Growth in Brazil, 1964–90*, Washington: World Bank, 1995; and Fundação Getúlio Vargas, *Conjuntura Econômica* [Rio de Janeiro], various issues.

Table 9. Major Permanent Crops: Area Harvested, Production, Mean Productivity, Production Value, and Major Producing States, 1993[1]

Main Product	Area Harvested (hectares)	Production (1,000 tons)	Mean Productivity (kilograms per hectare)	Production Value (millions of CR$)	Major Producing State
Apples[2]	25,652	3,494	136,200	18,706	Santa Catarina
Avocados[2]	15,112	423	28,004	2,766	São Paulo
Bananas[3]	520,014	558	1,073	39,994	Bahia
Cocoa (beans)	734,124	341	464	25,933	Bahia
Cashew nuts	726,140	77	106	5,600	Piauí
Coconut[2]	231,660	837	3,615	15,987	Bahia
Coffee (beans)	2,259,332	2,558	1,131	189,529	Minas Gerais
Cotton, seed (arboreous)	137,333	8	57	388	Ceará
Grapes	60,200	787	13,079	30,839	Rio Grande do Sul
Guavas[2]	8,479	1,392	164,172	2,737	São Paulo
Hevea (coagulated latex)	51,626	54	1,048	3,989	São Paulo
Lemons[2]	43,967	7,220	164,214	12,637	São Paulo
Mangoes[2]	53,107	1,610	30,316	6,548	São Paulo
Oranges[2]	800,505	93,986	117,408	223,355	São Paulo
Palm oil (nuts)	69,714	657	9,421	4,866	Pará
Papayas[2]	26,322	1,081	41,069	21,844	Bahia
Passion fruit[2]	32,539	3,004	92,324	7,943	Pará
Peaches[2]	18,954	1,273	67,173	6,153	Rio Grande do Sul

Table 9. (Continued) Major Permanent Crops: Area Harvested, Production, Mean Productivity, Production Value, and Major Producing States, 1993[1]

Main Product	Area Harvested (hectares)	Production (1,000 tons)	Mean Productivity (kilograms per hectare)	Production Value (millions of CR$)	Major Producing State
Pepper (black)	23,572	42	1,793	2,652	Pará
Sisal	179,105	126	703	3,327	Bahia
Tangerines[2]	48,586	4,891	100,663	10,397	São Paulo
Yerba maté (green leaves)	18,841	227	12,066	2,466	Rio Grande do Sul

1 Includes only those products with area harvested of more than 100,000 hectares or production value of more than CR$2 billion (for value of the cruzeiro *real*—see Glossary).
2 Production expressed in millions of fruits, and mean productivity expressed in fruits per hectare.
3 Production expressed in millions of bunches, and mean productivity expressed in bunches per hectare.

Source: Based on information from Fundação Instituto Brasileiro de Geografia e Estatística, Directoria de Pesquisas, Departmento de Agropecuária, *Agricultural Production Survey* [Rio de Janeiro], 1995.

Table 10. Major Temporary Crops: Area Harvested, Production, Mean Productivity, Production Value, and Major Producing States, 1993[1]

Main Product	Area Harvested (hectares)	Production (1,000 tons)	Mean Productivity (kilograms per hectare)	Production Value (millions of CR$)	Major Producing State
Beans (grain)	3,884,341	2,478	638	102,930	Paraná
Cassava	1,810,895	21,837	12,058	140,049	Pará
Corn (grain)	11,870,763	30,051	2,531	283,455	Paraná
Cotton, seed (herbaceous)	922,593	1,127	1,221	28,245	Paraná
Garlic	17,441	87	4,984	12,004	Santa Catarina
Onions	71,910	929	12,914	17,844	São Paulo
Pineapples[2]	39,719	835	21,012	15,044	Paraíba
Potatoes	162,063	2,368	14,608	30,509	Paraná
Rice (paddy)	4,411,315	10,108	2,291	154,100	Rio Grande do Sul
Soybeans (grain)	10,635,300	22,575	2,122	232,973	Rio Grande do Sul
Sugarcane	3,864,488	244,344	63,227	317,622	São Paulo
Tobacco (leaves)	372,912	658	1,763	22,916	Rio Grande do Sul
Tomatoes	53,726	2,348	43,706	48,701	São Paulo
Wheat	1,462,741	2,156	1,474	38,467	Paraná

[1] Includes only those products with production value more than CR$10 billion (for value of the cruzeiro *real*—see Glossary).
[2] Production expressed in millions of fruits, and mean productivity expressed in fruits per hectare.

Source: Based on information from Fundação Instituto Brasileiro de Geografia e Estatística, Directoria de Pesquisas, Departmento de Agropecuária, *Agricultural Production Survey* [Rio de Janeiro], 1995.

Table 11. Number of Livestock and Poultry by Region, 1992 (in thousands)

Region	Cattle	Buffalo	Horses	Goats	Sheep	Hogs	Poultry
Center-West	48,788	127	954	164	418	3,341	30,787
North	15,847	877	550	267	328	4,216	30,437
Northeast	26,912	117	1,780	10,928	7,974	9,752	109,947
South	25,451	195	1,208	452	10,848	11,085	271,280
Southeast	37,443	107	1,837	350	387	6,139	197,174
TOTAL[1]	154,441	1,423	6,329	12,160	19,956	34,532	639,625

[1] Figures may not add to totals because of rounding.

Source: Based on information from Fundação Instituto Brasileiro de Geografia e Estatística, Directoria de Pesquisas, Departamento de Agropecuária, *Livestock and Poultry Production Survey* [Rio de Janeiro], 1995.

Table 12. Monetary Units, 1942–94

Monetary Unit	Date Created	Relation to Preceding Unit
Cruzeiro (Cr$)........................	October 5, 1942	Cr$1.00=1,000 reis
Cruzeiro novo (NCr$).................	February 8, 1967	NCr$1.00=Cr$1,000
Cruzeiro (Cr$)........................	May 15, 1970	Cr$1.00=NCr$1.00
Cruzado (Cz$)........................	February 28, 1986	Cz$1.00=Cr$1,000
Cruzado novo (NCz$).................	January 15, 1989	NCz$1.00=Cz1,000
Cruzeiro (Cr$)........................	March 16, 1990	Cr$1.00=NCz$1,000
Cruzeiro *real* (CR$)....................	August 1, 1993	CR$1.00=Cr$1,000
Real (R$)	July 1, 1994	R$1.00=CR$2,750

Source: Based on information from Donald V. Coes, *Macroeconomic Crises, Policies, and Growth in Brazil, 1964–90*, Washington, 1995, 172.

Table 13. Principal Components of the Balance of Payments, 1981–96
(in millions of United States dollars)

Year	Trade Balance	Net Services	Current Account	Capital Account	Interest Payments
1981	1,202	–13,135	–11,734	12,773	–9,161
1982	780	–17,083	–16,311	7,851	–13.494
1983	6,470	–13,415	–6,837	2,103	–11,008
1984	13,090	–13,215	45	253	–11,471
1985	12,486	–12,877	–241	–2,554	–11,259
1986	8,304	–13,694	–5,304	–7,108	–11,126
1987	11,172	–12,678	–1,436	–7,986	–10,318
1988	19,184	–15,104	4,174	–8,685	–12,085
1989	16,120	–14,800	1,564	–4,179	–12,016
1990	10,753	–15,369	–3,782	–4,715	–9,748
1991	10,579	–13,542	–1,407	–4,148	–8,621
1992	15,239	–11,339	6,143	25,271	–7,253
1993	13,341	–15,585	–592	10,115	–8,280
1994	10,466	–13,542	–1,689	14,294	–6,338
1995	–3,115	–11,339	–17,742	30,703	–8,158
1996	–5,539	–15,585	–24,347	n.a.[1]	–9,840

[1] n.a.—not available.

Source: Based on information from Fundação Instituto Brasileiro de Geografia e Estatística, *Estatísticas históricas do Brasil*, Section 11.6, Rio de Janeiro, 1981–86; Fundação Instituto Brasileiro de Geografia e Estatística, *Anuário estatístico do Brasil, 1986–88*, Rio de Janeiro, 1990; and Fundação Getúlio Vargas, *Conjuntura Econômica* [Rio de Janeiro], various issues, 1989–96.

Table 14. Public-Sector National Income Accounts, 1970–90

Year	Total Tax Receipts	Net Transfers[1]	Interest on Domestic Debt[2]	Interest on External Debt	Net Receipts of Public Sector	Total Noninterest Expenditures[3]	Net Public-Sector Saving	Noninterest Public-Sector Surplus
	1	2	3	4	5=1-2-3-4	6	7=5-6	8=1-2-6
1970	26.3	8.8	0.5	0.1	17.0	11.3	5.6	6.2
1971	25.2	7.8	0.4	0.1	17.0	11.2	5.7	6.2
1972	25.9	7.8	0.3	0.2	17.7	10.7	7.0	7.5
1973	25.0	7.8	0.4	0.1	16.7	10.0	6.7	7.2
1974	25.1	8.2	0.4	0.1	16.4	9.4	7.0	7.5
1975	25.2	9.4	0.4	0.2	15.2	10.2	5.0	5.6
1976	25.1	8.8	0.5	0.2	15.7	10.5	5.2	5.9
1977	25.6	8.7	0.5	0.2	16.2	9.4	6.7	7.4
1978	25.7	10.0	0.5	0.2	15.0	9.7	5.3	6.0
1979	24.7	9.7	0.6	0.3	14.1	9.9	4.2	5.1
1980	24.7	11.6	0.8	0.4	11.9	9.2	2.7	3.9
1981	24.7	10.9	1.1	0.3	12.4	9.3	3.1	4.4
1982	25.3	11.1	1.1	1.1	12.0	10.0	1.9	4.2
1983	25.1	11.0	1.6	1.6	10.9	9.7	1.2	4.4
1984	21.8	9.4	2.4	1.8	8.3	8.3	0.0	4.2
1985	22.5	8.8	3.4	1.5	8.8	9.9	–1.0	3.8
1986	25.4	9.4	3.6	1.4	11.0	10.7	0.3	5.2

Table 14. (Continued) Public-Sector National Income Accounts, 1970–90

Year	Total Tax Receipts	Net Transfers[1]	Interest on Domestic Debt[2]	Interest on External Debt	Net Receipts of Public Sector	Total Noninterest Expenditures[3]	Net Public-Sector Saving	Noninterest Public-Sector Surplus
1987	23.3	9.1	3.1	1.4	9.6	12.2	–2.5	2.0
1988	21.9	8.4	3.1	1.7	8.6	12.6	–4.0	0.9
1989	21.9	9.4	6.1	2.0	4.4	14.3	–9.9	–1.8
1990	27.4	10.0	1.9	2.1	13.4	15.6	–2.2	1.8

[1] Includes social security and other net transfers to private sector.
[2] Interest on domestic debt excludes monetary correction.
[3] Includes public-sector spending on wages and salaries and expenditure for goods and services.

Source: Based on information from Fundação Instituto Brasileiro de Geografia e Estatística, Departamento Nacional de Contas, Rio de Janeiro, 1992.

Table 15. Annual Inflation Rate, 1964–96
(in percent change in consumer price index)[1]

Year	Index	Year	Index
1964	83.9	1981	109.9
1965	37.0	1982	95.4
1966	37.6	1983	154.5
1967	24.3	1984	220.6
1968	23.5	1985	225.5
1969	20.0	1986	142.3
1970	19.0	1987	224.8
1971	19.2	1988	684.5
1972	15.6	1989	1,320.0
1973	15.7	1990	2,739.7
1974	33.6	1991	414.7
1975	29.0	1992	991.4
1976	45.0	1993	2,103.7
1977	42.7	1994	2,406.8
1978	38.7	1995	14.8
1979	53.9	1996	9.3
1980	100.2		

[1] The price index on which the series is based is the Indice Geral de Preços—Disponibilidade Interna (General Index of Prices—Internal Availability).

Source: Based on information from Fundação Getúlio Vargas, *Conjuntura Econômica* [Rio de Janeiro], various issues.

Table 16. Nominal Tariff Rate Average by Sector, Selected Years, 1980–94
(in percentages)

Sector	1980	1990	1991[1]	1992[1]	1993[1]	1994[1]
Agricultural and forestry products	16.4	12.7	11.0	9.9	9.1	n.a.[2]
Beverages	179.0	75.2	63.7	53.5	34.7	19.7
Chemicals	48.2	17.5	13.1	11.7	10.0	9.5
Clothing and footwear	181.2	38.3	33.6	27.0	20.3	16.4
Communications and electrical products	95.4	45.2	37.0	31.9	26.2	21.5
Food products	107.8	26.7	20.7	17.0	14.9	13.1
Furniture	148.2	38.6	31.7	24.7	20.0	20.0
Machinery and equipment	56.3	40.7	30.7	26.1	21.3	19.6
Metals	77.4	27.0	20.8	17.6	14.6	12.3
Mining	27.0	6.0	3.8	2.2	1.4	1.1
Nonmetallic mineral products	109.4	25.9	14.8	12.2	8.3	7.2
Paper and paper products	120.2	18.1	9.6	7.7	6.8	6.7
Perfumes and cosmetics	160.5	58.2	41.6	28.7	24.0	19.6
Pharmaceuticals	27.9	24.7	18.5	15.7	12.8	12.6
Plastics	203.8	39.2	35.3	30.0	21.5	18.8
Rubber and rubber products	107.3	51.4	36.7	29.3	20.7	15.2
Textiles	167.3	35.7	34.7	27.6	23.8	17.0
Tobacco products	184.6	79.1	69.5	60.0	37.3	19.1
Transportation equipment	101.9	47.0	37.0	31.4	25.7	21.3
Wood and wood products	125.3	21.1	11.3	10.7	10.2	9.9
Miscellaneous	87.0	43.9	35.0	28.5	22.4	17.3
Simple average	115.8	31.4	24.6	20.4	16.4	13.6
Standard deviation	51.7	17.7	15.2	12.6	9.3	6.9

[1] Projected.
[2] n.a.—not available.

Source: Based on information from Honório Kume and Guida Piani, "A política de importação no período 1991–1994," Rio de Janeiro, 1991.

Table 17. Foreign Trade by Major Product, Selected Years, 1978–96[1]
(in millions of United States dollars)

Product	1978	1982	1986	1990	1996
Exports					
Primary products					
Coffee	1,947	1,858	2,006	1,102	1,719
Iron ore	1,028	1,847	1,615	2,409	2,693
Soybeans	1,050	1,619	1,253	1,609	3,743
Sugar	196	259	141	289	936
Other	1,757	2,655	2,265	3,342	3,094
Total primary products	5,978	8,238	7,280	8,751	12,185
Manufactured products					
Iron and steel	172	795	1,179	1,644	2,574
Machinery	566	1,191	1,471	2,474	2,211
Orange juice	333	575	678	1,468	1,389
Transportation equipment	828	1,718	1,568	2,181	2,464
Other	4,605	7,407	9,999	14,318	26,103
Total manufactured products	6,504	11,686	14,895	22,085	34,741
Other	177	251	173	578	821
Total exports	12,659	20,175	22,348	31,414	47,747
Imports					
Chemicals	893	1,003	1,352	1,691	6,677
Fertilizers	309	239	325	319	426
Fuels and lubricants	4,483	10,457	3,540	5,363	6,906
Grain	702	848	823	251	2,105
Other	7,296	6,848	8,004	12,782	37,172
Total imports	13,683	19,395	14,044	20,406	53,286
TRADE BALANCE	–1,024	780	8,304	11,008	–5,539

[1] Free on board. Figures may not add to totals or balances because of rounding.

Source: Based on information from Fundação Getúlio Vargas, *Conjuntura Econômica* [Rio de Janeiro], various issues; and Fundação Instituto Brasileiro de Geografia e Estatística, *Estatísticas históricas do Brasil*, Rio de Janeiro, 1964–97.

Table 18. Party Members in the National Congress, Selected Years, 1987–97

Party Delegation	1987[1]	1990	1991[1]	1992	1993	1994	1995[1]	1996	1997
Chamber of Deputies									
Arena[2]/PDS[3]/PPR[4]/PPB[5]	32	32	42	45	69	67	53	89[6]	79
MDB[7]/PMDB[8]	260	131	108	98	101	96	107	96	94
PCB[9]/PPS[10]	3	3	3	3	3	3	2	2	2
PC do B[11]	3	6	5	5	7	6	10	10	10
PDC[12]	5	15	22	19	n.a.[13]	n.a.	n.a.	n.a.	n.a.
PDT[14]	24	38	46	40	36	35	33	25	23
PFL[15]	118	90	84	86	87	89	89	99	105
PL[16]	6	13	15	18	14	16	13	9	10
PP[17]	0	0	0	0	37	45	36	n.a.	n.a.
PRN[18]	0	31	40	26	16	4	1	0	0
PSB[19]	1	8	11	10	10	10	15	12	11
PSDB[20]	0	60	38	40	45	48	62	83	97
PT[21]	16	17	35	36	35	36	49	50	51
PTB[22]	18	28	38	30	26	29	31	28	23
Other	1	23	16	47	17	19	12	10	8
Total Chamber of Deputies	487	495	503	503	503	503	513	513	513

Table 18. (Continued) Party Members in the National Congress, Selected Years, 1987–97

Party Delegation	1987[1]	1990	1991[1]	1992	1993	1994	1995[1]	1996	1997
Federal Senate									
Arena/PDS/PPR/PPB	5	3	3	4	9	10	6	5[6]	6
MDB/PMDB	44	22	27	26	27	27	22	24	22
PDC	1	7	4	3	n.a.	n.a.	n.a.	n.a.	n.a.
PDT	2	5	5	6	4	5	6	3	2
PFL	16	13	15	17	17	14	19	22	24
PL	1	0	0	0	0	0	1	0	0
PP	0	0	0	0	4	4	5	n.a.	n.a.
PRN	0	3	3	5	5	3	0	0	0
PSB	2	2	1	1	1	1	1	2	3
PSDB	0	12	10	9	9	11	10	14	14
PT	0	0	1	1	1	1	5	5	5
PTB	1	4	8	8	4	4	5	4	4
Other	0	4	4	1	0	1	1	2	1
Total Federal Senate	72	75	81	81	81	81	81	81	81

[1] Result of election the previous year.
[2] Aliança Renovadora Nacional (National Renewal Alliance).
[3] Partido Democrático Social (Democratic Social Party).
[4] Partido Progressista Renovador (Progressive Renewal Party).
[5] Partido Progressista Brasileiro (Brazilian Progressive Party).
[6] Merged with PP and PPR to form PPB in September 1995.
[7] Movimento Democrático Brasileiro (Brazilian Democratic Movement).

[8] Partido do Movimento Democrático Brasileiro (Brazilian Democratic Movement Party).
[9] Partido Comunista Brasileiro (Brazilian Communist Party).
[10] Partido Popular Socialista (Popular Socialist Party).
[11] Partido Comunista do Brasil (Communist Party of Brazil).
[12] Partido Democrático Cristão (Christian Democratic Party).
[13] Merged with PDS to form PPR in April 1993; n.a.—not available.
[14] Partido Democrático Trabalhista (Democratic Labor Party).
[15] Partido da Frente Liberal (Liberal Front Party).
[16] Partido Liberal (Liberal Party).
[17] Partido Progressista (Progressive Party).
[18] Partido da Reconstrução Nacional (National Reconstruction Party).
[19] Partido Socialista Brasileiro (Brazilian Socialist Party).
[20] Partido da Social Democracia Brasileira (Brazilian Social Democracy Party).
[21] Partido dos Trabalhadores (Workers' Party).
[22] Partido Trabalhista Brasileiro (Brazilian Labor Party).

Source: Based on official electoral data from the Chamber of Deputies and Federal Senate provided by David V. Fleischer.

Table 19. Election Results for the National Congress and for Governors, November 1982, and Composition of Electoral College, January 1985, by Party

	PDS[1]	PMDB[2]	PDT[3]	PTB[4]	PT[5]	Total
National Congress						
Federal deputies						
Number	235	200	23	13	8	479
Percentage	49.0	41.8	4.8	2.7	1.7	100.0
Number of votes[6]	17,780	17,674	2,393	1,829	1,449	41,125
Percentage of votes	43.2	43.0	5.8	4.5	3.5	100.0
Senators[7] (number)	45	22	1	1	0	69
Governors[8] (number)	13	9	1	0	0	23
Electoral college						
Delegates[9] (number)	81	51	6	0	0	138
Composition[10]	361	273	30	14	8	686

[1] Partido Democrático Social (Democratic Social Party).
[2] Partido do Movimento Democrático Brasileiro (Brazilian Democratic Movement Party). Merged with Progressive Party (Partido Progressista—PP) in February 1992.
[3] Partido Democrático Trabalhista (Democratic Labor Party).
[4] Partido Trabalhista Brasileiro (Brazilian Labor Party).
[5] Partido dos Trabalhadores (Workers' Party).
[6] In thousands. Excludes 5,286,684 blank and 2,058,459 void ballots.
[7] Includes forty-four senators elected in 1978 and three new seats elected from Rondônia. At the end of 1983, the PMDB acquired its twenty-second seat, because the alternate elected in 1978 had since left Arena for the PP and then the PMDB. Thus, the PDS lost its two-thirds majority.
[8] Only twelve PDS governors were elected directly. Governor of Rondônia was appointed through 1987.
[9] Includes six delegates representing the majority party in each of the twenty-two state assemblies. Because of a tie in Mato Grosso do Sul, the PDS and PMDB each got three delegates.
[10] Includes federal deputies, senators, and delegates. Met on January 15, 1985.

Source: Based on information from preliminary election statistics reported by Brazil, Superior Electoral Court, *Diário da Justiça* [Brasília], November 28, 1983, 18630–86.

Table 20. *Direct Elections for Governor by State and Party, 1982, 1986, 1990, and 1994: Winning Parties*

State	1982	1986	1990	1994[1]
Acre	PMDB[2]	PMDB	PDS[3]	*PPR*[4], PMDB
Alagoas	PDS	PMDB	PSC[5]	PMDB
Amapá	n.a.[6]	n.a.	PFL[7]	*PSB*[8], PTB[9]
Amazonas	PMDB	PMDB	PMDB	PPR
Bahia	PDS	PMDB	PFL	*PFL*, PMN[10]
Ceará	PDS	PMDB	PSDB[11]	PSDB
Espírito Santo	PMDB	PMDB	PDT[12]	*PT*[13], PSD[14]
Goiás	PMDB	PMDB	PMDB	*PMDB*, PP[15]
Maranhão	PDS	PMDB	PFL	*PFL*, PPR
Mato Grosso	PDS	PMDB	PFL	PDT
Mato Grosso do Sul	PMDB	PMDB	PTB	PMDB
Minas Gerais	PMDB	PMDB	PTB	PP, *PSDB*
Pará	PMDB	PMDB	PMDB	PPR, *PSDB*
Paraíba	PDS	PMDB	PMDB	*PMDB*, PDT
Paraná	PMDB	PMDB	PMDB	PDT
Pernambuco	PDS	PMDB	PFL	PSB
Piauí	PDS	PMDB	PFL	PFL, *PMDB*
Rio de Janeiro	PDT	PMDB	PDT	*PSDB*, PDT
Rio Grande do Norte	PDS	PMDB	PFL	PMDB
Rio Grande do Sul	PDS	PMDB	PDT	*PMDB*, PT
Rondônia	n.a.	PMDB	PTR	*PMDB*, PDT
Roraima	n.a.	n.a.	PTB	*PTB*, PSDB
Santa Catarina	PDS	PMDB	PFL	PPR, *PMDB*
São Paulo	PMDB	PMDB	PMDB	*PSDB*, PTB
Sergipe	PDS	PFL	PFL	PDT, *PSDB*
Tocantins	n.a.	PDC[16]	PMDB	PPR
Federal District	n.a.	n.a.	PTR[17]	PTB, *PT*

[1] Nine states elected governors in the first round (October 3, 1994), and eighteen states elected governors in the second round (November 15, 1994). Italicized party won.
[2] Partido do Movimento Democrático Brasileiro (Brazilian Democratic Movement Party).
[3] Partido Democrático Social (Democratic Social Party).
[4] Partido Progressista Renovador (Progressive Renewal Party).
[5] Partido Social Cristão (Social Christian Party).
[6] n.a.—not available.
[7] Partido da Frente Liberal (Liberal Front Party).
[8] Partido Socialista Brasileiro (Brazilian Socialist Party).
[9] Partido Trabalhista Brasileiro (Brazilian Labor Party).
[10] Partido da Mobilização Nacional (National Mobilization Party).
[11] Partido da Social Democracia Brasileira (Brazilian Social Democracy Party).
[12] Partido Democrático Trabalhista (Democratic Labor Party).
[13] Partido dos Trabalhadores (Workers' Party).
[14] Partido Social Democrático (Social Democratic Party).
[15] Partido Progressista (Progressive Party).
[16] Partido Democrático Cristão (Christian Democratic Party). Elected in 1988.
[17] Partido Trabalhista Renovador (Workers Renewal Party).

Source: Based on official electoral data provided by David V. Fleischer.

Table 21. Municipal Elections in the 100 Largest Cities, 1988, 1992, and 1996

Party	1988		1992		1996	
	Percentage of Votes	Electorate	Percentage of Votes	Electorate	Percentage of Votes	Electorate
PDC[1]	5	870,195	3	741,047	n.a.[2]	n.a.
PDS/PPB[3]	10	1,371,263	7[4]	6,822,597	11	8,462,240
PDT[5]	17[6]	8,403,612	15[7]	4,167,710	15	3,783,676
PFL[8]	9	2,373,601	7	1,822,170	8[6]	6,346,293
PL[9]	2	294,793	0	0	2	257,567
PMDB[10]	20	4,211,092	29[11]	9,420,266	16[4]	3,687,305
PRN[12]	2	373,098	1	92,062	0	n.a.
PSB[13]	3	857,004	4	1,021,615	8[14]	2,528,380
PSDB[15]	8	3,065,788	13	3,307,923	21	4,495,374
PT[16]	12[17]	9,269,506	12[18]	4,297,722	9[19]	2,357,134

Table 21. (Continued) Municipal Elections in the 100 Largest Cities, 1988, 1992, and 1996

Party	1988		1992		1996	
	Percentage of Votes	Electorate	Percentage of Votes	Electorate	Percentage of Votes	Electorate
PTB[20]	12	2,529,370	5	1,375,581	6	1,248,537
Other	0	0	4	550,629	4	452,744
TOTAL	100	33,619,322	100	33,619,322	100	33,619,322

1 Partido Democrático Cristão (Christian Democratic Party). Merged with PDS/PPB in 1993.
2 n.a.—not available.
3 Partido Democrático Social (Democratic Social Party)/Partido do Povo Brasileiro (Brazilian People's Party).
4 Won São Paulo.
5 Partido Democrático Trabalhista (Democratic Labor Party).
6 Won Rio de Janeiro.
7 Lost Rio de Janeiro.
8 Partido da Frente Liberal (Liberal Front Party).
9 Partido Liberal (Liberal Party).
10 Partido do Movimento Democrático Brasileiro (Brazilian Democratic Movement Party).
11 Won Rio de Janeiro.
12 Partido da Reconstrução Nacional (National Reconstruction Party).
13 Partido Socialista Brasileiro (Brazilian Socialist Party).
14 Won Belo Horizonte.
15 Partido da Social Democracia Brasileira (Brazilian Social Democracy Party).
16 Partido dos Trabalhadores (Workers' Party).
17 Won São Paulo.
18 Lost São Paulo.
19 Lost Belo Horizonte.
20 Partido Trabalhista Brasileiro (Brazilian Labor Party).

Source: Based on information from Superior Electoral Court provided by David V. Fleischer.

Table 22. Presidential Election, November 15, 1989: First-Round Results

Candidate	Party	Number of Votes	Percentage of Votes Cast
Fernando Collor de Mello	PRN[1]	20,611,030	28.5
Luis Inácio "Lula" da Silva	PT[2]	11,622,321	16.1
Leonel Brizola.	PDT[3]	11,167,665	15.5
Mário Covas.	PSDB[4]	7,790,381	10.8
Pedro Maluf.	PDS[5]	5,986,585	8.3
Afif	PL[6]	3,272,520	4.5
Ulysses Guimarães.	PMDB[7]	3,204,996	4.4
Roberto Freire.	PCB[8]	769,117	1.1
Aureliano.	PFL[9]	600,821	0.8
R. Caiado.	PSD[10]	488,893	0.7
A. Camargo	PTB[11]	379,284	0.5
Other	n.a.[12]	1,732,273	2.6
Total valid votes.	n.a.	67,625,886	n.a.
Blank	n.a.	1,176,367	1.6
Void	n.a.	3,487,963	4.8
Total votes cast[13].	n.a.	72,290,216	100.0
Abstention	n.a.	9,784,502	n.a.
ELECTORATE	n.a.	82,074,718	n.a.

[1] Partido da Reconstrução Nacional (National Reconstruction Party).
[2] Partido dos Trabalhadores (Workers' Party).
[3] Partido Democrático Trabalhista (Democratic Labor Party).
[4] Partido da Social Democracia Brasileira (Brazilian Social Democracy Party).
[5] Partido Democrático Social (Democratic Social Party).
[6] Partido Liberal (Liberal Party).
[7] Partido do Movimento Democrático Brasileiro (Brazilian Democratic Movement Party).
[8] Partido Comunista Brasileiro (Brazilian Communist Party).
[9] Partido da Frente Liberal (Liberal Front Party).
[10] Partido Social Democrático (Social Democratic Party).
[11] Partido Trabalhista Brasileiro (Brazilian Labor Party).
[12] n.a.—not applicable.
[13] Figures may not add to totals because of rounding.

Source: Based on information from Superior Electoral Court provided by David V. Fleischer.

Table 23. Presidential Election, December 17, 1989, by Size of Municipal Electorate: Second-Round Results

Second-Round Results	Municipalities by Size of Electorate (1,000s)								
	Above 200	100 to 200	50 to 100	20 to 50	10 to 20	5 to 10	2 to 5	Fewer Than 2	Total Brazil[1]
Percentage of votes cast									
Fernando Collor de Mello	39.2	44.0	48.1	55.4	59.4	61.9	62.6	60.2	49.9
Luis Inácio "Lula" da Silva	55.0	50.2	45.9	38.6	34.8	32.6	32.1	34.6	44.2
Blank	0.9	1.1	1.3	1.7	1.9	2.0	1.9	1.7	1.4
Void	5.0	4.8	4.7	4.3	3.9	3.6	3.5	3.6	4.4
Total[1]	100.0	100.0	100.0	100.0	100.0	100.0	100.0	100.0	100.0
Number of votes cast	23,667,147	6,061,773	6,854,092	11,516,793	10,568,698	7,651,427	3,693,667	247,104	70,260,701
Number of municipalities	40	49	113	449	956	1,371	1,329	268	4,575
Percentage of voters[1]	33.7	8.6	9.8	16.4	15.1	10.9	5.3	0.4	100.0

[1] Figures may not add to totals because of rounding.

Source: Based on information from Superior Electoral Court provided by David V. Fleischer.

Table 24. Composition of the Federal Senate, Chamber of Deputies, and State Assemblies by Party, 1991 and 1995

Party	Federal Senate		Chamber of Deputies		State Assemblies	
	1991	1995[1]	1991	1995	1991	1995
PCB[2]/PPS[3]	0	1	3	2	3	3
PC do B[4]	0	0	5	10	8	8
PDS[5]-PDC[6]/PPR[7] ...	7	6	65	53	133	113
PDT[8]	5	6	47	33	91	88
PFL[9]	15	19	82	89	171	159
PL[10]	0	1	16	13	51	50
PMDB[11]	22	22	108	107	214	205
PMN[12]	0	0	1	4	6	18
PRN[13]	3	0	40	1	73	2
PRP[14]	0	0	0	1	0	7
PSB[15]	1	1	11	15	17	34
PSC[16]	0	0	6	3	13	19
PSD[17]	0	0	1	3	2	20
PSDB[18]	10	10	37	62	74	93
PT[19]	1	5	35	49	83	92
PTB[20]	8	5	38	31	79	72
PTR[21]-PST[22]/PP[23] ..	0	5	4	36	25	54
PV[24]	0	0	0	1	0	4
Other	4	0	4	0	6	4
TOTAL	76	81	503	513	1,049	1,045

[1] Three seats sub judice.
[2] Partido Comunista Brasileiro (Brazilian Communist Party).
[3] Partido Popular Socialista (Popular Socialist Party).
[4] Partido Comunista do Brasil (Communist Party of Brazil).
[5] Partido Democrático Social (Democratic Social Party).
[6] Partido Democrático Cristão (Christian Democratic Party).
[7] Partido Progressista Renovador (Progressive Renewal Party).
[8] Partido Democrático Trabalhista (Democratic Labor Party).
[9] Partido da Frente Liberal (Liberal Front Party).
[10] Partido Liberal (Liberal Party).
[11] Partido do Movimento Democrático Brasileiro (Brazilian Democratic Movement Party).
[12] Partido da Mobilização Nacional (National Mobilization Party).
[13] Partido da Reconstrução Nacional (National Reconstruction Party).
[14] Partido Revolucionário do Proletariado (Revolutionary Party of the Proletariat).
[15] Partido Socialista Brasileiro (Brazilian Socialist Party).
[16] Partido Social Cristão (Social Christian Party).
[17] Partido Social Democrático (Social Democratic Party).
[18] Partido da Social Democracia Brasileira (Brazilian Social Democracy Party).
[19] Partido dos Trabalhadores (Workers' Party).
[20] Partido Trabalhista Brasileiro (Brazilian Labor Party).
[21] Partido Trabalhista Renovador (Workers Renewal Party).
[22] Partido Social Trabalhista (Social Workers Party).
[23] Partido Progressista (Progressive Party).
[24] Partido Verde (Green Party).

Source: Based on official electoral data provided by David V. Fleischer.

Table 25. Presidential Election, October 3, 1994: First-Round Results

Candidate	Party	Number of Votes	Percentage of Electorate[1]	Percentage of Votes Cast[1]	Percentage of Valid Votes[1]
Fernando Henrique Cardoso	PSDB[2]-PFL[3]-PTB[4]	34,365,895	36.3	44.1	54.3
Luis Inácio "Lula" da Silva	PT[5]-PSB[6]-PC do B[7]-PPS[8]-PV[9]-PSTU[10]	17,122,384	18.1	22.0	27.0
Enéas Ferreira Carneiro	Prona[11]	4,671,540	4.9	6.0	7.4
Orestes Quêrcia....	PMDB[12]-PSD[13]	2,772,242	2.9	3.6	4.4
Leonel Brizola.....	PDT[14]	2,015,853	2.1	2.6	3.2
Esperidão Amin....	PPR[15]	1,739,926	1.8	2.2	2.8
Carlos Gomes......	PRN[16]	387,756	0.4	0.5	0.6
Hernani Fortuna...	PSC[17]	238,209	0.3	0.3	0.4
Total valid votes....		63,313,805	n.a.[18]	n.a.	100
Blank		7,192,255	7.6	9.2	n.a.
Void		7,444,197	7.9	9.6	n.a.
Total votes cast.....		77,950,257	n.a.	100	n.a.
Abstention		16,832,153	17.8	n.a.	n.a.
ELECTORATE.....		94,782,410	100	n.a.	n.a.

[1] Figures may not add to totals because of rounding.
[2] Partido da Social Democracia Brasileira (Brazilian Social Democracy Party).
[3] Partido da Frente Liberal (Liberal Front Party).
[4] Partido Trabalhista Brasileiro (Brazilian Labor Party).
[5] Partido dos Trabalhadores (Workers' Party).
[6] Partido Socialista Brasileiro (Brazilian Socialist Party).
[7] Partido Comunista do Brasil (Communist Party of Brazil).
[8] Partido Popular Socialista (Popular Socialist Party).
[9] Partido Verde (Green Party).
[10] Partido Social Trabalhista Unificada (Unified Social Workers Party).
[11] Partido da Redefinição da Ordem Nacional (National Order Redefinition Party).
[12] Partido do Movimento Democrático Brasileiro (Brazilian Democratic Movement Party).
[13] Partido Social Democrático (Social Democratic Party).
[14] Partido Democrático Trabalhista (Democratic Labor Party).
[15] Partido Progressista Renovador (Progressive Renewal Party).
[16] Partido da Reconstrução Nacional (National Reconstruction Party).
[17] Partido Social Cristão (Social Christian Party).
[18] n.a.—not applicable.

Source: Based on information from final electoral data of Superior Electoral Court, November 15, 1994, provided by David V. Fleischer.

Table 26. Party Blocs in the National Congress, 1995

Bloc and Party	Seats in Federal Senate	Seats in Chamber of Deputies
Pro-government		
PFL[1]	19	89
PSDB[2]	10	62
PTB[3]	5	31
Total pro-government	34	182
Potential government allies		
PL[4]	1	13
PMDB[5]	22	107
PP[6]	5	36
PPR[7]	6	53
Total potential government allies	34	209
Undefined		
PMN[8]	0	4
PRN[9]	0	1
PRP[10]	0	1
PSC[11]	0	3
PSD[12]	0	3
Total undefined	0	12
Opposition		
PC do B[13]	0	10
PDT[14]	6	33
PPS[15]	1	2
PSB[16]	1	15
PT[17]	5	49
PV[18]	0	1
Total opposition	13	110
TOTAL	81	513

[1] Partido da Frente Liberal (Liberal Front Party).
[2] Partido da Social Democracia Brasileira (Brazilian Social Democracy Party).
[3] Partido Trabalhista Brasileiro (Brazilian Labor Party).
[4] Partido Liberal (Liberal Party).
[5] Partido do Movimento Democrático Brasileiro (Brazilian Democratic Movement Party).
[6] Partido Progressista (Progressive Party).
[7] Partido Progressista Renovador (Progressive Renewal Party).
[8] Partido da Mobilização Nacional (National Mobilization Party).
[9] Partido da Reconstrução Nacional (National Reconstruction Party).
[10] Partido Revolucionário do Proletariado (Revolutionary Party of the Proletariat).
[11] Partido Social Cristão (Social Christian Party).
[12] Partido Social Democrático (Social Democratic Party).
[13] Partido Comunista do Brasil (Communist Party of Brazil).
[14] Partido Democrático Trabalhista (Democratic Labor Party).
[15] Partido Popular Socialista (Popular Socialist Party).
[16] Partido Socialista Brasileiro (Brazilian Socialist Party).
[17] Partido dos Trabalhadores (Workers' Party).
[18] Partido Verde (Green Party).

Source: Based on official electoral data provided by David V. Fleischer.

Table 27. Regional Strength of Parties by Blocs in the Chamber of Deputies, 1995
(in percentages of region's votes)

Bloc and Party	Center-West	North	North-east	South	South-east	Brazil
Pro-government						
PFL[1]	7.3	12.3	33.8	13.0	9.5	17.3
PSDB[2]	7.3	7.7	13.9	3.9	16.8	12.1
PTB[3]	7.3	9.2	1.3	7.8	7.8	6.0
Total pro-government	21.9	29.2	49.0	24.7	34.1	35.4
Potential government allies						
PL[4]	2.4	1.5	1.3	0.0	5.0	2.5
PMDB[5]	26.9	26.2	19.9	22.0	17.9	20.9
PP[6]	17.1	9.2	4.0	7.8	6.1	7.0
PPR[7]	7.3	23.2	4.6	15.6	8.9	10.1
Total potential government allies	53.7	60.1	29.8	45.4	37.9	40.5
Undefined						
PMN[8]	0.0	0.0	2.0	0.0	0.6	0.8
PRN[9]	2.4	0.0	0.0	0.0	0.0	0.2
PRP[10]	0.0	0.0	0.0	0.0	0.6	0.2
PSC[11]	0.0	1.5	1.3	0.0	0.0	0.6
PSD[12]	0.0	0.0	0.7	0.0	1.1	0.6
Total undefined	2.4	1.5	4.0	0.0	2.3	2.4
Opposition						
PC do B[13]	4.9	1.5	1.3	1.3	2.2	2.0
PDT[14]	4.9	1.5	4.6	13.0	7.2	6.6
PPS[15]	2.4	0.0	0.0	0.0	0.6	0.4
PSB[16]	0.0	3.1	6.7	0.0	1.7	2.9
PT[17]	9.8	3.1	4.6	15.6	13.4	9.6
PV[18]	0.0	0.0	0.0	0.0	0.6	0.2
Total opposition	22.0	9.2	17.2	29.9	25.7	21.7
TOTAL	100.0	100.0	100.0	100.0	100.0	100.0
Number of seats	(41)	(65)	(151)	(77)	(179)	(513)

1 Partido da Frente Liberal (Liberal Front Party).
2 Partido Social Democracia Brasileira (Brazilian Social Democracy Party).
3 Partido Trabalhista Brasileiro (Brazilian Labor Party).
4 Partido Liberal (Liberal Party).
5 Partido do Movimento Democrático Brasileiro (Brazilian Democratic Movement Party).
6 Partido Progressista (Progressive Party).
7 Partido Progressista Renovador (Progressive Renewal Party).
8 Partido da Mobilização Nacional (National Mobilization Party).
9 Partido da Reconstrução Nacional (National Reconstruction Party).
10 Partido Revolucionário do Proletariado (Revolutionary Party of the Proletariat).

[11] Partido Social Cristão (Social Christian Party).
[12] Partido Social Democrático (Social Democratic Party).
[13] Partido Comunista do Brasil (Communist Party of Brazil).
[14] Partido Democrático Trabalhista (Democratic Labor Party).
[15] Partido Popular Socialista (Popular Socialist Party).
[16] Partido Socialista Brasileiro (Brazilian Socialist Party).
[17] Partido dos Trabalhadores (Workers' Party).
[18] Partido Verde (Green Party).

Source: Based on official electoral data provided by David V. Fleischer.

Table 28. Military Expenditures (ME), Armed Forces (AF), Gross National Product (GNP), Central Government Expenditures (CGE), and Population, 1984–95

Year	ME (millions of US dollars; constant 1994)	AF (1,000s)	GNP (millions of US dollars; constant 1994)	CGE (millions of US dollars; constant 1994)	Population (millions)	ME/GNP (percentages)	ME/CGE (percentages)	ME per Capita (US dollars; constant 1994)	AF per 1,000 Population (soldiers)	GNP per Capita (US dollars; constant 1994)
1984...	3,630	459	432,300	131,300	134.3	0.8	2.8	27	3.4	3,220
1985...	3,843	496	468,500	186,900	136.8	0.8	2.1	28	3.6	3,424
1986...	4,789	527	510,300	192,100	139.5	0.9	2.5	34	3.8	3,657
1987...	5,494	541	532,600	258,800	142.3	1.0	2.1	39	3.8	3,744
1988...	7,559	319	530,900	196,200	145.0	1.4	3.9	52	2.2	3,662
1989...	8,402	319	554,200	219,400	147.7	1.5	3.8	57	2.2	3,753
1990...	9,078	295	532,200	197,700	150.1	1.7	4.6	60	2.0	3,546
1991...	7,194	295	537,100	148,300	152.3	1.3	4.9	47	1.9	3,526

Table 28. (Continued) Military Expenditures (ME), Armed Forces (AF), Gross National Product (GNP), Central Government Expenditures (CGE), and Population, 1984–95

Year	ME (millions of US dollars; constant 1994)	AF (1,000s)	GNP (millions of US dollars; constant 1994)	CGE (millions of US dollars; constant 1994)	Population (millions)	ME/GNP (percentages)	ME/CGE (percentages)	ME per Capita (US dollars; constant 1994)	AF per 1,000 Population (soldiers)	GNP per Capita (US dollars; constant 1994)
1992 . . .	6,674	296	74,200	188,100	154.5	1.2	3.5	43	1.9	3,716
1993 . . .	8,296	296	602,100	246,600	156.7	1.4	3.4	53	1.9	3,844
1994 . . .	7,365	296	625,500	237,900	158.7	1.2	3.1	46	1.9	3,940
1995 . . .	10,900	285	656,500	276,800	160.7	1.7	3.9	68	1.8	4,084

Source: Based on information from United States Arms Control and Disarmament Agency, *World Military Expenditures and Arms Transfers 1996*, Washington, 1996, 62.

Table 29. Major Army Equipment, 1997

Type and Description	Country of Origin	In Inventory
Medium battle tanks		
Leopard 1A4	Germany	88
Light tanks		
M–3A1	United States	150
M–41B/C	United States	296
Armored personnel carriers		
EE–11 Urutu	Brazil	219
M–59	United States	20
M–113	United States	584
Armored reconnaissance vehicles		
EE–9 Cascavel	Brazil	409
M–8	United States	30
Mortars		
81mm	n.a.[1]	n.a.
M–30	n.a	217
120mm	n.a.	85
Recoilless launchers		
57mm M–18A1	n.a.	240
75mm M–20	n.a.	20
105mm	n.a.	n.a.
106mm M–40A1	n.a.	n.a.
Light antitank guided weapons		
Cobra	United States	300
Aérospatiale Milan 3 (600-meter Eryx and 2,000-meter Euromissile)	France	n.a.
Air defense weapons		200
20mm, 35mm	n.a.	n.a.
35mm GDF–001	n.a.	n.a.
40mm L–60/–70 (some with BOFI)[2]	n.a.	n.a.
Roland II SAM	France	2
Artillery		
Towed	n.a.	504
155mm M–114	n.a.	98
105mm M–101/–102 (including 320 Model 56 pack)	n.a.	353
Special 105mm M–7/–108	n.a.	74
Coastal 57mm, 75mm, 120mm, 150mm, 152mm, 305mm	n.a.	240
Medium-range launchers		
SS–06 108mm	n.a.	n.a.
Astros II	Brazil	4
Helicopters		
Aérospatiale SA–365K Dauphins	France	36

Table 29. (Continued) Major Army Equipment, 1997

Type and Description	Country of Origin	In Inventory
Aérospatiale AS–550 Fennec	France	15
Aérospatiale AS–350L–1 Esquilos (armed)	France	26
Aérospatiale AS–355	France	16

[1] n.a.—not available.
[2] Bofors Optronic Fire-Control Instrument.

Source: Based on information from *The Military Balance, 1997–1998*, London, 1997, 209.

Table 30. Major Naval Equipment, 1997

Type and Description	Country of Origin	In Inventory
Navy		
Aircraft carrier		
Minas Gerais (Colossus-class)	Britain	1
Missile destroyers		
Mato Grosso-class	United States	3
Missile frigates	Britain, Germany, United States	18
Corvettes		
Inhaúma-class	n.a.[1]	5
Submarines		
Humaitá (Oberon)-class	Britain	3
Tupi-class (Type 209/1400)	Germany	3
Patrol and coastal combatants	n.a.	35
Mine countermeasures vessels		
Aratú-class	Germany	6
Amphibious	United States	4
Support and miscellaneous	n.a.	26
Lighthouse tenders and auxiliary hydrographic vessels		
River-class	Britain	3
Naval Aviation		
Naval helicopters (armed)	n.a.	54
Sikorsky S–70A Black Hawk	United States	4
SH–3B antisubmarine warfare	United States	6
SH–3D antisubmarine warfare	United States	7
SH–3G/H antisubmarine warfare	United States	6
Lynx HAS–21 attack	Britain	5
Lynx MK–21A	Britain	9
AS–332 utility	France	5

Table 30. (Continued) Major Naval Equipment, 1997

Type and Description	Country of Origin	In Inventory
AS–350 armed utility	France	12
AS–355 armed utility	France	9
TH–57 training	United States	13
Marines		
Reconnaissance		
EE–9 Mk IV Cascavels	Brazil	6
Amphibious armored vehicles		
Transport landing vehicle, tracked personnel (LVTP–7A1)	n.a.	11
Armored personnel carriers		
M–113	United States	28
EE–11 Urutu	Brazil	5
Towed artillery		
105mm	n.a.	31
M–101	United States	15
L118	n.a.	18
155mm	n.a.	
M–114	United States	6
Mortars		
Self-propelled, 81mm	United States	2
Rocket launchers		
3.5-inch, M–20, 89mm	United States	n.a.
Recoilless launchers		
M–40A1, 106mm	United States	8
Air defense guns		
L/70 40mm with BOFI[2]	n.a.	6

[1] n.a.—not available.
[2] Bofors Optronic Fire-Control Instrument.

Source: Based on information from *The Military Balance, 1997–1998*, London, 1997, 210; and George Palaczi-Horvath, "Brazil: Choices for a Navy with a Tight Budget," *Naval Forces*, 17, No. 1, 1996, 42–49.

Table 31. Major Air Force Equipment, 1997

Type and Description	Country of Origin	In Inventory
Fighters		
F–103E/D (Mirage IIIE/DBR)	United States	16
Ground-attack fighters		
F–5E/–B/–F	United States	46
AMX	Brazil	32
Counterinsurgency aircraft		
AT–26 (EMB–326)	Brazil	58
Reconnaissance aircraft		
RC–95	United States	4
RT–26	United States	10
Learjet 35 Reconnaissance/VIP	United States	12
RC–130E	United States	3
Transports		
C–130H	United States	9
KC–130H	United States	2
KD–137	United States	4
C–91	United States	12
C–95A/B/C	United States	18
C–115	United States	17
VC–91	United States	1
VC/VU–93	United States	12
VC–96	United States	2
VC–97	United States	5
VU–9	United States	5
Boeing 737–200	United States	2
VH–4 helicopters	United States	3
C–115	United States	7
C–95A/B/C	United States	86
EC–9 (VU–9)	United States	6
Helicopters		
Aérospatiale AS–332 (armed)	France	6
Aérospatiale AS–355	France	8
Bell 206	United States	4
HB–350B	United States	27
OH–6A	United States	4
OH–13	United States	25
Trainers		
C–95A/B/C	United States	97
AT–26	United States	38
EMB–110	Brazil	97
EMB–ALX (AT–29)	Brazil	100
T–23	Brazil	25

Table 31. (Continued) Major Air Force Equipment, 1997

Type and Description	Country of Origin	In Inventory
T–25	Brazil	98
T–27 (Tucano)	Brazil	61
AMX–T	Brazil	14
Air-to-air missiles		
AIM–9B Sidewinder	United States	n.a.
R–530	United States	n.a.
Magic 2	France	n.a.
Liaison/observation		
T–27	Brazil	8
U–7	Brazil	31
UH–1H (armed)	United States	29
C–42	United States	50
Cessna 208	United States	3
U–42	United States	30
Antisubmarine warfare		
S–2	United States	5
S–2A	United States	7
S–2E	United States	6
Marine reconnaissance/search and rescue		
EMB–110B	Brazil	11
EMB–111	Brazil	20

Source: Based on information from *The Military Balance, 1997–1998*, London, 1997, 210.

Table 32. Number of Fellowships Granted by the National Council for Scientific and Technological Development, 1995

Fellowships	In Brazil	Abroad	Total
Undergraduate (*iniciação científica*)	18,790	n.a.[1]	18,790
Graduate, nondegree (*aperfeiçoamento*)	2,397	n.a.	2,397
Master's (M.A.) degree students (*mestrado*)	10,960	5	10,965
Doctoral (Ph.D.) degree students	4,965	1,475	6,440
Postdoctoral fellowships	89	293	382
Senior training (*estágios senior*)	n.a.	21	21
Salary supplement for faculty and full-time researchers (*bolsas de pesquisa*)	3,594	n.a.	3,594
TOTAL	25,906	n.a.	25,906

[1] n.a.—not available.

Source: Based on information provided by Simon Schwartzman.

Table 33. Signed Contracts of the Funding Authority for Studies and Projects, 1996[1]

Signed Contracts	Number of Contracts	Total Value (US$1,000)	Percentage	Average Value (US$1,000)
Loans				
To industry: Support Program for Technological Development of Industry[2]	1	180,939	50.0	3,547
To consulting firms: Support Program for Users of Consulting Services[3]	10	33,758	9.3	3,375
To any firm: Support Program for Total Quality Management[4]	26	76,626	21.1	2,947
Total loans	87	291,323	80.4	3,348
Grants to National Fund for Scientific and Technological Development[5]	491	61,003	16.8	124.2
Grants to World Bank Sector Loan to the Program in Support of Scientific and Technological Development[6]	128	9,896	2.7	77.3
TOTAL	706	362,222	100.0	513

[1] Financiadora de Estudos e Projetos (Finep). Figures refer to contracts that may span several years, and not to expenditures.
[2] Programa de Apoio ao Desenvolvimento Tecnológico da Indústria Nacional (ADTEN).
[3] Programa de Apoio aos Usuários de Serviços de Consultória (AUSC).
[4] Programa de Apoio à Gestão de Qualidade (AGQ).
[5] Fundo Nacional de Desenvolvimento Científico e Tecnológico (FUNDCT).
[6] Programa de Apoio ao Desenvolvimento Científico e Tecnológico (PADCT).

Source: Based on information from Financiadora de Estudos e Projetos, *Diretoria operacional da Finep*, 1997.

Table 34. Fellowships of the Council for Advanced Professional Training Granted in 1991 and 1995[1]

Fellowships	In Brazil (spontaneous demand)[2]	In Brazil (other)	Abroad
Undergraduate	889[3]	n.a.[4]	n.a.
Graduate, nondegree	n.a.	11[3]	82[3]
Master's (M.A.) degree	10,307	1,517	64
Doctoral (Ph.D.) degree	3,596	2,895	958
Postdoctoral	n.a.	n.a.	67
"Sandwich"[5] programs, M.A.and Ph.D. levels	n.a.	n.a.	104
For retired professors	289[3]	n.a.	n.a.
Other	n.a.	n.a.	103[3]
TOTAL	12,042	3,395	1,756

[1] Coordenação Fundação de Aperfeiçoamento de Pessoal de Nível Superior (CAPES).
[2] "Spontaneous demand" refers to grants given to people who apply individually, as opposed to grants given to institutions and agency projects. For example, CAPES has a fellowship program designed for teachers in the federal universities, but the program also accepts applicants from the general public.
[3] Figures for 1991.
[4] n.a.—not available.
[5] "Sandwich" fellowships are those given for students in graduate programs in Brazil to spend a year or similar period in a foreign institution.

Source: Based on information from Coordenação para o Aperfeiçoamento de Pessoal de Nível Superior (CAPES), *Relatório de atividades* [São Paulo], 1990 and 1991; and Fundação Coordenação de Aperfeiçoamento de Pessoal de Nivel Superior, *Relatório de atividades* [São Paulo], 1997.

Table 35. Budget of the National Council for Scientific and Technological Development by Main Line of Activity, 1980–95 (in millions of United States dollars)

Year	Fellowships	Grants[1]	Institutes	Administration	Other[2]	Total
1980	43.5	23.8	27.0	41.8	4.4	140.5
1981	50.0	23.5	31.8	44.9	2.6	152.8
1982	75.8	39.8	36.1	36.7	2.4	190.8
1983	78.5	32.4	31.0	33.1	3.7	178.7
1984	75.1	26.5	28.3	33.9	6.2	169.9
1985	100.7	47.6	37.9	38.4	6.0	230.5
1986	105.1	56.7	39.4	31.0	8.4	240.6
1987	216.9	57.6	68.0	75.1	5.2	422.8
1988	302.2	59.1	62.6	60.0	5.6	489.5
1989	303.5	43.2	109.9	62.5	29.2	547.9
1990	242.7	56.7	69.3	49.7	20.2	438.6
1991	311.5	26.6	41.3	35.3	20.0	434.7
1992	259.6	10.2	41.1	23.3	14.2	348.4
1993	347.6	41.3	49.9	30.6	14.3	483.7
1994	459.7	19.9	48.4	28.8	27.0	583.8
1995	498.2	34.6	88.1	38.5	21.0	687.7

[1] Includes special projects.
[2] Includes debt-service payments, fringe benefits to employees (for food, nursery, and transportation), and persons working for other government agencies.

Source: Based on information from Brazil, Ministry of Science and Technology, *Relatório de atividades* [Brasília], 1995, 169, 172–73.

Table 36. Expenditures for Science and Technology in the State of São Paulo, 1996

Institution	Expenditures (in Brazilian *reais* (R$))[1]
DCET/Funcet[2]	500
FAPESP[3]	230,667
Universities	
University of São Paulo[4]	767,488
Campinas State University[5]	338,176
Unesp[6]	363,072
Institutes	
IPT[7]	42,398

[1] For value—see Glossary.
[2] Departamento de Ciência e Tecnologia (Department of Science and Technology)/Fundo Estadual de Desenvolvimento Científico e Tecnológico (State Foundation for Scientific and Technological Development).
[3] Fundação de Apoio à Pesquisa de Estado de São Paulo (São Paulo Federation to Support Research).
[4] Universidade de São Paulo (USP).
[5] Universidade Estadual de Campinas.
[6] Universidade Estadual Paulista (São Paulo State University).
[7] Instituto de Pesquisas Tecnológicas (Institute for Technological Research).

Source: Based on information from São Paulo Federation to Support Research (Fundação de Apoio à Pesquisa de São Paulo—FAPESP) and São Paulo State Secretary of Science, Technology, and Economic Development, 1997.

Table 37. Education Obtained by the Higher Education Professorate, 1983
(in percentages)

Level of Education	Federal Institutions	State Institutions	Municipal Institutions	Private Institutions	Total
No undergraduate degree . . .	0.28	0.06	0.13	0.15	0.17[1]
Undergraduate	19.29	21.41	18.09	26.87	23.11[1]
Specialization . . .	31.32	33.03	63.95	49.65	41.50[1]
Master's (M.A.) degree	30.43	19.18	13.88	17.1	21.53[1]
Doctoral (Ph.D.) degree	18.68	26.31	3.95	6.24	13.69[1]
Number of individuals	48,959	28,248	6,843	71,726	155,776
M.A. degrees granted	56.7	31.2	n.a.[2]	12.1	100.0
Ph.D. degrees granted	35.6	57.9	n.a.	6.4	100.0

[1] As given. Figures do not appear to be totals.
[2] n.a.—not available.

Source: Based on information from Brazil, Ministério da Educação, Serviço de Estatística da Educação e Cultura (SSEC), Brasília, 1997; and Brazil, Ministério da Educação, Council for Advanced Professional Training (Conselho para o Aperfeiçoamento de Pessoal de Nível Superior—CAPES), Brasília.

Bibliography

Chapter 1

Abreu, João Capistrano de. *Chapters of Brazil's Colonial History, 1500–1800.* Trans., Arthur Brakel. New York: Oxford University Press, 1997.

Albuquerque, Manoel Maurício de. *Pequena história da formação social brasileira.* 3d ed. Rio de Janeiro: Edições Graal, 1981.

Alden, Dauril, ed. *Colonial Roots of Modern Brazil.* Berkeley: University of California Press, 1973.

Alden, Dauril, ed. "Late Colonial Brazil, 1750–1808." Pages 284–343 in Leslie Bethell, ed., *Colonial Brazil.* New York: Cambridge University Press, 1987.

Alden, Dauril, ed. "The Population of Brazil in the Late Eighteenth Century: A Preliminary Survey," *Hispanic American Historical Review,* 43, 1963, 173–205.

Alden, Dauril, ed. *Royal Government in Colonial Brazil: With Special Reference to the Administration of the Marquis of Lavradio, Viceroy, 1769–1779.* Berkeley: University of California Press, 1973.

Alves, Maria Helena Moreira. *State and Opposition in Military Brazil.* Austin: University of Texas Press, 1985.

Appleby, David P. *The Music of Brazil.* Austin: University of Texas Press, 1983.

Arquidiocese de São Paulo. Igreja Católica. *Projeto "Brasil—nunca mais."* 10th ed. Petrópolis, Brazil: Editora Vozes, 1988.

Arruda, Antônio de. *A Escola Superior de Guerra: História de sua doutrina.* 2d ed. São Paulo: Edições GRD, 1983.

Assis, José Carlos de. *A chave do tesouro: Anatomia dos escândalos financeiros: Brasil, 1974–1983.* Rio de Janeiro: Paz e Terra, 1983.

Assis, José Carlos de. *Os mandarins da república: Anatomia dos escândalos na administração pública, 1968–84.* Rio de Janeiro: Paz e Terra, 1984.

Bandeira, Luiz Alberto Moniz. *Brasil—Estados Unidos: A rivalidade emergente, 1950–1988.* Rio de Janeiro: Editora Civilização Brasileira, 1989.

Bandeira, Luiz Alberto Moniz. *Estado nacional e política internacional na América Latina: O continente nas relações Argentina—Brasil.* Brasília: Editora Universidade de Brasília, 1993.

Bandeira, Luiz Alberto Moniz. *O governo João Goulart: As lutas sociais no Brasil, 1961–1964.* Rio de Janeiro: Editora Civilização Brasileira, 1977.

Bandeira, Luiz Alberto Moniz. *Presença dos Estados Unidos no Brasil: Dois séculos de história.* Rio de Janeiro: Editora Civilização Brasileira, 1973.

Barbosa, Lívia. *O jeitinho brasileiro: A arte de ser mais igual que os outros.* Rio de Janeiro: Editora Campus, 1992.

Barman, Roderick J. *Brazil: The Forging of a Nation, 1798–1852.* Stanford: Stanford University Press, 1988.

Bastide, Roger. *The African Religions of Brazil: Toward a Sociology of the Interpenetration of Civilizations.* Baltimore: Johns Hopkins University Press, 1978.

Bello, José Maria. *A History of Modern Brazil, 1889–1964.* Stanford: Stanford University Press, 1966.

Beloch, Israel, and Alzira Alves de Abreu, eds. *Dicionário histórico-biográfico brasileiro, 1930–1983.* 4 vols. Rio de Janeiro: Editora Forense-Universitária, 1984.

Beloch, Israel, and Alzira Alves de Abreu, eds. "Ernesto Geisel." Pages 1450–59 in Israel Beloch and Alzira Alves de Abreu, eds., *Dicionário histórico-biográfico brasileiro, 1930–1983,* 2. Rio de Janeiro: Editora Forense-Universitária, 1984.

Benevides, Maria Victoria de Mesquita. *O governo Kubitschek: Desenvolvimento econômico e estabilidade política, 1956–1961.* Rio de Janeiro: Paz e Terra, 1976.

Bethell, Leslie, ed. *The Cambridge History of Latin America.* 2 vols. Cambridge: Cambridge University Press, 1986.

Bethell, Leslie, ed. *Colonial Brazil.* Cambridge: Cambridge University Press, 1987.

Binzer, Ina von. *Os meus romanos: Alegrias e tristezas de uma educadora alemã no Brasil.* São Paulo: Paz e Terra, 1982.

Black, Jan Knippers. *United States Penetration of Brazil.* Philadelphia: University of Pennsylvania Press, 1977.

Boxer, Charles R. *The Golden Age of Brazil, 1695–1750.* Berkeley: University of California Press, 1964.

Boxer, Charles R. *Salvador de Sá and the Struggle for Brazil and Angola, 1602–1686.* London: Athlone Press for University of London, 1952.

Brandi, Paulo. *Vargas, da vida para a história.* Rio de Janeiro: Zahar Editores, 1983.

Brigagão, Clóvis. *A militarização da sociedade.* Rio de Janeiro: Zahar Editores, 1985.

Britto, Antônio, and Luís Claudio Cunha. *Assim morreu Tancredo.* Porto Alegre, Brazil: L and PM Editores, 1985.

Bruneau, Thomas C. *The Political Transformation of the Brazilian Catholic Church.* New York: Cambridge University Press, 1974.

Burkholder, Mark A., and Lyman L. Johnson. *Colonial Latin America.* 2d ed. New York: Oxford University Press, 1994.

Burns, E. Bradford. *A History of Brazil.* 3d ed. New York: Columbia University Press, 1993.

Burns, E. Bradford. *Nationalism in Brazil: A Historical Survey.* New York: Praeger, 1968.

Burns, E. Bradford. *Perspectives on Brazilian History.* New York: Columbia University Press, 1967.

Burns, E. Bradford. *The Unwritten Alliance: Rio-Branco and Brazilian-American Relations.* New York: Columbia University Press, 1966.

Bushnell, David, and Neill Macaulay. *The Emergence of Latin America in the Nineteenth Century.* New York: Oxford University Press, 1988.

Calmon, Pedro. *História do Brasil.* 9 vols. Rio de Janeiro: Editora Olympio, 1959.

Camargo, Aspásia, and Walder de Góis. *Meio século de combate: Diálogo com Cordeiro de Farias.* Rio de Janeiro: Editora Nova Fronteira, 1981.

Camargo, Aspásia, et al. *O golpe silencioso: As origens da república corporativa.* Rio de Janeiro: Editora Rio Fundo, 1989.

Canale, Dario, Francisco Viana, and José Nilo Tavares. *Novembro de 1935: Meio século depois.* Petrópolis, Brazil: Editora Vozes, 1985.

Carone, Edgard. *O Estado Novo, 1937–1945.* São Paulo: Difel/Difusão Editorial, 1976.

Carone, Edgard. *A primeira república, 1889–1930.* São Paulo: Difusão Européia do Livro, 1969.

Carone, Edgard. *A quarta república, 1945–1964: Documentos.* São Paulo: Difel/Difusão Editorial, 1980.

Carone, Edgard. *A república nova, 1930–1937.* São Paulo: Difusão Européia do Livro, 1974.

Carone, Edgard. *A república velha: Evolução política.* São Paulo: Difusão Européia do Livro, 1975.

Carone, Edgard. *A república velha: Instituições e classes sociais.* São Paulo: Difusão Européia do Livro, 1972.

Carone, Edgard. *A segunda república, 1930–1937.* São Paulo: Difusão Européia do Livro, 1973.

Carone, Edgard. *O tenentismo: Acontecimentos, personagens, programas.* São Paulo: Difel/Difusão Editorial, 1975.

Carrato, José Ferreira. *Igreja, iluminismo e escolas mineiras colonais.* São Paulo: Editora Nacional, 1968.

Carvalho, José Murilo de. "Armed Forces and Politics in Brazil, 1930–1945," *Hispanic American Historical Review*, 62, No.2, May 1982, 193–223.

Carvalho, José Murilo de. *Os bestializados: O Rio de Janeiro e a república que não foi.* São Paulo: Companhia das Letras, 1987.

Carvalho, José Murilo de. *A construção da ordem: A elite política imperial.* Rio de Janeiro: Editora Campus, 1980.

Carvalho, José Murilo de. "Forças Armadas e política, 1930–1945." Pages 109–50 in Centro de Pesquisa e Documentacão de História Contemporânea do Brasil (CPDOC), *A revolucão de 30, seminário internacional.* Brasília: Editora Universidade de Brasília, 1982.

Carvalho, José Murilo de. "As forças armadas na primeira república: O poder desestablizador." Pages 183–234 in Boris Fausto, ed., *História geral da civilização brasileira.* São Paulo: Difel/Difusão Editorial, 1977.

Carvalho, José Murilo de. *A formação das almas: O imaginário da república no Brasil.* São Paulo: Companhia das Letras, 1990.

Castello Branco, Manoel Thomaz. *O Brasil na II Grande Guerra.* Rio de Janeiro: Editora Biblioteca do Exército, 1960.

Castro, Celso. *O espírito militar: Um estudo de antropologia social na Academia Militar das Agulhas Negras.* Rio de Janeiro: Jorge Zahar Editores, 1990.

Cavaliero, Roderick. *The Independence of Brazil.* London: I. B. Tauris for British Academic Press; distributed by St. Martin's Press, 1993.

Centro de Pesquisa e Documenta de História Contemporânea do Brasil (CPDOC). *A revolução de 30, seminário internacional.* Brasília: Editora Universidade de Brasília, 1982.

Cervo, Amado Luiz. *O parlamento brasileiro e as relações exteriores, 1826–1889.* Brasília: Editora Universidade de Brasília, 1981.

Cervo, Amado Luiz. *As relações históricas entre o Brasil e a Itália: O papel da diplomacia.* Brasília: Editora Universidade de Brasília, Instituto Italiano di Cultura, 1991.

Cervo, Amado Luiz, and Clodoaldo Bueno. *O desafio internacional: A política exterior do Brasil de 1930 à nossos dias.* Brasília: Editora Universidade de Brasília, 1994.

Cervo, Amado Luiz, and Clodoaldo Bueno. *História da política exterior do Brasil.* São Paulo: Editora Ática, 1992.

Chagas, Carlos. *A guerra das estrelas, 1964–1984: Os bastidores das sucessões presidenciais.* Porto Alegre, Brazil: L and PM Editores, 1985.

Chiavenatto, Julio José. *Genocídio americano: A guerra do Paraguai.* São Paulo: Editora Brasiliense, 1979.

Chilcote, Ronald H. *The Brazilian Communist Party: Conflict and Integration, 1922–1972.* New York: Oxford University Press, 1974.

Cobbs, Elizabeth A. *The Rich Neighbor Policy: Rockefeller and Kaiser in Brazil.* New Haven: Yale University Press, 1992.

Coelho, Edmundo Campos. *Em busca de identidade: O exército e a política na sociedade brasileira.* Rio de Janeiro: Editora Forense-Universitária, 1976.

Conniff, Michael L. "Populism in Brazil, 1925–1945." Pages 67–91 in Michael L. Conniff, ed., *Latin American Populism in Comparative Perspective.* Albuquerque: University of New Mexico Press, 1982.

Conniff, Michael L. "The Tenentes in Power: A New Perspective on the Brazilian Revolution of 1930," *Journal of Latin American Studies,* 10, No. 1, May 1978, 61–82.

Conniff, Michael L. *Urban Politics in Brazil: The Rise of Populism, 1925–1945.* Pittsburgh: University of Pittsburgh Press, 1981.

Conniff, Michael L., and Frank D. McCann, eds. *Modern Brazil: Elites and Masses in Historical Perspective.* Lincoln: University of Nebraska Press, 1989.

Conrad, Robert. *The Destruction of Brazilian Slavery, 1850–1888.* Urbana: University of Illinois Press, 1972.

Corréa, Carlos Humberto. *Militares e civis num governo sem rumo: O governo provisório revolucionário de Desterro, 1893–1894.* Florianópolis, Brazil: Editora Universidade Federal de Santa Catarina, Editora Lunardelli, 1990.

Costa, Emilia Viotti da. *The Brazilian Empire: Myths and Histories.* Chicago: University of Chicago Press, 1985.

Costa, Emilia Viotti da. "1870–1889." Pages 161–213 in Leslie Bethell, ed., *Brazil: Empire and Republic, 1822–1930.* Cambridge: Cambridge University Press, 1989.

Costa, João Cruz. *A History of Ideas in Brazil.* Berkeley: University of California Press, 1964.

D'Araújo, Maria Celina Soares. *O segundo governo Vargas, 1951–1954: Democracia, partidos e crise política.* Rio de Janeiro: Zahar Editores, 1982.

Davidoff, Carlos. *Bandeirantismo: Verso e reverso.* São Paulo: Editora Brasiliense, 1986.

Davis, Shelton H. *Victims of the Miracle: Development and the Indians of Brazil.* Cambridge: Cambridge University Press, 1977.

De Carli, Gileno. *Visão da crise, 1961–1964.* Brasília: Editora Universidade de Brasília, 1980.

Dean, Warren. *The Industrialization of São Paulo, 1880–1945.* Austin: University of Texas Press, 1969.

Dean, Warren. *Rio Claro: A Brazilian Plantation System, 1820–1920.* Stanford: Stanford University Press, 1976.

Della Cava, Ralph. *Miracle at Joaseiro: A Political and Economic History of a Popular Religious Movement in Brazil, 1889–1934.* New York: Columbia University Press, 1970.

Denys, Odylio. *Ciclo revolucionário brasileiro: Memórias.* Rio de Janeiro: Editora Nova Fronteira, 1980.

Devevan, William M., ed. *The Native Population of the Americas in 1492.* Madison: University of Wisconsin Press, 1976.

Diacon, Todd A. *Millenarian Vision, Capitalist Reality: Brazil's Contestado Rebellion, 1912–1916.* Durham: Duke University Press, 1991.

Dias, Maria Odila Leita da Silva. *Power and Everyday Life: The Lives of Working Women in Nineteenth-Century Brazil.* Cambridge, United Kingdom: Policy Press, 1995.

Dimenstein, Gilberto, et al. *Brazil: War on Children.* London: Latin American Bureau, 1991.

Dimenstein, Gilberto, et al. *O complô que elegeu Tancredo.* Rio de Janeiro: Editora JB, 1985.

Dreifuss, René A. *1964: A conquista do estado: Ação política, poder e golpe de classe.* Petrópolis, Brazil: Editora Vozes, 1981.

Dreifuss, René Armand. *O jogo da direita na nova república.* Petrópolis, Brazil: Editora Vozes, 1989.

Drosdoff, Daniel. *Linha dura no Brasil: O governo Médici, 1969–1974.* São Paulo: Editora Global, 1986.

Drummond, José Augusto. *O movimento tenentista: A intervenção política dos oficiais jovens, 1922–1935.* Rio de Janeiro: Edições Graal, 1986.

Duarte, Paulo de Queiroz. *Os Voluntários da Pátria na Guerra do Paraguai.* Rio de Janeiro: Editora Biblioteca do Exército, 1981.

Dulles, John W.F. *President Castello Branco: Brazilian Reformer.* College Station: Texas A and M University Press, 1981.

Dulles, John W.F. *Vargas of Brazil: A Political Biography.* Austin: University of Texas Press, 1967.

Dutra, Francis A. *A Guide to the History of Brazil, 1500–1822: The Literature in English.* Santa Barbara, California: ABC-Clio, 1980.

Eakin, Marshall C. *Brazil: The Once and Future Country.* New York: St. Martin's Press, 1997.

Fausto, Boris. *A Revolução de 1930: Historiografia e história.* São Paulo: Editora Brasiliense, 1970.

Fausto, Boris. *Trabalho urbano e conflito social, 1890–1920.* São Paulo: Difel/Difusão Editorial, 1976.

Fernandes, Heloisa Rodrigues. *Política e segurança, força pública do estado do São Paulo: Fundamentos histórico-sociais.* São Paulo: Editora Alfa-Omega, 1974.

Fontes, Lourival, and Glauco Carneiro. *A face final de Vargas: Os bilhetes de Getúlio.* Rio de Janeiro: Edições O Cruzeiro, 1966.

Forman, Shepard. *The Brazilian Peasantry.* New York: Columbia University Press, 1975.

Fragoso, Augusto Tasso. *Os franceses no Rio de Janeiro.* Rio de Janeiro: Editora Biblioteca do Exército, 1950.

Freyre, Gilberto. *The Mansions and the Shanties: The Making of Modern Brazil.* New York: Knopf, 1963.

Freyre, Gilberto. *The Masters and the Slaves: A Study in the Development of Brazilian Civilization.* Abridged ed. New York: Knopf, 1956.

Freyre, Gilberto. *New World in the Tropics: The Culture of Modern Brazil.* New York: Knopf, 1959.

Freyre, Gilberto. *Order and Progress: Brazil from Monarchy to Republic.* New York: Knopf, 1970.

Frota, Lélia Coelho. *Ataíde.* Rio de Janeiro: Editora Nova Fronteira, 1982.

Góes, Walder de. *O Brasil do General Geisel: Estudo do processo de tomada de decisão no regime militar-burocrático.* Rio de Janeiro: Editora Nova Fronteira, 1978.

Góes, Walder de, and Aspásia Camargo. *O drama da sucessão e a crise do regime.* Rio de Janeiro: Editora Nova Fronteira, 1984.

Gomis, Angela Maria de Castro, ed. *O Brasil de JK.* Rio de Janeiro: Editora da Fundação Getúlio Vargas-Centro de Pesquisa e Documenta de História Contemporânea do Brasil (CPDOC), 1991.

Gomis, Angela Maria de Castro, ed. *Regionalismo e centralização política: Partidos e constituinte nos anos 30.* Rio de Janeiro: Editora Nova Fronteira, 1980.

Graham, Lawrence S., and Robert H. Wilson, eds. *The Political Economy of Brazil: Public Policies in an Era of Transition.* Austin: University of Texas Press, 1990.

Graham, Richard. *Britain and the Onset of Modernization in Brazil, 1850–1914.* Cambridge: Cambridge University Press, 1972.

Graham, Richard. "1850–1870." Pages 113–60 in Leslie Bethell, ed., *Brazil: Empire and Republic, 1822–1930.* New York: Cambridge University Press, 1989.

Graham, Richard. *Patronage and Politics in Nineteenth-Century Brazil.* Stanford: Stanford University Press, 1990.

Graham, Richard, ed. *Brazil and the World System.* Austin: University of Texas Press, 1991.

Hahner, June E. *Civilian-Military Relations in Brazil, 1889–1898.* Columbia: University of South Carolina Press, 1969.

Hahner, June E. *Emancipating the Female Sex: The Struggle for Women's Rights in Brazil, 1850–1940.* Durham: Duke University Press, 1990.

Haines, Gerald K. *The Americanization of Brazil: A Study of U.S. Cold War Diplomacy in the Third World, 1945–1954.* Wilmington, Delaware: Scholarly Resources, 1989.

Hall, Michael M., and Marco Aurélio Garcia. "Urban Labor." Pages 161–91 in Michael L. Conniff and Frank D. McCann, eds., *Modern Brazil: Elites and Masses in Historical Perspective.* Lincoln: University of Nebraska Press, 1991.

Haring, Clarence H. *Empire in Brazil: A New World Experiment with Monarchy.* Cambridge: Harvard University Press, 1966.

Hayes, Robert Ames. *The Armed Nation: The Brazilian Corporate Mystique.* Tempe: Center for Latin American Studies, Arizona State University, 1989.

Hemming, John. *Amazon Frontier: The Defeat of the Brazilian Indians.* Cambridge: Harvard University Press, 1987.

Hemming, John. "How Brazil Acquired Roraima," *Hispanic American Historical Review,* 70, No. 2, 295–325.

Hemming, John. "Indians and the Frontier." Pages 145–89 in Leslie Bethell, ed., in *Colonial Brazil.* New York: Cambridge University Press, 1987.

Hemming, John. *Red Gold: The Conquest of the Brazilian Indians, 1500–1760.* Cambridge: Harvard University Press, 1978.

Hilton, Stanley E. *Brazil and the Great Powers, 1930–1939: The Politics of Trade Rivalry.* Austin: University of Texas Press, 1975.

Hilton, Stanley E. *1932: A guerra civil brasileira: História da revolução constitucionalista de 1932.* Rio de Janeiro: Editora Nova Fronteira, 1982.

Hilton, Stanley E. *A rebelião vermelha.* Rio de Janeiro: Editora Record, 1986.

Hirst, Mônica. *Brasil-Estados Unidos na transição democrática.* Rio de Janeiro: Paz e Terra, 1985.

Hogan, James E. "Antonio Francisco Lisboa, 'O Aleijadinho': An Annotated Bibliography," *Latin American Research Review,* 9, No. 2, 1974, 83–94.

Hogan, James E. "The Contemporaries of Antonio Francisco Lisboa: An Annotated Bibliography," *Latin American Research Review,* 9, No. 2, 1974, 138–45.

Holanda, Sérgio Buarque de. *Raízes do Brasil.* 2d ed. Rio de Janeiro: Editora Olympio, 1948.

Holanda, Sérgio Buarque de. *Visão do paraíso: Os motivos edênicos no descobrimento e colonização do Brasil.* São Paulo: Editora Nacional, 1969.

Holanda, Sérgio Buarque de, ed. *História geral da civilização brasileira.* São Paulo: Difusão Européia do Livro, 1960.

Holloway, Thomas H. *Policing Rio de Janeiro: Repression and Resistance in a Nineteenth-Century City.* Stanford: Stanford University Press, 1993.

Huggins, Martha K. *From Slavery to Vagrancy in Brazil: Crime and Social Control in the Third World.* New Brunswick: Rutgers University Press, 1985.

Ireland, Rowan. *Kingdoms Come: Religion and Politics in Brazil.* Pittsburgh: University of Pittsburgh Press, 1991.

Janotti, Maria de Lourdes Mônaco. *Os subversivos da república.* São Paulo: Editora Brasiliense, 1986.

Johnson, Harold B. "Portuguese Settlement, 1500–1580." Pages 1–38 in Lesley Bethell, ed., *Colonial Brazil.* New York: Cambridge University Press, 1987.

Josephy, Alvin M., Jr., ed. *America in 1492: The World of the Indian Peoples Before the Arrival of Columbus.* New York: Knopf, 1992.

Karasch, Mary C. *Slave Life in Rio de Janeiro, 1808–1850.* Ann Arbor, Michigan: University Microfilms, 1974.

Keith, Henry. "Armed Federal Interventions in the States During the Old Republic." Pages 51–77 in Henry H. Keith and Robert A. Hayes, eds., *Perspectives on Armed Politics in Brazil.* Tempe: Center for Latin American Studies, Arizona State University, 1976.

Keith, Henry, and Robert A. Hayes, eds. *Perspectives on Armed Politics in Brazil.* Tempe: Center for Latin American Studies, Arizona State University, 1976.

Kolinski, Charles J. *Independence or Death! The Story of the Paraguayan War.* Gainesville: University of Florida Press, 1965.

Krischke, Paulo, J., ed. *Brasil: Do "milagre" à "abertura".* São Paulo: Editora Cortez, 1983.

Krischke, Paulo J., and Scott Mainwaring, eds. *A igreja nas bases em tempo de transição, 1974–1985.* Porto Alegre, Brazil: L and PM Editores, CEDEC, 1986.

Labaki, Amir. *1961: A crise da renùncia e a solução parlamentarista.* São Paulo: Editora Brasiliense, 1986.

Lacombe, Américo Jacobina. *Brasil: Período nacional*, 3. Mexico City: Programa de História de America, Editorial Cultura, 1956.

Lagôa, Ana. *SNI: Como nasceu, como funciona.* São Paulo: Editora Brasiliense, 1983.

Lange, Francisco. *O Brasil monárquico*, Book 2. *História geral da civilização brasileira*, 5. São Paulo: Difel/Difusão Editorial, 1972.

Lapa, José Roberto do Amaral. *A Bahia e a carreira da india.* São Paulo: Editora Nacional, 1968.

Lapa, José Roberto do Amaral. *Economia colonial.* São Paulo: Editora Perspectiva, 1973.

Leacock, Ruth. *Requiem for Revolution: The United States and Brazil, 1961–1969.* Kent, Ohio: Kent State University Press, 1990.

Leite, Serafim. *Novas páginas de história do Brasil.* São Paulo: Editora Nacional, 1965.

Levine, Robert M. "Elite Perceptions of the *Povo.*" Pages 209–24 in Michael L. Conniff and Frank D. McCann, eds., *Modern Brazil: Elites and Masses in Historical Perspective.* Lincoln: University of Nebraska Press, 1991.

Levine, Robert M. *Pernambuco in the Brazilian Federation, 1889–1937.* Stanford: Stanford University Press, 1978.

Levine, Robert M. *Vale of Tears: Revisiting the Canudos Massacre in Northeastern Brazil, 1893–1897.* Berkeley: University of California Press, 1992.

Levine, Robert M. *The Vargas Regime: The Critical Years, 1934–1938.* New York: Columbia University Press, 1970.

Lewin, Linda. *Politics and Parentela in Paraíba: A Case Study of Family-Based Oligarchy in Brazil.* Princeton: Princeton University Press, 1987.

Lima Sobrinho, Barbosa. *A verdade sobre a Revolução de Outubro 1930.* 2d ed. São Paulo: Editora Alfa-Omega, 1975.

Linz, Juan J. "The Future of an Authoritarian Situation or the Institutionalization of an Authoritarian Regime: The Case of Brazil." Pages 233–54 in Alfred Stepan, ed., *Authoritarian Brazil: Origins, Policies, and Future.* New Haven: Yale University Press, 1973.

Lockhart, James, and Stuart B. Schwartz. *Early Latin America: A History of Colonial Spanish America and Brazil.* New York: Cambridge University Press, 1983.

Love, Joseph L. *Rio Grande do Sul and Brazilian Regionalism, 1882–1930.* Stanford: Stanford University Press, 1971.

Love, Joseph L. *São Paulo in the Brazilian Federation, 1889–1937.* Stanford: Stanford University Press, 1980.

Lowenstein, Karl. *Brazil under Vargas.* New York: Macmillan, 1942.

Lugon, Clóvis. *A república "comunista" cristã dos Guaranis, 1610–1768.* Rio de Janeiro: Paz e Terra, 1977.

Lynch, F.C. "Admiral Lord Cochrane: A Hero for Today's Professionals," *Proceedings of the United States Naval Institute,* February 1975, 63–73.

Lyra, Heitor. *História da queda do império.* 2 vols. São Paulo: Editora Nacional, 1964.

McCann, Frank D. "The Brazilian Army and the Problem of Mission, 1939–1964," *Journal of Latin American Studies* [London], 12, No. 1, May 1980, 107–26.

McCann, Frank D. "The Brazilian Army and the Pursuit of Arms Independence, 1899–1979." Pages 171–93 in Benjamin F. Cooling, ed., *War, Business, and World Military-Industrial Complexes.* Port Washington, New York: Kennikat Press, 1981.

McCann, Frank D. "Brazilian Foreign Relations in the Twentieth Century." Pages 1–23 in Wayne A Selcher, ed., *Brazil in the International System: The Rise of a Middle Power.* Boulder, Colorado: Westview Press, 1981.

McCann, Frank D. *The Brazilian-American Alliance, 1937–1945.* Princeton: Princeton University Press, 1973.

McCann, Frank D. "The Military." Pages 47–80 in Michael L. Conniff and Frank D. McCann, eds., *Modern Brazil: Elites and Masses in Historical Perspective.* Lincoln: University of Nebraska Press, 1991.

McCann, Frank D. *A nação armada: Ensaios sobre a história do exército brasileiro.* Recife, Brazil: Editora Guararapes, 1982.

Macaulay, Neill. *Dom Pedro: The Struggle for Liberty in Brazil and Portugal.* Durham: Duke University Press, 1986.

Macaulay, Neill. *The Prestes Column: Revolution in Brazil.* New York: New Viewpoints, 1974.

Machado, Lourival Gomes. "Arquitetura e artes plásticas." Pages 106–20 in Sérgio Buarque de Holanda, ed., *História geral da civilização brasileira,* 2. São Paulo: Difusão Européia do Livro, 1960.

Magalhães, Raymond. *Deodoro: A espada contra o império.* 2 vols. São Paulo: Editora Nacional, 1957.

Mainwaring, Scott. *The Catholic Church and Politics in Brazil, 1916–1985.* Stanford: Stanford University Press, 1986.

Martins, Paulo Guilherme. *Um dia na vida do Brasilino.* 8th ed. São Paulo: Editora Brasiliense, 1964.

Matta, Roberto da. *Carnavais, malandros e heróis: Para uma sociologia do dilema brasileiro.* 4th ed. Rio de Janeiro: Zahar Editores, 1983.

Matta, Roberto da. *Explorações: Ensaios de sociologia interpretativa.* Rio de Janeiro: Rocco, 1986.

Matta, Roberto da. *O que faz o Brasil, Brasil?* Rio de Janeiro: Rocco, 1986.

Mattos, Carlos de Meira. *Geopolítica e teoria de fronteiras: Fronteiras do Brasil.* Rio de Janeiro: Editora Biblioteca do Exército, 1990.

Mattos, Carlos de Meira. *Uma geopolítica pan-amazônica.* Rio de Janeiro: Editora Olympio, 1980.

Mauro, Frédéric. *O Brasil no tempo de Dom Pedro II, 1831–1889.* São Paulo: Companhia das Letras, 1991.

Mauro, Frédéric. *Do Brasil à América.* São Paulo: Editora Perspectiva, 1975.

Mauro, Frédéric. *Nova história e nôvo mundo.* São Paulo: Editora Perspectiva, 1969.

Mauro, Frédéric. "Political and Economic Structures of Empire, 1580–1750." Pages 39–66 in Leslie Bethell, ed., *Colonial Brazil.* New York: Cambridge University Press, 1987.

Maxwell, Kenneth R. *Conflicts and Conspiracies: Brazil and Portugal, 1750–1808.* Cambridge: Cambridge University Press, 1973.

Meggers, Betty J. *Amazonia: Man and Culture in a Counterfeit Paradise.* Chicago: Aldine, Atherton, 1971.

Meireles, Denise Maldi. *Guardiães da fronteira: Rio Guaporé, século XVIII.* Petrópolis, Brazil: Editora Vozes, 1989.

Metcalf, Alida C. *Family and Frontier in Colonial Brazil: Santana de Parnaíba, 1580–1822.* Berkeley: University of California Press, 1992.

Ministério da Guerra. *Almanac do Ministério da Guerra, 1930.* Rio de Janeiro: Imprensa Militar, 1930.

Ministério da Guerra. *Almanac do Ministério da Guerra, 1931.* Rio de Janeiro: Imprensa Militar, 1931.

Ministério da Guerra. *Relatório sucinto das actividades do Ministerio da Guerra durante o ano de 1962, apresentado ao Excelentissímo Senhor Presidente da República.* Rio de Janeiro: SMG Imprensa do Exército, 1963.

Monteiro, Duglas Teixeira. *Os errantes do novo século: Um estudo sobre o surto milenarista do Contestado.* São Paulo: Livraria Duas Cidades, 1974.

Moraes, João Quartim de. *A esquerda militar no Brasil: Da conspiração republicana à guerrilha dos tenentes.* São Paulo: Edições Siciliano, 1991.

Moraes, João Quartim de. *A tutela militar.* Rio de Janeiro: Editora Revista dos Tribunais, 1987.

Moreira, Marcílio Marques. *The Brazilian Quandary.* New York: Priority Press, 1986.

Mota, Carlos Guilherme. *Ideologia da cultura brasileira, 1933–1974: Pontos de partida para uma revisão histórica.* São Paulo: Editora Ática, 1980.

Mota, Carlos Guilherme. *Nordeste 1817: Estruturas e argumentos.* São Paulo: Editora Perspectiva, 1972.

Mota, Carlos Guilherme, ed. *Brasil em perspectiva.* São Paulo: Difusão Européia do Livro, 1969.

Mota, Lourenço Dantas. *A nova república: O nome e a coisa.* São Paulo: Editora Brasiliense, 1985.

Moura, Gerson. *O alinhamento sem recompensa: A política externa do Governo Dutra.* Rio de Janeiro: Centro de Pesquisa e Documentação de História Contemporânea do Brasil (CPDOC), 1990.

Nabuco, Joaquim. *Abolitionism: The Brazilian Antislavery Struggle.* Urbana: University of Illinois Press, 1977.

Norton, Luís. *A Corte de Portugal no Brasil.* São Paulo: Editora Nacional, 1979.

Novais, Fernando A. *Portugal e Brasil na crise do antigo sistema colonial, 1777–1808.* São Paulo: Editora Hucitec, 1979.

Novais, Fernando A. "A proibição das manufacturas no Brasil e a política econômica portuguesa do fim do século XVIII," *Revista de história* [São Paulo], 32, No. 67, 1966, 145–66.

Oliveira, Eliézer Rizzo de, Geraldo L. Cavagnari Filho, João Quartim de Moraes, and René Armand Dreifuss. *As Forças*

Armadas no Brasil. Rio de Janeiro: Editora Espaço e Tempo, 1987.

Oliveira, Lúcia Lippi, Eduardo Rodrigues Gomes, and Maria Celina Whately. *Elite intelectual e debate político nos anos 30: Uma bibliografia comentada de Revolução de 1930.* Rio de Janeiro: Fundação Getúlio Vargas, 1980.

Oliveira, Lúcia Lippi, Mônica Pimenta Velloso, and Ângela Maria Castro Gomes. *Estado novo: Ideologia e poder.* Rio de Janeiro: Zahar Editores, 1982.

Patai, Daphne. *Brazilian Women Speak: Contemporary Life Stories.* New Brunswick: Rutgers University Press, 1988.

Peixoto, Artur Vieira. *Floriano: Biografia do Marechal Floriano Peixoto; Memórias e documentos.* Rio de Janeiro: Ministério da Educação, 1939.

Pinheiro, Paulo Sérgio de M.S. *Escritos indignados: Polícia, prisões e política no estado autoritário (no 20º aniversário do Regime de Exceção, 1964–1984).* São Paulo: Editora Brasiliense, 1984.

Pinheiro, Paulo Sérgio de M.S. *Estratégias da ilusão: A revolução mundial e o Brasil, 1922–1935.* São Paulo: Companhia das Letras, 1991.

Pinto, Virgílio Noya. "Balanço das transformações econômicas no Século XIX." Pages 125–45 in Carlos Guilherme Mota, ed., *Brasil em perspectiva.* São Paulo: Difusão Européia do Livro, 1969.

Pomer, León. *A guerra do Paraguai: A grande tragédia rioplatense.* São Paulo: Editora Gobal, 1980.

Portela, Fernando. *Guerra de guerrilhas no Brasil.* 7th ed. São Paulo: Editora Global, 1986.

Prado, João F. de Almeida. *D. João VI e o início da classe dirigente no Brasil.* São Paulo: Editora Nacional, 1968.

Prado Júnior, Caio. *The Colonial Background of Modern Brazil.* Berkeley: University of California Press, 1971.

Proença Júnior, Domício, ed. *Uma avaliação da indústria bélica brasileira: Defesa, indústria e tecnologia.* Rio de Janeiro: Grupo de Estudos Estratégicos, Forum de Ciência e Cultura, Universidade Federal do Rio de Janeiro, 1993.

Queiroz, Maurício Vinhas de. *Messianismo e conflito social: A guerra sertaneja do Contestado, 1912–1916.* 2d ed. São Paulo: Editora Ática, 1977.

Queiroz, Suely Robles Reis de. *Os radicais da república: Jacobinismo: Ideologia e ação, 1893–1897.* São Paulo: Editora Brasiliense, 1986.

Rachum, Ilan. "Nationalism and Revolution in Brazil, 1922–1930: A Study of Intellectual, Military, and Political Protesters and of the Assault on the Old Republic." Ph.D. dissertation. New York: Columbia University, 1970.

Reber, Vera Blinn. "The Demographics of Paraguay: A Reinterpretation of the Great War, 1864–1870," *Hispanic American Historical Review*, 68, No. 2, May 1988, 289–319.

Ribeiro, Darcy. *O povo brasileiro.* São Paulo: Companhia das Letras, 1995.

Riedinger, Edward A. *Como se faz um presidente: A campanha de J.K.* Rio de Janeiro: Editora Nova Fronteira, 1988.

Rodrigues, José Honório. *Independência, revolução e contrarevolução: As Forças Armadas.* Rio de Janeiro: Editora Francisco Alves, 1975.

Rouquié, Alain, ed. *The Military and the State in Latin America.* Berkeley: University of California Press, 1987.

Rouquié, Alain, ed. *Les partis militaires au Brésil.* Paris: Presses de la Fondation Nationale des Sciences Politiques, 1980.

Russell-Wood, A.J.R., ed. *From Colony to Nation: Essays on the Independence of Brazil.* Baltimore: Johns Hopkins University Press, 1975.

Russell-Wood, A.J.R., ed. "Preconditions and Precipitants of the Independence Movement in Portuguese America." Pages 3–40 in A.J.R. Russell-Wood, ed., *From Colony to Nation: Essays on the Independence of Brazil.* Baltimore: Johns Hopkins University Press, 1975.

Schmitter, Philippe C. *Interest Conflict and Political Change in Brazil.* Stanford: Stanford University Press, 1971.

Schneider, Ronald M. *Order and Progress: A Political History of Brazil.* Boulder, Colorado: Westview Press, 1991.

Schneider, Ronald M. *The Political System of Brazil: Emergence of a "Modernizing" Authoritarian Regime, 1964–1970.* New York: Columbia University Press, 1971.

Schwartz, Stuart B. "Free Labor in a Slave Economy: The Lavradores de Cana of Colonial Bahia." Pages 147–97 in Dauril Alden, ed., *Colonial Roots of Modern Brazil.* Berkeley: University of California Press, 1973.

Schwartz, Stuart B. "Plantations and Peripheries, ca. 1580–ca.1750." Pages 67–144 in Leslie Bethell, ed., *Colonial Brazil.* New York: Cambridge University Press, 1987.

Schwartz, Stuart B. *Sovereignty and Society in Colonial Brazil: The High Court of Bahia and its Judges, 1609–1751.* Berkeley: University of California Press, 1973.

Schwartz, Stuart B. *Sugar Plantations in the Formation of Brazilian Society: Bahia, 1550–1835.* Cambridge: Cambridge University Press, 1985.

Schwartzman, Simon. *São Paulo e o estado nacional.* São Paulo: Difel, 1975.

Seckinger, Ron. *The Brazilian Monarchy and the South American Republics, 1822–1831: Diplomacy and State Building.* Baton Rouge: Louisiana State University Press, 1984.

Shoumatoff, Alex. *The Capital of Hope.* New York: Coward, McCann and Geoghegan, 1980.

Silva, Hélio. *1889: A república não esperou o amanhecer.* Rio de Janeiro: Editora Civilização Brasileira, 1972.

Silva, Hélio. *1930: A revolução traída.* Rio de Janeiro: Editora Civilização Brasileira, 1966.

Silva, Hélio. *1933: A crise do tenentismo.* Rio de Janeiro: Editora Civilização Brasileira, 1968.

Silva, Hélio, and Maria Cecília R. Carneiro. *O pensamento político de Vargas.* Porto Alegre, Brazil: L and PM Editores, 1980.

Silva, Maria Beatriz Nizza da. *Cultura e sociedade no Rio de Janeiro, 1808–1821.* São Paulo: Editora Nacional, 1977.

Silveira, Joel, and Thassilo Mitke. *A luta dos pracinhas: A Força Expedicionária Brasileira—FEB na II Guerra Mundial.* 3d ed. Rio de Janeiro: Editora Record, 1993.

Simonsen, Roberto C. *História econômica do Brasil, 1500–1820.* 2 vols. São Paulo: Editora Nacional, 1944.

Skidmore, Thomas E. *Black into White: Race and Nationality in Brazilian Thought.* Durham: Duke University Press, 1993.

Skidmore, Thomas E. *Politics in Brazil, 1930–1964: An Experiment in Democracy.* New York: Oxford University Press, 1967.

Skidmore, Thomas E. *The Politics of Military Rule in Brazil, 1964–85.* New York: Oxford University Press, 1988.

Smith, Joseph. *Unequal Giants: Diplomatic Relations Between the United States and Brazil, 1889–1930.* Pittsburgh: University of Pittsburgh Press, 1991.

Soares, Álvaro Teixeira. *Diplomacia do império no Rio da Prata.* Rio de Janeiro: Editora Brand, 1955.

Soares, Álvaro Teixeira. *História da formação das fronteiras do Brasil.* Rio de Janeiro: Editora Biblioteca do Exército, 1973.

Sodré, Nelson Werneck. *História militar do Brasil.* Rio de Janeiro: Editora Civilização Brasileira, 1965.

Souza, Maria do Carmo Campello de. *Estado e partidos políticos no Brasil, 1930 à 1964.* São Paulo: Editora Alfa-Omega, 1976.

Stein, Stanley J. *Vassouras: A Brazilian Coffee County, 1850–1900; The Roles of Planter and Slave in a Plantation Society.* Princeton: Princeton University Press, 1985.

Stein, Stanley J., and Barbara H. Stein. *The Colonial Heritage of Latin America: Essays on Economic Dependence in Perspective.* New York: Oxford University Press, 1970.

Stepan, Alfred C. *The Military in Politics: Changing Patterns in Brazil.* Princeton: Princeton University Press, 1971.

Stepan, Alfred C. *Rethinking Military Politics: Brazil and the Southern Cone.* Princeton: Princeton University Press, 1988.

Stepan, Alfred C., ed. *Authoritarian Brazil: Origins, Policies, and Future.* New Haven: Yale University Press, 1973.

Stepan, Alfred C., ed. *Democratizing Brazil: Problems of Transition and Consolidation.* New York: Oxford University Press, 1989.

Stumpf, André Gustavo, and Merval Pereira Filho. *A segunda guerra: Sucessão de Geisel.* São Paulo: Editora Brasiliense, 1979.

Tanenbaum, Barbara A., ed. *Encyclopedia of Latin American History and Culture,* 5. New York: Charles Scribner's Sons, 1996.

Topik, Steven C. *The Political Economy of the Brazilian State, 1889–1930.* Austin: University of Texas Press, 1987.

Topik, Steven C. *Trade and Gunboats: The United States and Brazil in the Age of Empire.* Stanford: Stanford University Press, 1996.

Toplin, Robert B. *The Abolition of Slavery in Brazil.* New York: Atheneum, 1972.

Tôrres, João Camilo de Oliveira. *Os construtores do império: Ideais e lutas do Partido Conservador Brasileiro.* São Paulo: Editora Nacional, 1968.

Tôrres, João Camilo de Oliveira. *Interpretação da realidade-brasileira: Introdução à história das idéias políticas no Brasil.* 2d ed. Rio de Janeiro: Editora Olympio, 1973.

Valença, José Rolim. *Modinha: Raizes da música do povo.* São Paulo: Empresas Dow, 1985.

Vasconcellos, Genserico de. *Historia militar do Brasil: Introdução da influencia do factor militar na organização da nacionalidade—a campanha de 1851/1852.* Rio de Janeiro: Imprensa Militar, 1922.

Vasconcellos, Sylvio. *Vila Rica: Formação e desenvolvimento, residências.* Rio de Janeiro: Ministério da Educação e Cultura, Instituto Nacional do Livro, 1956.

Vinhosa, Francisco Luiz Teixeira. *O Brasil e a Primeira Guerra Mundial.* Rio de Janeiro: Instituto Histórico e Geográfico Brasileiro, 1990.

Vinhosa, Francisco Luiz Teixeira. "Brasil sede da monarquia: Brasil Reino." Pt. 2 of Vicente Tapajós, ed., *História administrativa do Brasil,* Brasília: Fundação Centro de Formação do Servidor Público, 1984.

Wagley, Charles. *An Introduction to Brazil.* Rev. ed. New York: Columbia University Press, 1971.

Warren, Harris G. *Paraguay and the Triple Alliance: The Postwar Decade, 1869–1878.* Austin: University of Texas Press, 1978.

Weis, W. Michael. *Cold Warriors and Coups d'État: Brazilian-American Relations, 1945–1964.* Albuquerque: University of New Mexico Press, 1993.

Weschler, Lawrence. *A Miracle, A Universe: Settling Accounts with Torturers.* New York: Penguin Books, 1990.

Whigham, Thomas L., and Barbara Potthast. "Some Strong Reservations: A Critique of Vera Blinn Reber's *The Demographics of Paraguay: A Reinterpretation of the Great War, 1864–1870,*" *Hispanic American Historical Review,* 70, No. 1990, 667–78.

Wirth, John D. *Minas Gerais in the Brazilian Federation, 1889–1937.* Stanford: Stanford University Press, 1977.

Wirth, John D. *The Politics of Brazilian Development, 1930–1954.* Stanford: Stanford University Press, 1970.

Wolfe, Joel. *Working Women, Working Men: São Paulo and the Rise of Brazil's Industrial Working Class, 1900–1955.* Durham: Duke University Press, 1993.

Chapter 2

Albuquerque, Roberto Cavalcanti de. "A situação social: O que diz o passado e o que promete o futuro." Pages 387–410 in

Instituto de Pesquisa Econômica Aplicada (IPEA), *Perspectivas da economia brasileira, 1992.* Brasília: 1991.

Almanaque Abril, Abril 92. São Paulo: Editora Abril, 1992.

Andrews, George Reid. *Blacks and Whites in São Paulo, Brazil: 1888–1988.* Madison: University of Wisconsin Press, 1992.

Amnesty International. *Brazil: Authorized Violence in Rural Areas.* London: 1988.

Amnesty International. *Brazil: Torture and Extrajudicial Execution in Urban Brazil.* New York: 1990.

Anderson, Anthony B., ed. *Alternatives to Deforestation: Steps Toward Sustainable Use of the Amazon Rain Forest.* New York: Columbia University Press, 1990.

Andrade, Manoel Correa de. *A terra e o homem no Nordeste.* 4th ed. São Paulo: Livraria Editora Glencias Humanas, 1980.

Aragão, Murillo de. *Grupos de pressão no Congresso Nacional: Como a sociedade pode defender licitamente seus direitos no poder legislativo.* São Paulo: Maltese, 1994.

Bacha, Edmar L., and Herbert Klein S., eds. *Social Change in Brazil, 1945–1985: The Incomplete Transition.* Albuquerque: University of New Mexico Press, 1989.

Baer, Werner. *The Brazilian Economy: Growth and Development.* 3d ed. New York: Praeger, 1989.

Baer, Werner. *A industrialização e o desenvolvimento econômico no Brasil.* 2d ed. rev. Rio de Janeiro: Fundação Getúlio Vargas, 1975.

Bandeira, Moniz. *Estado nacional e política internacional na América Latina: O continente nas relacões Argentina-Brasil, 1930–1992.* São Paulo: Editora Ensaio, 1993.

Barbosa, Lívia. *O jeitinho brasileiro: A arte de ser mais igual que os outros.* Rio de Janeiro: Editora Campus, 1992.

Barcellos, Caco. *Rota 66.* São Paulo: Editora Globo, 1992.

Barros, Ricardo Paes de, and Rosane Mendonça. "Geração e reprodução da desigualdade de renda no Brasil." Pages 471–90 in Instituto de Pesquisa Econômica Aplicada (IPEA), *Perspectivas da economia brasileira, 1994.* Rio de Janeiro: 1993.

Becker, Bertha K. "Repensando a questão ambiental no Brasil a partir da geografia política." Pages 127–52 in Maria do Carmo Leal, ed., *Saúde, ambiente e desenvolvimento.* São Paulo, Hucitec, 1992.

Bodea, Miguel. *Trabalhismo e populismo no Rio Grande do Sul.* Porto Alegre, Brazil: Universidade Federal do Rio Grande do Sul, 1992.

Borges, Vavy Pacheco. *Tenentismo e revolucão brasileira.* São Paulo Editora Brasiliense, 1992.

Brisco, John. *Brazil: The New Challenge of Adult Health.* Washington: World Bank, 1990.

Browder, John O. "Alternative Rainforest Uses." Pages 58–95 in Joseph S. Tulchin, ed., *Economic Development and Environmental Protection in Latin America.* Washington: Woodrow Wilson Center Press, 1991.

Buarque, Cristovam. *A revolução na esquerda e a invenção do Brasil.* Rio de Janeiro: Paz e Terra, 1992.

Caldeira, Teresa. "Desventuras dos direitos humanos no Brasil," *Novos Estudos CEBRAP* (Centro Brasileiro de Análise e Planejamento) [São Paulo], No. 30, 1991.

Camargo, José Márcio, and Fábio Giambiagi, eds. *Distribuição de renda no Brasil.* São Paulo: Paz e Terra, 1991.

Cardoso, Fernando Henrique. *A construção da democracia: Estudos sobre política.* São Paulo: Editora Siciliano, 1994.

Carpenter, Mark. *Brazil: An Awakening Giant.* Minneapolis: Dillon Press, 1987.

Castro, Antônio Barros de. *7 ensaios sobre a economia brasileira.* 2d ed. Rio de Janeiro: Editora Forense-Universitaria, 1972.

Cervo, Amado Luiz, and Clodoaldo Bueno. *História da política exterior do Brasil.* São Paulo: Editora Ática, 1992.

Coelho, João Gilberto Lucas, and Antônio Carlos Nantes de Oliveira. *A nova constituição: Avaliação do texto e perfil dos constituintes.* Rio de Janeiro: Revan, INESC, 1989.

Comisssão Interministerial para Preparacão da Conferencia das Nações Unidas Sobre Meio Ambiente Desenvolvimento (CIMA). *The Challenge of Sustainable Development: The Brazilian Report for the United Nations Conference on Environment and Development.* Brasília: Press Secretariat of the Presidency of the Republic, 1992.

Crespo, Samyra, and Pedro Leitão. *O que o brasileiro pensa sobre o meio ambiente.* Rio de Janeiro: Museu de Astronomia e Ciências Afins (MAST). Centro de Tecnologia Mineral (Cetem), Instituto de Estudos da Religião (Iser), 1993.

Cunha, Euclides da. *Rebellion in the Backlands.* Chicago: University of Chicago Press, 1957.

Cunha, Manuela Carneiro da. *História dos Índios do Brasil.* São Paulo: Companhia das Letras, Fundação de Apoio á Pesquisa de São Paulo (Fapesp), Secretária Municipal de Cultura de São Paulo, 1992.

Davis, Shelton H. *Victims of the Miracle: Development Against the Indians of Brazil.* Cambridge: Cambridge University Press, 1976.

Dimenstein, Gilberto. *A guerra dos meninos: Assassinatos de menores no Brasil.* São Paulo: Editora Brasiliense, 1990.

Faria, Vilmar E. "Desenvolvimento, urbanização e mudanças na estrutura do emprego: A expêriencia brasileira dos últimos trinta anos." Pages 118–63 in Bernardo Sorj and Maria Herminia T. Almeida, eds., *Sociedade e política no Brasil pós-64.* São Paulo: Editora Brasiliense, 1983.

Figueiredo, Argelina Cheibub. *Democracia ou reformas?: Alternativas democráticas à crise política.* Rio de Janeiro: Paz e Terra, 1993.

Figueiredo, Marcus Faria. *A decisão do voto: Democracia e racionalidade.* São Paulo: Editora Sumaré, 1991.

Flores, Mário César. *Bases para uma política militar.* Campinas, Brazil: Editora de Unicamp, 1992.

Fontaine, Pierre-Michel, ed. *Race, Class and Power in Brazil.* Los Angeles: Center for Afro-American Studies, University of California, 1985.

Freyre, Gilberto. *The Mansions and the Shanties: The Making of Modern Brazil.* New York: Knopf, 1963.

Freyre, Gilberto. *The Masters and the Slaves: A Study in the Development of Brazilian Civilization.* 2d English-language ed. New York: Knopf, 1963.

Furtado, Celso. *The Economic Growth of Brazil: A Survey from Colonial to Modern Times.* Berkeley: University of California Press, 1963.

Goldemberg, José. "Looking Inside Brazil: The Challenges Facing Brazil's Education System," *World Outlook,* No. 14, 1992, 52–57.

Goldemberg, José. *Relatório sobre a educação no Brasil.* São Paulo: Instituto de Estudos Avançados, Coleção Documentos, 1993.

Goodman, David, and Michael Redclift. *From Peasant to Proletarian.* New York: St. Martin's Press, 1982.

Grimes, Barbara F., ed. *Ethnologue: Languages of the World.* 12th ed. Dallas: Summer Institute of Linguistics, 1992.

Guimarães, Roberto P. *The Ecopolitics of Development in the Third World: Politics and Environment in Brazil.* Boulder, Colorado: Lynne Rienner, 1991.

Hahner, June E. *Emancipating the Female Sex: The Struggle for Women's Rights in Brazil, 1850–1940.* Durham: Duke University Press, 1990.

Haines, Andrew. "Brazil: Progress in Decentralizing Health Care," *Lancet,* 341, No. 8857, 1993, 1403.

Haines, Andrew. "Health Care in Brazil," *British Medical Journal,* 306, No. 6876, 1993, 503–6.

Haverstock, Nathan. *Brazil in Pictures.* Minneapolis: Lerner, 1987.

Hecht, Susanna, and Alexander Cockburn. *The Fate of the Forest: Developers, Destroyers, and Defenders of the Amazon.* London: Verso, 1989.

Hirschman, Albert O. *Journeys Toward Progress.* Garden City, New York: Doubleday, 1965.

Hogan, Daniel, and Paulo Vieira da Cunha, eds. *Dilemas sócio-ambientais e desenvolvimento sustentável.* Campinas, Brazil: Editora da Unicamp, 1992.

Human Rights Watch. *Rural Violence in Brazil: An Americas Watch Report.* New York: 1991.

Instituto Brasileiro de Geografia e Estatística (IBGE). *Anuário estatístico, 1991.* Rio de Janeiro: 1992.

Instituto Brasileiro de Geografia e Estatística (IBGE). *Anuário estatístico do Brasil 1993.* Rio de Janeiro: 1993.

Instituto Brasileiro de Geografia e Estatística (IBGE). *Atlas do Brasil.* Rio de Janeiro: 1990.

Instituto Brasileiro de Geografia e Estatística (IBGE). *Censo demográfico de 1991: Resultados preliminares.* Rio de Janeiro: 1993.

Instituto Brasileiro de Geografia e Estatística (IBGE). *Enciclopédia dos municípios do Brasil.* Rio de Janeiro: 1957.

Instituto Brasileiro de Geografia e Estatística (IBGE). *Estatísticas históricas do Brasil.* Rio de Janeiro: 1990.

Instituto Brasileiro de Geografia e Estatística (IBGE). *Geografia do Brasil.* 5 vols. Rio de Janeiro: 1977.

Instituto Brasileiro de Geografia e Estatística (IBGE). *Geografia do Brasil.* 5 vols. Rio de Janeiro: 1989.

Inter-American Development Bank. *Basic Socioeconomic Data.* Washington: 1996.

Jaguaribe, Hélio, ed. *Sociedade, estado e partidos políticos da atualidade brasileira.* São Paulo: Paz e Terra, 1992.

Klink, Carlos, Adriana Moreira, and Otto Thomas Solbrig. "Ecological Impact of Agricultural Development in the Brazilian Cerrados." Pages 112–35 in Michael D. Young, and Otto T. Solbrig, eds., *The World's Savannas: Economic Driving Forces, Ecological Constraints and Policy Options for Sustainable Land Use.* Man and the Biosphere Series, No. 12. Paris: UNESCO, 1993.

Krieger, Gustavo, Luiz A. Novaes, and Tales Faria. *Todos os sócios do presidente.* São Paulo: Scritta Editorial, 1992.

Lamounier, Bolivar. *Ouvindo o Brasil: Uma análise da opinião pública brasileira hoje.* São Paulo: Editora Sumaré, 1992.

Leacock, Seth, and Ruth Leacock. *Spirits of the Deep: A Study of an Afro-Brazilian Cult.* Garden City, New York: Doubleday, 1972.

Leal, Maria do Carmo, ed. *Saúde, ambiente e desenvolvimento.* São Paulo: Editora Hucitec, 1992.

Lewis, Marcia A., and André Médici. "Private Payers of Health Care in Brazil: Characteristics, Costs, and Coverage," *Health Policy,* 10, No. 4, 1995, 362–75.

Lutzemberger, José. "Environment and Development: A View from Brazil." In Heraldo Munoz, ed., *Environment and Diplomacy in the Americas.* Boulder, Colorado: Lynne Rienner, 1992.

Martine, George. "Brazil." Pages 31–46 in Charles B. Nam, William J. Serow, and David F. Sly, eds., *International Handbook on Internal Migration.* New York: Greenwood Press, 1990.

Martine, George, ed. *População, meio ambiente e desenvolvimento: Verdades e contradições.* Campinas, Brazil: Editora da Unicamp, 1993.

Martine, George, Kaizô Beltrão, Ana Amélia Camarano, and Ricardo Neupert. "A urbanização no Brasil: Retrospectiva, componentes e perspectiva." Pages 99–159 in *Para a década de 90: Prioridades e perspectivas de políticas públicas,* 3. Brasília: Instituto de Pesquisa Econômica Aplicada/Instituto de Planejamento, 1990.

Martins, José de Souza. *Expropriação e violencia: A questão política no campo.* 3d ed. revised and expanded. São Paulo: Editora Hucitec, 1991.

Mendes, Cândido. *A democracia desperdiçada: Poder e imaginação social.* Rio de Janeiro: Editora Nova Fronteira, 1992.

Merrick, Thomas, and Douglas Graham. *Population and Economic Development in Brazil: 1800 to the Present.* Baltimore: Johns Hopkins University Press, 1979.

Moran, Emílio. *Through Amazonian Eyes: The Human Ecology of Amazonian Populations.* Iowa City: University of Iowa Press, 1993.

Mueller, Charles. "Centro-Oeste: Evolução, situacão atual e perspectivas do desenvolvimento sustentável." Pages 89–128 in João Paulo dos Reis Velloso, ed., *A ecologia e o novo padrão de desenvolvimento no Brasil.* São Paulo: Nobel, 1992.

Mueller, Charles Curt. "Dinâmica, condicionantes e impactos socio-ambientais da expansão de fronteira agrícola no Brasil," *Revista de Administração Pública* [Rio de Janeiro], 26, No. 3, July–September 1992, 64–87.

Muricy, Carmen M. *The Brazilian Amazon: Institutions and Publications.* Albuquerque: SALALM Secretariat, General Library, University of New Mexico, 1991.

Neumanne, José. *A república na lama: Uma tragédia brasileira.* São Paulo: Geração Editorial, 1992.

Oliveira, Evangelina Xavier Gouveia de, et al. *Brasil, uma visão geográfica nos anos 80.* Rio de Janeiro: Instituto Brasileiro de Geografia e Estatística (IBGE), 1988.

Oliveira, Francisco de. "A economia brasileira: Crítica à razão dualista." Pages 5–78 in *Questionando a economia brasileira.* São Paulo: Centro Brasileiro de Análise e Planejamento (CEBRAP), 1975.

Oliveira, Francisco de. *Elegia para uma religião: Sudene, Nordeste—Planejamento e conflito de classes.* Rio de Janeiro: Paz e Terra, 1977.

Pan American Health Organization. *AIDS Surveillance in the Americas.* Washington: 1996.

Pan American Health Organization. *Condiciones de salud en las Américas.* Washington: 1994.

Pan American Health Organization. *Health Statistics from the Americas.* Scientific Publication No. 556. Washington: 1995.

Parker, Eugene. *The Amazon Caboclo: Historical and Contemporary Perspectives.* Studies in Third World Societies, No. 32. Williamsburg, Virginia: College of William and Mary, 1985.

Parker, Richard. *Bodies, Pleasures, and Passions: Sexual Culture in Contemporary Brazil.* Boston: Beacon, 1990.

Patarra, Neide, and Diana Sawyer. *Relatório do Brasil para a Conferência Internacional sobre População e Desenvolvimento.* Brasília: Ministério das Relações Exteriores, 1993.

Pathfinder International. *Saude reprodutiva do adolescente: Pesquisa em cinco cidades, Brasil, 1987–89.* Salvador, Bahia: Policrom, 1991.

Payne, Leigh Ann. "Working Class Strategies in the Transition to Democracy in Brazil," *Comparative Politics,* 23, No. 2, January 1991, 221–38.

Peliano, Ana Maria, ed. *O mapa da fome III: Indicadores sobre a indigencia no Brasil (classificação absoluta e relativa por municipios).* Documento de política, No. 17. Brasília: IPEA, 1971.

Pesquisa Nacional por Amostra de Domicílios (PNAD). *Síntese de indicadores, 1993.* Ministério do Planejamento e Orçamento, Fundação Instituto Brasileiro de Geografia e Estatística (IBGE), Diretoria de Pesquisas, Departamento de Emprego e Rendimento. Rio de Janeiro: O Departamento, 1996.

Pinotti, José Aristodemo. *The Health Transition in Brazil.* São Paulo: CAPAIS, 1989.

Plonski, Guilherme Ary, ed. *Cooperación empresa-universidad en Iberoamérica.* São Paulo: Programa Iberoamericano de Ciência y Tecnologia para el Desarrollo, 1993.

Prado Júnior, Caio. *The Colonial Background of Modern Brazil.* Berkeley: University of California Press, 1971.

Proença Júnior, Domício, ed. *Uma avaliação da indústria bélica brasileira: Defesa, indústria e tecnologia.* Rio de Janeiro: Grupo de Estudos Estratégicos/Forum de Ciência e Cultura/Universidade Federal do Rio de Janeiro, 1993.

Reale, Miguel. *De Tancredo à Collor.* São Paulo: Siciliano, 1992.

Ribeiro, Darcy. *O Brasil como problema.* Rio de Janeiro: F. Alves, 1995.

Ribeiro, Darcy. *O povo brasileiro: A formacão e o sentido do Brasil.* São Paulo: Companhia das Letras, 1995.

Rocha, Sonia, and Hamilton Tolosa. "Metropolização da pobreza: Uma análise núcleo-periferia." Pages 101–29 in Instituto de Pesquisa Econômica Aplicada (IPEA), *Perspectivas da economia Brasileira, 1994.* Rio de Janeiro: 1993.

Rodrigues, Roberto do Nascimento. "O Brasil: Rumo a um novo padrão demográfico." Pages 117–26 in Maria do Carmo Leal, ed., *Saúde, ambiente e desenvolvimento.* São Paulo: Editora Hucitec, 1992.

Roosevelt, Ann Curtenius. *Amazonian Indians from Prehistory to the Present: Anthropological Perspectives.* Tucson: University of Arizona Press, 1994.

Saffioti, Heleieth I.B. *Mulher brasileira: Opressão e exploração.* Rio de Janeiro: Achiamé, 1984.

Saffioti, Heleieth I.B. *Violencia de genero: Poder e impotencia.* Rio de Janeiro: Revinter, 1995.

Santos, Breno dos. *Amazônia: Potencial mineral e perspectivas de desenvolvimento.* São Paulo: Queiroz, 1981.

Santos, Roberto Araújo de Oliveira. *História econômica da Amazônia, 1800–1920.* São Paulo: Queiroz, 1980.

Sawyer, Donald. "Frontier Expansion and Retraction in Brazil." Pages 180–203 in Marianne Schmink and Charles H. Wood, eds., *Frontier Expansion in Amazônia.* Gainesville: University of Florida Press, 1984.

Sawyer, Donald, and George Martine. *Educação e transição demográfica: População em idade escolar no Brasil.* Série de Relatório de Pesquisa, No. 2B. Brasília: Ministério de Educação e Cultura, Instituto Nacional de Estudos Pedagógicos (MEC, INEP), 1993.

Schmink, Marianne, and Charles H. Wood. *Contested Frontiers in Amazônia.* New York: Columbia University Press, 1992.

Schmink, Marianne, and Charles H. Wood, eds. *Frontier Expansion in Amazonia.* Gainesville: University of Florida Press, 1984.

Schmitter, Philippe C. *Interest Conflict and Political Change in Brazil.* Stanford: Stanford University Press, 1971.

Schneider, Ronald M. *Brazil: Culture and Politics in a New Industrial Powerhouse.* Boulder, Colorado: Westview Press, 1996.

Shott, Thomas S. *Performance, Specialization, and International Integration of Science in Brazil: Changes and Comparisons with Other Latin American Countries and Israel.* Rio de Janeiro: Fundação Getúlio Vargas, 1994.

Silva, José Francisco Graziano da. *Estrutura agrária e produção de subsistência na agricultura brasileira.* São Paulo: Editora Hucitec, 1978.

Silva, José Francisco Graziano da. *Progresso técnico e relações de trabalho na agricultura.* São Paulo: Editora Hucitec, 1981.

Silva, Nelson do Valle. "Human Development in Brazil, 1960–1988." Paper presented at United Nations Development Programme Human Development Report Seminar, December 1990.

Skidmore, Thomas E. *Politics in Brazil: 1930–1964, An Experiment in Democracy.* New York: Oxford University Press, 1967.

Smith, Nigel J.H. *Man, Fishes, and the Amazon.* New York: Columbia University Press, 1981.

Smith, Nigel J.H. *Rainforest Corridors: The Transamazon Colonization Scheme.* Berkeley: University of California Press, 1982.

Smith, Thomas Lynn. *Brazil: People and Institutions.* Baton Rouge: Louisiana State University Press, 1963.

Sorj, Bernardo, and Maria Herminia T. Almeida, eds. *Sociedade e política no Brasil pós-64.* São Paulo: Editora Brasiliense, 1983.

Stepan, Alfred, ed. *Authoritarian Brazil: Origins, Policies, and Future.* New Haven: Yale University Press, 1973.

Steward, Julian Haynes, ed. *Handbook of South American Indians.* Washington: GPO, 1946–59.

Stoll, David. *Is Latin America Turning Protestant? The Politics of Evangelical Growth.* Berkeley: University of California Press, 1990.

Suassuna, Luciano, and Luiz Costa Pinto. *Os fantasmas da Casa da Dinda.* São Paulo: Editora Contexto, 1992.

Tanenbaum, Barbara A., ed. *Encyclopedia of Latin American History and Culture,* 5. New York: Charles Scribner's Sons, 1996.

Tavares, Maria da Conceição. *Da substituição de importações ao capitalismo financeiro.* 4th ed. Rio de Janeiro: Zahar Editores, 1975.

Tendler, Judith. *New Lessons from Old Projects: The Workings of Rural Development in Northeast Brazil.* Washington: World Bank, 1993.

Trindade, Hélgio, ed. *Reforma eleitoral e representação política no Brasil dos anos 90.* Porto Alegre, Brazil: Editora da Universidade Federal de Rio Grande do Sul, 1992.

United Nations. Population Division. *Urban Agglomerations, 1992.* New York: 1992.

United Nations Development Programme (UNDP). *Human Development Report 1995.* New York: Oxford University Press, 1995.

United States. Central Intelligence Agency. *The World Factbook 1996.* Washington: CIA, 1997 (World-Wide Web homepage URL: http://www.odci.gov).

Valadares, Tadeu. "Deforestation: A Brazilian Perspective." Pages 38–53 in Joseph S. Tulchin, ed., *Economic Development and Environmental Protection in Latin America.* Washington: Wilson Center, 1991.

Valdes, Teresa, Enrique Gomariz, and Jacqueline Pitanguy, eds. *Mulheres latinoamericanas em dados: Brasil.* Madrid: Instituto de la Mujer, Ministerio de Asuntos Sociales, Federación Latinoamericana de Ciencias Sociales (FLACSO), 1993.

Vasconcelos, E., ed. *Gerenciamento da tecnologia: Um instrumento de competitividade industrial.* São Paulo: Editora Edgard Blücher, 1992.

Velho, Otávio G.C.A. *Capitalismo autoritário e campesinato: Um estudo comparativo a partir da fronteira em movimento.* São Paulo: Difel/Difusão, 1976.

Viola, Eduardo. *A expansão do ambientalismo multisetorial e a globalização da ordem mundial, 1985–1992.* Documento de Trabalho, No. 16. Brasília: Instituto Sociedade, População e Natureza (ISPN), 1992.

Viola, Eduardo. "O movimento ambientalista no Brasil, 1971–1991: Da denúncia e conscientização para a institucionalização e o desenvolvimento sustentável." Pages 45–59 in Mirian Goldenberg, ed., *Ecologia, ciência e política.* Rio de Janeiro: Revan, 1992.

Viola, Eduardo, and Hector Leis. "Desordem global da biosfera e nova ordem institucional: O papel organizador do ecologismo," *Lua Nova* [São Paulo], No. 20, 1990.

Wagley, Charles. *Amazon Town: A Study of Man in the Tropics.* New York: Oxford University Press, 1976.

Wagley, Charles. *An Introduction to Brazil.* Rev. ed. New York: Columbia University Press, 1971.

Wagley, Charles, ed. *Man in the Amazon.* Gainesville: University of Florida Press, 1973.

Weffort, Francisco. *Qual democracia?* São Paulo: Companhia das Letras, 1992.

Wilheim, Jorge. *Problemas ambientais urbanos.* Documento de Trabalho, No. 24. Brasília: Instituto Sociedade, População e Natureza (ISPN), 1993.

Winter, Nevin O. *Brazil and Her People of Today: An Account of the Customs, Characteristics, Amusements, History, and Advancement of the Brazilians, and the Development and Resources of Their Country.* Boston: Page, 1910.

Wood, Charles H., and José Alberto Magno de Carvalho. *The Demography of Inequality in Brazil.* Cambridge: Cambridge University Press, 1988.

World Bank. *Brazil: A Poverty Assessment.* New York: Oxford University Press, 1995.

World Bank. *World Development Report, 1993.* New York: Oxford University Press, 1993.

Chapter 3

Abreu, Marcelo de Paiva. "Brazilian Public Foreign Debt Policy, 1931–1945," *Brazilian Economic Studies,* No. 4, Rio de Janeiro: Instituto de Pesquisa Econômica Aplicada (IPEA), 1978.

Abreu, Marcelo de Paiva. "A dívida pública externa do Brasil, 1824–1931," *Estudos Econômicos,* May 1985, 15, No. 2, 167–89.

Abreu, Marcelo de Paiva. "Equações de demanda de importações revisitadas: Brasil, 1960–1985," *Texto para discussão.* No. 148. Rio de Janeiro: Pontifícia Universidade Católica (PUC), 1987.

Abreu, Marcelo de Paiva, ed. *A ordem do progresso: Cem anos de política econômica republicana, 1889–1989.* Rio de Janeiro: Editora Campus, 1990.

Albuquerque, Roberto Cavalcanti de. "A situação social: O que diz o passado e o que promete o futuro." Pages 387–410 in

Instituto de Pesquisa Econômica Aplicada (IPEA), *Perspectivas da economia brasileira, 1992.* Brasília: 1991.

Almeida dos Reis, José Guilherme. "Salario mínimo e distribuição de renda." Pages 41–53 in Instituto de Pesquisa Econômico Aplicada/Institito Nacional de Pesquisa (IPEA/Inpes), *Perspectivas da economia brasileira, 1989.* Rio de Janeiro: 1989.

"Amazonia: A World Resource at Risk," *National Geographic Magazine.* August 1992 (map).

Arida, Persio, and André Lara-Resende. "Inertial Inflation and Monetary Reform," in John Williamson, ed., *Inflation and Indexation: Argentina, Brazil and Israel.* Cambridge: MIT Press, 1985.

Bacha, Edmar L., and Herbert Klein S. *Social Change in Brazil, 1945–1985: The Incomplete Transition.* Albuquerque: University of New Mexico Press, 1989.

Bacha, Edmar L., and Lance Taylor. *Brazilian Income Distribution in the 1960s: Facts, Model, Results, and the Controversy.* No. 34. Cambridge: Harvard Institute for International Development Theory, Harvard University, 1977.

Baer, Werner. *The Brazilian Economy: Growth and Development.* 3d ed. New York: Praeger, 1989.

Baer, Werner. *The Brazilian Economy: Growth and Development.* 4th ed. Westport, Connecticut: Praeger, 1995.

Baer, Werner. *The Brazilian Economy: Its Growth and Development.* Columbus: Grid, 1979.

Baer, Werner. *Industrialization and Economic Development in Brazil.* Homewood, Illinois: Irwin, 1965.

Banco Central do Brasil. *Boletim do Banco Central do Brasil* [Brasília], 12, No. 2, February 1976.

Banco Central do Brasil. *Boletim do Banco Central do Brasil* [Brasília], 29, No. 9, September 1993.

Barbosa, Fernando de Holanda, and Mario Henrique Simonsen. *Plano Cruzado: Inércia versus inépcia.* Rio de Janeiro: Editora Globo, 1989.

Barros, Mendonça de, José Roberto, Afonso Celso Pastore, and Juarez A.B. Rizzieri. "A evolução recente da agricultura brasileira." Pages 16–27 in José Roberto Mendonça de Barros and Douglas Graham, eds., *Estudos sobre a modernização da agricultura brasileira*. Série IPE No. 9. São Paulo: Instituto de Pesquisa Económicas (IPE), 1977.

Barros, Ricardo Paes de, and Rosane Mendonça. "Geração e reprodução da desigualdade de renda no Brasil." Pages 471–90 in Instituto de Pesquisa Econômica Aplicada (IPEA), *Perspectivas da economia brasileira, 1994*. Rio de Janeiro: 1993.

Barros, Ricardo Paes de, et al. "Welfare, Inequality, Poverty, and Social Conditions in Brazil in the last Three Decades," Paper presented at the Brookings Institution Conference, July 15–17, 1992. Washington: 1992.

Batista, Jorge Chami. *Debt and Adjustment Policies in Brazil*. Boulder, Colorado: Westview Press, 1992.

Batista Júnior, Paulo Nogueira. *Da crise internacional à moratória brasileira*. Rio de Janeiro: Paz e Terra, 1988.

Batista Júnior, Paulo Nogueira. *Mito e realidade da dívida externa, brasileira*. Rio de Janeiro: Paz e Terra, 1983.

Bergsman, Joel. *Brazil: Industrialization and Trade Policies*. London: Oxford University Press, 1970.

Bittermann, Henry. *The Refunding of International Debt*. Durham: Duke University Press, 1973.

Bonelli, Regis, and Guilherme Luis Sedlacek. "Distribuição de renda: Evolução no último quarto de século." Pages 123–55 in Guilherme Luis Sedlacek and Ricardo Paes de Barros, eds., *Mercado de trabalho e distribuição de renda: Uma coletânea*. Rio de Janeiro: Instituto Nacional de Pesquisa/Instituto de Pesquisa Econômica Aplicada (Inpes/IPEA), 1989.

Bresser Pereira, Luiz Carlos. *Development and Crisis in Brazil, 1930–1983*. Boulder, Colorado: Westview Press, 1984.

Bresser Pereira, Luiz Carlos. *Economic Crisis and State Reform in Brazil: Toward a New Interpretation of Latin America*. Boulder, Colorado: Lynne Rienner, 1996.

Bruneau, Thomas C., and Philippe Faucher, eds. *Authoritarian Capitalism: Brazil's Contemporary Economic and Political Development*. Boulder, Colorado: Westview Press, 1981.

Burns, E. Bradford. *A History of Brazil*. 3d ed. New York: Columbia University Press, 1993.

Calogeras, João Pandia. *La politique monétaire du Brésil*. Rio de Janeiro: Imprimerie Nationale, 1910.

Camargo, José Márcio, and Fábio Giambiagi, eds. *Distribuição de renda no Brasil*. São Paulo: Paz e Terra, 1991.

Cardoso, Eliana A. "The Burden of Exchange Rate Adjustment in Brazil," *Quarterly Review of Economics and Business,* 21, 1981, 168–81.

Cardoso, Eliana A. "Celso Furtado Revisited: The Post-War Years," *Economic Development and Cultural Change,* 39, 1981, 117–28.

Cardoso, Eliana A. "The Great Depression and Commodity Exporting LDC's: The Case of Brazil," *Journal of Political Economy,* 89, 1981, 1239–50.

Cardoso, Eliana A. "Minidevaluations and Indexed Wages: The Brazilian Experience in the Seventies," *Journal of Development Economics,* 33, 1980, 453–65.

Cardoso, Eliana A. "A Money Demand Equation for Brazil," *Journal of Development Economics,* 36, 1983, 183–93.

Cardoso, Eliana A. "Nineteenth-Century Exchange Rates in Brazil: An Econometric Model," *Journal of Development Studies,* 19, 1983, 170–78.

Cardoso, Eliana A., and Rudiger Dornbusch. "Brazil after 1982: Adjusting or Accommodating?" Pages 129–53 in J. Williamson and Daniel Dantas, eds., *Latin American Adjustment to the Debt Crisis: How Much Has Happened?* Washington: Institute for International Economics, 1990.

Cardoso, Eliana A., and Rudiger Dornbusch. "Brazilian Debt Crises: Past and Present." Pages 106–39 in Barry J. Eichengreen and Peter H. Lindert, *The International Debt Crisis in Historical Perspective.* Cambridge: MIT Press, 1989.

Cardoso, Eliana A., and Rudiger Dornbusch. "Brazil's Tropical Plan," *American Economic Review,* 77, No. 3, 1987, 288–92.

Cardoso, Eliana A., and Rudiger Dornbusch. "Deficit Finance and Monetary Dynamics in Brazil and Mexico," *Journal of Development Economics,* 37, 1992, 173–97.

Cardoso, Eliana A., and Rudiger Dornbusch. "From Inertia to Megainflation: Brazil in the 1980s." Pages 143–77 in Michael Bruno and Stanley Fischer, eds., *Lessons of Economic Stabilization and Its Aftermath.* Cambridge: MIT Press, 1991.

Cardoso, Eliana A., and Rudiger Dornbusch. "The Macroeconomics of the Brazilian External Debt." Pages 269–392 in Jeffrey Sachs and Albert Fishlow, eds., *Developing Country Debt and Economic Performance,* 2. Chicago: Chicago University Press, 1990.

Cardoso, Eliana A., and Albert Fishlow. "Brazilian Debt: A Requiem for Muddling Through." Pages 194–318 in Sebastian Edwards, Rudiger Dornbusch, and F. Larrain, eds., *Debt Adjustment and Recovery*. Oxford: Basil Blackwell, 1989.

Cardoso, Eliana A., and Albert Fishlow. "The Macroeconomics of the Brazilian External Debt." Pt. 3 of Jeffrey Sachs, ed., *Developing Country Debt and Economic Performance*, 2. Chicago: National Bureau of Economic Research, University of Chicago Press, 1990.

Cardoso, Fernando Henrique, and Enzo Faletto. *Dependency and Development in Latin America*. Trans., Marjory Mattingly Urquidi. Berkeley: University of California Press, 1979.

Carreira, Liberato de Castro. *Historia financeira e orçamentaria do Imperio do Brasil desde à sua fundação*. Rio de Janeiro: Imprensa Nacional, 1989.

Castro, Antônio Barros de, and Francisco Eduardo Pires de Souza. *A economia brasileira em marcha forçada*. Rio de Janeiro: Paz e Terra, 1985.

Cavalcanti, Carlos Brandão. *Transferência de recursos ao exterior e substituição de dívida externa por dívida interna*. Rio de Janeiro: Banco Nacional de Desenvolvimento Econômico e Social (BNDES), 1988.

Chacel, Julian M., Pamela S. Falk, and David V. Fleischer, eds. *Brazil's Economic and Political Future*. Boulder, Colorado: Westview Press, 1988.

Chaffee, Wilber A. *Desenvolvimento: Politics and Economy in Brazil*. Boulder, Colorado: Lynne Rienner, 1997.

Cline, William. *Economic Consequences of a Land Reform in Brazil*. Amsterdam: North Holland, 1970.

Coes, Donald V. *Economic Crises, Policies, and Growth in Brazil, 1964–90*. Washington: World Bank, 1994.

Coes, Donald V. *Macroeconomic Crises, Policies, and Growth in Brazil, 1964–90*. Washington: World Bank, 1995.

Coes, Donald V. "Macroeconomic Stabilisation and Trade Liberalisation: Brazilian Experience and Choices," *World Economy*, 17, No. 4, July 1994, 433–50.

Coes, Donald V. "Trade Agreements in the Americas: Brazil." Latin America Trade and Finance, Working Paper. Washington: World Bank, 1992.

Conniff, Michael L., and Frank D McCann, eds. *Modern Brazil: Elites and Masses in Historical Perspective.* Lincoln: University of Nebraska Press, 1989.

Cruz, Paulo Davidoff. *Dívida externa e política econômica: A experiencia brasileira nos anos setenta.* São Paulo: Editora Brasiliense, 1984.

Cysne, Rubens Penha. *Política macroeconômica no Brasil, 1964–66 e 1980–84.* Rio de Janeiro: Fundação Getúlio Vargas, 1985.

Dean, Warren. *The Brazilian Economy, 1880–1945.* Austin: University of Texas Press, 1969.

Dean, Warren. *The Industrialization of São Paulo, 1880–1945.* Austin: University of Texas Press, 1969.

Delfim Netto, Antônio. *O problema do café no Brasil.* Rio de Janeiro: Fundação Getúlio Vargas, 1979.

Diaz Alejandro, Carlos. "Some Aspects of the 1982–1983, Brazilian Payments Crisis," *Brookings Papers on Economic Activity,* No. 1. 1983, 515–52.

Dinsmoor, James. *Brazil: Responses to the Debt Crisis.* Washington: Inter-American Development Bank, 1990.

Donnelly, John T. "External Financing and Short-Term Consequences of External Debt Servicing for Brazilian Economic Development, 1947–1968," *Journal of Developing Areas,* April 1973, 411–30.

Dornbusch, Rudiger. "External Debt, Budget Deficits, and Disequilibrium Exchange Rates." Pages 12–24 in Gordon W. Smith and John T. Cuddington, eds., *International Debt and the Developing Countries.* Washington: World Bank, 1985.

Dornbusch, Rudiger, and Mario Henrique Simonsen. *Inflation Stabilization with Incomes Policy Support.* New York: Group of Thirty, 1987.

Dornbusch, Rudiger, and Mario Henrique Simonsen, eds. *Inflation, Debt, and Indexation.* Cambridge: MIT Press, 1983.

Dornbusch, Rudiger, Frederico Sturzenegger, and Holger Wolf. "Extreme Inflation: Dynamics and Stabilization," *Brookings Papers on Economic Activity,* No. 2, 1990, 1–84.

Dunham, Gilbert G. "Challenges to Privatization in Brazil," *World Outlook,* No. 19, Winter 1995, 85–112.

Economist Intelligence Unit. *Country Profile: Brazil, 1994–95.* London: 1995.

"Energy Map of Latin America," *Major Pipelines of the World* [London], 62, No. 3, March 1995 (map).

Erickson, Kenneth. "Brazil." Pages 50–70 in Howard J. Wiarda and Harvey F. Kline, eds., *Latin American Politics and Development.* Boulder, Colorado: Westview Press, 1985.

Evans, Peter. "Declining Hegemony and Assertive Industrialization: U.S.-Brazil Conflicts in the Computer Industry," *International Organization,* 43, No. 2, Spring, 1989, 207–38.

Evans, Peter. *Dependent Development: The Alliance of Multinational, State, and Local Capital in Brazil.* Princeton: Princeton University Press, 1979.

Faro, Clovis de, ed. *Plano Collor: Avaliações e perspectivas.* Rio de Janeiro: Livros Técnicos e Científicos Editora, 1990.

Fishlow, Albert. "Brazilian Size Distribution of Income." Pages 148–76 in Alejandro Foxley, ed., *Income Distribution in Latin America.* Cambridge: Cambridge University Press, 1976.

Fishlow, Albert. "The Debt Crisis: Round Two Ahead?" Pages 50–74 in Richard E. Feinberg and Valleriana Kallab, eds., *Adjustment Crisis in the Third World.* Washington: Overseas Development Council, 1984.

Fishlow, Albert. "Lessons of the 1890s for the 1980s." Pages 112–35 in Ronald Findlay, ed., *Debt, Stabilization, and Development.* Oxford: Basil Blackwell, 1988.

Fishlow, Albert. "Some Reflections in Post-1964 Economic Policy." Pages 30–50 in Alfred Stepan, ed., *Authoritarian Brazil: Origins, Policies, and Future.* New Haven: Yale University Press, 1973.

Fishlow, Albert. "Tale of Two Presidents." Pages 55–70 in Alfred C. Stepan, ed., *Democratizing Brazil: Problems of Transition and Consolidation.* New York: Oxford University Press, 1989.

Fox, M. Louise, and Samuel A. Moreley. "Who Paid the Bill? Adjustment and Poverty in Brazil, 1980–95." PRE Working Paper No. 648. Washington: World Bank, 1991.

Fraga, Arminio. *German Reparations and Brazilian Debt: A Comparative Study.* Essays in International Finance. Princeton: University Press, 1986.

Furtado, Celso. *The Economic Growth of Brazil: A Survey from Colonial to Modern Times.* Berkeley: University of California Press, 1971.

Furtado, Celso. *Formação econômica do Brasil.* 7th ed. São Paulo: Editora Nacional, 1967.

Goldsmith, Raymond. *Desenvolvimento financeiro sob um século de inflação: Brasil, 1850–1984.* São Paulo: Harper and Row do Brasil, 1986.

Goodman, David. "Rural Economy and Society." Pages 50–75 in Edmar Bacha and Herbert Klein, eds., *Social Change in Brazil, 1945–1985: The Incomplete Transition.* Albuquerque: University of New Mexico Press, 1989.

Graham, Richard. *Britain and the Onset of Modernization in Brazil, 1850–1914.* Cambridge: Cambridge University Press, 1968.

Haddad, Claudio. *Crescimento do produto real no Brasil, 1900–1947.* Rio de Janeiro: Fundação Getúlio Vargas, 1978.

Hewlett, Sylvia Ann. *The Cruel Dilemmas of Development: Twentieth-Century Brazil.* New York: Basic Books, 1980.

Hoffmann, Helga. "Poverty and Prosperity in Brazil." Pages 20–49 in Edmar Bacha and Herbert Klein, eds., *Social Change in Brazil, 1945–1985: The Incomplete Transition.* Albuquerque: University of New Mexico Press, 1989.

Horta, Maria Helena. "Sources of Brazilian Export Growth in the 70s," *Brazilian Economic Studies,* 9, 1985, 164–65.

Instituto Brasileiro de Geografia e Estatística (IBGE). *Anuário estatístico, 1991.* Rio de Janeiro: 1992.

Instituto Brasileiro de Geografia e Estatística (IBGE). *Anuário estatístico, 1992.* Rio de Janeiro: 1993.

Instituto Brasileiro de Geografia e Estatística (IBGE). *Estatísticas históricas do Brasil,* Rio de Janeiro: 1986.

Instituto Brasileiro de Geografia e Estatística (IBGE). *Estatísticas históricas do Brasil.* 2d. ed. Rio de Janeiro: 1990.

Instituto Brasileiro de Geografia e Estatística (IBGE). *Estatísticas históricas do Brasil: Séries econômicas, demográficas e sociais de 1550 a 1988.* Série estatísticas retrospectivas, No. 3. 2d ed., rev. Rio de Janeiro: 1990.

Instituto de Pesquisa Econômica Aplicada (IPEA). *Perspectivas da economia brasileira, 1992.* Brasília: 1991.

Knight, Peter, and R. Moran. *Brazil: Poverty and Basic Needs.* Washington: World Bank, 1981.

Kume, Honório, and Guida Piani. "A política de importação no período 1991–1994." Research paper. Rio de Janeiro: Fundação Centro de Estudos do Comércio Exterior, 1991.

Lamounier, Bolivar, and Alkimar Moura. "Economic Policy and Political Opening in Brazil." Pages 80–102 in Jonathan Hartlyn and Samuel A. Morelly, eds., *Latin American Political Economy: Financial Crisis and Political Change.* Boulder, Colorado: Westview Press, 1986.

Langoni, Carlos. *Distribuição da renda e desenvolvimento econômico do Brasil.* Rio de Janeiro: Editora Expressão e Cultura, 1973.

Leff, Nathaniel. *Underdevelopment and Development in Brazil.* London: Allen and Unwin, 1982.

Longo, Carlos. "Processo orçamentário," *Revista de Economia Política* [São Paulo], 11, No. 2, April–June 1991.

Lopes, Francisco. *O choque heterodoxo.* Rio de Janeiro: Editora Campus, 1986.

Lozardo, Ernesto, ed. *Déficit público brasileiro: Política econômica e ajuste estrutural-organização.* Rio de Janeiro: Paz e Terra, 1987.

Macedo, Roberto B. "A Critical Review of the Relation Between Post-1964 Wage Policy and the Worsening of Brazil's Income Distribution in the 1960's," *Explorations in Economic Research,* 4, 1977, 117–40.

Macedo, Roberto B. "Wage Indexation and Inflation: The Recent Brazilian Experience." Pages 164–97 in Rudiger Dornbusch and Mario Henrique Simonsen, eds., *Inflation, Debt, and Indexation.* Cambridge, Massachusetts: MIT Press, 1983.

Malan, Pedro, et al. *Política econômica externa e industrialização no Brasil.* Relatórios de Pesquisa. Rio de Janeiro: Instituto de Pesquisa Econômica Aplicada/Instituto Nacional de Pesquisa (IPEA/Inpes), 1977.

Marquês, Maria Silvia Bastos. "Estratégia de ajustamento externo: 1983–1986." Pages 115–33 in Paulo Nogueira Batista Júnior, ed., *Novos ensaios sobre o setor externo da economia brasileira.* Rio de Janeiro: Fundaçao Getúlio Vargas, 1988.

Marques Moreira, Marcilio. *The Brazilian Quandary.* New York: Twentieth Century Fund, 1986.

Martino, Orlando D., ed. *Mineral Industries of Latin America.* Washington: GPO, 1988.

Merrick, Thomas. "Population since 1945." Pages 52–75 in Edmar L. Bacha and Herbert S. Klein, eds., *Social Changes in Brazil, 1945–1985: The Incomplete Transition.* Albuquerque: University of New Mexico Press, 1989.

Ministério da Infra-Estrutura. *Balanço energético nacional, 1990.* Brasília: 1990.

Ministério das Minas e Energia. *Anuário mineral brasileiro, 1991,* Brasília: 1991.

Ministério das Minas e Energia. *Balanço energético nacional, 1993.* Brasília: 1993.

Modiano, Eduardo. *Da inflação ao cruzado.* Rio de Janeiro: Editora Campus, 1986.

Moraes, Pedro Bodin. "Equações de demanda de importações," *Texto para discussão.* Rio de Janeiro: Pontifícia Universidade Católica (PUC), 1985.

Moreira, Marcílio Marques. *The Brazilian Quandary.* New York: Priority Press Publications, 1986.

Morley, Samuel A. *Labor Markets and Inequitable Growth: The Case of Authoritarian Capitalism in Brazil.* Cambridge: Cambridge University Press, 1982.

Mueller, Charles Curt. *Das oligarquia agrárias ao predomínio urbano-industrial: Um estudo do processo de formação de políticas agrícolas no Brasil.* Série PNPE, No. 9. Rio de Janeiro: Instituto de Pesquisa Econômica Aplicada/Instituto Nacional de Pesquisa (IPEA/Inpes), 1983.

Mueller, Charles Curt. "Dinâmica, condicionantes e impactos socio-ambientais da expansão da fronteira agrícola no Brasil," *Revista de Administração Pública* [Rio de Janeiro], 26, No. 3, July–September 1992, 65–87.

Neuhaus, Paulo, ed. *Economia brasileira: Uma visão histórica.* Rio de Janeiro: Editora Campus, 1980.

Nicholls, William H. "A economia agrícola brasileira: Desempenho e política recente." Pages 76–94 in Claudio Contador, ed., *Tecnologia e desenvolvimento agrícola.* Série monográfica, No. 17. Rio de Janeiro: Instituto de Pesquisa Econômica Aplicada/Instituto Nacional de Pesquisa (IPEA/Inpes), 1975.

Nogueira Batista, Paulo. *Mito e realidade da dívida externa Brasileira.* Rio de Janeiro: Paz e Terra, 1983.

Novais, Fernando A. "O Brasil nos quadros do antigo sistema colonial." Pages 121–44 in Carlos G. Mota, ed., *Brasil em perspectiva,* 19th ed. Rio de Janeiro: Editora Bertrand Brasil, 1990.

Oliveira, João do Carmo. "Deficits dos orçamentos públicos no Brasil: Conceitos e problemas de mensuração." Pages 245–78 in Ernesto Lozardo, ed., *Déficit público brasileiro: Política econômica e ajuste estructural-organização.* Rio de Janeiro: Paz e Terra, 1987.

Oliveira, João do Carmo. "Tranferência de recursos da agricultura no Brasil, 1950–74," *Pesquisa e Planejamento Econômico* [Rio de Janeiro], 14, No. 3, 1984.

Paes de Barros, Ricardo, and José G.A. dos Reis. "Educação e desigualdade de salarios." Pages 15–35 in Instituto de Pesquisa Econômica Aplicada/Instituto Nacional de Pesquisa (IPEA/Inpes), *Perspectivas da economia brasileira, 1989.* Rio de Janeiro: 1989.

Parkin, Vincent. *Chronic Inflation in an Industrialising Economy: The Brazilian Experience.* Cambridge: Cambridge University Press, 1991.

Pastore, José, et al. *Mudança social e probreza no Brasil.* São Paulo: Fundação Instituto de Pesquisas Econômicas (FIPE)/Pioneira, 1983.

Payne, Leigh Ann. *Brazilian Industrialists and Democratic Change.* Baltimore: Johns Hopkins University Press, 1993.

Pechman, Clarice. *O dolar paralelo no Brasil.* Rio de Janeiro: Paz e Terra, 1984.

Pelaez, Carlos, and Wilson Suzigan. *Historia monetária do Brasil: Análise da política, comportamento e instituições monetárias.* Série Monográfica. Rio de Janeiro: Instituto de Pesquisa Econômica Aplicada (IPEA), 1976.

Pfeffermann, Guy Pierre, and Richard Webb. "The Distribution of Income in Brazil," *World Bank Staff Working Paper,* No. 356, September 1979.

Piorkowski, Anne. "Brazilian Computer Import Restrictions: Technological Independence and Commercial Reality," *Law and Policy in International Business,* 17, No. 3, 1985, 619–45.

Rangel, Inácio. *A inflação brasileira.* Rio de Janeiro: Tempo Brasileiro, 1963.

Ravallion, Martin, and Gaurav Datt. *Growth and Redistribution Components of Changes in Poverty Measures.* LSMS Working Paper No. 83. Washington: World Bank, 1991.

Redclift, Michael. "Sustainable Energy Policies for the Brazilian Amazon," *Energy Policy,* 22, May 1994, 427–31.

Resende, André Lara, and Francisco L. Lopes. "Sobre as causas recentes da aceleração inflacionária," *Pesquisa e Planejamento Econômico* [Rio de Janeiro], 11, No. 3, December 1981.

Rezende, Fernando, José R. Afonso, Renato Villela, and Ricardo Varsano. "A questão fiscal." Pages 161–85 in Instituto de Pesquisa Econômica Aplicada/Instituto Nacional de Pesquisa (IPEA/Inpes), *Perspectivas da economia brasileira, 1989*. Rio de Janeiro: 1989.

Rocha, Sonia. "Pobreza metropolitana: Balanço de uma década." Pages 140–60 in Instituto de Pesquisa Econômica Aplicada (IPEA), *Perspectivas da economia brasileira, 1992*. Brasília: 1991.

Rocha, Sonia, and Hamilton Tolosa. "Metropolização da pobreza: Uma análise núcleo-periferia." Pages 186–208 in Instituto de Pesquisa Econômica Aplicada (IPEA), *Perspectivas da economia brasileira, 1994*. Rio de Janeiro: 1993.

Rocha, Sonia, and Hamilton Tolosa. "Probreza metropolitana e políticas sociais." Pages 43–65 in Instituto de Pesquisa Econômica Aplicada/Instituto Nacional de Pesquisa (IPEA/Inpes), *Perspectivas da economia brasileira, 1989*. Rio de Janeiro: 1989.

Roett, Riordan. *Brazil: Politics in a Patrimonial Society*. New York: Praeger, 1984.

Romao, Mauricio Costa. "Distribuição de renda, probreza e desigualdades regionais no Brasil." Pages 53–75 in José Camargo and Fábio Giambiagi, eds., *Distribuição de renda no Brasil*. Rio de Janeiro: Paz e Terra, 1991.

Romeu, Nilton, and Otávio Franco. "Desequilíbrio do setor de energia e condicionantes econômicos e financeiros da política energética nacional." Pages 35–53 in Instituto de Pesquisa Econômica Aplicada/Instituto Nacional de Pesquisa (IPEA/Inpes), *Para a década de 90: Prioridades e perspectivas de políticas públicas*, 2. Brasília: 1989.

Salazar-Carillo, Jorge, and Roberto Fendt, eds. *The Brazilian Economy in the Eighties*. New York: Pergamon Press, 1985.

Sedlacek, Guilherme Luis. "Evolução da distribuição de renda entre 1984 e 1987." Pages 50–65 in Instituto de Pesquisa Econômica Aplicada/Instituto Nacional de Pesquisa (IPEA/Inpes), *Perspectivas da economia brasileira, 1989*. Rio de Janeiro: 1989.

Sedlacek, Guilherme Luis, and Ricardo Paes de Barros, eds. *Mercado de trabalho e distribuição de renda: Uma coletanea.* Serie Monográfica. Rio de Janeiro: Instituto de Pesquisa Econômica Aplicada/Instituto Nacional de Pesquisa (IPEA/Inpes), 1989.

Silva, José Cláudio F. da. "Origens, evolução e estágio atual da crise econômica." Pages 116–34 in Instituto de Pesquisa Econômica Aplicada (IPEA), *Perspectivas da economia brasileira, 1992.* Brasília: 1991.

Simonsen, Mario Henrique. "Brasil." Pages 49–75 in Rudiger Dornbusch and F.L.C.H. Helmers, eds., *The Open Economy: Tools for Policy Makers in Developing Countries.* New York: Oxford University Press for the World Bank, 1988.

Simonsen, Mario Henrique. *Brasil 2002.* Rio de Janeiro: APEC-Bloch, 1972.

Simonsen, Mario Henrique. "The Developing Country Debt Problem." Pages 40–55 in Gordon W. Smith and John T. Cuddington, eds., *International Debt and the Developing Countries.* Washington: World Bank, 1985.

Simonsen, Mario Henrique. "Indexation: Current Theory and the Brazilian Experience." Pages 50–70 in Rudiger Dornbusch and Mario Henrique Simonsen, eds., *Inflation, Debt, and Indexation.* Cambridge: MIT Press, 1983.

Simonsen, Roberto C. *Evolução industrial do Brasil e outros estudos.* São Paulo: Editora Nacional, 1973.

Skidmore, Thomas E. *Politics in Brazil, 1930–1964: An Experiment in Democracy.* New York: Oxford University Press, 1967.

Skidmore, Thomas E. *The Politics of Military Rule in Brazil, 1964–1985.* New York: Oxford University Press, 1988.

Stepan, Alfred C., ed. *Authoritarian Brazil: Origins, Policies, and Future.* New Haven: Yale University Press, 1973.

Suzigan, Wilson. *Indústria brasileira: Origem e desenvolvimento.* São Paulo: Brasiliense, 1986.

Suzigan, Wilson. "Industrial policy and the challenge of competitiveness." Pages 45–63 in Werner Baer and Joseph S. Tulchin, eds., *Brazil and the Challenge of Economic Reform.* Washington: Woodrow Wilson Center Press, 1993.

Taylor, Lance, et al. *Models of Growth and Distribution in Brazil.* New York: Oxford University Press, 1980.

Trebat, Thomas J. *Brazil's State-Owned Enterprises: A Case Study of the State as Entrepreneur.* Cambridge: Cambridge University Press, 1983.

Tyler, William G. *The Brazilian Industrial Economy.* Lexington, Massachusetts: Lexington Books, 1981.

Tyler, William G. *Manufactured Export Expansion and Industrialization in Brazil.* Kieler Studien, No. 134. Tübingen, Germany: Mohr, 1976.

Versiani, Flávio R. *A década de 20 na industrialização brasileira.* Rio de Janeiro: Instituto de Pesquisa Econômica Aplicada/Instituto Nacional de Pesquisa (IPEA/Inpes), 1987.

Versiani, Flávio R., and José Roberto Mendonça de Barros, eds. *Formação econômica do Brasil.* São Paulo: Edição Saraiva, 1978.

Villela, Anibal V., and Wilson Suzigan. *Política do governo e crescimento da economia brasileira, 1889–1945.* Série monográfica, No. 10. Rio de Janeiro: Instituto de Pesquisa Econômica Aplicada/Instituto Nacional de Pesquisa (IPEA/Inpes), 1973.

Weisskopf, Richard. "The Growth and Decline of Import Substitution in Brazil Revisited," *World Development,* 8, No. 9, September 1980, 647–76.

Welch, John H. *Capital Markets in the Development Process: The Case of Brazil.* Pittsburgh: University of Pittsburgh Press, 1993.

Wells, John. "Brazil and the Post-1973 Crisis in the International Economy." Pages 79–103 in Rosemary Thorp and Lawrence Whitehead, eds., *Inflation and Stabilization in Latin America.* New York: Holmes and Meier, 1978.

Werneck, Rogério L.F. *Empresas estatais e política macroeconômica.* Rio de Janeiro: Editora Campus, 1987.

Werneck, Rogério L.F. "Estrangulamento externo e investimento público." Pages 108–29 in Persio Arida, ed., *Dívida externa, recessão e ajuste estrutural: O Brasil diante da crise.* Rio de Janeiro: Paz e Terra, 1983.

Werneck, Rogério L.F. "The Uneasy Steps Toward Privatization in Brazil." Pages 149–80 in William Glade, ed., *Privatization of Public Enterprises in Latin America.* San Francisco: ICS Press, 1991.

Williamson, John. *The Progress of Policy Reform in Latin America,* Washington: Institute for International Economics, 1990.

Wileman, J.P. *Brazilian Exchange: The Study of an Inconvertible Currency.* New York: Greenwood Press, 1969.

World Bank. *Brazil: Economic Memorandum.* Washington: 1984.

World Bank. *Brazil: Financial Systems Review.* A World Bank Country Study. Washington: 1985.

World Bank. *Brazil: Industrial Policies and Manufactured Exports.* A World Bank Country Study. Washington: 1983.

World Bank. *Brazil: Public Spending on Social Programs: Issues and Options.* Report No. 7086–BR. Washington: 1988.

World Bank. *World Development Report, 1992.* New York: Oxford University Press, 1992.

(Various issues of the following publications were also used in the preparation of this chapter: *Anuário estatístico do Brasil* [Rio de Janeiro]; *Boletim do Banco Central* [Brasília]; *Conjuntura econômica* [Rio de Janeiro]; *International Financial Statistics*; and *World Development Report.*)

Chapter 4

Abdenur, Roberto. "O Brasil e a nova realidade asiática: Uma estratégia de aproximação," *Revista de Política Externa* [São Paulo], 2, No. 3, 1993, 43–69.

Abdenur, Roberto. "A política externa brasileira e o 'sentimento de exclusão.'" Pages 31–45 in Gelson Fonseca Júnior and S.N.H. Castro, eds. *Temas de política externa.* Rio de Janeiro: Paz e Terra, 1994.

Abdenur, Roberto. *Textos de política externa.* Brasília: FUNAG, 1994.

Abranches, Sérgio H.H. "Presidencialismo de coalização: O dilema institucional brasileiro," *Dados* [Rio de Janeiro], 31, No. 1, 1988, 5–34.

Abranches, Sérgio H.H. "Strangers in a Common Land: Executive/Legislative Relations in Brazil." Pages 86–109 in Siegfried Marks, ed., *Political Constraints on Brazil's Economic Development.* New Brunswick, New Jersey: Transaction Books, 1993.

Abranches, Sérgio H.H., and Gláucio Ary Dillon Soares. "As funções do legislativo," *Revista de Administração Pública* [São Paulo], 7, No. 1, 1973, 73–98.

Abreu, Alzira Alves de, and José Luciano de Mattos Dias, eds. *O futuro do Congresso Brasileiro.* Rio de Janeiro: Fundação Getúlio Vargas, 1995.

Abrucio, Fernando Luiz. "Os barões da federação," *Lua Nova* [São Paulo], 33, 165–83.

Adler, Emanuel. *The Power of Ideology: The Quest for Technological Autonomy in Argentina and Brazil.* Studies in International Political Economy, No. 16. Berkeley: University of California Press, 1991.

Aguiar, Neuma, ed. *The Structure of Brazilian Development.* New Brunswick, New Jersey: Transaction Books, 1979.

Albuquerque, José Augusto Guilhon, ed. *Sessenta anos de política external brasileira, 1930–1990.* São Paulo: Cultura Editores, 1996.

Aleixo, José Carlos Brandi. "Fundamentos e linhas gerais da política externa no Brasil," *Revista Brasileira de Ciência Política* [Brasília], 1, No. 1, March 1989, 7–43.

Almeida, Luciano Martins de, ed. *O Brasil e as tendências econômicas e políticas contemporâneas.* Brasília: Fundação Alexandre Gusmão, 1995.

Alvarez, Sônia E. *Engendering Democracy in Brazil: Women's Movements in Transition Politics.* Princeton: Princeton University Press, 1990.

Alves, Branca Moreira. *Ideologia e feminismo: A luta da mulher pelo voto no Brasil.* Petrópolis, Brazil: Editora Vozes, 1980.

Alves, Maria Helena Moreira. *State and Opposition in Military Brazil.* Austin: University of Texas Press, 1985.

Amaral, Roberto. "A esquerda e a nova conjuntura internacional: Análise a uma esperança frustrada." Pages 245–67 in Roberto Amaral, ed. *FHC: Os Paulistas no poder.* Niteroi, Brazil: Casa Jorge Editorial, 1995.

Ames, Barry. "The Congressional Connection, the Structure of Politics, and the Distribution of Public Expenditures in Brazil's Competitive Period," *Comparative Politics,* 19, 1987, 147–71.

Ames, Barry. "Electoral Rules, Constituency Pressures, and Pork Barrel: Bases of Voting in the Brazilian Congress, *Journal of Politics,* 57, No. 2, 1995, 406–33.

Ames, Barry. *Political Survival: Politicians and Public Policy in Latin America.* Berkeley: University of California Press, 1987.

Ames, Barry. "The Reverse Coattails Effect: Local Party Organization in the 1989 Brazilian Presidential Elections," *American Political Science Review*, 88, No. 1, March 1994, 95–111.

Ames, Barry. *Rhetoric and Reality in a Militarized Regime: Brazil since 1964.* Beverly Hills, California: Sage, 1973.

Amorim, Celso Luiz Nunes. "O leviatã e o 'chip'," *Revista Brasileira de Ciência Política* [Brasília], 1, No. 1, 1989, 125–44.

Aragão, Murillo de. *Grupos de pressão no Congresso Nacional: Como a sociedade pode defender licitamente seus direitos no poder legislativo.* São Paulo: Maltese, 1994.

Assis, José Carlos de. *Os mandarins da República: Anatomia dos escândalos da administração pública.* Rio de Janeiro: Paz e Terra, 1984.

Avelar, Lúcia. *O segundo eleitorado: Tendências do voto feminino no Brasil.* Campinas, Brazil: Editora da Unicamp, 1989.

Azevedo, Luiz, and Adacir Reis. *Roteiro da impunidade: Uma radiografia dos sistemas de corrupção.* São Paulo: Scritta Editorial, 1994.

Baaklini, Abdo I. *The Brazilian Legislature and the Political System.* Westport, Connecticut: Greenwood Press, 1992.

Baaklini, Abdo I., and Antonio Carlos Pojo do Rego. "O presidencialismo na política brasileira," *Revista Brasileira de Ciência Política* [Brasília], 1, No. 1, March 1989, 165–91.

Bacchus, Wilfred A. *Mission in Mufti: Brazil's Military Regimes, 1964–1985.* Westport, Connecticut: Greenwood Press, 1990.

Bacha, Edmar L., and Herbert S. Klein, eds. *A transição incompleta: Brasil desde 1945.* 2 vols. Rio de Janeiro: Paz e Terra, 1986.

Baer, Werner. *The Brazilian Economy: Growth and Development.* New York: Praeger, 1983.

Baer, Werner, and Joseph S. Tulchin, eds. *Brazil and the Challenge of Economic Reform.* Washington: Woodrow Wilson Center Press, 1993.

Baer, Werner, Richard Newfarmer, and Thomas Trebat. "On State Capitalism in Brazil: Some New Issues and Questions," *Inter-American Economic Affairs*, 30, No. 3, Winter 1976, 69–91.

Baloyra, Enrique A. "From Moment to Moment: The Political Transition in Brazil, 1977–1981." Pages 9–53 in Wayne A. Selcher, ed., *Political Liberalization in Brazil: Dynamics, Dilem-*

mas, and Future Prospects. Boulder, Colorado: Westview Press, 1986.

Baloyra, Enrique A., ed. *Comparing New Democracies: Transition and Consolidation in Mediterranean Europe and the Southern Cone.* Boulder, Colorado: Westview Press, 1987.

Bandeira, Moniz. *Brasil—Estados Unidos: A rivalidad emergente, 1950–1988.* Rio de Janeiro: Editora Civilização Brasileira, 1989.

Bandeira, Moniz. *Brizola e o trabalhismo.* Rio de Janeiro: Editora Civilização Brasileira, 1979.

Bandeira, Moniz. *Estado nacional e política internacional na América Latina: O continente nas relações Argentina-Brasil.* São Paulo: Editora Ensaio, 1993.

Bandeira, Moniz. *O governo João Goulart: As lutas sociais no Brasil, 1961–1964.* Rio de Janeiro: Editora Civilização Brasileira, 1977.

Bandeira, Moniz. *Presença dos Estados Unidos no Brasil: Dois séculos de história.* Rio de Janeiro: Editora Civilização Brasileira, 1973.

Barbosa, Rubens. *América Latina em perspectiva: A integração regional, da retórica à realidade.* São Paulo: Editora Aduaneiras, 1991.

Barboza, Mario Gibson. *Na diplomacia: O traço todo da vida.* Rio de Janeiro: Editora Record, 1992.

Barros, Alexandre de Souza Costa. "The Brazilian Military: Professional Socialization, Political Performance, and State Building." Ph.D. dissertation. Chicago: University of Chicago, 1978.

Barros, Alexandre de Souza Costa. "A formulação e implementação da política externa brasileira: O Itamaraty e os novos atores." Pages 29–42 in Heraldo Muñoz and Joseph Tulchin, eds., *A América Latina e a política mundial.* São Paulo: Editora Convívio, 1986.

Beloch, Israel, and Alzira Alves de Abreu, eds. *Dicionário histórico-biográfico brasileiro, 1930–1983.* 4 vols. Rio de Janeiro: Forense-Universitaria, 1984.

Benevides, Maria Victória. *O governo Kubitschek: Desenvolvimento econômico e estabilidade política, 1956–1961.* Rio de Janeiro: Paz e Terra, 1976.

Benevides, Maria Victória. *O PTB e o trabalhismo: Partido e sindicato em São Paulo: 1945–1964*. São Paulo: Editora Brasiliense, 1989.

Benevides, Maria Victória. *A UDN e o udenismo: Ambigüidades do liberalismo brasileiro, 1945–1965*. Rio de Janeiro: Paz e Terra, 1981.

Bernard, Jean-Pierre A., et al. *Guide to the Political Parties of South America*. Harmondsworth, United Kingdom: Penguin Books, 1973.

Bierrenbach, Flávio Flores da Cunha. *Quem tem mêdo da Constituinte?* Rio de Janeiro: Paz e Terra, 1986.

Black, Jan Knippers. "Brazil's Limited Redemocratization," *Current History*, 91, February 1992, 85–89.

Black, Jan Knippers. "Challenging the Divine Right of Generals in Latin America: Brazil, Bolivia, and Peru," *Comparative Social Research*, 4, 1981, 319–52.

Black, Jan Knippers. "The Military and Political Decompression in Brazil," *Armed Forces and Society*, 6, No. 4, Summer 1980, 625–37.

Black, Jan Knippers. *United States Penetration of Brazil*. Philadelphia: University of Pennsylvania Press, 1977.

Bodea, Miguel. *Trabalhismo e populismo no Rio Grande do Sul*. Porto Alegre, Brazil: Universidade Federal do Rio Grande do Sul, 1992.

Brener, Jayme. "Tucano abatido: Embraer perde concorrência bilionária nos EUA para Raytheon, empresa responsável pelo Sivam no Brasil," *Istoé* [São Paulo], June 28, 1995, 26.

Bruneau, Thomas C. *The Church in Brazil: The Politics of Religion*. Austin: University of Texas Press, 1982.

Bruneau, Thomas C., and William E. Hewitt. "Patterns of Church Influence in Brazil's Political Transition," *Comparative Politics*, 22, No. 1, October 1989, 39–61.

Bruneau, Thomas C., and Philippe Faucher, eds. *Authoritarian Capitalism: Brazil's Contemporary Economic and Political Development*. Boulder, Colorado: Westview Press, 1981.

Buarque, Cristovam. *A revolução na esquerda e a invenção do Brasil*. Rio de Janeiro: Paz e Terra, 1992.

Bunker, Stephen G. "Policy Implementation in an Authoritarian State: A Case from Brazil," *Latin American Research Review*, 18, No. 1, 1983, 33–58.

Bunker, Stephen G. *Underdeveloping the Amazon: Extraction, Unequal Exchange, and the Failure of the Modern State.* Urbana: University of Illinois Press, 1985.

Burdick, John. *Looking for God in Brazil: The Progressive Catholic Church in Urban Brazil's Religious Arena.* Berkeley: University of California Press, 1993.

Burns, E. Bradford. *Nationalism in Brazil: A Historical Survey.* New York: Praeger, 1968.

Burns, E. Bradford. "Tradition and Variation in Brazilian Foreign Policy," *Journal of Interamerican Studies and World Affairs,* 9, No. 2, 1967, 195–212.

Burns, E. Bradford. *The Unwritten Alliance: Rio Branco and Brazilian-American Relations.* New York: Columbia University Press, 1966.

Bursztyn, Marcel. *O país das alianças: Elites e continuísmo no Brasil.* Petrópolis, Brazil: Editora Vozes, 1990.

Bursztyn, Marcel. *Poder dos donos: Planejamento e clientelismo no Nordeste.* Petrópolis, Brazil: Editora Vozes, 1985.

Cachel, Julian M., Pamela S. Falk, and David V. Fleischer, eds. *Brazil's Economic and Political Future.* Boulder, Colorado: Westview Press, 1988.

Caldeira, Jorge. *Mauá: Empresário do Império.* Rio de Janeiro: Campanhia de Letras, 1995.

Camargo, Aspásia, and Eli Diniz, eds. *Continuidade e mudança no Brasil da nova república.* São Paulo: Vértice, 1989.

Camargo, Aspásia, and Walder de Gós. *Meio século de combate: Diálogo com Cordeiro de Farias.* Rio de Janeiro: Editora Nova Fronteira, 1981.

Camargo, Sônia. *Autoritarismo e democracia na Argentina e Brasil: Uma década de política exterior, 1974–1984.* São Paulo: Editora Convívio, 1988.

Cammack, Paul. "Clientelism and Military Government in Brazil." Pages 53–75 in Christopher Clapham, ed., *Private Patronage and Public Power.* New York: St. Martin's Press, 1982.

Campos, Roberto. *A lanterna na popa: Memórias.* Rio de Janeiro: Topbooks, 1994.

Cardoso, Fernando Henrique. "Associate-Dependent Development in Democratic Theory." Pages 299–326 in Alfred E. Stepan, ed., *Democratizing Brazil: Problems of Transition and Consolidation.* New York: Oxford University Press, 1988.

Cardoso, Fernando Henrique. "Associate-Dependent Development: Theoretical and Practical Implications." Pages 142–76 in Alfred E. Stepan, ed., *Authoritarian Brazil: Origins, Policy, and Future.* New Haven: Yale University Press, 1973.

Cardoso, Fernando Henrique. *Autoritarismo e democratização.* Rio de Janeiro: Paz e Terra, 1975.

Cardoso, Fernando Henrique. *A construção da democracia: Estudos sobre política.* São Paulo: Editora Siciliano, 1994.

Cardoso, Fernando Henrique. *Mãos à obra, Brasil: Proposta de governo.* [s.n.]: Brasília, 1994.

Cardoso, Fernando Henrique. "Partidos e deputados em São Paulo: O voto e a representação política." Pages 45–74 in Fernando Henrique Cardoso and Bolivar Lamounier, eds., *Os partidos e as eleições no Brazil.* Rio de Janeiro: Paz e Terra, 1975.

Cardoso, Fernando Henrique, and Enzo Faletto. *Dependency and Development in Latin America.* Berkeley: University of California Press, 1979.

Cardoso Silva, Vera Alice, and Lucila de Almeida Neves. *Tancredo Neves: A trajetória de um liberal.* Petrópolis: Editora Vozes, 1985.

Carmagnani, Marcello, ed. *Federalismos latinoamericanos: México/Brasil/Argentina.* Mexico City: Fondo de Cultura Económica, 1995.

Carvalho, Getúlio. *Petrobrás: Do monopólio aos contratos de risco.* Rio de Janeiro: Editora Forense-Universitária, 1977.

Carvalho, José Murilo de. "Armed Forces and Politics in Brazil, 1930–1945," *Hispanic American Historical Review,* 62, No. 2, May 1982, 193–223.

Carvalho, José Murilo de. *A construção da ordem: A elite política imperial.* Brasília: Editora Universidade de Brasília, 1981.

de Castro, Ferreira. *Itamar: O Homem que redescobriu o Brasil: A trajetória política de Itamar Franco e os bastidores de seu governo.* Rio de Janeiro: Editora Record, 1995.

Cava, Ralph della. "The 'People's Church,' the Vatican, and Abertura." Pages 143–67 in Alfred C. Stepan, ed., *Democratizing Brazil: Problems of Transition and Consolidation.* New York: Oxford University Press, 1988.

Cerqueira, Silas. "Brazil." Pages 150–235 in Jean-Pierre A. Bernard, et al., *Guide to the Political Parties of South America*. Harmondsworth, United Kingdom: Penguin, 1973.

Cervo, Amado Luiz. *As relações históricas entre o Brasil e a Itália: O papel, da diplomacia*. Brasília: Editora Universidade de Brasília, Instituto Italiano di Cultura, 1991.

Cervo, Amado Luiz, and Clodoaldo Bueno. *O desafio internacional: A política exterior do Brasil de 1930 à nossos dias*. Brasília: Editora da Universidade de Brasília, 1994.

Cervo, Amado Luiz, and Clodoaldo Bueno. *História da política exterior do Brasil*. São Paulo: Editora Ática, 1992.

Cervo, Amado Luiz, and Clodoaldo Bueno. *A política externa brasileira, 1822–1985*. São Paulo: Editora Ática, 1986.

Chacon, Vamireh. *Estado e povo no Brasil: As experiências do estado novo e da democracia populista, 1937–1964*. Brasília: Câmara dos Deputados, 1977.

Chacon, Vamireh. *Parlamento e parlamentarismo: O Congresso Nacional na história do Brasil*. Brasília: Câmara dos Deputados, 1982.

Chacon, Vamireh. *Vida e morte das constituições brasileiras*. Rio de Janeiro: Forense Editora-Universitária, 1987.

Chagas, Carlos. *A guerra das estrelas, 1964–1984: Os bastidores das sucessões presidenciais*. Porto Alegre, Brazil: L and PM Editores, 1985.

Chagas, Carlos. *113 dias de angústia: Impedimento e morte de um presidente*. Porto Alegre, Brazil: L and PM Editores, 1979.

Chalmers, Douglas, Maria do Carmo Campelo de Souza, and Atílio Borón, eds. *The Right and Democracy in Latin America*. New York: Praeger, 1992.

Chilcote, Ronald H. *The Brazilian Communist Party: Conflict and Integration, 1922–1972*. New York: Oxford University Press, 1974.

Chilcote, Ronald H., and Joel C. Edelstein, eds. *Latin America: The Struggle for Dependency and Beyond*. Cambridge, Massachusetts: Schenkman, 1974.

Cintra, Antônio Octávio. "Traditional Brazilian Politics: An Interpretation of Relations Between Center and Periphery." Pages 127–66 in Neuma Aguiar, ed., *The Structure of Brazilian Development*. New Brunswick, New Jersey: Transaction Books, 1979.

Cobbs, Elizabeth A. *The Rich Neighbor Policy: Rockefeller and Kaiser in Brazil.* New Haven: Yale University Press, 1992.

Cohen, Youssef. "Democracy from Above: The Political Origins of Military Dictatorship in Brazil," *World Politics,* 40, 1987, 30–45.

Cohen, Youssef. *The Manipulation of Consent: The State and Working-Class Consciousness in Brazil.* Pittsburgh: University of Pittsburgh Press, 1989.

Cohen, Youssef. *Popular Support for Authoritarian Regimes: Brazil under Médici.* Ann Arbor: University of Michigan Press, 1979.

Colby, Gerald, and Charlotte Dennett. *Thy Will Be Done: The Conquest of the Amazon, Nelson Rockefeller and Evangelism in the Age of Oil.* Dunmore, Pennsylvania: Harper-Collins, 1995.

Collier, David, ed. *The New Authoritarianism in Latin America.* Princeton: Princeton University Press, 1979.

Conca, Ken. *Manufacturing Insecurity: The Rise and Fall of Brazil's Military Industrial Complex.* Boulder, Colorado: Lynne Rienner, 1997.

Conca, Ken. "Technology, the Military, and Democracy in Brazil," *Journal of Interamerican Studies and World Affairs,* 34, No. 1, 1992, 141–77.

Conniff, Michael L. *Urban Politics in Brazil: The Rise of Populism, 1925–1945.* Pittsburgh: University of Pittsburgh Press, 1981.

Conniff, Michael L., and Frank D. McCann, eds. *Modern Brazil: Elites and Masses in Historical Perspective.* Lincoln: University of Nebraska Press, 1989.

Conselho Brasileiro de Relações Internacionais. *Mercosul: Desafios a vencer.* Paper presented at Seminário Mercosul: Desafios a Vencer, October 1993. São Paulo: Bartia Gráfica, 1994.

Correa, Luiz Felipe de Seixas. "As relações internacionais do Brasil em direção ao ano 2000." Pages 219–54 in Gelson Fonseca Júnior and Valdemar Carneiro Leão, eds., *Temas de política externa brasileira.* Brasília: Fundação Alexandre Gusmão, Editora Ática, 1989.

Couto, Claudio Gonçalves. *O desafio de ser governo: O PT na prefeitura de São Paulo.* Rio de Janeiro: Paz e Terra, 1995.

Dagnino, Evelina, ed. *Os anos 90: Política e sociedade no Brasil.* São Paulo: Editora Brasiliense, 1990.

Daland, Robert T. *Exploring Brazilian Bureaucracy: Performance and Pathology*. Washington: University Press of America, 1981.

Dantas, Francisco Clementino de Santiago. *Política externa independente*. Rio de Janeiro: Editora Civilização Brasileira, 1962.

D'Araújo, Maria Celina Soares. *O segundo governo Vargas, 1951–1954: Democracia, partidos e crise política*. Rio de Janeiro: Zahar Editores, 1982.

D'Araújo, Maria Celina Soares. *Sindicatos, carisma e poder: O PTB de 1945–1965*. Rio de Janeiro: Fundação Getúlio Vargas, 1996.

D'Araújo, Maria Celina Soares, Gláucio Ary Dillon Soares, and Celso Castro. *Visões do golpe: A memória militar sobre 1964*. Rio de Janeiro: Relume-Dumará, 1994.

Dassin, Joan R. "The Brazilian Press and the Politics of Abertura," *Journal of Interamerican Studies and World Affairs*, 26, No. 3, August 1984, 385–414.

Dassin, Joan R., ed. *Torture in Brazil*. New York: Random House, 1986.

Delgado, Lucília de Almeida Neves. *PTB: Do getúlismo ao reformismo, 1945–1964*. São Paulo: Editora Marco Zero, 1989.

Departamento Intersindical de Assessoria Parlamentar. "Perfil e propostas do governo FHC," *Boletim do DIAP* [Brasília], No. 1, January 1995.

Dimenstein, Gilberto, and Josias Souza. *A história real: Trama de uma sucessão*. São Paulo: Editora Ática, 1994.

Dimenstein, Gilberto, et al. *O complô que elegeu Tancredo*. Rio de Janeiro: Editora JB, 1985.

Diniz, Eli. *Voto e máquina política: Patronagem e clientelismo no Rio de Janeiro*. Rio de Janeiro: Paz e Terra, 1982.

Diniz, Eli, Renato Boschi, and Renato Lessa. *Modernização e consolidação democrática no Brasil: Dilemas da nova república*. São Paulo: Vértice, 1989.

Drake, Paul W., and Eduardo Silva, eds. *Elections and Democratization in Latin America, 1980–1985*. San Diego: University of California Press, 1986.

Dreifuss, René Armand. *O jogo da direita na nova república*. Petrópolis: Editora Vozes, 1989.

Dreifuss, René Armand. *1964: A conquista do estado: Ação política, poder e golpe de classe*. Petrópolis, Brazil: Editora Vozes, 1981.

Dulci, Otávio Soares. *A UDN e o anti-populismo no Brasil.* Belo Horizonte, Brazil: Editora Universidade Federal de Minas Gerais, 1986.

Erickson, Kenneth Paul. *The Brazilian Corporative State and Working-Class Politics.* Berkeley: University of California Press, 1977.

Eugster, Markus. *Der brasilianische Verfassungsgebungsprozess von 1987–88.* Bern: Verlag Paul Haupt, 1995.

Evans, Peter. *Dependent Development: The Alliance of Multinational, State, and Local Capital in Brazil.* Princeton: Princeton University Press, 1979.

Evans, Peter, "Informática: Metamorfose da dependência," *Novos Estudos CEBRAP* (Centro Brasileiro de Análise e Planejamento) [São Paulo], 15, 1986, 14–31.

Faoro, Raymundo. *Os donos do poder: Formação do patronato político brasileiro.* 2 vols. 6th ed. Rio de Janeiro: Editora Globo, 1984.

Faoro, Raymundo. *Existe um pensamento político brasileiro?* São Paulo: Editora Ática: 1994.

Fausto, Boris. *História do Brasil.* São Paulo: Editora da Universidade de São Paulo, 1995.

Ferreira, Oliveiros, "Política externa e liberdade de manobra," *Política e Estratégia* [São Paulo], 3, No. 1, 1985, 70–95.

Fiechter, Georges-André. *Brazil since 1964: Modernization under a Military Regime.* New York: John Wiley, 1975.

Figueira, Archibaldo. *Lobby: O fico da UDR.* Porto Alegre, Brazil: Editora Sagra, 1987.

Figueiredo, Argelina Cheibub. *Democracia ou reformas?: Alternativas democráticas à crise política.* Rio de Janeiro: Paz e Terra, 1993.

Figueiredo, Marcus Faria. *A decisão do voto.* São Paulo: Editora Sumaré, 1991.

Figueiredo, Marcus Faria, and José Antônio Borges Cheibub. "A abertura política de 1973 à 1981: Quem disse o que, quando: Inventário de um debate," *BIB: Boletim Informativo e Bibliográfico de Ciências Sociais* [Rio de Janeiro], No. 14, 1982, 22–61.

Filho Expedito. *Fernando Henrique Cardoso: Crônica de uma vitória.* Série Nos. Bastidores da Company. Rio de Janeiro: Editora Objetiva, 1994.

Fishlow, Albert. "The United States and Brazil: The Case of the Missing Relationship," *Foreign Affairs*, 60, No. 4, Spring 1982, 904–23.

Fleischer, David V. "Brazil at the Crossroads: The Elections of 1982 and 1985." Pages 299–327 in Paul W. Drake and Eduardo Silva, eds., *Elections and Democratization in Latin America, 1980–1985*. San Diego: University of California Press, 1986.

Fleischer, David V. "The Brazilian Congress: From 'Abertura' to 'New Republic.'" Pages 97–133 in Wayne A. Selcher, ed., *Political Liberalization in Brazil: Dynamics, Dilemmas, and Future Prospects*. Boulder, Colorado: Westview Press, 1986.

Fleischer, David V. "The Brazilian Municipal Elections of October 3, 1996." (http://www.brasil.emb.nw.dc.us/munelt96.htm)

Fleischer, David V. "The Constituent Assembly and the Transformation Strategy: Attempts to Shift Political Power from the Presidency to the Congress." Pages 210–58 in Lawrence S. Graham and Robert H. Wilson, eds., *The Political Economy of Brazil: Public Policies in an Era of Transition*. Austin: University of Texas Press, 1990.

Fleischer, David V. "Constitutional and Electoral Engineering in Brazil: A Double-Edged Sword, 1964–1982," *Inter-American Economic Affairs*, 37, 1984, 3–36.

Fleischer, David V. "A evolução do bipartidarismo brasileiro, 1966–1979," *Revista Brasileira de Estudos Políticos* [Belo Horizonte], 51, July 1980, 155–85.

Fleischer, David V. "Manipulações casuísticas do sistema eleitoral durante o período militar, ou como usualmente o feitiço se voltava contra o feiticeiro." Pages 154–97 in Gláucio A.D. Soares and Maria Celina D'Aráujo, eds., *21 anos de regime militar: Balanços e perspectivas*. Rio de Janeiro: Fundação Getúlio Vargas, 1994.

Fleischer, David V. "Parties, Elections, and 'Abertura' in Brazil." Pages 79–96 in Robert Wesson, ed., *New Military Politics in Latin America*. New York: Praeger, 1982.

Fleischer, David V. "Renovação política-Brasil 1978: Eleições parlamentares sob a égide do 'Pacote de Abril,'" *Revista de Ciência Política* [Brasília], 32, 1982, 57–82.

Fleischer, David V., ed. *Da distensão à abertura: As eleições de novembro de 1982.* Brasília: Editora Universidade de Brasília, 1988.

Fleischer, David V., ed. *Os partidos políticos no Brasil.* 2 vols. Brasília: Editora Universidade de Brasília, 1981.

Flynn, Peter. *Brazil: A Political Analysis.* Boulder, Colorado: Westview Press, 1978.

Flynn, Peter. "Collor, Corruption, and Crisis: Time for Reflection," *Journal of Latin American Studies,* 25, No. 2, May 1993, 351–71.

Fonseca, Gelson Júnior, and Valdemar Carneiro Leão, eds. *Temas de política externa brasileira.* Brasília: Fundação Alexandre Gusmão, Editora Ática, 1989.

Fontaine, Roger W. *Brazil and the United States.* Washington: American Enterprise Institute, 1975.

"Formação militar: O ensino no Exército," *Revista do Exército Brasileiro* [Rio de Janeiro], 127, No. 2, April–June 1990, 68–77.

Fragoso, João Luís Ribeiro. "Notas sobre a política externa brasileira dos anos 50–70," *Estudos Afro-Asiáticos* [Rio de Janeiro], 10, 1984, 5–29.

Fragoso, João Luís Ribeiro. "As reformulações na política externa brasileira nos anos 70," *Estudos Afro-Asiáticos* [Rio de Janeiro], 5, 1981, 41–53.

Friedman, Steven, and Riaan de Villiers, eds. *Comparing Brazil and South Africa: Two Transitional States in Political and Economic Perspective.* Johannesburg: Centre for Policy Studies/ Foundation for Global Dialogue, 1996.

Frota, Luciara Silveira de Aragão. *Brasil-Argentina e a política das grandes potências 1945–1995.* Brasília: Gráfica Regional, 1995.

FUNAG. *A palavra do Brasil nas Nações Unidas, 1946–1995.* Brasília: Fundação Alexandre Gusmão, 1995.

Garner, Lydia M. "Unresolved Issues in Brazil: Challenges to the Political Leadership in the 1990s," *Journal of Third World Studies,* 9, February 1992, 59–79.

Gay, Robert. *Popular Organization and Democracy in Rio de Janeiro: A Tale of Two Favelas.* Philadelphia: Temple University Press, 1994.

Geddes, Barbara. *Politicians' Dilemma: Building State Capacity in Latin America.* Berkeley: University of California Press, 1994.

Geddes, Barbara, and Artur Ribeiro Neto. "Institutional Sources of Corruption in Brazil," *Third World Quarterly*, 33, 1989, 319–47.

Góes, Walder de. *O Brasil do General Geisel: Estudo do process de tornada de decisão no regime militar-burocrático.* Rio de Janeiro: Editora Nova Fronteira, 1978.

Góes, Walder de, and Aspásia Camargo. *O drama da sucessão e a crise do regime.* Rio de Janeiro: Editora Nova Fronteira, 1984.

Gonçalves, Reinaldo. *O abre-alas: A nova inserção do Brasil na economia mundial.* Rio de Janeiro: Relume Dumara, 1994.

Gouvea, Gilda Portugal. *Burocracia e elites burocráticas no Brasil.* São Paulo: Editora Paulicéia, 1995.

Graham, Lawrence S., and Robert H. Wilson, eds. *The Political Economy of Brazil: Public Policies in an Era of Transition.* Austin: University of Texas Press, 1990.

Graham, Richard, ed. *Brazil and the World System.* Austin: University of Texas Press, 1991.

Guerreiro, Ramiro Saraiva. *Lembranças de um empregado do Itamaraty.* São Paulo: Siciliano, 1992.

Gurgel, Antonio P., and David Fleischer. *O Brasil vai às urnas: Retrato da campanha presidencial.* Brasília: Editora Thesaurus, 1990.

Hagopian, Frances. "After Regime Change: Authoritarian Legacies, Political Representation, and the Democratic Future of South America," *World Politics*, 45, No. 3, 1993, 464–500.

Hagopian, Frances. "Democracy by Undemocratic Means? Elites, Political Pacts, and Regime Transition in Brazil," *Comparative Political Studies*, 23, July 1990, 147–70.

Hagopian, Frances. *Traditional Politics and Regime Change in Brazil.* New York: Cambridge University Press, 1996.

Hagopian, Frances, and Scott Mainwaring. "Democracy in Brazil: Problems and Prospects," *World Policy Journal*, 4, Summer 1987, 485–514.

Haguette, Teresa Maria Frota. O *cidadão e o estado: A construção da cidadania brasileira, 1940–1992.* Fortaleza, Brazil: Edições Universidade Federal do Ceará, 1994.

Haines, Gerald K. *The Americanization of Brazil: A Study of U.S. Cold War Diplomacy in the Third World, 1945–1954.* Wilmington, Delaware: Scholarly Resources, 1989.

Hewlett, Sylvia Ann. *The Cruel Dilemmas of Development: Twentieth-Century Brazil.* New York: Basic Books, 1980.

Hewlett, Sylvia Ann, and Richard S. Weinert, eds. *Brazil and Mexico: Patterns in Late Development.* Philadelphia: Institute for the Study of Human Issues, 1982.

Hill, Lawrence F. *Diplomatic Relations Between the United States and Brazil.* Durham: Duke University Press, 1932.

Hilton, Stanley E. *O Brasil e a crise internacional, 1930–1945.* Rio de Janeiro: Editora Civilização Brasileira, 1977.

Hilton, Stanley E. *Brazil and the Great Powers, 1930–1939: The Politics of Trade Rivalry.* Austin: University of Texas Press, 1975.

Hippolito, Lúcia. *De raposas e reformistas: O PSD e a experiência democrática brasileira, 1945–64.* Rio de Janeiro: Paz e Terra, 1985.

Hirst, Mônica. "Pesos y medidas de política externa brasileña." Pages 25–50 in Juan Carlos Puig, ed., *América Latina: Políticas exteriores comparadas.* Buenos Aires: Grupo Editorial Interamericano, 1984.

Hirst, Mônica, "Tempos e contratempos da política externa brasileira." Pages 245–61 in C.A. Plastino and R. Bouzas, eds., *A América Latina e a crise internacional.* Rio de Janeiro: Edições Graal, 1985.

Hirst, Mônica. "Transição democrática e política externa: A experiência do Brasil." Pages 207–18 in Heraldo Muñoz and Joseph Tulchin, eds., *A América Latina e a política mundial: Uma perspectiva latino-americana das relações internacionais.* São Paulo: Editora Convívio, 1986.

Hunter, Wendy. *Politicians on the Advance: Eroding Military Influence in Brazil.* Chapel Hill: University of North Carolina, 1997.

Hurrell, Andrew. "The International Dimensions of Democratization in Latin America: The Case of Brazil." Pages 146–74 in Lawrence Whitehead, ed., *The International Dimensions of Democratization: Europe and the Americas.* Oxford: Oxford University Press, 1996.

Iglesias, Francisco. *Constituintes e constituições brasileiras.* São Paulo: Editora Brasiliense, 1986.

Institute of Latin American Studies. *Brazil: The Struggle for Modernization.* London: Institute of Latin American Studies, 1993.

Ireland, Rowan. *Kingdoms Come: Religion and Politics in Brazil.* Pittsburgh: University of Pittsburgh Press, 1992.

Jaguaribe, Hélio. "O Brasil e o sistema internacional contemporâneo." Pages 65–84 in J. Marcovitch, ed. *Cooperação internacional: Estratégia e gestão.* São Paulo: EDUSP, 1994.

Jaguaribe, Hélio. *O nacionalismo na realidade brasileira.* Rio de Janeiro: Instituto Superior de Estudos Brasileiros, 1958.

Jaguaribe, Hélio. *Novo cenário internacional.* Rio de Janeiro: Editora Guanabara, 1986.

Jaguaribe, Hélio, ed. *Sociedade, estado e partidos políticos da atualidade brasileira.* Rio de Janeiro: Paz e Terra, 1992.

Jenks, Margaret Sarles. "Political Parties in Authoritarian Brazil." Ph.D. dissertation. Durham: Department of Political Science, Duke University, 1979.

Keck, Margaret E. *The International Politics of the Brazilian Amazon.* New York: Columbia University Press, 1991.

Keck, Margaret E. "The 'New Unionism' in the Brazilian Transition." Pages 252–96 in Alfred C. Stepan, ed., *Democratizing Brazil: Problems of Transition and Consolidation.* New York: Oxford University Press, 1988.

Keck, Margaret E. *PT: A lógica e a diferença: O Partido dos Trabalhadores na construção da democracia brasileira.* São Paulo: Editora Ática, 1991.

Keck, Margaret E. *The Workers' Party and Democratization in Brazil.* New Haven: Yale University Press, 1992.

Keith, Henry H., and Robert A. Hayes, eds. *Perspectives on Armed Politics in Brazil.* Tempe: Center for Latin American Studies, Arizona State University, 1976.

Kinzo, Maria D'Alva Gil. *Legal Opposition Politics under Authoritarian Rule in Brazil: The Case of the MDB, 1966–79.* London: Macmillan, 1988.

Kinzo, Maria D'Alva Gil. *Radiografia do quadro partidário brasileiro.* São Paulo: Konrad Adenauer Sifung, 1993.

Kinzo, Maria D'Alva Gil. *Representação política e sistema eleitoral no Brasil.* São Paulo: Edições Símbolo, 1980.

Kinzo, Maria D'Alva Gil, ed. *Brazil: The Challenges of the 1990s.* London: Tauris/Institute of Latin American Studies, 1993.

Kinzo, Maria D'Alva Gil, and Victor Blumer-Thomas, eds. *Growth and Development: Cardoso's 'Real' Challenge.* London: Institute of Latin American Studies, 1995.

Krieger, Gustavo, Luiz A. Novaes, and Tales Faria. *Todos os sócios do presidente.* São Paulo: Scritta Editorial, 1992.

Kucinski, Bernardo. *Abertura: A história de uma crise.* São Paulo: Brasil Debates, 1982.

Kucinski, Bernardo. *Brazil: State and Struggle.* London: Latin American Bureau, 1982.

Lafer, Celso. *O Brasil e a crise mundial.* São Paulo: Editora Perspectiva, 1984.

Lafer, Celso. *O Brasil no mundo pós-Guerra Fria: A economia mundial em transformação.* Rio de Janeiro: Fundação Getúlio Vargas, 1994.

Lafer, Celso. "Novas dimensões da política externa brasileira," *Revista Brasileira de Ciências Sociais* [Fortaleza], 1, No. 3, 1987, 73–82.

Lafer, Celso. *Paradoxos e possibilidades sobre a ordem mundial e sobre a política externa do Brasil num sistema internacional em transformação.* Rio de Janeiro: Editora Nova Fronteira, 1982.

Lafer, Celso. *Política externa brasileira: Três momentos.* São Paulo: Konrad Adenauer Stiftung, 1993.

Lafer, Celso. *O sistema político brasileiro.* São Paulo: Editora Perspectiva, 1975.

Lafer, Celso, and Felix Peña. *Argentina e Brasil no sistema de relações internacionais.* São Paulo: Duas Cidades, 1973.

Lagôa, Ana. *SNI: Como nasceu, como funciona.* São Paulo: Editora Brasiliense, 1983.

Lamounier, Bolivar. "Apontamentos sobre a questão democrática brasileira." Pages 104–40 in Alain Rouquié, et al., eds., *Como renascem as democracias.* São Paulo: Editora Brasiliense, 1985.

Lamounier, Bolivar. "Authoritarian Brazil Revisited: The Input of Elections." Pages 43–79 in Alfred Stepan, ed., *Authoritarian Brazil: Origins, Policies, and Future.* New Haven: Yale University Press, 1973.

Lamounier, Bolivar. "Brazil Towards Parlamentarism?" Pages 149–81 in Arturo Valenzuela and Juan Linz, eds., *Presidentialism and Parlamentarism: Does It Make a Difference?* Baltimore: Johns Hopkins University Press, 1995.

Lamounier, Bolivar. *A democracia brasileira no liminar do século 21.* São Paulo: Konrad Adenauer Stiftung, 1996.

Lamounier, Bolivar. "As eleições de 1982 e a abertura política em perspectiva." Pages 121–33 in Hélgio Trindade, ed., *Brasil em perspectiva: Dilemas da abertura política.* Porto Alegre, Brazil: Sulina, 1982.

Lamounier, Bolivar. "Opening Through Elections: Will the Brazilian Case Become a Paradigm?" *Government and Opposition,* 19, No. 2, Spring 1984, 167–77.

Lamounier, Bolivar. *Ouvindo o Brasil: Uma análise da opinião pública brasileira hoje.* São Paulo: Editora Sumaré, 1992.

Lamounier, Bolivar. *Partidos e utopias: O Brasil no limiar dos anos 90.* São Paulo: Edições Loyola, 1989.

Lamounier, Bolivar, ed. *De Geisel a Collor: O balanço da transição.* São Paulo: Instituto de Estudos Econômicos, Sociais e Políticos de São Paulo/Conselho Nacional de Pesquisas (IDESP/CNPq), 1990.

Lamounier, Bolivar, ed. *Voto de desconfiança: Eleições e mudança política no Brasil, 1970–1979.* Petrópolis, Brazil: Editora Vozes, 1980.

Lamounier, Bolivar, and Rachel Meneguello. *Partidos políticos e consolidação democrática: O caso brasileiro.* São Paulo: Editora Brasiliense, 1986.

Lamounier, Bolivar, and Amaury de Souza. "Changing Attitudes Toward Democracy and Institutional Reform in Brazil." Pages 295–326 in Larry Diamond, ed., *Political Culture and Democracy in Developing Countries.* Boulder, Colorado: Lynne Rienner, 1993.

Lamounier, Bolivar, and Maria Teresa Sadek R. Souza. *Depois da transição: Democracia e eleições no governo Collor.* São Paulo: Edições Loyola, 1991.

Landers, Clifford R. "The União Democrática Nacional in the State of Guanabara: An Attitudinal Study of Party Membership." Ph.D. dissertation. University of Florida, 1971. Ann Arbor: Xerox University Microfilms, 1973.

Lara, Maurício. *Campanha de rua.* São Paulo: Geração Editorial, 1994.

Lavareda, José Antônio. *A democracia nas urnas: Processo partidário eleitoral brasileiro.* Rio de Janeiro: Editora Rio Fundo, 1991.

Leacock, Ruth. *Requiem for Revolution: The United States and Brazil, 1961–1969.* Kent, Ohio: Kent State University Press, 1990.

Leal, Victor Nunes. *Coronelismo: The Municipality and Representative Government in Brazil.* Cambridge: Cambridge University Press, 1977.

Levinson, Jerome, and Juan de Onis. *The Alliance That Lost Its Way.* Chicago: Quadrangle Books, 1970.

Lewin, Linda. *Politics and Parentela in Paraíba: A Case Study of Family-Based Oligarchy in Brazil.* Princeton: Princeton University Press, 1987.

Lima, Maria Regina Soares de. "Brazil's Response to the 'New Regionalism'." Pages 50–75 in Gordon Mace and Jean-Philippe Thérien, eds., *Foreign Policy and Regionalism in the Americas.* Boulder, Colorado: Lynne Rienner, 1996.

Lima, Maria Regina Soares de, and Gerson Moura. "Relações internacionais e política externa brasileira: Uma resenha bibliográfica," *BIB: Boletim Informativo e Bibliográfico de Ciências Sociais* [Rio de Janeiro], 13, 1982, 5–36.

Lima, Maria Regina Soares de, and Gerson Moura. "A trajetória do pragmatismo: Uma análise da política externa brasileira," *Dados* [Rio de Janeiro], 25, No. 3, 1982, 349–63.

Lima, Venício Artur de. "Brazilian Television and the 1989 Presidential Elections: Constructing a President." Pages 97–117 in Thomas E. Skidmore, ed., *Television, Politics, and the Transition to Democracy in Latin America.* Baltimore: Johns Hopkins University Press, 1993.

Lima Júnior, Olavo Brasil de. *Democracia e instituições políticas no Brasil dos anos 80.* São Paulo: Edições Loyola, 1993.

Lima Júnior, Olavo Brasil de. *Os partidos políticos brasileiros: A experiência federal e regional, 1945–1964.* Rio de Janeiro: Edições Graal, 1983.

Lima Júnior, Olavo Brasil de. "A reforma das instituicões políticas: A experiência brasileira e o aperfeiçoamento democrático," *Dados* [Rio de Janeiro], 36, No. 1, 1993, 89–117.

Lima Júnior, Olavo Brasil de, ed. *O balanço do poder: Formas de dominação e representação.* Rio de Janeiro: Rio Fundo Editora, 1990.

Lima Júnior, Olavo Brasil de, ed. *Sistema eleitoral brasileiro.* Rio de Janeiro: Rio Fundo Editora, 1991.

Lima Júnior, Olavo Brasil de, Rogério Augusto Schmidt, and Jairo Marconi Nicolau. "A produção brasileira recente sobre partidos, eleições e comportamento político: Balanço bibliográfico," *BIB: Boletim Informativo e Bibliográfico de Ciências Sociais* [Rio de Janeiro], No. 34, 1992, 3–36.

Linz, Juan J., and Alfred Stepan, eds. *The Breakdown of Democratic Regimes*, 3. Baltimore: Johns Hopkins University Press, 1978.

Lopes, Roberto. *Rêde de intrigas.* Rio de Janeiro: Editora Record, 1994.

Macaulay, Neill. *The Prestes Column: A Revolution in Brazil.* New York: New Viewpoints, 1974.

Mace, Gordon, and Jean-Philippe Thérien, eds. *Foreign Policy and Regionalism in the Americas.* Boulder, Colorado: Lynne Rienner, 1996.

Mainwaring, Scott. "Brazil: Weak Parties, Feckless Democracy." Pages 354–98 in Scott Mainwaring and Timothy Scully, eds., *Building Democratic Institutions: Parties and Party Systems in Latin America.* Stanford: Stanford University Press, 1995.

Mainwaring, Scott. "Brazilian Party Underdevelopment in Comparative Perspective," *Political Science Quarterly*, 107, 1992, 677–707.

Mainwaring, Scott. *The Catholic Church and Politics in Brazil, 1916–1985.* Stanford: Stanford University Press, 1986.

Mainwaring, Scott. *The Party System and Democratization in Brazil.* Stanford: Stanford University Press, 1997.

Malloy, James M. *The Politics of Social Security in Brazil.* Pittsburgh: University of Pittsburgh Press, 1979.

Malloy, James M., and Mitchell A. Seligman, eds. *Authoritarians and Democrats: Regime Transitions in Latin America.* Pittsburgh: University of Pittsburgh Press, 1987.

Manwaring, Max G. "Brazilian Security in the New World Disorder: Implications for Civilian Military Relations." Pages 125–50 in Richard L. Millett and M. Gold-Biss, eds., *Beyond Praetorianism: The Latin American Military in Transition.* Boulder, Colorado: Lynne Rienner, 1996.

Marchal, Odile, Hervé Théry, and Philippe Waniez. "La géographie électorale du Brésil après l'élection présidentielle de 1989," *Cahiers des sciences humaines* [Paris], 28, 1992, 535–54.

Margolis, Maxine. *Little Brazil: An Ethnography of Brazilian Immigrants in New York City.* Princeton: Princeton University Press, 1993.

Mariano, Ricardo, and Antônio F. Pierucci. "O envolvimento dos Pentencostais na eleição de Collor," *Novos Estudos CEBRAP* (Centro Brasileiro de Análise e Planejamento) [São Paulo], 34, 1992, 92–106.

Mariz, Cecília Loreta. *Coping with Poverty: Pentecostals and Christian Base Communities in Brazil.* Philadelphia: Temple University Press, 1994.

Markoff, John, and Sílvio R.D. Baretta. "Brazil's Abertura: Transition from What to What?" Pages 43–65 in James M. Malloy and Mitchell A. Seligman, eds., *Authoritarians and Democrats: Regime Transitions in Latin America.* Pittsburgh: University of Pittsburgh Press, 1987.

Martinez-Alier, Verena, and Armando Boito Júnior. "The Hoe and the Vote: Rural Labourers and the National Election in Brazil in 1974," *Journal of Peasant Studies,* 4, No. 3, April 1977, 147–70.

Martinez-Lara, Javier. "Building Democracy in Brazil: The Politics of Constitutional Change, 1985–1993." Ph.D. dissertation. London: St. Antony's College, Oxford University, 1994.

Martins, Carlos Estevam. "A evolução da política externa brasileira na década 64/74," *Estudos CEBRAP* (Centro Brasileiro de Análise e Planejamento) [São Paulo], No. 12, 1975, 53–98.

Martins, Luciano. *Estado capitalista e burocracia no Brasil pós-64.* Rio de Janeiro: Paz e Terra, 1985.

Martins, Luciano. "The 'Liberalization' of Authoritarian Rule in Brazil." Pages 72–4 in Guillermo A. O'Donnell, Philippe C. Schmitter, and Laurence Whitehead, eds. *Transitions from Authoritarian Rule: Latin America.* Baltimore: Johns Hopkins University Press, 1986.

McCann, Frank D. *The Brazilian-American Alliance.* Princeton: Princeton University Press, 1973.

McCann, Frank D. "Brazilian Foreign Relations in the Twentieth Century." In Wayne A. Selcher, ed., *Brazil in the International System: The Rise of a Middle Power.* Boulder, Colorado: Westview Press, 1981.

McDonald, Ronald H., and Mark J. Ruhl. *Party Politics and Elections in Latin America.* Boulder, Colorado: Westview Press, 1989.

McDonough, Peter. *Power and Ideology in Brazil.* Princeton: Princeton University Press, 1981.

McDonough, Peter. "Repression and Representation in Brazil," *Comparative Politics,* 15, No. 1, October 1982, 73–99.

McNally, Leonard. "Brazil: The Effects of Modernization and Political Policy," *Revue de Droit International de Sciences Diplomatiques et Politiques* [Geneva], 59, No. 3, June–September 1981, 177–200.

Mello E. Silva, Alexandra. *A política externa de JK: Operação Panamericana.* Rio de Janeiro: Fundação Getúlio Vargas/Centro de Pesquisa e Documenta de História Contemporânea do Brasil (CPDOC), 1992.

Melo Franco, Afonso Arinos de. *Planalto: Memórias.* Rio de Janeiro: Editora Olympio, 1968.

Mendes, Cândido. *A democracia desperdiçada: Poder e imaginação social.* Rio de Janeiro: Editora Nova Fronteira, 1992.

Menezes, Adolfo Justo Bezerra de. *Asia, Africa e a política independente do Brasil.* Rio de Janeiro: Zahar Editores, 1961.

Mericle, Kenneth S. "Corporatist Control of the Working Class: Authoritarian Brazil since 1964." Pages 303–38 in James M. Malloy, ed., *Authoritarianism and Corporatism in Latin America.* Pittsburgh: University of Pittsburgh Press, 1977.

Mir, Luiz. *A revolução impossível: A esquerda e a luta armada no Brasil.* São Paulo: Edotpra Best Seller, 1994.

Miyamoto, Shiguenoli. *Geopolítica e poder no Brasil.* São Paulo: Papirus, 1995.

Miyamoto, Shiguenoli. "Geopolítica, poder e relações internacionais," *A Defesa Nacional* [Rio de Janeiro], 712, 1984, 51–71.

Moises, José Alvaro. *Os brasileiros e a democracia: Bases sócio-políticas da legitimidade democrática.* São Paulo: Editora Ática, 1995.

Moises, José Alvaro. *Cidadania e participação: Ensaio sobre o referendo, o plebiscito e a iniciativa popular legislativa na nova Constituição.* São Paulo: Editora Marco Zero, 1990.

Moises, José Alvaro. "Democratização e cultura política de massas no Brasil," *Lua nova: Revista de Cultural Política* [São Paulo], No. 26, 1992, 5–51.

Moises, José Alvaro, ed. *O futuro do Brasil: A América Latina e o fim da guerra fria.* Rio de Janeiro: Paz e Terra, 1992.

Moises, José Alvaro, and José Augusto Guilhon Albuquerque, eds. *Dilemas da consolidação da democracia.* Rio de Janeiro: Paz e Terra, 1989.

Monclaire, Stéphane. "Le quasi-impeachment du Président Collor: Questions sur la 'consolidation de la démocratie' brésilienne," *Revue française de science politique* [Paris], 44, No. 1, 1994, 23–48.

Morais, Fernando. *Chatô: O rei do Brasil: A vida de Assis Chateaubriand, um dos brasileiros mais poderosos deste século.* São Paulo: Campanhia das Letras, 1994.

Moura, Gerson. *Autonomia e dependência: A política externa brasileira de 1935 à 1942.* Rio de Janeiro: Editora Nova Fronteira, 1980.

Moura, Gerson. *Sucessos e ilusões: Relações internacionas do Brasil durante e após a Segunda Guerra Mundial.* Rio de Janeiro: Fundação Getúlio Vargas, 1991.

Muñoz, Heraldo, and Joseph Tulchin, eds. *A América Latina e a política mundial.* São Paulo: Editora Convívio, 1986.

Nascimento, Elimar Pinheiro do. "L'affaire Collor de Mello: Renúncia e impeachment no presidencialismo brasileiro." *Cahiers du Centre d'Études Politiques Brésiliennes* [Paris], No. 15–16, July–October 1992.

Neumanne, José. *A república na lama: Uma tragédia brasileira.* São Paulo: Geração Editorial, 1992.

Nery, Sebastião. *As 16 Derrotas que abalaram o Brasil.* Rio de Janeiro: Editora Francisco Alves, 1975.

Nichols, Gary A. "Toward a Theory of Political Party Disunity: The Case of the National Democratic Union Party of Rio de Janeiro." Ph.D. dissertation. New Orleans: Tulane University, 1974.

Nicolau, Jairo Marconi. *Multipartidarismo e democracia: Um estudo sobre o sistema partidário brasileiro, 1985–94.* Rio de Janeiro: Fundação Getúlio Vargas, 1996.

Noblat, Ricardo. *Céu dos favoritos: O Brasil de Sarney a Collor.* Rio de Janeiro: Editora Rio Fundo, 1990.

Nunes, Edson de Oliveira. "Bureaucratic Insulation and Clientelism in Contemporary Brazil: Uneven State-Building and the Taming of Modernity." Ph.D. dissertation. Berkeley:

Department of Political Science, University of California, 1984.

Nunes, Edson de Oliveira. "Legislativo, política, e recrutamento de elites no Brasil," *Dados* [Rio de Janeiro], No. 17, 1978, 53–78.

Nunes, Edson de Oliveira, and Barbara Geddes. "Dilemmas of State-Led Modernization in Brazil." Pages 103–45 in John D. Wirth, Edson de Oliveira Nunes, and Thomas E. Bogenschild, eds., *State and Society in Brazil.* Boulder, Colorado: Westview Press, 1987.

O'Donnell, Guillermo A. "Challenges to Democratization in Brazil," *World Policy Journal,* 5, Spring 1988, 281–300.

O'Donnell, Guillermo A. *Modernization and Bureaucratic-Authoritarianism: Studies in South American Politics.* Politics of Modernization Series, No. 9. Berkeley: Institute of International Studies, University of California, 1973.

O'Donnell, Guillermo A., and Fábio Wanderley Reis, eds. *A democracia no Brasil: Dilemas e perspectivas.* São Paulo: Vértice, 1988.

O'Donnell, Guillermo A., Philippe C. Schmitter, and Laurence Whitehead, eds. *Transitions from Authoritarian Rule: Latin America.* Baltimore: Johns Hopkins University Press, 1986.

Oliveira, Eliézer Rizzo de. *De Geisel à Collor: Forças Armadas, transição democrática.* Campinas, Brazil: Editora Papirus, 1994.

Oliveira, Eliézer Rizzo de, ed. *Militares, pensamento e ação política.* Campinas, Brazil: Papirus, 1987.

Oliveira, Eliezer Rizzo de, Wilma Peres Costa, and João Quartim de Moraes. *A tutela militar.* São Paulo: Vértice, 1987.

Oliveira, Eliézer Rizzo de, Geraldo L. Cavagnari Filho, João Quartim de Moraes, and René Armand Dreifuss. *As Forças Armadas no Brasil.* Rio de Janeiro: Editora Espaço e Tempo, 1987.

Onis, Juan de. "Brazil on the Tightrope Toward Democracy," *Foreign Affairs,* 68, No. 4, 1989, 127–43.

Overholt, William H., ed. *The Future of Brazil.* Boulder, Colorado: Westview Press, 1978.

Packenham, Robert A. "The Changing Political Discourse in Brazil, 1964–1985." Pages 135–73 in Wayne A. Selcher, ed., *Political Liberalization in Brazil: Dynamics, Dilemmas, and Future Prospects.* Boulder, Colorado: Westview Press, 1986.

Palaczi-Horvath, George. "Brazil: Choices for a Navy with a Tight Budget." *Naval Forces*, 17, No. 1, 1996, 42–49.

Parker, Phyllis R. *Brazil and the Quiet Intervention, 1964.* Austin: University of Texas Press, 1979.

Payne, Leigh Ann. *Brazilian Industrialists and Democratic Change.* Baltimore: Johns Hopkins University Press, 1993.

Payne, Leigh Ann. "Working Class Strategies in the Transition to Democracy in Brazil," *Comparative Politics*, 23, No. 2, January 1991, 221–38.

Pereira Bresser, Luiz Carlos. *O colapso de uma aliança de classes.* São Paulo: Editora Brasiliense, 1978.

Pereira Bresser, Luiz Carlos. *O PMDB e as eleições de 1986.* São Paulo: Fundação Pedroso Horta, 1987.

Pereira Bresser, Luiz Carlos. *A sociedade estatal e a tecnoburocracia.* São Paulo: Editora Brasiliense, 1981.

Pereira, Osny Duarte. *Constituinte: Anteprojeto da Comissão Afonso Arinos.* Brasília: Editora Universidade de Brasília, 1987.

Perry, William. *Contemporary Brazilian Foreign Policy: International Strategy of an Emerging Power.* Beverly Hills, California: Sage, 1976.

Pinheiro Neto, João. *Jango: Um depoimento pessoal.* Rio de Janeiro: Editora Record, 1995.

Porcile, Gabriel. "The Challenge of Cooperation: Argentina and Brazil, 1939–1955," *Journal of Latin American Studies*, 27, No. 1, 1995, 129–160.

Power, Timothy J. "Elites and Institutions in Conservative Transitions to Democracy: Ex-Authoritarians in the Brazilian National Congress," *Studies in Comparative International Development*, 31, No. 3, 1996, 56–84.

Power, Timothy J. "Parties, Puppets and Paradoxes: Changing Attitudes Toward Party Institutionalization in Postauthoritarian Brazil," *Party Politics*, 3, No. 2, 1997, 189–219.

Power, Timothy J. "Politicized Democracy: Competition, Institutions and 'Civil Fatigue' in Brazil," *Journal of Interamerican Studies and World Affairs*, 33, Fall 1991, 75–112.

Power, Timothy J., and Mark J. Gasiorowski. "Institutional Design and Democratic Consolidation in the Third World," *Comparative Political Studies*, 30, No. 2, 1997, 123–55.

Power, Timothy J., and Timmons Roberts. "Compulsory Voting, Invalid Ballots, and Abstention in Brazil," *Political Research Quarterly*, 48, No. 3, 1995, 795–826.

Prezeworski, Adam, José Alvaro Moises, and José Augusto Guilhon Albuquerque, eds. *Dilemas da consolidação da democracia.* Rio de Janeiro: Paz e Terra, 1989.

Purcell, Susan Kaufman, and Riordan Roett, eds. *Brazil under Cardoso.* Boulder, Colorado: Lynne Rienner, 1997.

Quadros, Jânio. "Brazil's New Foreign Policy," *Foreign Affairs*, 40, No. 1, October 1961, 19–27.

Queiroz, Antônio Augusto de. "Radiografia do novo Congresso," *Boletim do DIAP* [Brasília], No. 10, October, 1994.

Reale, Miguel. *De Tancredo à Collor.* São Paulo: Edições Siciliano, 1992.

Rego, Antonio Carlos Pojo do. "O lobby nordestino: Novos padrões de atuação política no Congresso brasileiro," *Revista de Informação Legislativa* [Brasília], No. 21, January–March 1984, 349–72.

Reis, Eliza Pereira, et al. *Cultura e política: Visões do passado e perspectivas contemorâneas.* São Paulo: Editora Hucitec/ ANPOCS, 1996.

Reis, Fábio Wanderley, ed. *Os partidos e o regime: A lógica do processo eleitoral brasileiro.* São Paulo: Símbolo, 1978.

Remmer, Karen. "New Wine or Old Bottlenecks? The Study of Latin American Democracy," *Comparative Politics*, 23, No. 4, 1991, 479–95.

Ribeiro, Darcy. *O povo brasileiro.* São Paulo: Companhia das Letras, 1995.

Ricupero, Rubens. *Visões do Brasil: Ensaios sobre a história e a inserção internacional do Brasil.* Rio de Janeiro: Editora Record, 1995.

Rochon, Thomas R., and Michael Mitchell. "Social Bases of the Transition to Democracy in Brazil," *Comparative Politics*, 21, No. 3, 1989, 307–22.

Rodrigues, José Honório. *Brasil e África: Outro horizonte.* Rio de Janeiro: Nova Editora Fronteira, 1982.

Rodrigues, José Honório. *The Brazilians: Their Character and Aspirations.* Austin: University of Texas Press, 1967.

Rodrigues, José Honório. *Interesse nacional e política externa.* Rio de Janeiro: Editora Civilização Brasileira, 1966.

Rodrigues, Leôncio Martins. *CUT: Os militantes e a ideologia.* Rio de Janeiro: Paz e Terra, 1990.

Rodrigues, Leôncio Martins. "Eleições, fragmentação partidária e governabilidade," *Novos Estudos CEBRAP* [São Paulo], 41, 1995, 78–90.

Rodrigues, Leôncio Martins. *Partidos e sindicatos.* São Paulo: Editora Ática, 1990.

Rodrigues, Leôncio Martins. *Quem é quem na Constituinte.* São Paulo: OESP-Maltese, 1987.

Roett, Riordan. *Brazil in the Sixties.* Nashville: Vanderbilt University Press, 1972.

Roett, Riordan. *Brazil: Politics in a Patrimonial Society.* New York: Praeger, 1992.

Roett, Riordan. "The Transition to Democratic Government in Brazil," *World Politics,* 38, No. 2, January 1986, 371–82.

Roninger, Luis. "Caciquismo and Coronelismo: Contextual Dimensions of Patron Brokerage in Mexico and Brazil," *Latin American Research Review,* 22, No. 2, 1987, 71–99.

Rosenbaum, H. Jon, and William G. Tyler, eds. *Contemporary Brazil: Issues in Economic and Political Development.* New York: Praeger, 1972.

Rosenn, Keith S. "Brazil's New Constitution: An Exercise in Transient Constitutionalism for a Transitional Society," *American Journal of Comparative Law,* 38, Fall 1990, 773–802.

Rosenn, Keith S. *Foreign Investment in Brazil.* Boulder, Colorado: Westview Press, 1991.

Rosenn, Keith S., ed. *Whither Brazil: The Consolidation of Democracy in Brazil after the Impeachment of President Collor.* Coral Gables: University of Miami Press, 1995.

Rouquié, Alain, et al., eds. *Como renascem as democracias.* São Paulo: Editora Brasiliense, 1985.

Sader, Emir. *1994: Idéias para uma alternativa de esquerda à crise brasileira.* Rio de Janeiro: Relume Dumará, 1993.

Sader, Emir, and Ken Silverstein. *Without Fear of Being Happy: Lula, the Workers' Party, and the 1989 Elections in Brazil.* New York: Verso, 1991.

Santilli, Márcio. *Eleições, 1994.* Brasília: Instituto Socioambiental, 1994.

Santos, Wanderley Guilherme dos. *Crise e castigo: Partidos e generais na política brasileira.* São Paulo: Vértice, 1987.

Santos, Wanderley Guilherme dos. *Poder e política: Crônica do autoritarismo brasileiro.* Rio de Janeiro: Editora Forense-Universitária, 1978.

Santos, Wanderley Guilherme dos. *Razões da desordem.* Rio de Janeiro: Rocco, 1993.

Santos, Wanderley Guilherme dos. *Regresso: Anatomia da crise.* São Paulo: Editora Vértice, 1994.

Santos Júnior, Theôtonio dos. "Brazil: Origins of a Crisis." Pages 415–90 in Ronald H. Chilcote and Joel C. Edelstein, eds., *Latin America: The Struggle with Dependency and Beyond.* Cambridge, Massachusetts: Schenkman, 1974.

Sardenberg, Ronaldo Mota. "A estratificação internacional nos anos 90." Pages 255–72 in Gelson Fonseca Júnior and Valdemar Carneiro Leão, eds., *Temas de política externa brasileira.* Brasília: Fundacão Alexandre Gusmão, Editora Ática, 1989.

Sarles, Margaret. "Maintaining Political Control Through Parties: The Brazilian Strategy," *Comparative Politics,* 15, No. 1, October 1982, 41–72.

Sarney, José. "Brazil: A President's Story," *Foreign Affairs,* 65, No. 1, Fall 1986, 105–16.

Sartori, Giovanni, "Nem presidencialismo, nem parlamentarismo," *Novos Estudos CEBRAP* (Centro Brasileiro de Análise e Planejamento), 35, 1993, 3–20.

Scartezini, Antônio Carlos. *Dr. Ulysses: Uma biografia.* São Paulo: Editora Marco Zero, 1993.

Schmitter, Philippe C. *Interest Conflict and Political Change in Brazil.* Stanford: Stanford University Press, 1971.

Schneider, Ben Ross. "Brazil under Collor: Anatomy of a Crisis," *World Policy Journal,* 8, Spring 1991, 321–47.

Schneider, Ben Ross. "Framing the State: Economic Policy and Political Representation in Post-Authoritarian Brazil." Pages 213–55 in John D. Wirth, Edson de Oliveira Nunes, and Thomas E. Bogenschild, eds., *State and Society in Brazil.* Boulder, Colorado: Westview Press, 1987.

Schneider, Ben Ross. *Politics Within the State: Elite Bureaucrats and Industrial Policy in Authoritarian Brazil.* Pittsburgh: University of Pittsburgh Press, 1991.

Schneider, Ronald M. *Brazil: Culture and Politics in a New Industrial Powerhouse.* Boulder, Colorado: Westview Press, 1996.

Schneider, Ronald M. *Brazil: Foreign Policy of a Future World Power.* Boulder, Colorado: Westview Press, 1976.

Schneider, Ronald M. "Brazil's Political Future." Pages 217–60 in Wayne A. Selcher, ed., *Political Liberalization in Brazil: Dynamics, Dilemmas, and Future Prospects.* Boulder, Colorado: Westview Press, 1986.

Schneider, Ronald M. *Order and Progress: A Political History of Brazil.* Boulder, Colorado: Westview Press, 1991.

Schneider, Ronald M. *The Political System of Brazil: Emergence of a "Modernizing" Authoritarian Regime, 1964–1970.* New York: Columbia University Press, 1971.

Schoultz, Lars, William C. Smith, and Augusto Varas, eds. *Security, Democracy, and Development in U.S.-Latin American Relations.* Miami: North-South Center, University of Miami, 1994.

Schwartzman, Simon. *Bases do autoritarismo brasileiro.* Rio de Janeiro: Editora Campus, 1975.

Schwartzman, Simon. *São Paulo e o estado nacional.* São Paulo: Difusão Editorial, 1975.

Segatto, José Antônio. *Reforma e revolução: As vicissitudes políticas do PCB, 1954–1964.* Rio de Janeiro: Editora Civilização Brasileira, 1995.

Seitenfus, Ricardo Antônio da Silva. "A política externa brasileira: Da marginalidade à responsabilidade, 1930–90." Pages 117–48 in Jacques Marcovitch, ed., *Cooperação internacional: Estratégia e gestão.* São Paulo: Editora da Universidade de São Paulo, 1994.

Selcher, Wayne A. "Brazil and the Southern Cone Subsystem." Pages 87–120 in G. Pope Atkins, ed., *Latin America in the International Political System.* Boulder, Colorado: Westview Press, 1990.

Selcher, Wayne A. *Brazil's Multilateral Relations: Between First and Third Worlds.* Boulder, Colorado: Westview Press, 1978.

Selcher, Wayne A., ed. *Brazil in the International System: The Rise of a Middle Power.* Boulder, Colorado: Westview Press, 1981.

Selcher, Wayne A., ed. *Political Liberalization in Brazil: Dynamics, Dilemmas, and Future Prospects.* Boulder, Colorado: Westview Press, 1986.

Serra, José. *Orçamento no Brasil: As raízes da crise.* São Paulo: Editora Atual, 1994.

Share, Donald, and Scott Mainwaring. "Transitions Through Transaction: Democratization in Brazil and Spain." Pages 175–215 in Wayne A. Selcher, ed., *Political Liberalization in Brazil: Dynamics, Dilemmas, and Future Prospects.* Boulder, Colorado: Westview Press, 1986.

Sikkink, Kathryn. *Ideas and Institutions: Developmentalism in Brazil and Argentina.* Ithaca: Cornell University Press, 1991.

Silva, Luiz D. *PSB: O socialismo pragmático: Uma análise política e histórica.* Recife, Brazil: Editora de Pernambuco, 1989.

Skidmore, Thomas E. *Politics in Brazil: 1930–1964, An Experiment in Democracy.* New York: Oxford University Press, 1967.

Skidmore, Thomas E. *The Politics of Military Rule in Brazil, 1964–85.* New York: Oxford University Press, 1988.

Skidmore, Thomas E., ed. *Television, Politics, and the Transition to Democracy in Latin America.* Baltimore: Johns Hopkins University Press, 1993.

Smith, William C. "The Political Transition in Brazil: From Authoritarian Liberalization and Elite Conciliation to Democratization." Pages 179–240 in Enrique A. Baloyra, ed., *Comparing New Democracies: Transition and Consolidation in Mediterranean Europe and the Southern Cone.* Boulder, Colorado: Westview Press, 1987.

Soares, Gláucio A.D. *Colégio eleitoral, convenções partidárias, e eleições diretas.* Petrópolis, Brazil: Editora Vozes, 1984.

Soares, Gláucio A.D. "Elections and the Redemocratization of Brazil." Pages 273–98 in Paul W. Drake and Eduardo Silva, eds., *Elections and Democratization in Latin America, 1980–1985,* San Diego: University of California Press, 1986.

Soares, Gláucio A.D. *Sociedade e política no Brasil.* São Paulo: Difel/Difusão Editorial, 1973.

Soares, Gláucio A.D., and Maria Celina D'Araújo, eds. *21 anos de regime militar: Balanços e perspectivas.* Rio de Janeiro: Fundação Getúlio Vargas, 1994.

Soares, Gláucio Ary Dillon, and Nelson do Valle. "O Charme discreto do socialismo moreno," *Dados* [Rio de Janeiro], 28, No. 2, 1985, 253–73.

Soares, Rosinethe Monteiro, and Abdo I. Baaklini. *O poder legislativo no Brasil.* Brasília: Câmara dos Deputados, 1975.

Sola, Lourdes, ed. *O estado da transição: Política e economia na nova república.* São Paulo: Vertice, 1988.

Sola, Lourdes, ed. *Estado, mercado e democracia: Política e economia comparada.* São Paulo: Paz e Terra, 1993.

Sola, Lourdes, and Leda M. Paulani, eds. *Licões da década de 80.* São Paulo: Editora da USP, 1995.

Souza, Amaury de. "The Nature of Corporative Representation: Leaders and Members of Organized Labor in Brazil." Ph.D. dissertation. Cambridge: Massachusetts Institute of Technology, 1975.

Souza, Amaury de. "O Sistema Político-partidário." Pages 157–98 in Hélio Jaguaribe, ed., *Sociedade, estado e partidos políticos da atualidade brasileira.* Rio de Janeiro: Paz e Terra, 1992.

Souza, Amaury de, and Bolivar Lamounier. "La elaboración de la nueva constitución brasileña," *Síntesis* [Madrid], 11, 1990, 245–64.

Souza, Celina. "Political and Financial Decentralization in Brazil," *Local Government Studies,* 20, No. 4, 1994, 588–609.

Souza, Maria do Carmo Campello de. *Estados e partidos políticos no Brasil, 1930 à 1964.* São Paulo: Editora Alfa-Omega, 1976.

Staubhaar, Joseph, Organ Olsen, and Maria Cavallari Nunes. "The Brazilian Case: Influencing the Voter." Pages 118–36 in Thomas E. Skidmore, ed., *Television, Politics, and the Transition to Democracy in Latin America.* Baltimore: Johns Hopkins University Press, 1993.

Stepan, Alfred C. *Os militares: Da abertura à nova república.* Rio de Janeiro: Paz e Terra, 1986.

Stepan, Alfred C. *The Military in Politics: Changing Patterns in Brazil.* Princeton: Princeton University Press, 1971.

Stepan, Alfred C. "Political Leadership and Regime Breakdown: Brazil." Pages 110–37 in Juan Linz and Alfred Stepan, eds., *The Breakdown of Democratic Regimes.* Baltimore: Johns Hopkins University Press, 1978.

Stepan, Alfred C. *Rethinking Military Politics: Brazil and the Southern Cone.* Princeton: Princeton University Press, 1988.

Stepan, Alfred C., ed. *Authoritarian Brazil: Origins, Policies, and Future.* New Haven: Yale University Press, 1973.

Stepan, Alfred C., ed. *Democratizing Brazil: Problems of Transition and Consolidation.* New York: Oxford University Press, 1989.

Stumpf, André Gustavo, and Merval Pereira Filho. *A segunda guerra: Sucessão de Geisel.* São Paulo: Editora Brasiliense, 1979.

Suassuna, Luciano, and Luiz Antônio Novães. *Como Fernando Henrique foi eleito presidente: Os acordos secretos, o PT de salto alto.* São Paulo: Editora Contexto, 1994.

Suassuna, Luciano, and Luiz Costa Pinto. *Os fantasmas da Casa da Dinda.* São Paulo: Editora Contexto, 1992.

Tabak, Fanny. *A mulher brasileira no Congresso Nacional.* Brasília: Câmara dos Deputados, 1989.

Tachinardi, Maria Helena. *A guerra das patentes: O conflito Brasil x EUA sobre propriedade intelectual.* São Paulo: Paz e Terra, 1993.

Tavares, Cristina, and Milton Seligman. *Informática: A batalha do século XXI.* Rio de Janeiro: Paz e Terra, 1984.

Topik, Steven C. *Trade and Gunboats: The United States and Brazil in the Age of Empire.* Stanford: Stanford University Press, 1996.

Trindade, Antônio Augusto Cançado. "Posições internacionais do Brasil no plano multilateral," *Revista Brasileira de Estudos Políticos,* 52, 1981, 147–219.

Trindade, Hélgio. *Integralismo: O facismo brasileiro na década de 30.* São Paulo: Difel/Difusão Editorial, 1974.

Trindade, Hélgio. "O radicalismo militar em 64 e a nova tentação fascista." Pages 123–41 in Gláucio A.D. Soares and Maria Celina D'Araújo, eds., *21 anos de regime militar: Balanços e perspectivas.* Rio de Janeiro: Fundação Getúlio Vargas, 1994.

Trindade, Hélgio, ed. *Brasil em perspectiva: Dilemas da abertura política.* Porto Alegre, Brazil: Sulina, 1982.

Trindade, Hélgio, ed. *Reforma eleitoral e representação política no Brasil dos anos 90.* Porto Alegre, Brazil: Editora Universidade Federal do Rio Grande do Sul, 1992.

Valenzuela, Arturo, and Juan Linz, eds. *Presidentialism and Parlamentarism: Does It Make a Difference?* Baltimore: Johns Hopkins University Press, 1995.

Vasconcellos, Gilberto. *Itamar: O predestinado.* Brasília: Agência Quality, 1993.

Velloso, João Paulo dos Reis, ed. *Governabilidade, sistema político, e violência urbana.* Rio de Janeiro: Editora Olympio, 1994.

Velloso, João Paulo dos Reis, ed. *Modernização política e desenvolvimento.* Rio de Janeiro: Editora Olympio, 1990.

Viana, Hélio. *História diplomática do Brasil.* São Paulo: Melhoramentos, 1958.

Vidal, J.W. Bautista. *Soberania e dignidade: Raizes da sobrevivência*. Petrópolis, Brazil: Editora Vozes, 1991.

Vizentini, Paulo Gilberto Fagundes. *Relaçôes internacionais e desenvolvimento: O nacionalismo e a política externa independente: 1951–1961*. Petrópolis, Brazil: Editora Vozes, 1995.

Von Mettenheim, Kurt. "The Brazilian Voter in Democratic Transition, 1974–1982," *Comparative Politics*, 23, October 1990, 23–44.

Von Mettenheim, Kurt. *The Brazilian Voter: Mass Politics in Democratic Transition, 1974–1986*. Pittsburgh: University of Pittsburgh Press, 1995.

Wagley, Charles. *An Introduction to Brazil*. New York: Columbia University Press, 1971.

Wallerstein, Michael. "The Collapse of Democracy in Brazil: Its Economic Determinants," *Latin American Research Review*, 5, No. 3, 1980, 3–40.

Weffort, Francisco. *O populismo na política brasileira*. Rio de Janeiro: Paz e Terra, 1978.

Weffort, Francisco. *Por que democracia?* São Paulo: Editora Brasiliense, 1984.

Weffort, Francisco. *Qual democracia?* São Paulo: Companhia das Letras, 1992.

Weis, W. Michael. *Cold Warriors and Coups d'État: Brazilian-American Relations, 1945–1964*. Albuquerque: University of New Mexico Press, 1993.

Welch, Cliff. "Rivalry and Unification: Mobilizing Rural Workers in São Paulo on the Eve of the Brazilian 'Golpe' of 1964," *Journal of Latin American Studies*, 27, No. 1, 1995, 161–88.

Wesson, Robert. *The United States and Brazil: Limits of Influence*. New York: Praeger, 1981.

Wesson, Robert, ed. *New Military Politics in Latin America*. New York: Praeger, 1982.

Wesson, Robert, and David V. Fleischer. *Brazil in Transition*. New York: Praeger, 1983.

Weyland, Kurt. "Obstacles to Social Reform in Brazil's New Democracy," *Comparative Politics*, 29, No. 1, 1996, 1–22.

Weyland, Kurt. "The Rise and Fall of President Collor and Its Impact on Brazilian Democracy," *Journal of Interamerican Studies and World Affairs*, 35, No. 1, 1993, 1–37.

Wilhelmy, Manfred. "Brasil: Cambio político y continuidad internacional." Pages 13–29 in Heraldo Muñoz, ed., *Las políticas exteriores latinoamericanas frente a la crisis*. Buenos Aires: Grupo Editorial Latinoamericano, 1985.

Wirth, John D., Edson de Oliveira Nunes, and Thomas E. Bogenschild, eds. *State and Society in Brazil*. Boulder, Colorado: Westview Press, 1987.

Wohlcke, Manfred. *Brasilien: Diagnose einer Krise*. Munich: Ebenhausen Institut, 1994.

Worcester, Donald E. *Brazil: From Colony to World Power*. New York: Scribner's, 1973.

Zaverucha, Jorge. "The Degree of Military Political Autonomy During the Spanish, Argentine, and Brazilian Transitions," *Journal of Latin American Studies*, 25, No. 2, May 1993, 283–99.

Zirker, Daniel. "The Legislature and Democratic Transition in Brazil." Pages 89–112 in David Close, ed. *Legislatures in the New Democracies in Latin America*. Boulder, Colorado: Lynne Rienner, 1995.

Chapter 5

Abraham, Itty. "Security, Technology, and Ideology: 'Strategic Enclaves' in Brazil and India, 1945–1989." Ph.D. dissertation. Urbana: University of Illinois, 1993.

Alves, Maria Helena Moreira. *State and Opposition in Military Brazil*. Latin American Monographs, No. 63. Austin: University of Texas Press, 1985.

Andrade, John. *World Police and Paramilitary Forces*. New York: Stockton Press, 1985.

Andrade, Roberto Pereira de. *A construção aeronáutica no Brasil, 1910–1976*. São Paulo: Editora Brasiliense, 1976.

Anthony, Ian. *The Naval Arms Trade*. Oxford: Oxford University Press, 1990.

Arnt, Ricardo, ed. *O armamentismo e o Brasil: A guerra deles*. São Paulo: Editora Brasiliense, 1985.

Arquidiocese de São Paulo. *Brasil, nunca mais*. 10th ed. Petrópolis, Brazil: Editora Vozes, 1985.

Bacchus, Wilfred A. "Development under Military Rule: Factionalism in Brazil," *Armed Forces and Society*, 12, No. 3, Spring 1986, 401–18.

Bacchus, Wilfred A. "Long-Term Military Rulership in Brazil: Ideologic Consensus and Dissensus, 1963–1983," *Journal of Political and Military Sociology*, 13, Spring 1985, 99–123.

Bandeira, Moniz. *Brasil-Estados Unidos: A rivalidade emergente, 1950–1988*. Rio de Janeiro: Editora Civilização Brasileira, 1989.

Bandeira, Moniz. *Estado nacional e política internacional na América Latina: O continente nas relações Argentina-Brasil, 1930–1992*. São Paulo: Editora Ensaio, 1993.

Barcellos, Caco. *Rota 66*. São Paulo: Editora Globo, 1992.

Barros, Alexandre de Souza Costa. "Back to the Barracks: An Option for the Brazilian Military?" *Third World Quarterly*, 7, No. 1, January 1985, 63–77.

Barros, Alexandre de Souza Costa. "Brazil." Pages 73–87 in James Everett Katz, ed., *Arms Production in Developing Countries: An Analysis of Decision Making*. Lexington, Massachusetts: Lexington Books, 1984.

Barros, Alexandre de Souza Costa. "The Brazilian Military: Professional Socialization, Political Performance, and State Building." Ph.D. dissertation. Chicago: University of Chicago, 1978.

Bittencourt, Emilio L.A. "The 'Abertura' in Brazil: The Day-After of the Brazilian Intelligence 'Monster'." Paper presented at 33d Annual Convention of the International Studies Association, Atlanta, April 1992.

Bittencourt, Getúlio. *A quinta estrela: Como se tenta fazer um presidente no Brasil*. São Paulo: Editora Ciências Humanas, 1978.

Black, Jan Knippers. "The Military and Political Decompression in Brazil," *Armed Forces and Society*, 6, No. 4, Summer 1980, 625–38.

Bonturi, Orlando. *Brazil and the Vital South Atlantic*. Washington: National Defense University, 1988.

Borges, Vavy Pacheco. *Tenentismo e revolução brasileira*. São Paulo: Editora Brasiliense, 1992.

Branco, Robert J. *The United States and Brazil: Opening a New Dialogue*. Washington: National Defense University Press, 1984.

Brigagão, Clóvis. *O mercado da segurança: Ensaios sobre economia política da defesa*. Rio de Janeiro: Editora Nova Fronteira, 1984.

Brigagão, Clóvis. *A militarização da sociedade.* Rio de Janeiro: Zahar Editores, 1985.

Brzoska, Michael, and Thomas Ohlson, eds. *Arms Production in the Third World.* London: Taylor and Francis, 1986.

Brzoska, Michael, and Thomas Ohlson, eds. *Arms Transfers to the Third World, 1971–85.* New York: Oxford University Press, 1987.

Carus, W. Seth. "Trends and Implications of Missile Proliferation." Paper presented at the Annual Meeting of the International Studies Association, April 1990.

Castro, Therezinha de. "Diretrizes geopolíticas do Brasil," *A Defesa Nacional* [Lisbon], 693, January–February 1981, 33–47.

Caubet, Christian G. "Diplomacia, geopolítica e direito na Bacia do Prata," *Política e Estratégia* [São Paulo], 2, No. 2, April–June 1984, 337–46.

Caubet, Christian G. "Por uma (nova?) epistemologia da geopolítica," *Política e Estratégia* [São Paulo], 2, No. 4, October–December 1984, 628–47.

Celiberti, Lilian, and Lucy Garrido. *Meu quarto, minha cela.* Porto Alegre, Brazil: L and PM Editores, 1989.

Child, Jack. *Geopolitics and Conflict in South America: Quarrels Among Neighbors.* New York: Praeger, 1985.

Child, Jack, and Phillip Kelly, eds. *Geopolitics of the Southern Cone and Antarctica.* Boulder, Colorado: Lynne Rienner, 1988.

Chow, Brian G. *An Evolutionary Approach to Space Launch Commercialization.* Santa Monica, California: Rand, National Defense Research Institute, 1993.

Coelho, Edmundo Campos. *Em busca da identidade: O exército e a política na sociedade brasileira.* Rio de Janeiro: Editora Forense-Universitária, 1976.

Coelho, Edmundo Campos. "A instituição militar no Brasil: Um ensaio bibliográfico," *BIB: Boletim Informativo e Bibliográfico de Ciências Sociais* [Rio de Janeiro], 19, First semester 1985, 5–19.

Collier, David, ed. *The New Authoritarianism in Latin America.* Princeton: Princeton University Press, 1979.

Comblin, Joseph. *A ideologia da segurança nacional: O poder militar na América Latina.* Rio de Janeiro: Editora Civilização Brasileira, 1980.

Conca, Ken. *Manufacturing Insecurity: The Rise and Fall of Brazil's Military-Industrial Complex.* Boulder, Colorado: Lynne Rienner, 1996.

Costa, Thomaz Guedes da. "A idéia de medidas de confiança a mútua (CBMs) em uma visão brasileira," *Contexto Internacional* [Rio de Janeiro], 14, No. 2, July–December 1992, 297–308.

Costa, Thomaz Guedes da. "A indústria de material bélico no Brasil," *A Defesa Nacional* [Lisbon], 703, September–October 1982, 111–31.

Costa, Thomaz Guedes da. "A integração internacional e o impacto sobre a política de defesa do Brasil e a segurança regional." Paper presented at 16th annual meeting of the Associação de Pós-graduação em Ciências Sociais (ANPOCS), Caxambu, Brazil, October 1992.

Crawley, Eduardo. *A House Divided: Argentina, 1880–1980.* London: Hurst, 1984.

Dagnino, Renato P. "A indústria de armamentos brasileira: Uma tentativa de avaliação." Ph.D. dissertation. Campinas, Brazil: Universidade Estadual de Campinas, 1989.

Dagnino, Renato P. "P e D militar e desenvolvimento na América Latina," *Política e Estratégia* [São Paulo], 2, No. 3, July–September 1984, 429–45.

Daskal, Steven. "Brazilian Defense," *Defense and Diplomacy*, September 1989.

Donato, Hernani. *Dicionário das batalhas brasileiras.* São Paulo: Instituicão Brasileira de Difusão Cultural, 1987.

Dreifuss, René Armand. *1964: A conquista do estado: Ação política, poder e golpe de classe.* Petrópolis, Brazil: Editora Vozes, 1981.

Dreifuss, René Armand. "O mar e a marinha no contexto das tendências de estruturação do novo cenário mundial," *Premissas* [Campinas], 4, August 1993, 50–66.

Dreifuss, René Armand, and Otávio Soares Dulci. "As forças armadas e a política." Pages 87–117 in Bernardo Sorj and Maria Hermínia Tavares de Almeida, eds., *Sociedade e política no Brasil pós-1964.* São Paulo: Editora Brasiliense, 1983.

English, Adrian J. *The Armed Forces of Latin America: Their Histories, Development, Present Strength, and Military Potential.* New York: Jane's, 1985.

English, Adrian J. "Brazil: A Super Power in the Making," *Defence* [London], 18, No. 9, September 1987, 545–50.

Estado Maior do Exército. *Historia do Exército Brasileiro: Perfil militar do um povo.* 3 vols. Brasília: Gráfica da Fundação IBGE, 1972.

Figueiredo, Eurico de Lima. *Os militares e a democracia: Análise estrutural de ideologia do Pres. Castelo Branco.* Rio de Janeiro: Edicões Graal, 1980.

Fitch, J. Samuel. "Military Professionalism, National Security, and Democracy: Lessons from the Latin American Experience," *Pacific Focus,* 6, 1989, 99–147.

Flank, Steven M. "Reconstructing Rockets: The Politics of Developing Military Technology in Brazil, India, and Israel." Ph.D. dissertation. Cambridge: Massachusetts Institute of Technology, 1993.

Fleischer, David V. "US-Brazil Defense Relations: Collor's First Year." Paper presented at the 16th International Congress of the Latin American Studies Association, Washington, April 1991.

Flores, Mário César. *Bases para uma política militar.* Campinas, Brazil: Editora de Unicamp, 1992.

Flores, Mário César. "O papel da coerção militar nas próximas décadas," *Política Externa* [São Paulo], 2, No. 2, September 1993, 59–67.

Flynn, Peter. "Collor, Corruption, and Crisis: Time for Reflection," *Journal of Latin American Studies,* 25, No. 2, May 1993, 351–71.

Fragoso, Augusto Tasso. *História da guerra entre a tripice aliança e o Paraguai.* 5 vols. Rio de Janeiro: Biblioteca do Exército Editora, 1956–60.

Franko-Jones, Patrice. *The Brazilian Defense Industry: A Case Study of Public-Private Collaboration.* Boulder, Colorado:Westview Press, 1992.

Franko-Jones, Patrice. "'Public Private Parnership': Lessons from the Brazilian Armaments Industry," *Journal of Interamerican Studies and World Affairs,* 29, No. 4, Winter 1987–88, 41–68.

Füllgraf, Frederico. *A bomba pacífica: O Brasil e outro cenários da corrida nuclear.* São Paulo: Editora Brasiliense, 1988.

Góes, Walder de. *O Brasil do General Geisel: Estudo do processo de tomada de decisão no regime militar-burocrático.* Rio de Janeiro: Editora Nova Fronteira, 1978.

Goodman, Louis W., Johanna Mendelson, and J. Rial, eds. *The Military and Democracy: The Future of Civil-Military Relations in Latin America.* Lexington, Massachusetts: Lexington Books, 1990.

Hayes, Robert Ames. *The Armed Nation: The Brazilian Corporate Mystique.* Tempe: Center for Latin America Studies, Arizona State University, 1989.

Hilton, Stanley E. "The Armed Forces and Industrialists in Modern Brazil: The Drive for Military Autonomy, 1889–1954," *Hispanic American Historical Review,* 62, No. 4, November 1982, 629–73.

Hilton, Stanley E. "The Brazilian Military: Changing Strategic Perceptions and the Question of Mission," *Armed Forces and Society,* 13, No. 3, Spring 1987, 329–52.

Howarth, H.M.F. "Brazil's Defense Industry: Ambitious and Growing Fast," *International Defense Review,* September 1985, 1413–32.

Hunter, Wendy Ann. "Back to the Barracks? The Military in Post-Authoritarian Brazil." Ph.D. dissertation. Berkeley: University of California, 1992.

Hunter, Wendy Ann. *Eroding Military Influence in Brazil: Politicians Against Soldiers.* Chapel Hill: University of North Carolina Press, 1997.

Huntington, Samuel P. *Political Order in Changing Societies.* New Haven: Yale University Press, 1968.

Huntington, Samuel P. *The Soldier and the State: The Theory of Politics of Civil-Military Relations.* New York: Random House, 1964.

Hurrell, Andrew. "Brazil as a Regional Power: A Study in Ambivalence." Pages 16–48 in Iver B. Neumann, ed., *Regional Great Powers in International Politics.* New York: St. Martin's Press, 1992.

International Institute for Strategic Studies. *The Military Balance, 1997–98.* London: Brassey's, 1997.

Katz, James Everett, ed. *Arms Production in Developing Countries: An Analysis of Decision Making.* Lexington, Massachusetts: Lexington Books, 1984.

Keegan, John, ed. *World Armies.* 2d ed. Detroit: Gale Research, 1983.

Klare, Michael T. "The Arms Trade: Changing Patterns in the 1980s," *Third World Quarterly,* 9, No. 4, October 1987, 60–76.

Kolcum, Edward H. "Aerospace in South America: Pt. 1 - Industry," *Aviation Week and Space Technology,* August 1987, 40–60.

Kolinski, Charles J. *Independence or Death! The Story of the Paraguayan War.* Gainesville: University of Florida Press, 1965.

Kramer, Paulo. "As relações militares Brasil-Estados Unidos," *Política e Estratégia* [São Paulo], 4, No. 1, January–March 1986, 44–53.

Lagôa, Ana. *SNI: Como nasceu, como funciona.* São Paulo: Editora Brasiliense, 1983.

Lamazière, Georges, and Roberto Jaguaribe. "Beyond Confidence-Building: Brazilian-Argentine Nuclear Cooperation," *Disarmament,* 15, No. 3, 1992, 102–17.

Leventhal, Paul L., and Sharon Tanzer, eds. *Averting a Latin American Nuclear Arms Race: New Prospects and Challenges for Argentine-Brazilian Nuclear Cooperation.* London: Macmillan, Nuclear Control Institute, 1992.

Lieuwen, Edwin. *Generals vs. Presidents: Neo-Militarism in Latin America.* London: Pall Mall Press, 1964.

Lima de Sigueira, Deoclécito. *Fronteiras: A patrulha aérea e o adeus do arco e flecha.* Rio de Janeiro: Revista Aeronáutica Editores, 1986.

Linz, Juan J., and Alfred Stepan, eds. *The Breakdown of Democratic Regimes,* 3. Baltimore: Johns Hopkins University Press, 1978.

Loveman, Brian, and Thomas M. Davies, Jr., eds. *The Politics of Antipolitics: The Military in Latin America.* Lincoln: University of Nebraska Press, 1978.

Lowenthal, Abraham F., and J. Samuel Fitch, eds. *Armies and Politics in Latin America.* Rev. ed. New York: Holmes and Meier, 1986.

Malheiros, Tania. *Brasil, a bomba oculta: O programa nuclear brasileiro.* Rio de Janeiro: Gryphus, 1993.

Marcella, Gabriel. "The Latin American Military, Low Intensity Conflict, and Democracy," *Journal of Interamerican Studies and World Affairs,* 32, No. 1, Spring 1990, 45–82.

Mattos, Carlos de Meira. *Brasil: Geopolítica e destino.* Rio de Janeiro: Editora Olympio, 1975.

Mattos, Carlos de Meira. *Estratégias militares dominantes: Sugestões para uma estratégia militar brasileira.* Rio de Janeiro: Editora Biblioteca do Exército, 1986.

Mattos, Carlos de Meira. "O pensamento estratégico brasileiro," *A Defesa Nacional* [Lisbon], March 1991.

McCann, Frank D. *The Brazilian-American Alliance, 1937–1945.* Princeton: Princeton University Press, 1973.

McCann, Frank D. "The Brazilian Army and the Problem of Mission, 1939–1964," *Journal of Latin American Studies,* 12, No. 1, May 1980, 107–26.

McCann, Frank D. "The Brazilian Army at the Outset of the 1990s." Paper delivered at International Congress of the Latin American Studies Association, Washington, April 1991.

McCann, Frank D. "The Brazilian Army, 1889–1985: Conservative or Revolutionary?" Paper presented at 17th International Congress of the Latin American Studies Association, Los Angeles, September 1992.

McCann, Frank D. "The Formative Period of Twentieth-Century Brazilian Army Thought, 1900–1922," *Hispanic American Historical Review,* 64, No. 4, November 1984, 737–65.

McCann, Frank D. "Origins of the 'New Professionalism' of the Brazilian Military," *Journal of Interamerican Studies and World Affairs,* 21, November 1979, 505–22.

McDonough, Peter. *Power and Ideology in Brazil.* Princeton: Princeton University Press, 1981.

Maxwell, Kenneth. *Conflicts and Conspiracies: Brazil and Portugal, 1750–1808.* Cambridge: Cambridge University Press, 1973.

Miyamoto, Shiguenoli. "Do discurso triunfalista ao pragmatismo ecuménico: Geopolítica e política externa no Brasil pós-64." Ph.D. dissertation. São Paulo: Universidade de São Paulo, 1985.

Moraes, João Quartim de. *A esquerda militar no Brasil: Da conspiração republicana à guerrilha dos tenentes.* São Paulo: Edições Siciliano, 1991.

Morris, Michael A. *Expansion of Third World Navies.* New York: St. Martin's Press, 1987.

Morris, Michael A. *International Politics and the Sea: The Case of Brazil.* Boulder, Colorado: Westview Press, 1979.

Morris, Michael A., and Victor Millín, eds. *Controlling Latin American Conflicts: Ten Approaches.* Boulder, Colorado: Westview Press, 1983.

Nordlinger, Eric A. *Soldiers in Politics: Military Coups and Governments.* Englewood Cliffs, New Jersey: Prentice Hall, 1977.

Noticiário do Exército [Rio de Janeiro], No. 8958, April 19, 1995, 2.

Nunn, Frederick M. *Yesterday's Soldiers: European Military Professionalism in South America, 1890–1940.* Lincoln: University of Nebraska Press, 1983.

O'Brien, Philip, and Paul Cammack, eds. *Generals in Retreat: The Crisis of Military Rule in Latin America.* Manchester, United Kingdom: 1985.

O'Donnell, Guillermo A. "Challenges to Democratization in Brazil," *World Policy Journal*, 5, Spring 1988, 281–300.

O'Donnell, Guillermo A. *Modernization and Bureaucratic-Authoritarianism: Studies in South American Politics.* Politics of Modernization Series, No. 9. Berkeley: Institute of International Studies, University of California, 1973.

O'Donnell, Guillermo A., and Philippe C. Schmitter. *Transitions from Authoritarian Rule: Tentative Conclusions about Uncertain Democracies.* Baltimore: Johns Hopkins University Press, 1986.

O'Donnell, Guillermo A., Philippe C. Schmitter, and Laurence Whitehead, eds. *Transitions from Authoritarian Rule: Prospects for Democracy.* Baltimore: Johns Hopkins University Press, 1986.

Oliveira, Eliézer Rizzo de. *De Geisel à Collor: Forças Armadas, transição e democracia.* São Paulo: Papirus Editora, 1994.

Oliveira, Eliézer Rizzo de, Geraldo L. Cava Gnari Filho, João Quartini de Moraes, and René Armand Dreifus. *As Forças Armadas no Brasil.* Rio de Janeiro: Espaço e Tempo, 1987.

Philip, George. *The Military in South American Politics.* London: Croom Helm, 1985.

Pinheiro, Paulo Sérgio. *Democracia e violencia: Reflexões para a Constituinte.* Rio de Janeiro: Paz e Terra, 1986.

Pinheiro, Paulo Sérgio. *Crime, violencia e poder.* São Paulo: Brasiliense, 1983.

Pires, Sergio de Ary. "Missão das Forças Armadas," *Revista do Exército Brasileiro* [Rio de Janeiro], 128, No. 3, July–September 1991, 7–9.

Proença Júnior, Domício. "Informática e indústria bélica," *Política e Estratégia* [São Paulo], 3, No. 3, July–September 1985, 481–94.

Proença Júnior, Domício, ed. *Indústria bélica brasileira: Ensaios.* Rio de Janeiro: Grupo de Estudos Estratégicos/Forum de Ciência e Cultura da UFRJ (Universidade Federal do Rio de Janeiro), 1994.

Proença Júnior, Domício, ed. *Uma avaliação da indústria bélica brasileira: Defesa, indústria e tecnologia.* Rio de Janeiro: Grupo de Estudos Estratégicos, 1993.

República Federativa do Brasil. *Constituição, 1988.* Brasília: Centro Gráfica do Senado Federal, 1994.

Revuelta, Klaus Wolff-Casado. "The Brazilian Defence Industry: Partner or Competitor to the Established Western Defence Industries?" *Military Technology* [Bonn], 8, No. 10, October 1985, 92–119.

Roett, Riordan. *Brazil: Politics in a Patrimonial Society.* 4th ed. New York: Praeger, 1992.

Roett, Riordan, and Scott D. Tollefson. "Brazil's Status as an Intermediate Power," *Third World Affairs* [London], 1986, 101–12.

Roett, Riordan, and Scott D. Tollefson. "Federative Republic of Brazil." Pages 250–60 in George E. Delury, ed., *World Encyclopedia of Political Systems and Parties.* New York: Facts on File, 1986.

Rosa, Luiz Pinguelli. *A política nuclear e o caminho das armas atômicas.* Rio de Janeiro: Zahar Editores, 1985.

Rouquié, Alain. *O estado militar na América Latina.* São Paulo: Alfa-Omega, 1984.

Saldanha da Gama, Arthur Oscar. *A Marinha do Brasil na Primeira Guerra Mundial.* Rio de Janeiro: CAPEMI Editora e Gráfica, 1982.

Saldanha da Gama, Arthur Oscar. *A Marinha do Brasil na Segunda Guerra Mundial.* Rio de Janeiro: CAPEMI Editora e Gráfica, 1982.

Sanders, Ralph. *Arms Industries: New Suppliers and Regional Security.* Washington: National Defense University, 1990.

Sanders, Thomas G. "Brazilian Geopolitics: Securing the South and North," *Latin America*, No. 23, 1987.

Saravia, Maria Gomes. "A opção européia e o projeto de Brasil: Potência emergente," *Contexto Internacional* [Rio de Janeiro], 6, No. 11, January–June 1990.

Scheper-Hughes, Nancy. *Death Without Weeping: The Violence of Everyday Life in Brazil*. Berkeley: University of California Press, 1993.

Schilling, Paulo R. *O expansionismo brasileiro: A geopolítica do General Golbery e a diplomacia do Itamarati*. São Paulo: Editora Global, 1981.

Selcher, Wayne A. "Brazil and the Southern Cone Subsystem." Pages 73–99 in G. Pope Atkins, ed., *South America into the 1990s: Evolving International Relationships in a New Era*. Boulder, Colorado: Westview Press, 1990.

Selcher, Wayne A. *Brazil in the International System: The Rise of a Middle Power*. Boulder, Colorado: Westview Press, 1981.

Selcher, Wayne A. *Brazil's Multilateral Relations: Between First and Third Worlds*. Boulder, Colorado: Westview Press, 1978.

Selcher, Wayne A. "Current Dynamics and Future Prospects of Brazil's Relations with Latin America: Toward a Pattern of Bilateral Cooperation," *Journal of Interamerican Studies and World Affairs*, 28, No. 2, Summer 1986, 67–99.

Selcher, Wayne A. "Emerging Patterns of Interactions and Influence Relationships: Possible Consequences of Brazilian Continental Policy." Pages 35–47 in G. Poke Atkins, ed., *South America into the 1990s*. Boulder, Colorado: Westview Press, 1988.

Silva, Golbery do Couto e. *Conjuntura política nacional: O poder executivo e geopolítica do Brasil*. Rio de Janeiro: Editora Olympio, 1981.

Silva, Golbery do Couto e. *Planejamento estratégico*. 2d ed. Brasília: Editora Universidade de Brasília, 1981.

Silveira, Flavio Eduardo. "Golpe militar? Não é apenas uma chantagem," *Utopia* [Rio de Janeiro], 3, No. 10, 1993, 4–5.

Skidmore, Thomas E. *Politics in Brazil, 1930–1964: An Experiment in Democracy*. New York: Oxford University Press, 1967.

Skidmore, Thomas E. *The Politics of Military Rule in Brazil, 1964–85*. New York: Oxford University Press, 1984.

Sodré, Nelson Werneck. *Do Estado Novo à ditadura militar: Memórias de um soldado.* 2d ed. Petrópolis, Brazil: Editora Vozes, 1988.

Solingen, Etel. "Macropolitical Consensus and Lateral Autonomy in Industrial Policy: The Nuclear Sector in Brazil and Argentina," *International Organization,* 47, No. 2, Spring 1993, 263–98.

Solingen, Etel. "Technology, Exports, and Countertrade: Brazil as an Emerging Nuclear Supplier." Pages 211–35 in William C. Potter, ed., *International Nuclear Trade and Nonproliferation: The Challenge of the Emerging Suppliers.* Lexington, Massachusetts: Lexington Books, 1990.

Stepan, Alfred C. *The Military in Politics: Changing Patterns in Brazil.* Princeton: Princeton University Press, 1971.

Stepan, Alfred C. *Rethinking Military Politics: Brazil and the Southern Cone.* Princeton: Princeton University Press, 1988.

Stepan, Alfred C., ed. *Authoritarian Brazil: Origins, Policies, and Future.* New Haven: Yale University Press, 1973.

Stepan, Alfred C., ed. *Democratizing Brazil: Problems of Transition and Consolidation.* New York: Oxford University Press, 1989.

Stockholm International Peace Research Institute. *SIPRI Yearbook of World Armaments and Disarmament, 1995.* Philadelphia: Taylor and Francis, 1996.

Stumpf, André Gustavo, and Merval Pereira Filho. *A Segunda Guerra: Sucessão de Geisel.* São Paulo: Editora Brasiliense, 1979.

Tollefson, Scott D. "Brazilian Arms Transfers, Ballistic Missiles, and Foreign Policy: The Search for Autonomy." Ph.D. dissertation. Washington: Paul H. Nitze School of Advanced International Studies, Johns Hopkins University, 1991.

Tollefson, Scott D. "From Collor to Itamar: Resurgent Nationalism and Civil-Military Relations in Brazil." Paper presented at Middle Atlantic Council of Latin American Studies, State College, Pennsylvania, April 1993.

Tollefson, Scott D. "U.S. Security Relations with Brazil: Implications for Civil-Military Relations in Brazil." Paper presented at the 17th International Congress of the Latin American Studies Association, Los Angeles, September 1992.

Totten, James. *As relações militares entre o Brasil e os Estados Unidos.* Rio de Janeiro: Escola Superior de Guerra, 1965.

United States. Arms Control and Disarmament Agency. *World Military Expenditures and Arms Transfers, 1996.* Washington: GPO, 1996.

United States. Department of State. *Country Reports on Human Rights Practice for 1995: Hearing Before the Subcommittee on International Operations and Human Rights.* 104th, 2d Session, House of Representatives, Committee on International Relations, and Subcommittee on International Operations and Human Rights. Report submitted to United States Congress, March 26, 1996. Washington: GPO, 1996.

United States. General Accounting Office. *The Drug War: Extent of Problems in Brazil, Ecuador, and Venezuela.* Report submitted to United States Congress, 102d, 2d Session, Senate, Committee on Governmental Affairs, Permanent Subcommittee on Investigations. Publication No. GAO/NSIAD-92-226. Washington: GPO, June 1992.

Varas, Augusto. *Militarization and the International Arms Race in Latin America.* Boulder, Colorado: Westview Press, 1985.

Vaz, Alcides Costa. "Condicionantes das posições brasileiras frente ao desarmamento, regimes de controle de exportações e segurança regional," *Premissas* [Campinas], 4, August 1993, 3–18.

Wesson, Robert, ed. *The Latin American Military Institution.* New York: Praeger, 1986.

Wiederspahn, Henrique Oscar. *Campanha de Ituzaingo: Ensaio de historia militar sulamericana em torna da Batalha de Ituzaingo ou de Passo do Rosario, na guerra de 1825 a 1828 entre o Imperio do Brasil e as Provincias Unidas do Rio da Prata.* Rio de Janeiro: Biblioteca do Exército-Editora, 1961.

Williams, John Hoyt. "Brazil: A New Giant in the Arms Industry," *Atlantic Monthly,* August 1984, 24–27.

Williams, John Hoyt. "Brazil: Giant of the Southern Cone," *National Defense,* November 1982, 16–20.

Williams, John Hoyt. "Brazilian Weapons," *National Defense,* September 1986, 57–64.

Wolf, Charles, Gregory Hildebrandt, Michael Kennedy, Donald Putnam Henry, Katsuaki Tersawa, K.C. Yeh, Benjamin Zycher, Anil Bamezai, and Toshiya Hayashi. *Long-Term Economic and Military Trends, 1950–2010.* Santa Monica, California: Rand, 1989.

Zagorski, Paul. "The Brazilian Military under the New Republic," *Review of Latin American Studies,* 1, No. 2, 1988, 45–64.

Zaverucha, Jorge. "Civil-Military Relations During the Process of Transition: Spain, Argentina, and Brazil." Ph.D. dissertation. Chicago: University of Chicago, 1991.

Zaverucha, Jorge. "The Degree of Military Political Autonomy During the Spanish, Argentine, and Brazilian Transitions," *Journal of Latin American Studies,* 25, No. 2, May 1993, 283–99.

Zirker, Daniel. "The Civil-Military Mediators in Post-1985 Brazil," *Journal of Political and Military Sociology,* 19, Summer 1991, 47–73.

Zirker, Daniel, and Marvin Henberg. "Amazônia: Democracy, Ecology, and Brazilian Military Prerogatives in the 1990s," *Armed Forces in Society,* 20, No. 2, Spring 1994, 259–81.

(Various issues of the following publications were also used in the preparation of this chapter: Foreign Broadcast Information Service, *Latin America Daily Report*; Information Services Latin America (ISLA); Info-South Data-Base [University of Miami, North-South Center]; *Jane's Defence Weekly* [London]; *Latin America Weekly Report* [London]; *New York Times*; *Veja* [Rio de Janeiro]; and *Washington Post.* In addition, other newspapers from both the United States and Brazil were utilized.)

Chapter 6

Abraham, Itty. "Security, Technology, and Ideology: 'Strategic Enclaves' in Brazil and India, 1945–1989." Ph.D. dissertation. Urbana: University of Illinois, 1993.

Adler, Emanuel. *The Power of Ideology: The Quest for Technological Autonomy in Argentina and Brazil.* Studies in International Political Economy, No. 16. University of California Press, 1991.

Alves, Péricles Gasparini. "Access to Outer Space Technologies: Implications for International Security." Research Paper No. 15. Geneva: United Nations Institute for Disarmament Research, 1992.

Andrade, Roberto Pereira de. *A construção aeronáutica no Brasil, 1910–1976.* São Paulo: Editora Brasiliense, 1976.

Azevedo, Fernando de. *As ciências no Brasil.* 2d ed. 2 vols. Rio de Janeiro: Editora UFRJ (Universidade Federal do Rio de Janeiro), 1994.

Azevedo, João Lúcio de. *Agricultura.* Background paper prepared for the Brazilian Science and Technology Policy Project. São Paulo: Fundação Getúlio Vargas, 1993.

Bailey, Kathleen C. *Strengthening Nuclear Non-Proliferation.* Boulder, Colorado: Westview Press, 1993.

Barbieri, José Carlos. *Conselho Nacional de Desenvolvimento Científico e Tecnológico.* Background paper prepared for the Brazilian Science and Technology Policy Project. São Paulo: Fundação Getúlio Vargas, 1993.

Bastos, Maria Inês. "How International Sanctions Worked: Domestic and Foreign Political Constraints on the Brazilian Informatics Policy," *Journal of Development Studies* [London], 30, No. 2, January 1994, 380–404.

Bastos, Maria Inês. "State Autonomy and Capacity for Science and Technology Policy Design and Implementation in Brazil." Pages 68–108 in Maria Inês Bastos and C. Cooper, eds., *The Politics of Technology in Latin America.* London: Routledge, 1995.

Bastos, Maria Inês. *Winning the Battle to Lose the War: Brazilian Electronics Policy under US Threat of Sanctions.* Ilford, Essex, United Kingdom: Frank Case, 1994.

Ben-David, Joseph. *The Scientist's Role in Society: A Comparative Study.* Englewood Cliffs, New Jersey: Prentice Hall, 1971.

Biato, Francisco, et al. *Estudos analíticos do setor de ciência e tecnologia no Brasil: Relatório final.* Projeto Ministério de Ciência e Tecnologia, Academia Brasileira de Ciência, United Nations Development Programme. Brasília: 1992–93.

Botelho, Antônio José. "The Brazilian Society for the Progress of Science (SBPC) and the Professionalization of Brazilian Scientists," *Social Studies of Science,* No. 20, 1990, 473–502.

Botelho, Antônio José. "Struggling to Survive: The Brazilian Society for the Progress of Science (SBPC) and the Authoritarian Regime, 1964–1980," *Historia Scientiarum: International Journal of the History of Science Society of Japan* [Tokyo], No. 38, 1989, 46–63.

Brazil. Ministério da Ciência e Tecnologia. *Relatório de atividades, 1992–94.* Brasília: 1994.

Brisolla, S. *Indicadores quantitativos de ciência e tecnologia no Brasil.* Background paper prepared for the Brazilian Science and Technology Policy Project. São Paulo: Fundação Getúlio Vargas, 1993.

Bulloch, Chris. "Brasilsat: A Good Investment that Justifies Its Cost," *Space Markets* [Geneva], No. 2, Summer 1986, 112–14.

Cabral, Milton. *A questão nuclear.* Relatório de Comissão Parlamentar de Inquérito do Senado Federal sobre o Acordo Nuclear do Brasil com a República Federal da Alemanha. Brasília: Senado Federal, Centro Gráfico, 1983.

Campos, Ernesto de Souza. *História da Universidade de São Paulo.* São Paulo: Editora Universidade de São Paulo, 1954.

Cavagnari, Geraldo L. *P e D militar: Situação, avaliação e perspectivas.* Background paper prepared for the Brazilian Science and Technology Policy Project. São Paulo: Fundação Getúlio Vargas, 1993.

Chow, Brian G. *An Evolutionary Approach to Space Launch Commercialization.* Santa Monica, California: Rand/National Defense Research Institute, 1993.

Conca, Ken. "Technology, the Military, and Democracy in Brazil," *Journal of Interamerican Studies and World Affairs,* 34, No. 1, Spring 1992, 141–77.

Coutinho, G. Luciano, and Wilson Suzigan. *Desenvolvimento tecnológico da indústria e a constituição de um sistema nacional de inovação no Brasil: Convênio Unicamp/IPT, relatório síntese.* Campinas, Brazil: Editora da Unicamp (Universidade Estadual de Campinas).

Coordenação para o Aperfeiçoamento de Pessoal de Nível Superior (Capes), *Relatório de Atividades* [São Paulo], 1990 and 1991.

Dagnino, Renato P. "P e D militar e desenvolvimento na América Latina," *Política e Estratégia* [São Paulo], 2, No. 3, July–September 1984, 429–45.

Dagnino, Renato P. "To the Barracks or into the Labs? Military Programmes and Brazilian S and T Policy," *Science and Public Policy,* 20, No. 6, December 1993, 389–435.

Dagnino, Renato, and Domicio Proença Júnior. *The Brazilian Aeronautics Industry.* Working Paper No. 23. Geneva: World Employment Programme Research/ILO, 1989.

Erber, Fábio Stefano. "The Development of the Electronics Complex and Government Policies in Brazil," *World Development,* 13, No. 3, 1985, 293–309.

Erber, Fábio Stefano. "The Political Economy of Technological Development: The Case of Brazil's Informatics Policy." Pages 196–224 in Maria Inês Bastos and C. Cooper, eds., *The Politics of Technology in Latin America.* London: Routledge, 1995.

Erber, Fábio Stefano, and Leda U. Amaral. *Os centros de pesquisa das empresas estatais: Um estudo de três casos.* Background paper prepared for the Brazilian Science and Technology Policy Project. São Paulo: Fundação Getúlio Vargas.

Felício, José Eduardo Martins. "Os regimes de contrôle das technologias avançadas e a inserção do Brasil na nova equação do poder internacional." Pages 263–82 in Gelson Fonseca Júnior, Valdemar Carneiro Leão, and Sérgio Henrique Nabuco de Castro, eds., *Temas de política externa Brasileira.* Rio de Janeiro: Paz e Terra, 1994.

Fernandes, Ana Maria. "The Scientific Community and the State in Brazil: The Role of the Brasilian Society for Advancement of Science, 1948–1980." Ph.D. dissertation. London: St. Antony's College, Oxford University, 1987.

Ferraz, João Carlos, Howard Rush, and Ian Miles. *Development, Technology, and Flexibility: Brazil Faces the Industrial Divide.* New York: Routledge, 1992.

Ferri, Mário G., and Shozo Motoyama. *História das ciências no Brasil.* 3 vols. São Paulo: Editora Universidade São Paulo, 1979–1981.

Findlay, Trevor, ed. *Chemical Weapons and Missile Proliferation: With Implications for the Asia/Pacific Region.* Boulder, Colorado: Lynne Rienner, 1991.

Fitch, J. Samuel. "The Decline of US Military Influence in Latin America," *Journal of Interamerican Studies and World Affairs,* 35, No. 2, Summer 1993, 1–49.

Flank, Steven M. "Reconstructing Rockets: The Politics of Developing Military Technology in Brazil, India, and Israel." Ph.D. dissertation. Cambridge: Massachusetts Institute of Technology, 1993.

Frischtak, Cláudio, and E.A. Guimarães. "O sistema nacional de inovação." Paper prepared for V Forum Nacional, May 1993. São Paulo: May 1993.

Füllgraf, Frederico. *A bomba pacífica: O Brasil e outros cenários da corrida nuclear.* São Paulo: Editora Brasiliense, 1988.

Gall, Norman. "Atoms for Brazil, Dangers for All," *Foreign Policy,* 23, Summer 1976, 155–201.

Goldemberg, José. *O que é energia nuclear.* São Paulo: Editora Brasiliense, 1980.

Goldemberg, José. *Relatório sobre a educação no Brasil.* São Paulo: Instituto de Estudos Avançados, Coleção Documentos, 1993.

Guimarães, Reinaldo. "O fomento nos anos 90: Possibilidades e requisitos." Paper presented at 45th Annual Reunion of SBPC, "Retomada do fomento: Voltar aos anos 70," Recife, July 1993.

Hilton, Stanley E. "The Armed Forces and Industrialists in Modern Brazil: The Drive for Military Autonomy, 1889–1954," *Hispanic American Historical Review,* 62, No. 4, November 1982, 629–73.

Hirst, Mônica, and Héctor Eduardo Bocco. "Cooperação nuclear e integração Brasil-Argentina," *Contexto Internacional* [Rio de Janeiro], 4, No, 9, January–June 1989, 63–78.

Hudson, Rexford A. "The Brazilian Way to Technological Independence: Foreign Joint Ventures and the Aircraft Industry," *Inter-American Economic Affairs,* 37, No. 2, Autumn 1983, 23–43.

Jane's Information Group. *Jane's Spaceflight Directory, 1988–89.* Alexandria, Virginia: 1989.

Krasno, Jean. "Brazil's Secret Nuclear Program," *Orbis,* 48, No. 3, Summer 1994, 425–37.

Lamazière, Georges, and Roberto Jaguaribe. "Beyond Confidence-Building: Brazilian-Argentine Nuclear Cooperation," *Disarmament,*15, No. 3, 1992, 102–17.

Leventhal, Paul L., and Sharon Tanzer, eds. *Averting a Latin American Nuclear Arms Race: New Prospects and Challenges for Argentine-Brazilian Nuclear Cooperation.* London: Macmillan (for Nuclear Control Institute), 1992.

Lucena, Carlos F.P. *A situação atual e o potencial da área de computação no Brasil.* Background paper prepared for the Brazilian Science and Technology Policy Project. São Paulo: Fundação Getúlio Vargas, 1993.

Malavolta, Euripides. "As ciências agrícolas no Brasil." Pages 105–49 in Mário G. Ferri and Shozo Motoyama, eds., *História das ciências no Brasil.* 3 vols. São Paulo: Editora Universidade de São Paulo, 1979, 1981.

Malheiros, Tania. *Brasil, a bomba oculta: O programa nuclear brasileiro.* Rio de Janeiro: Gryphus, 1993.

Marcovitch, Jacques. *Centros de excelência em P e D no Brasil: Lições da crise: Instabilidade e desempenho em C e T.* Estudos analíticos do setor de ciência e tecnologia. Brasília: Ministério da Ciência e Tecnologia, 1992.

Martins, G., and R. Queiroz. "O perfil do pesquisador brasileiro," *Revista Brasileira de Tecnologia* [São Paulo], 18, No. 6, September 1987.

Meyer-Stamer, Jörg. *Technology, Competitiveness and Radical Policy Change: The Case of Brazil.* London and Portland, Oregon: Frank Cass, in association with the German Development Institute, 1997.

Navias, Martin. "Ballistic Missile Proliferation in the Third World," *Adelphi Papers,* No. 252, Summer 1990.

Nunes, Marcia B., Nadja V. de Souza, and Simon Schwartzman. "Pós-graduação em engenharia: A experiência da Coppe." Pages 72–97 in Simon Schwartzman, ed., *Universidades e instituições científicas no Rio de Janeiro.* Brasília: CNPq, Coordenação Editorial, 1982.

Pirard, Theo. "Buy, Buy Brazil," *Satellite Communications,* March 1988, 33–37.

Plonski, Guilherme Ary, ed. *Cooperación empresa-universidad en Iberoamérica.* São Paulo: Programa Iberoamericano de Ciência y Tecnologia para el Desarrollo, 1993.

Redick, John R. "Nuclear Confidence-Building in Latin America." Pages 116–45 in *Verification Report 1993: Yearbook on Arms Control and Environmental Agreements.* London: Verification Technology Information Centre, 1993.

Redick, John R., Julio C. Carasales, and Paulo S. Wrobel. "Nuclear Rapprochement: Argentina, Brazil, and the Nonproliferation Regime," *Washington Quarterly,* 18, No. 1, Winter 1995, 107–22.

Rosa, Luiz Pinguelli. *A política nuclear e o caminho das armas atômicas.* Rio de Janeiro: Zahar Editores, 1985.

Rosa, Luiz Pinguelli, ed. *A política nuclear no Brasil.* São Paulo: Greenpeace, 1991.

Schmitz, Hubert, and José Cassiolato, eds. *Hi-Tech for Industrial Development: Lessons from the Brazilian Experience in Electronics and Automation.* London: Routledge, 1992.

Schwartzman, Simon. "Brazil: Scientists and the State: Evolving Models and the 'Great Leap Forward'." Pages 171–88 in Etel Solingen, ed. *Scientists and the State: Domestic Structures and the International Context.* Ann Arbor: University of Michigan Press, 1994.

Schwartzman, Simon. "Changing Roles of New Knowledge." Pages 230–360 in Peter Wagner, Björn Wittrock, Carol Weiss, and Hellmutt Wollman, eds., *Social Sciences and Modern States.* Cambridge: Cambridge University Press, 1991.

Schwartzman, Simon. "Coming Full-Circle: For a Reappraisal of University Research in Latin America," *Minerva* [London], 34, No. 4, Winter 1986, 456–76.

Schwartzman, Simon. *The Future of Higher Education in Brazil.* Latin American Program Working Papers, No. 197. Washington: Woodrow Wilson Center Press, 1992.

Schwartzman, Simon. "High Technology Versus Self-Reliance: Brazil Enters the Computer Age." Pages 67–82 in Julian Chacel, Pamela S. Falk, and David V. Fleischer, eds., *Brazil's Economic and Political Future.* Boulder, Colorado: Westview Press, 1988.

Schwartzman, Simon. "The Power of Technology," *Latin American Research Review,* 24, No. 1, 1989, 209–21.

Schwartzman, Simon. *A Space for Science: The Development of the Scientific Commnunity in Brazil.* University Park: Pennsylvania State University Press, 1991.

Schwartzman, Simon, ed. *Universidades e instituições científicas no Rio de Janeiro.* Brasília: CNPq, Coordenação Editorial, 1982.

Schwartzman, Simon, and Maria Helena Magalhães Castro, eds. "Nacionalismo, iniciativa privada e o papel da pesquisa tecnológica no desenvolvimento industrial: Os primórdios de um debate," *Dados* [Rio de Janeiro] 28, No. 1, 1985, 89–111.

Schwartzman, Simon, Eduardo Krieger, Fernando Galembeck, Eduardo Augusto Guimarães, and Carlos Osmar Bertero. *Science and Technology in Brazil: A New Policy for a Global World.* São Paulo: Fundação Getúlio Vargas, 1994.

Shott, Thomas S. *Performance, Specialization, and International Integration of Science in Brazil: Changes and Comparisons with Other Latin America Countries and Israel.* Rio de Janeiro: Fundação Getúlio Vargas, 1994.

Silva, Marco Antonio Felício da. "Necessidade de nuclearização das forças armadas brasileiras," *A Defesa Nacional* [Lisbon], 712, March–April 1984, 109–29.

Solingen, Etel. "Brazil: Domestic Adjustment and International Response." Pages 123–52 in Raju G.C. Thomas and Bennett Ramberg, eds., *Energy and Security in the Industrializing World.* Lexington, Kentucky: University Press of Kentucky, 1990.

Solingen, Etel. "Brazil: Technology, Countertrade, and Nuclear Exports." Pages 111–51 in William C. Potter, ed., *International Nuclear Trade and Nonproliferation: The Challenge of the Emerging Suppliers.* Lexington, Massachusetts: Lexington Books, 1990, 111–51.

Solingen, Etel. *Industrial Policy, Technology, and International Bargaining: Designing Nuclear Industries in Argentina and Brazil.* Stanford: Stanford University Press, 1996.

Solingen, Etel. "Macropolitical Consensus and Lateral Autonomy in Industrial Policy: The Nuclear Sector in Brazil and Argentina," *International Organization,* 47, No. 2, Spring 1993, 263–98.

Solingen, Etel. "The Political Economy of Nuclear Restraint," *International Security,* 19, No. 2, Fall 1994, 126–69.

Solingen, Etel. "Technology, Exports, and Countertrade: Brazil as an Emerging Nuclear Supplier." Pages 211–35 in William C. Potter, ed., *International Nuclear Trade and Nonproliferation: The Challenge of the Emerging Suppliers.* Lexington, Massachusetts: Lexington Books, 1990.

Spector, Leonard S. *Nuclear Proliferation Today.* New York: Random House, 1984.

Spector, Leonard S. *The Undeclared Bomb: The Spread of Nuclear Weapons, 1987–1988.* Cambridge, Massachusetts: Ballinger, 1988.

Spector, Leonard S., and Jacqueline R. Smith. *Nuclear Ambitions: The Spread of Nuclear Weapons, 1989–1990.* Boulder, Colorado: Westview Press, 1990.

Stepan, Nancy. *Beginnings of Brazilian Science: Oswaldo Cruz, Medical Research and Policy, 1890–1920.* New York: Science History, 1976.

Tigre, Paulo Bastos. *Liberalização e capacitação tecnológica: O caso da informática pós-reserva de mercado no Brasil.* São Paulo: 1993.

Tigre, Paulo Bastos. *Technology and Competition in the Brazilian Computer Industry.* New York: St. Martin's Press, 1983.

Tollefson, Scott D. "Brazilian Arms Transfers, Ballistic Missiles, and Foreign Policy: The Search for Autonomy." Ph.D. dissertation. Washington: Paul H. Nitze School of Advanced International Studies, Johns Hopkins University, 1991.

United States. General Accounting Office. *Nuclear Nonproliferation: Export Licensing Procedures for Dual-Use Items Need to Be Strengthened.* Publication No. GAO/NSIAD–94–119. Washington: GPO, April 1994.

United States. Office of Technology Assessment. *Proliferation of Weapons of Mass Destruction: Assessing the Risks.* Publication No. QTA–ISC–559. Washington: GPO, August 1993.

Vargas, Milton, ed. *História da técnica e da tecnologia no Brasil.* São Paulo: Editora Unesp (Universidade Estatual Paulista) da Fundação para o Desenvolvimento da Universidade Estadual Paulista (Fundunesp), 1994.

Vasconcelos, E., ed. *Gerenciamento da tecnologia: Um instrumento de competitividade industrial.* São Paulo: Editora Edgard Blücher, 1992.

Vaz, Alcides Costa. "Condicionantes das posições brasileiras frente ao desarmamento, regimes de contrôle de exportações e segurança regional," *Premissas* [Campinas], 4, August 1993, 3–18.

Wilson, Andrew, ed. *Interavia Space Directory, 1989–90.* Alexandria, Virginia: Jane's Information Group, 1989.

Wrobel, Paulo Sérgio. "O Brasil e o TNP: Resistência à mudança?" *Contexto Internacional* [Rio de Janeiro], 18, No.1, 1996, 143–55.

Wrobel, Paulo Sérgio. "A diplomacia nuclear brasileira: A não-proliferação nuclear e o tratado de Tlatelolco," *Contexto Internacional* [Rio de Janeiro], 18, No. 1, 1993, 27–56.

(Various issues of the following publications were also used in the preparation of this chapter: *Financial Times* [London] and *New York Times.*)

Glossary

adelantado—In the sixteenth century, the Spanish crown awarded the office of *adelantado* to selected individuals who, at their own expense, undertook the discovery and conquest of new overseas territories. *Adelantados* served as executive officers to govern a region, to act as head of military forces at distant frontier posts, or to command a military expedition.

Alliance for Progress—Established in 1961 at a hemispheric meeting in Punta del Este, Uruguay, under the leadership of President John F. Kennedy as a long-range program to help develop and modernize Latin American states through multisector reforms, particularly in health and education. Involved various forms of foreign aid, including development loans offered at very low or zero interest rates, from the United States to all states of Latin America and the Caribbean, except Cuba.

Andean Group—An economic group, the Andean Common Market, created in 1969 by Bolivia, Chile, Colombia, Ecuador, Peru, and Venezuela as a subregional market to improve its members' bargaining power within the Latin American Free Trade Association (LAFTA) and to encourage increased trade and more rapid development. LAFTA, which dated from 1960, was replaced in 1980 by the Latin American Integration Association (Asociación Latinoamericana de Integración—ALADI), which advocated a regional tariff preference for goods originating in member states. Chile left the Andean Group in 1976. The threat that Peru might withdraw from the pact had receded by August 1992.

audiencia—A high court of justice, exercising some administrative and executive functions in the colonial period.

balance of payments—An annual statistical summary of the monetary value of all economic transactions between one country and the rest of the world, including goods, services, income on investments, and other financial matters, such as credits or loans.

bandeirantes—Colonial Portuguese expeditions made up of adventurers, named after the Portuguese word for flag (*bandeira*) because they traveled under the *bandeira* of their leader, who took with him kin, friends, slaves, and friendly Amerindians.

campesino—A Latin American Indian farmer or farm laborer.

capital goods—A factor of production category consisting of manufactured products used in the process of production.

Carta di Lavoro—This electoral model involves "functional representation" by corporate groups; that is, instead of having direct elections for the national legislature by districts or by proportional representation, elections are indirect within corporate management and labor unions.

central bank—Usually a federal government-related institution that is entrusted with control of the commercial banking system and with the issuance of the currency. Responsible for setting the level of credit and money supply in an economy and serving as the banker of last resort for other banks. Also has a major impact on interest rates, inflation, and economic output.

clientelism—Personal relationships that link patrons and clients together in a system in which jobs, favors, and protection are exchanged for labor, support, and loyalty.

"coattails"—The process whereby presidential candidates transfer votes and "pull in" candidates of the same party or coalition who are running for governor, senator, and so forth. Thus, "reverse coattails" occurs when candidates for governor, senator, and so forth transfer votes and "pull in" their respective candidates for president.

Common Market of the South (Mercado Comum do Sul—Mercosul)—An organization established on March 26, 1991, when the Treaty of Asunción was signed by Argentina, Brazil, Paraguay, and Uruguay for the purpose of promoting regional economic cooperation. Chile was conspicuously absent because of its insistence that the other four countries first had to lower their tariffs to the Chilean level before Chile could join. Mercosul became operational on January 1, 1995. Chile became an associate member that month and agreed to join as a full member on June 25, 1996. Bolivia was admitted into Mercosul in March 1997. Mercosul is more commonly known by its Spanish acronym, Mercosur (Common Market of the South—Mercado Común del Sur).

comparative advantages—The relative efficiencies with which countries can produce a product or service.

consumer durables—Consumer items or durable goods (*q.v.*)

used for several years, such as automobiles, appliances, or furniture.

consumer price index (CPI)—A statistical measure of sustained change in the price level weighted according to spending patterns.

Contadora Support Group—A diplomatic initiative launched by a January 1983 meeting on Contadora Island off the Pacific coast of Panama, by which the "Core Four" mediator countries of Colombia, Mexico, Panama, and Venezuela sought to prevent through negotiations a regional conflagration among the Central American states of Costa Rica, El Salvador, Guatemala, Honduras, and Nicaragua. The governments of Argentina, Brazil, Peru, and Uruguay formed the Contadora Support Group in 1985 in an effort to revitalize the faltering talks. The Contadora process was effectively superseded by direct negotiations among the Central American states.

coronelismo—Derives from the honorary title of colonel (*coronel*; pl., *coroneis*) in the National Guard that was customarily conferred on a locally dominant political boss, usually a substantial landowner or local justice of the peace. The term eventually became applied to local strongmen or political bosses, especially in rural areas and particularly in poorer Northeastern states. *Coronelismo* thus was a classic boss system under which control of patronage and minor funds was centralized in the *coronel*, who would dispense favors in return for political loyalty.

corporatism—The belief that society was, as political scientist Philippe C. Schmitter stated, made up of "a natural hierarchy of social groups, each with its ordained place and its own set of perquisite responsibilities." As a sociopolitical philosophy, corporatism found its most developed expression in Italy under Benito Mussolini. Corporatism is antithetical to both Marxist and liberal democratic political ideals. A corporatist would organize society into industrial and professional corporations that serve as organs of political representation within a hierarchical, centralized polity controlled by the state. A corporatist society is elitist, patrimonial, authoritarian, and statist. Some social science theorists have argued that Latin political tradition has had a fundamental corporatist feature, but others argue that it is but one of many cultural influences in the region.

cruzado—On February 28, 1986, the Brazilian cruzado, equal

to 1,000 cruzeiros, was introduced, and the Cruzado Plan to fight inflation was announced. The new cruzado (cruzado novo), equal to 1,000 old cruzados, was introduced on January 15, 1989.

cruzeiro (Cr$)—The old national currency, consisting of 100 centavos, which replaced the mil-reis on November 1, 1942. The cruzeiro novo was created on February 8, 1967, to replace the cruzeiro. After August 1968, the cruzeiro novo was adjusted by small amounts at frequent intervals, often every week or two. On May 15, 1970, the currency reverted to the cruzeiro, which remained in effect until 1986 when it was replaced by the cruzado (*q.v.*). The cruzeiro was reinstituted on March 16, 1990.

cruzeiro *real* (CR$)—On August 1, 1993, the cruzeiro *real*, equal to 1,000 cruzeiros, was introduced, as the national currency. It was replaced on July 1, 1994, by the *real* (*q.v.*).

current account—Current account balance is the difference between (a) exports of goods and services as well as inflows of unrequited transfers but exclusive of foreign aid and (b) imports of goods and services as well as all unrequited transfers to the rest of the world.

debt service—Cash requirement to meet annual interest and principal repayment obligations on total external debt.

degredados—Usually refers to minor Portuguese criminals exiled to Brazil in the sixteenth century as their punishment.

dependency theory—A theory that seeks to explain the continuing problems of Latin American underdevelopment and political conflict by positing the existence of an imperialistic, exploitative relationship between the industrialized countries and the developing nations of Latin America and other developing regions.

d'Hondt method—Also known as the highest-average method of determining the allocation of seats to political parties after an election. It was devised by the Belgian Victor d'Hondt to be used in electoral systems based on proportional representation. In addition to Portugal, the method has been adopted by Austria, Belgium, Finland, and Switzerland. Under this method, voters do not choose a candidate but vote for a party, each of which has published a list of candidates. The party winning the most votes in a constituency is awarded the area's first seat, which goes to the candidate at the top of the winning party's list. The total vote of this party is then divided by two, and this amount is compared with the totals of other parties. The party with the greatest number of votes at this point receives the next seat to be awarded. Each time a party wins a seat, its total is divided by the number of seats it has won plus one. This process continues until all the seats in a constituency are awarded. The d'Hondt method slightly favors large parties. Because there is no minimum threshold for winning a seat, however, small parties can also elect representatives.

durable goods—Goods or consumer durables (*q.v.*) that have a life extending more than three years, such as automobiles, appliances, and manufacturing equipment.

Ecclesiastical Base Communities (Comunidades Eclesiais de Base—CEBs)—Grassroots groups consisting of mostly poor Christian lay people through which advocates of liberation theology (*q.v.*) mainly work. Members of CEBs meet in small groups to reflect on scripture and discuss its meaning in their lives. They are introduced to a radical interpretation of the Bible, one employing Marxist terminology to analyze and condemn the wide disparities between the wealthy elite and the impoverished masses in most underdeveloped countries. This reflection often leads members to organize and improve their living standards through cooperatives and civic-improvement projects.

Economic Commission for Latin America and the Caribbean (ECLAC)—A United Nations regional economic commission established on February 25, 1948, as the Economic Commission for Latin America (ECLA). More commonly known in Latin America as Comisión Económica para América Latina (CEPAL). In 1984 ECLAC expanded its operations and title to include the Caribbean. Main functions are to initiate and coordinate policies aimed at promoting economic development. In addition to the countries of Latin America and the Caribbean, ECLAC's forty-one members include Britain, Canada, France, the Netherlands, Portugal, Spain, and the United States. There are an additional five Caribbean associate members.

elasticity—Usually refers to price elasticity, the ratio of the responsiveness of quantity demanded, or supplied, to a change in price.

European Community (EC—also commonly called the Community)—Established on April 8, 1965, the EC comprised three communities: the European Coal and Steel Community (ECSC), the European Economic Community (EEC), and the European Atomic Energy Community (Euratom). Each community was a legally distinct body, but from 1967 the communities shared common governing institutions. The EC formed more than a framework for free trade and economic cooperation; the signatories to the treaties governing the communities agreed in principle to integrate their economies and ultimately to form a political union. Belgium, France, Italy, Luxembourg, the Netherlands, and the Federal Republic of Germany (West Germany) were charter members of the EC. Britain, Denmark, and Ireland joined on January 1, 1973; Greece became a member on January 1, 1981; and Portugal and Spain entered on January 1, 1986. In November 1993, the EC was subsumed under a new organization, the European Union (EU—*q.v.*).

European Economic Community (EEC)—*See* EC.

European Union (EU)—Successor organization to the European Community (EC—*q.v.*), officially established on November 1, 1993, when the Treaty on European Union went into effect. The goal of the EU is a closer economic union of its member states and the European Monetary Union, a greater unity in matters of justice and domestic affairs, and the development of a common foreign and security policy. To the members of the EC, the EU added Austria, Finland, and Sweden, effective January 1, 1995.

export-led growth—An economic development strategy that emphasizes export promotion as the engine of economic growth. Proponents of this strategy emphasize the correlation between growth in exports and growth in the aggregate economy.

extreme poverty—Those who live below the poverty line, defined as half or less of the family income needed for a minimal level of food and shelter.

factors of production—Land (or natural resources), labor, capital goods, sometimes entrepreneurship, and other resources used in the production of goods and services.

fiscal year (FY)—Coincides with calendar year.

General Agreement on Tariffs and Trade (GATT)—A 123-member international organization created on October 30, 1947, to provide a continuing basis for nations to negotiate and regulate commercial policies and promote international trade on a nondiscriminatory basis. Principal activity multinational negotiation for tariff reductions. Seventh and last round of negotiations, held on April 15, 1994, was Uruguay Round, with the aim of liberalizing the world market and promoting intellectual property. GATT was subsumed by World Trade Organization (WTO) on January 1, 1995.

general price index (GPI)—A statistical measure of sustained change in the price level (rate of inflation) weighted according to spending patterns.

Gini index or coefficient—A measure of inequality in a country's wealth distribution. It contrasts actual income and property distribution with perfectly equal distribution. The value of the coefficient, or index, can vary from 0 (complete equality) to 1 (complete inequality). Brazil's Gini index in 1991 was 0.6366.

gross domestic product (GDP)—The broadest measure of the total value of goods and services produced by the domestic economy during a given period, usually a year. GDP has mainly displaced a similar measurement, the gross national product (GNP—*q.v.*). GDP is obtained by adding the value contributed by each sector of the economy in the form of profits, compensation to employees, and depreciation (consumption of capital). The income arising from investments and possessions owned abroad is not included, hence the use of the word "domestic" to distinguish GDP from GNP. Real GDP adjusts the value of GDP to exclude the effects of price changes, allowing for measurement of actual yearly increases or decreases in output. Real GDP is the value of GDP when inflation has been taken into account.

gross national product (GNP)—Total market value of all final goods (those sold to the final user) and services produced by an economy during a year, plus the value of any net changes in inventories. Measured by adding the gross domestic product (GDP—*q.v.*), net changes in inventories, and the income received from abroad by residents less payments remitted abroad to nonresidents. Real GNP is the value of GNP when inflation has been taken into account.

Henriques—Militia units named after Henrique Dias, a black Brazilian guerrilla leader who led black troops against the Dutch in Pernambuco in the 1640s.

human development index (HDI)—A measurement of human

progress introduced by the United Nations Development Programme (UNDP) in its *Human Development Report 1990*. By combining indicators of real purchasing power, education, and health, the HDI provides a more comprehensive measure of development than does the GNP (*q.v.*) alone.

import-substitution industrialization—An economic development strategy and a form of protectionism that emphasizes the growth of domestic industries by restricting the importation of specific manufactured goods, often by using tariff (*q.v.*) and nontariff measures, such as import quotas. Theoretically, capital would thus be generated through savings of foreign-exchange earnings. Proponents favor the export of industrial goods over primary products and foreign-exchange considerations. In the post-World War II period, import-substitution industrialization was most prevalent in Latin America. Its chief ideological proponents were the Argentine economist Raúl Prebisch and the Economic Commission for Latin America (*q.v.*). Main weaknesses in Latin America: the domestic markets in the region were generally too small; goods manufactured domestically were too costly and noncompetitive in the world market; most states in the region had an insufficient variety of resources to build a domestic industry; and most were also too dependent on foreign technology.

indexation—Automatic adjustment of remuneration in accordance with changes in a specific price index.

informal economy—Unofficial or underground sector of economic activity beyond government regulation and taxation, to include street vendors, some domestic servants, and unskilled workers in urban areas.

Inter-American Development Bank (IADB)—Also known as Banco Interamericano de Desarrollo (BID). A forty-six-member bank established on December 30, 1959, to promote economic and social development in Latin America.

Inter-American Treaty of Reciprocal Assistance of 1947. *See* Rio Treaty.

intermediate goods—Goods purchased for resale or for use in producing final goods for consumers, or inventories consisting of raw materials, semifinished goods, and finished goods not yet sold to the final consumer. The gross national product (*q.v.*) does not include sales of intermediate goods or services.

International Bank for Reconstruction and Development

(IBRD)—Formal name for the World Bank Group (*q.v.*) which was conceived at the Bretton Woods Conference on July 22, 1944, and began operations in June 1946. Its primary purpose is to provide technical assistance and loans at market-related rates of interest to developing countries at more advanced stages of development.

International Monetary Fund (IMF)—Established on December 27, 1945, the IMF began operating on March 1, 1947. The IMF is a specialized agency affiliated with the United Nations that takes responsibility for stabilizing international exchange rates and payments. The IMF's main business is the provision of loans to its members when they experience balance of payments difficulties. These loans often carry conditions that require substantial internal economic adjustments by the recipients. The IMF's capital resources comprise Special Drawing Rights (a new form of international reserve assets) and currencies that the members pay under quotas calculated for them when they join. These resources are supplemented by borrowing. In 1995 the IMF had 179 members.

international reserves—Some reserves, in the form of gold, currencies of other countries, and Special Drawing Rights, that every country holds to serve as "international money" when a nation faces balance of payments (*q.v.*) difficulties.

International Telecommunications Satellite Organization (Intelsat)—Created in 1964 under a multilateral agreement, Intelsat is a nonprofit cooperative of 134 countries that jointly own and operate a global communications satellite system.

Kardecian spiritualism—Allen Kardec (a pseudonym) founded Kardecism, a spiritualist religion, in mid-nineteenth-century France. Imported into Brazil at the end of the nineteenth century, the religion was adopted by members of Brazil's upper classes eager to identify with French culture. It centers on séances in which the dead return through mediums and give the living advice.

Latin American Free Trade Association (LAFTA)—A regional group founded by the Montevideo Treaty of 1960 to increase trade and foster development. LAFTA's failure to make meaningful progress in liberalizing trade among its members or to move toward more extensive integration prompted the leaders of five Andean states to meet in Bogotá in 1966. This meeting led to the creation in 1969 of the Andean Group (*q.v.*)—consisting of Bolivia, Chile, Colombia, Ecuador, Peru, and Venezuela—to serve as a subregional structure within LAFTA. LAFTA was replaced in 1980 by the Latin American Integration Association (Asociación Latinoamericana de Integración—ALADI), which advocated a regional tariff preference for goods originating in member states. ALADI has since declined as a major Latin American integration effort in favor of regional efforts, such as the Common Market of the South (*q.v.*).

League of Nations—An international organization whose covenant arose out of the Paris Peace Conference in 1919. It was created for the purpose of preserving international peace and security and promoting disarmament by obligating nations to submit their conflicts to arbitration, judicial settlement, or to the League Council for consideration. By not signing the Treaty of Versailles, the United States refused to join. Although the fifty-three-member body considered sixty-six disputes and conflicts between 1920 and 1939, it proved ineffective against German, Italian, Japanese, and Soviet aggression in the 1930s. Formally disbanded in April 1946, its functions were transferred to the United Nations.

liberation theology—An activist movement led by Roman Catholic clergy who trace their inspiration to Vatican Council II (1965), when some church procedures were liberalized, and the Latin American Bishops' Conference in Medellín, Colombia (1968), which endorsed greater direct efforts to improve the lot of the poor. Advocates of liberation theology—sometimes referred to as "liberationists"—work mainly through Ecclesiastical Base Communities (*q.v.*).

marginality—A concept used to explain the poor political, economic, and social conditions of individuals within a society, social classes within a nation, or nations within the larger world community. Refers often to poverty-stricken groups left behind in the modernization process. They are not integrated into the socioeconomic system, and their relative poverty increases. Marginality is sometimes referred to as dualism or the dual-society thesis.

Mercosul—*See* Common Market of the South.

mestiço (mestizo) or *mameluco*—Person of mixed racial origin.

Missile Technology Control Regime (MTCR)—A twenty-five-member organization established in April 1987 to counter missile proliferation by controlling the export of key missile technologies and equipment.

moderating power (*poder moderador*)—The constitutional function of the emperor during Brazil's monarchy era to oversee or moderate the political system by intervening at times of political crisis or institutional deadlock. From the fall of the monarchy in 1889 to the 1964 military coup, the military assumed and delegated the moderating power on an extra-legal basis. Political scientist Alfred A. Stepan uses the term to describe the moderator model of civil-military relations in the sense of "arbiter."

monetarists—Advocates of monetarism, an economic policy based on the control of a country's money supply. Monetarists assume that the quantity of money in an economy determines its economic activity, particularly its rate of inflation. A rapid increase in the money supply creates rising prices, resulting in inflation. To curb inflationary pressures, governments need to reduce the supply of money and raise interest rates. Monetarists believe that conservative monetary policies, by controlling inflation, will increase export earnings and encourage foreign and domestic investments. Monetarists generally have sought support for their policies from the International Monetary Fund (*q.v.*), the World Bank Group (*q.v.*), and private enterprise, especially multinational corporations.

nonparticipatory methodology—Unlike the "start from scratch" methodology used in 1987–88 (involving twenty-four subcommittees, eight committees, including a drafting committee, two rounds of floor votes, and extensive popular hearings in the committee stages), the nonparticipatory methodology in the constitutional revision made in 1993–94 was very streamlined, with no hearings or committees. It involved only the reporter's reports article by article, including or excluding the proposed changes, and then a floor vote.

North American Free Trade Agreement (NAFTA)—A free-trade agreement comprising Canada, Mexico, and the United States. NAFTA was approved by the United States House of Representatives in November 1993. NAFTA exceeds 360 million consumers, whose countries have a combined output of US$6 trillion.

Organization of American States (OAS)—Established by the Ninth International Conference of American States held in Bogotá on April 30, 1948, and effective since December 13, 1951. Has served as a major inter-American organization to promote regional peace and security as well as economic and social development in Latin America. Composed of thirty-five members, including most Latin American states and the United States and Canada. Determines common political, defense, economic, and social policies and provides for coordination of various inter-American agencies. Responsible for implementing the Inter-American Treaty of Reciprocal Assistance (Rio Treaty) (*q.v.*), when any threat to the security of the region arises.

personalism—The dominance of a charismatic personality in the political life of a nation. Loyalty is to a political leader rather than to institutions, organizations, or ideals.

plebiscite—A device of direct democracy whereby the electorate can pronounce, usually for or against, some measure put before it by a government. Also known as a referendum.

political culture—The orientation of the citizens of a nation toward politics, and their perceptions of political legitimacy and the traditions of political practice.

"popular" sectors—A term similar to popular culture, referring to the masses of working-class, underemployed, and unemployed citizens.

positivism—The theory that genuine knowledge is acquired by science and that metaphysical speculation has no validity. Positivism, based largely on the ideas of the French philosopher Auguste Comte, was adopted by many Latin American intellectuals in the late nineteenth and early twentieth centuries.

primary goods or products—Raw materials, such as ores, logs, and agricultural products, or other products with a high content of natural resources.

primary sector—Agriculture, extractive activities, and fishing.

real (pl., *reais*; R$)—On July 1, 1994, Brazil's sixth currency in nine years, the dollar-linked *real* (pronounced hay-OW), equal to 2,750 cruzeiro *reais*, replaced the cruzeiro *real* (CR$—*q.v.*). During the transition from the cruzeiro *real* to the *real*, Real Value Units (Unidades Reais de Valor—URVs) acted as a temporary currency, beginning on March 1, 1994, with one URV equal to one *real* or CR$2,750. URVs began gradually replacing indexes used to adjust wages, prices, taxes, contracts, and interest and utility rates. The URV was also part of an economic stabilization plan, the *Real* Plan (Plano *Real*), under which prices were gradually converted from cruzeiro *reais* to URVs. The URV is, by definition, the inflation rate itself. The URV rate is calculated as the average of a basket (*cesta*) of price indexes. The fluctuation band mechanism set by the Central Bank (*q.v.*) in March 1995 provided for bank intervention in the interbank exchange markets whenever the buying floor rate of R$0.88 per dollar and the ceiling selling rate of R$0.93 per dollar were affected by the market rates. The Central Bank restructured the *real's* trading ban on January 15, 1997, to a range of 1.0430 to 1.0480 per dollar, after the currency fell through its previous band. The dollar/*real* rate on April 13, 1998, was R$1.140.

real exchange rate—The value of foreign exchange corrected for differences between external and domestic inflation.

Rio Treaty (Inter-American Treaty of Reciprocal Assistance)—A regional alliance, signed in Rio de Janeiro in 1947, that established a mutual security system to safeguard the Western Hemisphere from aggression from within or outside the zone. Signatories include the United States and twenty Latin American republics. In 1975 a special conference approved, over United States objections, a Protocol of Amendment to the Rio Treaty that, once ratified, would establish the principle of "ideological pluralism" and would simplify the rescinding of sanctions imposed on an aggressor party.

slash-and-burn agriculture—Method of cultivation whereby areas of the forest are burned and cleared for planting, the ash providing some fertilization. Area is cultivated for several years and then left fallow for a decade or longer. These practices by subsistence farmers could destroy almost half of world's remaining 2.08 billion hectares of tropical forests, according to a study released by Consultative Group on International Agricultural Research (CGIAR) in August 1996.

structuralists—Advocates of structuralism, an economic policy that blames chronic inflation primarily on foreign trade dependency, insufficient local production, especially in agriculture, and political struggles among entrenched vested interests over government contracts. Structuralists advocate encouraging economic development and modernization through Keynesian and neo-Keynesian policies of governmental stimulative actions, accompanied by organizational reforms. Structuralists contend that monetarist (*q.v.*) policies retard growth and support the status quo.

sustainable development—Development that meets the needs of the present generation without compromising the ability of future generations to meet their own.

tariff—A tax levied by a government in accordance with its tariff schedule, usually on imported products, but sometimes also on exported goods. May be imposed to protect domestic industries from competitive imported goods and/or to generate revenue. Types include ad valorem, variable, or some combination.

tenentismo—A reform movement among junior army officers that began in the early 1920s and played a significant role in bringing Getúlio Dorneles Vargas (president, 1930–45, 1951–54) to power.

terms of trade—The ratio of a country's index of average export prices and average import prices. In international economics, the concept of "terms of trade" plays an important role in evaluating exchange relationships between nations. The terms of trade shift whenever a country's exports will buy more or fewer imports. An improvement in the terms of trade occurs when export prices rise relative to import prices. The terms of trade turn unfavorable in the event of a slump in export prices relative to import prices.

Third Worldism—An ideology that began in 1947 in which mostly developing nations not committed to either the East or the West in the Cold War professed policies of "neutralism" and "nonalignment." Since the 1970s, Latin American states have moved increasingly from a position of political and economic alignment with the United States to one of sympathy with Third Worldism.

Treaty of Tlatelolco—On being ratified by Cuba in April 1995, the treaty took effect, binding the thirty-three Latin American and Caribbean signatory nations to the peaceful use of nuclear power. Under the treaty, Latin America became the world's first region to prohibit nuclear weapons. The treaty covers all of Latin America, including the Caribbean, from the Mexican border with the United States to Antarctica. It bans the testing, use, manufacture, production, or acquisition of nuclear weapons. Each participating country must negotiate accords with the International Atomic Energy Agency (IAEA) to facilitate verification.

Treaty of Tordesillas—Under a papal bull issued in 1493, Spain was awarded lands west and south of the line of demarcation, and Portugal received lands east and south. Dissatisfied with this arrangement, however, Portugal and Spain concluded the Treaty of Tordesillas of June 4, 1494, to establish a new line of demarcation 370 leagues west of the Cape Verde Islands, placing all of Africa, India, and later, Brazil, within Portugal's sphere.

United Nations Development Programme (UNDP)—A thirty-six-member organization, established on November 22, 1965, to provide technical assistance to stimulate economic and social development.

value-added tax (VAT)—An incremental tax applied to the value added at each stage of the processing of a raw material or the production and distribution of a commodity. It is calculated as the difference between the product value at a given stage and the cost of all materials and services purchased as inputs. The value-added tax is a form of indirect taxation, and its impact on the ultimate consumer is the same as that of a sales tax.

vertical integration—Merging into a single ownership of firms producing in successive stages of a production process, whether it be forward toward the finished goods market or backward toward raw material producers.

World Bank—Informal name used to designate the World Bank Group of four affiliated international institutions: the International Bank for Reconstruction and Development (IBRD—*q.v.*), the International Development Association (IDA), the International Finance Corporation (IFC), and the Multilateral Investment Guarantee Agency (MIGA). The IBRD, established in 1945, has the primary purpose of providing loans to developing countries for productive projects. The IDA, a legally separate loan fund administered by the staff of the IBRD, was established in 1960 to furnish credits to the poorest developing countries on much easier terms than those of conventional IBRD loans. The IFC, founded in 1956, supplements the activities of the IBRD through loans and assistance designed specifically to encourage the growth of productive private enterprises in less developed countries. MIGA, founded in 1988, insures private foreign investment in developing countries against various noncommercial risks. The president and certain senior officers of the IBRD hold the same positions in the IFC. The four institutions are owned by the governments of the countries that subscribe their capital. To participate in the World Bank Group, member states must first belong to the IMF (*q.v.*). In 1995 the World Bank included 178 member-countries. By the early 1990s, the Latin American and Caribbean region had received more loan aid through the World Bank Group than any other region.

yellow cake—The U308 uranium concentrate used by nuclear power plants in Angra dos Reis in Rio de Janeiro State. It is a radioactive substance made from a low-grade uranium ore.

Index

Contributors

Werner Baer is Professor of Economics at the University of Illinois at Urbana-Champaign.

Donald V. Coes is Associate Director of the Latin American Institute and Professor of International Management at the University of New Mexico in Albuquerque.

David V. Fleischer is Professor of Political Science at the University of Brasília (Universidade de Brasília) in the Federal District.

Rex A. Hudson is Senior Research Specialist in Latin American Affairs with the Federal Research Division of the Library of Congress.

Maria Helena Magalhães Castro is a researcher with the Brazilian Institute of Geography and Statistics (Fundação Instituto Brasileiro de Geografia e Estatística—IBGE) in Rio de Janeiro and Assistant Professor at the Institute of Philosophy and Social Sciences (Instituto de Filosofia e Ciências Sociais) of the Federal University of Rio de Janeiro (Universidade Federal do Rio de Janeiro—UFRJ).

Frank D. McCann is Professor of History at the University of New Hampshire in Durham.

Charles C. Mueller is Professor of Economics at the University of Brasília. He is also a member of the Institute for the Study of Society, Population, and Nature (Instituto Sociedade, População e Natureza—ISPN), also in the Federal District.

Donald Sawyer is a sociologist and President of the ISPN.

Simon Schwartzman is President of the IBGE and Coordinator for Technical Cooperation at the IBGE.

Scott D. Tollefson is Assistant Professor in the Department of National Security Affairs of the Naval Postgraduate School in Monterey, California.

Jaklen Muoi Tuyen received an M.A. in Latin American Studies from the University of California/Los Angeles (UCLA) in 1996 and a Master of Public Health from Yale University in 1998. She completed a summer internship with the Federal Research Division of the Library of Congress under the sponsorship of the Hispanic Association of Colleges and Universities (HACU).

Published Country Studies

(Area Handbook Series)

550–65	Afghanistan	550–36	Dominican Republic and Haiti
550–98	Albania	550–52	Ecuador
550–44	Algeria	550–43	Egypt
550–59	Angola	550–150	El Salvador
550–73	Argentina		
550–111	Armenia, Azerbaijan, and Georgia	550-113	Estonia, Latvia, and Lithuania
550–169	Australia	550–28	Ethiopia
550–176	Austria	550–167	Finland
550–175	Bangladesh	550–173	Germany
550–112	Belarus and Moldova	550–153	Ghana
550–170	Belgium	550–87	Greece
550–66	Bolivia	550–78	Guatemala
550–20	Brazil	550–174	Guinea
550–168	Bulgaria	550–82	Guyana and Belize
550–61	Burma	550–151	Honduras
550–50	Cambodia	550–165	Hungary
550–166	Cameroon	550–21	India
550–159	Chad	550–154	Indian Ocean
550–77	Chile	550–39	Indonesia
550–60	China	550–68	Iran
550–26	Colombia	550–31	Iraq
550–33	Commonwealth Caribbean, Islands of the	550–25	Israel
		550–182	Italy
550–91	Congo	550–30	Japan
550–90	Costa Rica	550–34	Jordan
550–69	Côte d'Ivoire (Ivory Coast)	550–114	Kazakstan, Kyrgyzstan, Tajikistan, Turkmenistan, and Uzbekistan
550–152	Cuba		
550–22	Cyprus	550–56	Kenya
550–158	Czechoslovakia	550–81	Korea, North

550–41 Korea, South
550–58 Laos
550–24 Lebanon
550–38 Liberia
550–85 Libya

550–172 Malawi
550–45 Malaysia
550–161 Mauritania
550–79 Mexico
550–76 Mongolia

550–49 Morocco
550–64 Mozambique
550–35 Nepal and Bhutan
550–88 Nicaragua
550–157 Nigeria

550–94 Oceania
550–48 Pakistan
550–46 Panama
550–156 Paraguay
550–185 Persian Gulf States

550–42 Peru
550–72 Philippines
550–162 Poland
550–181 Portugal
550–160 Romania
550–115 Russia

550–37 Rwanda and Burundi
550–51 Saudi Arabia
550–70 Senegal
550–180 Sierra Leone
550–184 Singapore

550–86 Somalia
550–93 South Africa
550–95 Soviet Union
550–179 Spain
550–96 Sri Lanka

550–27 Sudan
550–47 Syria
550–62 Tanzania
550–53 Thailand
550–89 Tunisia

550–80 Turkey
550–74 Uganda
550–97 Uruguay
550–71 Venezuela
550–32 Vietnam

550–183 Yemens, The
550–99 Yugoslavia
550–67 Zaire
550–75 Zambia
550–171 Zimbabwe